PRE-OWNED ASSETS AND ESTATE PLANNING

THIRD EDITION

PRE-OWNED ASSETS
AND ESTATE PLANNING

EMMA CHAMBERLAIN

CHRIS WHITEHOUSE

SWEET & MAXWELL

 THOMSON REUTERS

Published in 2009 by
Thomson Reuters (Legal) Limited
(Registered in England and Wales, Company No. 1679046.
Registered Office and address for service:
100 Avenue Road, London, NW3 3PF)
trading as Sweet and Maxwell

Typeset by DC Graphics Design Limited, Swanley Village, Kent

Printed and bound in Great Britain by CPI Antony Rowe, Chippenham,
Wiltshire

For further information on our products and services, visit
www.sweetandmaxwell.co.uk

No natural forests were destroyed to make this product;
only farmed timber was used and replanted

A CIP catalogue record for this book is available from the British Library
ISBN 978-0-414-04011-3

CONTENTS

PART I: SETTING THE SCENE

PART II: HOW THE LEGISLATION WORKS

PART III: PLANNING IN PRACTICE: REACTIVE PLANNING

PART IV: PLANNING IN PRACTICE: PROACTIVE PLANNING

APPENDIX I: THE LEGISLATION

APPENDIX II: MATERIAL ISSUED BY HMRC

PREFACE

It seemed a good idea at the time: a "thinking outside the box" solution to IHT avoidance. Leave the IHT loopholes but charge the taxpayer income tax as the "price" for his temerity in avoiding IHT and at the same time bring into charge past IHT avoidance schemes going back to 1986. So was born POAT, a tax, the sole function of which is to act as a deterrent to the avoidance of another tax. It is a tax wholly devoid of principle with the charging provisions reflecting areas of avoidance (land/chattels) and even particular schemes (settled intangibles/**Eversden**).

With its absence of a motive defence and its labyrinthine list of exclusions and exemptions it is both a trap for the unwary and an administrative nightmare: unloved and often misunderstood by both taxpayers and HMRC.

Subsequent amendments to the POAT legislation have been illuminating: take the attempt to close the reverter to settlor loophole which was framed in such general terms as to catch wholly innocuous arrangements but in revising the election machinery succeeded in undermining the imposition of the reservation of benefit rules. Of course, one can sympathise with the Parliamentary draftsmen: a rickety structure of this type is vulnerable to any wind of change.

It is surely in the interests of both taxpayer and HMRC that this misguided experiment be repealed and IHT, if it is to be retained at all, put on a sound legislative footing. This would recognise that POAT was after all an ill-thought out and fundamentally lazy attempt to deal with problems in another tax. Indeed the recent dramatic fall in IHT yield may suggest a more radical solution: abolish IHT altogether and replace it with a capital gains tax on death. POAT could go at the same time.

As with "Trust Taxation" we are indebted to our Australian secretary Elouise Dale who despite the loss of the Ashes not only dealt with the manuscript but oversaw the entire project.

The law is stated at 1 October 2009.

EMC
CJW
5 Stone Buildings
Lincoln's Inn

PREFACE TO THE SECOND EDITION

The pre-owned assets charge duly came into force on 6 April 2005 with a whimper rather than a bang. Widespread ignorance concerning the scope of the tax continues as do uncertainties over the details: whether commercial loans within the family are capable of satisfying the contribution condition is a good illustration.[1]

We have included in the book the bulk of the preface to the first edition, above all to reflect our feelings some 12 months ago. With the passage of time we remain convinced that the tax is a mess: legislate in haste repent in leisure is certainly true in this case as with other taxes rushed through by recent Labour administrations. Long term it seems unlikely that the charge will prevent the development of new IHT avoidance schemes—the demand is there, not least because IHT is perceived to be unfair.

Thanks are due to Catherine Aldred for again struggling with the manuscript and to the team at Sweet and Maxwell: as ever models of restraint! One of our number has defected: after years spent clarifying concepts of capital transfer tax and then inheritance tax, Barry McCutcheon has retired to enjoy the delights of Portugal where the weather is warm; the wine is good and the taxes uncollected. We wish him well.

The law is stated at 1 October 2005.

EMC
CJW
5 Stone Buildings
Lincoln's Inn

---

[1] See AppII-D36

EXTRACTS FROM PREFACE TO THE FIRST EDITION

The days when tax avoidance was viewed as a game played out between taxpayer and Revenue subject to well established rules of conduct have long since gone. The growth of a tax avoidance industry promoting schemes that were frequently artificial; rarely anything other than complex and which displayed a high level of ingenuity in using the legislation against the intention of its promoters has unsurprisingly provoked a fierce reaction from Government and Revenue. We now live in an age when fire will be fought with fire and the old certainties are no more. No longer is it possible to say that legislation to stop tax avoidance will not affect past schemes or that tax is only payable if the case falls within the clear words of the legislation.

The subject matter of this book—the Pre-Owned Assets Charge—offers a case study in tax avoidance and the reaction against it. IHT avoidance, widespread and often "artificial", has been met by a novel charge: rather as Canning called into being a New World to redress the balance of the Old, so income tax has been summoned to cover up the cracks in IHT. From the original announcement on December 10, 2003, Ministers have not wavered from two principles: firstly that this novel solution was going to happen (in modern terminology it was "non negotiable") and, secondly, that a major objective was to bring back within the tax net past transactions. In some cases, such transactions had been carried out over 17 years ago. Objections based on retrospective taxation were to be fiercely resisted. Within these parameters the consultation process was then distinguished by great willingness on the part of Ministers and the Revenue to amend and clarify the original detail and to exclude "hard" cases. (Typically these were situations when the new charge would be unnecessary since the taxpayer would in any event suffer an IHT charge or where the reservation of benefit legislation was not intended to apply.)

While the Revenue and Government's willingness to entertain amendments as the Schedule passed through Parliament was wholly admirable, the resultant mutilation of the original Finance Bill legislation was not pretty to behold and Sch.15 is unsurprisingly something of a mess. Further, such legislation "on the hoof" inevitably carries within it the seeds of its own destruction and is unlikely to stop the spiral of avoidance/anti-avoidance legislation. Perhaps good will eventually emerge if it encourages a future Government finally to address the reform of death duties. Inheritance tax has been in a sorry state since the wholesale mutilation of Capital Transfer Tax by Tory Governments in the 80s. This book has been written with the intention of explaining the new legislation and considering how it affects existing arrangements and its impact upon future tax saving strategies.

For a number of taxpayers the introduction of the POA charge will lead them to rue ever having sought to avoid IHT. To deal with such cases it is unfortunate that the legislation does not afford a complete fiscal unscrambling. Realisation of the mess that they have ended up in will lead some taxpayers to question the scheme that they had purchased (usually for much fine gold!). Signing papers without appreciating their full impact may well lead to a trickle of cases before the courts seeking to set the whole thing aside on the basis of mistake.

There is, however, another side to the coin. Rising property values not accompanied by corresponding adjustment to the IHT rates brought many taxpayers into the IHT net during the late 90s for the first time. This fuelled a demand for an "arrangement" that would prevent a large portion of the property value being taken up in a windfall tax charge. It was a desire to share this increased prosperity (if that is the correct word to describe a property boom) with children and family that fuelled the glut of IHT schemes. Nothing has been done to deal with the real sense of injustice resulting in a flat rate tax of 40 per cent once the £263,000 nil rate band has been used up.

The POA charge is an aggressive response to such schemes which is unlikely to be wholly successful in dousing the fires of discontent. As such it is likely to be viewed in the future as merely a further step in the ongoing tussle between a cash strapped Exchequer and reluctant taxpayers. It was more a knee jerk reaction than a well thought out response to the fundamental problem which lies in the structure of IHT.

TABLE OF CASES

TABLE OF STATUTES

TABLE OF STATUTORY INSTRUMENTS

PART I: SETTING THE SCENE

This Part outlines the reasons for the introduction of the Pre-Owned Assets Regime and provides a general introduction to Inheritance Tax, the reservation of benefit legislation and the 2006 changes to the tax treatment of settlements.

Chapter 1

INTRODUCTION

The Finance Act 2004 (FA 2004) s.84 and Sch.15 introduced an entirely new tax   **1–01** charge known as "the pre-owned assets" charge ("the Regime"). The Regime charges individuals to income tax on an annual basis in respect of benefits they enjoy—or, in some cases, are capable of enjoying—from certain kinds of property which they have owned at some time after March 17, 1986. The charge is intended to perform two functions: first, as a fine on individuals who have escaped the clutches of the IHT reservation of benefit provisions by what HMRC regard as unacceptable means; and secondly, as a general deterrent to individuals considering inheritance tax schemes because they now run the risk of other such fines being introduced in the future.[1] It will be helpful to consider why the Government came to the view that such a radical measure was in order.

Inheritance tax and the Finance Act 1986

It all goes back to the Finance Act 1986, which, apart from rechristening capital   **1–02** transfer tax as inheritance tax (IHT), introduced both the potentially exempt transfer ("PET") regime and the reservation of benefit rules. Unlike the capital transfer tax regime, which did not allow tax-free gifts in excess of the nil rate band threshold but had no reservation of benefit rules, the PET regime was intended to encourage timely giving by allowing lifetime gifts to be IHT free provided that the donor survived seven years. However, the donor had to give up all benefit from the gift. One could give freely, but the gift had to be without any strings which allowed, or might allow, the donor to enjoy the gifted property in the future (and nor must the taxpayer in fact benefit from the gifted property).[2]

Not surprisingly, after the introduction of the PET regime and the reservation of benefit provisions, tax advisers devised methods by which individuals could make PETs of property which, without infringing the reservation of benefit provisions, they could still continue to enjoy or have the potential to enjoy. This, of course, was only to be expected. Normally when new anti-avoidance legislation is introduced there is a cat-and-mouse game between taxpayers and HMRC, with HMRC incrementally cracking down on loopholes and gambits until the legislation is sufficiently watertight to achieve its end. This is how matters initially proceeded with the reservation of benefit rules

---

[1] It is possible to see the Regime as a (rather arbitrary) wealth tax, but the authors think it operates more as a fine than as a wealth tax.

[2] The relevant legislative provisions are in FA 1986 s.102; SI02ZA; SI02A-C and Sch.20.

Ingram—HMRC's first defeat

1–03 HMRC's first significant defeat was in the *Ingram* case,[3] following which they introduced, in the traditional manner, narrowly targeted anti-avoidance legislation in relation to disposals of land made after March 8, 1999.

Eversden—the straw that broke the camel's back

1–04 The *Eversden* case—discussed in more detail below[4]—was first decided in the taxpayer's favour by a Special Commissioner in 2001. Prior to that decision, the planning technique which the Revenue challenged in *Eversden*, and which was capable of being used in a variety of circumstances, had been employed on a relatively limited basis, but the Commissioner's decision encouraged more widespread use, particularly in relation to the family home. HMRC appealed and Lightman J. in 2002 also found for the taxpayer. This led to a number of "*Eversden*" schemes being developed, marketed and implemented. Matters were made even worse for HMRC when the Court of Appeal in 2003 unanimously upheld Lightman J.'s decision.

This forced HMRC's hand and the Finance Act 2003 introduced anti-avoidance provisions designed to defeat *Eversden* schemes implemented by disposals made after June 19, 2003. Needless to say, advisers scrutinised these new anti-avoidance provisions with a view to identifying any remaining loopholes. Their motivation for doing so was perhaps even stronger than usual: by now taxpayers had become accustomed to circumventing the reservation of benefit provisions and expected to continue to be able to do so. After all, their advisers had always come up with something in the past—why should they not do so now? Advisers, for their part, had found devising ways round the reservation of benefit provisions a remunerative area. There was clearly a continuing demand. All that was needed was a product.

The authors concluded that the new provisions did their job rather well and that the various attempts being suggested for outflanking them were, on the whole, unlikely to succeed. Others, however, reached different conclusions and a whole series of "post-*Eversden*" schemes—discussed in **Ch.16**—appeared to brighten the lives of taxpayers intent on having access to property which they had given away.

1–05 As HMRC were well aware, "*Eversden* schemes" were merely one of a number of IHT "arrangements" on the market and which were designed to circumvent the reservation of benefit rules. Of these, the so-called Home Loan (or Double Trust) Scheme had been widely marketed[5] and in addition chattel gifts and leaseback, reversionary leases, and cash gifts were employed. The Revenue was also aware that the new anti-*Eversden* legislation was under close scrutiny and that, almost inevitably, *Eversden* Mark II schemes would appear. In the Standing Committee debates[6] on the introduction of the Regime, Ms Dawn Primarolo, the Paymaster General, stated that HMRC had tried twice to tighten up the reservation

---

[3] The *Ingram* case and "*Ingram* arrangements" are considered in **Chs 2** and **14**.

[4] See **Chs 2** and **16**.

[5] It has been suggested that 30,000 of these have been implemented, but this figure is thought to be an underestimate.

[6] *Hansard*, Standing Committee Debates, May 28, 2004, col.256.

of benefit rules and that "it has encouraged more ingenious schemes"; the implication being that HMRC thought or, at any rate, feared that these "more ingenious schemes" were effective. Hence, as a result it is thought of ministerial prompting, HMRC decided to adopt an entirely new *technical* approach. Further, having been shocked by the perceived scale of IHT avoidance, they decided that not only must a shot be fired across taxpayers' bows, but also a shot must be fired *into* taxpayers' bows, i.e. that a wholly new *philosophical* approach was needed.

Too much of a bad thing

The need for a new philosophical approach was made crystal clear by Ms Dawn **1–06** Primarolo in her opening remarks to the Standing Committee concerning the need for the pre-owned assets charge. Having referred to the figures mentioned above—30,000 taxpayers, billions of pounds of assets (*not* tax)—she said (the italics are the authors):

> "Faced with such figures, the Committee will not be surprised to hear that the Government decided to take action. *It is not enough to tackle new arrangements and future avoidance.* The Government wanted to send a clear message that artificial avoidance of that kind is not acceptable. Those who devise and market such schemes, and the people who take advantage of them, *need to understand that and not assume that* avoidance *is risk-free.* Such schemes have grown so rapidly because they are regarded as a one-way bet. The essential point is that nothing really changes. For example, let us consider somebody who wants to ensure that the house they live in is not part of their taxable estate, but they want to remain living there. They see their adviser, sign a series of papers and pay a substantial fee, even though there might be a relatively small amount of work in it. The client goes home, the paperwork is filed and the arrangements are designed to unscramble when the client dies and have no lasting effect. The only real effect is inheritance tax savings that can run into hundreds of thousands of pounds or more. Given that perception of risk and rewards, it is not surprising that people and advisers have found such schemes increasing attractive. *The clause gives notice that that is a false perception.*
>
> People who have used such schemes, or who contemplate others like them in the future, are right to think that they will get any inheritance tax saving that their scheme is able to assure, *but they are wrong to think that that protects them against any future tax charge. That is at the heart of the changes under schedule 15.*"[7]

This is an important statement, in a number of ways. First and foremost, it sets out the Government's new philosophical approach—taxpayers can now find that they are to be fined for having avoided IHT—and makes it clear that this "is at the heart" of the new legislation. Secondly, it greatly oversimplifies the characterisation of the kind of arrangements people entered into. While it is probably fair to say that people who entered into *Eversden* arrangements did not substantially alter their affairs, that was certainly not true of other arrangements, notably so-called "*Ingram*" schemes which had significant capital gains tax consequences.[8] This is an important point if, as Dawn Primarolo stated, the kind

---

[7] *Hansard*, Standing Committee Debates, May 28, 2004, col.238.

[8] See, for instance, the taxpayers' arguments in *Wolff v Wolff* [2004] STC 1633 accepted by the High Court that they did not realise that in a reversionary lease scheme they would cease to have the right to occupy their house at the end of the deferral period.

of schemes which were objectionable were those which involved no real change in the taxpayer's situation. Thirdly, although one can have some sympathy with the view that avoidance of IHT had reached such proportions that a solution was required which would put people altogether off the idea of trying to avoid the tax in the future, that does not necessarily justify the particular solution that she proposed. This is because any solution should not only do what it sets out to do (viz prevent IHT avoidance), but should also satisfy other criteria among which are: first, it should not catch individuals who are not successful tax avoiders; secondly, it should not complicate excessively an already over-complicated system; thirdly, it should not impose excessive compliance requirements and fourthly there should be certainty about its scope and effects. In short, the solution must be technically efficacious and perceived to be "fair". If it is not, any philosophical justification becomes irrelevant. If the tax system is perceived by "ordinary" people to be unfair the practical consequence is that they will not comply with it and that tax evasion will increase. The authors consider that in many ways the Regime has been effective in stopping IHT schemes in respect of the family home. However, the Regime has certainly complicated the tax system and in some cases has adversely affected taxpayers with no IHT avoidance motive. Some examples of the unfairness of this legislation are set out at **1–15** et seq. Rather than introducing the POAT Regime it might have been better for the Government to consider ways of making IHT a fairer and less unpopular tax. It is often perceived as a tax on the middle classes, whose wealth is tied up in their family home: an asset which they cannot give away during their lifetime without reservation of benefit problems. The truly wealthy can avoid IHT by making lifetime gifts or investing in business or agricultural property.[9]

Implementing the Regime

1–07 The Chancellor's Autumn Statement of December 10, 2003 announced that measures would be taken to tackle tax avoidance, including the avoidance of IHT. On the following day, a consultation document ("The Tax Treatment of Pre-Owned Assets") was published. For the first time it was made clear that what was being proposed was an income tax charge on (broadly) the benefit derived from the continued use of assets by a former owner. As a consultation document it was flawed: instead of an analysis of the problem and a number of suggested solutions it merely gave scanty details of a brand new tax charge. Little wonder that all those who contributed to the consultation exercise urged the Government to adopt a different solution.[10] The die had already been cast, however, as had been made clear in the press release of the previous day which referred to the charge being introduced by legislation in the Finance Bill 2004 with consultation being confined to "the detailed workings of this measure".

There is no evidence that at this stage any one had sat down and thought through the implications of the proposed income tax charge: instead it has all the

---

[9] For a discussion of the IHT regime and whether the current policy can be justified, see the recent Mirrlees Report: R. Boadway, E. Chamberlain, C. Emmerson, Taxation of Wealth and Wealth Transfers (OUP). See also N. Lee "Inheritance tax—an equitable tax no longer: time for abolition?" (2007) 27 (4) *Legal Studies* 678–708.

[10] Most obviously to amend the IHT legislation on gifts with reservation to stop up the loopholes.

hallmarks of a "bright idea" which was seized upon by a government which had become irritated beyond measure by the activities of the tax avoidance industry.[11]

A technically misconceived approach

The starting point in evaluating the Regime technically is to realise that it is built **1–08** on shaky foundations,[12] because it involves the grafting of a minicode—the Regime—onto another minicode—the reservation of benefit rules—which was itself ineptly grafted onto the basic IHT (formerly CTT) legislation. It will be surprising if this does not produce problems for both the taxpayer and the Revenue.

The consequences of the inept grafting of the reservation of benefit rules onto the IHT legislation is already a matter of public record. Two examples suffice: first, *Eversden* schemes which took advantage of the inadequate integration into the reservation of benefit rules of the IHT exemptions for transfers of value and the effect in that context of s.49(1) of the Inheritance Tax Act 1984; and secondly, the fact that no one can predict with any certainty the effect for the reservation of benefit rules of what should be a straightforward transaction, namely the settling by an individual of property on trusts under which he retains an interest in possession.[13]

The grafting of the Regime onto the IHT legislation generally, and the reservation of benefit rules in particular, can only lead to problems. Innocent taxpayers may fall within the ambit of the Regime because it does not adopt the approach used in the past to combat tax avoidance—viz introducing narrowly targeted provisions. Instead it operates by taxing anything that is not expressly excluded from the scope of the charging provisions; for example, any disposal of land whether by sale, gift or exchange, is caught where the taxpayer continues to occupy the land **unless** it falls within a specific exclusion or exemption. Since it is obviously difficult successfully to exclude every type of innocent transaction, the scope for collateral damage on innocent taxpayers is considerable

---

[11] This has become an all too predictable pattern: a hasty and ill-conceived measure is announced and, despite objections, put on the statute book. There then follows a period of "tidying up" the defects and anomalies. See the equally unhappy history of Stamp Duty Land Tax and the tax scheme disclosure rules. Not only does this make for bad legislation in policy terms; it seemed in 2004 at odds with the declared objectives of the "plain English" rewrite. Indeed we have now had the situation when a tranche of legislation has been rewritten in plain English and put on the statute book only for a schedule to be repealed and anti-avoidance provisions with respect to that same rewritten legislation introduced in "old style" English. Pity indeed the poor practitioner. No doubt such drafting leads to yet more loopholes for the sophisticated tax avoider to exploit but it is hardly a sensible way to operate a tax system. The rationale for rewriting vast tracts of the legislation in plain English was in any event questionable (much of it involved distinctly worse drafting) but when it was mixed in with old style drafting and parts of it almost immediately repealed the result was chaos. It is therefore a relief that the rewrite programme is coming to an end after the Corporation Tax legislation is rewritten.

[12] IHTA 1984 s.49 is a key provision providing that a qualifying interest in possession beneficiary is treated for the purposes of the tax as beneficially entitled to the property in the trust fund—for the operation of this deeming in relation to liabilities (both trust and personal) see *St Barbe Green v IRC* [2005] STC 288. Note that as from March 22, 2006 it is not generally possible to create new qualifying interests in possession to which s.49(1) applies.

[13] See **Ch.19**.

notwithstanding HMRC's best efforts.[14] Amendments to the Regime—dealing with both ingenious schemes and wronged taxpayers—were inevitable.[15]

Compliance with the requirements of the Regime is a significant problem.[16] To some extent this is the product of the approach adopted in 2004. The tax charge under the Regime is to income tax but involves deeming the taxpayer to have the necessary income and uses terms and concepts from the IHT legislation. Further its introduction was not intended to produce a substantial income tax yield but to deter IHT avoidance. Little wonder therefore that those responsible for the collection of income tax have little interest in and are largely ignorant of POAT. But a similar malaise afflicts those responsible for the administration and collection of IHT: after all this is an income tax charge and therefore nothing to do with them. POAT, it can be said, is unloved and, it appears, unwanted in the corridors of HMRC.

One cannot help but think that narrowly targeted IHT anti-avoidance legislation would have been a better option. It is true that tax planners have over the years developed various approaches to outflank the reservation of benefit provisions, but this was only to be expected in the years following the ill-thought out introduction of those provisions. Narrowly targeted anti-avoidance provisions—the HMRC's traditional approach—had closed off most of the loopholes and, in the authors' view, the remaining ones could have been dealt with in the same way leaving everyone knowing more or less where they stood. The possibility of the legislation hitting unintended targets would have been minimal. That approach, alas, was not adopted.

A rush to implement

1–09   The problems of the Regime were exacerbated by its rushed implementation. The original proposals in the consultation document were substantially amended by the time that the 2004 Finance Bill was published, whilst no fewer than 45 amendments were made at Committee Stage of the Bill, and a further 18 at Report Stage. While HMRC were admirable in their willingness to consult on detail, the fundamental problem remained: by taxing everything not expressly excluded innocent transactions are caught.

1–10   Even at the eleventh hour, all was chaos and disorder: the first set of Regulations were only published at the very last moment given that they had to come into force on April 6, 2005 (the start date for the POA charge) and followed not one but two ministerial statements[17] made on consecutive days because the contents of the second (an extension of double charges relief) had been inadvertently omitted from the first! The guidance notes were rushed out in an attempt to quell a rising tide of press concerns about the new tax.[18] The operation of the election into GWR[19] provides an even more graphic illustration of the confusion and

---

[14] For some examples of this collateral damage, see **Ch.21** (equity release schemes) and **Ch.6** (intangibles). There is no motive defence—see **1–14**.

[15] These amendments themselves may produce further anomalies: note especially the attempt to combat the use of reverter to settlor arrangements in FA 2006, s.80: see A2.119–A2.132 and **8.19** and **7.24** for the very arbitrary effect on foreign domiciliaries.

[16] See **Ch.13** (administration).

[17] These are in **Appendix I**.

[18] For the guidance notes, see A2.01 et seq.

[19] See **Ch.11**.

ignorance at the heart of the Regime. It seems not to have been appreciated that the form of election required Parliamentary approval (via the laying of a statutory instrument) and so this was not done until after the deadline for electing in respect of existing schemes had passed. The resulting confusion has never been cleared up. Even the regulations required to make a valid election were not issued until after the deadline for making the election so that no valid election could in fact be made![20]

Broad structure—the "Holy Trinity" approach

The broad structure of the Regime in Sch.15 is to establish a separate charging **1–11** system for each of three different kinds of property:

i   land (see paras 3–5);

ii   chattels (see paras 6–7);

iii intangible property comprised in a settlor—interested settlement (see para.8).

Certain conditions, which vary according to the type of property concerned, must be satisfied before the Regime can apply. In the case of land and chattels certain transactions (called "excluded transactions") are outside the charge (see para.10). Further, even if the conditions are satisfied, there are a number of exemptions which may prevent the Regime from applying (see para.11). Since its introduction the main effect of the Regime has been to stop IHT schemes involving the family home.

Two tier structures: three into two will go

It is important to note at the outset that more than one charging system can apply **1–12** to an arrangement. Hence if X sells part of his house to a wholly owned company at full market value and continues to occupy it, this is a disposal of an interest in land for the purposes of the Regime and he is liable to pay income tax despite the fact that there is no IHT saving. If the company shares are settled into a trust from which he can benefit, prima facie (depending on how the trust is set up) the Regime is capable of applying both to his occupation of the house (para.3) and to the shares held in the settlement (under para.8 intangibles charge). (Of course in this example it is possible that the various exclusions and exemptions in paras 10 and 11 will take X out of the charge altogether and these are discussed later in **Chs 5** and **7**.) Whilst it is true that there are provisions aimed at preventing double taxation arising in such a case, the point to bear in mind is that each situation must be carefully analysed to arrive at its consequences under the Regime.

---

[20] See **13**.

Guiding principles

1–13 The Regime is based on the following guiding principles:

  i   the value of property which is subject to IHT in the hands of the taxpayer should not be subject to the Regime;

  ii   property and transactions which are outside the IHT net either by reason of qualifying for favoured IHT treatment or by reason of what HMRC regard as "acceptable" IHT planning should not be caught by the Regime; and

  iii land, chattels and settled intangible property not caught in the IHT net and to which no favoured treatment is given by the Regime are subject to the Regime.

No motive test or commercial transaction defence

1–14 It is worth stressing that there is no motive test under the Regime, i.e. a taxpayer cannot escape the ambit of the Regime by establishing that the arrangement was not implemented with a view to avoiding IHT but was instead entirely motivated by other considerations.[21] Nor is there a general exclusion from the POA charge in the case of bona fide commercial transactions.[22]

Equity release schemes

1–15 A good illustration of the absence of any motive requirement is afforded by the following example. Mrs A owns her house worth £300,000. She has no other significant assets, so IHT saving is not an issue: all she is concerned about is ensuring that she can go on living in her house and has cash to fund her living expenses and to pay for improvements that might be required. With this in mind she might:

  a)   sell the entire house to her children at full market value and rely upon them to allow her to continue in occupation;

  b)   sell part of her house at full market value either to her children or to a commercial provider with the right to continue in occupation (a so-called equity release scheme); or

  c)   borrow on the security of the house either from a commercial provider or from her children.

Is the Regime capable of applying to Mrs A in any of these circumstances? It is irrelevant that she is not motivated by a wish to avoid IHT since, as noted, the Regime takes no account of motive. All that is required is a disposal and continued

---

[21] The Low Incomes Tax Reform Group provided a series of illustrations showing the impact of the POA charge on "ordinary family arrangements entered into without any thought of tax avoidance". These are discussed at **1–16**.

[22] Contrast the "bad bargain" exclusion from IHT in IHTA 1984, s.10. Para.10(1) provides for only a limited exclusion.

occupation. Nor will the so-called de minimis exemption necessarily help given that the value of the occupation benefit may exceed £5,000.[23]

Bizarrely on the above facts, the Regime will not apply to her if she does (a) or (c) but will apply to her if she does (b) with her children (but not with a commercial provider) after March 6, 2005. In the case of (a) this is an excluded transaction and in the case of (c) no disposal of her land has taken place at all. However, in the case of (b) there is only an exemption contained in reg.5 of the 2005 SI for sales of part to a commercial provider or to a connected person before March 7, 2005. Where is the logic (or justice) in these distinctions? Are they not simply a trap for the unwary?[24]

Are "ordinary innocent" transactions caught?

Is there any truth in the assertion that ordinary taxpayers who have no inheritance **1–16** tax motive will be unwittingly caught by the Regime and may not even realise that income tax is due?[25] The Government consistently justified the introduction of the pre-owned assets regime as affecting only tax avoiders who should be punished for their sins.

Consider *Examples 1.1* and *1.2* which are taken from the Low Incomes Tax Reform Group website.

Example 1.1

A mother and father help their daughter and son-in-law with the purchase of a new house. Time passes and the son-in-law vanishes from the scene. The daughter falls ill and six years later the mother and father move into the house to help look after the grandchildren.

In these circumstances it would appear to the authors that unless the cash gift was made before April 6, 1998[26] or the parents move in more than seven years after the cash gift, then the parents are caught under the Regime. The fact that the daughter's circumstances have changed does not protect the parents.

It may be that the de minimis exemption will apply (two £5,000 exemptions each for the mother and father so that there is no charge). However, this still requires the mother and father to obtain valuations to establish this point. If they elect into reservation of benefit, the daughter and son-in-law as donees are responsible on their deaths for payment of any inheritance tax due. Will the daughter have to sell the house?

Example 1.2

In 2000, a mother and daughter decide to live together on the death of the father. The mother gives cash to her daughter and eventually they decide to buy a property jointly. The daughter later marries and moves out.

---

[23] The de minimis provision is considered at **Ch.9**.

[24] See further **Ch.21** and in particular **21–35** for a summary of the highly complicated provisions which now apply in relation to sales for full value/at an undervalue/sales of part/sales of whole.

[25] The example considered at **1–15** involving the sale of part of Mrs A's house is surely a wholly (IHT) innocent transaction.

[26] On this matter, see **5–21** and **5–24**. An outright cash gift will not normally present reservation of benefit problems (see **2–26** and **7–44**).

The authors' view is that there is no reservation of benefit for the mother (cash gift—no tracing[27]), but there is a POA charge for the mother once the daughter moves out, even though she has no control over this.[28] Again the de minimis exemption may apply. If the mother had loaned the cash to the daughter then the position would be uncertain but the authors' view is that no POA charge arises: see **3–12**.

1–17 Consider also the following:

Example 1.3

(1) In 2002 a husband settles the matrimonial home which he occupies on interest in possession trusts for his wife and then on discretionary trusts for himself and his children.[29] There is no POA charge while the trust owns only the home because the exclusion in para.10(1)(c) provides protection and this is the case both before and after the death of W. However, if the couple later downsize so that a smaller replacement home is built and the trustees invest the balance of the sale proceeds in shares, para.10 does not protect the intangibles, whether these are held before or after W's death. H is therefore caught by the POA charge on the cash/shares element. The fact that W suffers inheritance tax on her death (given that the trust had been created before March 22, 2006 so that her interest was "qualifying") so that there is no inheritance tax avoidance is irrelevant.

(2) In 2007 H settles the matrimonial home which he occupies on non-qualifying interest in possession trusts for his wife, but H is a default beneficiary only if W and all his children die. This is a chargeable transfer into a property trust.[30] There is no IHT charge on W's death but the trust is within the relevant property regime, so entry and exit charges apply. This transaction has the protection of para.10(1)(c) even though the spouse does not take a qualifying interest in possession and while H is in occupation of the property there is a reservation of benefit and therefore protection under para.11(5). However, the trustees downsize and eventually the trust holds cash/shares/other intangibles as well as a smaller replacement property. There is still no POA charge on the replacement home. However, there is a POA charge on the intangibles element. This is because the para.10 protection does not operate in respect of intangibles and the para.11 exemption is no longer in point because H's reservation of benefit has ceased given that H retains only a remainder interest.[31]

---

[27] See **Ch.21**.

[28] See **21–14**.

[29] This is not a reservation of benefit by H because the gift to W prevents a reservation of benefit—see the *Eversden* decision and **Ch.16**. Hence the protections in para.11 would not apply.

[30] The FA 2006 changes in the IHT treatment of settlements are considered in **Ch.11**.

[31] This assumes H receives no benefit from the shares. All he has is a remainder interest which is a carve out. A deemed PET arises in respect of the cessation of his reservation of benefit on the intangibles.

Example 1.4

In 1999 Bruce gives his partner John cash. John purchases a house. John and Bruce then occupy the property in 2000. They register their civil partnership in 2006. Bruce is subject to the POA charge because the contribution condition is breached. The fact that they register a civil partnership in 2006 does not protect Bruce from a POA charge after that date. Bruce should have purchased a **share** in the house with John (because then he would have had protection under para.11(8)).[32] The same is true of transactions between couples who later marry—the fact they marry later does not "cure" the POA problem. One might argue that since Bruce made a substantial gift and occupied property he should be caught by the charge, but such transactions are relatively common between unmarried couples or same sex partners who will be completely unaware that what they have done results in an income tax charge. One solution might be to relieve them from the charge once they marry or register a partnership or simply to exempt transfers between cohabitees from the Regime altogether given that they are subject to a more adverse IHT regime than married couples. A more radical answer would be to introduce a motive test in the legislation (so that it only catches arrangements entered into with the intention of avoiding IHT).

Statutory links with IHT

Although the POA Regime is freestanding, it is intimately linked with IHT in a number of ways: **1–18**

(a) not only is property which is comprised in an individual's estate for IHT purposes outside the scope of the Regime, but so is other property not comprised in the individual's estate but from which property which is comprised in his estate derives its value (see para.11(1)). This prevents the same value being subject both to IHT and to the Regime[33];

(b) subject to certain qualifications, property which falls to be treated as property subject to a reservation in relation to the individual is outside the scope of the Regime so that the same property is not subject to both IHT and to the Regime (see para.11(5)(a)). Furthermore, it is open to a person to opt out of the Regime in relation to property by electing to subject himself to the reservation of benefit rules in relation to that property. He thus has the choice of the lesser of two evils[34];

(c) the territorial scope of the Regime is framed by reference to the territorial scope of IHT in some respects—there are notable mismatches—and the IHT deemed domicile provisions apply to the POA charge: an income tax![35];

---

[32] For the position of sharing arrangements, see **Ch.21**.

[33] See **Ch.7**.

[34] See Sch.15, **21–23**: this election is considered in detail in **Ch.11**. Some, but not all, of the statutory exemptions to reservation of benefit also apply to exclude the POA charge (notably situations where the taxpayer pays full consideration for his benefit and "sharing arrangements"—see **Ch.7**).

[35] See **Chs 8 and 24**.

(d) favoured treatment given to posthumous transactions is linked to the IHT favoured treatment given to such transactions so this remains a fruitful area for planning[36];

(e) certain reliefs and exemptions are framed by reference to IHT reliefs and exemptions; and

(f) a number of IHT definitions apply for the purpose of the Regime.

Definitions

1–19 The following terms are defined (as for IHT) as follows:

(a) "interest in land" has the same meaning as in Ch.4 of Pt VI of the 1984 Act[37];

(b) "land" is defined as for IHT[38];

(c) "property" has the wide IHT meaning in s.272 of the 1984 Act and so includes rights and interests of any description other than a settlement power[39]; and

(d) "settlement" and "settled property" have the same meanings as in the 1984 Act.[40]

As will be seen, the use of some of these IHT definitions may give rise to problems.

"Chattel" and "intangible property" are defined as follows:

(a) "chattel" means any tangible moveable property (or, in Scotland, corporeal moveable property)[41]; and

(b) "intangible property" means any property other than chattels or interests in land.[42] "Intangible property" is thus a default term in that it applies to all property other than chattels and interests in land and includes cash.

Associated operations

1–20 The IHT associated operations provisions[43] are of limited relevance under the Regime. They apply in relation to the "excluded liability" provisions, but otherwise do not apply for the purposes of the Regime (though they can be indirectly relevant in that they may apply for the purposes of determining whether or not property is subject to a reservation). In particular, although the Regime uses the term "disposition" it does not adopt the extended IHT definition of that

---

[36] See **Ch.7–49**.
[37] See Sch.15, para.1.
[38] See Sch.15, para.1.
[39] See Sch.15, para.1.
[40] See Sch.15, para.1.
[41] See Sch.15, para.1.
[42] See Sch.15, para.1.
[43] See IHTA 1984, s.268.

term whereby a disposition includes a disposition effected by associated operations.[44] Indeed, the Regime generally uses the term "disposal" rather than "disposition".

Valuation

The value of any property is the price which the property might reasonably be expected to fetch if sold in the open market at that time, but that price shall not be assumed to be reduced on the ground that the whole property is to be placed on the market at one and the same time.[45] This is the same as the basic IHT valuation rule.[46] Note, however, that unlike IHT, the Regime does not contain any specific rules for valuing property. This may cause compliance difficulties if say, a half share in the property is being gifted or the taxpayer only occupies part of a property.[47] Similar problems can arise where the asset in question is a life policy. Certain valuation issues arise in relation to rental values under the Regime discussed in **Ch.21** and at **3–20**.

1–21

Starting date, retrospectivity and "retroactivity"

The only time limit for the application of the Regime is that it does not operate in respect of arrangements put into effect before March 18, 1986, which is also the cut-off date for the application of the reservation of benefit provisions.[48]

1–22

Strenuous representations were made that the Regime was retrospective and should catch only arrangements put into effect after December 9, 2003 (December 10, 2003 being the date on which it was announced that the Regime was to be introduced). The matter was raised in the Standing Committee debates on the 2004 Finance Bill with Opposition amendments seeking to restrict its operation to the date when the charge was announced, or failing that, when the *Ingram* anti-avoidance legislation took effect or, failing that, when the *Eversden* anti-avoidance legislation took effect. These amendments were all rejected by the Government.

In the Standing Committee debates[49] Dawn Primarolo rejected the view that the Regime was retrospective on the basis that although it affected structures put into place before its introduction, it imposed a charge only on benefits enjoyed after April 5, 2005. The Regime, she asserted, was therefore retroactive, but not retrospective.

It was acknowledged by the Government that unwinding arrangements effected prior to the introduction of the Regime may be difficult, if not impossible. The

---

[44] See IHTA 1984, s.272.

[45] Sch.15, para.15; see also the rules concerning "excluded liabilities" in paras 11(6) and (7).

[46] See IHTA 1984, Pt VI.

[47] See *CIR v Arkwright* [2004] EWHC 1720 (Ch); [2004] S.T.C. 1323 for certain valuation issues and **3–20** for a discussion of the charge on land.

[48] Sch.15, paras 3(2)(a), 3(3), 6(2)(a), 6(3) and 8(2). However, the legislation inadvertently created a further limitation since outright cash gifts made before April 6, 1998 (more than 7 years before the POA charge takes effect) are ignored since they cannot satisfy the contribution condition (see Sch.15, para.10(2)(c) and **5–24**, A2.70).

[49] *Hansard*, Standing Committee A, May 28, 2004, col.261.

Regime accordingly provides taxpayers with the ability to "opt out" and, in effect, into IHT.

The point was made in the Standing Committee debates—given that transactions that took place as long ago as 1986 could be caught under the Regime—that taxpayers would be faced with considerable difficulties in tracking down relevant information. The Paymaster General dismissed such concerns on the basis that such taxpayers would have had to keep records for IHT purposes. While this may be correct insofar as the circumstances of the donor taxpayers are concerned, transactions entered into by donees in respect of which they were under no obligation to keep any records can also be extremely important for Regime purposes, and the difficulties involved in retrieving such information may be significant: see **3–27** and **Ch.13**.[50]

Human rights

1–23   The Finance Act 2004 carried with it a statement by the Chancellor of Exchequer under s.19(1)(a) of the Human Rights Act 1998 that in his view the provisions of the Act were compatible with the Convention rights. In the House of Commons debates it was mentioned that a group of "eminent lawyers" were considering taking the introduction of the Regime to the European Court of Justice.[51]

The Joint Committee on Human Rights in Parliament was requested to investigate the matter and in June 2004 produced a report on Sch.15. The Committee criticised the fact that the explanatory notes did not contain any express consideration of the Human Rights implications of the Bill and examined concerns that the provisions amounted to retrospective taxation and were therefore in breach of art.1 to the ECHR Protocol.

Article 1 gives the right to peaceful enjoyment of possessions and provides that no one shall be deprived of his possessions "except in the public interest". However, it is expressly provided that this shall not impair the right of the state to secure the payment of taxes. Thus any interference with property rights to secure the payment of taxes must strike a balance between public interest and the protection of an individual's fundamental rights. Retrospective legislation might be regarded as requiring a clearer public interest. The Committee recognised that for such interference to be lawful it must also satisfy the requirements of accessibility and enforceability, i.e. the law must be intelligible and enable the individual to organise his affairs knowing with reasonable certainty the consequences of his actions.

The Committee accepted that the charge was not directly retrospective in that it was not levied in respect of the benefit enjoyed in previous years albeit it does impose a liability in respect of future benefits by reference to past arrangements. The Committee concluded that the provisions were sufficiently accessible and foreseeable and that the interference was proportionate,[52] i.e. it struck a fair

---

[50] Although such difficulties have been relieved to some extent by the fact that cash gifts made prior to April 1998 are not caught by the Regime and therefore do not have to be traced.

[51] *Hansard*, Finance Bill debates, July 7, 2004, col.876.

[52] See, for example, *National Provincial Building Society v UK* [1997] STC 1466, where it was held that a taxation measure which had been enacted with retroactive effect did not violate Art.1 because the interference was justified.

balance between the demands of the general interest of the community and the individual's fundamental rights.[53]

However, this view was reached on the premise that the income tax charge was **1–24** only imposed in respect of a benefit derived from continued use of assets which have been disposed of in order *to avoid liability to inheritance tax* and therefore the tax cannot be characterised as an arbitrary confiscation. This is by no means the case and one could certainly argue that the imposition of income tax on innocent non-tax avoidance arrangements is an arbitrary imposition. The Committee seemed to believe that the Regime was clear in its application—it did not discuss the very real compliance issues for the taxpayer arising out of the ambiguity and uncertainty of the Regime in a number of areas. Further, the occupier of the property or user of chattels could be left without any ability to pay income tax under the Regime for the privilege of continuing in occupation. While the taxpayer can elect into the inheritance tax regime, this does not put him in the position that he would have been if he had never entered into the transaction.[54] Again this was not discussed. As we will see, *Ingram* schemes in particular may be very hard hit by the provisions in that the donee now faces both an inheritance tax charge (if the donor elects into reservation of benefit) and a capital gains tax charge.

The charge to income tax

The charge to income tax was originally to be under Sch.D, Case VI, but, as a **1–25** result of the rewritten legislation, under the Income Tax (Trading and Other Income) Act 2005 the charge is under Ch.V, Pt VIII of that Act.

Authors' approach

Given the structure of the Regime, the best approach is first to consider how **1–26** chargeable occasions may arise and then against that background review the provisions which take property out of the Regime. Before doing so, however, it will be appropriate to review briefly some key IHT provisions.

---

[53] The Committee criticised Sch.15 merely on the basis that the benefit of the exclusions in para.10 should not be confined just to spouses but should be extended to homosexual couples and thus the Act discriminated on the grounds of sexual orientation. This was rectified for same sex couples who registered a civil partnership when the Civil Partnership Act 2005 came into force on December 5, 2005. This does not, however, protect past transactions.

[54] See, for example, the discussion in *Eversden* planning at **16–51**. Recent Labour Governments have a poor record in introducing retrospective tax legislation: consider the introduction of the revised public access requirement for conditionally exempt property in 1998 and the anti flip flop capital gains tax legislation in 2003 and the abolition of source ceasing in FA 2008, Sch.7 which affected even those accounts where the source had been ceased. The Government's attitude can be summed up in the Paymaster General's defence of the 2003 legislation in the Committee Stage Debates at that time:

"If taxpayers have found a way of not paying that charge when the legislation clearly states that they should, they are playing with fire and can expect any Government to act...those who play with fire must expect to have their fingers burnt when the Government restore the legislation."

CHAPTER 2

IHT, RESERVATION OF BENEFIT AND QUALIFYING INTERESTS IN POSSESSION

2–01   The Regime is intended to prevent taxpayers from circumventing the reservation of benefit rules and so avoiding the payment of IHT. In certain key areas it operates by reference to the reservation of benefit provisions. Accordingly, it will be helpful to consider a few essential IHT provisions briefly, before analysing the Regime.[1]

INHERITANCE TAX GENERALLY

2–02   Inheritance tax is charged on an individual who makes a transfer of value (typically a gift) during his lifetime and on his estate at death. Various exemptions and reliefs are available to prevent certain kinds of transactions from giving rise to a charge. For example, gifts between spouses and civil partners are normally outside the scope of IHT,[2] as are certain family maintenance dispositions[3] and gifts of modest amounts.[4] Some of these exemptions and reliefs are incorporated into the Regime and where that is done the terms of the IHT exemption or relief will be discussed.

The charge on death

2–03   IHT charged on death is intimately linked with the reservation of benefit provisions. It is therefore important to understand exactly how this charge operates. IHT is chargeable on a person's death as if immediately before he died he made a transfer of value and the value transferred thereby was equal to the value of his estate at that time.[5] For this purpose a person's estate is the aggregate of all the property to which he is beneficially entitled, except that immediately before his death his estate does not include excluded property.[6] Since for IHT purposes a person entitled to a qualifying interest in possession in settled property

---

[1]   For greater detail on the reservation of benefit provisions, see *Dymond's Capital Taxes*, Ch.5A.
[2]   IHTA 1984, s.18.
[3]   IHTA 1984, s.11.
[4]   IHTA 1984, s.19 (annual exemption); s.20 (small gifts) and s.21 (normal expenditure out of income). In the latter case the exemption can be used to make substantial IHT savings given that there is no prescribed ceiling on the payments: see *Bennett v IRC* [1995] STC 54.
[5]   IHTA 1984, s.4(1).
[6]   IHTA 1984, s.5(1).

is treated as beneficially entitled to the property in which his interest subsists, on the death of such a person the settled property will form part of his estate and be subject to IHT.[7]

Calculating the charge on death

Calculating the IHT payable for the deceased's estate involves the following: **2–04**

(a) valuing all property in his estate immediately before his death (on the definition of "property" see IHTA 1984, s.272 and see **1–21**);

(b) the estate may be swollen by trust property in which the deceased had enjoyed a qualifying interest in possession[8] and by the value of property in which the deceased had reserved a benefit (qualifying interests in possession and reservation of benefit are discussed further below);

(c) excluded property is left out of account[9];

(d) the value of business and agricultural property may be reduced by either 100 per cent or 50 per cent: this is business property relief ("BPR") and agricultural property relief ("APR")—see further in **Ch.25**;

(e) liabilities are deducted from the value of the property in the estate provided that such liabilities are incurred "for a consideration in money or money's worth" (IHTA 1984, s.5(5)).[10] IHT is calculated on the net value of the estate with the nil rate band applying (in 2009/10) up to £325,000[11] and thereafter tax being charged at a flat rate of 40 per cent[12];

(f) property must be valued at "the price which the property might reasonably be expected to fetch if sold in the open market"[13] immediately before death. In this connection note the following:

   (i) no discount is allowed for the fact that all the property is put onto the market at the same time;

---

[7] IHTA 1984, s.49(1). Again this is subject to the excluded property rules. Primary responsibility for payment of the tax is on the trustees of the settlement. For the treatment of liabilities, see *St Barbe Green v IRC* [2005] STC 288.

[8] Note, however, that if the reverter to settlor relief is available then although the property is comprised in the estate of the deceased its value is untaxed: see generally **Ch.18**.

[9] IHTA 1984, s.5(1) and for the meaning of excluded property see IHTA 1984, s.5 and s.48.

[10] Note that special rules apply to artificial debts; see FA 1986, s.103: In general a liability secured on property will be deducted from the value of that property: see IHTA 1984, s.162(4), but for business property relief see ibid., s.110.

[11] For 2009/10. It will rise to £350,000 in 2010/11.

[12] If the deceased had made chargeable transfers or PETS within seven years of his death these may exhaust his IHT nil rate band since they are cumulated with his estate at death for the purpose of calculating the tax payable. In the event that tax is payable on lifetime transfers as a result of death within seven years primary responsibility for that tax rests with the donee: IHTA 1984, s.199(1)(b) and for the contingent liability of the deceased's personal representatives, see ibid., s.199(2); 204(8) and for their right of recovery s.211(3).

[13] IHTA 1984, s.160.

(ii) in certain cases a change in value of the assets resulting from the death may be taken into account (e.g. loss of goodwill in an owner-occupied business)[14];

(iii) in general the IHT value will become the CGT acquisition cost of a legatee inheriting the assets of the deceased[15]; and

(iv) if liabilities exceed the deceased's "free estate" they cannot be used to reduce the value of settled property in which he had a qualifying interest in possession.[16]

Reservation of benefit

2–05 The fundamental provision in the reservation of benefit minicode which determines whether an individual has reserved a benefit is s.102(1) FA 1986 , the essential part of which is as follows:

" . . . this section applies where, on or after 18th March 1986, an individual disposes of any property by way of gift and either—

(a) possession and enjoyment of the property is not bona fide assumed by the donee at or before the beginning of the relevant period; or
(b) at any time in the relevant period the property is not enjoyed to the entire exclusion, or virtually to the entire exclusion, of the donor and of any benefit to him by contract or otherwise;

and in this section 'the relevant period' means a period ending on the date of the donor's death and beginning seven years before that date, or, if it is later, on the date of the gift."

For this purpose, by the Finance Act 1986, Sch.20, para.6(1)(c), a benefit which a donor obtained by virtue of associated operations of which the disposal by way of gift is one, are to be treated as a benefit to him by contract or otherwise.

2–06 Notice two key points. First, that what activates the provisions is a "**gift**" made by an individual. There is no definition of gift which will presumably bear its normal meaning as a transfer of property with donative intent. In any event, the use of "gift" as the triggering event distinguishes the reservation of benefit minicode from the rest of the IHT legislation where the key event is the making of a transfer of value. It is thought that in certain circumstances there can be a

---

[14] IHTA 1984, s.171.
[15] This will only be the case if the value has been "ascertained" for IHT purposes which will not be the case, e.g. if the assets passed to the deceased spouse, qualified for 100% APR or BPR or if the deceased's estate fell within his IHT nil rate band. See TCGA 1992, s.274 and *Tax Bulletin* April 1995, p.209. There is no uplift in the CGT base cost for reservation of benefit property which is taxed on the death of the donor.
[16] This is the effect of *St Barbe Green v IRC* [2005] STC 288. Presumably liabilities on free estate will not be available to reduce the value of reservation of benefit property which is included in the free estate unless (possibly) the liability is charged on such reserved benefit property. It was accepted in this case that the value of trust property is the net value **after** deducting trust liabilities.

transfer of value for IHT purposes which is not a gift and this dichotomy may be exploited by taxpayers.[17]

Secondly, that what can trigger the rules once a gift has been made is that the property is not enjoyed to the entire exclusion of the donor. This can mean de facto enjoyment. In particular, once a gift has been made it is never safe for the donor to enjoy benefits in the property (i.e. there is no seven-year period after which the slate is wiped clean).

Let-outs

The legislation provides that certain disposals by way of gift which would **2–07** otherwise result in property being subject to the reservation of benefit provisions are taken outside the ambit of those provisions. For example, s.102(5) of the Finance Act 1986 takes a disposal of property by way of gift which qualifies for the IHT spouse or civil partner exemption outside the provisions.[18] Some of these let-outs are incorporated into the Regime so that a transaction which qualifies for favoured treatment under the reservation of benefit provisions generally also does so for the purposes of the Regime.[19] Where this is the case, the let-outs from the reservation of benefit provisions are discussed in detail.

Where the conditions in s.102(1) are satisfied, the property in question is prima facie "property subject to a reservation" and so caught by the reservation of benefit provisions. In certain cases, anti-avoidance legislation has the effect that property may be caught even though these requirements are not satisfied. Conversely, there are various ameliorating provisions that mean that even if s.102(1) requirements are satisfied or the anti-avoidance provisions are prima facie infringed there is not a reservation of benefit problem.

Full consideration[20]

A key let-out is provided by FA 1986, Sch.20 para.6(1)(a) which provides that in **2–08** the case of land and chattels the:

> "retention or assumption by the donor of actual occupation of the land or actual enjoyment of an incorporeal right over the land or actual possession of the chattel shall be disregarded if it is for full consideration in money or money's worth".

---

[17] For the view of HMRC, see IHTM 14315. Note that FA 2006 introduced a new s.102ZA into the GWR legislation deeming a beneficiary with a qualifying interest in possession to make a gift when that interest terminates.

[18] It was this exemption which was exploited in the *Eversden* case, discussed in **Ch.16**. HMRC also take the view that there can be a gift without a transfer of value: see IHTM 14315.

[19] A good example is "sharing arrangements" considered in detail in **Ch.21**.

[20] See also **7–39**. For the view of HMRC see IHTM 14341 where it is stated that:

> "it is unlikely that any such arrangement could be overturned if the taxpayer can demonstrate that it resulted from
>
> a. a bargain negotiated at arm's length
> b. by parties who were independently advised and
> c. which followed the normal commercial criteria in force at the time it was negotiated".

Example 2.1

(a) Jake gives his house "Marigold" to his daughter Sissie. He continues to occupy the property under an assured shorthold tenancy paying a full market rent. He is outside the reservation of benefit provisions.

(b) As in (a) above but Sissie and her family also occupy the property and Jake merely uses the converted loft space. If he now wishes to escape the GWR provisions by paying a full rent it is thought that this will be calculated by reference only to the loft space which he occupies (i.e. that he need not pay a rent for the whole property).

(c) Bill gave a 50 per cent share in his house to his brother Ben some years ago (for such "sharing arrangements", see **Ch.21**). Ben has now left and moved to Manila. Bill wishes to pay full consideration to avoid the GWR rules applying to the gifted half share, but what is full consideration for the use of Ben's 50 per cent share in the property? No guidance is given in the legislation but to be "on the safe side" 50 per cent of a rent for the whole would undoubtedly suffice.

2–09 The following points should be noted about the full consideration let-out.

(a) The consideration must be full throughout the occupation of the property by the donor. If at any stage less than full consideration is paid he will reserve a benefit. Hence normal commercial rent reviews should be incorporated into any tenancy agreement and should be observed.

(b) Whereas the POA legislation sets out in some detail the terms of the lease on which the "rental value" of the property is arrived at,[21] FA 1986 gives no guidance on how "full consideration" is to be determined. It must, however, involve a consideration of all the terms of any letting so that if the donor takes over responsibility for repairing, insuring the property, etc this will reduce the amount to be paid in rent. This flexibility is not available under the POA legislation.

(c) The full consideration let-out provides the basis for a widely used chattel scheme involving a gift and leaseback of the chattels. Its attraction is that the actual rent paid in such cases is relatively small.[22]

(d) Whilst full consideration will commonly involve the payment of rent the requirement may also be satisfied by the payment of a premium: for instance Jake in *Example 2.1* does not want the uncertainties of a series of assured shorthold tenancies with the risk in the future of substantial rent increases which he might not be able to afford. Accordingly he negotiates a lease for his life with Sissie for which he pays a commercial premium.[23]

(e) The POA charge does not apply where this let-out applies to the GWR rules.[24] Note that if the donor ceases to pay full consideration but continues

---

[21] Sch.15, paras 4(2) and 5(1).
[22] See further **Ch.20**.
[23] For the taxation of rent and any premium paid on the grant of a lease, see ITTOIA 2005, Pt 3. A lease for life granted for full consideration is not a settlement for IHT (and POAT) purposes: see IHTA 1984, s.43(3).
[24] Sch.15, para.11(3)(5(d).

to use or enjoy the property he thereby falls within the GWR legislation **but remains outside the POA charge.**[25]

The donor's spouse / civil partner

One point should be noted in passing concerning the scope of the provisions, **2–10** namely that there is nothing in s.102(1) which makes property which the donor's spouse or civil partner (but not the donor) is capable of enjoying or from which he or she benefits "property subject to a reservation" in relation to the donor.[2626] On the contrary, the legislation confers favourable treatment on some gifts to spouses and civil partners. This approach is also adopted for the purposes of the Regime but only in relation to outright gifts or where the interest in possession trust for the spouse holds land or chattels.[2727]

Example 2.2

Silas establishes a discretionary trust under which the beneficial class:

(a) includes Silas. He is therefore caught by the reservation of benefit rules and is outside the POA charge.[28] If Silas is not a named beneficiary but the trustee has power to add any person (including Silas) as a beneficiary it is thought that the position is the same although the contrary is arguable; or

(b) alternatively Silas is wholly excluded from benefit but his wife can benefit under the trust. Silas is not within the reservation of benefit rules nor the POA charge.

Ingram *and* Eversden

Two IHT cases—*Ingram* and *Eversden*—are particularly important for the **2–11** purposes of the Regime and it will be helpful to review them briefly.

---

[25] See further **7–39** for further discussion of what constitutes full consideration.

[26] A benefit to the donor's spouse is, however, relevant under FA 1986, Sch.20, para.7. Also, the fact that the donor's spouse has a right may have adverse implications for the donor under FA 1986, s.102A.

[27] See **5–05** and contrast **6–02**.

[28] See *IRC v Eversden* [2002] STC 1109 before Lightman J. where it was accepted by both parties that this was the case. The effect of settlor-interested trusts falling within the reservation of benefit rules is that the para.8 charge on settled intangible property will be inapplicable. Note that there is no reservation if (i) the settlor retains a life interest in his settlement or (ii) if he retains a remainder interest in circumstances where the "carve-out" principle applies.

2–12 Lady Ingram owned real property which she wished to give to her children and grandchildren subject to retaining the right to occupy the property during her life. To achieve this she transferred the property to her nominee. The next day, acting on her directions, he granted her a 20-year rent free lease and on the following day transferred the property, encumbered by the lease, to trustees who immediately executed declarations of trust whereby the property became held for the benefit of her children and grandchildren, to the exclusion of Lady Ingram.

Following her death, the Revenue issued a determination that, under the reservation of benefit rules, the property was deemed to be comprised in her estate immediately before she died. The House of Lords found unanimously for Lady Ingram's executors. The lease was valid, but even if it was not, the property given away was the encumbered reversion. Their Lordships stressed that it was important to identify precisely what property had been given away by the donor and what (if anything) he had retained. Continued enjoyment of the latter did not amount to a reservation in the former (arrangements of the type adopted in this case are known as "shearing" operations). Not long after the House of Lords' decision, anti-avoidance legislation, intended to nullify the effect of the decision in relation to land was introduced (now FA 1986, s.102A–C[30]).

THE *EVERSDEN* CASE[31]

2–13 In 1988 Mrs S settled the family home, which she then owned, upon trust to hold the same for herself as to five per cent absolutely and as to 95 per cent upon the trusts of a settlement under which her husband, Mr S, was the life tenant. After his death the trust fund was to be held upon discretionary trusts for a class of beneficiaries which included Mrs S.

During their joint lives Mr and Mrs S occupied the family home—Mr S under the terms of the settlement, and Mrs S by virtue of her retained interest as a tenant in common. After Mr S's death in 1992 Mrs S continued to occupy the family home. In 1993 the trustees sold the house and, out of the proceeds, including Mrs S's five per cent share, acquired a replacement property and an investment bond. Thereafter Mrs S had a five per cent interest in the replacement property and the bond. She died in 1998 having, in the interim, been in sole occupation of the replacement property, but having received no benefit from the bond.

The Revenue argued that the entirety of the replacement property (and the bond) should, under the reservation of benefit provisions, be included in her estate immediately before she died by reason of her enjoyment of it.

The Court of Appeal unanimously rejected the Revenue's appeal. The case was argued solely on the application of s.102(5) of the Finance Act 1986 which provided that a disposal of property which was a spouse exempt transfer was outside the scope of the reservation of benefit rules. The Revenue sought to restrict the size of gift to which the spouse exemption applied by arguing there

---

[29] [1995] STC 564: on appeal [1997] 4 All ER 395; [1997] STC 1234, CA; reversed [1999] STC 37 (HL) and see **14–02**.

[30] Discussed at **14–09**.

[31] *Essex (Executors) v IRC* [2002] STC (SCD) 30; affirmed sub nom. *IRC v Eversden (Greenstock's Executors)* [2002] STC 1109 *affirmed*; [2003] STC 822 (CA).

was a mismatch in the legislation between "gift" and "transfer of value". Although when Mrs S created the settlement she may have made a transfer of value to her husband of her 95 per cent interest, for the purpose of the reservation of benefit provisions she also made a series of gifts consisting of the equitable interests given to the various beneficiaries under the settlement and the exemption in s.102(5) was confined to the gift (of the life interest) which she made to her husband.

Carnwath L.J., with whom Brooke L.J. and Nelson J. agreed, rejected the Revenue's argument. *Ingram* was concerned solely with the nature of the interest retained by the donor and was decided in a different context. The same applied to the *Perpetual Trustee*[32] case. Neither was concerned with and neither addressed the position of successive interests forming part of a gift into a settlement. Carnwath L.J. held that it was not possible to introduce conceptual subtleties into s.102(5) without distorting the language.

Given s.49(1),[33] Mrs S had clearly made a transfer of value of the whole of the settled property to her husband and to him alone. Section 102(5) applied to that transfer, and so Mrs S did not reserve a benefit. There was nothing in s.102 to modify the effect of s.49(1). If this caused problems then he concluded that they were for Parliament to correct.[34]

ANTI-EVERSDEN LEGISLATION

The Revenue heeded Carnwath L.J.'s comments and the Finance Act 2003, s.185 **2–14** introduced ss.102(5A)–(5C) into FA 1986 in order to reverse the Court of Appeal's decision. These provisions had effect in relation to disposals made on or after June 20, 2003. *Eversden* schemes put in motion before then were thus unaffected by the new provisions.

Section 102(5A) provides that s.102(5)(a) (the spouse exemption) does not apply if or, as the case may be, to the extent that the four conditions are satisfied:

(a) the property becomes settled by virtue of the gift;

(b) by reason of the donor's spouse (who is referred to as "the relevant beneficiary") becoming beneficially entitled to an interest in possession in the settled property, the disposal is or, as the case may be, is to any extent within the spouse exemption because of s.49(1)[35];

(c) sometime after the disposal during the donor's lifetime the relevant beneficiary's interest in possession comes to an end; and

(d) on the occasion when the interest in possession comes to an end, the relevant beneficiary does not become entitled to the settled property or to another interest in possession in the settled property.

---

[32] *Comr for Stamp Duties for New South Wales v Perpetual Trustee Co Ltd* [1943] AC 425, PC.

[33] to the effect that a qualifying interest in possession beneficiary is treated as beneficially entitled to the settled property: see **2–03** above.

[34] For a fuller discussion see **Ch.16** and Appendix III–B.

[35] Note that this will not generally happen on or after March 22, 2006 as a result of the changes in the IHT treatment of settlements made by FA 2006: see **2.31** et seq.

For this purpose: (i) the disposal of an interest is treated as the termination of that interest; and (ii) references to any property or to an interest in any property include references to part of any property or interest.[36]

Section 102(5B) then provides that to the extent that s.102 applies by virtue of s.102(5A), s.102 has effect as if the disposal by way of gift had been made immediately after the relevant beneficiary's interest in possession came to an end.

These anti-avoidance provisions were thus targeted directly at *Eversden* schemes. Tax planners were not slow in responding and a number of schemes were put forward as "Eversden Mark II Schemes".

Application of reservation of benefit provisions generally

2–15 Whether the reservation of benefit provisions apply in a particular case is generally outside the scope of this book, but the application of the provisions in certain cases in connection with the Regime is discussed in various contexts. When the provisions do apply, they have two consequences.

Clawback on death: s.102(3)

2–16 Section 102(3) provides that if, immediately before the death of the donor, there is any property which in relation to him is property subject to a reservation then, to the extent that the property would not otherwise form part of the donor's estate at that time, that property shall be treated as property to which he is beneficially entitled.[37] This is important in two ways.

Property comprised in the donor's estate

2–17 First, the fact that s.102(3) does not operate with respect to property which **already** forms part of the deceased's estate immediately before he dies is hardly surprising because the reservation of benefit provisions are designed to prevent individuals from enjoying property which has ceased to form part of their estate. If the property is still part of his estate, there is no reason to apply the reservation of benefit provisions to it. A benefit can be reserved in excluded property but because it is excluded it will not be taxed as part of the individual's estate on death (see *Example 7.45*). Note, however, that just because property is deemed to be part of someone's estate on death under the reservation of benefit provisions this does not mean it is **actually** comprised in the deceased's estate: see **2–23** below for problems that can arise.

---

[36] FA 1986, s.102(5C).

[37] It follows that property subject to a reservation in relation to an individual does not form part of his estate until immediately before his death (assuming that the reservation is then continuing). This view is not affected by s.102(4): see below.

Secondly, s.102(3) is not itself a charging provision. It merely deems the deceased   **2–18**
to be beneficially entitled to the reserved benefit property in question immediately
before his death. The charge on death is then imposed on the property deemed to
be comprised in a person's estate, not only on property to which he is actually
beneficially entitled.[38][38] That rule, however, is subject to one important
qualification, namely that, immediately before a person's death his estate does
not include any excluded property. So, where the property which is subject to a
reservation is excluded property no charge will be imposed on a person's death
in respect of it, notwithstanding that under s.102(3) he was treated as beneficially
entitled to it immediately before he died. Whether or not property subject to a
reservation is excluded property can in some cases be a difficult question in
theory though, as matters stand, not in practice.[39]

The position in respect of non-settled property is straightforward. Assume X,   **2–19**
who is not domiciled in the UK for IHT purposes, dies having reserved a benefit
in respect of a house in Florida. As non-UK situs property the house treated as
owned by X is excluded property and no problems arise. Of course, if on his
death X had been domiciled or deemed domiciled in the United Kingdom when
he died the property would not have been excluded property.

Change the facts and assume that the house was owned by a settlement which
X had created when he was domiciled outside the UK. If he dies domiciled
abroad the position will be exactly as it was in the first example. But what if X
dies domiciled in the United Kingdom, e.g. under the IHT deemed domicile
rules?[40] In that case which rules apply for determining whether or not the house
is excluded property for the purposes of the reservation of benefit rules? If the
fact that the house is settled property is ignored, the house will be prevented by
X's deemed domicile from being excluded property. If, on the other hand, account
is taken of the fact that the house is settled property and the rules for determining
whether or not settled property is excluded property are applied, the house will
remain excluded property notwithstanding that X has become domiciled in the
UK.[41] It is believed that the latter approach is correct and no charge arises on
death. The point is discussed further in **Ch.24**.

Exemptions

The fact that s.102(3) operates to claw back property into the deceased's estate   **2–20**
does not necessarily mean that such property will be subject to IHT on the
deceased's death.[42] Such a result will be avoided if the property qualifies for a
relief such as business property relief. See **2–22** below.

---

[38] IHTA 1984, s.4.

[39] Excluded property is defined in IHTA 1984, s.6 and, in the context of settlements and interests
in settled property, see IHTA 1984, s.48(1) and (3).

[40] See IHTA 1984, s.267.

[41] IHTA 1984, s.267 provides that non UK situs property comprised in a settlement is excluded
property provided that the settlor was non-UK domiciled when he made the settlement.

[42] It may, for instance, fall within his IHT nil rate band.

Lifetime cessation of reservation: s.102(4)

2–21 Section 102(4) provides that if, at any time before the end of the "relevant period"[43] any property ceases to be property subject to a reservation, the donor is treated as having at that time made a disposition of the property by a disposition which is a PET.[44]

> ### Example 2.3
>
> Silus sets up a discretionary trust under which he can benefit. Accordingly he reserves a benefit in the trust property. Subsequently the trustees exclude him from all benefit so that the reservation of benefit cases. Silus accordingly makes a deemed PET under s.102(4).

Business relief and agricultural relief

2–22 In certain cases the rules governing the availability of business property relief and agricultural property relief are relaxed so that property which is subject to a reservation may qualify for relief on the basis that a notional transfer by the donee can include the donor's ownership and occupation periods in determining whether relief is due.[45]

A possible misunderstanding

2–23 The reservation of benefit rules sometimes give rise to a misunderstanding, the view being mistakenly taken that where an individual reserves a benefit he is (for IHT purposes) treated as though he had never given the property away. This is incorrect. The rules operate by clawing the property back into his estate immediately before he died, or by providing for a notional PET if he ceases to reserve a benefit, but they do not operate by deeming the property never to have left his estate.

It accordingly follows that:

(a) as a matter of general law the property is comprised in the estate of the donee so that IHT will be payable on the donee's death and there is no relief for any IHT that may also be paid on the donor's death;

(b) there is no CGT uplift on the death of the donor even though the reservation of benefit rules result in an IHT charge on the property.[46]

(c) it is the donee who is primarily liable to pay any IHT owing on the reservation property resulting from the death of the donor[47];

---

[43] "The relevant period" means a period ending on the date of the donor's death and beginning seven years before that date or, if it is later, on the date of the gift: FA 1986, s.102(1).

[44] Note that the property is **not** treated as forming part of the taxpayer's estate. For HMRC's view on the inter-relationship between s.102(4) and excluded property.

[45] FA 1986, Sch.20, para.8.

[46] See Taxation of Chargeable Gains Act 1992, s.62 for the CGT rules on death.

[47] IHTA 1984, s.200(1)(c); 204(9); 211(3) and see **Ch.11** and **13–15**.

(d) the property is not treated as forming part of the donor's estate for IHT purposes while he is alive;

(e) because property subject to a reservation is in the ownership of the donee it will not qualify for e.g. the spouse exemption on the donor's death because it will not then become comprised in that spouse's estate.[48]

AVOIDING THE RESERVATION OF BENEFIT RULES

Inevitably taxpayers will seek to reduce their estates for IHT purposes by making PETs of property whilst at the same time wishing to retain benefits (e.g. use or income) from the property gifted. In some cases the taxpayer may be content simply to know that he will be able to obtain benefits from the gifted property if the need arises.   **2–24**

It is a testimony to the success of such arrangements that the Government felt it necessary to introduce the pre-owned assets charge. What therefore were the arrangements entered into by tax payers which have led to this new tax?

The Home Loan (Double Trust) Scheme: which was probably the single most common arrangement affected by the POA legislation.[49]   **2–25**

The use of cash gifts: an apparent weakness in the reservation of benefit legislation is that whilst there are tracing provisions which may apply if the original property given is switched into a new property, these rules do not apply to an outright gift of cash. Hence if Albert were to give his son Sidney £400,000 which Sidney uses to purchase a house for occupation by Albert it is not considered that there is any reservation of benefit in the house.[50] Not surprisingly, the Regime therefore includes detailed provisions to catch cash contributions. They will still escape inheritance tax but instead suffer the POA charge.   **2–26**

Reversionary lease arrangements: these are considered in **Ch.15**. It is widely thought that they are not caught by the anti-*Ingram* legislation provided that **either** the property had been owned more than seven years before the arrangement was entered into **or** that it had been purchased for full consideration at any time.[51]   **2–27**

Chattel schemes: these avoided the reservation rules either by a shearing arrangement or by satisfying the full consideration exemption. They are considered in **Ch.20**.   **2–28**

---

[48] For the spouse exemption, see IHTA 1984, s.18. For HMRC's views, see IHTM 14303:
". . . the GWR rules are fictitious treatments created only for the purposes of preventing IHT avoidance. They do not affect the actual devolution of the property in real life so the gift property does not actually pass on death under the will or intestacy." For a consideration of whether the spouse exemption could apply in the context of a home loan scheme where the election has been made, see **17–62** and A2.90.

[49] HMRC have attacked some of these arrangements on the basis that they fall within the reservation of benefit net. As with reversionary leases (discussed below) this raises difficult compliance issues for taxpayers. See **Ch.17**.

[50] See **Chs.21** and **23**.

[51] HMRC's view on reversionary lease arrangements changed. Originally the view was taken that arrangements entered into on or after March 9, 1999 were caught by the anti-*Ingram* legislation and so were not within POAT. Subsequently, however, it was accepted that when the property had been owned for at least seven years GWR did not apply but POAT could. This depressing saga is considered in **Ch.15** and see A2.57.

2–29 ***Ingram* land schemes:** these have been caught by the reservation of benefit legislation since 1999 but pre–1999 arrangements are a target of the Regime.[52]

2–30 ***Eversden* schemes:** similar motivation. New schemes are within the 2003 legislation but "revenge" on past schemes has an attraction.[53]

QUALIFYING AND NON-QUALIFYING INTERESTS IN POSSESSION

2–31 The definition of a "qualifying interest in possession" is important both for IHT and POA purposes. In the case of IHT, the beneficiary entitled to the income of a trust (usually the life tenant) is treated as owning that portion of the capital of the trust fund:

> "a person beneficially entitled to an interest in possession in settled property shall be treated for the purposes of the Act as beneficially entitled to the property in which the interest subsists."[54]

This rule is a fiction because in no real sense is the interest in possession beneficiary the owner of the capital in the fund. For IHT purposes, however, the capital forms part of his estate, so that on a chargeable occasion inheritance tax is charged on the trust fund at his rates. The settlement itself is not a separate taxable entity (contrast the rules for relevant property trusts), although primary liability for any tax falls upon the trustees.[55]

2–32 For POA purposes a person with a qualifying interest in possession is entitled to certain protections contained in para.11(1) and discussed in **Ch.17**.

Position after March 2006

2–33 However, not all interests in possession are "qualifying". As a result of changes effected by FA 2006, *inter vivos* interest in possession settlements set up after March 21, 2006 will only be qualifying if the interest is a disabled person's interest within IHTA 1984, s.89B. A non-qualifying interest in possession settlement is taxed in accordance with the relevant property regime and the fictional entitlement posited by s.49(1) does not apply.[56]

It remains possible to set up a qualifying interest in possession trust by will (this is an "IPDI")[57] and the definition of a qualifying interest in possession extends to an interest in possession to which an individual was entitled on March 22, 2006 and (in limited circumstances) to a successive interest in possession in that settlement (a "transitional serial interest").[58]

2–34 The 2006 change in the IHT treatment of settlements was achieved by:

> (i) the amendment of the definition of a qualifying interest in possession in IHTA 1984, s.59 (see new s.59(1)) and note that the relevant property

---

[52] See **Ch.14**.
[53] See **Ch.15**.
[54] IHTA 1984, s.49(1).
[55] IHTA 1984, s.201.
[56] i.e. under IHTA 1984, Pt III Ch. III: see s.59(2) as amended by FA 2006, Sch.20, para.20.
[57] "Immediate Post Death Interest": see IHTA 1984, s.49A inserted by FA 2006, Sch.20, para.5.
[58] IHTA 1984, s.49B–E inserted by FA 2006, Sch.20, para.5.

charge now applies to "certain settlements in which interests in possession ('iip') subsist";

(ii) the amendment of s.49(1) to exclude iips arising after March 21, 2006 with only three exceptions (this section provides for the iip beneficiary to be treated as beneficially entitled to the property in which the interest subsists);

(iii) the amendment of s.5 (definition of estate) to exclude the value of an interest in possession ;

(iv) the amendment of the PET definition in s.3A: the old definition continues to apply to transfers of value made before March 22, 2006. The new definition—effective for transfers on and after that date—is in s.3A(1A). This preserves the status of the transfer which arises on the ending of a qualifying interest in possession provided that either the settlement then ends or the property becomes held (1) on bereaved minor trusts or (2) on interest in possession trusts which qualify as transitional serial interests or (3) on a disabled person's trust.

The main impact of the change is in the tax treatment on the creation of settlements **2–35** inter vivos since, unless the trust is one for a disabled person, the settlor will make an immediately chargeable transfer for IHT purposes. The practical consequences are:

(i) that PETS are now generally limited to outright gifts. Settled gifts involve an immediately chargeable transfer;

(ii) lifetime trusts are likely in the future to be limited to:

- gifts up to the amount of the settlor's available IHT nil rate band (£325,000 for 2009–10). Bear in mind that both spouses (including civil partners) can establish nil rate band trusts and that gifts inter se (e.g. to enable both to set up such trusts) are spouse exempt[59];

- gifts into trust of property attracting 100 per cent relief (or of excluded property) so that no IHT is payable on the creation of the trust[60];

- a gift into a bare trust (not a settlement for IHT purposes) which will still takes effect as a PET.

Example 2.4

(1) Under the Toulouse trust, which was set up in 1999 by Monsieur X, he is entitled to an interest in possession. On his death his son, Francois, takes an interest in possession with remainder over to a chocolate charity. X has a qualifying interest in possession and no POA charge arises because of the protection in para.11(1). IHT is payable on his death if he is still entitled to the iip. If his interest ends before October 6, 2008 Francois will, in turn, become entitled to a qualifying interest in possession (a TSI) and X will make a PET. If, however, X's interest ends in 2009, Francois' interest will not be qualifying, X will make a

---

[59] IHTA 1984, s.18.
[60] See IHTA 1984, Pt V, Chs I and II.

chargeable transfer and the trust will henceforth be taxed as a relevant property settlement. If X's iip ends during his lifetime the POA treatment will depend on whether X continues to benefit from the trust property and if so in what circumstances. For example, if X's iip ends, the trust holds only a house but if the house is not occupied by X then no POA charge arises. If on termination of X's IIP, the trust holds intangibles and X remains a potential beneficiary then POA may still be avoided *if* X's interest constitutes a reservation of benefit.

(2) Facts as above except that Monsieur X settles the property into an iip trust for himself in 2007. This is not a qualifying iip and so X makes an immediately chargeable transfer and the trust will suffer 10 yearly and exit charges. Depending on the terms of the trust, X may not reserve a benefit (e.g. if he is only entitled to the income and has no access to the capital it is likely to be regarded as a carve-out). In these circumstances none of the protections in para.11 apply. There is no IHT charge on X's death, but POA is due if the trust holds intangibles.

(3) Mindful of the attentions of his creditors, Nasty put his assets into a life interest trust for his wife in 2007. Mrs Nasty does not enjoy a qualifying interest in possession because the trust was set up after March 21, 2006 and Mrs Nasty is not disabled. The trust is taxed as a relevant property settlement. There is no tax on Mrs Nasty's death because she is not deemed to own the assets. For POA purposes, if Nasty is a discretionary beneficiary of the trust then he reserves a benefit, IHT is due on his death and the protections in para.11(5) apply. If he is merely a default beneficiary and does not reserve a benefit (because his interest is carved-out) then POA could apply if the trust holds intangibles, but not if it holds land or chattels. In the latter cases the protection in para.10(1)(c) applies, even though Mrs Nasty does not take a qualifying interest in possession.

PART II: HOW THE LEGISLATION WORKS

This part considers in detail the Pre-Owned Assets legislation in FA 2004, Sch.15. In this Part references to paras are to the provisions of Sch.15. There are three distinct charging regimes as follows:

- land (para.3);
- chattels (para.6); and
- intangible property held in a settlor interested trust (para.8).

In addition, certain transactions are excluded from the charge on land and chattels (these are considered in **Ch.5**) and there are a number of blanket exemptions from the charge (see **Ch.7**). The income tax charge may also be avoided if an election is made under paras 21 or 22 to subject the property to the reservation of benefit rules—in effect to bring it back into the IHT net—and this is considered in **Ch.11**.

CHAPTER 3

THE PARAGRAPH 3 CHARGE ON LAND

WHEN THE CHARGE APPLIES

Paragraph 3 applies when two conditions are satisfied. The first condition is that **3–01**
in any year of assessment, an individual occupies any land, whether alone or
together with other persons. The second is that either the individual disposes of
an interest in the land—"the disposal condition" **or** (broadly) he provides
consideration for the acquisition of an interest in the land by another—"the
contribution condition". Each of these conditions is discussed in turn.

Occupation

The first condition requires **occupation of the land**. "Occupation" is not defined **3–02**
and HMRC have set out—in some detail—their view of how it is to be interpreted:
see, in particular A2.43 and A2.71 in the guidance notes and in an exchange of
correspondence with CIOT/STEP. In practice this is one of the thorniest areas in
this problematic tax! The dictionary meaning for the word includes "to fill up";
"to take or maintain possession"; "to reside in or use as owner or tenant".[1] There
are a number of rating cases on occupation and more recently a VAT case.[2] The
authors consider that occupation requires the taxpayer to use or be physically
present in the property for at least part of the year. On this basis:

(a) more than one property may be occupied (e.g. a main residence and second
home);

(b) a property may be occupied by a person if his possessions are stored there
although only, it is thought, if such storage amounted to the **exclusive** use
(i.e. so that he had the right to use that part of the property as he chose) so

---

[1] See Longmans Dictionary of the English Language. "Occupation" is also relevant in the context
of the main residence relief for CGT purposes (see TCGA 1992 s.222) and in the area of landlord and
tenant law. HMRC consider that "in this context (i.e. for POA purposes) "occupation" is construed
quite widely". Given that there is nothing unique about the POA use of the word (save that it is the
basis for the para.3 charge!) presumably such a wide construction should apply for *e.g.* s.102B(4)
sharing arrangements (when occupation by the donee prevents a possible charge under the reservation
of benefit rules).

[2] See, for example, *RCC v Principal and Fellows of Newnham College* [2008] STC 1225 where
the meaning of occupation in the context of a VAT leaseback scheme was considered by the House of
Lords.

that no one else was in occupation (for instance if I leave a suitcase or my books at Aunt Dorothy's flat I can hardly be said to occupy the flat); and

(c) a right to occupy (for instance under an *Ingram* lease) or the power to occupy: e.g. by possessing a key which is not exercised probably does not amount to occupation.

An important point following from "occupation" requiring physical use of the property is that a person receiving or entitled to receive rents from a property is not in occupation.

3–03   It is thought that a common-sense approach must be applied.

Example 3.1

(1) X has a key to her elderly mother's flat "for emergencies". From time to time X visits to check that her mother is okay. X does not occupy the property.

(2) On Y's divorce, his father agrees to store his possessions. Y is not in occupation of his father's property.[3]

(3) Z lives in America but he has a key to his mother's house in the UK where many of his possessions are kept and where he grew up. He comes to the UK for a few weeks each year when he uses the property as his base. Z is arguably in occupation for POA purposes, especially if he has free access to visit when he wishes. But contrast the position if Z merely visits his mother—perhaps staying for a few days—when in the UK as her guest. In this situation Z is not considered to be in occupation of the property.

(4) Q receives rent from property. He is not in occupation.

The *Newnham* case shows that mere physical presence may not by itself be sufficient for the purposes of VATA 1994 Sch.10, para.3(A)(7). There must be some right to occupy even if not an exclusive right or a right to occupy the whole.[4] However, for IHT purposes de facto occupation—without any enforceable right—can constitute a reservation of benefit and the authors consider that this suffices for POA purposes although the contrary is arguable. The *Newnham* case was concerned with the particular wording and background to the relevant VAT legislation with the House of Lords deciding that, for these purposes, mere physical presence was not occupation.

3–04   It does not matter on what basis the individual occupies the land. For instance it may be mere de facto occupation; or under a gratuitous licence; or under a rack rent lease. All that is relevant in relation to this threshold test is the fact of occupation.[5] HMRC accept that:

> "if the person's occupation or use of the property is only very limited in its nature or duration it may not come within the provisions of para.3".

---

[3]   Contrast A2.43 where HMRC comment that "the chargeable person would be regarded as in occupation…if they used (the relevant property) for storage". This is, without more, not thought to be correct.

[4]   HMRC Business Brief 33/09 in the light of the Newnham decision confirms this: see [2009] SWTI 1882.

[5]   In *Ingram* arrangements (14–02) occupation is by virtue of a retained lease which limits the property disposed of by the taxpayer and so affects the DV/V calculation: see **14–14**.

In effect therefore they have introduced a de minimis exclusion along the lines of the provision in the reservation of benefit legislation.[6]

Here are a couple of examples of difficult issues that may arise.

(a) Gerontius, an infirm donor, in principle caught by the Regime, has the right to occupy the whole but only occupies a very small part of the house, never venturing into more than (say) three rooms. In these circumstances, will he be taxed on only a proportion of the appropriate rental value?

(b) The disposal was of (say) Gruesome Grange and the Lodge but the occupation was merely of the Lodge and did not affect the main house.

HMRC comment as follows:

"in a case where a former owner of property was residing in part of it and had possession of the means of access to the rest of it **and used it from time to time** . . . we would regard him as occupying the whole property for the purpose of para.3 . . . on the other hand where a former owner of property occupies a self contained part of it and has no access to the remainder which is occupied by others it would seem reasonable to regard the "relevant land" . . . as being confined to the self-contained part." (emphasis supplied).[7]

Applying this guidance to the two problems noted above leads to the following conclusions:

(a) Gerontius will be within para.3 in relation to the part actually occupied but given that he never ventures into the rest of the building—although possessing the means of access—it is thought the POA charge will not extend to those other parts;

(b) so far as Gruesome Grange is concerned the POA charge is limited to the Lodge occupied. Incidentally it should not matter whether there is actual occupation of the main house by another: the key point is that the Lodge is separate and the donor does not **in fact** occupy the big house.

Notice also that the legislation refers to the occupation of relevant land whether **3–05** alone or with other persons. Even if the occupation is non exclusive there is no express reduction in the rental value and benefit taxed.[8]

There are also problems in reaching the correct valuation in the event that the disposal is by more than one owner (e.g. by husband and wife) of the land, which could cause problems under self-assessment. These are discussed in **Ch.13**.

---

[6] The same guidance is used: see A2.43 and RI 55 (*Tax Bulletin*, November 1993). In the context of the reservation of benefit legislation a donor's gift may be subject to a reservation if the property in question "is not enjoyed to the entire exclusion **or virtually to the entire exclusion** of the donor" (FA 1986, s.102(1)(b)). Limited benefits are therefore permitted to the donor. In the POA legislation the introduction (as a matter of practice) of this de minimis exclusion is in addition to the annual exemption of £5,000 which may exclude from charge benefits exceeding the de minimis threshold.

[7] See A2.71–A.2.

[8] See, however, **20** et seq. for a further discussion of how the chargeable amount on which the taxpayer pays income tax is reached. Of course if it is accepted that occupation is of part only the property there may be difficulties in determining what rent that part would command.

Example 3.2

(a) Generous gave his daughter £300,000 in 2000 which she used to purchase a flat overlooking the Thames at Brentford lock. Consider the following alternative possibilities:

    (i) Generous could use the property at any time: in fact he occupies it for the "season" (June–September) each year. The POA charge applies and he is treated as in occupation for the entire tax year for the purpose of calculating that charge; or

    (ii) Generous pays occasional visits to the flat: e.g. for babysitting, when he often stays overnight. HMRC consider this not to be caught by POA: his occupation is de minimis (see guidance notes, para.4.6 at A2.43).

(b) If, instead, the money was used by the daughter to buy a holiday home in the Algarve, actually used on an occasional basis by both Generous and his daughter, but available for their use throughout the year, then the POA charge applies with Generous being treated as occupying for the entire year. Contrast the position if the property was commercially let for six months of the year: now the charge would be limited to the remaining six months.[9]

3–06 As already noted, a POA charge will not arise merely because the taxpayer is in occupation of land. It is also necessary for either the disposal or the contribution condition to be satisfied. These conditions are discussed below. Although it is only necessary for the taxpayer to satisfy either one of the disposal or contribution conditions, in some cases there is an overlap between the two and both conditions are satisfied. It will be important to know which condition is satisfied because the exclusions in para.10 (excluding the taxpayer from a POA charge) are not the same in relation to the disposal and contribution conditions.

The disposal condition

3–07 The "disposal condition"[10] is that:

(a) at any time after March 17, 1986 the individual owned an interest:

    (i) in the land; **or**

    (ii) in other property the proceeds of the disposal of which were directly or indirectly applied by another person towards the acquisition of an interest in the land; **and**

(b) the individual has disposed of all, or part of, his interest in the relevant land or the other property, otherwise than by an excluded transaction.

---

[9] If Generous had purchased the property jointly with his daughter (e.g. they each put in £100,000 with the daughter's share being money provided by Generous) then there would be no POA charge on Generous as a result of the exemption for sharing arrangements: see Sch.15, para.11(8) and **Ch.21–14**.

[10] See Sch.15, paras 3(2)(a) and (b).

Paragraphs 3(2)(a)(i) and (b) cover direct acquisitions, i.e. cases where X previously owned and disposed[11] of the land which he now occupies. Paragraphs 3(2)(a)(ii) and (b), on the other hand, cover representative acquisitions, i.e. cases where the land in question was acquired by someone other than X using the proceeds from the disposal (by whatever person) of property previously owned by X. So, if X gives Y Blackacre and Y sells Blackacre and buys Whiteacre, the disposal condition in paras (a)(ii) and (b) is satisfied.[12] It does not seem that the property previously owned, which is disposed of, has to be land: it could, for instance, be shares. Accordingly, if X gives shares to Y and Y sells the shares to buy Whiteacre, the disposal condition is satisfied. However, if X gives cash to Y and Y uses the cash to buy Whiteacre it is the contribution, not the disposal condition, that is satisfied.

The references to "proceeds of the disposal" suggest that an exchange of **3–08** property (e.g. swapping Redacre for Blackacre) is not caught by the disposal condition. This would cover, for example, X giving Redacre to Y, Y then exchanging Redacre for Blackacre with a third party and Blackacre then being occupied by X. It is thought that in the absence of a sale there are no "proceeds" to be directly or indirectly applied.

Note that the disposal condition embraces sales and gifts of the whole or part of the land. It also covers sales of part or whole at an undervalue. This is discussed later in the context of calculating the POA charge. However, although a sale of the whole land for full consideration will satisfy the disposal condition, it will nevertheless be outside the POA charge if the exclusion in para.10(1) is satisfied.

New interests

For these purposes, a disposition which creates a new interest in land out of an **3–09** existing interest in land is to be taken to be a disposal of part of the existing interest.[13] The draftsman has introduced the term "disposition" for this purpose, in contradistinction to "disposal", but it is difficult to see to what effect. In particular, the extended IHT definition of "disposition"[14] does not apply.

The contribution condition

The second condition, the "contribution condition",[15] is that at any time after **3–10** March 17, 1986 the individual has directly or indirectly provided, otherwise than by an excluded transaction, any of the consideration given by another person for the acquisition of:

(a) an interest in the land; **or**

---

[11] Otherwise than by an excluded transaction.

[12] Note that the HMRC guidance notes have been amended to confirm that if a donor sells Blackacre and gives the cash to donee and donee buys Whiteacre in which donor lives, the donor has satisfied the contribution, not the disposal condition. The disponor satisfies the disposal condition only if he disposes of an interest in land or property other than cash: whether the land is the land actually occupied or the disposal is of other property which is then sold and replaced by the property occupied by the disponer: see A2.04 as amended.

[13] Sch.15, para.3(4).

[14] IHTA 1984, s.272.

[15] Set out in Sch.15, para.3(3).

(b) an interest in any other property the proceeds of the disposal of which were directly or indirectly applied by another person towards the acquisition of an interest in the land.[16]

Limb (a) of this condition is presumably intended to cover directly funded acquisitions, and involves cash gifts, i.e. where X provides Y with the funds to acquire Blackacre. Limb (b) covers indirectly funded acquisitions, i.e. where X provides Y with the funds to acquire Blackacre, which Y acquires and subsequently sells, using the proceeds of sale to acquire Whiteacre which X then occupies. However, the words "directly or indirectly provided" apply to both limbs and it is hard to see why if X gives Y cash to buy Blackacre which Y then sells and uses the proceeds to buy Whiteacre this is not also within (a) as indirect provision. Note that it is not necessary for X to have the intention of occupying Whiteacre when he gave the cash to Y. X can make an unfettered gift to Y and still be caught by the contribution condition if later Y buys a house that is occupied by X.

Scope of the contribution condition

3–11 The contribution condition is not limited to cash contributions, but extends to the situation when A gave Blackacre to B which he exchanged for Whiteacre (then occupied by A). As noted above, it is difficult to see how such an exchange falls within the representative acquisition limb of the disposal condition so that unless within the contribution condition an exchange would fall outside the POA net. In determining the scope of the contribution condition, note also the following:

(a) The legislation does not refer to "cash" consideration but to **the provision of any of the consideration** given by another person for the acquisition of an interest in the relevant land. It is thought:

(i) that for consideration to be provided there must be an element of bounty on the part of the provider **but**

(ii) it can encompass any form of property.

CIR v Leiner[117] (an income tax case) confirms that the term "provided" requires an element of bounty.

(b) Para.10 distinguishes between excluded transactions which apply to the disposal condition and those applicable to the contribution condition.[18] In para.10(2)(c) "an outright gift of money (in sterling or other currency)" is in the circumstances there prescribed an excluded transaction for the contribution condition. Were the contribution condition limited to cash contributions the express limitations of this provision would be unnecessary. The other excluded transactions in para.10(2) merely refer to "consideration".

(c) If the contribution condition may be satisfied by gifts other than cash there is an overlap with the disposal condition. Taking the example considered

---

[16] Outright cash gifts made before April 6, 1998 are ignored as a result of the wording of para.10(2)(c). See **5–24** and A2.70.

[17] 41 TC 589.

[18] See **Ch.7**.

above, if X gives Y Blackacre and Y sells Blackacre and buys Whiteacre (which he occupies) then it would appear that:

(i) X satisfies the disposal condition (there is a representative acquisition: see para.**3–05** above);

(ii) he satisfies the contribution condition since Blackacre is consideration for the acquisition of Whiteacre.[19]

Loans

The position of loans has been subject to considerable debate. Initially HMRC   **3–12** considered that any loan could amount to the provision of consideration for POA purposes. However, the amended guidance notes now state:

> "HMRC do not regard the contribution condition...as being met where a lender resides in a property purchased by another with money loaned to him by the lender. Our view is that since the outstanding debt will be part of his estate for IHT purposes it would not be reasonable to consider that the loan falls within the contribution condition."[20]

Perhaps a more technical justification is that a loan cannot constitute "provision" because it has to be repaid: there is no element of bounty. Even if the loan from lender (X) is interest free there is no provision of consideration by X for the acquisition of the property by Y. Y has provided consideration by his promise to repay X. The interest foregone by X does not enable Y to buy the property. Hence where property prices are likely to increase, a father may consider it worthwhile to lend funds to his son to enable the son to purchase a property for father to occupy. There would, of course, be little security for the father in these circumstances and no principal private residence relief would be available on a subsequent sale, but the increased value of the property would fall outside the father's estate for IHT purposes and the father would not pay a POA charge.

Note that the question of whether loans constitute consideration is a different issue from the question of whether a loan to a company that then buys a house can be regarded as "derived property" for the purposes of the para.11(1) exemption. This is discussed further at **7–20**.

Tracing

Some of the problems raised by the disposal and contribution conditions have   **3–13** been reflected in the more recent legislation found at FA 2008, Sch.7, in relation to remittances and foreign domiciliaries. In both cases it is not always clear how far to take the tracing of cash and sale proceeds. For example, if A gives cash to B who then gives it to C who buys a house for A to occupy, one might say that A

---

[19] This overlap may present problems if e.g. the conditions of para.10(1)(a) are satisfied in respect of the disposal of Blackacre (i.e. it was an excluded transaction) and so the disposal condition is not met. There is of course no equivalent excluded transaction in respect of the contribution condition, although it may be that there has been no provision of consideration by X if the original disposal of Blackacre was on arm's length terms.

[20] See A2.05.

satisfied the contribution condition and POAT was due if this was all in contemplation at the time of the original gift, i.e. the two steps formed part of a single arrangement. But if A gives cash to B who gives cash or other property to C and these are separate gifts not conditional on each other or in contemplation at the time, the authors' view is that the POA charge does not apply because there is not sufficient direct or indirect "provision": see **3–33**.[21]

Difficult problems arise in relation to trusts. For example, a settlor (A) may be non-UK resident and give cash to a trust. The cash is used to buy shares. Many years later[22] the trustees sell the shares and subscribe cash for shares in a wholly owned company which then buys a house for A to live in after he has become UK resident. Does this satisfy the contribution condition? The authors consider it does. There is indirect provision, albeit not by the trustees.[23]

Second-hand companies

3–14 Second-hand companies have become a way of circumventing the POA charge both for houses and chattels. Assume that company Holdco owns a house. Holdco has been owned for many years by a third party. X gives cash to Y (or a trust) who then purchases all the shares of Holdco from the third party. X occupies the property. In these circumstances the disposal condition is not satisfied (there has been no disposal of an interest in land); the contribution condition is not satisfied because X has provided no consideration for the acquisition of an interest in land but only for the acquisition of company shares. The company shares are not subject to the POA charge provided they are not held in a trust (otherwise the para.8 charge may apply).

Similar options can be considered for the foreign domiciliary who needs to use relevant foreign income to purchase a house in the UK and wants to avoid a taxable remittance. The purchase of shares of an offshore company where the company already owns the house may avoid a taxable remittance under s.809L. However, the other disadvantages of owning property through a holding company must always be considered. For example, there is no principal private residence relief; and there is the risk of a shadow director charge.

The interaction of the disposal and contribution conditions

3–15 As will be seen below,[24] the legislation provides for five excluded transactions in relation to the contribution condition, and five excluded transactions in relation to the disposal condition. Four of the excluded transactions which apply to the contribution condition also apply to the disposal condition, but there is one excluded transaction which is only applicable to the contribution condition and one excluded transaction which is only applicable to the disposal condition. It may therefore be important to know which of the two conditions is relevant. The

---

[21] Similar problems arise in relation to the question of whether a remittance has occurred if, for example, A gives income to his adult son B who then settles it into a trust for A and the trustees remit the funds to the UK. Contrast the tracing rules in FA 1986 Sch.20, para.2 and para.5.

[22] The 7-year exclusion in para.10 arguably does not apply to cash gifts into trust: see **5–23**.

[23] See also **3–29**.

[24] See **Ch.5**.

question is most likely to arise in cases where the owner of the land acquired it from someone other than the person who occupies it.

Example 3.3

(a) Reg sells his house—"Inglenooks"—to his son Sid for its market value of £450,000. If Reg continues to occupy Inglenooks then:

    (i) as he has not made a gift, the reservation of benefit rules are inapplicable;

    (ii) if the sale falls within para.10(1) as "a transaction such as might be expected to be made at arm's length between persons not connected with each other" the POA charge is also inapplicable.[25]

(b) If in the future Sid sells the house and with the proceeds purchases "Gory Grange" which Reg occupies, then whilst the reservation of benefit position is unaltered, what of the POA charge? Again no change since the disposal condition is not met (the sale of Inglenooks was an excluded transaction so that there is no question of the representative acquisition limb being satisfied). Reg did not give or "provide" Sid with the cash or other property to buy the house so that neither is the contribution condition met.

(c) Assume that Jason falls within the disposal condition in respect of "Fairwinds", the house which he occupies in Cheshire. Assume, however, that this house is replaced by the donee with "Tradewinds". Jason's POA position is as follows:

    (i) if Fairwinds is sold and the proceeds used to purchase Tradewinds he falls within the representative acquisition limb of the disposal condition: see **3–07**;

    (ii) if the properties are exchanged it is thought that he is now outside the disposal but not the contribution condition, so that the POA charge applies.

(d) George lends his son £500,000 to buy "Farthings". He charges no interest and takes security for the loan over the property. George has not "provided" consideration used for the purchase of the property since no element of bounty is involved.[26] Were George to occupy Farthings therefore it is not thought that the POA charge will apply.

(e) By contrast with George, Gilbert is a generous father. His son borrows £500,000 from the bank to acquire "Nutley" and George pays off that debt as a Christmas present. If he occupies Nutley it may be said that he has indirectly provided consideration for its purchase even if when the son took out the loan it had not been agreed that Gilbert would pay it off. More difficult is the situation where rather than paying off the debt Gilbert pays the interest each month. It is difficult to see that he has provided any of the consideration used for the purchase of the property— even indirectly—if he is merely servicing the debt. If Gilbert had paid

[25] Para.10(1) is considered below.
[26] See *IRC v Plummer* [1979] 3 All E.R. 775 and **3–12**.

the interest on the loan from the start it might be said that consideration had been "provided" on bounteous terms, but as noted at **3–07**, in the authors' view paying interest on a loan is not provision of the consideration used to acquire an interest in land, because it is the loan not the interest which results in the acquisition.

(f) Astute buys Bridge Farm, a rundown farmhouse in Northumberland, for £75,000. His father gives him £250,000 which is used to effect massive improvements and repairs to the property. If the father then occupies Bridge Farm he is not within the POA charge since he has not provided monies for "**the acquisition of**" the property, only for its improvement. Similarly if Astute uses his own cash to buy the land and main house, and his father pays for the building of a second property on the land which he then occupies, it is not thought that there is a POA charge.

(g) Judy gives her daughter Debbie £100 which she uses to buy premium bonds. Debbie wins the jackpot and with the winnings buys, inter alia, a large property overlooking the Mersey at Birkenhead. If Judy occupies this property then even if it is the case that she provided the monies used for its purchase the POA charge will not apply, assuming that the £100 gift falls within either the IHT annual £3,000 exemption or the £250 gifts exemption (see Sch.15, para.10(2)(e)).

Guarantees

3–16 It should be noted that where a person (A) acts as a guarantor in respect of a loan made to another person (B) by a third party in connection with B's acquisition of any property, the mere giving of the guarantee is not regarded as the provision by A of consideration for B's acquisition of the property.[27] This prevents the guarantor of a loan from being treated as providing any of the funds lent. Even if the guarantee was called on later it is not clear that the guarantor would at that time be treated as providing consideration for the acquisition of property if this was not in contemplation at the time of the acquisition.

THE CHARGE[28]

3–17 Where para.3 applies to the individual in respect of the whole or any part of a year of assessment, an amount equal to "the chargeable amount" is treated as his income and is chargeable to income tax. If the land is only occupied for part of a tax year (e.g. 3 months) and the taxpayer has no right to occupy for longer periods, only a portion of rental value for the year is taxed (and of course, this amount may be exempt under the de minimis provisions considered in **Ch.9**. The annual exemption of £5,000 is not pro rated but applies for the whole year or any part when the taxpayer is subject to the POA charge).

[27] Sch.15, para.17.
[28] paras 4 and 5, Sch.15.

Definitions

There are seven definitions that have to be considered before one can determine **3–18** the taxable benefit on which the individual will pay income tax! These are set out in para.4 and are:

1. the chargeable amount: being the appropriate rental value less certain payments made;

2. the appropriate rental value: being R x DV/V;

3. the rental value (R) being the rent which would have been payable if the property had been let at an annual rent equal to the annual value;

4. the valuation date;

5. DV being the value at the valuation date of the interest disposed of;

6. V being the market value of the relevant land at the valuation date; and

7. annual value: being broadly the rent that would be obtained from a standard residential letting of the entire land.

Each of these will be considered in turn.

The chargeable amount

For any taxable period—i.e. any year of assessment or part thereof during which **3–19** para.3 applies[29]—the chargeable amount is the "appropriate rental value", less the amount of any payments made by the individual in pursuance of any legal obligation to the land's owner in respect of his occupation.[30]

The appropriate rental value is defined as such proportion of the rental value (R) as is found by the following formula:

$$R \times \frac{DV}{V}$$

Valuation and rental value

The DV definition varies slightly according to whether it is the disposal condition **3–20** or contribution condition which is in point.[31] However, in all cases regard is to be had to certain common factors. Of these the least involved is "**the valuation**

---

[29] Sch.15, para.4(5).

[30] Sch.15, para.4(1). Reducing the chargeable amount by making payments to the landlord under a legal obligation has implications which are considered elsewhere. For instance it will not affect the operation of the de minimis exemption (see **9–03**); it may be especially valuable in *Ingram* cases (see **14–15**) but difficult to apply in deferred leases (see **15–06**). "Rent" paid will attract an income tax charge on the landlord albeit with a deduction for the usual landlord expenses. The income tax charge when rent is paid may therefore be less than POA tax on the deemed benefit of the gross rent. Moreover the donee is assessed on rent paid while the donor is assessed to POAT if no rent is paid. If the donee is a lower rate taxpayer payment of rent may result in less tax being paid.

[31] This is considered further at **3–10** and **3–34**.

date", which, in relation to a taxable period, simply means such date as may be prescribed[32] in the Regulations. This has been set in relation to a taxable period as April 6 in the relevant year of assessment or, if later, the first day of the taxable period.[33]

Example 3.4

(a) Priscilla entered into a home loan scheme on April 1, 2003, which falls within the POA charge for tax years 2005–6 et seq. The valuation date is April 6, 2005 and the value thus obtained will be used in computing the tax charge for that year and each of the following four tax years (viz 2006/7; 2007/8; 2008/9; 2009/10). A further valuation will be needed on April 6, 2010.

(b) On May 1, 2006, Bill first occupies property bought by his son using cash that Bill gave him on September 6, 2005. Accordingly, he falls within the POA charge for the first time on May 1, 2006 which is therefore the valuation date (it is the first day of the taxable period). However, thereafter the value is fixed by the "valuation date at the last five year anniversary".[34] The five-year anniversary is defined as the fifth anniversary of April 6 in the tax year in which POA first applied. Therefore it appears (although the legislation is not wholly clear) that the next valuation date is April 6, 2011 for the purposes of calculating the charge for periods from May 1, 2011.

The "rental value" of the land for the taxable period is defined as the rent which would have been payable for that period if the property had been let to the individual at an annual rent equal to the annual value.[35] This leads on to the meaning of "annual value". The rental value is determined for the first five years by reference to the annual value in the first year of assessment in which the POA Regime applies to the taxpayer. Thereafter it is determined by working out the annual value at each five-year anniversary (which will always be April 6).

If there is an interruption in the person's use and occupation of the property or the POA charge does not apply (e.g. the taxpayer becomes non-UK resident) and then the POA charge applies again when he resumes UK residence, the new five-year anniversary is the first date from when the provisions apply again. So if A is within the POA charge on April 6, 2005, then becomes non-resident from 2008/9 and resumes UK residence on June 6, 2014, there is no POA charge for the period of non-residence, and a new valuation is made on June 6, 2014 and this is the start of the next five years. The next five-year anniversary would appear to be April 6, 2019.

---

[32] Sch 15, para.4(5). By para.4(5)(a), regulations may in relation to any valuation date provide for a valuation of the land or any interest therein by reference to an earlier valuation date to apply subject to any prescribed adjustments. See **Ch.12** for further information.

[33] (SI 2005/724), reg.2 (**Ch.12**)

[34] (SI 2005/724), reg.4(1)(b) and (3).

[35] FA 2004, Sch.15, para.4(3). By para.4(5)(b), regulations may, in relation to any year of assessment, provide for a determination of the rental value of any land by reference to any earlier year of assessment to apply subject to any prescribed adjustments. By reg.2 of SI 2005/724 the prescribed valuation date is April 6 in the relevant year of assessment or, if later, the first day of the taxable period and by reg.4(2) that value is retained for the next four tax years: for a detailed consideration of the Regulations, see **Ch.12**.

Annual value

The annual value is the rent which might reasonably be expected to be obtained **3–21** on a letting from year to year if:

(a) the tenant undertook to pay all taxes, rates and charges usually paid by a tenant; **and**

(b) the landlord undertook to bear the costs of the repairs and insurance and the other expenses (if any) necessary for maintaining the property in a state to command that rent.

For this purpose, the rent is taken to be the amount that might reasonably be **3–22** expected to be so obtained in respect of a letting of the land and is to be calculated on the basis that the only amounts that may be deducted in respect of services provided by the landlord are amounts in respect of the cost to the landlord of providing a service other than the repair, insurance or maintenance of the premises.[36] Hence if the landlord provides services for the maintenance of the common parts in a block of flats, and the cost of this is reflected in the rent, then this may be deducted in calculating rental value.

Accordingly, the calculation of rent for these purposes will be based upon that payable under a relatively standard form residential tenancy. In the event that the individual makes some payments in respect of his occupation these may be deducted from the appropriate rental value in arriving at the chargeable amount.[37] Note that when calculating the rental value one fixes the rent taking into account the actual condition of the property. For example, in some *Ingram* and reversionary lease schemes, an elderly donor occupies the house by virtue of his retained interest. The rental value is the rent due (**assuming vacant possession**) under a standard shorthold tenancy. However, in some cases the properties are unmodernised and would not be attractive to tenants. The market rent is therefore often quite low as compared with the capital value of the property. It is therefore always important to obtain a proper rental valuation from a qualified letting agent.

Also, bear in mind that the POA charge will not apply if the taxpayer is in occupation of the land but outside the reservation of benefit charge because he is paying "full consideration in money or money's worth". This exemption is dealt with at **7–39**.[38]

Appropriate rental value

As noted above the appropriate rental value is found (when the disposal condition **3–23** is met) by multiplying the rental value for the taxable period by the fraction:

$$\frac{\text{value at the valuation date of the interest in the land disposed of (DV)}}{\text{value of the land at the valuation date (V)}}$$

---

[36] FA 2004, Sch.15, paras 5(1)–(3).

[37] See **3–12**.

[38] Note that whilst the rent calculation is spelt out in some detail for para.3 purposes the same is not true of the full consideration let-out to reservation of benefit. The two may very well be different— see **Ch.7**.

i.e. $R \times DV/V$

The value for DV and V are to be taken at April 6 in the relevant year of assessment or, if later, the first day of the taxable period, and that value is then retained for the next four tax years but thereafter assessed at April 6 on each five-year anniversary—see above, and for a detailed consideration of the Regulations, see **Ch.12**.

Example 3.5

Assume that X effected an *"Ingram"* scheme in 1996 by giving away the freehold interest in a land subject to a lease over it which he reserved to himself. At the valuation date (April 6, 2005) the land is worth £1,000,000 and the encumbered freehold is worth £600,000. Assume the rental value is £20,000. (The rental value is surprisingly low but the agents have said that with vacant possession they could not obtain more than this due to the unmodernised kitchen and poor quality floorboards!) This rental value is then reduced by 40 per cent as follows:

$$£20,000 \times £600,000/£1,000,000 = £12,000$$

The appropriate rental value is therefore £12,000. Assuming X pays nothing for his occupation, then £12,000 is also the chargeable amount. If X paid £8,000 under a legal obligation, the chargeable amount is reduced to £4,000. Note from the above that the value of what X retains is not relevant. It is the value of what he has given away valued at the valuation date that is relevant. Nor does it matter that the chargeable amount is now less than £5,000 (the annual exemption). The appropriate rental value is over £5,000 and therefore POA is charged on the remaining chargeable amount. (see para.13(2), Sch.15).

3–24   The legislation broadly defines DV as the value at the valuation date of the interest disposed of. However, the DV value may not be easily ascertainable.

Example 3.6

Tony and Rebecca are married and owned property as tenants in common in equal shares. Tony carried out an *Eversden* scheme in 1999 which involved him settling his half share on interest in possession trusts and part of that interest has now been terminated in favour of their children.[39] Tony has suffered an income tax charge from April 6, 2005, but what is the value (the DV) of the interest he settled on trust for his wife? Is it an arithmetical one-half share or discounted to allow for the fact that she is in occupation and retains one-half? Until the DV has been established Tony cannot self-assess.[40] The authors consider that it is the discounted value.

Cash sales at an undervalue ("non-exempt sales")

3–25   The legislation also caters for sales of the *whole interest in the land* at an undervalue so as to reflect the fact that the proceeds from the sale will have been

---

[39] See **Ch.16** for a consideration of *Eversden* schemes.
[40] See **Chs 13** and **16** for further comments and A2–77 which accepts that a discount may be appropriate.

(indeed may still be) comprised in the value of the vendor's estate. It does so by providing that where the disposal of an interest in land is a "non-exempt" sale, the annual rent is reduced to take account of the consideration paid. In effect the POA charge is limited to the undervalue element.

"Non-exempt sale" is somewhat bewilderingly defined in relation to a disposal by a person of his interest in land as a sale which, although it was not an excluded transaction, was a sale of his *whole* interest in the property for a consideration paid in money in any currency.[41] This exemption is intended to cover sales at an undervalue for cash. (Sales for full consideration will normally be excluded transactions—see **5–10** onwards.) The definition of non-exempt sale is, however, flawed because it only covers sales of the whole interest, not sales of part (for any value), and it does not cover exchanges of property but only cash sales.[42]

In the case of non-exempt sales the annual rent is reduced to take account of the undervalue by multiplying the annual rent by the following fraction[43]: **3–26**

$$\frac{\text{the ``appropriate proportion'' of the value at the valuation}}{\text{value of the land}}$$
$$\text{date of the interest in the land disposed of}$$

The "appropriate proportion" is[44]:

$$\frac{\text{value of the interest in land at the time of the}}{\text{value of the interest in land (MV) at the time of sale}}$$
$$\text{sale (MV) } less \text{ the amount paid (P)}$$

Example 3.7

Assume X sold for £800,000 land worth £1,000,000 and that the rental value is £50,000. The appropriate proportion is[45]:

(MV – P)/MV, i.e. (£1,000,000 – £800,000)/£1,000,000 = 20%

The rental value of £50,000 is then multiplied by 20% = £10,000

Link up with reservation of benefit

In many cases a non-exempt sale will involve an element of gift[46] leaving the taxpayer at risk of being within the reservation of benefit rules if he continues to **3–27**

---

[41] Sch.15, para.4(4).

[42] These points are discussed further at **3–22**, onwards. On a policy level it will be remembered that the purpose of the POA charge is to catch cases which were intended to be caught by the reservation of benefit rules but which had—for whatever reason—slipped through that net. HMRC's practice in the case of undervalue sales is only to apply the reservation of benefit charge to the gift element in the transaction. If, for instance, Jack sells his house for £50,000 (a quarter of its true value) to his son and continues to occupy the property then he is caught by the GWR legislation as to 75% of the property: see IHTM 14316. The £50,000 paid is, of course, comprised in his estate anyway. What is odd is why the relief for sales at an undervalue is limited to sales of the whole interest rather than part.

[43] Sch.15, para.4(2)(a).

[44] Sch.15, para.4(4).

[45] MV-P / MV.

[46] This will not be the case if the taxpayer has simply made a bad bargain.

use the property which he has sold. HMRC practice is then to apply the reservation of benefit provisions to the gifted element in the property. In terms of *Example 3.6* therefore the gifted element (in value terms) is of course 1/5, the same as the appropriate portion for the purpose of the POA charge. It therefore follows that if that proportion of the property is within the reservation of benefit rules so far as X is concerned then the POA charge ought not to apply, as a result of the exemption in paras 11(3) and 11(5). In many cases this will result in non-exempt sales being outside the POA charge altogether since the proportion of the property for which cash consideration has been furnished is relieved by para.4(2) and the balance by the reservation of benefit exemption. The one difficulty with this interpretation is that the para.11(3) exemption is on its face limited to cases where there is a reservation of benefit in the relevant property and, of course, the reservation is in part only of the relevant property. The authors, however, consider that this will not prevent the exemption from applying.[47]

Cash limitation

3-28 This non-exempt sale relief is expressly made available only to cash sales, though why this should be so is not clear.[48] This limitation is capable of producing some unfairness. For example, no relief will be available in respect of an exchange. Assume X transfers Blackacre worth £1,000,000 to Y in consideration of Y transferring to X Whiteacre worth £800,000 and X continues to occupy Blackacre. The annual value of Blackacre, without any reduction, is £50,000. In fairness this should be reduced to £10,000, but no such reduction will be available. Instead, X will pay tax on £50,000 and prima facie be liable for IHT on the value of Whiteacre which forms part of his estate. This, however, assumes that the undervalue element is not treated as a gift with reservation and hence protected from a POA charge under para.11(3). In practice HMRC accept that the undervalue is subject to reservation of benefit so the POA charge is limited to the percentage equal to the consideration received for Blackacre, i.e. 80 per cent of £50,000.

It might also be argued that as Whiteacre is part of X's estate, it derives its value from Blackacre and thus the exemption in para.11(1)(b) applies such that there should be a reduced income tax charge on X's occupation of Blackacre.[49] However, it is difficult to construe para.11(1) in this way.[50]

The position is also difficult where there is a part exchange at an undervalue with a cash adjustment, i.e. instead of Y transferring Whiteacre worth £800,000 to X he transfers Greenacre worth £200,000 to X and also pays X £500,000. HMRC's approach in practice is set out at A2.113. The annual rent is reduced to take account of the cash payment of £500,000. The undervalue element is treated as a gift with reservation and so protected under para.11(3) so the POA charge is limited to the exchanged property worth £200,000 (25 per cent) only. Such transactions are not uncommon in family situations where parties exchange properties or provide partial consideration.

---

[47] See **21-35** for a summary of the position on sales.
[48] It may be that, given that transactions as long ago as March 1986 are relevant, HMRC wished to avoid valuation difficulties.
[49] See **7-15**.
[50] For a fuller discussion, see **21-35**.

Unlike an arm's length sale which is an excluded transaction under para.10(1), a **3–29** transaction can only qualify as a non-exempt sale if it is a sale of the whole interest in the property; the disponer cannot retain any right or interest over the land.[51] Hence the non-exempt sale rules will not be relevant in relation to sales of part for cash at an undervalue nor to schemes where, for example, X carved out a lease for himself and then sold the freehold at an undervalue. Nor to reversionary lease schemes which might involve some sort of sale at an undervalue. In all such cases the non-exempt sale provisions are of no assistance because the disponer has not disposed of his entire interest in the land.

Example 3.8

A retains a lease for 15 years and sells the freehold reversion to B for what he believes to be full consideration. It turns out that the price paid by B is an undervalue and therefore the sale is not an excluded transaction. However, it is not a non-exempt sale (because the sale is of part only) and therefore none of the purchase price received by A can be taken into consideration. Again, this is capable of producing unfairness.[52]

A common problem is where sales of part occur at an undervalue. Assume that a mother wishes to raise cash on her property. She sells 50 per cent of her house worth £1m to her daughter for £100,000. The market value of a 50 per cent share is £400,000. Hence there is an undervalue of £300,000. There is no POA charge on the undervalue element. However, arguably there is a POA charge to the extent of one-quarter of the value of the property disposed of. If the rental value is £50,000 and the DV/MV figure is £20,000 then the chargeable amount would be one quarter of this, i.e. £5,000 within the annual exemption.

This leads to the question: Do the provisions on non-exempt sales have any **3–30** practical application? In most cases an undervalue sale will be caught by the reservation of benefit rules assuming that it will contain an element of gift. Hence the undervalue element will be outside the POA charge and it is the purpose of the non-exempt sale provisions to exclude the balance of the value (i.e. that attributable to the consideration paid) from charge.

Conclusions

The non-exempt sale provisions are something of a mess. When they apply—viz **3–31** to a sale of the taxpayer's whole interest in the property for a cash consideration—they will normally result in no POA charge applying given that (a) the value of the property attributable to the cash received is not charged and (b) the balance will normally fall within the reservation of benefit exemption. However, no relief is given for a sale of part of the taxpayer's property under para.10(1) when it is for full value, nor for a sale of part at an undervalue under the non-exempt sale

---

[51] Compare the wording in 10(1)(a).

[52] The possible application of the non-exempt sale provisions in the context of home loan schemes is considered at **17–18**. Equity release schemes and sales generally are discussed in **Ch.21**.

rules or a sale of the whole for anything other than cash. Perhaps this is a form of consistency! Assume, for instance, that A sells a half share in his house to son B for £300,000 when its market value is £400,000. A continues to occupy the property with B and presumably there is no reservation of benefit in the gifted portion (1/4) because of the s.102B(4) exemption for sharing arrangements. The remaining portion of the property (3/4) is, however within the POA net.[53]

Funded acquisition

3–32   Where the disposal condition is met because the individual funded the acquisition as discussed in 3–07, above, the appropriate rental value is found by multiplying the rental value for the taxable period by the fraction[54]:

$$\frac{\text{such part of the value of the land as can reasonably be attributed to the property originally disposed of by the individual (or, where the disposal was a non-exempt sale, the appropriate proportion of that value)}}{\text{value of the land}}$$

"Non-exempt" sale and "the appropriate proportion" have the same meanings as were discussed above.[55]

Tracing problems

3–33   It is not difficult to anticipate both theoretical and practical problems in applying the "reasonably attributed test". What happens if e.g. Albert gives his son Ben land worth £100,000, Ben retains the land for a few years after which it is compulsorily acquired for £1,000,000 with Ben using £200,000 of the proceeds to buy a country cottage for occupation by Albert? What part of the value of the cottage at the valuation date can reasonably be attributed to the land Albert gave to Ben? How is Albert to self-assess? HMRC would doubtless argue that the whole value is attributable.

A harder situation would arise if when the land is worth £300,000 Ben develops it, subsequently selling it for £2,500,000 and using £200,000 of the proceeds to buy Albert the country cottage. These uncertainties in the scope of the charge in a tax collected under self-assessment demonstrate the difficulties of applying this legislation. Presumably any taxpayer should ensure he makes detailed disclosure on his tax return as to how he has done the reasonable attribution calculation and the basis of the values reached.

In other cases funds will have become mixed to such an extent that it will be difficult, if not impossible, to determine with any precision how much the taxpayer contributed to the land. The rule, rather than the exception, will be that

---

[53]   This raises the question of how the para.11(3) exemption is to be applied when para.11(5)(c) only applies to part of the relevant property.

[54]   See Sch.15, para.4(2)(b).

[55]   Sch.15, para.4(4).

individuals will either be unable to retrieve relevant information or will be able to do so only with considerable difficulty and often at no little cost.[56]

Contribution condition

Where the contribution condition is satisfied, the appropriate rental value is found by multiplying the rental value for the taxable period by the fraction[57]:   **3–34**

$$\frac{\text{such part of the value of the land as can reasonably be attributed to the consideration provided by the individual}}{\text{value of the land}}$$

Tracing problems

Again, it is not difficult to anticipate both theoretical and practical problems in applying the "reasonably attributed test". What happens if, e.g. Charles gives his daughter Dorothy £50,000 "to invest wisely". Dorothy invests £25,000 in ICI shares and £25,000 in Biotech Ltd. The ICI shares languish but the Biotech Ltd shares have grown tenfold in value. Five years later Dorothy sells all the shares and uses the £25,000 from the ICI shares and £125,000 from the Biotech Ltd shares (the permutations are endless) to buy a cottage in Wales for Charles to occupy. What part of the value of the cottage at the valuation date can reasonably be attributed to the consideration provided by Charles?   **3–35**

It is likely that individuals will often be unable to obtain relevant information or will be able to do so only with considerable difficulty and often at no little cost. Even if they can obtain the necessary information as to how the gifted cash was used, it is still not clear how the "reasonably attributed" test should be applied.

As noted at **3–06**, it does not seem necessary for Charles to have made the gift with the intention that Dorothy ultimately will use the funds to acquire an interest in land for his occupation. All that is required is to show that Charles provided the consideration and that it was actually used by Dorothy to acquire an interest in the land. Unless more than seven years has elapsed between the date of the gift and the date when Charles occupies[58], there is a POA charge if the consideration for the cottage is derived from the gifted cash. A more difficult question is what happens if Dorothy has died leaving her estate to her child who then buys a house for Charles' occupation. In these circumstances is the contribution condition satisfied? The legislation does not say that the person who buys the house must be the same as the person who received the consideration. Equally it is thought that there must be some limit to the words "directly or indirectly provided".[59]

Note that the special rules for non-exempt sales do not apply to cases where the contribution condition is met.

---

[56] The same problems arise when the cash contribution condition is met: see **3–34** below.
[57] Sch.15, para.4(2)(c).
[58] For the seven-year defence, see **5–24** and para.10(2)(c).
[59] See also **3–11**.

Determining the chargeable amount—relevance of payments made

3–36 It is only **after** determining the appropriate rental value according to the above rules that any payments made in pursuance of a legal obligation by the individual concerned to the owner of the land are taken into account in determining the chargeable amount on which the individual pays income tax.[60] Note that the deduction is limited to payments made by the chargeable person during the taxable period. Assume, therefore, that the appropriate rental value is £10,000 p.a. and to avoid a POA charge Jason agrees to pay £30,000 to cover occupation for five years. This premium will reduce, to zero, the chargeable amount in the year when it is paid but the balance (£20,000) will not reduce the POA charge in later years.

Making payments to avoid the POA charge will be a consideration for a number of taxpayers. Note:

(a) such payments cannot be structured to link-in with the de minimis exemption: see **Ch.9**;

(b) taxpayers who have effected *Ingram* schemes may find such payments especially attractive: see **14–17**;

(c) there is difficulty in applying the deduction in the case of reversionary leases given that payments have to be to "the owner of the relevant land"; In this case it is the freehold owner: see **Ch.15**;

(d) in the case of home loan schemes such payments will be circular, i.e. they will be made to the trust in which the payer is life tenant: see **17–47**;

(e) whilst payments made can reduce the POA income tax charge on the payer they will normally be taxed as rent in the hands of the recipient.

Example 3.9

Thoughtful is caught by the POA charge because in 2001 he gave his son £500,000 to buy a flat which Thoughtful now occupies. The chargeable amount for 2005–6 is £16,000. The flat needs substantial repairs and the service charge has recently trebled. These are some of the consequences if Thoughtful were to pay his son rent of £16,000.

(a) It would prevent Thoughtful suffering a POA charge.

(b) The son would be able to deduct—in arriving at his income tax charge on the £16,000 rent—the normal business expenses (repairs and service charge) which he incurs.

(c) An incidental effect is that Thoughtful is reducing his estate to the tune of £16,000 for IHT purposes.

(d) The son may only be a basic rate taxpayer in which case the total tax paid may be lower than if Thoughtful was assessed to POAT on the chargeable amount. (If one of them falls into the 50 per cent income tax

---

[60] See **9–03** for how this process impacts upon the de minimis exemption.

rate band from 2010/11 it will be even more important to ensure that the tax liability falls on the lower rate taxpayer.)

Link-up with reservation of benefit and full consideration

The fact that payments must be made pursuant to a legal obligation means that **3–37** voluntary payments which may come within the IHT ameliorating provisions in the Finance Act 1986, Sch.20, para.6(1)(a) will not be taken into account for this purpose. This, however, should not generally matter because if the para.6(1)(a) full consideration let-out is available the para.3 charge will not apply.[61] Bear in mind in this connection that "full consideration" for the purposes of para.6(1)(a) may be quite different from the annual value that is relevant under para.4.[62]

Example 3.10

Chris gave his house to his son Johnny in 2000. As part of the arrangements made then, Chris paid a premium for the right to continue in occupation for seven years. This is full consideration for IHT purposes and therefore there is no reservation of benefit (FA 1986, Sch.20, para.6). Such a payment is not a payment that could ever reduce the chargeable amount for the purposes of the Regime, but since Chris has the para.6 protection he is also given exemption from an income tax charge under para.11(5)(d). If Chris pays nothing for his continued occupation after 2007 or less than full consideration then he has reserved a benefit in the property and therefore there is still no POA income tax charge since he is protected by para.11(5)(a).[63]

Would it be possible to take advantage of any disparity between the "chargeable **3–38** amount" for POA purposes and "full consideration" in the GWR context? Might the taxpayer benefit from electing into the GWR rules and then paying "full consideration" so as to avoid a future charge under these provisions?[64]

---

[61] However, many of the schemes were of course, structured to fall outside the reservation of benefit rules and so full consideration payments are irrelevant and cannot be protected under para.15(5)(d) (see, for instance, *Ingram* schemes and reversionary leases).

[62] See **Ch.21**.

[63] See **Ch.7** for exemptions under the Regime.

[64] See **Ch.11**.

CHAPTER 4

THE PARAGRAPH 6 CHARGE ON CHATTELS

WHEN THE PROVISIONS APPLY

4–01 Paragraph 6 applies where an individual is in possession of, or has the use of, a chattel, whether alone or together with other persons and either one of two conditions is met.

The threshold test is that the individual must be in possession of, or have the use of, the chattel.[1] "Possession" and "use" are not defined and so bear their normal meaning. Compare, in the reservation of benefit legislation, the requirement that the donee has not assumed "possession and enjoyment of the property"[2]. It is considered that a mere legal right to have possession of the chattel is not enough: control of the chattel must be assumed by the individual (or, presumably, his agent). If goods are stored (e.g. at a warehouse) it is considered that they are in the possession of the person responsible for the storage.

The disposal condition

4–02 The first condition, "the disposal condition", is that:

(a) at any time after March 17, 1986, the individual, whether alone or jointly with others, owned

　(i) the chattel; or

　(ii) any other property the proceeds of the disposal of which were directly or indirectly applied by another person towards the acquisition of the chattel; and

(b) the individual disposed of all, or part of, his interest in the chattel or the other property, otherwise than by an excluded transaction.[3]

Limb (a)(i) and (b) cover direct acquisitions, i.e. cases where X previously owned and disposed[4] of the chattel which he now uses or enjoys. Limb (a)(ii) and (b), on the other hand, cover representative acquisitions, i.e. cases where the chattel

---

[1] Compare the land charge under para.3 which depends upon "occupation".
[2] FA 1986, s.102(1)(a). See *Dymond's Capital Taxes* at 5.406.
[3] Sch.15, para.6(2).
[4] Otherwise than by an excluded transaction.

in question was acquired by someone other than X using the proceeds from the disposal[5] (by whatever person) of property previously owned by X. So, if X gives Y a violin and Y sells the violin and buys a painting which X then possesses, the disposal condition in limb (a)(ii) and (b) is satisfied.

It does not appear that the property sold has to be a chattel. Hence in the above example X could give shares to Y who sells them and buys a picture that X uses and the disposal condition would be satisfied.

The contribution condition

The second condition is "the contribution condition". It is that at any time after **4–03** March 17, 1986 the individual has directly or indirectly provided, otherwise than by an excluded transaction, any of the consideration given by another person for the acquisition of:

(a) the chattel; or

(b) any other property the proceeds of the disposal of which were directly or indirectly applied by another person towards the acquisition of the chattel.[6]

As with disposals of land, a disposition which creates a new interest in a chattel out of an existing interest in a chattel is to be taken to be a disposal of part of the existing interest.[7]

Relationship between the disposal and contribution condition

The same points apply in relation to the contribution and disposal conditions and **4–04** their overlap as are discussed in relation to land at **Ch.3** at 3–07 to 3–13 and the reader is referred to these paragraphs. As with land the contribution condition is not limited to cash contributions.

As with the charge for land, second-hand companies may be a way of circumventing the chattels charge (see **3–14**).

THE CHARGE

Where para.6 applies to the individual in respect of the whole or part of a year of **4–05** assessment, an amount equal to "the chargeable amount" is treated as income of his chargeable to income tax.[8] The main difference between the land and chattels charge is not in respect of the conditions necessary for the POA charge to apply but rather in how the charge is calculated once the conditions are satisfied. The charge as it applies to chattels does not look at market rental values at all but adopts a much harsher approach. In brief, the taxable benefit is found by multiplying the market value of the chattel (or the DV/MV equation if part of the chattel remains in the taxpayer's estate) by the official rate of interest. Hence

---

[5]   Otherwise than by an excluded transaction.
[6]   Sch.15, para.6(3).
[7]   Sch.15, para.6(4).
[8]   Sch.15, para.6(5).

there is no need to obtain rental values. So, to take a simple example, if X gives cash to his son who buys chattels for X to use and the chattels are worth £1m at the valuation date, then if the official rate of interest is five per cent the taxable benefit is £50,000 and income tax is paid on this sum. This is likely to be much higher than the rental value which typically is less than one per cent of the chattel's value in the case of most chattels.

The calculation of the charge is examined in more detail below.

The chargeable amount

4–06 For any taxable period, i.e. the year of assessment or part thereof during which para.6 applies[9]—the chargeable amount is the "appropriate amount", less the amount of any payments made by the individual in pursuance of any legal obligation to the chattel's owner in respect of the individual's possession or use.[10] The relevance of such payments is discussed at 4–16. If possession and use is only for part of a tax year, the chargeable amount is reduced accordingly.

The appropriate amount varies according to whether it is the disposal condition or contribution condition which is in point. However, in all cases regard is had to three considerations. The first is "the valuation date" which, in relation to a taxable period, simply means such date as may be prescribed.[11] The second is the value of the chattel. For this purpose regulations may, in relation to any valuation date, provide for a valuation of the chattel or any interest in it by reference to an earlier valuation date subject to any prescribed adjustments.[12] The third is the amount of the interest that would be payable for the taxable period if interest were payable at the prescribed rate on an amount equal to the value of the chattel at the valuation date.[13] For convenience, this will be called "the prescribed interest" and has been fixed in the Regulations as being the official rate of interest at the valuation date. On April 6, 2005 and 2006 it was five per cent per annum.[14] On April 6, 2007 and 2008 it was 6.25 per cent. On April 6, 2009 it was 4.75 per cent.

Assume X is, as the settlor of a discretionary trust, allowed by the trustees to use a chattel worth £400,000. The chargeable amount for 2005/6 (if none of the exemptions apply) was £400,000 x 5 per cent = £20,000. In 2008/9 it was £400,000 x 6.25 per cent = £25,000. For 2009/10 the lower rate of 4.75 per cent is taken and the chargeable amount reduces to 4.75 per cent x £400,000 = £19,000.

Note that if interest rates rise during the course of 2009/10 this is irrelevant to the charge. It is always the official rate of interest as at April 6 that is taken unless the POA charge only begins during the course of that year, in which case it is the official rate of interest when the POA charge starts for that year of assessment and thereafter the official rate of interest at April 6 for future years of assessment.

---

[9] Sch.15, para.7(4).

[10] Sch.15, para.7(1).

[11] Sch.15, para.7(4). See **Ch.12** for the Regulations. By para.4 of SI 2005/724 this has been set, in relation to a taxable period, as April 6 in the relevant year of assessment or, if later the first day of the taxable period (see *Example 3.4*).

[12] Sch.15, para.7(3). In the event reg.4 provides that the initial value will be used for the next four tax years: see further, **Ch.12**.

[13] Sch.15, para.7(2).

[14] See further (SI 2005/724), reg.3 (**Appendix I**).

As noted above, there is a significant difference between the way in which the benefit to the individual is calculated under the chattel rules and under the provisions dealing with land. Under the latter, a market rent is arrived at on the basis of empirical evidence (the letting of comparable properties). For chattels, however, such comparable evidence is largely lacking. Hence the taxpayer is treated as benefiting on the basis of a percentage of the market value of the chattel.[15] In effect the charge is a percentage of capital value and more akin to a wealth tax.

Valuation

It was accepted that valuing chattels is a particularly difficult art. Values may **4–07** fluctuate year on year as particular items come in and out of fashion and insurance values are rarely the same as the values realised in an auction.[16] The regulations therefore adopt a pragmatic approach. Valuations are only required every five years (with the first valuation being obtained at April 6, 2005 or the date when POAT first applies if later). If the chattel is sold during the course of the five years and a cheaper replacement chattel is purchased then a revaluation is required at that time. However, unlike land, even if the same chattel is retained and used throughout the five-year period, the taxable benefit will vary over the five-year period simply because the official rate of interest varies. This is in contrast to land, where both the market capital value and the rental value are fixed at the start of the five-year period. In the case of chattels, only the capital value of the chattel is fixed for five years.

Position if a retained interest

Where the individual previously owned the chattel so satisfying the disposal **4–08** condition, as with land, the appropriate amount is found by multiplying the prescribed interest (N) for the taxable period by the fraction[17]:

$$\frac{\text{value of interest in the chattel disposed of (DV)}}{\text{value of the chattel (V)}}$$

Thus, if the person possessing or using the chattel retained an interest in it, the amount on which he is charged is reduced.[18] Assume X effected an *"Ingram"* scheme by giving away the freehold interest in a chattel subject to a lease over it which he has reserved to himself.[19] At the valuation date the market value of the chattel is worth £400,000 and the encumbered freehold worth (April 6, 2005)

---

[15] See the Consultation Document of December 11, 2003 which referred to the taxed benefit being at market rent "where market evidence allows (e.g. for real property) and a specified percentage of capital value . . . in other cases (such as art or antiques)".

[16] Fixing a value for a five-year period with no possibility of a revaluation will result in some taxpayers gaining and others losing!

[17] FA 2004, Sch.15, para.7(2)(a). The figure is expressed in the legislation as N x DV/V.

[18] Compare the similar position under the para.3 charge on land: see **3–20**. The valuation date is the same.

[19] For *Ingram* chattel schemes, see **Ch.20**. The use of the terms leasehold and freehold interests in the case of chattels is to be preferred to bailment and ownership.

£300,000. The official rate of interest at April 6, 2005 was five per cent and therefore N (prescribed interest) is £20,000. The calculation is therefore:

$$£20,000 \times £300,000/£400,000 = £15,000$$

Cash sales at an undervalue

4-09 As with disposals of land, the legislation also caters for sales at an undervalue so as to reflect the fact that the proceeds from the sale may be comprised in the value of the vendor's estate. It does so by providing that where the disposal of an interest in a chattel is a "non-exempt" sale, the annual rent is reduced to take account of the undervalue.

"Non-exempt sale" is then defined as a sale which, although not an excluded transaction, was a sale of his *whole* interest in the chattel for a consideration paid in money in any currency.[20] By referring to a sale that is not an excluded transaction the draftsman appears to be flagging up a sale at an undervalue.

In such a case the "appropriate amount" is reduced to take account of the undervalue by multiplying it by the following fraction:[21]

$$\frac{\text{the appropriate proportion of the value of the interest in the chattel disposed of}}{\text{value of the chattel}}$$

In relation to such a sale, "the appropriate proportion" is[22]:

$$\frac{\text{value of the interest in the chattel at the time of the sale less the amount paid}}{\text{value of the interest in the chattel at the time of the sale}^{23}}$$

This is expressed in the legislation as:

$$MV - PP$$

Example 4.1

Assume X sold a painting worth £1,000,000 for £800,000. The appropriate proportion is:

$$£200,000 \ (£1,000,000 - £800,000)/£1,000,000 = 1/5$$

The appropriate amount is then arrived at under para.7(2) by the formula:

$$\frac{N \times DV}{V}$$

- **N** is the prescribed interest (5 per cent) applied to the value of the chattel at the valuation date. In this case 5 per cent x £1,000,000 = £50,000.

---

[20] Sch.15, para.7(3). The wording is the same in relation to non-exempt sales of land: see generally **3-27** where the policy behind this provision is considered.

[21] Sch.15, para.7(2)(a).

[22] Sch.15, para.7(3).

[23] Sch.15, para.7(2)(a).

- **DV** is the appropriate proportion of the value of the interest in the chattel disposed of at the valuation date. Taking the 1/5 proportion and the value as £1,000,000 DV is £200,000.

- **V** is the value of the chattel at the valuation date (£1,000,000).

Notice that in the above example it has been assumed that the values at the time of disposal remain unaltered at the valuation date. However, the relevant date for the purpose of calculating the charge is always the valuation date, not the date of disposal.

Cash limitation

The non-exempt sale relief is only available in respect of cash sales. As with land, **4–10** this limitation may result in some unfairness. For example, no relief will be available in respect of an exchange.

Example 4.2

X transfers his Van Gogh worth £1,000,000 to Y in consideration of Y transferring to X a Rembrandt worth £800,000. Without any reduction, the chargeable amount in respect of the use of the Van Gogh is £50,000. In fairness this should be reduced to £10,000, but no such reduction will be available under the non-exempt sale relief.

See **3–25** et seq. for further consideration of the non-exempt sales rules.

Property limitation

The relief is available only if the donor has disposed of his *whole* interest in the **4–11** chattel. If X grants a lease to Y over a chattel at an undervalue no account will be taken of the consideration received by X. Again, this appears capable of producing unfairness. See also **3–29** for further comments.

Note that a non-exempt sale (i.e. a sale of the whole interest at an undervalue) will commonly involve a gift with reservation and that the non-exempt sale protection will afford an exemption from the POA charge for the sale element.

In summary the alternatives are:

(a) a sale at undervalue: no POAT because non-exempt sale relief on cash and reservation of benefit on undervalue element;

(b) an exchange at undervalue: POA charge on consideration element only; reservation of benefit on undervalue element;

(c) an exchange at undervalue but incorporating a cash payment: non-exempt sale relief on the cash so no POA on this; POA payable on exchange consideration; no POA charge on undervalue gift element because reservation of benefit applies.

Funded acquisitions

4-12 Where the disposal condition is satisfied by the individual funding the acquisition as discussed in **4-02**, above, the appropriate amount is found by multiplying the prescribed interest for the taxable period by the fraction[24]:

$$\frac{\text{such part of the value of the chattel as can reasonably be}}{\text{attributed to the property originally disposed of by}}$$
$$\frac{\text{the individual (or, where the disposal was a}}{\text{non-exempt sale, the appropriate proportion}}$$
$$\frac{\text{of that value)}}{\text{value of the chattel}}$$

"Non-exempt" sale and "the appropriate proportion" have the same meanings as were discussed above.[25] Values are taken at the "valuation date".

Tracing problems

4-13 It is not difficult to foresee both theoretical and practical problems in applying the "reasonably attributed test". What happens if, e.g., Ernest gives his son Frank shares worth £25,000 in E F Ltd, the family company for which they both work? The company prospers and five years later is sold, Frank receiving £3,000,000 for his shares. He purchases an organ for £350,000 which is installed in Ernest's house. What part of the value of the chattel can reasonably be attributed to the shares Ernest gave to Frank?[26]

Contribution condition

4-14 When the contribution condition is satisfied, the appropriate amount is found by multiplying the prescribed interest for the taxable period by the fraction[27]:

$$\frac{\text{such part of the value of the chattel as can reasonably be}}{\text{attributed to the consideration provided by}}$$
$$\frac{\text{the individual}}{\text{value of the chattel at the valuation date}}$$

Values are, of course, to be taken at the valuation date.

Tracing problems in applying the contribution condition

4-15 Again, it is not difficult to anticipate both theoretical and practical problems in applying the "reasonably attributed test". What happens if, e.g. George lends his daughter Henrietta £75,000 to start up an internet business? Henrietta's business

---

[24] Sch.15, para.7(2)(b).
[25] Sch.15, para.7(3).
[26] See generally **3-33** for a consideration of these "tracing" problems.
[27] See Sch.15, para.7(2)(c).

takes off and six years later she sells it for £3,000,000. She repays George and purchases a yacht for £500,000 which George is free to use any time he wants. Without George's initial loan Henrietta could not have gone into business. What part (if any) of the value of the yacht at the valuation date can reasonably be attributed to the funding provided by George?[28]

Relevance of payments made

It is only after determining the appropriate amount according to the above rules **4–16** that any payments made in pursuance of a legal obligation by the individual concerned to the owner of the chattel are taken into account. This is important in relation to the annual £5,000 exemption.[29]

The fact that payments must be made pursuant to a legal obligation means that voluntary payments made to satisfy the IHT ameliorating provisions in the Finance Act 1986, Sch.20, para.6(1)(a) (full consideration let out) will not be taken into account for this purpose. This, however, may not matter because if the para.6(1)(a) full consideration let-out is available the pre-owned assets charge does not apply.[30] However, it may not always be possible to avoid the POA charge on chattels simply by paying full rent or consideration for use because the latter requires the reservation of benefit rules to be in point. For example, if a chattels *Ingram* scheme has been effected then the reservation of benefit rules do not apply so the full consideration let-out does not count and it is the POA charge that has to be considered. It is only if there would *otherwise be a reservation of benefit if full consideration is **not** paid that para 6(1)(a) can help avoid the POA charge*.

Note that the deduction allowed is only for payments made by the chargeable person to the owner of the chattel. It is common in sale and leaseback arrangements for the terms of the lease to impose a burden on the donor/tenant to insure the chattel. Such payments, not being made to the owner, would not be deductible under para.7(1). Accordingly, if the particular arrangement is caught[31] by the POA charge it will be sensible to amend the terms of the lease so that the donee owner insures and is reimbursed under the lease by the donor/tenant. Of course it may be difficult to amend the terms of the lease without inadvertently creating a reservation of benefit problem by conferring a benefit on the donor. For example, if the donor is released from an existing obligation under the lease this may result in a reservation of benefit and the IHT benefits of the scheme will be lost.

---

[28] Note the seven-year defence: see (**5–12**) and that consequently outright cash gifts made before April 6, 1998 are ignored. It is thought that as with land a loan—even on commercial terms—may satisfy the contribution condition. See also **Ch.13** for a full discussion of the problems of compliance under self-assessment.

[29] See **Ch.9**.

[30] For this exemption, see **7–39**. For a discussion of its application to chattel schemes (which is somewhat surprising given that one of the main purposes of the pre-owned assets charge was said to be to catch arrangements where there was no ready market), see **Ch.20**.

[31] As discussed at **Ch.20** it seems that these arrangements will not generally be caught. Either the full consideration exemption will be available or they will fall foul of the reservation of benefit rules.

Scope of the chattels charge

4–17 As will be discussed in **Ch.20**, two main chattels schemes have been used in IHT planning. The most common—a gift and arm's length leaseback—is not caught by para.6, leaving the scope of this charge extremely limited. So for example if X gave his pictures to his son in 2004 and now rents them back, paying full consideration each year (which is likely to include the costs of security and insurance) then there is no reservation of benefit and no POA charge because of the protection in para.11(5), as discussed in **Ch.7**.

CHAPTER 5

EXCLUDED TRANSACTIONS OVERVIEW

Excluded transactions are defined in para.10. Note carefully the following points: **5–01**

(a) Excluded transactions are relevant in preventing a charge arising under either para.3 (land) or para.6 (chattels). **They have no application to the charge on settled intangible property in para.8 and cannot provide any defence to such a charge.**

(b) Paragraph 10 deals separately with exclusions which prevent the **disposal** conditions[1] from being satisfied and exclusions preventing the **contribution conditions**[2] from being met. Paragraph 10(1) deals with the former, para.10(2) with the latter.

Dealing separately with the disposal and contribution conditions means that there is a degree of repetition in the legislation, i.e. certain of the exclusions for the disposal condition are repeated almost word for word for the contribution condition. However, not all the exclusions that apply to one condition apply to the other; this difference reinforces the view that the disposal and contribution conditions may on occasion overlap but should be interpreted as covering separate situations: see **3–15**.

The exclusions may be summarised as follows: **5–02**

Exclusion	Disposal condition	Contribution condition
Certain arm's length sales	10(1)(a)	N/A
Transfers to spouse / civil partner	10(1)(b)	10(2)(a)
Iip trust for spouse / civil partner	10(1)(c): requires a "gift"	10(2)(b) requires property to become settled on acquisition
Occupation 7 years after cash gifts	N/A	10(2)(c)
Section 11 IHTA 1984	10(1)(d)	10(2)(d)
Sections 19 or 20 IHTA 1984	10(1)(e)	10(2)(e)

[1] Paragraph 3(2)—being the disposal condition for land—refers to the disposal of land being "otherwise than by an excluded transaction". See also para.6(2) which is in similar terms for disposals of chattels.

[2] See para.3(3)—the contribution condition for land—referring to a provision of consideration "otherwise than by an excluded transaction". Paragraph 6(3) is in similar terms in relation to the chattel condition.

It will be noted from the above that para.10(1)(a) deals with an excluded transaction only relevant to the disposal condition ("**an arm's length sale**") and para.10(2)(c) with an excluded transaction relevant only to the contribution condition ("**the seven-year defence**"). These two "limited" excluded transactions will be looked at later in this chapter.

5–03   Excluded transactions prevent one of the pre-conditions for the land or chattels charge from being satisfied. By contrast, the exemptions from charge (which are relevant to charges under the settlement provisions of para.8 as well as to the charges under paras 3 and 6 in relation to land and chattels)[3] and are found in para.11, provide for certain exemptions from charge when the pre-conditions of the charge have been satisfied. Hence the correct procedure (taking the charge on land as an illustration) is first to consider whether there is an excluded transaction under para.10 and, only if the answer is no, then consider whether an exemption from charge under para.11 or para.13 applies.

Example 5.1

In 2005 A sells his entire interest in his house to a qualifying interest in possession trust for himself. Full market value is paid and the transaction is on fully arm's length terms. He continues to live in the house. This transaction satisfies the basic conditions for the land charge in para.3 in that there is a disposal and continued occupation of land, but since it is an excluded transaction there is no need to consider the position further. It does not matter that there may be "an excluded liability" affecting the house, nor that A's interest in possession is a qualifying interest in possession and therefore para.11(1) applies so as to provide protection. Hence even if his interest in possession later terminates so that the para.11(1) exemption is no longer available this does not matter for POAT purposes because para.10(1)(a) still gives protection.[4]

By contrast, if in 2005 A had sold his house to a qualifying interest in possession trust for himself at an undervalue there would be no protection under para.10(1)(a) and one would then need to consider whether A fell within one of the exemptions. Prima facie the exemption in para.11(1) applies (see **Ch.7**) since the house is part of A's estate, but if the house is subject to an excluded liability or A's interest in possession later ends there could be a POA problem.

If A had sold the house after March 21, 2006 to a newly established interest in possession trust for himself there would be no POA protection under para.11(1) since the interest in possession is not qualifying. Hence A would then be entirely reliant on the protections in para.10. Similarly, if A sold his house to his wife (whether or not at full market value) but left the purchase price outstanding as a debt, the transaction is excluded under para.10(1)(b) and again it does not matter that there is an excluded liability nor whether the sale takes place before or after the inheritance tax changes in the treatment of settlements in FA 2006. Hence the para.10 exclusions are more generous than the para.11 exemptions, not least because apart from para.10(1)(c) and 10(2)(b), once a para.10 exclusion is obtained on a

---

[3] See **Ch.7**.
[4] For a discussion of arm's length sales in the context of home loan schemes, see **17–17**.

particular transaction it is permanent: the taxpayer does not need to worry what happens later.

The excluded transactions are curious in two ways. First, they do not apply at all **5–04** to intangible settled property. Suppose an *Eversden* pre-June 20, 2003 trust holds cash or an insurance bond plus a house; the spouse retains a qualifying interest in possession[5] and the settlor a remainder interest. There is no reservation of benefit (a) because the transaction is protected by FA 1986, s.102(5)[6] and (b) because at least in relation to the intangibles the settlor seems to have effected a carve-out by retaining only a remainder interest.[7] The settlor is in occupation of the house. While the spousal interest in possession continues he will not be within the POA charge so far as the house is concerned, but will be subject to the para.8 charge on the insurance bond. So someone who effected an uncompleted *Eversden* scheme on different types of assets may find themselves in an odd position with POA on intangibles and no POA on the real estate. Indeed anyone who settles property on interest in possession trusts for their spouse needs to consider POAT since it will apply as soon as the trust holds intangibles, whether or not the interest in possession for the spouse has ended. The POA position for spousal interest in possession trusts set up after March 2006 is discussed below at **5–09**.

Secondly, there appears to be no power to extend the number of excluded transactions by statutory instrument.[8] This may explain the rather odd approach in respect of the relief given for sales of part.[9]

EXCLUDED TRANSACTIONS COMMON TO BOTH THE DISPOSAL AND CONTRIBUTION CONDITIONS

There are **four** transactions that are excluded transactions for the purpose of both **5–05** the disposal and contribution conditions.[10]

Spouse/civil partner exemption—para.10(1)(b) and para.10(2)(a)

A transfer of property by an individual is an excluded transaction (so that the **5–06** disposal condition is not met) if the property is transferred to his spouse or (with effect from December 5, 2005) civil partner (or where the transfer has been ordered by a court, to his former spouse or former civil partner).[11] The transfer can be by any means, i.e. it need not be by way of gift, nor need it satisfy any conditions other than those stated. Hence it must be to the spouse direct not into

---

[5] See **2–31** and **7–06** for consideration of qualifying and non-qualifying interests in possession

[6] And since the scheme was effected prior to June 20, 2003, it remains protected for inheritance tax purposes as far as the settlor is concerned even if the spousal interest in possession is later ended. Note though that if the interest in possession is ended after March 22, 2006, the spouse rather than the donor will be treated as reserving a benefit if the spouse can still benefit after the termination of the spousal interest in possession: see **5–13**.

[7] This is discussed further in **Ch.22**.

[8] See Sch.15, para.14 and **Ch.12**.

[9] See **Ch.21** and **12–13**.

[10] It is clear that what may initially have been an excluded transaction may subsequently cease to be excluded: see para.10(3) in the context of a spouse's interest in possession coming to an end. It appears that HMRC does not accept that the converse is true: see **5–08**.

[11] See Sch.15, para.10(1)(b).

a trust for the spouse. This relief is thus considerably wider than both the IHT spouse exemption and the CGT relief for disposals between spouses.[12] Note that, unlike the IHT exemption, the spouse's/civil partner's domicile is irrelevant.[13] "Spouse" for this purpose means a person who is legally married.[14] A marriage ceases only on the grant of a decree absolute.[15] A civil partner is a person in a civil partnership registered, pursuant to the Civil Partnership Act 2004.

5–07   The provision by a person of consideration for another's acquisition of any property is an excluded transaction (so that the contribution condition is not met) if the other person was his spouse or civil partner (or, where the transfer has been ordered by the court, his former spouse or former civil partner).[16] So, if X buys a house in his civil partner's name the disposal condition will not be satisfied and the provision by X of the funds will be an excluded transaction in relation to the contribution condition. Hence no POA charge arises.

The legislation gives no let-out if the prohibited transaction has taken place prior to marriage.

Example 5.2

In 2004 Bruce gives his partner Fiona cash to purchase a house. Fiona and Bruce then occupy the property in 2005. Bruce is subject to the POA charge because the contribution condition is breached. The fact that they marry in 2006 does not protect Bruce from a POA charge after that date. Bruce should have purchased a **share** in the house with Fiona (because then he would have had protection under para.11(8)).[17]

The spouse exemption may provide only limited protection in respect of certain transactions.

Example 5.3(1)

In 1998 H transfers a house he occupies into a company he wholly owns in consideration of the issue of shares. He has satisfied the disposal condition. However, para.11(1) will protect him from a POA charge while he still owns the company shares. Assume that he gives the company shares to his wife. He is no longer protected under para.11 and the gift of shares to his wife would not appear to protect the earlier disposal of the land. To avoid a POA charge one would have to show that the transfer of the land in consideration of the issue of shares was an excluded transaction under para.10(1)(a), being one "such as might be expected to be made" between unconnected persons.

Nevertheless the spouse exemption leaves open some useful planning options.

---

[12] For IHT purposes there is a limited £55,000 spouse exemption where property passes from a UK domiciled spouse to his foreign domiciled spouse. In the case of CGT, transfers between spouses take place on a no-gain no-loss basis, but only if the spouses are living together. By contrast the POA exclusion applies where the spouses are separated but not yet divorced.

[13] Although in practice if a gift to a foreign domiciled spouse is made and the donor continues to benefit, the reservation of benefit provisions will be in point and hence there will be no POA problem anyway due to para.11(5)(a).

[14] *Holland v IRC* [2003] STC (SCD) 43.

[15] *Fender v St John Mildmay* [1938] A.C. 1.

[16] See Sch.15, para.10(2)(a).

[17] For the position of sharing arrangements, see **Ch.21**.

Example 5.3(2)

In 2007 a husband sells his main home to his wife in consideration of an IOU. The debt is left outstanding, is interest free and is repayable on the last of them to die. SDLT is payable on the consideration paid, i.e. the loan. The transfer between spouses takes place on a no-gain no-loss basis for capital gains tax purposes so there is no tax payable even if the gain is not protected by principal private residence relief. The transfer is not subject to reservation of benefit to the extent that there is any gift or undervalue element due to FA 1986, s.102(5)(a), provided both spouses have the same domicile or the wife (the purchasing spouse) is domiciled in the UK. No POA charge arises on H's subsequent occupation even if the wife is not domiciled here or leaves the property to someone else on her death because of the protection in para.10(1)(b). The house itself is devalued by the debt. The husband assigns or gives the debt to his children (a PET) and survives seven years. On the last of them to die the debt is deducted from the value of the house. This scheme is discussed further at **21–30**.

Spouse/civil partner entitled to an interest in possession

Disposal condition

A disposal by an individual is an excluded transaction if it was a disposal by way **5–08** of gift by virtue of which the property became settled property in which the individual's spouse, former spouse, civil partner or former civil partner is beneficially entitled to an interest in possession.[18] It is not necessary for the spouse/civil partner to be domiciled in the UK (contrast the inheritance tax exemption), but the transfer must be by way of gift. A disposal by an individual is also an excluded transaction if the transfer is for the benefit of a former spouse/ civil partner in accordance with a court order. The spouse does not need to take a *qualifying* interest in possession. Therefore a gift to an interest in possession trust set up after March 21, 2006 can still be an excluded transaction.

However:

> "a disposal is not an excluded transaction . . . if the interest in possession of the spouse or former spouse has come to an end otherwise than on the death of the spouse or former spouse".

Does this mean that the transaction ceases to be excluded at that point with an income tax charge only for future periods, or is the transaction retrospectively re-categorised so that it is treated as never having been an excluded transaction at all? The authors believe that the first view must be correct and this is now confirmed in the guidance notes.[19],[20] However, if the spousal interest comes to an end on the spouse/civil partner's death then the POA charge will not apply to the donor. (By contrast if the gift is made on interest in possession trusts for a spouse after June 19, 2003, then the reservation of benefit charge **will** apply on the death of the spouse if the settlor continues to benefit.)

---

[18] See also **16–33** for further comments.
[19] See A2.08 and A2.111.
[20] See Sch.15, paras 10(1)(c) and (3).

In the first edition of this book the authors expressed the view that if the trust was not initially interest in possession for the spouse but the spousal interest subsequently arose, the disposal would at that point become an excluded transaction. HMRC have said in the guidance notes at 1.3.1 that "the spouse must take an interest in possession from the outset".[21]

Example 5.4

In 2005 John settled his house on interest in possession trusts for himself and then interest in possession trusts for his wife Carolyn. They both occupy the house. In 2007 the trustees terminate John's interest in possession and Carolyn takes an interest in possession (which is qualifying because it is a transitional serial interest and therefore spouse exempt for inheritance tax purposes). HMRC consider that the transaction can never be an excluded transaction for POA purposes. It is not clear that HMRC are correct in this view.

Unlike the para.10(1)(c) exclusion for outright "transfers" between spouses, where the transfer is to a trust it must be by way of gift.[22]

Contribution condition

5–09 Similarly, the provision of consideration for the acquisition of any property is an excluded transaction if on its acquisition the property became settled property in which the contributor's spouse or former spouse is beneficially entitled to an interest in possession. Hence there is no objection to e.g. X settling cash on the trustees of settlement under which his spouse has an interest in possession who then acquires a house in which X subsequently lives, so long as his spouse continues to have an interest in possession in the house.

Example 5.5

(1) In July 2003 John gives cash to a trust in which his wife Emma has a revocable qualifying interest in possession. Emma is UK domiciled. Note at that point the transaction is not an excluded transaction because the settled property comprises intangibles. It is assumed the transaction can become excluded once the trustees purchase the house, otherwise para.10(2)(b) would be meaningless. Accordingly the trust purchases a house that both John and Emma occupy. John is protected by para.10(2)(b) from any income tax charge under POAT. There is also no reservation of benefit because of s.102(5) of the Finance Act 1986 (spouse exempt gift).

In July 2004, Emma dies. Her interest in possession ends (with IHT being payable) and the home is now held on continuing trusts for her children (and inheritance tax may or may not be paid depending on values), but John still occupies the property. There is no income tax charge under the Regime

---

[21] See A2.10.

[22] Although presumably a sale at an undervalue would qualify as a gift to the extent of the undervalue—see **Ch.16**. It is clear that the gift must result in the property becoming settled. It is not, however, certain that the spouse had to enjoy an interest in possession **at that time**. The authors incline to the view that if the spousal interest subsequently arises the disposal will thereupon become an excluded transaction.

because her interest ended on her death. Paragraph 10(1)(c) protection continues to apply. However, this does not protect John from a later IHT charge, since he is treated as having reserved a benefit under s.102(5A)(c) given that the initial gift into trust was made after June 19, 2003. The fact that Emma is dead does not matter. A reservation of benefit arises at her death and the home will be taxed on John's death unless he ceases to occupy it more than seven years before his death.

What if Emma's interest ended while she was alive? In these circumstances there would be no protection under para.10(1)(c) from an income tax charge on John because of para.10(3),[23] but since John will have reserved a benefit (see ss.102(5A)(c) and 102(5B)) he is protected from an income tax charge by virtue of para.11(5)(a).[24] However, if Emma's interest in possession is ended after March 22, 2006, then she is treated as reserving a benefit for inheritance tax purposes by virtue of FA 1986, s.102ZA if she continues to benefit from the property. The result is that both John and Emma can end up with a reservation of benefit problem.[25]

(2) If, however, John had made the gift of cash into the trust prior to the introduction of the anti-*Eversden* legislation on June 20, 2003, then even though Emma's interest was terminated after this date, ss.102(5A) and (5B), FA 1986 do not apply to John so there is no reservation of benefit by him. Hence unless Emma's interest is terminated on her death, John is subject to an income tax charge under the Regime once her interest ends. If Emma's qualifying iip is terminated after March 21, 2006 she has a reservation of benefit problem.

(3) Suppose her interest is **not** ended but the house is sold and the trustees hold cash. In these circumstances from the date of sale there is an intangibles charge on John under para.8 even though no inheritance tax planning may have been intended at all.

The position after March 22, 2006

The spouse exemption for interest in possession trusts produces further **5–10** complications in respect of trusts set up on or after March 22, 2006. Paragraph 10 states that the spouse/civil partner must become "beneficially entitled to an interest in possession". It does not require the spouse/civil partner to take a qualifying interest in possession. Interest in possession is not defined, even by reference to the IHT legislation but there is no suggestion that the interest in possession taken must be one in which the person is treated as beneficially entitled to the underlying trust capital. Therefore if A transfers his house to an interest in possession trust for his spouse on or after March 22, 2006 and it is occupied by A and his spouse, that is still a protected transaction for POA purposes so long as the spousal interest in possession continues until the spouse's death.

However, the inheritance tax consequences are quite different from the position if the transaction had been effected prior to March 22. First, there could be an

---

[23] Although see **5–21** and **5–23** for a consideration of the exclusion for cash gifts and whether such gifts need to be to an individual or can be settled.

[24] See **Ch.7**.

[25] See further **5–11** below.

entry charge on setting up the relevant property settlement (20 per cent over his unused nil rate band). The spouse exemption is not available because the property does not become comprised in the estate of the spouse.

Secondly, there is no protection from reservation of benefit if A continues to occupy the property because s.102(5) can only provide such protection if the transfer of value is spouse exempt.

Thirdly, there are 10-year anniversary charges on the settled property.

Fourthly, there is no inheritance tax payable on the death of the spouse because the property is not comprised in her estate. The inheritance tax charge arises on the death of A if the reservation of benefit continues.

5–11   A further complication in relation to the spousal interest in possession trust is that from March 22, 2006, any termination of the spousal interest where the spouse has a qualifying interest in possession can raise reservation of benefit problems by virtue of FA 1986, s.102ZA. This provides that where an individual has a qualifying interest in possession which is ended on or after March 22, 2006 by the trustees, that individual is deemed to make a gift for inheritance tax purposes in the underlying settled property. All this may mean is that in some cases a reservation of benefit problem can arise for both donor and spouse or a reservation of benefit problem can arise for the spouse and a POA problem for the donor. The range of problems is considered at **5–12** below.

Summary of interest in possession trusts and the spouse exemption: the POA, reservation of benefit and inheritance tax treatment

5–12   It will be helpful to consider the range of possible scenarios that can arise in relation to this exclusion depending on when the original disposal took place and when the spousal interest in possession is terminated. Each will be considered in turn. In all cases it is assumed that the spouse/civil partner is domiciled in the UK (which is important for IHT purposes) and that the property settled is land.

The first four scenarios outline the position where the settlement was made prior to June 20, 2003 (the date when the anti-*Eversden* legislation was introduced).

The second set of scenarios considers the position when the settlement is made between June 20, 2003 and March 21, 2006.

The final set of scenarios considers the position if the spousal trust is set up on or after March 22, 2006 (when the IHT settlement legislation changed).

5–13   *Trust established prior to June 20, 2003*

1.   In 2002

H settled his house on interest in possession trusts for his spouse W and continues to occupy the house. W's interest in possession is ended in 2004 when the children take on interest in possession trusts.

Tax consequences:

(a)   Exempt gift on settlement by H because of the spouse exemption. No inheritance tax payable. Spouse takes qualifying interest in possession.

(b) PET by W on termination of her interest in 2004. Children have qualifying interest in possession.

(c) No reservation of benefit by H or W. (H not caught by *Eversden* legislation because property settled prior to 2003 even though W's interest terminated in July 2004, i.e. after changes in June 2003. W not caught by s.102ZA because termination occurred prior to March 22, 2006.)

(d) POA charge on H from April 2005 (when POAT came into force).

2. In 2002

    H settled his house on interest in possession trusts for his spouse W and continues to occupy the house. W's interest in possession is ended in May 2007 when children take on interest in possession trusts. Both H and W continue to occupy the property.

    Tax consequences:

    (a) Exempt gift on settlement by H because of the spouse exemption. No inheritance tax payable. Spouse takes qualifying interest in possession.

    (b) PET by W on termination of her interest in May 2007. Children have qualifying interests in possession under the transitional serial interest rules.

    (c) No reservation of benefit by H. (H not caught by *Eversden* legislation because property settled prior to 2003.)

    (d) Reservation of benefit by W since her interest terminated after March 2006 and caught by s.102ZA.

    (e) POA charge on H from May 2007. Protection from POA until then.

    Note: in the above example there is a POA charge on H and a reservation of benefit by W!

3. In 2002

    H settled his house on interest in possession trusts for his spouse W and continues to occupy the house. W's interest in possession is ended in March 2009 when children take on interest in possession trusts. H and W continue to benefit.

    Tax consequences:

    (a) Exempt gift on settlement by H because of the spouse exemption. No inheritance tax payable. Spouse takes qualifying interest in possession.

    (b) Chargeable transfer by W on termination of her interest in March 2009. Children have non-qualifying interests in possession. Inheritance tax may be payable at 20 per cent if value of settled property exceeds W's nil rate band.

    (c) 10-year charges arise in the future since the settlement is in the relevant property regime.

(d) No reservation of benefit by H. (H not caught by *Eversden* legislation because property settled prior to 2003.)

(e) Reservation of benefit by W since her interest terminated after March 2006 and she is caught by s.102ZA.

(f) POA charge on H from March 2009 (when W's interest ends).

Note: in the above example there is a POA charge on H and a reservation of benefit by W!

4. In 2002

H settled his house on interest in possession trusts for his spouse W and continues to occupy the house. W's interest in possession ended on her death in March 2009 when the children took on interest in possession trusts.

Tax consequences:

(a) Exempt gift on settlement by H because of the spouse exemption. No inheritance tax payable. Spouse takes qualifying interest in possession.

(b) Chargeable transfer by W on termination of her interest on her death in 2009. Inheritance tax payable.

(c) Children have non-qualifying interests in possession and 10-year charges arise in the future.

(d) No reservation of benefit by H. (H not caught by anti-*Eversden* legislation because property settled prior to 2003.)

(e) No POA charge on H since W's interest ended on death.

5–14 *Trust set up between June 20, 2003 and March 22, 2006*

5. In 2004

H settled his house on qualifying interest in possession trusts for his spouse W and continues to occupy the house. W's interest in possession is ended in 2005 when the children take on interest in possession trusts.

Tax consequences:

(a) Exempt gift on settlement by H because of the spouse exemption. No inheritance tax payable. Spouse takes qualifying interest in possession.

(b) PET by W on termination of her interest in 2005. Children take qualifying interests in possession.

(c) Reservation of benefit by H but only after W's interest terminated. (H caught by anti-*Eversden* legislation once W's interest is terminated because property settled after June 20, 2003 and he is a beneficiary of the trust.)

(d) W not caught by s.102ZA because termination occurred prior to March 22, 2006. Hence no reservation of benefit by W.

(e) No POA charge on H because he has reserved a benefit. H is therefore protected under para.11(3); see **Ch.7**.

6. In 2004

H settled his house on qualifying interest in possession trusts for his spouse W and continues to occupy the house. W's interest in possession is ended in May 2007 when the children take on interest in possession trusts. Both H and W continue to benefit.

Tax consequences:

(a) Exempt gift on settlement by H because of the spouse exemption. No inheritance tax payable. Spouse takes qualifying interest in possession.

(b) PET by W on termination of her interest in May 2007. Children have qualifying interests in possession under the transitional serial interest rules.

(c) Reservation of benefit by H from May 2007. Until then protected from POA and reservation of benefit. (H caught by anti-*Eversden* legislation because property settled prior to 2003.)

(d) Also reservation of benefit by W since her interest terminated after March 2006 and therefore a deemed gift for inheritance tax purposes caught by s.102ZA.

(e) No POA charge on H due to reservation of benefit protection.

Note: in the above example there is an inheritance tax charge on H's death and on W's death under the reservation of benefit rules!

7. In 2004

H settled his house on interest in possession trusts for his spouse W and continues to occupy the house. W's interest in possession is ended inter vivos in March 2009. Children take on interest in possession trusts. W continues to benefit.

Tax consequences:

(a) Exempt gift on settlement by H because of the spouse exemption. No inheritance tax payable. W takes qualifying interest in possession.

(b) Chargeable transfer by W on termination of her interest in March 2009. Children have non-qualifying interests in possession. Inheritance tax may be payable at 20 per cent if value of settled property exceeds W's nil rate band.

(c) 10 year charges on the settlement arise in the future.

(d) Reservation of benefit by H. (H caught by anti-*Eversden* legislation because property settled prior to 2003.)

(e) Reservation of benefit by W: her interest terminated after March 2006 and therefore caught by s.102ZA.

(f) No POA charge on H due to reservation of benefit protection—para.11(5).

Note: in the above example there is an inheritance tax charge on H's death and on W's death under the reservation of benefit rules!

8. In 2004

H settled his house on interest in possession trusts for his spouse W and continues to occupy the house. W's interest in possession ends on her death in March 2009 when the children take on interest in possession trusts.

Tax consequences:

(a) Exempt gift on settlement by H because of the spouse exemption. No inheritance tax payable. W takes a qualifying interest in possession.

(b) Chargeable transfer by W on termination of her interest on death in 2009. Inheritance tax payable.

(c) Children have non-qualifying interests in possession and 10-year charges on the settlement arise in the future.

(d) Reservation of benefit by H. (H caught by anti-*Eversden* legislation because property settled prior to 2003.)

(e) No POA charge on H since W's interest ended on death and in any event protection available under para.11(5).

Note that both H and W suffer inheritance tax charges!

5–15 *Trust set up on or after March 22, 2006*

9. In 2007

H settled his house on interest in possession trusts for his spouse W and continues to occupy the house. W's interest in possession continues until her death.

Tax consequences:

(a) No spouse exemption on gift by H to trust because no qualifying interest in possession. Inheritance tax payable if value of settled property exceeds H's unused nil rate band.

(b) No inheritance tax payable on spouse's death—she did not have a qualifying interest in possession.

(c) Ten-year charges on the settlement.

(d) Reservation of benefit by H under s.102A while he occupies house. Protection from ROB under s.102(5) not available because gift is not spouse exempt. Inheritance tax is therefore chargeable on H's death (before or after W).

(e) No POA charge due to reservation of benefit and therefore H has protection under para.11(5). In any event the gift into the interest in possession trust is protected from a POA charge by virtue of para.10.

10. **In 2007**

H settled his house on non-qualifying interest in possession trusts for his spouse W and continues to occupy the house. W's interest in possession is ended inter vivos in May 2009 when children take on interest in possession trusts. Both H and W continue to benefit.

Tax consequences:

(a) No spouse exemption on gift by H to trust because W does not take a qualifying interest in possession. Inheritance tax is payable if value of settled property exceeds H's unused nil rate band.

(b) No inheritance tax payable on spouse's death or on termination of her interest in possession and no reservation of benefit problem for W because she did not have a qualifying interest in possession. Section 102ZA does not apply to her. No chargeable transfer or PET on termination of W's interest in possession since this is a relevant property settlement.

(c) Ten-year charges on the settlement.

(d) Reservation of benefit by H under s.102A while he occupies house. Protection under s.102(5) is not available because the gift into trust is not spouse exempt. Inheritance tax is therefore chargeable on H's death (before or after W).

(e) No POA charge due to reservation of benefit and therefore H has protection under para.11(5). In any event the gift into interest in possession trust is protected from a POA charge by virtue of para.10 albeit only while W's interest in possession continues.

11. **In 2007**

H settled **a share of** his house on non-qualifying interest in possession trusts for his spouse W and continues to occupy the house with W. W's interest in possession is ended inter vivos in May 2009 when the children take on interest in possession trusts. Both H and W continue to benefit.

Tax consequences:

(a) No spouse exemption on gift by H to trust because W does not have a qualifying interest in possession. Inheritance tax is payable if the value of the settled property exceeds H's unused nil rate band.

(b) No inheritance tax payable on spouse's death or on termination of her interest in possession and no reservation of benefit problem for W because she did not have a qualifying interest in possession. Section 102ZA does not apply. No chargeable transfer or PET on termination of W's interest in possession since this is a relevant property trust.

(c) Ten-year charges on the settlement.

(d) Reservation of benefit by H under s.102A while he occupies house. Inheritance tax on H's death before or after W and before or after termination of her interest in possession. No inheritance tax protection against reservation of benefit under s.102B(4) (joint occupation) because the donee here is a trust and the trustees are not in occupation. W is not deemed to be the donee because she did not take a qualifying interest in possession. Nor is there protection against reservation of benefit under s.102(5) since there is no spouse exemption.

(e) No POA charge due to reservation of benefit and therefore H has protection under para.11(5). In any event the gift into interest in possession trust is protected from POA under para.10 albeit only while W's interest in possession continues.

12. In 2007

H settled a share of rented property on non-qualifying interest in possession trusts for his spouse W and W receives rent from her share of the house. W's interest in possession continues until death. H can also benefit from the trust.

Tax consequences:

(a) No spouse exemption available on gift by H to trust because no qualifying interest in possession taken by W. Inheritance tax is payable if value of the settled property exceeds H's unused nil rate band.

(b) No inheritance tax on spouse's death or on earlier termination of her interest in possession and no reservation of benefit issue for W—she has no qualifying interest in possession. Section 102ZA therefore does not apply on any inter vivos termination of her interest and the settled property is not part of her estate on death.

(c) Ten-year charges on the settlement.

(d) No reservation of benefit by H: property is rented out even if he benefits from the rent and can benefit under the trust: s.120B(3) provides protection. No inheritance tax on the settled property on H's death before or after W.

(e) No POA charge due to protection under para.10 and in any event let property is outside the POA regime.

No POA charge arises and no inheritance tax is due on the settled property on H or W's deaths. For further discussion of this arrangement, see Ch.21.

A disposal by an individual is an excluded transaction if the disposal was a **5–16** disposition within the relief afforded to family maintenance dispositions by s.11 of the IHTA 1984.[26]

Similarly the provision of consideration by a disposition falling within s.11 is an excluded transaction so that the contribution condition is not met.[27] Such transactions are not transfers of value under the inheritance tax legislation and obtain a similar protection under the Regime. (However, note that a gift which is an exempt transfer under s.11 can still be caught by the reservation of benefit rules.) This exclusion will cover dispositions for the maintenance of a spouse or former spouse (and civil partners), dispositions for the maintenance education and training of children and dispositions for dependent relatives which are reasonable provision for the relative's care or maintenance. A dependent relative means (a) a relative of the donor or of his spouse/civil partner who is incapacitated by old age or infirmity from maintaining himself; or (b) the donor's mother/ father or either parent of the spouse/civil partner of the donor whether or not such parent is incapacitated.

A disposition of a capital sum (for example a cash sum settled into trust **5–17** following divorce) can be a disposition within s.11 but only insofar as it genuinely provides for the maintenance of the disponee. In earlier editions of this book it was not thought that this exclusion could be of much relevance given the restrictive view taken by HMRC of maintenance. If the cash was used to purchase a house for a child it was felt unlikely that HMRC would accept this was for the "maintenance" of the child. However, there have been two recent reported cases on this exemption: *McKelvey v RCC*[28] and *Phizackerley v RCC*.[29] In *McKelvey* a daughter who lived with and looked after her widowed mother who was 85, fell ill with terminal cancer. She gave two houses to her mother in March and May 2003. The combined value of the two properties was £169,000. Neither the daughter or her mother lived in the properties but the mother benefited from the rental income. The daughter died within seven years of the gift and even though the houses were not sold and not in the event needed for the mother, the executors successfully argued that most of the gift was exempt under s.11. The intention of the donor had been to provide for her mother and HMRC were not entitled to take into account events after the donor's death.

Example 5.6

As part of the financial settlement on divorce Carolyn settles cash into trust for her children in order to fund school fees. She retains a remainder interest. This will result in a para.8 charge on Carolyn because the para.10 exclusions do not apply to intangibles.[30] If the trust used the cash to purchase a property

---

[26] See Sch.15, para.10(1)(d).
[27] See Sch.15, para.10(2)(d).
[28] [2008] STC (SCD) 944.
[29] [2007] STC (SCD) 328.
[30] Unless it can be said that the para.8 charge is inapplicable to the interest carved-out and kept by Carolyn because this remainder interest is not settled property and does not apply to the interests set up for the children: see **6–14**. Alternatively it might be argued that a trust set up pursuant to a court order is not a gift anyway and involves no element of bounty. Therefore nothing has been "provided" and para.8 cannot apply.

in which Carolyn also lives it is unlikely that this would fall within the definition of "maintenance"[31] and therefore obtain protection under para.10. Carolyn would have to rely on para.11(5)(a) (reservation of benefit) for protection from the POA charge. She reserved a benefit by living in the house.

Annual and small gifts exemptions

5–18   A disposal by an individual is an excluded transaction if the disposal is an outright gift to another individual and is, for IHT purposes, a transfer of value that is wholly exempt by virtue of the annual exemption or the small gifts exemption.[32] Gifts to trustees (other than bare trustees) will thus not qualify. There is a similar exclusion from the contribution condition where the provision of the consideration is an outright gift within either s.19 or s.20 of IHTA 1984.[33]

Curiously whilst gifts within s.20 (small gifts exemption) are outside the reservation of benefit rules,[34] there is no exemption for gifts falling within the annual exemption, i.e. the reservation of benefit rules are capable of applying in such cases as they are to gifts that are excluded under s.11.

These exemptions might be of use if, for example, a father gives a son shares worth £6,000 using two annual IHT exemptions. The son sells the shares and with the cash sets up a new business which does well. He later uses the sale proceeds of the business to buy a house for his father's occupation.

EXCLUDED TRANSACTION APPLICABLE ONLY TO THE DISPOSAL CONDITION

Arm's length sales

5–19   This is one of the most important exclusions because the intention is to exclude normal commercial sales from the POA charge. It only applies in relation to the **disposal condition**, not the contribution condition.

Under both the land charge and the chattels charge, the disposal is an excluded transaction if it was of the individual's *whole* interest in the property, except for any right expressly reserved by him over the property, either:

(a) by a transaction made at arm's length with a person not connected with him; or

(b) by a transaction such as might be expected to be made at arm's length between persons not connected with each other.[35]

The arm's length or equivalent transaction test is the same as that in s.10(1)(a) and (b) of the IHTA 1984. As with s.10 and the inheritance tax legislation generally, the definition of "connected persons" under the Regime and hence

---

[31] See *Phizackerley* [2007] STC (SCD) 328 when a gift of a residence was not maintenance.
[32] See Sch.15, para.10(1)(e).
[33] See Sch.15, para.10(2)(e).
[34] See FA 1986, s.102(5)(b).
[35] See Sch.15, para.10(1)(a).

under para.10 is modified so that "relative" is extended to include uncle, aunt, nephew and niece as well as brother, sister, ancestor or lineal descendant.[36]

It will be noted that the exclusion does not cover a sale of a half share in a property or a sale of the whole but at an undervalue. This omission excluded from protection a variety of common transactions, particularly commercial equity release schemes. After some pressure, the Paymaster General introduced a Regulation giving limited relief for sales of part[37] and this is discussed in more detail in **Ch.12**.[38]

HMRC confirms in the guidance notes (see A2.49) that a donor's whole interest means whatever interest he owns: so if a vendor owns only half the property and sells that half for full consideration he can come within the exclusion. It is also accepted that the wording in para.10(1)(a) which refers to a disposal of his whole interest "except for any right expressly reserved by him over the property" can encompass a transaction whereby the owner carves out a lease and then sells the freehold subject to that lease at market value. However, "a truly arm's length transaction must take account of the [marriage] value."

Importance of arm's length exclusion

Paragraph 10(1) is a key provision which is considered further in **Ch.21** on equity release arrangements within the family and in **17–18** in the context of home loan schemes. So far as the latter are concerned it is generally considered that the necessary arm's length element will be missing and that such arrangements do not therefore amount to excluded transactions. For instance, the fact that the loan is left outstanding indefinitely is not the sort of arm's length transaction one would "expect" to make with an unconnected party.   **5–20**

Note also that para.10(1)(a) only protects transactions which are otherwise within the disposal condition. If Michael gives his partner Susan cash in 2003 and Susan then buys the entirety of Michael's interest in the property this will be an excluded transaction for the purposes of the disposal condition but not for the purposes of the contribution condition and therefore Michael will be subject to the POA Regime.[39] If Michael sells his house for full market value to Susan and Susan then sells that house and invests the proceeds in another property which is occupied by Michael that is still not in breach of the contribution condition because it has not been "provided", i.e. there is no bounty

---

[36] See Sch.15, para.2. The definition of connected persons in the inheritance tax legislation is in s.270 and apart from extending the meaning of relative as set out above cross-refers to TCGA 1992, s.286. Under the Regime the definition of connected person is found in Sch.15, para.2, extending the meaning of relative as above and referring to TA 1988, s.839. The definition of connected persons is the same for s.286 and s.839; hence the following are included as connected persons: husband and wife (or civil partner); issue; brother, sister, grandparents and great grandparents, settlor and trustee; trustees of settlements set up by the same settlor and certain company and partnership arrangements. Note that cohabitees are not connected persons.

[37] The statement is in **Appendix I** where the Regulation (SI 2005/724) is also set out.

[38] See also HMRC guidance at A2.50.

[39] Contrast the position on sales of part discussed in **Ch.12** and **Ch.21**.

EXCLUDED TRANSACTION APPLICABLE ONLY TO THE CONTRIBUTION CONDITION

The seven-year defence

5–21   The provision by a person of consideration for another's acquisition of land or chattels is an excluded transaction (so that the contribution condition is not met) if it constituted an outright gift of money (in any currency) by the individual to the other person and was made at least seven years before the earliest date on which:

· (a) in the case of land, the individual occupies the land, whether alone or together with any person[40]; and

(b) in the case of a chattel, the individual is in possession of, or has the use of, the chattel, whether alone or together with other persons.[41]

So, if X gives Y £100,000 which Y uses to purchase a house and X does not occupy the house until at least seven years after the cash gift, the contribution condition will not be satisfied. This provision incorporates into the land and chattels charging codes the same time limit as applies to a PET.[42]

5–22   The aim is to ease compliance. Thus where someone has made a gift of cash seven years ago and has not yet occupied land or used chattels purchased by the donee the donor does not need to be concerned about the Regime. Note though that the exclusion does not apply unless there is an outright gift of money so that there are still potential compliance problems. The exclusion will also apply if the donor made the gift at any time before April 6, 1998 even if he occupied the land or used the chattels within seven years of the gift: see **5–24**.

Example 5.7

(1) Eric gave Ernie shares worth £100,000 in 1987. Ernie mixed the shares with his own portfolio and sold all the shares for £200,000 in 1997. He used the resulting cash to buy a house which Eric then occupies. Eric is not within any of the para.10 exclusions even though the occupation took place more than seven years after the gift. The gift was of shares not cash. However, Eric may be caught by the reservation of benefit provisions (because the tracing provisions apply) in which case the Regime does not apply because of the exemption under para.11(5).[43]

(2) By contrast, if Eric had given cash to Ernie in 1987 who then immediately used it to purchase a house for Eric's occupation, Eric would not be caught by either POA or reservation of benefit. The tracing provisions for reservation of benefit purposes do not apply to the cash and the gift by Eric occurred prior to 1998 so cannot be caught by the POA Regime in **Ch.23**.

---

[40]   See Sch.15, para.10(2)(c) and para.3(1)(a).
[41]   See Sch.15, para.10(2)(c) and para.6(1)(a).
[42]   See also the prior independent transaction exclusion for lease carve-outs in the anti *Ingram* legislation: see FA 1986, s.102A(5).
[43]   See **Ch.7**.

(3) If Eric had lent the funds to Ernie and then written off the debt later that is not exempt as an outright gift of money.

Cash gifts to trusts

Does the gift of cash have to be outright to an individual rather than a cash gift to **5–23** a trust to come within para.10(2)(c)? The different wording used in para.10(2)(e) in relation to the annual exemption (which expressly refers to gifts to individuals) suggests that an outright gift to an individual is not required.[44] In their guidance at A2.10 HMRC indicate that "other person" means the person referred to in paras 3(3) and 6(3). This could include trustees not just individuals although HMRC may not accept that gifts of cash to trusts can be excluded transactions.

Example 5.8

In May 1997 John gives cash of £100,000 to an interest in possession trust set up for his wife Carolyn. The trust uses that cash to purchase a house in which John lives. Carolyn's interest in possession is terminated in 2005. Is the transaction an excluded transaction?

It cannot be an excluded transaction under para.10(2)(b) because his wife's interest in possession has ended. The property is not subject to the reservation of benefit provisions because the gift into trust for his spouse was made before June 20, 2003.[45] Therefore it does not have protection under para.11(3) and (5)(a). However, one would argue that it is an excluded transaction under para.10(2)(c). It is an outright gift of money to "a person" albeit not to an individual. This would mean that gifts of cash into spousal trusts pre-June 20, 2003 are not caught if the cash was subsequently used to purchase a house which the couple occupied after seven years or if the gift was made pre-April 6, 1998.

Such transactions are uncommon. Gifts of cash to other sorts of trusts are likely to be outside the Regime anyway because they are within the reservation of benefit provisions. However, if for some reason reservation of benefit does not apply, a gift of cash to an irrevocable discretionary trust could in the authors' view still be considered an outright gift (even if the donor is a discretionary beneficiary) and therefore provide protection where the donor occupies a house owned by the trustees.

Cash gifts pre-April 6, 1998

The actual wording in para.10 refers to (inter alia) the gift being made "at least **5–24** seven years before the earliest date on which the chargeable person met the condition in para.3(1)(a)". Hence the condition in para.3(1)(a) cannot be met (i.e. there cannot be a chargeable person) until April 6, 2005 (when the Schedule takes effect). On this basis HMRC has confirmed that cash gifts made before

---

[44] In the Independent Taxation Manual outright gift in the context of income tax is defined as a gift not subject to conditions and not able to revert to the donor in any circumstances whatsoever.
[45] See **Ch.16**.

April 6, 1998 are not caught by the Regime even if the donor occupies the property within seven years.[46]

It appears that if the occupation has occurred within seven years of the gift and the gift was made after April 5, 1998 it will be caught even if the occupation arose prior to April 2005. It is also thought that if a person goes into occupation within seven years and then moves out but re-occupies later, even if seven years has expired, he will be outside the protection of the exclusion.

The exclusion is similar to the approach adopted in the anti-*Ingram* legislation in 1999: where the lease is carved-out more than seven years before the gift of the freehold then such a transaction is (after 1999) not caught by the reservation of benefit rules (although it is caught by the POA Regime).

5–25   In summary, the excluded transactions contained in para.10 are important but limited in scope; it will be seen from the above examples that they do not provide protection for a number of transactions (particularly in relation to intangibles) where inheritance tax avoidance may not have been in contemplation.

---

[46] See A2.10.

CHAPTER 6

INTANGIBLE PROPERTY COMPRISED IN A SETTLOR-INTERESTED SETTLEMENT: PARAGRAPH 8

Introduction

Paragraph 8 can apply only to intangibles. It does not apply to land or chattels **6–01** whether or not caught under the para.3 or para.6 charge. Moreover it applies only to intangibles held within a settlement. Intangibles is defined to include cash, equities, insurance products and indeed all property other than land or chattels.

Three conditions must be satisfied in order for a para.8 charge to arise. First, the terms of a settlement, as they affect any property comprised in the settlement, are such that any income arising from that property would be treated as the income of the settlor by virtue of ITTOIA 2005, s.624.[1]

Secondly, the property in the settlement must at any time in the tax year comprise intangible property.

Thirdly, the intangible property in the trust is or represents property which the individual either settled or added to the settlement after March 17, 1986.[2] Note that it only includes property held directly by the trustees, not cash or intangibles owned by any holding company. This is relevant in relation to foreign domiciliaries (see **Ch.8**).

Curiously, although para.8 is framed by reference to s.624, the term "settlement" is given the meaning it has for IHT purposes, not the meaning it has under s.620(1) for the purposes of s.624. For IHT purposes no bounty is required. HMRC regard this as significant. However, para 8 requires the chargeable person to have "settled or added to" the settlement and therefore this distinction may be of less relevance than HMRC realise: see **6–11** below.

Although the charge only applies to settled property, in three ways it is significantly harsher than the charge on land or chattels. First, none of the para.10 exclusions can apply to intangible property. As the example below demonstrates, this can be particularly unfortunate where the spouse/civil partner has an interest in possession in the settlement. Secondly, under the valuation provisions the charge is fixed by reference to the capital value of the property on April 6, 2005 (or the date the charge first applies if later) and has to be revalued each year rather than every five years.[3] This can be problematic where, for example, the settled property is an insurance policy or shares in an unquoted company. Thirdly,

---

[1] As a result of the Tax Law Rewrite, from April 6, 2005 this section replaced TA 1988, s.660A.

[2] See Sch.15, paras 8(1)(a) and (2). This is the date marking the introduction of the reservation of benefit rules.

[3] See further **Ch.12**.

the charge is a fixed percentage of capital values. Only limited relief is given for the fact that the settlor will also pay income tax on any actual income generated by the settlement and no account is taken of the fact that the trust may never generate income at all. It is tax on "hypothetical" income.

Spouse and civil partner ignored

6–02 For this purpose s.624 is applied ignoring any benefit or possible benefit to the settlor's spouse or civil partner from the settlement.[4] Thus a settlor cannot be caught simply because his spouse can benefit.

Example 6.1

On May 18, 2003 John settles property on qualifying interest in possession trusts for his wife Emma. He is excluded from all benefit. The trust holds cash. John is not caught by para.8 even though his spouse can benefit. However, if John can potentially benefit under the settlement (e.g. under the terms of an overriding power of appointment) then even though the settled property is within Emma's estate for IHT purposes he is subject to income tax under para.8.[5]

It is therefore necessary to review all trusts set up after March 17, 1986 in which the settlor retains some interest. Although such trusts may not have been set up for inheritance tax reasons, if they hold any property other than land or chattels, the settlor will be within para.8. There is no let out or exclusion just because the spouse retains an interest in possession. The consequences of this can be severe as explained later.

6–03 As noted above, land or chattels comprised in a settlement do not fall within para.8 (see para.8(1)(a)). If the settlor does not occupy the land or use or enjoy the chattels, then neither paras 3 nor 6 can apply. Hence trustees of a settlement otherwise within para.8 may consider selling their intangible investments and purchasing tangible assets in the form of let land or chattels. In Example 6.1 since the spouse took an interest in possession and this has not yet been ended, if the trustees now sell the intangible property and purchase land occupied by John this would not matter because the transaction is an excluded transaction.[6] There is no reservation of benefit issue. The property remains part of Emma's estate for inheritance tax purposes. If the trustees buy let land there is no POA charge anyway even if Emma's interest in possession is then ended.

The property test and sub-funds

6–04 What matters is that the settlement is settlor-interested in relation to the property in question, not that the settlement is settlor-interested generally.

---

[4] See Sch.15, para.8(1)(b).

[5] Note that as a result of the anti-*Eversden* legislation if the settlement had been set up after June 19, 2003 and Emma's interest terminated to enable the property to be held on discretionary trusts, John would at that point reserve a benefit, hence there is no POA charge: see **Ch.16**.

[6] See para.10(1)(c) and **5–11**.

Example 6.2

Assume X is the settlor of a settlement with two sub-funds. Sub-fund A, from which the settlor can benefit, contains land, while sub-fund B, from which the settlor cannot benefit, contains intangible property. The settlement as a whole is settlor-interested, but that does not matter. What matters is that the settlement is not settlor-interested in relation to sub-fund B and is not within para.8 in relation to sub-fund A while it holds only tangible property. (Compare this with the capital gains tax treatment prior to April 6, 2008 when the settlor would have been taxed on all the gains arising from the property in both funds under TCGA 1992, s.77 where he could benefit from any part of the trust.)

Absence of income

As noted already, the fact that no actual income arises does not prevent an income **6–05** tax charge under the Regime.[7] Hence if the trust holds non-income producing shares, e.g. offshore funds, the POA charge can still arise. At a 4.75% official rate of interest the effective rate of tax is 1.9% of the capital value (40% x 4.75 x capital value).

Paragraph 8 requires that the terms of the settlement as they affect any property comprised in the settlement are such that any income arising from the property would be treated as income of the settlor. It may be that income arises to the settlement which would be treated as the income of the settlor under s.624 but otherwise than by reason of the terms of the settlement, e.g. where the settlor waives dividends on shares he owns personally and other shares are owned by a settlement for (say) grandchildren from which he and his spouse are excluded. If the dividend declared multiplied by the number of shares in issue exceeds the company's distributable reserves, i.e. the waiver enables the trust to receive a greater dividend than would otherwise be possible, s.624 can apply. However, in this case the Regime does not apply because the income does not arise *from* the settled property: it arises as a result of the waiver.

An entirely different approach

Paragraph 8 adopts an entirely different approach to that adopted under the para.3 **6–06** land provisions and the para.6 chattels provisions, in a number of ways.

Psychic income and the comfort factor

First, under the para.3 and para.6 provisions there must be some element of **6–07** actual benefit to the taxpayer. Under para.8, on the other hand, the mere possibility of benefiting is sufficient to invoke the charge.

---

[7] See **6–20** for the limited relief if income tax is suffered by the settlor on income which does arise in the settlement.

6–08 Secondly, as noted earlier, none of the "excluded transaction" let-outs in para.10 can apply to prevent para.8 from operating.[8] Accordingly, the favoured treatment available to transfers to spouses is unavailable: as noted earlier, if X settles intangible property on trusts under which his spouse has an interest in possession which is subject to a power of appointment which can be exercised in favour of a class of beneficiaries including X then para.8 will apply. If the settlement initially owns a house (outside the para.8 charge) which is later sold and for one month cash is held before further land is purchased then the para.8 charge applies for that month.[9]

The "no bounty" rule

6–09 If the income tax definition of "settlement" applied, an arm's length transaction would not be caught under para.8, not because of any provision in the Regime but because of income tax case law. Under a string of cases, culminating in *IRC v Plummer*,[10] it is well established that what would otherwise be a settlement for the purposes of s.624 will be prevented from being a settlement if it lacks any element of bounty. So, entirely commercial arrangements which involve intangible property being held in trust will be outside s.624. A good example is where partners in a firm, in order to provide funding to purchase the shares of a deceased partner, take out insurance policies on their own lives and then settle them on trusts under which the policies are held for all the partners. The arrangement is entirely commercial and in no way intended to benefit any partner gratuitously. If the s.620(1) definition of "settlement" applied, such an arrangement would prima facie fall outside the terms of para.8 in relation to each of the partners. The relevant definition of settlement for POA purposes, however, is the IHT definition, which is not subject to any such "no bounty" limitation and in the above example the partner has clearly "settled" something on trust, even if he had no gratuitous intention.

The section in the HMRC guidance notes on partnership life insurance policies at A2.63 states their view that where "the partner retains a benefit for themselves, for example they can cash in the policy during their lifetime", although it is not a gift with reservation for inheritance tax purposes because the arrangement is commercial, the trust is a settlement for inheritance tax purposes and a charge to tax under para.8 will arise. Such policies are used not only by partners but also by shareholders in a private company. Even though under the terms of the policy only business owners can normally benefit, the terms of the trust under which the policy is held often provide that should the settlor leave the business the benefits will revert to him automatically. Under other trust arrangements the settlor remains one of the potential beneficiaries in whose favour the trustees can appoint, for example if he leaves the business. It is possible that the life policy may have very little value—it is often a term policy and if the life assured is in good health the de minimis exemption should apply. However, the possibility of a para.8 charge will require the taxpayer to effect a revaluation each year.

---

[8] Excluded transactions are considered in **Ch.5**.
[9] Of course the benefit may fall within de minimis: see **Ch.9**.
[10] [1980] AC 896; [1979] STC 793.

Similar problems arise in relation to pension policies. Individual trusts of **6–10** retirement annuity and personal pension policies will typically provide for the retirement benefits to be held for the absolute benefit of the individual member with death benefits held on discretionary trusts. There is no reservation of benefit problem by virtue of SP 10/86 but could they be caught by POA? It was thought that the POA Regime would not apply to approved pension arrangements on the basis that the retirement benefits themselves are not settled property and even if the death benefits are held for the member's estate this is not sufficient to bring the trust within para 8. HMRC's view is unknown.[11]

Although the inheritance tax definition of settlement is adopted, para.8 requires **6–11** the settled property on which POA is charged to be or represent property "which the chargeable person settled or added to the settlement after 17 March 1986". Hence where X has sold a house to the trust leaving the purchase price outstanding as a loan, it would not appear that he has settled or added anything to the trust (other than the initial £10 he may have put in to set it up in pilot form). Hence in the case of a home loan scheme, where the house is later sold and the property trust holds cash subject to a debt it is arguable that no POA charge arises.

The charge does not apply to intangible property owned by a company which **6–12** is in turn owned by a trust since such property is not comprised in a settlement. The shares of the company itself will be settled property and potentially caught by POA. However, in the case of foreign domiciliaries, such shares will generally be protected under para.12 anyway (see **Ch.8**). Hence if the trustees of a trust established by a foreign domiciliary own an offshore holding company which in turn holds UK shares, there is no POA charge on the UK shares, and the holding company's shares should be protected by the para.12(3) relief (see **Ch.8**).

Practical scope: relevance of exemptions

Although none of the "excluded transactions" provisions apply in relation to **6–13** para.8, all of the para.11 exemptions apply, and this is likely to restrict the operation of para.8 in practice for two reasons.[12]

The settlor has a qualifying interest in possession

First, where the settlor has a qualifying interest in possession in intangible **6–14** property, the exemption given to property already comprised within the settlor's IHT estate will prevent para.8 from applying.

Trustees can benefit the settlor under non-Eversden trusts

Secondly, where the settlor does not have a qualifying interest in possession but **6–15** is capable of benefitting under the trust because, e.g. he is a member of a discretionary class of beneficiaries in whose favour the trustees can exercise a power of appointment, the settlor is likely to have reserved a benefit in respect of

---

[11] See the approach adopted in relation to discounted gift schemes: **Ch.22** and for the approach of HMRC, see A2.61.
[12] See **Ch.7** for a consideration of these exemptions.

the settlement so that the exemption given under para.11(5)(a) prevents para.8 from applying.

Trustees can benefit the settlor under Eversden trusts

6–16 If the settlement is one under which the property is held under an *Eversden* arrangement (see **Ch.16**) on discretionary trusts under which the settlor can benefit, the property will not be caught by the reservation of benefit rules and therefore para.8 will apply. *Eversden* arrangements were the primary target of para.8.

Settlor has a reversionary interest

6–17 If the settlor has settled property on trusts such that he retains a reversionary interest, the carve-out principle will prevent the reservation of benefit provisions from applying.[13] The only relief available which will reduce (although not eliminate) the para.8 charge is given by para.11(1)(b) as restricted by para.11(2).[14] However, it is possible that reverter to settlor trusts are not in fact caught by the Regime. The analysis of HMRC in relation to certain insurance schemes which employ such trusts appears to be that where the settlor retains rights in respect of discounted gift schemes, such rights are not settled property and therefore para.8 does not apply. HMRC does not accept that this approach can be adopted in relation to reverter to settlor trusts which hold other intangibles such as shares or cash.[15]

THE CHARGE

6–18 Where para.8 applies in respect of the whole or part of a year of assessment an amount equal to "the chargeable amount" is treated as the individual's income chargeable to income tax.[16]

The chargeable amount

6–19 For any taxable period—i.e. the year of assessment or part thereof during which para.8 applies[17]—the chargeable amount is N minus T where N is what we will call "the prescribed interest" and T is what we will call "the tax allowance". For this purpose:

(a) **"the prescribed interest"** is the amount of interest that would be payable for the taxable period if interest were payable at the prescribed rate (now 4.75 per cent) on an amount equal to the value of the intangible property at

---

[13] See, for instance, *Re Cochrane* [1906] 2 I.R. 200 and see **22–02**.
[14] See **7–08**.
[15] See A2.61.
[16] See Sch.15, para.8(3).
[17] See Sch.15, para.9(3).

the valuation date.[18] The "valuation date", in relation to a year of assessment, being such date as may be prescribed and under the Regulations means April 6, 2005 or the first day on which the taxpayer becomes chargeable under the Regime if later.[19]

(b) "**the tax allowance**" is the amount of any income tax or CGT payable by the individual in respect of the taxable period by virtue of ss.461 and 624 of ITTOIA 2005; ss.720–730 of the Income Tax Act 2007[20]; and s.77 (now repealed) and s.86 of the Taxation of Chargeable Gains Act 1992 so far as that tax is attributable to the relevant intangible property.[21] The use of the word "payable" means that the "allowance" is available whether that tax is actually paid or not and even if it is reimbursed by the trustees. However, if the chargeable person is a remittance basis user and the foreign income of the trust is unremitted and no tax is paid because of the foreign domicile defence in s.648, it is thought that the tax allowance is nil. No tax is payable until the income is remitted.

The prescribed rate has varied since the Regime was first introduced. On April 6, 2005 the rate was five per cent. This operated for two years. Then on April 6, 2007 the rate was 6.25 per cent which operates for the next two years (although the official rate of interest has reduced to 4.75 per cent from March 1, 2009 it is the rate at April 6 in the relevant tax year that is relevant). On April 6, 2009 the rate was 4.75 per cent. The effect of this can be seen in Example 6.3 (2) below.

No tax credits

The chargeable amount on which tax under the Regime is levied is reduced only **6–20** by the amount of any tax that is payable under the other provisions (s.624, s.77, etc). It would, arguably, be fairer for *the tax due* under the Regime to be reduced by a tax credit. This matter was raised in the Standing Committee debates where the Government made the point that both the charge under the existing rules in (then) TA 1988, s.739, etc. and the charge under the Regime were freestanding charges imposed by reference to separate codes and were therefore justified in their own right. In the Government's view, any relief at all was generous!

---

[18] See Sch.15, para.9(1).

[19] See Sch.15, para.9(3). See reg.2.

[20] In practice since the para.8 charge cannot apply to assets owned by a holding company in trust; usually the transfer of assets charge is limited to income of these underlying assets rather than income at the trust level, since ITTOIA, s.624 will generally apply to such income. Hence it is unlikely ss.720–730 will be of much relevance since it will be tax **attributable to the income of the shares and other assets** held by the holding company and these assets are not relevant property. In a few circumstances where the settlement is not bounteous and therefore the trust income is not caught by ITTOIA, s.624 the transfer of assets provisions may be relevant. However, there seems no scope for deducting the tax paid under the transfer of assets provisions in respect of income produced by the underlying assets of a holding company against the chargeable amount levied on the taxpayer in respect of the holding company shares ("the relevant property").

[21] See Sch.15, para.9(1).

Example 6.3

(1) Waldo is the UK resident and domiciled settlor of a non-resident settlor-interested settlement. Assume that the value of the intangible property in the settlement is £1,300,000. In tax year 2005–2006 the trustees receive income of £50,000 which is taxed on Waldo under s.624 and realise capital gains of £100,000 which are deemed to be Waldo's gains by virtue of s.86 of the Taxation of Chargeable Gains Act 1992. Waldo's circumstances are such that £20,000 is payable in income tax on the £50,000 and £40,000 in CGT on the £100,000. The tax allowance is thus £60,000. The chargeable amount in 2005/06 is five per cent of £1.5 million = £65,000. This will be reduced by the tax allowance to £5,000 (with the result that the chargeable amount is within the £5,000 annual exemption; see **Ch.9**).

(2) Fred is the UK resident and domiciled settlor of a UK resident trust which holds tracker funds. He is caught by the POA charge. The funds were worth £100,000 in April 2005. Assume no income or gains arise. The chargeable amount for POA purposes is 5 per cent x £100,000 = £5,000. This is within the annual exemption and so no POA arises.

On April 6, 2006 the funds are worth £120,000. The chargeable amount is £6,000. POA is payable on the whole £6,000.

On April 6, 2007 the valuation is £90,000 but the prescribed rate of interest is 6.25 per cent. The chargeable amount is £5,625 and POA is due.

On April 6, 2009 the valuation is £105,000 and the rate is 4.75 per cent. The chargeable amount is £4,987.50 and no POA is due since it falls within the annual exemption.

Difficulties in valuation

6–21 There are particular difficulties in valuing intangibles. For example, how are insurance policies meant to be valued under the Regime? There is nothing to suggest that one takes the surrender value or follows the treatment set out in the inheritance tax legislation.[22]

Suppose a settlor effected an insurance policy on his life written on trusts under which he can benefit before March 18, 1986. The reservation of benefit rules were not then in force. For the last 20 years he has been paying the premiums on that policy. FA 1986, s.102(6) provides an exemption from reservation of benefit in respect of premiums paid post March 17, 1986 where the policy was taken out before March 18 and the premiums increase at a pre-arranged rate.[23]

However, premiums paid since March 17, 1986 are arguably within the POA Regime although one could argue that there is no **addition** to the settled property by payment of the premiums, only a **preservation** of the settled property. A

---

[22] See, for instance, IHTA 1984, s.167.
[23] A2.78.

similar problem arose in relation to the IHT changes in 2006 and a specific exemption was introduced.[24]

Operation of relieving provisions

Assume that the settlor has retained a remainder interest under a settlement **6–22** which falls within para.8 (as in a classic reverter to settlor trust[25]) and that such reverter to settlor trusts are within the para.8 charge. The IHT position is as follows:

(a) the settlor is not caught by reservation of benefit because the remainder interest is considered to be property which was never given away (it is a "carve-out"); and

(b) the remainder interest is taxed as part of the settlor's estate.[26]

So far as the para.8 charge is concerned the remainder interest (comprised in the settlor's estate) derives its value from the relevant property (the intangibles comprised in the settlement). An exemption from charge is therefore given under para.11(2), which provides that "the chargeable amount in para.9 is to be reduced by such proportion as is reasonable to take account of the inclusion of the (remainder interest) in his estate".

Example 6.4

In 1987 Julia settled property on interest in possession trusts for her mother. She retained a reversionary interest so that on her mother's death the property will revert to Julia. The trust property initially comprised a house occupied by her mother. In 2006 her mother moved out and the trust sells the house in June 2009 and then holds cash of £1 million. For the purposes of para.8 the chargeable amount is 4.75 per cent of £1 million = £47,500. It is this sum which falls to be reduced by reference to para.11(2). For instance, if the remainder interest was worth £100,000 (i.e. one tenth of the value of the trust fund), then a ten per cent reduction in the chargeable amount would leave a sum chargeable of £42,750 (4.75 per cent x £900,000).

This small reduction may result in the settlor wishing to make the election in para.22 (i.e. to opt into the reservation of benefit rules) or possibly re-organising the trust so that it is no longer within para.8. For example, the cash could be invested in land again or Julia could assign her remainder interest to her spouse.[27]

---

[24] See IHTA 1984, s.46A.

[25] See **Ch.18**.

[26] It is not excluded property for IHT purposes: see IHTA 1984, s.48(1)(b). In practice the value of the interest may be small, e.g. if it is subject to overriding powers of appointment vested in the trustees.

[27] The anti-avoidance provisions on reverter to settlor trusts introduced in FA 2006 are discussed in **Ch.18** and at **7–24** and **8–19**, but are not relevant in this situation.

Anomalies

6–23 It is also somewhat surprising that where the settlor retains an interest in the settlement but his spouse still has a continuing interest in possession he is nevertheless subject to an income tax charge under para.8. Why not introduce an exclusion in the same way as for land and chattels so that the charge is only applicable if the spousal interest has terminated? After all, the property is within the spouse's estate for IHT purposes if the spouse enjoys a qualifying interest in possession and the settlor already pays income tax on any actual income produced.

In summary, death benefit policies taken out by business owners, pre-March 1986 trusts, pension policies, interest in possession trusts for the spouse/civil partner and reverter to settlor trusts holding intangibles remain problematic areas with HMRC apparently being unwilling to introduce any relieving provisions from POA.

CHAPTER 7

MAIN EXEMPTIONS UNDER THE REGIME

INTRODUCTION

As we have explained elsewhere, the principle behind the Regime is to tax any **7–01** transaction that falls within the disposal/contribution condition where there is continued use, benefit or occupation unless there is a specific exclusion or exemption. As explained in **Ch.1** this means that some innocent transactions are caught. This chapter considers three main exemptions which, if they apply, prevent any of the three charging codes under the Regime (for land, chattels and settled intangible property) from operating. Note that unlike excluded transactions (discussed in **Ch.5**) they apply to settled intangible property as well as to land and chattels. However, for reasons we will see, it is generally preferable for the taxpayer if a transaction is excluded under para.10 rather than exempt under para.11.

These three exemptions are as follows.

1. **The ownership exemption**. This is contained in para.11(1), Sch.15 and exempts property from the Regime if its value is comprised in the donor's estate for IHT purposes. Furthermore exemption is also given if other property is in the donor's estate which derives its value from (say) the relevant land or chattels. The rationale for the exemption is that if the donor pays IHT then he should not also pay income tax. In fact, as we will see, this exemption does not always work in the way intended and can leave innocent transactions caught by the POA Regime. Equally schemes designed to avoid IHT can in some cases escape the POA charge. The important point to note at this stage is that the exemption applies if the property is in the person's estate for inheritance tax purposes even if it is not actually taxed on that person's death (for instance because the value falls within his IHT nil rate band or qualifies for the spouse exemption). This exemption covers property owned by the donor personally and settled property in which the donor retains a **qualifying** interest in possession. After March 22, 2006 new qualifying interests in possession are increasingly rare.[1]

2. **The reserved benefit exemption**. This exemption is found in paras 11(3) and (5) and exempts property which is subject to a reservation of benefit and therefore within the IHT net. Furthermore, there is an exemption

---

[1] See **7–06**.

where property which derives its value from the relevant property is subject to a reservation (see paras 11(3)(b) and 5). Again the principle is clear—where the donor pays IHT he should not also have to pay income tax under the Regime. In addition, if the property would be subject to a reservation of benefit but for some statutory let-out in the inheritance tax legislation, then the intention is that the same statutory let-out should apply to exempt the taxpayer from POA.[2] In other words, as the Government has decided that certain transactions should qualify for favoured treatment under the reservation of benefit rules, the same should apply under the Regime. An important point to note at this stage is that property which is subject to a reservation of benefit is not as such in the person's estate for inheritance tax purposes while he is alive.[3] This can be significant when looking at the excluded liability provisions.

3. **The posthumous arrangements exemption**. This is found in para.16 of Sch.15 and aims to ensure that a person effecting a deed of variation and similar transactions should not be regarded as the disponer for the purposes of the Regime. (see **7–19**).

FIRST EXEMPTION—THE OWNERSHIP EXEMPTION

7–02 This provides that, subject to the qualifications considered at **7–19**, below, none of the three charging codes applies to an individual at a time when **for IHT purposes** his estate includes the relevant property.[4]

The purpose of this exemption is straightforward enough—property already within a person's estate for inheritance tax purposes is already prima facie within the scope of IHT. Were the Regime also to apply to it, there would be an element of double taxation.

Meaning of "IHT estate"

7–03 For IHT purposes the estate of a person includes all the property to which he is beneficially entitled.[5] In this connection two points should be borne in mind.

---

[2] In fact this policy is not always followed since not all exemptions from the reservation of benefit charge are carried over into the Regime (for instance there is no carry over of the FA 1986, s.102A(5) seven-year lease exemption).

[3] This is discussed further in **Ch.2**.

[4] See Sch.15, para.11(1)(a). "**Relevant property**" means in relation to paras 3 and 6 where the disposal condition in para.3(2) or para.6(2) is met, the property disposed of; and where the contribution condition in para.3(3) or para.6(3) is met, the property representing the consideration directly or indirectly provided. In relation to para.8 it means intangible property which is or represents property which the chargeable person settled, or added to the settlement after March 17, 1986; Sch.15, para.8(2) and para.11(9). The problems arising from this definition are discussed in **7–48** below.

[5] See IHTA 1984, s.5(1).

Property already comprised within an individual's free estate will not normally **7–04**
be subject to the Regime anyway (because he is unlikely to have disposed of
(say) the land or provided the funds for another person to buy it), so this provision
is likely to be most relevant where an individual has a qualifying interest in
possession in settled property. For IHT purposes such an individual is treated as
being beneficially entitled to the settled property in which his interest subsists,
regardless of the term of his interest and therefore the exemption in para.11(1)
can apply.[6]

However, where the interest in possession is one to which the individual
became entitled on or after March 22, 2006, it cannot be a qualifying interest in
possession for inheritance tax purposes even though it gives an entitlement to
income unless it is one of the following:

(a) an immediate post death interest;

(b) a disabled person's interest; or

(c) a transitional serial interest.[7]

If the interest in possession is not a qualifying interest in possession then the **7–05**
value of the settled property in which the interest subsists is ignored for
inheritance tax purposes albeit the person is entitled to the income. Indeed even
the actuarial value of the life interest is excluded from a person's estate for
inheritance tax purposes.[8] In summary, a qualifying iip is either an iip that arose
before March 22, 2006 or one of the new types of qualifying iips that arose after
March 21 and are set out in **7–06** below. If it is not a qualifying interest in
possession then the ownership exemption cannot apply and the taxpayer must
rely either on the para.10 exclusions, on the reserved benefit exemption, or on
one of the reliefs given in para.12 to avoid a POA charge.

*The new types of qualifying interests in possession that can arise after
March 22, 2006*

An **immediate post death interest** is an interest in possession arising immediately **7–06**
on the death of a person and in a settlement created by will or arising on an
intestacy. It is unlikely to be relevant in the context of the POA Regime.

A **disabled person's interest** is defined in IHTA 1984, s.89B and comprises
the following.

(i) An interest in possession which a disabled person is treated as enjoying
under a trust falling within s.89. This covers the "deemed" interest in
possession set up under a pre-2006 disabled trust. The person is not
actually entitled to the income for income tax purposes but is deemed to be
entitled to the property for inheritance tax purposes!

---

[6] See IHTA 1984, s.49(1).
[7] See **Ch.2**; 2–33 and IHTA 1984, ss.49(1A) and 49A–D.
[8] See IHTA 1984, s.5(1).

(ii) An interest in possession which is deemed to arise under a self settlement made on or after March 22, 2006 by a person with a condition expected to lead to a disability. Again this is a deemed interest in possession.[9]

(iii) An interest in possession in a settlement to which a disabled person becomes entitled on or after March 22, 2006. In this case the settlement contains an actual entitlement to income (i.e. this is not a case of a deemed interest in possession) and note that the settlement can be established either by will or inter vivos by any person.[10]

(iv) A self settlement (as in (ii) above) which gives an actual interest in possession to a disabled person.

A **transitional serial interest** ("TSI") is defined in IHTA 1984, s49B–E. Four conditions must be satisfied for there to be a TSI.

1. *Condition 1*: the settlement commenced before March 22, 2006 and immediately before that date "the property then comprised in the settlement was property in which" a person had an interest in possession ("the prior interest"). Note that it does not matter if the person who had the pre-March 2006 interest in possession was a company or an individual: the successor can still take a transitional serial interest although if a company's interest in possession terminated this would not be a PET.

2. *Condition 2*: that the prior interest ends on or after March 22, 2006 but before October 6, 2008 (extended from April 6, 2008 by FA 2008, s.141). Note that the prior interest can end inter vivos or on death. It does not matter if the prior interest is ended by the beneficiary assigning[11] or surrendering it or that it ends by exercise of the trustees' overriding powers of appointment or advancement.

3. *Condition 3*: on the termination of the prior interest someone immediately becomes entitled to an interest in possession in the settled property.

4. *Condition 4*: the person with the current interest does not have a disabled person's interest and s.71A does not apply.

Example 7.1

Under the Baggins trust, set up in 2001, Bilbo was entitled to an interest in possession on March 22, 2006. On January 1, 2007 he surrendered that interest as a result of which his cousin Frida became entitled to a life interest in the trust fund. The IHT position is as follows:

(i) Bilbo had been entitled to a qualifying interest in possession and Frida became entitled to a TSI;

---

[9] See IHTA 1984, s.89A inserted by FA 2006, Sch.20, para.6.

[10] IHTA 1984, s.89B(1)(c) inserted by FA 2006, Sch.20, para.6.

[11] s.51 provides that where A assigns his interest in possession to B it is treated as coming to an end even though the life interest in fact continues (with B having an interest *pur autre vie*). Hence condition 2 is satisfied.

(ii) Frida is therefore treated as owning the capital in the settlement and Bilbo made a PET when his interest terminated.[12]

In general a TSI must arise before October 6, 2008: Condition 2 in IHTA 1984, **7–07** s.49C(3) provides that the prior interest (viz the interest in possession in existence on March 22, 2006) must come to an end "at a time on or after March 22, 2006 but before October 6, 2008" and the current interest (the TSI) must arise at that time. It follows that the prior interest in possession can be superseded only once. A second successive interest in possession even if arising during the transitional period will not be a TSI.

Section 49D, however, contains a limited extension of the time limit but only **7–08** if the following conditions are met:

(i) the settlement must have commenced before March 22, 2006 and immediately before that date "F" was beneficially entitled to an interest in possession in the trust property ("the previous interest") (Condition 1);

(ii) the previous interest came to an end on or after October 6, 2008[13] on the death of F (Condition 2);

(iii) immediately before F died E was the spouse or civil partner of F (Condition 3);

(iv) on F's death E became entitled to an interest in possession in the settled property ("the successor interest") (Condition 4);

(v) s.71A does not apply to the property in which the successor interest subsists and the successor interest is not a disabled person's interest (Condition 5).

If the above conditions are met then E's interest in possession is a transitional serial interest and accordingly the spouse exemption will apply on F's death.[14]
Note especially the following: **7–09**

(i) this TSI can arise at any time: the only limiting factors are that it must be on the death (not inter vivos termination) of the previous interest and the beneficiary must be the surviving spouse or civil partner;

(ii) it is not necessary for the marriage/civil partnership to have been in place on March 22, 2006.

In general the POA exclusion in para.10(1)(c) for settled gifts whereby the **7–10** settlor's spouse / civil partner was given an interest in possession will protect the donor anyway without the need for exemption in para.11(1), except in relation to intangibles.[15]

Example 7.2

In December 2005 Andrew settled his house on a qualifying interest in possession trust for his civil partner Paul and remains a discretionary beneficiary. Paul retained the interest in possession until his death in June

---

[12] See the PET definition in IHTA 1984, s.3A(1A): the transfer constitutes a gift to another individual within (1A)(c)(i).

[13] If it ended before this date s.49C applied.

[14] See IHTA 1984, s.18.

[15] para.10(1)(c) is considered at **5–11**.

2009. By that time the settled property comprised a house worth £500,000 in which they both lived and cash of £400,000.

Position on Paul's death

On Paul's death, Andrew took an interest in possession in the property which is qualifying, being a transitional serial interest. There is no inheritance tax on Paul's death because the transfer to Andrew is exempt under the spouse/civil partner exemption (s.18). There is no POA charge on Andrew in respect of the house before or after Paul's interest terminates even if Andrew does not then take an interest in possession because of the exclusion in para.10(1)(c). Nor does the POA charge apply to Andrew in respect of the cash **while Paul is alive**. Although the para.10 exclusion does not apply to intangibles, this is a post *Eversden* spousal interest in possession trust and Andrew has reserved a benefit. Therefore while Paul is alive Andrew is protected under para.11(5).[16]

Position after Paul's death

If Andrew takes a qualifying interest in possession on Paul's death what then is the inheritance tax and POA position? The property will be subject to inheritance tax on Andrew's death because he has a qualifying interest in possession. It is comprised in his estate for inheritance tax purposes and therefore the para.11(1) exemption prima facie applies. However, para.11(11)(12) as inserted by FA 2006, s.80 has the effect that even though Andrew takes a qualifying interest in possession and will suffer inheritance tax on his death, for POA purposes the para.11(1) exemption is disapplied by 11(12).[17] The result is that Andrew is now liable to pay the POA charge.

Here are Andrew's options.

(a) Take the property outright (assuming, of course, that the trustees are agreeable and prepared to exercise a relevant power in his favour).

(b) Surrender his qualifying interest in possession in favour of discretionary trusts. In these circumstances at "the subsequent time" (see para.11(12)) although the intangibles are not comprised in his estate for inheritance tax purposes under s.49, he still reserves a benefit and then the protection in para.11(5) applies to prevent a POA charge! The property will still be subject to inheritance tax on his death but under the reservation of benefit rules rather than under s.49. However, the termination of his qualifying interest in possession is an immediately chargeable transfer. Assuming he has a full unused nil rate band (which is the relevant nil rate band to use— see IHTA 1984, ss.52 and 80) and the value of the intangibles is £400,000, if his interest in possession is ended in say £325,000 worth of intangibles no inheritance tax is payable. From that point on there is no POA charge in respect of the £325,000. He retains a qualifying interest in possession in the balance of £75,000 which is within the POA Regime but there is no taxable benefit because the chargeable amount falls within the annual £5,000 exemption (see **Ch.9**).

---

[16] See **7–30** and **5–12**.

[17] The scope of the s.80 amendment to the POA legislation is considered at **7–24**.

(c) Retain his qualifying interest in possession (thereby ensuring a capital gains tax uplift on his death) but elect into the reservation of benefit provisions. This would then prevent the POA charge applying, without effecting his IHT position (he will be taxed on the settled property as a result of s.49).

The policy behind paras 11(11) and (12) is discussed further at **7–23** below, but the golden rule is to check that the donor, being the person entitled to the qualifying interest in possession who is relying on the para.11(1) exemption, has always either owned the property outright or had a qualifying interest in possession in it. If at any point it had ceased to be comprised in the donor's estate for IHT purposes and he now has a qualifying interest in possession in the property, there is a POA problem unless paras 10 or 12 apply. Note that in the above example Andrew does not suffer any POA charge on the land because this remains protected by para.10.

Prior to March 22, 2006 the para.11(1) exemption was useful in circumstances **7–11** where the donor wished to protect his home from care fee claims.

Example 7.3

Algy is elderly and frail. In 2005 he decided to transfer his only asset, a house worth £200,000, into an interest in possession trust for himself and then for his wife Emma. His two sons were appointed trustees and they took over the management of the house. He also thought that this arrangement will better protect the house and prevent it being sold later to pay for his and Emma's nursing home fees. He continues living in the house. The disposal and occupation conditions are satisfied and the disposal is not an excluded transaction under para.10. However, while Algy retains a qualifying interest in possession in the house it is an exempt transaction under para.11(1)(a). No POA income tax is payable by Algy.

Note the following.

1. The fact that Algy has no inheritance tax saving motive in the transaction does not matter. The gift into trust in 2005 was a non-event for inheritance tax purposes because he retained a qualifying interest in possession, but it is a relevant disposal for POA purposes.

2. In the above example Algy is exempt from POA income tax under para.11(1). However, it is not a once and for all exemption. If his interest in possession ceases while he is alive and he continues to occupy the house then para.3 applies unless he can at that time claim another exemption or cease to occupy the property.[18] Note that the position would be different if the original disposal was an excluded transaction: see *Example 7.4*.

3. The para.11(1) exemption applies although the property may not be subject to IHT on Algy's death because it passes to his spouse and so is exempt.

---

[18] For instance, that he is reserving a benefit by his continued occupation so that he is within the para.11(3) exemption.

7–12 The operation of the ownership exemption has become more complicated since March 22, 2006 because of the interaction of a number of different provisions. The following is a relatively simple example raising complex problems!

Example 7.4

In 2009, Bertie decides to give his only asset—a house worth £200,000—into an interest in possession trust for himself. His motivation is to avoid the house being used to pay care home fees. His interest in possession is not a qualifying interest in possession and the transfer into trust is a chargeable transfer for inheritance tax purposes. In this case the value of the house is within his nil rate band so no inheritance tax is payable. The property is not part of his estate for inheritance tax purposes under s.49 and therefore the para.11(1) exemption cannot apply for POA purposes.

Does Bertie reserve a benefit for inheritance tax purposes? If he does then the property is taxed on his death as part of his estate (with no spouse exemption and no capital gains tax uplift), but no POAT arises during his lifetime.[19]

In any event, the settled property is subject to 10-year and exit charges under the relevant property regime. If he does not reserve a benefit, there is no inheritance tax charge on his death but there is POAT during his lifetime.

The answer to the reservation of benefit point will partly depend on the terms of the trust and partly on the nature of the asset originally settled. If the terms of the trust are such that Bertie has an interest in possession but no rights to capital then under general principles he has not reserved a benefit under FA 1986, s102 because this is a carve-out for reservation of benefit purposes. He retains the income and only gives away the capital.

However, as Bertie made a gift of an interest in land the anti-*Ingram* rules in FA 1986, s.102A must be considered. These treat him as reserving a benefit if he retains any significant right or interest that entitles him to occupy the land. Hence he **does** reserve a benefit as he has the right to occupy the gifted land. Since he reserves a benefit and the property is taxed on his death (albeit without any capital gains tax uplift), para.11(5) gives him protection from a POA charge.

If the house is later sold (e.g. Bertie goes into a nursing home and the trustees decide to sell it to produce income) and the trustees hold cash, does he still reserve a benefit in the cash or does his reservation of benefit cease at that point on the basis that there is a carve-out for s.102 purposes and s.102A no longer applies? If that is correct a POA charge would arise from that time. It is thought that the effect of s.102C(4) and Sch.20, para.5(1) is such that once the settlement ceases to hold land, the settlement is governed by the reservation of benefit rules in s.102 rather than s.102A. Hence there is no reservation of benefit if the terms of the trust can be construed as a carve-out by Bertie where he has retained the income and given away the capital. Protection from a POA charge under para.11(5) would then cease. Bertie would have to pay the POA charge. It is unlikely that either Bertie or the trustees will be aware of all these possible variations!

---

[19] See para.11(5).

As noted previously, it is generally better for a transaction to be an excluded **7–13**
transaction under para.10 rather than exempt under para.11. *Example 7.2*
illustrated the problems that can arise if para.11(1) ownership exemption is
required.

Example 7.5

In 2007 Jamie sold his house at full market value to an interest in possession
trust funded by his father under which he is the life tenant. It does not matter
in these circumstances if Jamie's interest in possession is later terminated
and he continues in occupation. The transaction is an excluded one under
para.10(1)(a) and this exclusion applies for all time.[20] There is no reservation
of benefit because the house is not gifted but sold and the cash remains part
of Jamie's estate for inheritance tax purposes. Jamie has a non-qualifying
interest in possession and is not subject to inheritance tax on his death on the
value of the trust fund which is taxed under the relevant property regime.

Excluded property

For IHT purposes, a person's estate includes, except immediately before he dies, **7–14**
excluded property to which he is beneficially entitled, including settled excluded
property in which he has a qualifying interest in possession.[21] The fact that the
property may not be subject to tax on his death is irrelevant.

Example 7.6

Andreas, a foreign domiciliary, transfers his house to a Jersey company
wholly owned and funded by him in exchange for shares. He continues to
occupy the property. The disposal[22] and occupation conditions are satisfied.
However, because he wholly owns the company shares and the shares derive
their value from the property (see **7–17** below), he is not subject to a POA
income tax charge. The fact that he will not pay inheritance tax on those
shares when he dies if he is still not domiciled in the UK because they are
non-UK situated property is irrelevant. The property is part of his estate
while he is alive.[23]

---

[20] See **5–19**.

[21] See IHTA 1984, ss.51(1) and 49(1).

[22] Or possibly contribution condition—even if one can argue the disposal is within para.10(1) he
still funded the company.

[23] This is discussed further in **Ch.8** There is a misconception that excluded property is outside a
person's estate for inheritance tax purposes. IHTA 1984, s.5(1) expressly states that a person's estate
does not include excluded property at the moment before his death (implying therefore that it is in his
estate at all other times) and s.3(2) states that in determining the amount of a transfer of value "no
account shall be taken of the value of excluded property which ceases to form part of a person's
estate" thereby confirming that although a gift of excluded property can be ignored as a transfer of
value such property was nevertheless comprised in the donor's estate.

Derived property in relation to the ownership exemption

7–15 Paragraph 11(1) does not just cover situations where the donor's estate includes the relevant property. Paragraph 11(1)(b) provides that the Regime does not apply to an individual in respect of relevant property if that individual's estate includes property which *derives* its value from that relevant property.[24]

This exemption is more subtle than the first. It means that although an individual does not directly own the relevant property or have an interest in possession in it, an exemption will apply if other property to which he is beneficially entitled derives its value from the relevant property. In *Example 7.6* the shares were in Andreas' estate and derived their value from the house.

Loan rather than share capital

7–16 Suppose in Example 7.6 that the company was funded by loans rather than by share capital. Both the shares and the loans are in Andreas' estate but can one argue that the loans as well as the shares derive their value from the relevant land? If not the value of the shares will be substantially less than the value of the relevant property and hence there will be a reduced exemption. It is believed that the correct answer is that the shares and the loan together are comprised in Andreas' estate and between them indirectly derive their value from the house. The loan does not merely derive its value from the contractual undertakings that oblige the borrowing company to make repayment. On that basis we consider para.11(1)(b) offers full protection against a POA charge. However, HMRC do not take this view.[25] But HMRC do accept that a loan to fund the acquisition of property does not represent the provision of consideration for the purposes of the contribution condition. Hence if Andreas lends £1m to a wholly owned company and the company purchases property for his occupation, then HMRC accept that the contribution condition is not satisfied and no POA charges can arise even though the loan does not (on HMRC's view) derive its value from the house. If Andreas later assigned the loan, no POA charge would appear to arise. Where Andreas funds a trust in which he takes a qualifying interest in possession and the trust then lends to a wholly owned company to purchase the house, the contribution condition is not satisfied in relation to the para.3 charge on land Because he has funded the trust. The fact that the trust lends to the company does not mean that the contribution condition is not met. It is also satisfied. in relation to the intangibles charge because Andreas has settled funds into trust. Hence the para.9 charge could apply but the para.11(1) exemption means that Andreas is protected from a POA charge while he retains a qualifying interest in possession.[26]

The "substantially less" rule

7–17 It may be that the value of the derivative property—in the example just given, the shares—is less than the value of the relevant property (the land). If the value of the

---

[24] Sch.15, para.11(1)(b). For the meaning of "Relevant property" see n.4.
[25] See A2.11 and A2.105.
[26] See A2.05.

derivative property is "substantially less" than the value of the relevant property, then the amount on which tax is charged under the Regime[27] is reduced by such proportion as is reasonable to take account of the inclusion of the derivative property in his estate.[28] At 4.7 of the guidance notes (see A2.45), HMRC offer guidance as to the meaning of "substantially less". As was to be expected, the CGT taper relief rules have been followed so that "substantially less" means a reduction in value of 20 per cent or more. The last sentence is unclear "if the circumstances of a particular case suggest that the substantially less provision should be triggered by a reduction of more or less than 20 per cent it will be judged on its individual merits". Presumably HMRC are reserving the right to invoke the provisions even if the reduction in value is less than 20 per cent.

Example 7.7

Assume that X funded X Limited by subscribing cash in consideration of the issue of shares. He subsequently gave away 25 per cent of the shares to his brother Y and some time later the company purchased land which X now occupies. He owns 75 per cent of the ordinary shares of X Ltd and his brother Y owns the remaining 25 per cent. **If** X is within the contribution condition because he has "provided" cash to the company then he may have a POA problem.[29] (It would not make any difference if he provided the cash before April 1998 or had not occupied the land for seven years after transferring the cash to the company. This is because the subscription of shares by cash is not a gift and therefore cannot be an excluded transaction under para.10(2)(c).)[30]

The value of X's shares will be "substantially less" than the value of the land, so X will not be wholly outside the charge unless he can argue that the reserved benefit exemption applies on the 25 per cent (as to which see **7–30** below). The amount on which tax is charged will be reduced by 75 per cent. If, however, X had owned 85 per cent of the ordinary shares then the substantially less provisions should not apply and so he will be wholly outside the POA charge.

The above assumes of course that the contribution condition is satisfied in the first place. The authors' view, however, is that whether X lends cash to the company which purchases the house or X subscribes for shares in the company which purchases the house he occupies, the contribution condition is not satisfied because there is no element of bounty involved. Hence no POA charge can arise. Even if X later gives away the shares in the company to other individuals and **continues** to occupy the house no POA charge arises because the contribution condition is not satisfied and there is no reservation of benefit problem either (because X has given the company shares and not the house itself so he reserves no benefit in the gifted property). HMRC appear to accept the latter point.[31] The continued occupation of the house is not referable to the gift of shares. Hence some of the anomalies in relation to derived property which were discussed in the earlier editions of this book are, in the authors' opinion, no longer relevant.

7–18

---

[27] Strictly, the appropriate rental value in para.4, the appropriate amount in para.7 and the chargeable amount in para.9 (as the case may be); FA 2004, Sch.15, para.11(2).

[28] Sch.15, paras 11(1)(b) and (2).

[29] The authors consider that bounty is required for the contribution condition to be met—see **3–11**.

[30] See further on these exemptions to the cash contribution condition, **5–21**.

[31] See IHTM 14334, Example 4.

Excluded liabilities

7–19 There are three important qualifications to the ownership exemption. The first has already been discussed: property is not comprised in a person's estate for the purposes of the exemption if the donor takes a non-qualifying interest in possession. Secondly, even if the donor takes a qualifying interest in possession the ownership exemption is not available if para.11(11) applies. This is discussed further at **7–23** below. The third qualification is that the ownership exemption is not available if the value of the relevant property is reduced by an "excluded liability", except to the extent that the value of the property exceeds the amount of the excluded liability.[32] For this purpose a liability is an excluded liability if:

(a) the creation of the liability; **and**

(b) any transaction by virtue of which the person's estate came to include the relevant property or any derivative property or by virtue of which the value of the property in his estate came to be derived from the relevant property were associated operations for IHT purposes.[33]

Taking a simple example, if the value of the property is £400,000 and there is an excluded liability of £100,000 the ownership exemption is intended to apply only to £300,000 and £100,000 is within the POA Regime.

The purpose of this provision is believed to be to nullify the effectiveness of "home loan" schemes; see the discussion of these schemes in **Ch.17**. The excluded liability rule only applies for the purposes of the ownership exemption in para.11(1). It does not apply in relation to the reservation of benefit exemption and this is discussed further below.

Problems in the definition

7–20 The definition of an excluded liability is not free from difficulties. For instance:.

(a) It is a liability "**affecting any property**". What is meant by "affecting" in this context? Presumably property is affected if there is a charge over it (certainly a fixed charge but what of a floating charge?). What if the relevant land is held in trust but there is no formal charge and the trustees have personal liability? In these circumstances one might argue that the excluded liability does not, as such, "affect" the land at all although as the trustees have a lien over the property to meet the liability in the authors' view it is therefore affected. Is a liability of a company a liability that affects the shares of the company or the underlying property of that company?

(b) Paragraph 11(7) requires that the creation of the liability and any transaction by which the property became comprised in the taxpayer's estate must be linked within the meaning of the associated operations rules. Accordingly a liability which pre-dates the ownership of the taxpayer will not generally be within the definition. Nor generally is a loan taken out on the security of the property after it has been acquired by the taxpayer an excluded liability.

---

[32] See Sch.15, para.11(6).
[33] Sch.15, para.11(7). Associated operations are defined in IHTA 1984, s.268.

(c) Paragraph 11(6) refers to "the amount of the excluded liability". Is this the commercial value of the debt or its face value?

Example 7.8

C entered into a home loan scheme.[34] The house is worth £2 million and the debt is repayable on C's death, is linked to the RPI and has a face value of £1.9 million. Its commercial value is discounted due to the fact that it is not repayable until C's death. Allowing for the fact that the debt is linked to the RPI, its market value would be (say) £1.2 million but increasing. In these circumstances the question is whether the excess value (which is treated as part of C's estate and therefore protected from the POA charge) under para.11(1) is:

(i) £100,000;

(ii) £800,000; or

(iii) some other figure such as £100,000 less accrued indexation?

Logic would dictate that one should take the commercial value of the debt in determining the reduction in a person's estate because in reality the property is only "affected" by this amount of debt. If this is correct, the POA charge would then increase as the commercial value of the debt increased towards the end of the donor's lifetime. However, the words "the amount (rather than the 'value') of the excluded liability" do not obviously suggest this result. HMRC have indicated that the correct value is the face value and any accumulations of interest are revalued every five years.[35]

(d) The liability must reduce the value of the person's estate. Hence if a foreign domiciliary funds a wholly owned non-UK company by share subscription which company lends to him in order to buy a house for his occupation, even assuming the contribution condition is satisfied at all (which is doubtful for the reasons in 7–17 above), the loan does not reduce the value of his total estate. The company shares derive their value from the debt and hence the value of the loan is comprised in his estate even though the shares are excluded property.

(e) If the individual lends to a wholly owned company which purchases the property for occupation by that individual there are three reasons why a POA charge should not arise: first, the contribution condition is not satisfied by a loan; secondly, if that is wrong, the ownership exemption in para.11(1) applies and the excluded liability rule does not apply because the debt does not reduce the value of his estate since the loan is still part of his estate; thirdly, unless the debt is secured on the house, it does not affect the house anyway so cannot be an excluded liability.

Some of these problems are further explored in **Ch.17** in the context of the home loan scheme.

What if the liability is fully commercial (e.g. a bank mortgage to purchase **7–21** property)? Is this an excluded liability? It is suggested that generally commercial

---

[34] For how home loan schemes operated, see **17–06**.
[35] See A2.15.

borrowing is not caught because it does not reduce the individual's estate: the liability incurred is in consideration of the borrowings received. Although the value of the asset is reduced, the value of his estate is the same. Some care, however, is required when unravelling home loan schemes.[36]

Example 7.9

Assume that "Westwinds" is a property now owned and occupied by David who had, in 1987, gifted the property to an old aunt. She had left the property to David on her death with a charge over it for an annuity payable to her housekeeper. The value of the property is £250,000 and the charge is for £120,000. The analysis is as follows:

(1) POAT will prima facie apply since David occupies Westwinds; and

(2) the disposal condition is satisfied since he had given the property to the aunt after March 17, 1986.

The property is in his estate and so prima facie covered by the ownership exemption. However, is the charge an excluded liability because if so only £130,000 of the value of the property is within the ownership exemption. It is thought that the annuity is not an excluded liability.

7–22 A more common situation is where part of the purchase price for the relevant land is funded with cash from the taxpayer and part with commercial borrowings.

Example 7.10

E settles cash of £200,000 into a qualifying interest in possession trust for himself in 2003. The trustees purchase a property worth £500,000, borrowing £300,000 commercially. There are other assets in the trust which can fund the interest charge on the borrowing which is secured on the house which E then occupies. In these circumstances, one would not expect a POA charge. There is no inheritance tax scheme and the borrowing is commercial and external.

  The loan is an excluded liability within para.11(7) as the loan taken out by the trustees and the purchase of the property are "associated operations" as defined in IHTA 1984, s.268. However, is the value of E's estate reduced by the loan? The legislation is unclear and the HMRC view as stated in A2.85 is unsatisfactory. Perhaps the best view is that as stated in 7–20 the borrowings do not reduce the value of E's estate. E's estate is £200,000 and the liability of £300,000 is in consideration of receiving cash of £300,000. His estate is neither increased nor decreased by the borrowings. An alternative view is that the consideration given for the property by E is only £200,000 and therefore only two-fifths of the value of the house appears to be relevant property within the definition of para.11(9).[37] The property representing the consideration provided is arguably two-fifths of the house. This is the view taken by HMRC.

7–23 The excluded liabilities restriction that operates in respect of direct ownership also operates in respect of derived value under para.11(2), regardless of whether

---

[36] See **Ch.17**.
[37] See **7–34**.

or not the "substantially less" rule applies.[38] So, the procedure is **first** to apply the excluded liabilities rule and **then** to apply the substantially less rule.

Example 7.11

Assume Y sets up an interest in possession trust for himself which owns shares in X Ltd. The shares are worth £750,000, but are subject to a mortgage of £250,000 which is an excluded liability. The company owns quoted investments worth £250,000 and a house, in which Y lives, worth £500,000. Accordingly, the shares derive two-thirds of their value from the house.

(a) Apply the **excluded liability** rule: £250,000 of the value of the shares is not treated as comprised in Y's estate for the purpose of the exemption. Y is chargeable under para.8 on £250,000.

The rules in respect of land also have to be applied.

(b) Shares worth £500,000 are comprised in the estate of Y of which two-thirds is attributable to the value of the house. Hence the tax charge is on relevant property having a value of £133,333 (one-third of £500,000).

Since (a) produces a higher chargeable amount than (b), para.18 requires (a) to be adopted.[39]

Reverter to settlor and paras 11(11) and 11(12) —"the s.80 problem"

After the POA Regime was introduced, taxpayers considered various ways of avoiding the tax and one of these involved the use of a reverter to settlor trust. **7–24**

Example 7.12

A effected an *Ingram* scheme in 1997. From April 2005 he was subject to the POA charge. In January 2005, his daughter who owned the freehold, settled it on qualifying interest in possession trusts for A, reverter to herself. The intention was to avoid a POA charge by ensuring that A took a qualifying interest in possession and he thereby obtained the benefit of the ownership exemption in para.11(1). There would be no charge on the freehold on A's death given that the property reverted to the daughter as settlor.[40]

With effect from December 5, 2005, the para.11(1) exemption does not apply if the taxpayer ceased to own the property and did not then take a qualifying interest in possession in the property but obtains a qualifying interest in possession subsequently. (See para.11(12) as enacted by FA 2006, s.80.) Hence in the above example, A's deemed ownership of the freehold is ignored for POA purposes and he is subject to the POA charge.

In fact FA 2006, s.80 goes much further than merely stopping reverter to settlor **7–25** schemes despite the explanatory note FB 2006 suggesting that the clause was simply intended to block such avoidance. The restriction on the scope of para.11(1) applies where at any time:

---

[38] See FA 2004, Sch.15, para.11(6).
[39] On para.18, see further **Ch.10**.
[40] Reverter to settlor trusts are discussed further in **Ch.18**.

(a) the relevant property has ceased to be comprised in the person's estate for inheritance tax purposes; **or**

(b) the person has directly or indirectly provided any consideration for the acquisition of the relevant property; and

(c) at any subsequent time the relevant property or any derived property is comprised in his estate for the purposes of IHTA 1984, s.49.

The width of this provision can be seen in *Example 7.2* and **7.12** above but is also relevant in the following circumstances.

Example 7.13

(1) B settles cash on a qualifying interest in possession trust for himself before March 22, 2006. The trustees purchase a property for his occupation or buy shares. Although the relevant property has never ceased to be comprised in his estate for inheritance tax purposes he has provided consideration for the acquisition of relevant property and the second condition is satisfied. Either the para.3 or para.8 charge would appear to apply despite the fact that the property is subject to inheritance tax on B's death.[41]

(2) C settles cash into a discretionary trust. He is foreign domiciled. The trust is then converted to a qualifying interest in possession trust prior to March 22, 2006 and the trustees purchase a house for his occupation. Both conditions above are satisfied. He has provided consideration and the property has ceased to be comprised in his estate and then become comprised in his estate for inheritance tax purposes when he later took a qualifying interest in possession. If the trust was converted after March 21, 2006 then he is not caught because the relevant property does not become comprised in his estate under s.49: the interest he takes is non-qualifying.

HMRC consider that B is not caught in Example (1) provided his qualifying interest in possession has subsisted in the relevant property throughout. C, however, is caught by para.11(11) and the ownership exemption will not apply unless the house is advanced to him outright. Alternatively if his qualifying interest in possession is terminated or he elects into POA he can once again obtain protection.

As the CIOT / STEP note makes clear, the potential difficulty with paras 11(11) and 11(12) is that they do not distinguish between reverter to settlor trusts and any trusts set up before March 22, 2006 where the settlor enjoys a qualifying interest in possession and would in that event be prima facie subject to inheritance tax on his death. HMRC justify their response to *Example 7.14(1)* above (i.e. that B is not subject to POA) on the basis that paras 11(11) and 11(12) cannot apply unless the consideration provided for the purchase of the property has left the donor's estate and then the property representing that consideration later becomes comprised in the donor's estate because B takes qualifying interest in possession (if B takes the property outright, no POA charge arises). The words "and at any subsequent time the relevant property or any derived property is comprised in his estate" do not actually state this. However, HMRC's view is that there is no FA

---

[41] See CIOT/STEP correspondence reproduced at A2.119.

2006, s.80 problem where cash or a house was settled on a qualifying interest in possession trust for the settlor and the settlor retains a qualifying interest in possession throughout the relevant period. The problem arises where the settlor did not retain a qualifying interest in possession at all times after the original disposal was made.

In practice, the FA 2006, s.80 charge is most likely to affect foreign domiciliaries **7–26** where it was common before March 2006 to settle cash into a discretionary trust which was then converted to a qualifying interest in possession trust. This was in order to avoid an inheritance tax problem (rather confusingly found in IHTA 1984, s.80) which provides that in the event the settlement starts off as a qualifying interest in possession trust and the settlor dies deemed UK domiciled, at that point the trust falls within the relevant property regime. Ensuring that the trust began as a discretionary trust before being converted to a qualifying interest in possession trust avoided this difficulty. The position of foreign domiciliaries is discussed further in **8–19**.

For UK domiciliaries the problem is most likely to arise (apart from in reverter **7–27** to settlor trusts) where they have set up a qualifying interest in possession trust for the spouse and then on the spouse's death, the settlor takes a qualifying interest in possession, e.g. some *Eversden* trusts may have been set up giving an interest in possession for the spouse but the spousal interest in possession has not yet been revoked and therefore the tax planning was not completed. The intention would be to avoid an inheritance tax charge on the spouse's death by letting the settlor take back an interest in possession (which will be a transitional serial interest and therefore qualifying). In these circumstances where the settled property comprises intangibles[42] the settlor either needs to take outright or elect into the reservation of benefit regime. An election should have no adverse consequences for the UK domiciled settlor and the capital gains tax uplift will still be available. The effect of an election when the settlor has a qualifying interest in possession is discussed further in **Ch.11**.

Section 80 is generally only a problem if the trust was set up before March 22, **7–28** 2006.[43] Trusts set up thereafter are not likely to give the settlor a qualifying interest in possession within s.49 so the s.80 difficulties cannot arise, although as explained in **Ch.11** the effect of s.80 is to provide another avoidance opportunity by deliberately making an election!

What is the solution if FA 2006, s.80 is a problem? There are four options. **7–29**

1. The settlor can be excluded from the trust altogether and cease to occupy any house if that is the relevant property. This is unlikely to be a practical solution and the termination of a qualifying interest in possession now will be a chargeable transfer unless beneficiaries take the property outright.

2. The settlor can receive the assets outright. Hence in *Example 7.2* above, Andrew could be advanced the house outright and the property will then be back in his estate for inheritance tax purposes. The POA charge then ceases to apply but a CGT charge may arise.

3. The qualifying interest in possession taken back by the settlor (in *Example 7.2*, Andrew) could be terminated and the property held on discretionary

---

[42] There would be no POA problem under FA 2006, s.80 if the settled property is land or chattels because the arrangement will be protected under para.10. Therefore the para.11 protections are not needed.

[43] See *Example 7.2*.

trusts. This will be a chargeable transfer but once the property ceases to be in the settlor's estate, sub-para (12) ceases to apply. (The wording in para.11(11) makes it clear that sub-para (12) only applies where "at any time...the relevant property is comprised in his estate...as a result of section 49".) Once the qualifying interest in possession is terminated then the disponer will generally reserve a benefit in the settled property under general principles (being a discretionary beneficiary) and the protections under para.11(5) will once again be available.

4. An election can be made into the reservation of benefit provisions. Generally where the settlor has a qualifying interest in possession and also elects this will have no adverse tax effects.[44]

SECOND EXEMPTION—RESERVED BENEFIT EXEMPTION

7–30   The second main exemption is contained in paras 11(3) and (5). None of the three charging codes applies to a person by reference to any relevant property[45] at a time when that property is either caught by the reservation of benefit legislation in respect of that person or would be so caught but for certain of the statutory exemptions in FA 1986.[46]

Assume that X gives his son a house which X continues to occupy in circumstances where the house is property subject to a reservation. In such a case, the property will be within the IHT net when X dies and so there is no need for the Regime to apply.

Derivative reserved benefit

7–31   Similarly the Regime does not apply to relevant property[47] from which reserved benefit property derives its value.[48]

Example 7.14

X gives cash to a trust under which he is a beneficiary (contribution condition satisfied) which then subscribes for shares in a company and the company acquires a house in which X lives. The house is relevant property. X reserves a benefit in the company shares (being the settled property). The reserved benefit property derives its value from the house. X has protection from a POA charge.

However, if the trust lent to the company to enable it to buy a house, then HMRC consider that the loan does not derive its value from the relevant property even if the company charged the loan on the house. As noted above,

---

[44] The FA 2006, s.80 change can pose particular problems for foreign domiciliaries. These are discussed in **Ch.8** and also at A2.131: see **Ch.11** and **11–11**.

[45] For the meaning of "Relevant property" see n.4 above.

[46] See Sch.15, para.11(3) and (5). The IHT reservation of benefit rules have been outlined in **Ch.2**. The position if part only of the relevant property is subject to a reservation is not clear cut: see, for instance, 137.151.

[47] The meaning of "relevant property" is set out in n.4 above.

[48] See Sch.15, paras 11(3)(b) and (5).

it is thought this view is wrong. Of course if the settlor has funded a trust which now holds company shares, these shares are intangible property and therefore the settlor may be subject to the para.8 charge, although if X was non-domiciled when he set up the trust, X will have protection separately under para.12 (discussed in **Ch.8**).

As suggested in *Example 7.8*, in the authors' view the POA regime does not **7–32** apply where X wholly owns the shares of a company which purchases a house in which he lives. Generally X will either have lent cash to the company to purchase the house or will have subscribed for shares in the wholly owned company. In either case the contribution condition is not satisfied because there is no bounty or provision. If X subsequently gave the shares to his son and **continued** to live in the house rent free then, as noted at **7–17** above, X does not reserve a benefit in the shares and the gift of shares is not referable to the benefit of occupying the house. Hence there would appear to be no reservation of benefit problem either. On the other hand, if the company directors allowed X to occupy the house for the first time after he had made the gift to the son, the position might be different. In that case a reservation of benefit might arise. Property which qualifies for the reserved benefit exemption and for the derived reserved benefit exemption falls into the following categories.

A. Property subject to a reservation

The basic category is property that would fall to be treated as property which in **7–33** relation to the individual is property subject to a reservation for IHT purposes.[49] Although the reason for using the phrase "would fall to be treated" is clear enough in relation to the three exemptions discussed below, because they make certain assumptions, the authors assume its use in relation to the first condition is based on the fact that "property subject to a reservation" is defined for IHT purposes by reference to the "relevant period",[50] e.g. the period of seven years ending with the death of the individual concerned, and at the juncture when the Regime is being applied the "relevant period" will normally not have arisen.

This requirement is less straightforward than it seems for the simple reason that HMRC and the taxpayer may not see eye-to-eye on the question of whether or not property is caught by the reservation of benefit rules. Until January 2007 there was, for instance, a difference of opinion between HMRC and many practitioners as to whether certain reversionary lease schemes were within the reservation of benefit rules.[51] Such differences of opinion may cause problems under self-assessment. The reservation of benefit exemption is not affected by the excluded liability rules.[52]

---

[49] See Sch.15, para.11(5)(a).

[50] See FA 1986, s.102(1).

[51] See the discussion in **Ch.15**. HMRC now accept that reversionary lease schemes whenever done are not caught by reservation of benefit provided the donor has owned the property for at least seven years or purchased it for full consideration. See guidance notes, A2–57.

[52] Note also that none of the exemptions in para.11(5) can apply unless the property is, or otherwise would be, subject to a reservation of benefit. This is relevant in the case of full consideration arrangements.

B. Property subject to a reservation of benefit but for certain exemptions

7–34 Paragraph 11(5)(b) provides that the Regime does not apply if the property would have been caught by the reservation of benefit rules but for certain exemptions given by FA 1986, s.102(5)(d)–(i).[53] These exemptions apply where[54] the disposal by way of gift is an IHT exempt transfer by reason of various provisions in the Inheritance Tax Act 1984, namely s.23 (gift to charities); s.24 (gifts to political parties); s.24A (gifts to housing associations); s.25 (gifts for national purposes, etc); s.27 (maintenance funds for historic buildings)[55]; and s.28 (employee trusts). This simply preserves the favoured IHT treatment available to such transfers. The draftsman has used the IHT legislation for ease of reference.[56]

Example 7.15

Chris gives a large house to a charity for the mentally handicapped in 2000. This is an exempt transfer. In 2006 the charity allows him to occupy part of the house. He pays less than a market rent but there is no reservation of benefit. The POA provisions do not apply.[57]

There is one noteworthy omission—gifts to spouses which are exempt from reservation of benefit are not exempt under para.11. They can only qualify as excluded transactions under para.10.

7–35 As was seen in **Ch.5** this gives rise to a number of anomalies because the POA legislation is not the same as the inheritance tax legislation. For example, the exclusions do not apply at all to gifts of intangibles into settled property for the spouse.

Example 7.16

In 2005 Chris settles shares on qualifying interest in possession trusts for his spouse Kate remainder on discretionary trusts under which he can benefit. Chris is subject to the POA charge. The reservation of benefit provisions do not apply while Kate's interest in possession continues to give Chris protection. Further it is not an excluded transaction because the relevant charge is under para.8 on intangible property.

However, if Kate's qualifying interest in possession is terminated so that the property is held on discretionary trusts, Chris is then treated as reserving

---

[53] On the assumption that the limitation in the reservation of benefit provisions concerning outright cash gifts did not prevent the provisions from applying; see FA 2004, Sch.15, para.11(8).

[54] See Sch.15, para.11(5)(b).

[55] This condition does not exclude the application of the Regime in relation to a maintenance fund for an historic building unless the property in question remains subject to trusts which comply with the requirements of IHTA 1984, Sch.4, para.3(1); Sch.15, para.11(10).

[56] It may be noted that the de minimis exemption ("or virtually to the entire exclusion of the donor") has not been replicated. However, the guidance notes suggest that in practice this exemption will prevent the property from being occupied (land) or used (chattels). Further, minimal use of the property (exceeding de minimis) will presumably fall within the £5,000 annual exemption.

[57] Of course the charity may be acting in breach of its charitable obligations by allowing him to occupy the property at an undervalue.

a benefit in the property (see s.102(5)(d)) and so the POA charge ceases to apply.[58]

Alternatively, if the trustees sold the shares at a time when Kate still enjoyed an interest in possession in the trust and purchased land occupied by Chris then Chris is not subject to the Regime any longer because the excluded transaction protection becomes available. The requirement under para.10(1)(c) is for a disposal of any property by way of gift into the spousal settlement. Provided the spousal interest continues it does not appear to matter that the initial settled property was shares not land.

Of course, if Chris had settled shares into interest in possession trust for Kate after March 2006 this is a non-qualifying interest in possession trust. Spouse exemption is not available and therefore there is no protection from reservation of benefit if Chris can benefit from the trust. Hence Chris is protected from a POA charge **at the outset** by the reserved benefit exemption irrespective of the type of settled property.[59]

C. Undivided shares in land

This category consists of property which would[60] fall within the reservation of **7–36** benefit rules but for the let-out in FA 1986, s.102B(4) in respect of the shared occupation of land by a donor and donee.[61] This ensures that POAT does not apply to land sharing arrangements blessed by the reservation of benefit provisions. This exemption is of limited scope but extremely important in practice. A typical case where it is in point would be where Mrs A gives a 50 per cent interest in her house to her daughter and both occupy the property sharing all outgoings. Not only does Mrs A not reserve a benefit in the gifted moiety but she is not caught by the pre-owned assets charge.[62]

The exemption also applies to such arrangements which came into being before March 9, 1999.[63] Those arrangements are not within s.102B, which has effect only in relation to disposals of an undivided share of an interest in land made on or after that date, but benefited from an earlier ministerial statement exempting them from the reservation of benefit rules.[64] Note that s.102B(3) has a let-out from reservation of benefit if the donor gives away a share in land which he does not occupy.

Example 7.17

Mrs A gives a 50 per cent interest in a let property to a trust and retains a (non-qualifying) interest in possession, entitling her to all the rent. In these circumstances there is no reservation of benefit assuming Mrs A is entitled

---

[58] See **5–11** for further examples.

[59] Note that para.10 provides proection if the settled property is land or chattels, even through the spouse's internet in possession is non-qualifying: see s.10.

[60] On the assumption that the limitation in the reservation of benefit provisions concerning outright cash gifts did not prevent the provisions from applying; see FA 2004, Sch.15, para.11(8).

[61] See FA 2004, Sch.15, para.11(5)(c).

[62] For a detailed consideration of the planning opportunities and pitfalls, see **21–05**.

[63] See FA 2004, Sch.15, para.11(5)(c).

[64] This statement is set out in **Ch.21**. It may be argued that this statement was wholly misconceived and that pre-March 1999 such arrangements were outside the reservation of benefit net because of the "carve-out" principle.

only to the income but not to the capital and there is no power to terminate her interest nor any POA charge because the relevant property is let property and therefore outside the scope of charge. If the trustees later sold the let property and held cash there is no reservation of benefit. However, there is a POA intangibles charge because neither the ownership nor the reservation of benefit exemptions apply. There is no inheritance tax on Mrs A's death because her interest in possession is non-qualifying. Current lifetime planning possibilities are discussed further in **Ch.19**.

D. Paragraph 6 let-outs

7–37 The fourth category is that the property would be caught by the reservation of benefit rules[65] but for the application of the exclusion of benefit provisions in FA 1986, s.102C(3) and Sch.20, para.6(1)(a)(b).[66] This category requires careful consideration and can be divided into two let-outs.

First let-out—full consideration let-out

7–38 The first let-out is that in determining whether any property is enjoyed to the entire or virtually to the entire exclusion of the donor:

(a) retention or assumption by the donor of the actual occupation of land or actual enjoyment of an incorporeal right over the land; and

(b) retention or assumption by the donor of actual possession of the chattel;

are disregarded if the retention or assumption is for full consideration.

This is a most important exemption since the full consideration provision has been widely used in practice as a way of avoiding the reservation of benefit provisions.

Example 7.18

A gives his house to his son B and continues to occupy the property under an agreement for full consideration: not only will he not fall foul of the reservation of benefit rules but the pre-owned assets charge will be equally inapplicable. Of course, it is important for him to be able to show that he is furnishing full consideration and the evidence of experts in the market should be obtained. Further it will be important to show that the arrangement is reviewed and the consideration adjusted in accordance with market conditions (in effect there should be "rent review clauses").

Many taxpayers who would wish to give away their house with a view to saving IHT cannot afford to pay a full rent for continued occupation or fear that they may not, in the future, be able to afford to pay that rent. Hence for the average taxpayer these arrangements are unavailable. Of course, instead

---

[65] See FA 2004, Sch.15, para.11(5)(d); on the assumption where the contribution condition in para.3(3) or 6(3) is satisfied that the limitation in the reservation of benefit provisions concerning outright cash gifts did not prevent the provisions from applying; see FA 2004, Sch.15, para.11(8), discussed below.

[66] See FA 2004, Sch.15, para.11(5)(d).

of paying a rent (with consequent risks of future upward increases at a time when the taxpayer may not have the finances available) a lease could be granted, say for the taxpayer's life, at a premium arrived at on an actuarial basis.[67] Provided that it can be shown that this is "full consideration", the exemption will apply. Bear in mind that any rent/premium paid will be subject to income tax in the hands of the recipient.

Paragraph 6(1)(a) is also important in the context of chattels where schemes have been set up on the basis of a gift and lease back. These are considered in detail in **Ch.18**.[68]

What is full consideration?

In a published letter dated March 18, 1987 the Revenue stated: **7–39**

> "Whether an arrangement is for full consideration will of course depend on the precise facts. But among the attributes of an acceptable arrangement will be the existence of a bargain negotiated at arm's length by parties who were independently advised and which follows the normal commercial criteria in force at the time it was negotiated."

It is important to be able to demonstrate that both parties have separate advisers and separate valuers. Records should be kept of the advice and valuations since the burden is on the taxpayer to be able to demonstrate that full consideration has been paid. In addition, it will be necessary to ensure that rent review clauses are inserted. In other words, the transaction must be exactly as it would be if it were with an unconnected party.

The easiest and safest type of full consideration arrangement is for the donor to enter into an assured shorthold tenancy for say one or two years with an option to renew because this is relatively common and the rent easy to establish. The donee would be responsible for landlord-type repairs and the donor would pay normal running expenses. This is very similar to the rent that would be paid under para.5(2).

Consideration is not defined in the legislation. It is certainly true that HMRC expect[69] (surely wrongly) that the consideration will necessarily take the form of rent:

> "While we take the view that such full consideration is required throughout the relevant period and therefore consider that the rent paid should be reviewed at appropriate intervals to reflect market changes we do recognise that there is no single value at which consideration can be fixed as full. Rather we accept that what constitutes full consideration in any case lies within a range of values reflecting normal valuation tolerances and that any amount within that range can be accepted as satisfying FA 1986 Schedule 20 para (6)(1a)."

---

[67] Provided that full consideration is paid, this will not create an IHT settlement under the lease for life provisions in IHTA 1984, s.43(3).

[68] The IHT legislation provides no guidance on how to arrive at "full consideration". However, it will depend upon the benefits enjoyed by the donor in the particular case. Contrast the provisions in the Regime dealing with "rental value" which provides fairly precise guidance as to the terms of the hypothetical lease. See **11–29** for a consideration of the effects of opting into the reservation rules and then paying full consideration.

[69] See *Tax Bulletin* No. 9, November 1993.

7–40 However, para.6(1)(a) draws no distinction between income and capital as full consideration. It does not use the word rent. Nor does para.11(5)(d). Hence the grant of a lease for say a term of years based on the life expectancy of donor (but for less than 21 years) for a full premium would be acceptable if it satisfied "normal commercial criteria". The donor could then be made responsible for capital repairs under the lease. One would need specialist valuation advice to ascertain the likely premium payable. This premium would be subject to income tax in the hands of the donees.

Arranging matters this way will mean that the upfront premium may well be lower than the total annual rent paid under an assured shorthold because the donor is responsible for capital repairs and the premium is discounted. SDLT will be payable on the premium although the amounts involved are likely to be small.

Obviously the premium payable will depend on the length of the lease and the obligations imposed on the donor. Furthermore, if the property is ever sold such that the lease is sold by the donor there is likely to be an income tax charge on him at that point since the lease will be for less than 50 years.

7–41 In any arrangements the donor must actually pay the premium or rent; he cannot leave it outstanding as a loan owed to the donees. HMRC have confirmed in their guidance notes at 4.4 (see A2–41):

> "If the chargeable person's occupation of the relevant land or enjoyment of the relevant chattel is for full consideration in money or money's worth i.e. a full market rent is paid by them for their continued occupation/enjoyment, their occupation, enjoyment is not a reservation of benefit for inheritance tax purposes. This treatment is extended to the income tax charge under the Schedule by virtue of para.11(5)(d). Any arrangement or transaction entered into on or after 18th March 1986 where the chargeable person pays full consideration for the enjoyment or occupation of the relevant asset will not be subject to the income tax charge".[70]

Again HMRC equate "full consideration" with "rent".

Example 7.19

(1) X gives his country mansion to his son and continues to occupy it, paying full consideration to avoid a reservation of benefit. The terms agreed are a lease for seven years under which X maintains the property and grounds and pays a premium. No POA charge arises because if X pays full consideration the let-out in para.11(5)(d) applies. If he does not pay full consideration he has reserved a benefit and the let-out in para.11(5)(a) applies.

(2) Instead of giving away his mansion, X grants a 199 year reversionary lease to his son retaining the freehold and hence the right to occupy for 20 years. There is no reservation of benefit. POA applies. X cannot pay full consideration along the lines of (1) above to avoid POA. The POA charge can be reduced only by X paying under a legal obligation on an annual basis a rent equivalent to the assured shorthold tenancy.

---

[70] Note, of course, that "full consideration" is only relevant if otherwise the reservation of benefit rules would apply. Hence the taxpayer who carried out an *Ingram* scheme will not be able to escape the POA charge by "full consideration" payments. He will need to make payments under para.4: see **14–17**.

(3) Y gives his chattels away, paying full consideration for their continued use (calculated as one per cent of capital value and the cost of insuring them). No POA charge arises; there is no reservation of benefit.

(4) Y effects an *Ingram* scheme over his chattels, retaining a lease and giving away the freehold. There is no reservation of benefit even if Y pays nothing and therefore para.11(5)(d) is irrelevant. The full consideration let-out is only relevant where reservation of benefit would **otherwise** apply. The result is that Y is subject to a POA charge and this is on the taxable benefit being 4.75 per cent of the value of the assets. The effective tax rate for a 40% taxpayer is 1.9%. Y can pay full consideration for the use of the chattels to reduce the POA charge but this will (almost certainly) be less than 4.75 per cent, so will not remove the POA charge.

(5) Z effected an *Eversden* scheme over a house in 2003. His wife's interest in possession was terminated, inter vivos, in 2005. There is no reservation of benefit by Z and therefore para.11(5)(d) is irrelevant. Z is within the POA charge; any sums he pays under a legal obligation will reduce the quantum of that charge.

From the above it can be seen that sometimes it is better to effect a transaction where there would be a reservation of benefit **unless full consideration is paid. The taxpayer is then able to bring himself within the para.11(5)(d) exemption. This is particularly the case for chattels where "full consideration" is generally much lower than the POA benefit.**

Second let-out—change in donor's circumstances: para.6(1)(b): hardship let-out

The second let-out, in para.6(1)(b), is that in certain cases occupation by the donor **7–42** of land is disregarded if conditions concerning inter alia changes in his circumstances are satisfied. This provision is severely restricted: e.g. the donor must have become unable to maintain himself through age, infirmity or otherwise and the occupation must represent reasonable provision by the donee (a relative) for the care and maintenance of the donor. It is not clear what happens if the donor pays full consideration for his occupation and then becomes infirm and is not able to continue the payments. Paragraph 6 of Sch.20 states that occupation by the donor of the land shall be disregarded if "it results from a change in the circumstances of the donor". In this case he has never ceased to occupy the land. Does it matter that the reason for his continued occupation changes? It is thought not.

Ambiguity in wording

In the first edition of this book we mentioned that there was some confusion as **7–43** to whether the full consideration exemption does in fact apply due to the use of the word "and" in para.11(5)(d) and the fact that s.102C itself does not refer to occupation of land for full consideration where the disposal took place after March 8, 1999. This is covered by s.102A(3) and 102B(3). Did the para.11(5)(d) exemption apply only if s.102C(3) and Sch.20, para.6 applied? Our previous view was that on a proper construction of the legislation the full consideration let-out must apply. Otherwise para.11(5)(d) would be limited just to gifts of land made on or after March 9, 1999 where the donor reoccupies due to hardship. The reference then to para.6 in para.11(5)(d) would be meaningless. Indeed since para.6(1)(b) (hardship let-out) and para.6(1)(a) (full consideration let-out) do not apply anyway to post-March 8, 1999 disposals of land (since these exemptions are incorporated separately in s.102A(3), s.102B(3) and s.102C(3)) arguably it would never be possible to satisfy both s.102C(3) and para.6 of Sch.20. The reference in para.11(5)(d) is simply to para.6 of Sch.20 without specifying whether this is referring to the hardship let-out or the full consideration let-out. Presumably the draftsman intended to refer to para.6 of Sch.20 in relation to chattels and ss.102A(3), B(3) and C(3) in relation to land.

The authors therefore came to the conclusion that "and" should be read disjunctively so that arrangements over any property where full consideration is paid or (in the case of land) the donor reoccupies due to hardship are covered.[71] As noted above, this view has been accepted in the guidance notes.[72]

Other matters concerning the reservation of benefit exemption

Cash gifts

7–44   The reservation of benefit property tracing provisions does not apply to property purchased with outright (i.e. non-settled) gifts of currency.[73] Accordingly, if X gives £100,000 to his son and his son of his own volition uses it to purchase property which X occupies the reservation of benefit provisions will not generally apply in respect of the purchased property (FA 1986, Sch.20, para.2). This is broadly confirmed in the guidance notes.[74]

POAT takes account of this by providing that if the para.3(3) or para.6(3) contribution condition is met the fact that the reservation of benefit provisions would not apply to the cash contribution anyway is ignored in deciding whether the three exemptions discussed above operate.[75]

Example 7.20

Rose gives her daughter £250,000 in 2000. In 2001 they decide they want to live together and they purchase a property worth £500,000, each contributing half the sale price. The contribution condition in para.3(3) will be met. Section 102B(4) is not directly applicable because Rose gave away cash, not an undivided share in land.

However, in determining whether the exemption in para.11(5)(c) applies, it is **assumed** that the reservation of benefit provisions apply: see **21–14**.

---

[71] The argument against this interpretation was that para.11(5)(d) did not refer to s.102A(3) and s.102B(3) which give favoured inheritance tax treatment to full consideration arrangements in respect of disposals of land post-March 8, 1999. If the draftsman had felt the need to specify s.102C(3) in para.11(5)(d) why did he not also cross-refer to these sections?

[72] See A2.41.

[73] See FA 1986, Sch.20, para.2(2)(b) and see **Ch.23**.

[74] See A2.38.

[75] See Sch.15, para.11(8): since the tracing limitation does not operate in respect of settled property, there is no need to disapply the limitation in relation to the para.8 charge on settled intangible property.

Example 7.21

Rose gives cash of £500,000 to her daughter in 2000. In 2001 her daughter purchases a property for Rose to occupy. Rose pays full consideration for her occupation. Paragraph 11(5)(d) is deemed to apply and there is no POA charge.

Excluded property

Assume X dies, having reserved a benefit in respect of excluded property held on discretionary trusts. Revenue practice in such a case is not to impose a charge on the property on the basis that, as excluded property, it does not form part of X's estate immediately before he died.[76] But this does not prevent the property from being reserved benefit property for the purposes of this exemption. Similarly, if X reserves a benefit in company shares but occupies a house owned by the company then he can generally rely on para.11(3)(b) (reservation of benefit in derived property) to give him exemption under the Regime in respect of his occupation of the land.   **7–45**

The "substantially less" rule[77]

The substantially less rule does not apply where the person directly reserves a benefit in the relevant property. It is only applicable in relation to derivative reserved benefit property: for example, where someone reserves a benefit in, say, company shares but occupies land owned by the company which had at one time been owned by him and which he disposed of to the company. In these circumstances if the person reserves a benefit in company shares whose value is "substantially less" than the relevant property, the rule discussed above at **7–17** applies.   **7–46**

The "excluded liabilities" rule

The excluded liabilities rule does not apply either to any property or any derived property in which the donor reserves a benefit. This may provide planning opportunities.   **7–47**

Example 7.22

In 2004 A sold his house to a qualifying interest in possession trust for himself as part of a home loan scheme so that the house is subject to an excluded liability.

In June 2006 A surrendered his interest in possession so that his sons became entitled to qualifying interests in possession in the property. He continues to live in the house. The reservation of benefit provisions now apply. The fact that the house is still affected by the excluded liability does not matter. A is therefore not subject to the POA charge. A may choose to pay full

---

[76] See **Ch.8**.
[77] Sch.15, para.11(4).

consideration for his occupation. This would be sufficient to take him out of the reservation of benefit regime and he would be protected from a POA charge by para.11(5)(d). If he ceases to pay full consideration no POA charge arises but he would then be treated as reserving a benefit in the property.

Problems with definition of relevant property

7–48 The term "relevant property" is defined in para.11(9) to mean in the case of the disposal condition the property originally disposed of or in the case of the contribution condition the property representing the consideration provided. The definition of relevant property in relation to land and chattels seems defective. In particular, it only appears to cover the original property disposed of in relation to the disposal condition. In the case of the contribution condition does the "property representing the consideration directly or indirectly provided" mean only the original property purchased with such consideration or the property for the time being representing such consideration thus including subsequent purchases using the proceeds of the first purchase? It is suggested that the latter is the correct construction. It does not help that different definitions of relevant property are adopted in para.11(13) [reverter to settlor trusts] and para.21(1)(a) [election].

Example 7.23

In 2005 A settles his house on qualifying interest in possession trusts for himself. The trustees dispose of the house and buy a new one for his occupation. The relevant property definition embraces the original property but not the new house in relation to the disposal condition. It seems impossible to conclude that the second house derives its value from the first house. Hence it is important to construe the contribution condition as including disposals of property where such property is sold and the proceeds are then invested in another asset occupied by the disponer. Only then can A obtain the protections under para.11. It appears HMRC agree with this view.

Another aspect is how the valuations work when only part of the property disposed of comprised relevant property.

Example 7.24

In 2008 A gives cash of £300,000 to his son and lends him £200,000. The son uses the £500,000 to purchase a house for A's occupation. Only the £300,000 is caught by the contribution condition because the loan is not a provision of consideration. Hence only three-fifths of the property is relevant property under para.11(9).

The property increases in value to £1m. The loan remains at £200,000. In these circumstances is the relevant property £800,000 or three-fifths of the market value, namely £600,000? The definition in para.11(9) would suggest the latter is correct.

The third exemption is an important one for taxpayers who have or may in the **7–49** future wish to carry out IHT planning using deeds of variation.

Paragraph 16 provides that any disposition made by a person in relation to an interest in the estate of a deceased person is to be disregarded for POA purposes, if under s.17 of the IHTA 1984 that disposition is not treated as a transfer of value for IHT purposes.[78] Section 17 provides that none of the following is a transfer of value:

(a) variations and disclaimers falling within s.142;

(b) dispositions made pursuant to precatory trusts within s.143;

(c) an election by a surviving spouse under s.47A of the Administration of Estates Act 1925; or

(d) the renunciation of a claim to legitimacy within the period mentioned in s.147(6).

The exemption does not extend to IHTA 1984, s.93 disclaimers, apparently on the basis that in order for a disclaimer to be legally effective it must be made before any benefit is taken from the entitlement and the person disclaiming is not as a matter of property law treated as having made a disposition. Hence it is assumed that any subsequent arrangements under which the person disclaiming occupies property that has been disclaimed would not be caught by POAT anyway because the basic disposal condition is not satisfied.

Tax trap—the missing transfer of value?

Although the draftsman's intention was to replicate the IHT favoured treatment **7–50** of, for instance, deeds of variation, in the first edition of this book we expressed a concern that the position in one case was not entirely free from doubt.

Example 7.25

X dies leaving his estate to his widow who within two years of X's death enters into a deed of variation under which, instead of taking X's estate absolutely, she settles it on trusts under which she retains an interest in possession with remainders over to her children. This is an effective deed of variation for IHT purposes, but does it qualify for favoured treatment under POAT? Under s.49A of the 1984 Act the widow will, by virtue of her qualifying interest in possession under the new settlement (which is an immediate post death interest), still be treated as owning X's estate with the result that she will not make a transfer of value. The question then arises as to whether s.17, which provides that a s.142 deed is not a transfer of value, will nevertheless be relevant for the purposes of obtaining protection under para.16.

On a narrow reading it is arguable that the deed is not a transfer of value because **7–51** of s.49(1) not by virtue of s.17 of the 1984 Act. Therefore, para.16 does not apply

---

[78] See Sch.15, para.16.

to protect the variation. If POAT did apply, then although it would not matter while the widow retained an interest in possession, it could become a problem if that interest were terminated and she continued to be able to benefit from the settlement.

In the first edition we expressed the view that this was not the correct interpretation. The variation is within s.142(1) if it is a variation made within two years of death and the other conditions are met. Section 17 then states that a variation or disclaimer to which s.142 applies is not a transfer of value. The fact that the variation may not be a transfer of value for some other reason as well would not appear to matter. HMRC have now confirmed that they agree with this interpretation:

> "We would agree that section 17 applies to all disclaimers or variations that come within section 142(1), even if the variation may not be a transfer of value in any event. As a result, I can confirm that all instruments of variation to which section 142(1) IHTA applies will come within the protection afforded by paragraph 16 of Schedule 15. We will supplement the guidance at 1.3.5 to make this clear."[79]

---

[79] See A2–69.

CHAPTER 8

TERRITORIAL SCOPE

This chapter considers the territorial exemptions and limitations given under **8–01** para.12 of Sch.15. It also discusses the interaction of paras 11 and 12 for foreign domiciliaries. The scope of the Regime is limited under para.12 by reference to a person's residence and domicile and to the situs of property. Subject to the application of these exemptions and limitations the POA charge is capable of applying to land, chattels and intangibles situated anywhere in the world and to settlor-interested settlements irrespective of where such settlements are established or their governing law. Note however that the intangibles charge can only ever apply to intangible property that is held directly by the trustees. The intangibles charge cannot apply to shares and cash held by an underlying company which is owned by the trustees, although of course the charge could apply to the holding company shares that are owned directly by the trustees.

BASIC RELIEFS

There are three basic reliefs: **8–02**

1. the non-residence relief under para.12(1): the Regime does not apply to non-UK residents at all wherever they are domiciled;

2. the situs relief under para.12(2): the Regime does not apply to persons not domiciled or deemed domiciled in the UK in respect of property situated outside the UK; and

3. the settled excluded property relief under para.12(3): the Regime does not apply to settled property which is excluded property for IHT purposes even if the person is resident and deemed domiciled in the UK.

Further exemptions

Before looking at each of these reliefs in detail it is important to appreciate that **8–03** the para.12 rules, if read in isolation, would give a distorted picture of the way the Regime operates in the case of foreign domiciliaries. As we will see, the para.12 rules must be read in conjunction with the para.11 exemptions discussed in **Ch.7**. Planning issues for foreign domiciliaries and typical POAT problems that can arise for them are discussed in **Ch.24**.

Paragraph 12(1): non-residents

8–04   The Regime does not apply to a person for any year of assessment during which he is not resident in the UK.[80]

Example 8.1

Desmond is potentially subject to the para.3 charge for tax year 2005–6 because he gave his son a substantial sum of money in 2002 which was used to buy the flat which Desmond occupies. On March 30, 2006, however, Desmond accepts a prestigious full-time job in eastern Europe and ceases to be UK resident. Accordingly he is not subject to the POA charge in 2006–7 even though he returns to England for a month over Christmas and New Year when he occupies the flat which is available for his use throughout the year.

FOREIGN DOMICILIARIES

8–05   There are two reliefs regulating the treatment of foreign domiciliaries. These provisions are similar to, but by no means identical to, the IHT rules. In addition to the ordinary law of domicile, the IHT deemed domicile rules apply for the purposes of both provisions and it will therefore be helpful to review these rules before considering the reliefs.[81]

Deemed domicile rules

8–06   By IHTA 1984, s.267 an individual is deemed to be domiciled in the United Kingdom for most IHT purposes even though he is domiciled elsewhere under general law if either one of two tests is satisfied, as follows.

Three-year rule

8–07   The individual will be deemed to be domiciled in the United Kingdom at any time if he was domiciled in the United Kingdom (as a matter of general law) within the three *years* immediately preceding that time.[82]

---

[80]   See Sch.15, para.12(1). "Residence" has its general meaning. For tax (and civil law) purposes, it may not always be easy to resolve a person's residence. HMRC booklet "Residence and Non-Residence" (IR 20) has been withdrawn. See now HMRC 6 which gives general but rather unhelpful guidance and the recent case law including *Gaines-Cooper v HMRC* [2007] STC (SCD) 23; *HMRC v Grace* [2009] STC 213; *Dubai Bank Ltd v Abbas* [1996] EWCA Civ 1342; *Shepherd v HMRC* [2006] STC 1821; *Cherney v Deripaska* [2007] EWHC 965 (Comm) and *OJSC Oil Company Yugraneft v Abramovich* [2008] EWHC 2613 (Comm). A person who is resident in another country for income tax purposes under the tie breaker provisions of a double tax treaty is also non resident for the purpose of the POA charge.

[81]   See Sch.15, para.12(4).

[82]   See IHTA 1984, s.267(1)(a).

Seventeen-year rule

The individual will be deemed to be domiciled in the UK at any time ("the **8–08** relevant time") if he was resident in the UK in not less than 17 of the 20 *years of assessment* ending with the year of assessment in which the relevant time falls. Residence for this purpose is determined as for income tax, but without regard to any dwelling-house available for the use of the person in question.[83]

The calendar year trap

Note that there is a trap here. The three-year rule is normally thought of as **8–09** applying to a person who emigrates from the UK, while the 17-year rule is normally thought of as applying to a foreign domiciliary who is a longstanding resident of the UK. While this will normally be correct, it is important to bear in mind that the 17-year rule can also apply to a UK domiciliary who emigrates from the UK, with potentially catastrophic results. Assume that Fred is a UK domiciliary who has lived in the UK all his life. On retiring, he emigrated to Spain, arriving there on January 1, 2009, at which time he became domiciled in Spain as a matter of general law. Under the three-year rule he ceased to be domiciled in the UK on January 1, 2012, but under the 17-year rule he will not cease to be domiciled in the UK until April 6, 2012.

The basic relief—para.12(2)

Where an individual is not domiciled in the UK for IHT purposes, the Regime **8–10** does not apply to him unless the property by reference to which the Regime operates is situated in the UK.[84]

Example 8.2

Tatiana, a foreign domiciliary who is not deemed domiciled in the UK, occupies foreign situs land owned by an offshore discretionary trust of which she is the settlor and beneficiary. Paragraph 12(2) prevents the Regime from applying to the land. But if Tatiana becomes domiciled in the UK the protection of para.12(2) will cease to be available. However, on the above facts, even after Tatiana becomes actually or deemed domiciled in the UK the para.12(3) exemption is available in respect of the settled property. Moreover since she reserves a benefit in the settled property she also has the protection of the reserved benefit exemption in para.11(5)(a).[85]

Comparison with IHT

The approach adopted under para.12(2) differs significantly from the IHT **8–11** approach to foreign situs property. Under IHT a basic distinction is drawn

---

[83] See IHTA 1984, s.267(1)(b).
[84] See Sch.15, para.12(2).
[85] See **7–30**.

between settled and non-settled property. Under the Regime, on the other hand, the relief in para.12(2) simply looks at the domicile of the individual and the situs of the Regime property, regardless of whether such property is owned by an individual, comprised in a settlement, or, indeed, owned by a company. Unlike the para.11(1) ownership exemption and the para.11(3) reserved benefit exemption,[86] the para.12(2) relief does not require a consideration of whether the property derives its value from other property at the different levels. All that is needed is to examine the particular item of property subject to the charge and then consider whether the property is situated in the UK and whether the person is UK domiciled.

Example 8.3

Tatiana (a foreign domiciliary) gave her UK house to a wholly owned company. This is a disposal for POAT purposes (even though there is no element of bounty).[87] She occupies the house. There is no para.9 POA charge on the company shares (despite being intangibles) because the shares are not settled property. However, para.12(2) provides no protection from a para.4 charge in respect of the disposal of land: the house is UK situated. In fact, there is no POA charge on Tatiana but this is due to the para.11(1) (derived ownership exemption); there is no para.12(2) protection. The fact that there is no IHT on the UK property on Tatiana's death because it is owned by an offshore company which is excluded property, does not prevent her from claiming protection under para.11(1).[88]

Example 8.4

If Tatiana had disposed of her Italian house to a wholly owned company the para.12(2) exemption would apply. Then protection under para.11(1) is not required. As noted later, this can be relevant to those foreign domiciliaries caught by FA 2006, s.80.[89] It is not necessary for Tatiana to be a remittance basis user to obtain protection under para.12(2). The FA 2008 changes are not relevant here. So long as she is neither domiciled nor deemed domiciled in the UK under general law, the fact that she may choose to be taxed on an

---

[86] See **Ch.7**.

[87] Note that if she lent the company money or subscribed for shares in the company to enable the company to purchase a house from a third party that she then occupied this would not fall within the contribution condition since there is no bounty and there is no disposal of land. Hence POA would not apply: see **3–12**; **7–20** and *Examples 7.8(e), 7.7* and *7.14*.

[88] See **7–14**.

[89] See **7–24** and **8–19**.

arising basis for capital gains tax and income tax purposes is irrelevant.[90] Once Tatiana becomes domiciled or deemed domiciled in the UK, however, the protection of para.12(2) will cease to apply. Hence, in Example 8.4, the Italian property will no longer be protected. However, as in Example 8.3, Tatiana should be able to rely on the para.11(1) ownership exemption at that point to prevent a POA charge. The property is in her estate for IHT purposes and therefore no POA charge arises provided paras 11(11)(12) are not in point—see below.

The settled property relief—para.12(3)

A more complex protection is given in para.12(3) which provides that: **8–12**

"in the application of this Schedule to a person who was at any time domiciled outside the UK for IHT purposes, no regard is to be had to any foreign *situs* property which is excluded property"

by reason of being comprised in a settlement made by a settlor who was not domiciled in the UK when he made the settlement.[91] This confers protection in relation to individuals who though domiciled abroad when setting up the trust subsequently become domiciled in the UK (whether deemed or under general law) and who are accordingly unable to shelter under the basic rule in para.12(2). As with para.12(2) it covers only foreign situs property (since UK property cannot be excluded). It protects only property owned directly by the trust rather than any underlying assets since it is only the property owned directly by the trustees that is the settled property and therefore excluded.

Returning to *Example 8.2* , although the relief under para.12(2) will cease to be available if Tatiana becomes domiciled in the UK the settled property relief will be available in respect of the company shares so long as she was domiciled abroad when she made the settlement. Note that unlike para.12(2) it therefore

---

[90] From April 6, 2008, to obtain the benefit of the remittance basis for foreign chargeable gains, foreign employment income or relevant foreign income an individual must claim to be taxed on a remittance basis unless he comes within certain limited exceptions. He is then a "remittance basis user". If he claims the remittance basis of taxation then he will lose all personal allowances and the annual capital gains tax exemption (from the first year of UK residence). In addition, if he has been UK resident in at least 7 out of the 9 tax years immediately preceding the tax year in question and is over 18, he must pay £30,000 for the privilege of retaining the remittance basis of taxation. He will continue to lose all personal allowances and the annual capital gains tax exemption. If he does not opt to pay the £30,000 charge he will pay tax on an arising basis (this has no bearing on his domicile status under general law). The £30,000 charge is in addition to any tax due on foreign income and games remitted to the UK. It is a tax charge on nominated unremitted income and gains rather than a stand-alone charge. There are ordering rules to ensure that if nominated income or gains is, in fact remitted when other untaxed income and gains remain unremitted, then that unremitted income and gains is deemed to be remitted before the nominated income and gains. The foreign domiciliary can opt in and out of the charge depending on the level of his overseas gains and income each year. The charge applies only to adults and so becomes payable in the year a person turns 18. Married couples may both have to pay the charge. The first £30,000 is due in January 2010 for 2008/9 and will apply to anyone who has been a UK resident continuously since 2001/2. If the £30,000 charge is paid from an offshore source direct to HMRC by cheque or electronic transfer, it will not itself be taxed as a remittance. If the £30,000 is repaid (e.g. the individual decides not to claim the remittance basis and amends his tax return) it will be taxed as a remittance at that point.

[91] For the definition of an excluded property settlement for IHT purposes, see IHTA 1984, s.48(3).

only protects property held at the trust level. Hence it is necessary to rely on paras 11(1)(b) and 11(3)(b) (derived ownership and derived reservation of benefit exemptions) to protect property held by the underlying companies.

It is not clear whether the settled property relief in para.12(3) applies only in respect of an individual who has **become** domiciled in the UK or can apply in cases where the individual has not yet become deemed or actually domiciled in the UK, but given the basic relief in para.12(2), nothing appears to turn on this. As noted above, para.12(2) relief can apply throughout all levels of the trust while para.12(3) can only apply to the settled property, i.e. the property held directly by the trustees.

Effect of para.12(3)

8–13   Paragraph 12(3) provides that excluded property is to be ignored for all Sch.15 purposes. Must one ignore excluded property for para.11 purposes? If so, the reliefs in para.11 might not be available. For example, if the effect of para.12(3) was that the company shares are ignored, then Tatiana cannot claim para.11 relief in respect of the property held by the underlying companies. Although the company shares derive their value from the property they hold, if the shares have to be ignored for para.11 purposes then the reserved benefit and ownership exemptions are not available. HMRC do not take this view.[92]

Comparison with IHT

8–14   The settled property relief in para.12(3) is similar but less generous than the IHT provisions that apply in determining whether property comprised in a settlement is excluded property, in two ways.

First, so far as IHT is concerned, favoured treatment depends only on the domicile of the settlor. Where the Regime is concerned, on the other hand, both the domicile of the settlor and the domicile of the individual who is potentially chargeable are relevant, though it appears that so far as the individual is concerned, all that matters is that he was not domiciled in the UK at some time, whether or not that time occurred during the year of assessment in which he is potentially within the POA charge.

Example 8.5

(a) Ron, a UK domiciliary, in 2001 gives his daughter (domiciled in France) £300,000. She settles this sum in a Jersey trust which uses it to purchase a flat in the Cote d'Azur. Ron lives there for six months of the year. The IHT/POA position is as follows:

   (i) the settlement being made by a non-UK domiciliary and comprising non-UK situs property falls within IHTA 1984, s.48(3) and is an excluded property settlement;

   (ii) so far as Ron is concerned, however, he is subject to the POA charge given that he is in occupation of land and satisfies the contribution

---

[92] See A2.114.

condition. As a UK domiciliary he is outside the protection of both paras 12(2) and 12(3).

(b) Tony, domiciled in Italy, puts his Sardinia property into a Swiss Trust and subsequently moves to the UK becoming domiciled here in due course. The settlement is, for IHT purposes, comprised of excluded property and because Tony was at one time non-UK domiciled he is protected from a POA charge by para.12(3).

Secondly, as emphasised already, the settled excluded property relief affords relief only in respect of settled property. Assume Max, a foreign domiciliary occupies foreign situs land owned by an offshore company all the shares in which are owned by trustees of a discretionary settlement made by him. So far as IHT is concerned, the relevant asset is the shares in the company which will be excluded property (because non situs) even if Max becomes domiciled in the UK. Under the Regime, on the other hand, there are two relevant assets—the shares and the land. If Max becomes domiciled in the UK the settled property relief will protect him in relation to the shares (being the settled foreign situs property which is excluded property), but it will not protect him in relation to the foreign situs land, because that land is not settled property. This reveals the limits of the para.12 reliefs: in a case like this it is likely, however, that Max is protected in respect of the land by a para.11 exemption because either he is deemed to own the property if he has a qualifying interest in possession or he reserved a benefit in it. The only difficulty is if FA 2006, s.80 applies to disapply the para.11 exemption and this is discussed in **8–19** below.

EXEMPT GILTS[93]

Unlike the IHT regime, POAT does not afford favoured treatment to exempt gilts **8–15** where the owner or settlor is UK domiciled. This is unlikely to be important in relation to non-settled exempt gilts since these will qualify for favoured IHT treatment only if owned beneficially by a person who is not ordinarily resident in the UK. Such a person will be outside the POA Regime anyway. Similarly in relation to settled exempt gilts the IHT relief is only available if the property is held on qualifying interest in possession trusts for the non-UK resident (and such a person is not within the POA charge anyway) or (broadly) if all the beneficiaries are non-UK resident.

Example 8.6

In 1997 A set up an interest in possession trust holding intangibles. He is UK domiciled and takes a qualifying interest in possession. He is within the POA charge since this is a settlor interested trust but the para.11(1) ownership exemption applies.

In 2008 he becomes non-UK resident. From that point POA ceases to apply to him until he becomes UK resident again. Whether or not the trust holds exempt gilts is irrelevant.

---

[93] IHTA 1984, s.6(2).

8–16 As explained in **Ch.7**, POAT does not apply to an individual in respect of property which is included in his IHT estate, whether this is property he owns, or property in which he has a qualifying interest in possession. Similarly, where he has a qualifying interest in possession or owns beneficially property which derives its value from other relevant property, there is no POA charge.

> ### Example 8.7
>
> Sergei, a foreign domiciliary, settles property on qualifying interest in possession trusts for himself and the settled property comprises an offshore company which in turn owns a UK house that he occupies. Paragraph 12(3) provides protection in respect of the offshore company shares and (provided that FA 2006, s.80 does not apply) para.11(1)(b) provides protection in respect of the house. (If the house was non-UK situated then para.12(2) would provide protection in respect of both the company shares and the house while Sergei is not domiciled or deemed domiciled here and there would be no need for para.11(1) protection.)

Reserved benefit exemption—paras 11(3)(a) and (5)(a)

8–17 POAT does not apply to an individual by reference to any property in which he has reserved a benefit or if he reserves a benefit in property which derives its value from relevant property.

> ### Example 8.8
>
> Sergei is now deemed domiciled in the UK, having set up in 2007 a relevant property trust comprising an offshore holding company holding UK land. He was not UK deemed domiciled at that time. Paragraph 12(3) provides protection in respect of the shares and para.11(3) in respect of the UK situated house provided the company shares derive their value from the house.[94]

Hierarchy of let-outs and exemptions

8–18 The legislation does not establish any hierarchy between the para.12 let-outs and the para.11 exemptions. In practice, it is simpler to apply the para.12 reliefs first because they are easier to apply conceptually than the para.11 exemptions and, unlike the para.11 exemptions, are not subject to any qualifications such as the excluded liability rule or the problems presented by FA 2006, s.80.

---

[94] For discussion on this point see **7–15**.

Section 80 is discussed at **7–24** and poses particular problems for foreign **8–19** domiciliaries although it will generally only apply to trusts where the settlor took an interest in possession prior to March 22, 2006 because thereafter few new interests in possession will be qualifying.

Example 8.9

(1) Sergei is neither deemed domiciled nor actually UK domiciled. In 2004 he settled cash into a discretionary trust. In 2005 this was converted into a qualifying interest in possession trust for Sergei and the trustees then purchased a house in the UK for occupation by Sergei. (The conversion to an interest in possession was done to avoid 10-year charges on the trustees which would have otherwise occurred given they own UK property.) The para.12 reliefs do not apply to the house because it is UK situated. Paragraph 11(1) (ownership exemption) ought to apply given that Sergei has a qualifying interest in possession. However, from December 2005 paras 11(11)(12) disapply the ownership exemption in para.11(1) while Sergei retains his qualifying interest in possession. If Sergei's interest in possession is ended this will involve him making an IHT chargeable transfer and thereafter the trustees will be subject to 10-year charges but there will be no POA charge on Sergei. However, on Sergei's death there will be a reservation of benefit in any UK situated property held directly by the trustees and IHT will be due.[95] There is no possibility of capital gains tax uplift and no spouse exemption even if his wife takes the property. If by the date of his death the UK property has been sold and instead the trustees own foreign situated assets then there would be no UK IHT (because the settled property is excluded) and no POA charge arises. Once the settled property is non-UK situated both the para.12(2) and para.12(3) reliefs are in point, although para.12(2) will be relevant only while Sergei is not domiciled or UK deemed domiciled.

(2) If the trustees sell the UK property in 2009 and invest the proceeds in an Italian house occupied by Sergei and he retains a qualifying interest in possession then although para.11 gives no protection, if the Italian house is owned directly by the trustees then both para.12(2) and (3) are in point and no POA charge arises. If the Italian house is owned through a holding company (not uncommon in relation to European property), then para.12(3) will protect the shares of the holding company but the Italian property is not protected by para.12(3) since it is not settled property; para 12(2) will protect Sergei from a charge on his occupation of the Italian property but only so long as he is not deemed or actually UK domiciled.

(3) If the trustees sell the UK property and invest in intangibles, e.g. shares, there is no POA charge if the trustees hold foreign shares because of the para.12 reliefs. If the trustees hold UK situated shares directly there will be a POA charge and the ownership exemption does not apply. If the

---

[95] FA 1986, s.102ZA, inserted by FA 2006.

trustees own UK shares but through an offshore company then para.12 reliefs will protect Sergei from a POA charge in respect of the offshore company shares. There is no para.12 protection in relation to the UK shares (since these are not excluded property). However, the intangibles charge in para.9 only applies to settled property held **directly** by the trustees. It does not apply to intangibles owned by an underlying company.

8–20 In summary if paras 11(11)(12) apply then even though the para.11 ownership exemption and reservation of benefit exemptions are disapplied, no POA charge can arise unless:

(a) Sergei retains his qualifying interest in possession, having not had this interest in possession throughout the period of the trust **or** the qualifying interest in possession trust has been funded by another trust which was not a qualifying interest in possession; and

(b) the trustees hold UK intangibles directly rather than through an offshore company; or

(c) the trustees hold UK land or UK chattels either directly or through an offshore company and he occupies the land or uses the chattels;

(d) the trustees hold foreign situated land or chattels that he occupies / uses through an offshore company and he is deemed UK domiciled so the para.12 protections do not apply to the land/chattels (although para.12(3) will protect the offshore company shares).

8–21 In practice the most likely time when POA will apply is in (c) above. In the case of (d) above the trustees may be able to arrange to hold the foreign situated land direct and thereby avoid the effect of para.11(11) and obtain the protection of para.12(3). This will not affect the IHT position adversely since the settlement continues to be excluded. In the case of (c) above, Sergei may prefer to pay the POA charge or pay rent under a legal obligation to the trustees rather than incur an immediate IHT charge on the ending of his interest in possession. The trustees could, of course, transfer the UK land to a foreign holding company and therefore avoid the charge on subsequent termination of his qualifying interest in possession (because at that point the settled property would be excluded property for IHT purposes). Once Sergei ceases to have an interest in possession, para.11(11) is not relevant and he obtains the protection of the reservation of benefit exemption.

8–22 However, a transfer even by gift of UK land to a connected company from the trustees will trigger SDLT on the market value of the property and so is likely to result in a 4 per cent SDLT charge. In addition Sergei may be concerned about shadow director charges under the benefit in kind legislation in ITEPA 2003. Another option for Sergei in the case of (c) above is to elect into the reservation of benefit provisions. If by the date of his death Sergei still retains his qualifying interest in possession then the reservation of benefit rules are disapplied by virtue of FA 1986, s.102(3). IHT is due on his death under general principles (as the holder of a qualifying interest in possession) but only if the settled property is still UK situated. If by then the UK property has been sold and the trustees hold non-UK situated property directly there is no IHT charge. Alternatively if on Sergei's death his qualifying interest in possession terminates and his spouse or civil partner takes a qualifying interest in possession[96] then spouse exemption is available. There will still be no IHT charge. Of course, Sergei may have missed the time limits for making an election: see **Ch.11** and A2–132.

If by Sergei's death the trustees have sold the UK land then whether or not he **8–23** elects and retains a qualifying interest in possession or his qualifying interest in possession is ended and he actually reserves a benefit no inheritance tax charge will arise because the settled property is excluded. However, generally if the UK land is to be retained by the trustees either directly or in an underlying holding company it is preferable that Sergei elects into the reservation of benefit regime and retains his interest in possession rather than that his interest in possession is actually terminated and he reserves a benefit: see **11–17**.

This is because:

(a) an inheritance tax charge is avoided if his interest in possession continues and moreover no 10-year charges arise in the future. By contrast if his qualifying interest in possession is ended and the trustees retain the UK property an inheritance tax charge arises as well as 10-year charges while the trustees hold UK property direct. Moving the UK property into an underlying company will raise capital gains tax issues as well as trigger SDLT charges;

(b) if Sergei dies with a qualifying interest in possession and the trustees own the UK house but Sergei has made an election into reservation of benefit s.102(3) disapplies the effect of the election. If his spouse takes the UK house outright or under a transitional serial interest, then spouse exemption may be available. This would not be the case if his qualifying interest in possession is ended and he reserves a benefit when the spouse exemption is not available even if his spouse takes outright.

The implications of this are discussed further in **Ch.24** in relation to houses occupied by foreign domiciliaries.

---

[96] This will be a transitional serial interest: see **7–06**.

CHAPTER 9

£5,000 ANNUAL EXEMPTION; DE MINIMIS AND MOTIVE

9–01 An individual is not chargeable in a year of assessment if the *aggregate* of:

a)   the appropriate rental value under para.4(2);

b)   the appropriate amount under para.7(2); and

c)   the chargeable amount under para.9;

does not exceed £5,000.[1]

Not a nil band

9–02 Assuming a notional five per cent "benefit" (this was the offical rate of interest when POAT was introduced), the broad effect of this exemption is to take out of the charge property worth up to £100,000. This figure does not, however, constitute an equivalent to the IHT nil rate band because if the £5,000 exemption is exceeded (even by £1) it is lost altogether.[2]

Tax trap: the ungenerous exemption

9–03 The exemption is less generous than it looks. Assume A falls within para.3 in respect of land worth £150,000, that the appropriate rental value is £7,500 and that A pays B £5,000 per year in rent. The amount on which A is actually chargeable is only £2,500 (£7,500 less £5,000) but the exemption operates by reference not to that amount but by reference to the appropriate rental value, i.e. £7,500. The exemption therefore does not apply at all. The exemption also operates in this way in relation to chattels.[3]

9–04 Note, by contrast, that where an individual pays income tax or CGT in respect of settled intangible property, the tax allowance he is given for the purposes of POAT (see **6–19**) reduces the para.8 chargeable amount.[4]

A married couple both of whom are within the POA charge (e.g. in respect of a property which they jointly occupy) will each have a £5,000 annual exemption.

---

[1] See Sch.15, paras 13(1)–(3). The figure proposed in the original consultation document had been £2,500. The £5,000 exemption has not increased since 2005.

[2] A similar position applies to the Stamp Duty Land Tax rate bands.

[3] The payment of consideration is irrelevant under para.8.

[4] Sch.15, para.9(1).

In such a case, property worth in the region of £200,000 may not be caught by the Regime.

Example 9.1

(a) Mr and Mrs X entered into a home loan scheme in 2003 which involved settling their house in Chichester on a joint life interest trust.[5] The property is worth £350,000 but is unmodernised and would only rent for around £800 pcm. Assuming that they are potentially within the POA charge the position is as follows:

    (i) given that they were joint owners, each has disposed of a 50 per cent interest in the property so that applying the DV/V formula to the annual rent of £9,600 each is treated as receiving benefits of £4,800[6];

    (ii) neither is subject to the POA charge since the appropriate rental value is within their de minimis £5,000 exemption.

(b) Mr and Mrs Y are in a similar position but in their case the property is worth £950,000. They had intended to pay rent each year in order to avoid the POA charge. Accordingly they occupy the property after April 6, 2005 until June 6, 2005 when they discover that the property would command a rent of £4,000 pcm. They promptly move out and the property is commercially let. Their POA position for 2005–6 is that:

    (i) they are within the charge for the occupation period of two months (but not thereafter);

    (ii) the apportioned value of that benefit is £8,000 which—as is the case of Mr and Mrs X—will be divided between them and again the £5,000 exemption will ensure that no POA charge arises. (Note therefore that the £5,000 exemption is not pro-rated even though they are within the Regime for only part of the tax year.)

De minimis occupation

In their guidance notes HMRC indicate that the POA charge will not apply in a **9–05** case where although land is occupied (or chattels possessed or used) such occupation is de minimis. For these purposes similar guidelines are to be adopted as are used for the purpose of determining whether a benefit has been reserved under the reservation of benefit legislation.[7] This appears to be a separate relief from the annual £5,000 exemption in that, if the occupation is de minimis, the taxpayer does not need to go to the trouble of obtaining valuations to ascertain whether the taxable benefit is under £5,000.

---

[5] Home loan (or double trust) schemes are considered in detail in **Ch.17**.
[6] It is arguable that DV (the value of the share sold) should be discounted to reflect joint ownership: see A2.77.
[7] See para.4.6 of the guidance notes (A2.43).

Motive and the annual exemption

9–06 Concerns have been expressed that individuals who enter into arrangements without any intention of avoiding IHT might find themselves caught by the pre-owned assets charge. Certainly there is no motive requirement. However, in some cases the £5,000 annual exemption will help: in others the general exemptions in para.11 (discussed in **Ch.7**) will assist in preventing any charge.

Take the example of Mrs A who owns her flat worth £200,000 and is concerned to ensure that the property will pass to her daughter Maisie. As she has no other significant assets, IHT saving is not an issue: all she is concerned about is ensuring that Maisie benefits from the flat. With this in mind she might:

(a) gift the flat to Maisie and rely upon her to allow her to continue in occupation; or

(b) transfer the flat into a settlement under which she retains an interest in possession[8] with remainder to Maisie. As compared to (a) Mrs A now has a right (under the settlement) to occupy. A gift of the property into such a trust after March 21, 2006 will be an immediate chargeable transfer for inheritance tax purposes because Mrs A cannot take a qualifying interest in possession unless she is disabled.

9–07 Is the Regime capable of applying to Mrs A in these circumstances? It is irrelevant that she is not motivated by a wish to avoid IHT since, as noted, the Regime takes no account of motive. Nor will the de minimis exemption help given that the value of the occupation benefit is likely to exceed £5,000. As can be seen Mrs A is not therefore in any sense a "special case" and the reason why the Regime will not apply follows from general principles. In both cases, because Mrs A's gift falls within the reservation of benefit rules, the Regime does not apply.[9] If the gift had been made into trust prior to March 22, 2006, then Mrs A would have taken a qualifying interest in possession and the ownership exemption in para.11(1) rather than the reservation of benefit exemption in para.11(3) would apply. See Examples 7.3 and 7.4 for further consideration of how the para.11 exemptions work in these circumstances.

Example 9.2

Jason is keen to raise money for a round the world cruise. His house is worth £500,000 and he wishes to raise £25,000 being the full market value—if not more than the full market value—for a five per cent share. His daughter agrees to buy a five per cent share in the property and pays him £25,000. Neither Jason nor his daughter are motivated by saving or avoiding IHT but the arrangement falls within the POA net.

(a) Because Jason is not selling his entire interest in the property the disposal is not an excluded transaction with para.10(1).[10]

---

[8] It is thought that although this involves a carve-out the reservation of benefit rules apply because of the anti-*Ingram* legislation in FA 1986, s.102A.

[9] See the para.11(5)(a) exemption from charge.

[10] See **5–19**.

(b) Nor does he fall within the exemption in para.5 of the Regulations given that the sale is to a connected person and occurs on or after March 7, 2005.[11]

(c) **However**, when it comes to calculating Jason's chargeable amount only five per cent of the rental value will be taken with the result that the sum is likely to fall within his de minimis £5,000 exemption.

The election and the annual exemption

If the benefits enjoyed by the taxpayer fall within the annual exemption he is not **9–08** able to make the election[12] because he is not "chargeable" under the Regime. Accordingly, the time limits for making the election are extended until such time as his taxable benefit exceeds £5,000. For a taxpayer currently within the Regime because he is in occupation of land and whose benefits fall within the annual exemption, the level of benefits is effectively frozen until 2010 as a result of reg.4.[13] Such taxpayers therefore have until January 31, 2012 to make an election.[14] There is no suggestion that the annual exemption will increase in line with RPI for the next five years but given the five-year freeze on valuations of land this is not unreasonable. However, the question of whether the annual exemption is available for intangibles and chattels must still be considered each year because of fluctuations in the official rate of interest.

Example 9.3

(1) X is subject to the chattels charge under para.7. The value of the chattels is £100,000 in April 2005 and this value remains fixed for the next five years (unless he ceases to use some of the chattels). In 2005/6 and 2006/7 the prescribed rate of interest is 5 per cent and the chargeable amount therefore falls within the annual exemption and no POAT is due. (The benefit "must not exceed" the £5,000 limit for the annual exemption to be available.)

From April 6, 2007 the rate of interest was 6.25 per cent and therefore the chargeable amount was £6,250 and POAT was payable on this for both 2007/8 and 2008/9 (since the rate of interest taken is that in force on April 6 of each year). From April 6, 2009 the rate of interest is 4.75 per cent so the chargeable amount now falls within the annual exemption for 2009/10 and no POAT is payable.

(2) Y is subject to the intangibles charge. The value of the settled property is £100,000 in April 2005 and £110,000 in April 2006. For the first year the chargeable amount falls within the annual exemption. For 2006/7 the chargeable amount is £5,500 but Y pays income tax of £1,000 on the trust income since the trust is settlor-interested, so the chargeable amount is still less than £5,000 and no POAT is due. For 2007/8 and 2008/9 the value of the settled property is £90,000 so the chargeable amount is

---

[11] This regulation is considered in detail in **Ch.12**.
[12] For the election, see **Ch.11**.
[13] See **12–08**.
[14] Of course they may still fall within the exemption after the April 2010 revaluation.

£5,625 less any capital gains tax or income paid by Y in respect of the settled property. (If the trust is UK resident then no capital gains tax will be payable by Y after April 2008[15] and capital gains tax paid by the trustees cannot reduce Y's POAT charge.)

9–09 The fact that the time limits for making the election do not run when the benefit falls within the annual exemption can be relevant where FA 2006, s.80 applies.[16]

Example 9.4

X, a foreign domiciliary set up a discretionary trust for himself in 2005. In January 2006 the trustees appointed a qualifying interest in possession on X. The trust owns a UK house that X occupies. The para.12 exemptions are not in point (see **8–19** and FA 2006 s.80) and para.11(1) and 11(3) exemptions are also not available while he retains an interest in possession. As set out in **8–20** onwards it may be preferable for X to retain his qualifying interest in possession and elect into the reservation of benefit regime. The POA charge is calculated from December 2005. If the taxable benefit was within the annual exemption for 2005/6, then the time limit for making the election does not expire until January 2008.

If X does not learn of the difficulties caused by FA 2006, s.80 until after the statutory deadline for making the election has passed this may be a case where HMRC allow a late election.[17]

---

[15] TCGA 1992, s.77 was repealed from April 6, 2008. If the trust is non-UK resident then X is chargeable to capital gains tax under s.86 and capital gains tax he pays can reduce the POAT charge even if he is reimbursed by the trustees.

[16] See **7–24**.

[17] See **Ch.11**.

CHAPTER 10

AVOIDANCE OF DOUBLE CHARGES

This chapter discusses double tax charges in three contexts: first, where the **10–01**
taxpayer is exposed to a double income tax charge on the same asset; secondly,
where the taxpayer is exposed to double inheritance tax charges because he
wishes to avoid an income tax charge under the Regime and thirdly where the
taxpayer is exposed to a double inheritance tax and income tax charge.

Double income tax charges

Schedule 15 makes provision to prevent the imposition of certain double charges
to income tax.

Employment benefits charge

It may be that in a year of assessment a person is chargeable to income tax in **10–02**
respect of his occupation of any land or his possession or use of any chattel under
both the benefits code in Pt 3 of ITEPA 2003 and under POAT. In that case the Pt
3 charge takes priority and displaces POAT, except to the extent that the amount
chargeable under POAT exceeds the amount treated as earnings under Pt 3.[1] It is
unlikely that the POAT charge will be greater than the charge under ITEPA.

Example 10.1

Charlotte is the beneficiary and settlor of an offshore trust which she
established with £1m. She is foreign domiciled but UK resident. The trust
has incorporated a company called Snape Limited. The company buys a
London house for £1 million. The contribution condition is satisfied as far as
para.3 is concerned.[2] She occupies the property. She is treated as the shadow
director of Snape Limited The charge under ss.97–113 ITEPA is on:

a)   annual value of the accommodation (meaning gross rateable value); plus

---

[1]   See Sch.15, para.19.
[2]   Contrast the position if Charlotte lent cash to a wholly owned company which then purchased the
property—arguably then the contribution condition is not satisfied and the POA charge cannot arise: see
Ch.3.

b) interest at the official rate on the amount by which the cost of providing accommodation exceeds £75,000 (s.106).

In practice the charge under (a) is low but under (b) the assessable benefit on which tax is paid will be £43,937.50 given an official rate of interest at 4.75 per cent (as at April 2009) annually.

There is no POA charge on the company shares as these are intangibles protected under para.12(3). She does, however, reserve a benefit in the house (since she gifted the cash to the trust which has acquired it through a company) and therefore the protection of the reservation of benefit exemption should be available.[3] If the trust has been set up in 2002 and was initially interest in possession for her spouse Alex but is now a discretionary trust for Charlotte, Alex and their children no reservation of benefit arises in respect of the company shares (the trust was established before the anti-*Eversden* legislation[4]) but the para.12(3) exemption would still be in point so there is no POAT on the company shares. It might be thought that there would be a reservation of benefit in respect of the house and therefore no POA charge on the house because the gift that is protected by FA 1986, s.102(5) is not the house but the cash gift to the interest in possession trust and the settled property (being the company shares) not the house is therefore protected from reservation of benefit. On the other hand there was no disposal of the house by way of exempt gift and although Charlotte is in occupation of the house, she would not appear to have a reserved a benefit. Hence beifore or after the termination of Alex's interest in possession there is a POAT charge on the house.

10–03   The rental value of the property under para.4 may well be less than 4.75 per cent (the official rate of interest) depending on where the property is situated and the condition of the property. Some houses with high capital values have a yield well below this amount.

10–04   A danger is that one person may be taxable under ITEPA and another under the Regime in respect of the same occupation because the liability arises in different ways.

Example 10.2

Suppose in the above example that Charlotte is not treated as a shadow director of the company but Luke (her son) is. In these circumstances the ITEPA charge is imposed on Luke (because Charlotte is a member of his household) but the POA charge (if any) is on Charlotte and there is no relief. It is better that Charlotte rather than Luke should be treated as a shadow director since she will then suffer the ITEPA charge but get POA relief.

Double income tax charges under the Regime

10–05   It may be that a person is chargeable under either para.3 or para.6 by reason of his occupation of land or his possession or use of a chattel and under para.8 by reference to intangible property which derives its value, whether in whole or in part, from that land or chattel.

---

[3]   See para.11(3).
[4]   See **Ch.5.**

Example 10.3

(1) Mr X (UK domiciled) subscribed for shares in X Ltd which in 2002 he settled on *Eversden* trusts under which his wife had an interest in possession. Her interest was subsequently terminated and the couple's children given qualifying interests in possession with Mr and Mrs X being capable of benefitting under overriding powers of the trustees. The company used the cash to purchase a property occupied by Mr X. Mr X does not reserve a benefit given that the arrangement was entered into before the 2003 amending legislation (his gift is protected by FA 1986, s.102(5) which precludes a benefit being reserved in either the shares or the house). For POAT purposes:

a. the para.9 charge in respect of intangibles applies to the shares given that the trust is settlor-interested;

b. the para.4 charge in respect of land is likewise capable of applying given that X provided the cash used by the company to purchase the shares.

Note (a) the possibility of an overlapping ITEPA 2003 charge on the benefit enjoyed by X if he is treated as a shadow director of the company, and (b) that if X had inherited the shares and had not lent cash to the company or subscribed shares to it, it is difficult to see how a para.4 charge could then apply given that neither the disposal nor contribution condition is met. However, a para.9 charge would apply to the shares.

(2) If the interest in possession of Mrs X had not been terminated and X occupies the land it appears that there is still a charge under para.4 in respect of the land and para.9 in respect of the intangibles: the transaction in shares cannot be an excluded transaction (the protections in para.10 do not apply for para.8 purposes) and para.10 cannot give protection in respect of the land because the spouse was not given an interest in possession in it under para.10(2)(b). (If, however, X had inherited the shares then no para.3 charge would arise.)

Double inheritance tax charges

An entirely separate problem in relation to the POA legislation may occur where **10–06** individuals wish to unravel or elect in relation to particular schemes. They are prepared to forfeit their inheritance tax savings in return for avoiding the income tax charge. The Government presented the election as a complete solution to persons in this position but in practice (as we will see in **Ch.11**) this is far from being the case. The potential double charge arises principally in respect of two schemes: first *Eversden* schemes and secondly home loan schemes. The matter is discussed in more detail in **Chs 16** and **17** respectively,[5] but the following points should be noted.

---

[5] See also **Ch.5**.

Eversden schemes

10–07 In the case of *Eversden* schemes it is the spouse who has made the PET but the settlor is the person who needs to receive back the property in order to avoid a POA charge.

Example 10.4

(1) Bruce settles his family home on qualifying interest in possession trusts for Fiona, his wife, in May 2002. In January 2003 her interest in possession is partially terminated and revocable interest in possession trusts for the children are appointed. Bruce remains in occupation of the home. Bruce faces a POA charge because the transaction ceases to be excluded with the termination of Fiona's interest.[6] The trustees therefore decide to appoint the property back to Bruce. This ensures that he will not suffer a POA charge. Fiona dies in May 2006. The PET she made in January 2003 when her interest in possession is terminated becomes fully chargeable to inheritance tax. It may be said that this was always a risk of the *Eversden* scheme. However, Bruce then dies in May 2008. The home is again charged to inheritance tax. No relief is available under the Double Charges Regulations 1987.[7]

(2) If Bruce had died before Fiona and left her the house in his will and then Fiona had died within seven years of her PET there is still no double charges relief because although the property is back within her estate for inheritance tax purposes at the time of her death, she did not acquire it from the transferee (namely the children who took the interest in possession) but from Bruce on his death. Therefore the conditions in para.4(3) of Inheritance Tax (Double Charges Relief) Regulations 1987 are not satisfied.

(3) If Bruce settled his family home on qualifying interest in possession trusts for Fiona his wife before June 20, 2003 and on or after March 22, 2006 Fiona's interest in possession is terminated in favour of interest in possession trusts for the children there is no reservation of benefit by Bruce because the trust is a pre-2003 trust. On termination of Fiona's interest in possession her children take qualifying interests in possession provided her interest is ended before October 5, 2008, so that the children can then take TSIs. This is a PET by Fiona. However, the termination of her qualifying interest in possession is treated as if she has made a gift for reservation of benefit purposes of the underlying property under FA 1986, s.102ZA. She therefore reserves a benefit if she remains in the property and does not pay a market rent. In addition, Bruce is subject to POAT from the date her interest in possession is terminated. (see **10–14**)

10–08 The same difficulty arises if an election under para.23 is made. Indeed in this instance there could be three inheritance tax charges on the same property!

---

[6] See para.10(1)(c); 10(3) and see **Ch.5**.
[7] These are in **Appendix I–C**.

Example 10.5

In Example 10.4 assume that Bruce makes an election in respect of the property. Bruce, Fiona and the children all die by 2007. Bruce will suffer inheritance tax on the house due to the election (it forms part of his death estate as a result of FA 1986, s.102(3)); Fiona pays inheritance tax on the failed PET and (if her interest in possession is terminated after March 22, 2006) under reservation of benefit; the children pay inheritance tax because the property remains part of their estates for inheritance tax purposes (they had enjoyed qualifying interests in possession in it at the time of their deaths)! In these circumstances an election appears a singularly unattractive option.

Home loan schemes

In **Ch.12** we discuss how relief has been given under the Regulations to avoid **10–09** double inheritance tax charges in relation to home loan schemes when an election is made. We discuss there the defects of reg.6 and how double charges can still arise. However, other double charge problems remain in relation to home loan schemes.

Many people wished to unravel the scheme entirely rather than elect and leave **10–10** two trusts in place.[8] Unravelling can be done in a number of ways (see **17–34** et seq.). In some cases the trustees of the Children's Trust which holds the IOU will advance the debt to the children absolutely who then give it to the settlor. Once the debt is back in the settlor's estate it ceases to reduce the value of his estate and is no longer a relevant excluded liability. However, this has the disadvantage of involving a PET by the children. Alternatively the trustees of the Children's Trust owning the debt advance the debt to the children contingently on surviving 30 days and the children then assign the benefit of their remainder interests to the settlor in that 30-day period. Reverter to settlor relief is available.[9] The property trustees can either leave the house in the interest in possession trust subject to the debt which is no longer a relevant excluded liability and therefore no POAT charge arises or they can advance the house subject to the debt to the settlor but without the settlor taking on any personal liability to pay the debt. This avoids SDLT issues. The house and debt are then back in the settlor's estate.

Prior to March 22, 2006, the children sometimes wrote off the debt in favour **10–11** of the property trustees. From that date, however, the children should not write off the debt in favour of the property trustees in case this is construed as an addition to the property trust which would be a chargeable transfer for inheritance tax purposes. (It is debateable whether this is in fact a problem if a house already in the interest in possession property trust for the release simply increases in value because of the removal of the charge. No property as such has been added.) If after March 22, 2006, the house is advanced to the settlor outright from the property trust and the children are advanced the debt from the Children's Trust and then the children write off the debt this would be a PET by the children.

Another concern is that if the original donor (Mr A) dies within seven years of **10–12** the gift of the IOU to the Children's Trust, there will be double inheritance tax charged—once on the failed PET he made when he originally gifted the debt to

---

[8] The difficulties of making the election in relation to home loan schemes are discussed further in **Chs 11** and **17**.

[9] See **17–38**.

the Children's Trust and again on the full value of the house with no deduction after the write off of the debt or if it has been advanced back to him.

10–13   Could relief be given on the basis of reg.4 of the 1987 Regulations?[10] That Regulation is concerned with PETs and death. Whether relief is available depends on the requirement in 4(2)(d) being met. This in turn depends on reg.4(3) under which the debt needs to have been treated as acquired by the transferor otherwise than for full consideration. The property acquired must either be the original gifted property (which it cannot be since the debt has disappeared) "or property directly or indirectly representing that property". One might argue that the house does indirectly represent the debt, because once the debt disappears, the value of the estate of Mr A is increased and this may be said to be attributable to the value of the property which he gifted (the debt) being returned to him albeit the debt itself has disappeared.

HMRC did not accept this construction of reg.4 and in July 2005 the Paymaster General introduced a new regulation to deal with the position where the debt had been released or written off.[11] The difficulty is that this only deals with the position where children write off the debt but not where the debt is transferred back to the settlor's estate so his house is no longer reduced by the debt for inheritance tax purposes. Where the 2005 Regulation applies on a write off of the debt, inheritance tax is levied on the transaction which produces the greatest amount of tax looking first at the value of the property unencumbered by the debt at death and secondly at the failed PET. Of course if on the settlor's death the house passes outright to his spouse anyway, the PET is still chargeable without double charges relief and on his spouse's death the full value of the property will be subject to inheritance tax.

10–14   As noted above sometimes the home loan scheme can be unravelled in a different way. For example, the debt could be assigned back to the donor by the children. This gets rid of the POA problem since the excluded liability which affects the house no longer reduces the donor's estate given that he now owns the debt. It will also generally avoid the risk of a double charge if the donor dies within seven years of the original gift because the debt is kept in existence and therefore is still deductible against the value of the house held by the property trust. It also has the advantage that if the house is left on interest in possession trusts for the spouse it remains reduced by the debt and the debt can be left to another member of the family (albeit then of course a chargeable transfer would arise on the settlor's death). However, even here one can still have a double charges problem. This is because if the original gift of the debt was to an accumulation and maintenance trust for the children and they then take a qualifying interest in possession before March 2006 (or have been appointed an interest in possession or have become absolutely entitled) there is no double charges relief. Under reg.4(3)(a) of the 1987 regulations the deceased donor has to acquire the debt from the transferee and in this case he acquires the debt from a beneficiary who was not the original transferee. No relief is available in this situation. Generally if the donor intends to leave everything to his spouse anyway (both the house in an interest in possession trust and his free estate) double charges relief will be irrelevant. The original PET he made will remain chargeable without any relief.

---

[10] See **Appendix I**.
[11] See **Appendix I**.

Ingram schemes[12]

Generally double inheritance tax charges for the donor are avoided where *Ingram*   **10–15**
schemes are unravelled (a) because the donor has usually survived seven years
from the original gift of the encumbered freehold anyway and (b) even if the gift
of the freehold reversion was made in the last seven years if it is now is back in
his estate double charges relief can be obtained. However, bear in mind that
double tax charges still remain in two respects: first, the donee has made a PET
if the freehold reversion is given back to the donor and secondly, the donee may
well suffer capital gains tax charges on a transfer back of the freehold reversion
to the donor. The Government offers the election under para.23 as a way round
the latter problem but in reality it does not provide any long-term solution because
of course an election does not remove the property consequences of the original
transaction.

Example 10.6

In 1998 John carved out a 15–year lease for himself and gave away the
freehold reversion on interest in possession trusts for his son Benjamin. John
does not wish to pay the POA income tax charge and therefore elects without
telling Benjamin. On his death the full value of the property is subject to
inheritance tax and is payable by Benjamin. However, if at any time Benjamin
dies the freehold reversion is subject to inheritance tax since it forms part of
his estate. In addition, on John's death there is no base cost uplift for capital
gains tax purposes. Hence Benjamin still faces the problem that if he disposes
of the freehold reversion he pays capital gains tax.

FA 2006, section 80

The problems raised by s.80 have been discussed at **7–24** and **8–19**. It is possible   **10–16**
to suffer both an inheritance tax on death and a POA charge during lifetime.

Example 10.7

In 1998 X set up an interest in possession trust for his wife and then on their
divorce in 2004 the trust was amended so that he took an interest in
possession. The trust owns intangibles (shares) so the para.10 protection is
not available. Section 80 applies and from December 5, 2005 the ownership
exemption in para.11(1) is disapplied. POAT is payable. In addition
inheritance tax is payable on the full value of the property on X's death if he
retains his interest in possession because it is a pre-March 2006 qualifying
interest in possession. If X elects then there is no POAT charge but on his
death the reservation of benefit provisions are disapplied by s.102(3) and
there is inheritance tax due under IHTA 1984, s.49. However if X misses the
deadline for making the election he is subject to income tax during his
lifetime and inheritance tax on his death.

---

[12] See **Ch.14**.

CHAPTER 11

OPT-OUT ELECTIONS INTO RESERVATION OF BENEFIT

11–01 A taxpayer who is otherwise caught by the pre-owned assets charge can avoid the payment of income tax by opting out of the Regime and into the IHT reservation of benefit provisions by means of an election. The position differs slightly according to whether the individual is chargeable in respect of land/chattels or settled intangible property. One point of general application is that the owner of the property, who will be the person primarily liable for any IHT resulting from the election having been made, has no say in the matter.[1] It is understood that at October 2009 only some 4900 elections had been made. The opt-out provisions have been bedevilled with problems from the outset[2] and illustrate the technical and logistical problems that affect the POA Regime.[3]

Land and chattel elections

11–02 To opt out of the charge on land and chattels the individual:

(a) must be chargeable[4] in any year of assessment (called "the initial year") under para.3 or para.6 by reference to his enjoyment of the property in question; and

(b) must not have been chargeable under para.3 or para.6, as the case may be, in respect of any previous year of assessment by reference to his enjoyment of the relevant property, or of any other property for which the relevant property has been substituted.[5]

If these conditions are satisfied he can elect that the Regime shall not apply to him by reference to the relevant property in the initial year and subsequent years of assessment and that instead, so long as he continues to enjoy that property or

---

[1] See IHTA 1984, s.204(9) and for a right to recover the tax, ibid. s.211(3).

[2] Note, for instance, the failure to make the requisite regulations in time for the January 31, 2007 deadline (see **11.13**) and the unintended effect of the 2006 amendments dealing with reverter to settlor trusts (see **11.25**).

[3] See HMRC Guidance at A2.26-A2.36; the STEP / CIOT Correspondence at A2.88-A2.96 and CIOT note on FA 2006, s.80 at A2.119 et seq.

[4] i.e. chargeable on the assumption that he did not opt out of the charge. It is thought that a purported election is of no validity unless the charging provisions of Sch.15 would otherwise apply. In a case where the taxpayer is uncertain whether the Schedule applies or not, he may consider making a precautionary election: see **17–53**.

[5] See Sch.15, para.21(1).

any substituted property the chargeable proportion of the property is to be treated for IHT purposes as property subject to a reservation to which ss.102(3) and (4) of the Finance Act 1986 shall apply.[6] For these purposes, a person "enjoys" property where land is concerned if he occupies the land and where a chattel is concerned if he has possession or the use of the chattel.[7] If a person is within the de minimis exemption under para.13 then it is not possible for that person to make an election because he is not chargeable at all under Sch.15 (see para.13(3)). In this case the time limits for making the election are effectively extended until such time as the taxable benefit exceeds the £5,000 level and he becomes chargeable.[8]

The chargeable proportion

The meaning of "the chargeable proportion" in relation to any property is **11–03** determined by reference to the formulae that apply for determining:

a) in a case involving land, the appropriate rental value; and

b) in a case involving chattels the appropriate amount.

These formulae are discussed in **Chs 3** and **4** respectively. For the purposes of the election, they are subject to two qualifications.[9] First, that the transactions to be taken into account in determining the numerator of the fractions involved include transactions after the time when the election takes effect as well as transactions before that time.[10] Secondly, that any reference in para.4(2) or para.7(2) to the valuation date is to be treated as a reference:

a) in the case of property falling within s.102(3), to the date of the death of the person; and

b) in the case of property falling within s.102(4), to the date on which the property ceases to be treated as property subject to a reservation.[11]

The reason for adopting the "chargeable proportion" test is to reflect the fact that, **11–04** in some cases, part of the value of the property in question will already be included in the individual's IHT estate. Assume X effected an "*Ingram*" scheme by giving away the freehold interest in a chattel subject to a lease over it which he has reserved to himself. At his death the chattel is worth £400,000 and the encumbered freehold £300,000. The chargeable proportion of the chattel would be:

$$\frac{£300,000}{£400,000}$$

[6] See Sch.15, para.21(2).
[7] See Sch.15, para.21(4). For difficulties over the meaning of occupation see **Ch.3**.
[8] For the £5,000 exemption, see **Ch.9**. This can be relevant where a taxpayer falls within the POA charge half way through the year. He may find that the chargeable amount is less than £5,000 in that part of the year and therefore the time limits for making an election have not yet started to run.
[9] See Sch.15, para.21(3).
[10] See Sch.15, para.21(3)(b).
[11] See Sch.15, para.21(3)(a).

so that only 75 per cent of the property would be treated as property subject to a reservation. This would broadly reflect the fact that the value of the lease was included in X's estate. (It is not clear how the loss of marriage value would be treated.)

11–05   It is not clear how the election mechanism deals with the position where part of the original gifted property is not within the Regime and part is.

Example 11.1

Andrew settles his house on interest in possession trusts for his wife Emma in 2000. Emma takes a qualifying interest in possession and the gift is spouse exempt. Subsequently her interest in possession is terminated in all but 20 per cent of the property. Hence the gift ceases to be an excluded disposal in relation to 80 per cent of the property and Andrew comes within the POA charge.[12] Andrew decides to make an election rather than to pay the income tax charge. In these circumstances is the chargeable proportion 100 per cent (being the DV/V figure) or 80 per cent? It is assumed the latter on the basis that he is chargeable only by reference to his enjoyment of the 80 per cent not by reference to his enjoyment of 100 per cent (see wording in para.21(1)(a)). Hence "the relevant property" on which he can elect is only 80 per cent.

What happens if in the above example Emma's interest in possession is terminated in the entire property and instead 20 per cent is appointed back to Andrew absolutely? Can he elect on just 80 per cent? Is Andrew chargeable in respect of the entire property not just the 80 per cent? The authors incline to the view that Andrew is chargeable under para.21 simply on the 80 per cent. This is because he is not chargeable under para.3 on the 20 per cent which he now owns and therefore cannot make an election on that part.

Intangible settled property election

11–06   To opt out of the charge on intangible settled property the individual:

(a) must be chargeable[13] in any year of assessment (called the "initial year") under para.8 by reference to the property in question ("the relevant property"); and

(b) must not have been chargeable under para.8 in respect of any previous year of assessment by reference to the relevant property or any property which the relevant property represents or is derived from.[14]

Where an individual is subject to the para.8 charge on settled intangible property he can elect that the Regime shall not apply to him in the initial year by reference to the relevant property or any property which represents or is derived from the relevant property. Instead the relevant property (and any representative or derivative property) shall be treated for IHT purposes as property subject to a reservation and ss.102(3) and (4) of the Finance Act 1986 shall apply so long as two conditions are satisfied, namely:

---

[12] For excluded transactions, see para.10(1)(c) and for the position when the spouse's interest is terminated inter vivos, para.10(3): see **5–11** et seq.

[13] If he did not opt out of the charge.

[14] Sch.15, para.22(1).

(a) the relevant property (or the representative or derivative property) remains comprised in the settlement; and

(b) any income arising under the settlement would be treated by virtue of ITTOIA 2005, s.624 as his income.[15]

Double trouble?

It is to be noted that the entirety of the property in respect of which the election is **11–07** made will be subject to the reservation of benefit regime, because the opt-out provisions for settled intangible property contain nothing equivalent to "the chargeable proportion" rule that operates in respect of land and chattels. In other words, there is no reduction for the value of any interest retained. In the first edition of this book the authors suggested that if X settled property on trusts under which he retained a reversionary interest and he opts out of the Regime by making an election there will be an element of double taxation. This was on the basis that first, the reversionary interest will not be excluded property for IHT purposes and so on his death will be comprised in his estate. Subject, for example, to the spouse exemption, it will then attract a charge to IHT on his death. Secondly, as a result of the election, the whole of the settled property would be subject to the reservation of benefit rules with the result that the value of the property prima facie subject to the IHT will exceed the value of the settled property.

It might be thought that the reversionary interest is in fact excluded from the **11–08** election because para.11(1) provides an exemption for that property in relation to the POAT charge, and therefore it is not necessary nor even possible to elect in respect of the reversionary interest. However, para.11(2) (the "substantially less" rule) does not mean the person is not actually chargeable under para.9 on the relevant property, only that the charge is reduced. Paragraph 22(1)(a) refers to a person being chargeable "by reference to any property" ("the relevant property") which *would* seem to include the reversionary interest. It is not, under the legislation, a separate piece of property which is excluded from the election.

Example 11.2

George, the settlor, has a remainder interest in a trust which holds cash. George will become absolutely entitled to the trust fund on the death of his mother who has an interest in possession. George does not elect. The cash is £1 million, the remainder interest is worth £50,000. He pays income tax on 4.75 per cent of £950,000.

If he elects, it appears that he pays IHT on his death on £1 million (the property subject to the reservation) and on £50,000 (the remainder interest already in his estate).

In practice it is believed that HMRC will not charge George to tax on both the value of the trust fund and his interest in it and instead that only one inheritance tax charge will be levied on the entire settled property. Contrast the position in Example 11.1 where there is no substantially less problem and therefore the taxpayer is not chargeable under the Regime in respect of the 20 per cent retained.

---

[15] Sch.15, paras 22(2) and (3).

The election—time limits

11–09 The election must be made on prescribed Form IHT 500[16] on or before the relevant filing date, which is January 31 in the year of assessment that immediately follows the initial year[17] or such later date as an officer of HMRC may allow. (These last words were inserted by FA 2007, s.66). Where the individual in question can show a reasonable excuse for the failure to make the election on or before the relevant filing date the election must be made on or before such later date as may be prescribed.[18] Once made, any election may be withdrawn or amended at any time during the individual's life before the relevant filing date.[19] So if X first becomes subject to POAT from April 6, 2009 (i.e. in tax year 2009/10), he has until January 31, 2011 to make the election. If an election is made prior to that date it can be withdrawn before January 31, 2011 so long as he has not died. The personal representatives of a deceased person cannot elect except in the limited circumstances provided for by FA 2006, s.80.[20] An election cannot be withdrawn or amended after the taxpayer's death. HMRC's guidance notes at 3.4 give details as to the very limited circumstances in which a late election will be accepted.[21] There is no right of appeal against a refusal to allow late elections but the refusal may be challenged by judicial review. It is possible to make a protective election: see **13–15**.

11–10 Subject to its being withdrawn or amended, the election takes effect for IHT purposes from the beginning of the initial year or, if later, the date on which the person would[22] have first become chargeable under the Regime by reference to the property to which the election relates.[23] There is therefore an element of "backdating".

Example 11.3

A gives cash to his son in 2003. In January 2009 he moves into a house bought by the son with the cash. He has occupied within seven years of the gift so is subject to the POA charge under para.3(3). A must make an election at the latest by January 31, 2010.

11–11 What is the position where someone is not chargeable under the Regime because of (say) a para.11 exemption but then subsequently becomes chargeable?

Example 11.4

A gives cash to his son in 2003 and moves into a house purchased by the son with the cash in the following year. Before April 6, 2005 the son settles the property on interest in possession trusts for A reverter to the son. Until December 2005 the property was protected from POA because it was part of

---

[16] Form 500 together with guidance notes for its completion is in **Appendix I**.
[17] Sch.15, para.23(2).
[18] Sch.15, para.23(3) as amended by FA 2007, s.66.
[19] Sch.15, para.23(5).
[20] See **11–15**.
[21] See A2.32 and note that a late election will be available if HMRC changes its guidance so that a POAT charge arises in circumstances where it had not been considered to arise previously. A similar approach is taken when the law is changed: see A2.34.
[22] But for the election.
[23] See Sch.15, para.23(6).

A's estate for inheritance tax purposes under para.11(1). However, FA 2006, s.80 provides that with effect from that date A is chargeable because his interest in possession is effectively ignored for the purposes of the ownership exemption. A should elect before January 31, 2007 unless the chargeable amount falls within the de minimis exemption for 2005/6.[24]

The form IHT500 is sent not to the taxpayer's local Inspector of Taxes but to the **11–12** Pre-Owned Assets Section, Capital Taxes in Nottingham. A copy of the election should be kept by the taxpayer. Separate forms must be completed for each previously owned asset. Capital Taxes will then inform the tax office that the election has been made and record the election. The intention is that at the point when someone dies a check can be made to see if they made the election. If they did, Capital Taxes will be able to inform the deceased's personal representatives accordingly and collect the inheritance tax! As already stated, no notification of the election needs to be sent to the donee (even though it is the latter who will have to pay the inheritance tax!).

Defective introduction of the election machinery

In the case of IHT schemes caught when POA came into force on April 6, 2005, **11–13** it was intended that an election had to be made no later than January 31, 2007. HMRC did not, however, appreciate that the election had to be made "in the prescribed manner" (para.23(2)) which means as "prescribed by regulations" (para.1). The necessary regulations were only laid before Parliament (prescribing Form 500) in October 2007 (SI 2007/3000) effective from November 14, 2007.[25] Nothing has been said officially about the absence of a valid election machinery until this date but it is strongly arguable that in the case of a taxpayer who:

a. made an "election" on or before January 31, 2007; and

b. has since died;

it is open to his PRs to say that the election was ineffective with the result that he was within the POA charge but outside the IHT charge. There will be cases (notably where the IHT planning succeeded because the taxpayer survived by seven years) where paying a couple of years income tax is a price worth paying for escaping the IHT net.

Can personal representatives elect?

In general it is not possible for the personal representatives of a chargeable person **11–14** to elect out of the POA Regime. This is sensible given that the resultant liability for IHT will usually fall not on the personal representatives but on the donee.

---

[24] For the changes in the treatment of reverter to settlor trusts made by FA 2006, s.80 see **18–21** and for the defective introduction of the election machinery in respect of existing arrangements, see **11–13** below.

[25] SI 2007/3000: the Regulations are in **Appendix I**.

Example 11.5

In 1998 A effected an *Ingram* scheme. He survived seven years and died in 2007 having made no POAT election. He leaves his lease (with four years to run) along with the rest of his estate to X and the freehold was given to his eldest son Y. Y is delighted. The IHT saving scheme has been successful. However, A has paid no POAT, and X is one of the executors who must pay the small amount of income tax due: X is reluctant to do this. If X was able to make an election then Y would have to pay IHT on the value of the freehold. It is unlikely that A would have wanted this. X cannot make a valid election.

11–15　In one bizarre situation only can PRs elect. This is if a chargeable person became subject to POAT as a result of the changes in FA 2006, s.80 (which came into effect from December 5, 2005) and dies before the day on which the Finance Act 2006 was passed (July 19, 2006) without having made an election. In those circumstances his PRs may make any election he could have made. If IHT is due as a result and would have been due at an earlier date, then it is treated instead as falling due at the end of the period of 14 days beginning with July 19, 2006.[26]

Example 11.6

Facts as in *Example 11.5* except that in order to avoid a POAT charge, A and Y decided to effect a reverter to settlor scheme. Accordingly in April 2005 Y settled his freehold interest on qualifying interest in possession trusts for A, reverter to Y. Under the law as it stood prior to December 5, 2005, this would have avoided IHT and POAT.[27] A dies unexpectedly on January 22, 2006. When they read s.80 his executors (who include X) realise that A is going to be subject to POAT from December 5, 2005 until his death in January because his interest in possession is ignored for the purposes of the POAT ownership exemption. Although there is only a tiny amount of POAT payable X and Y have never got on and X as an executor is delighted to make the election. The result is that the entire freehold is subject to IHT on A's death. IHT is due.

It is hard to see why the Government thought it worthwhile or sensible to pass this legislation. Anyone who died before July 10, 2006 would only have been subject to POAT as a result of s.80 for a maximum of eight months so the POA charge would have been very small. It is unlikely that any sensible executors would wish to inflict a large IHT bill on a donee in return for avoiding a tiny income tax liability. In some cases though where the donee has no interest in the deceased's estate at death, the executors may consider they are required to avoid the income tax charge and therefore make the election. A more sensible result might have been to enable the executors to recover any income tax liability from the donee.

---

[26] s.80 is set out in **Appendix I**.
[27] See **Ch.18**.

Factors to be taken into account in deciding whether to elect

Regard should be had to a number of factors in deciding whether or not to make **11–16** the election. In general it will be sensible to delay making the election until the last possible moment. This is because if the taxpayer were to die after having made the election but before that date then:

(a) it is not possible for the election to be revoked by his personal representatives;

(b) the saving in the POA charge is likely to be small whereas the IHT charge under the reservation of benefit rules may be considerable. A further factor to consider is whether the relevant IHT scheme has been effective in securing IHT benefits. If it has then the calculation involves comparing that benefit with the income tax costs each year. For instance, pre-March 9, 1999 *Ingram* schemes were effective in achieving IHT advantages.[28] It is therefore possible to calculate the IHT benefits (the PET of the freehold into trust is now exempt from charge since seven years will have elapsed). Reversionary lease schemes (whether effected before or after March 9, 1999) are in a similar position since HMRC accept they are not caught by GWR and are therefore within the POA regime. Home loan (or double trust) schemes are even more problematic with the guidance notes unhelpfully commenting that "assuming that none of them are subject to the inheritance tax reservation of benefit provisions then the income tax charge will apply". Of course, the taxpayer may decide to elect in order to ensure that whatever happens he will not be subject to the POA charge but the decision is difficult given that the taxpayer will not be able to weigh in the balance certain IHT savings against the income tax charge[29];

(c) the decision to elect, as noted above, affects donees, normally members of the family who may have a vested interest in the taxpayer *not* making the election (in simple terms it is they who will suffer the IHT charge when the taxpayer dies). They may be prepared to pay the POA charge and if they do so HMRC have confirmed that this will not lead to the original gift being caught by the reservation of benefit rules.[30]

Opting into reservation of benefit

It may be that opting into reservation of benefit has no adverse IHT implications **11–17** for one or more of the following reasons.

1. *Business/agricultural relief*: the property in question may qualify for 100 per cent business property relief or agricultural property relief by virtue of

---

[28] Assuming, of course, that the scheme was properly documented and established.

[29] See A2.87 where HMRC indicated that they would be issuing "updated technical guidance that will include material to identify the circumstances in which we consider a reservation of benefit in the loan exists". This has never happened but the authors believe that in cases where the loan is repayable on demand HMRC consider that there is a reservation of benefit.

[30] See FA 1986, s.102(1)(b) referring to "any benefit by contract or otherwise". One caveat is that the scheme must not have been entered into with this agreement in place. See A2.72.

para.8 of Sch.20 to the 1986 Act.[31] It is not entirely clear from the legislation that business property relief or agricultural property relief is available in respect of property which is subject to an election because the election does not in itself deem there to be a disposal by way of gift but simply states that the reservation of benefit provisions apply. Paragraph 21 states that "section 102(3) and (4) [of the Finance Act 1986] shall apply" but does not specifically refer to s.102(8) which brings in the provisions of Sch.20 and para.8. HMRC, however, accept that relief is available in appropriate cases.[32]

2. *Nil rate band*: the property when cumulated with the taxpayer's estate may fall within his unused IHT nil rate band (particularly bearing in mind that the taxpayer may have a transferable nil rate band if his spouse or civil partner has died leaving everything to him and given that the Conservatives plan to increase the nil rate band to £1 million).

3. *Full consideration let-out*: if the taxpayer pays full consideration for the use of land or chattels immediately on making the election there is no reservation of benefit (as a result of the full consideration let-out in FA 1986, Sch.20, para.6(1)(a)) and HMRC accept that there is no deemed PET under s.102(4). Contrast the position if he only started to pay full consideration at a later date when s.102(4) would apply and there is a deemed PET when he starts paying rent.[33]

Example 11.7

D effected an *Ingram* scheme.[34] He elects in to GWR and subsequently in April 2010 starts to pay full consideration for the use of his house. Has he made a deemed PET at that point (under s.102(4)) and is he protected from a reservation of benefit charge provided he continues to pay a market rent and survives seven years? There seems to be no express mechanism to achieve this in the legislation because the donor is still enjoying the property (albeit now paying rent) so that para.21(2)(b) would still apply. Although the let-outs in para.6, Sch.20 are not stated expressly to apply, HMRC have indicated that they consider the full consideration let-out in Sch.20 will apply so that there will be a deemed PET when he starts to pay full consideration. Note, however, that if *when the election is made* full consideration is paid they accept that the let-out will apply thereby ensuring that the taxpayer does not make a s.102(4) deemed PET.[35]

4. *Property already included in the taxpayer's estate by virtue of a qualifying interest in possession:* As noted in **Chs 7** and **8**, a person can be subject to the POA charge even if he has a qualifying interest in possession and would normally have the benefit of the ownership exemption. If the relevant property left the taxpayer's estate and only later did he obtain a qualifying interest in possession in it, then by virtue of FA 2006, s.80 the

---

[31] See **Ch.25**.
[32] See A2.89.
[33] See A2.89.
[34] For *Ingram* Schemes, see **Ch.14**.
[35] See A2.89.

POA charge applies unless an election is made.[36] Since generally the taxpayer will be subject to IHT anyway on his death because he has a qualifying interest in possession the election has no ill effects. In fact paras 21(2)(b)(ii) and 22(2)(b)(ii) make it clear that the reservation of benefit provisions do not apply if the chargeable person is beneficially entitled to an interest in possession and therefore the election is effectively ignored for IHT purposes. (See also **11–22** below for some more bizarre consequences.)

Example 11.8

Edwin settles his house on a qualifying interest in possession trust for his son in 2005. In 2007 Edwin occupies the house. The trustees appoint Edwin a qualifying interest in possession which involves a PET by the son being a transitional serial interest. Edwin will be subject to IHT on his death but be subject to the POA charge by virtue of FA 2006, s.80 inserting paras 11(11) (12) into FA 2004. If he elects, then he will no longer be subject to the POA charge. On his death, the reservation of benefit provisions in s.102(3) are disapplied because he has a qualifying interest in possession and the trustees will still obtain capital gains tax uplift on his death and spouse exemption if his spouse or civil partner takes the property outright. The election is, in effect, ignored for IHT purposes. As will be seen later, this can be relevant for home loan cases.

Position of non qualifying interests in possession: as a result of the FA 2006 **11–18** changes in the IHT treatment of settlements it will be rare for new "qualifying" interests in possession to arise in the future.[37] A non-qualifying interest in possession is a nothing for IHT purposes (the settlement will be taxed under the relevant property regime). Of course the relevant beneficiary will be beneficially entitled to the interest (e.g. he is entitled to income produced by the settlement) but for IHT purposes that interest is not part of his estate.[38] Paragraphs 21 and 22 were amended by FA 2006, s.80 as part of the attack on reverter to settlor trusts which were being used to circumvent the POAT charge.[39] Accordingly, even when the election is made, ss.102(3) and (4) (the reservation of benefit charging provisions) do not apply if the taxpayer is "beneficially entitled to an interest in possession in the property concerned". Note that the legislation does not refer to the taxpayer enjoying a "qualifying" interest in possession in the property albeit that the mischief concerned (the use of a reverter to settlor trust) required the taxpayer to enjoy a qualifying interest in possession. It is therefore arguable that the wording in paras 21 and 22 applies to non-qualifying interests in possession which, if right, has the very odd consequences set out in the following example.

Example 11.9

In 2009 Cunning settles intangibles on a life interest trust for himself, remainder for his children.

---

[36] See **11–25** et seq.
[37] See **2–31**.
[38] See IHTA 1984, s.5(1)(a)(ii); 5(1A) inserted by FA 2006.
[39] See **11–24** onwards.

1. *For IHT purposes* the arrangement will be treated as a carve-out (i.e. on the basis that the interest retained by Cunning in the income has never been given away) so that the reservation of benefit rules will not apply.

2. *For POAT purposes* the trust is settlor interested within para.8 so that Cunning must elect to avoid a POAT charge. If he elects then if the authors are right in their view that an interest in possession for the purposes of para.22 includes a non-qualifying interest then the reservation of benefit charging provisions (s.102(3) and (4)) will not apply (being disapplied by paras 21 and 22) and there is no inheritance tax on the termination of his non-qualifying interest in possession but because he has elected a POAT charge is avoided during his lifetime![40]

11–19 Even if there are adverse IHT implications, the taxpayer may still wish to elect out of the Regime in order to avoid the income tax charge. He may take the view that any resulting IHT liability will be the responsibility of the donee (the owner of the property) and not of his estate.[41]

Reasons for not electing into reservation of benefit

11–20 On the other hand, the taxpayer may prefer to pay POAT.

1. *Elderly/unwell taxpayer*: the taxpayer's life expectancy may be such that it is likely to be less expensive to pay the annual charge under the Regime than it is to bear IHT on the property.

2. *Tax burden on donee*: the taxpayer may not wish to burden the donee with the IHT on the property.

3. *Annual exemption*: the taxpayer may find that the taxable benefit falls within the annual exemption (see **Ch.9**).

4. As discussed in **Ch.10** double charges can result from making the election.

5. The election is not always clear in its effect, particularly in relation to home loan schemes.[42]

11–21 6. Is the spouse exemption available on elected property to prevent any charge arising as a result of s.102(3) deeming the property to be comprised in the taxpayer's estate at death? This depends on whether the spouse's estate is increased or property becomes comprised in that spouse's estate within the meaning of IHTA 1984, s.18. This is discussed in detail in relation to home loan schemes in **Ch.17**. However, problems can also arise in other situations.[43]

---

[40] A similar difficulty relating to non-qualifying interests in possession is caused by para.10(1)(c) discussed at **5–10**.

[41] The effect, however, is likely to be to increase the amount of IHT payable on his "free estate" given then the reservation of benefit property will benefit from a proportionate part of his nil rate band.

[42] See generally **11–22** but note that there are strong arguments that the election machinery is so defective in relation to home loan schemes that it does not result in the GWR rules applying!

[43] See A2.90.

Example 11.10

H has effected an *Eversden* scheme in relation to the house which he occupies. H falls within the POA charge and therefore elects. On H's death the house is worth £400,000. However, it does not pass to W and the value of her estate is not increased because the children have an interest in possession in the property. Hence the effect of the election is that the property is taxable on H's death by virtue of s.102(3). It is true that on W's death there should be no inheritance tax payable but the fact that the inheritance tax charge is triggered on the first rather than the last spouse's death will deter many couples from making an election.[44]

7. There are technical difficulties if the house is sold after an election has been made. Assume that a smaller replacement property is acquired by the trustees of an *Eversden* scheme. Accepting that the replacement property will be within the scope of the original election, what of the surplus cash which has been invested in intangibles? Does the para.8 charge apply on the basis that this is a settlor interested trust to which ITTOIA 2005, s.624 applies? Does a new election need to be made at that point under para.22 in relation to the intangibles?[45]

8. If the taxpayer moves out of the home having made an election then there is a deemed PET under s.102(4) by virtue of para.21(2)(b) because he has ceased to occupy the property. If he moves into a smaller property, say, a week later it is not clear whether he needs to elect again.

9. The election can result in unanticipated unfairness between members of the family. As noted in **11–08** it is the donee who picks up the inheritance tax charge if an election is made. The donor may well not have allowed for this inheritance tax liability in the overall division of his estate and his nil rate band may have been used up on later gifts. When a taxpayer makes an election his advisers should therefore encourage him to review his will and the general effect of the election on his family at the same time.

The election and the home loan (double trust) scheme

11–22 The effect of the election is thought to be that the full value of the property with no deduction for the debt will be treated as comprised in the taxpayer's estate on his death.[46] And, of course, that taxpayer during the seven-year period leading up to his death will, as part of the scheme, have made a PET of the debt. The element

---

[44] For a consideration of *Eversden* schemes generally, see **Ch.16**.

[45] See A2.91.

[46] In fact the matter is not straightforward. As life tenant of the property settlement which has purchased the house the taxpayer is treated as beneficially entitled to the property in that trust. The normal exemption from the POA charge in Sch.15, para.11(1)(a) is disapplied at least in part by the concept of an excluded liability (see paras 11(6) and (7)). For instance if the property in question is worth £500,000 and the debt £400,000 then it is intended that the POA charge will apply to £400,000 (the amount of the excluded liability) leaving £100,000 exempt. The provisions refer to the **amount** of the excluded liability" which presumably allows for the principal and any rolled-up interest and indexation. In any event it might be expected that the election would be for the amount of the excluded liability to be subject to the GWR rules rather than the property itself. It is thought that this confusion has led to the error in the guidance notes considered later.

of double charge (the value of the debt being charged twice) is intended to be dealt with by reg. 6 of SI 2005/724.[47] Unfortunately, the drafting leaves much to be desired since the double charges relief is only available if the gift (the failed PET) is "of property representing the proceeds of the disposal of the relevant property". This wording would apply if the taxpayer sold his house to the property trust and made a gift of his rights under the land contract (i.e. of the proceeds of the disposal). In most arrangements, however, this did not occur (because of the fear that it would involve the gift of an interest in land within the FA 1999 anti-*Ingram* legislation) and instead the taxpayer separately lent the trustees the money which was used to complete the land transaction and it was the benefit of this separate debt agreement that was given away.

11–23   The Regulations find it difficult to get to grips with the intricacies of the home loan scheme but the HMRC guidance notes are utterly hopeless! The matter is first dealt with at para.4.8 (under the heading Double Charges)[48] where the example is given of the sale of a house worth £500,000. It is stated that Mr G (the hypothetical taxpayer) is fully subject to the POA charge because the debt (the excluded liability) reduces the value of the house to nil. Accordingly he makes the GWR election. The home loan arrangement was entered into in June 2003 and Mr G dies within seven years in July 2007 at a time when the house has risen in value to £750,000. The notes then address the question of double charges and the operation of reg.6[49] on the basis that Mr G's estate is valued at £500,000 and there is a £263,000 nil rate band (presumably the figure for the estate is for assets having no connection with the property/home loan scheme). The alternative calculations which are then set out would seem to contain two fundamental mistakes:

(a) taxing the PET: it is assumed that the value of the PET to be taxed is £500,000 but frequently the debt was not to be repaid until Mr G was dead and so would have a discounted value: no allowance is made for this;

(b) taxing the GWR: the house has risen in value to £750,000 but we are not told that the debt has similarly increased. Accordingly on death three separate charges seem to be involved with different persons responsible for the payment of the resultant IHT:

 (i) free estate—the executors;

 (ii) the net value of the property settlement namely £750,000–£500,000 = £250,000 with the property settlement trustees being liable;

 (iii) the GWR (debt) with the trustees of the debt being liable.

The guidance notes, however, merely apportion the tax on the basis that the GWR applies to £750,000 (the value of the property, not of the debt).

11–24   Home loan schemes are next discussed in the notes in Sch.I A2.58 (under the heading "Lifetime Scheme Involving a Loan (Double Trust Scheme)") where it is stated that "there are a number of variants of this scheme . . . ". A2.60 expands on their views:

"The essence of many of these schemes involves the chargeable person(s) (the vendors) selling their home for full value to a newly formed trust (trust 1) with the

---

[47] The relevant provision is set out in **Appendix I**.
[48] See A2.46.
[49] See **Ch.12**.

sale proceeds left outstanding on loan. An IOU for the loan is gifted to a second trust (trust 2) for the benefit of the vendor's family. The vendor(s) continue to occupy the property under the terms of trust 1, and the loan is repayable to trust 2 on demand. HMRC's view on this is that since the loan was repayable on demand, there will be a GWR in respect of it, until such time as the trustees call in the loan. The reason for this is that if trust 2 had called in the loan, trust 1 would have been forced either to sell the home to repay the debt, or to seek finance from elsewhere. If the house were sold, then the vendor(s) would have been unable to occupy it under the terms of trust 1. In order to avoid the need for a sale, trust 1 would have had to find a third party willing to lend 100 per cent of the value of the property on the basis of a covenant by the trustees, and security over the house. Even if such borrowing could be obtained, which must be extremely doubtful, it would be prohibitively expensive. Trust 1 could only justify taking on such borrowing if they were financed by the vendor(s) (the life tenants) who would be benefiting from the property by residing in it. On the foregoing basis it is considered that the trustees of trust 2, in not calling in the loan, have enabled the vendor(s) to retain a significant benefit in it, and therefore that the debt was not enjoyed to the entire exclusion of any benefit to the vendor(s) by contract or otherwise. A variant of the scheme described above is where the terms of the loan provide that the debt is only repayable at a time after the death of the life tenant. Since, unlike the position with loans repayable on demand, the loan can not be called in by the loan trustees, it is generally thought that these schemes will not be caught as gifts with reservation."

The FA 2006 changes

These were intended to prevent reverter to settlor trusts being used to avoid the **11–25** POA charge. In brief, the gifted property was settled on interest in possession trusts for the donor (so that its value was back in his estate under IHTA 1984, s.49(1)) but with a resulting trust back to the donee / settlor (so that no IHT was payable on the donor's death under IHTA 1984, s.54(1)). Because the property was comprised again in the donor's estate, para.11(1) ousted the POA charge.[50] The POA charge was restored by amendments to para.11: see paras 11(11)–(13) inserted by FA 2006.[51] But the 2006 draftsmen also saw fit to amend the election machinery in paras 21 and 22.

His apparent purpose was to provide in these cases that if the election was **11–26** made then:

a. the property does not fall into the reservation of benefit net; *but instead*

b. the reverter to settlor exemption does not apply with the result that on the death of the taxpayer a full charge to IHT will apply as a result of s.49(1).

Why did the draftsman so deal with the matter? Arguably because if he had left this property subject to s.102(3)—i.e. the usual GWR deeming rule—then when it came to *value* the property s.54(1) would have applied to leave such value out of account.

That leads on to a consideration of how the draftsmen amended paras 21 and **11–27** 22. He did this by:

---

[50] Reverter to settlor trusts are considered in detail in **Ch.18**.
[51] These are considered at **7–24**.

a. in para.21(2)(b)(i) (and para.22(2)(b)(i)) excluding any property in which the chargeable person was "beneficially entitled to an interest in possession". But in the case of home loan schemes the taxpayer enjoys such a beneficial interest!;

b. then emphasising the position by excluding s.102(3) from applying if the chargeable person enjoyed a beneficial interest in possession (see paras 21(2)(b)(ii) and 22(2)(b)(i));

c. then excluding the reverter to settlor exemption by paras 21(2)(b)(iii) and 22(2)(b)(iii).

Note that there is no qualification in the above amendments (a) and (b): i.e. they do not merely exclude interest in possession property when otherwise the reverter to settlor exemption would apply. *They provide, it seems, a blanket exclusion from reservation of benefit for all home loan arrangements and other situations where the chargeable person has a qualifying or non-qualifying interest in possession.*[52]

What is the effect of s.102(3) applying?

11–28 Section 102(3) provides for reservation of benefit property to be subject to IHT on the death of the donor "to the extent that the property would not, apart from this section, form part of the donor's estate immediately before death". Is the effect of the election that this condition has to be met before a charge can arise? This question is considered in the context of home loan schemes at **17–55**. As noted above, new paras 21(2) and 22(2) may go further than this and provide that there is no reservation of benefit if the donor is beneficially entitled to an interest in possession in the property and has elected, even though neither the settled property nor the interest is part of his estate for IHT purposes.[53]

The impact of s.102(4)

11–29 If the election is exercised, the reservation of benefit may subsequently cease[54]: e.g. if the taxpayer ceases to occupy land. At that time FA 1986, s.102(4) will apply and there will be a deemed PET by the taxpayer.

There are, of course, other events which bring the reservation of benefit to an end: crucially if the taxpayer pays full consideration for his use or enjoyment of land and chattels so that FA 1986, Sch.20, para.6(1)(a) applies (although note the uncertainty as to whether the election enables Sch.20 to apply). This may have apparently bizarre results.

(a) In the case of land the rental value under the Regime may well be different from the full consideration required under FA 1986 (in particular it may be more!).

---

[52] See **11–22**, and further on home loan schemes, **Ch.17**.
[53] See **11–18**.
[54] Sch.15, para.21(2)(b); para.22(2)(b).

(b) In the case of chattels the proposed charge under the Regime is intended to be greater than the full consideration calculation. *Ingram* chattels schemes may be unscrambled with an election followed by the payment of full consideration which may be cheaper than suffering the para.6 charge (see further, **Ch.18**).

(c) If it is likely that the taxpayer will, e.g. cease to occupy land within para.3 it is important that he does not make the election and then shortly afterwards cease to occupy since that will result in a deemed PET arising.

(d) Unlike s.102(3), s.102(4) does not provide for an exemption from charge in a case where the property again becomes comprised in the donor's estate.[55]

Disposals of property and the election

The consequences if the taxpayer elects in respect of property A which is **11–30** subsequently sold and replaced by property B and a cash investment is considered in the CIOT / STEP Correspondence at A2–91.

---

[55] In practice the authors understand that no double charge will be claimed in this situation.

CHAPTER 12

REGULATIONS

Background

12–01 Schedule 15 gives powers for secondary legislation to be made in a number of areas:

(a) paras 4(5), 7(4) and 9(2) provide for regulations in relation to valuation issues;

(b) para.14 gives power for regulations to be issued conferring further exemptions from the charge to income tax imposed by paras 3, 6 and 8. (It appears, however, that this power is not wide enough to extend the number of excluded transactions.)

(c) Most importantly, para.20 gives the broadest possible powers to "make different provision for different cases and include transitional provisions and savings".

There is power also to prescribe different rates of charge in relation to property of different descriptions. Thus the Regulations can change the scope of the charging provisions if it is felt necessary. Given the extensive amendments to the original legislation at Committee and Report Stages in the Commons in 2004 and the controversy these produced, HMRC may well prefer to deal with any anomalies in future by secondary legislation, which is subject to less intense Parliamentary scrutiny.

12–02 The first Regulations were not issued until March 16, 2005—the latest possible date given that they needed to come into force on April 6, 2005.[56] Subsequently the following regulations have been made:

1. SI 2007/3000 laying down the form of the election to be made if the taxpayer wishes to opt-out of POAT into the reservation of benefit regime (see further **Ch 11**);

2. SI 2005/3441: these regulations afford relief for double charges to IHT and were made under the powers of FA 1986, s.104.

---

[56] See the Charge to Income Tax by Reference to Enjoyment of Property Previously Owned Regulations 2005: SI 2005/724 reproduced in **Appendix I**.

Matters dealt with by Regulations

Whilst the rules for establishing the benefit which is chargeable are set out in **12–03** Sch.15, the precise machinery for charging a taxpayer depends upon the nature of the asset in question. In the case of land, the "cash equivalent" of enjoyment in a particular tax year is derived from *market rent* that would be paid for use of the land over the taxable period (that is a tax year or any shorter period during which the taxpayer occupies the property) and in cases where an interest in the land has been retained valuing both the relevant land and the interest in the land that has been given away.[57]

In the case of chattels the "cash equivalent" of enjoyment in a particular tax year is found by applying a specified rate of return over the "taxable period" to the *capital* value of the gifted asset as at the valuation date.[58] As with land, other values are required if the taxpayer has retained an interest in the chattel.

In the case of intangible assets the "cash equivalent" is calculated, as with chattels, by applying a specified rate of return over the taxable period to the *capital* value of the intangibles in the settlement as at the valuation date.[59]

In each case there is provision for scaling down the benefit where the occupation, use or benefit only continues for part of the year or only part of the property is gifted (e.g. pre-March 1999 *Ingram* schemes where the freehold was gifted and a lease retained).

The key matters that the regulations needed to address therefore were: **12–04**

(a) what valuation date should be taken for the purpose of valuing the property given away and the relevant property used or enjoyed;

(b) how was it to be adjusted thereafter; and

(c) what rate of return should be specified for chattels and intangible assets.

The 2005 Regulations—SI 2005/724

Apart from the above, these Regulations cover two other matters: first, sales of **12–05** part and secondly, the double inheritance tax charge when an election is made in relation to home loan schemes.

Regulation 2: the prescribed valuation date

The "valuation date" in relation to land, chattels and intangibles is April 6 each **12–06** year or if the person first became subject to POA income tax charge during the tax year, the first day of the "taxable period".[60]

---

[57] See **Ch.3**
[58] See **Ch.4**.
[59] See **Ch.6**.
[60] reg.2.

Example 12.1

In 2000, John made a gift of cash to his daughter Emma. Emma used all that cash to buy a property and John first occupied the property on May 1, 2005. He will have to pay POA income tax in respect of his occupation (being caught by the contribution condition) and the property will be valued on May 1, 2005.

Regulation 3—prescribed rate of interest

12–07 This provides that the rate of interest used for calculating the charge on chattels and intangibles is the official rate of interest as at the beginning of the tax year. Subsequent changes are ignored until the next valuation date. Despite representations made during the consultation period, HMRC were unwilling to agree a rate of interest lower than the official rate on the basis that this rate is used in relation to employee benefits such as the occupation of company houses. (Of course, in those cases the charge is based on *cost* rather than current values.) The prescribed rate was five per cent in April 2005, 6.25 per cent in April 2007 and 4.75 per cent in April 2009. As noted in **Ch.6**, it is the prescribed rate at the beginning of the relevant tax year that is taken for the purposes of calculating the chargeable amount each tax year and as illustrated in **Ch.9** (annual exemption) even if the value of the relevant property remains the same, a taxpayer can fall in and out of the POA charge from tax year to tax year, depending on whether the chargeable amount is just over or under the £5,000 limit. If the official rate of interest increases again then a number of taxpayers currently within the annual exemption will fall outside it.

Regulation 4—valuation and rental value

12–08 This Regulation provides helpful and generally welcome provisions on valuation and rental values for land and chattels. It does *not* deal with intangibles where a revaluation is needed every year. It provides for a valuation as at April 6, 2005 in relation to schemes caught by the POA charge on April 6, 2005 and thereafter no revaluation is required until the next five-year anniversary unless the property is sold. In addition, rental values on land (which in April 2005 were low outside London) are fixed for five years. This is particularly favourable in relation to reversionary leases and *Ingram* schemes where the value of the interest in the land given away is highly likely to increase each year as the length of the lease kept by the taxpayer (or the value of the retained freehold) reduces.

12–09 If property falls in value, taxpayers have no option but to use the April 6, 2005 value but at least know what their taxable benefit for the next five years will be. Moreover it saves taxpayers from having to go to the expense of obtaining new valuations each year. Given the guidance from HMRC on the application of the case of *Langham v Veltema*, the taxpayer would be wise to ensure that he obtains a professional valuation and brings this to the attention of HMRC on his tax return.[61]

---

[61] See **Ch.13**.

Example 12.2

Andrew effected an *Ingram* scheme on March 8, 1999.[62] The value of the freehold interest in April 2005 was £600,000 and the market value of the entire land is £1 million. The rental value has been assessed as £60,000. Accordingly he pays income tax on a benefit of £60,000 x 600,000/1 million for the next five years (assuming that he continues to occupy the property).

Revaluations

Land and chattels are revalued, in general terms, every five years. Accordingly in **12–10** a straightforward case the initial valuation and rental value will be on April 6, 2005 (for all existing arrangements) and thereafter on April 6, 2010; April 6, 2015 and so on. The Regulations refer to the "first valuation date" as being "the date on which para 3 or para 6 first applied to the chargeable person in relation to the relevant land or chattel". In the above example, that was April 6, 2005 on the basis that the arrangement was then in place. In Example 12.1 above the first valuation date would be May 1, 2005. The revaluation is on the "five year anniversary" defined as "the fifth anniversary of 6 April in the year of assessment" in which the POA charge first applied. Accordingly even in Example 12.1 that will be April 6, 2010. If there is no valuation date at a five-year anniversary (for instance because, using Example 12.1, on April 6, 2010 John had ceased to occupy the property) then the date when the charge next applies to John (i.e. when he next occupies the property) is taken.

Example 12.3

Sam is caught by the POAT charge on April 6, 2005 but then:

1. on June 30, 2007, Sam ceases to occupy the property. The POAT charge ceases to apply;

2. he resumes occupation on September 30, 2009 when the charge again applies on the basis of April 6, 2005 valuations;

3. if he again ceases to occupy on April 4, 2010 resuming occupation on May 6, 2012 then that date becomes the valuation date with the five-year anniversary falling on April 6, 2017.

If someone who is caught by POA and pays income tax on the basis of rental **12–11** values of the particular property on April 6, 2005 subsequently moves to a property with reduced rental value, there seems to be no provision for reducing the rental value on which he is charged.

Example 12.4

A gave £300,000 to his son in April 2000. His son later uses all the cash to purchase a house contributing none of his own funds. A goes into occupation of the house in April 2002. He satisfies the contribution condition and is subject to the POA charge from April 6, 2005. The house is worth £1 million

---

[62] *Ingram* schemes are discussed in **Ch.14**.

on April 6, 2005. He pays income tax in 2005/6 by reference to the rental value of the house.

In 2007 his son sells the house and buys a new property for £500,000 into which A moves. In these circumstances there seems to be no mechanism for assessing A to income tax on the rental value of the new house. Does A really continue to pay income tax on a hypothetical rental value of the original £1 million house until 2010? Similar problems can arise if A moves into a discrete part of the house, letting the remainder. If he has not done this by April 6, 2005 is his charge not reduced for the next five years?

HMRC, in correspondence with CIOT / STEP,[63] commented in respect of the above example that a new valuation should be done which will apply for the remainder of the five-year cycle. This is on the basis that "relevant land" in para.4(5) means the land currently occupied by the taxpayer.

Regulation 5—exemptions from charge

12–12 Regulation 5 deals with the vexed question of equity release schemes by granting further exemptions (note not exclusions). As we have seen, POA income tax can prima facie apply when there is any disposal of land (or chattels) and the original owner continues to occupy the land or use the chattels. A gift is not required. No inheritance tax saving motive is necessary. Hence sales to commercial providers can be caught where the disponer continues in occupation.

Paragraph 10 of FA 2004, Sch.15[64] provides that where a person sells *the whole of his interest* in the land or chattels "apart from any rights expressly reserved by him over the property" in an arm's length transaction he is not caught by the POA charge even if the disposal is to a connected person. This provision does not cover sales of part.

Regulation 5 aims to correct this.

Example 12.5

On March 19, 1986 Rose sold a beneficial half share in her house at full market value to Carfax Limited, a bank, in order to raise cash; Rose is caught by the POA charge unless reg.5 applies.

12–13 Regulation 5 improves the position on sales of part of the home although the relief is not generous.

There are three possible exemptions.

1. If the transaction is made at arm's length with an *unconnected person*,[65] reg.5(1)(a) provides that a sale of part will be exempt whenever it is made. Hence equity release schemes with commercial providers (as in Example 12.5) are not caught *whenever made*. Nor would sales for cash between cohabitees be caught provided that they were on arm's length terms since they are not connected persons. However, if Rose in the above example

---

[63] See A2.73.
[64] See **Ch.5**.
[65] For the meaning of "connected persons" see Sch.15, para.2.

had sold half her house to her daughter Emma, she would not be protected under reg.5(1)(a) because her daughter is a connected person.

2. A sale of part made in an arm's length transaction is exempt from the POA charge if effected before March 7, 2005 even if made between connected parties (reg.5(1)(b)(ii)). Hence if Rose had sold a share of her house to her daughter Emma on arm's length terms before March 7, she is protected from the POA charge. If she effects the sale on or after March 7, 2005, however, she may suffer an income tax charge. There seems no reason for this restriction on the exemption.

The ministerial statement issued with the Regulations accepted[66] that past equity sales of part had not usually been done for tax avoidance reasons so it is hard to see why the position should suddenly be different from March 7, 2005, particularly given the SDLT charge on sales of land. They are not going to be a common method of inheritance tax planning.

Example 12.6

Carefree, a widower, wishes to raise money for a world cruise. Accordingly in February 2005 he sells a 20 per cent interest in his house to his rich son-in-law for £20,000. His continued occupation of the property does not give rise to a POA charge as a result of the reg.5 exemption. Contrast the position if the sale took place after March 6, 2005 when this protection is not available. Of course, it may be that the "benefit" to Carefree (being 20 per cent of the open market rent for the property) will not exceed the de minimis exemption of £5,000.

It is also odd as a matter of policy that a mortgage of land in favour of a connected **12–14** person (e.g. mother borrows from son) causes no POAT problems (because there is no disposal of land) while a sale of part of the land to the same connected person does cause a POA problem. It is possible for the mother who has borrowed the sums from her daughter to give part of the cash away—for example to her grandchildren without preventing the loan from being deductible in her estate on death. (s.103 of the Finance Act 1986 needs watching here.[67])

Curiously it would not appear to matter in Example 12.5 if before March 7, 2005 Rose had given cash to Emma which eventually facilitated the purchase by Emma of a property share from Rose. Regulation 5 simply says that paras 3 and 6 *do not apply where there has been a part disposal* falling within one of the three heads. Whether the disposal or contribution condition is satisfied, protection is still available. Contrast this with para.10 ("excluded transactions") where a gift of cash by Rose to Emma to enable Emma to buy Rose's entire interest in the house would not be protected from the POA charge since the contribution condition is satisfied.

Finally, reg.5(1)(b)(i) provides that a sale disposal of part on arm's length **12–15** terms "for a consideration not in money or in the form of readily convertible assets" will be exempt whenever made. The scope of this exemption is far from clear. The ministerial statement issued with the Regulations (as well as the HMRC guidance notes) suggest that this covers the position where a child moves into the house to care for an aged parent and acquires an equitable interest in the

---

[66] See **Appendix I**.
[67] See *Phizackerley v RCC* [2007] STC (SCD) 328.

shared home, presumably in consideration for providing caring services. In recent years, a number of cases have come before the courts in which it has been claimed that an interest in property has been acquired by the operation of either a construction trust or by equitable estoppel. It is presumably these cases that the regulation has in mind. However, it is unclear that such an arrangement is in fact protected by reg.5 because it is not necessarily a "transaction such as might be expected to be made at arms length between persons not connected with each other".[68]

12–16 The original guidance notes suggested that this Regulation could provide exemption for disposals of partnership interests.

> "C an existing partner brings his son D into the partnership. In return for D's agreement to take on most of the day to day running of the partnership C gives him a share in the partnership . . . it is accepted that D's agreement constitutes consideration in other than money or realisable assets and that the transaction is one that might be expected to be made at arms length."

This was later revised (see A2.52) as follows:

> "The treatment of a share of a partnership interest for Sch 15 purposes follows that applied for IHT purposes. In other words, we do not regard the partnership interest as transparent and the disposal of a share is unlikely to give rise to a Sch 15 charge in any circumstances."

It is true that as a matter of law a gift of a partnership interest is not a gift of the underlying assets within the partnership. There is a fundamental distinction between a firm's capital on the one hand and its individual assets on the other. C's proportionate interest in the capital may be equal to the value of the land or chattels but it is not the land or chattels itself.

12–17 The definition of readily convertible asset is contained in ITEPA 2003, s.702 and comprises assets which can be readily converted into cash such quoted shares. It is not clear what happens if the definition changes after a particular transaction has been done. If, for example, something that had not been a readily convertible asset and was therefore protected under para.5(1)(b) subsequently became a readily convertible asset would a transaction that was previously protected now lose such protection? Presumably not.[69]

12–18 Difficulties remain where land is held under one title but is physically discrete—for example, two fields. In these circumstances if the owner sells one of the two fields to his son for full value and continues to farm in partnership over that field (not necessarily paying a market rent) arguably he has a pre-owned assets problem unless he is protected under para.10(1)(a). Can it be treated as a sale of the whole if the son becomes beneficially and legally entitled to the entire field even though the father is selling only part of the entire farm? The father retains no interest (save as partner) in what has been sold.[70]

It remains curious that sales of the whole land at full value subject to a retained right such as a lease are protected as excluded transactions while sales of part are not protected. Indeed a sale of part at an undervalue (unlike sales of whole) does

---

[68] See A2.51 of the guidance notes which adds "the onus will be on the taxpayer to show that [the child]'s claim to a share of the property would meet with the approval of the Court".

[69] See A2.98.

[70] There is, of course, no reservation of benefit in this case since no gift is involved. Hence the protection of para.11(5)(d) is not available. For HMRC's view see A2.99.

not even receive relief from the POA charge as a non-exempt sale.[71] This is one of the most misconceived parts of Sch.15 and unfortunately is the area which is most likely to catch "normal" transactions carried out between members of the family who would not necessarily think of seeking professional tax advice in relation to such sales.

Regulation 6—avoiding a double charge

This Regulation, although part of the same statutory instrument, was issued under **12–19** the powers contained in s.104 of the Finance Act 1986 to extend double charges relief. The Double Charges Regulations 1987[72] aim to give relief from a double IHT charge in certain circumstances involving a reservation of benefit and reg.6 introduces a new relief. It makes provision for the avoidance of a double IHT charge in the event of an election being made in the case of home loan schemes.[73]

Example 12.7

A has entered into a home loan scheme and does not want to pay the income tax charge. Accordingly he makes an election. The intention of HMRC is that the election will ensure that the value of the house becomes part of his estate for IHT purposes without any deduction for the debt. If he dies within seven years of the gift of the debt, therefore, that PET becomes chargeable and yet the full value of the house is also taxed on his death. In effect, he pays inheritance tax twice on what is the same economic value. Regulation 6 aims to address this problem.

There are some difficulties with the wording of this relief although the intent of the legislation is clear. For example, relief would seem to be available only if the gift of the debt is to a settlement rather than outright, e.g. to the children. In most cases settlements were indeed used to hold the debt but this was not invariably the case. Furthermore the wording in reg.6(2)(a)(i) refers to someone making a gift of property representing the proceeds of the disposal of relevant property while some home loan schemes did not involve giving away the sale proceeds (for instance, where money was lent to the trustees to effect the purchase and it is the benefit of this debt which is gifted).

Despite reg.6, the election has continued to pose problems in relation to home loan schemes. These are discussed in detail in **Ch.11** (the election) and **Ch.17** (home loan schemes).

The 2005 Regulations in SI 2005/3441

These regulations are concerned with relieving a possible double charge to IHT **12–20** when, in order to avoid a POA charge, a home loan scheme has been dismantled. They were made under the powers in FA 1986, s.104 and are considered in **Ch.17** (home loan schemes).

---

[71] For non-exempt sale relief, see **3–25**.

[72] See **Appendix I**.

[73] Because of the nature of home loan schemes, double charges relief under the 1987 Regulations was not available: specifically the taxpayer did not reserve a benefit (as a result of the election) in the property given away.

Regulations in 2007 dealing with the election

12–21 The machinery for electing out of POA and into reservation of benefit was set out in these regulations which are considered at **Ch.11** (the election). Their late introduction has given rise to the problem which is considered at 11.13.

CHAPTER 13

ADMINISTRATION AND DISCLOSURE

Introduction

CAR (Charities, Assets and Residence) Inheritance Tax Nottingham Office has **13–01** overall responsibility for implementing the POA legislation and carrying out appropriate compliance checks. That is helpful because determining whether someone is subject to the POA Regime will often depend on an understanding of the IHT legislation. On the other hand, so far HMRC have seemed generally uninterested in raising any enquiry on a POAT issue or devoting any resources to the enforcement of POAT. This may be because the people who might be expected to know whether a POA liability is due are based in the Inheritance Tax Offices while POAT itself is an income tax charge which the taxpayer self-assesses on his tax return—a return that never gets sent to IHT offices. In many cases a POA charge may only come to light many years after it has first arisen: e.g. when a taxpayer has died and the executors send in the IHT return. In addition, the question of whether a POA charge arises in many cases depends on whether or not the taxpayer has reserved a benefit. The views of HMRC and the taxpayer may not always coincide on this point, but in any event it is not clear that HMRC are always correct in their view as to when a reservation of benefit arises. Of course, the Government did not expect taxpayers to pay the income tax charge and it is not thought to have raised any significant revenue. The real intention is to stop people carrying out "unacceptable" IHT schemes and make taxpayers who have already effected such schemes dismantle them. Surprisingly few elections have been made (less than 5,000). Given the thousands who carried out home loan, *Ingram* and *Eversden* schemes[74] it is assumed that the majority of taxpayers simply dismantled their IHT schemes. There are signs that this approach may be changing. The centralisation of returns for the top 5,000 high net worth taxpayers in the country will inevitably result in more specialised officers dealing with the wealthy with cross-over expertise coming from the IHT offices. In that case POAT may become a useful weapon in the HMRC armoury.

Under IR Code of Practice 10 on Information and Advice, the taxpayer is **13–02** entitled to ask for guidance as to the application of legislation and an interpretation on any particular point even if the transaction has not yet been completed provided that the query relates to the interpretation of legislation passed in the last four Finance Acts.[75] POAT was first enacted in FA 2004 but there were important revisions in 2006. Moreover queries over the application of POAT may arise out of uncertainties in the IHT legislation and in particular the FA 2006 changes. In these circumstances although the COP 10 procedure may not always be available it is likely to remain relevant until FA 2010 (although it cannot be used for tax avoidance purposes). For example, it may be important to know if

---

[74] It was estimated that 30,000 home loan schemes had been carried out but this is thought to be an underestimate.

[75] See the revision to the IHT clearance service for businesses announced by HMRC in August 2009 and which gives further details of the COP 10 procedure generally.

someone has a qualifying interest in possession for IHT purposes in order to understand whether the ownership exemption applies under para.11(1) for POAT purposes.

13–03 The area of compliance can be a difficult one. Suppose the taxpayer is advised that he is not caught by the POA Regime, e.g. because he can rely on a particular exemption and therefore does nothing. Subsequently it emerges that he was caught by the Regime and should have been paying income tax. He faces interest (even if not penalties) and he has now missed the time limit for the election which is January 31, in the tax year immediately following the year in which he first became chargeable under the Regime.[76] The classic example of this was in relation to reversionary leases where HMRC only accepted in January 2007 (a few days before the deadline for making the election) that pre- **and** post- FA 1999 reversionary lease schemes were outside the reservation of benefit provisions and therefore caught by POAT. In these circumstances the revised guidance makes it clear that the taxpayer would have a reasonable excuse for failing to make the election in time although the guidance does not explicitly refer to reversionary leases.[77]

13–04 POAT is, of course, an income tax charge and therefore subject to the rules for disclosure of tax avoidance schemes. These rules were introduced from August 1, 2004 and have been steadily expanded since. By contrast an IHT scheme is not yet disclosable. Of course in some cases a scheme will be devised primarily to avoid IHT but also by necessity be structured so as to avoid POAT. The question of whether such a scheme is disclosable can be a difficult one.[78]

Difficulties of self-assessment

13–05 The POA charge is part of the income tax system and taxpayers are required to self assess in the usual way. One of the objections to the proposed tax raised during the first consultation period was that taxpayers will not always be aware that they are chargeable. If they do not file tax returns there will be nothing to jog their memory and unless they are in the habit of receiving regular advice from professionals they are probably unaware that a transaction that they carried out in, say, 1987 is now caught by the Regime. The let out for outright cash gifts made prior to April 6, 1998 has relieved some of the worst problems but the authors find that issues continue to arise in relation to sales of land between family members.

Example 13.1

(1) Dan gave £400,000 cash to his son Michael in March 1987. Michael invested the cash in residential property which he let out in 1990. Dan later moved into the property. There is no reservation of benefit[79] but since Dan has occupied the property within seven years of making the gift it was originally thought that he was within the Regime. Dan has

---

[76] On the election, see **Ch.11**.
[77] See A2.32 and A2.57.
[78] See **13–17**.
[79] Because it is a gift of cash: see **Ch.23**.

forgotten all about the gift made 17 years ago. Fortunately HMRC have now confirmed that such gifts are not caught.[80]

(2) If Dan had given shares rather than cash to Michael and the shares were later sold and invested in property it is arguable that on Dan moving into the property a reservation of benefit arises at that point and therefore there is no POA charge.

Example 13.2

Dan gives £300,000 in cash in 1999 to his son James to help him start his own business. James contributes some small cash resources of his own. James works hard and does spectacularly well. He sells out within five years for £4 million and buys his father a house for £300,000 out of the sale proceeds. In these circumstances how is the charge to be calculated? Has Dan's cash gift been applied for the acquisition of the house or could one argue that none of it has, since James had enough surplus cash from the sale of the business? The sale proceeds were derived as much from James' own work as the initial cash contribution. How is a "reasonable attribution" to be made?

In the guidance notes HMRC state: **13–06**

"Each case will turn on its own facts and the value of the land disposed of and its ultimate sale price, the consideration provided and the independent financial resources of the recipient will all have to be taken into account when making a reasoned judgement as to the value reasonably attributable."[81]

But it is still not clear how the above scenario should be dealt with. In these circumstances what sort of disclosure should a taxpayer make to ensure that he is protected from a Taxes Management Act 1970, s.29 discovery enquiry after the one-year period has expired?

Example 13.3

Ralph is elderly and lives alone in a large house. He needs to raise cash and his son offers to buy a share in his house. Accordingly, Ralph sells a 50 per cent share in the house at full market value. The son may or may not occupy with Ralph. The cash forms part of Ralph's estate for IHT purposes. However, since Ralph has made a disposal of part of his house and he remains in occupation he satisfies the disposal condition. A POA charge will arise unless the rental value of the property (divided by 50 per cent) is less than £5,000 pa. (Note that one calculates the rental value of the whole property first assuming a normal shorthold tenancy and then one reduces this by 50 per cent to allow for the half retained, rather than calculating the rental value of what Ralph actually gave away, i.e. what he could obtain if he agreed to share his house with a lodger.)

Under Taxes Management Act 1970 a taxpayer must self-assess and deliver his **13–07** tax return by January 31 of the year following the year of assessment or three months from the date of the issue of the return if it is issued after October 31.

---

[80] See A2.10 and 70.
[81] See A2.40.

Thus for tax year 2005/06 (the first year when POAT operated) the taxpayer needed to deliver the tax return by January 31, 2007. However, from 2007/8 paper returns must be submitted by October 31, following the end of the tax year and electronic returns by January 31 (TMA ss.8,8A and 9 as amended by FA 2007, ss.88, 89). The requirement is for the return to disclose all the relevant information and for the taxpayer correctly to assess the tax due. HMRC may enquire into the return by issuing a formal notice. Up to 2007/8 the time limit was 12 months after the filing date: in the above example by January 31, 2008[82] (TMA 1970, ss.9, 19A). For 2007/8 and subsequent tax years, the time within which HMRC can issue a notice of enquiry changes to 12 months after the date on which the return was actually filed to encourage early filing. If HMRC make no enquiry during that period and the taxpayer has not amended his return, a self-assessment return becomes final on the expiry of that 12 months' enquiry period subject only to the possibility of a discovery assessment under TMA 1970, s.29 (as amended) or the taxpayer's right to make an error or mistake claim within five years from the normal filing date (TMA 1970, s.33).

Discovery assessments

13–08 A discovery assessment can be made under s.29 if HMRC "discovers" that income or capital gains that ought to be have been assessed have not been or that any relief has become excessive. However, if the taxpayer has made a self-assessment (i.e. delivered a return) the powers of HMRC are subject to limitations. (Note that if the taxpayer has simply ignored any POA charge and never submitted any return because he believes that he has no other taxable income the time limits below would not apply.) A discovery assessment can then only be made if there was fraud or negligence on the part of the taxpayer or his agent or the Revenue officer "could not have been reasonably expected on the basis of the information made available to him before that time, to be aware" of such failure of assessment or excessive claim for relief. The Court of Appeal decision in *Langham (Inspector of Taxes) v Veltema*[83] increased the possibility of HMRC making a successful discovery assessment under the Regime, at least in relation to valuation issues. The case related to a disputed valuation and the ultimate income tax liability under Sch.15 can also depend on the valuation of particular assets. The taxpayer had received property from a company and had disclosed the value of the benefit as £100,000 and paid tax on this basis. He did not send in the actual valuation. The Inspector raised no enquiry. In the event the company accounts were queried and a value was eventually agreed at £145,000 but after the enquiry period for the taxpayer had expired. The Court of Appeal overturned the High Court decision and held that the Inspector was entitled to make a discovery enquiry and therefore collect tax from the taxpayer on the additional benefit. As a result, a taxpayer has now to make the Inspector positively aware of an actual insufficiency in his self assessment for the information to be complete enough to prevent the making of a discovery assessment.[84]

---

[82] Or up to 15 months after the return was actually filed, if it was filed late: see *Tax Bulletin* Special Edition 3 (2000).
[83] [2004] EWCA Civ 193; [2004] STC 544.
[84] See also SP01/06.

Hence the taxpayer should set out in the white space of his return any areas 13–09
which may be open to a different interpretation. For example, if it is possible that
he could be within the POA Regime but he considers that for various technical
reasons he is outside it, this should be stated along with brief reasons. Professional
valuations should be obtained.

One difficulty is that HMRC has stated that where the same transaction is the 13–10
subject of an agreed valuation in a later related tax return (e.g. several parties
disposing of a jointly owned asset) and if it comes to light from examination of
the second return that the first return is insufficient then even if the first return
made full disclosure a discovery assessment can be raised.

Example 13.4

Elizabeth and Donald entered into a home loan scheme in 2003. They decide
not to elect but to pay the POA income tax bill. Don submits his 2005/6 tax
returns by January 2007. Full disclosure is made of the valuations they have
used and the rental value. No enquiry is raised into Donald's tax return by
January 2008 and he thinks that he has finality. However, Elizabeth's tax
return is enquired into by January 31, 2008 (or maybe she does not submit
her tax return or make sufficient disclosure so that HMRC raise a discovery
enquiry later). During the course of this enquiry it is discovered that there is
a valuation in respect of a related transaction. In these circumstances
Donald's tax return can be reopened.

The taxpayer may base his subsequent income tax liabilities under Sch.15 on that 13–11
valuation. Yet he will not have finality until after the time limits for making
discovery have elapsed. Valuation issues are therefore particularly difficult. It
was therefore welcome news when taxpayers realised that, at least in relation to
land and chattels, they only needed to revalue every five years although of course
a valuation can always be queried in respect of a subsequent year even if it has
not changed.

Other points are slightly easier. Where a taxpayer is doubtful as to whether he
is caught by the Regime in the first place he can put full details of his arguments
on the additional information pages of the return and presumably would then be
treated as having made full disclosure and be protected from a discovery
assessment. In any event at least until 2008 he could under the Code of Practice
10 obtain a ruling from HMRC in relation to the interpretation of Sch.15 and rely
on this.

Uncertainties over whether the POA Regime applies

Of course, even if a taxpayer does obtain finality in one tax year, this will not 13–12
prevent HMRC from raising an enquiry in later years if the taxpayer continues to
self assess on the basis that the Regime does not apply to him. Suppose HMRC
do not enquire into the taxpayer's return for 2005/6. In subsequent years he
continues to self assess on the basis that he is outside the POA Regime; HMRC
make an enquiry and it is established that the taxpayer was wrong to self assess
on the basis that no income tax was due under the Regime. Possibly a court case
clarifies the position or there is a change in legislation (such as FA 2006, s.80)
which is deemed to have always had effect.

In these circumstances the taxpayer will have missed the deadline for making the election (he first became chargeable under the POA Regime in 2005 and therefore needed to elect by January 31, 2007)[85] and will have to pay income tax going forward or else try to unravel the arrangement. It is for this reason that it may be worthwhile making a protective election, i.e. an election that is valid only in the event that income tax is due. If no income tax is due and the person is not chargeable then the election is not valid (although the taxpayer's executors may have some difficulty in convincing the relevant IHT office of this on the death of that taxpayer!).

13–13 Reversionary leases are a case in point. The guidance notes originally stated that post March 1999 reversionary lease schemes were not caught by POA because they were within the reservation of benefit rules. Many taxpayers disagreed with this view. In January 2007, just before the deadline for making the election HMRC accepted that they were wrong in their initial view giving advisers very little time to contact taxpayers to determine whether or not to make an election. Another difficulty arises if the taxpayer wrongly pays income tax on the basis that he was within the Regime when in fact he was not. This is particularly pertinent in relation to home loan schemes where HMRC accept that some work and some do not. If the taxpayer pays income tax only to find that in fact for various reasons the scheme does not achieve any inheritance tax savings it is not clear that he will obtain a refund of the income tax paid. It seems unlikely that an error or mistake claim under s.33 of TMA 1970 would be allowed.

The position of personal representatives

13–14 The Regime is likely to be a particular headache for personal representatives. For example, Ben dies not having paid income tax under Sch.15 because he believed that he was not within the Regime. HMRC investigate the matter after his death and consider that the Regime did apply. Income tax should have been paid. Obviously no election can now be made. Perhaps the IHT savings from the arrangement are secure but the income tax will be a liability of the estate (doubtless borne by residue). In these circumstances the personal representatives may find that they have a substantial income tax charge. Indeed, the matter may not come to light immediately after Ben's death. Suppose Ben is within the Regime because he made a gift of cash to his son in 1999 and then occupies a house purchased with that cash. He may not have been made aware of any problem. He dies in 2012. HMRC may not pick up the problem for some time. Fortunately, a back duty assessment on a deceased's personal representatives can only be made within three tax years of January 31 following the year of his death and only for fraudulent or negligent conduct by the deceased in any of the six years up to and including the year of his death.[86] FA 2008 changed this time limit with effect from April 1, 2010 so that an assessment cannot be made on the PRs more than four years (formerly three years) after the end of the tax year in which the deceased died.[87]

13–15 Personal representatives are under a duty to make additional enquires to establish whether the taxpayer made gifts of cash after April 6, 1998 and gifts of

---

[85] For the election, see **Ch.11**.
[86] TMA 1970, s.40.
[87] FA 2008, s.118; Sch.39, para.11 and SI 2009/403.

other assets after March 17, 1986 and if so what happened to the cash or property concerned.

There is another issue to consider on the death of the taxpayer. Suppose that he has made a valid election to come within the reservation of benefit rules in order to avoid POAT. In that event, the question of who pays the inheritance tax on his death in respect of that property will be decided in accordance with the normal IHT rules. The result is that it is the donee (the person in whom the property is vested) who is primarily liable to pay any tax arising out of the election; the donor's personal representatives only have a secondary liability (up to the value of the property under their control) and which arises to the extent that nobody else is liable for the tax or to the extent that it remains unpaid 12 months after the end of the month in which the taxpayer died.[88]

The donor's personal representatives should check whether an election has **13–16** been made and if it has been made, whether it is valid, i.e. whether the taxpayer was actually liable to POAT in the first place! In some cases people have been known to make elections when they were unnecessary. The election will be made to CAR (formerly Capital Taxes) in Nottingham who will then keep a record of the election which should be picked up automatically on the taxpayer's death even if the personal representatives make no enquiries themselves.[89] Difficulties could arise if a taxpayer made an election in (say) December 2006 and the donee refuses to pay the inheritance tax now due. The donee may argue that the election was not valid because it could not have been properly made until the required Regulation was passed[90]. HMRC do not accept this view but it has some merit. It may well suit both the donee and the beneficiaries of the free estate to argue the election was not valid because more nil rate band of the deceased is likely to be available on the death of the deceased. The PRs face a dilemma. Do they pay the income tax which would then be due (bearing in mind the above time limits on assessment) or argue with the donee that the election is valid? Much may depend on whether the deceased has survived the original gift by seven years (and therefore has an unused nil rate band again). If he has survived by seven years the beneficiaries of the free estate as well as the donee are likely to be united in arguing that the election is invalid.

DISCLOSURE[91]

The POA charge is to income tax and therefore within the rules for disclosure of **13–17** tax schemes. In brief, the rules are that a promoter of a scheme (a promoter includes accountants, tax advisers, solicitors and barristers who provide services relating to taxation) is required to provide details to the Anti-Avoidance Group (AAG) on a specified form of certain prescribed arrangements within a specified time limit. This regime was extended from August 1, 2006 by SI 2006/1543 so that it now covers income tax, corporation tax, CGT and SDLT. Separate disclosure regimes exist for VAT and for NI. Details must include a description of the scheme, including information about each element involved, the expected

---

[88] See IHTA 1984, s.204(1)(a) as limited by ibid. s.204(a) and note the PR's right of recovery if they do pay the tax in ibid. s.211(3).

[89] The election must be on Form 500: see **Appendix I**.

[90] See **11–03** for further discussion.

[91] FA 2004, ss.306–319.

tax consequences and the statutory provisions sought to be relied upon. HMRC will then register the scheme and allocate it a reference number. The promoter then gives that reference number to the taxpayer client who includes it on his tax return. If the client has devised the scheme himself or the scheme was provided by a foreign promoter who has not registered with HMRC or the promoter has not disclosed it on the basis of legal professional privilege, then the taxpayer will himself be required to disclosure the details of the scheme with his tax return. There are penalties for non-disclosure.

13–18   From August 1, 2006[92] arrangements must be disclosed (whether or not they involve financial or employment products) if income tax, corporation tax or CGT is being avoided. The conditions are:

(a) the arrangement will or might be expected to enable any person to obtain a tax advantage and it might reasonably be expected that any element of the arrangements giving rise to the tax advantage would be expected to be kept confidential from any competitor promoter or HMRC;

(b) the arrangement will or might be expected to enable any person to obtain a tax advantage and it might reasonably be expected that the arrangements are likely to command the payment of a fee, the amount of which is contingent on or attributable to a tax saving by a client with experience of purchasing sophisticated tax services (a premium fee);

(c) the tax advantage expected to be obtained arises to more than an incidental degree from the inclusion in the arrangement of one or more financial products, the promoter of the scheme is also a party to the arrangement (such as a bank or a security house) and the financial product is not offered on similar terms to those that can be obtained in the open market for a product that is the same or broadly similar;

(d) the arrangements are mass-marketed tax products, historically associated with unacceptable tax avoidance. Certain exceptions are specified, e.g. approved share incentive plans, enterprise management incentives, registered pension schemes, overseas pension schemes, enterprise investment schemes, venture capital trusts, accounts which satisfy the ISA regulations;

(e) the arrangements involve loss-making schemes of the type commonly used by high-wealth individuals to reduce their income tax or CGT liability; or

(f) the arrangements are leasing arrangements which concern the lease of high-value plant and machinery and which contain features commonly associated with avoidance.

FA 2004, s.308, together with SI 2004/1864 (as amended) requires that a promoter must, on or after August 1, 2004, disclose a notifiable scheme or arrangement to HMRC within five days of the earlier of making the proposal available for implementation or the date on which the promoter first became aware of any transaction forming part of the proposed arrangements. The first two conditions are the ones most likely to be relevant to POAT.

---

[92] Before then generally only arrangements involving employment and financial products that gave rise to a tax advantage needed to be disclosed and there were a number of filters to ensure that routine tax planning was excluded: see SI 2006/1543 which replaced SI 2004/1863.

PART III: PLANNING IN PRACTICE: REACTIVE PLANNING

This Part looks at the impact of the POA charge on arrangements which have already been implemented. It discusses whether the charge applies to the particular transactions and, if it does, what options are now open to the taxpayer.

CHAPTER 14

INGRAM SCHEMES

BACKGROUND

If an individual gives away his house (e.g. to his daughter) and continues to live **14–01** there, he is within the reservation of benefit rules. It is, however, possible to carve land up into different interests and the individual might, for instance, retain an interest which gave him a continued right of occupation and then give away the remaining interest in the land. What then will be the IHT consequences?

A key point to bear in mind is that the reservation of benefit rules apply to gifts of property in which the donor has reserved a benefit. If the taxpayer has effected the division of his land into different interests (a process usually referred to as a "shearing operation" or a "carve-out") then the question which arises is what property has he given away? Specifically, has he merely given the remainder interest in the land subject to the retained interest?

Divisions of land may be horizontal (as in the above example, when a single property is being carved into different slices) or vertical. In respect of the latter Lord Simmonds commented as follows:

> "[By retaining] something which he has never given, a donor does not bring himself within the mischief [of the reservation of benefit rules]—In the simplest analysis if A gives to B all his estates in Wiltshire except Blackacre, he does not except Blackacre out of what he has given: he just does not give Blackacre."[1]

Horizontal severances remained more problematic but the general consensus amongst advisers was that they could operate in such a way that the reservation of benefit rules were not infringed. Hence many such schemes were implemented after 1986, mainly in respect of landed estates and substantial properties.

The main attraction for taxpayers was that:

(a) the interest retained, which gave a continuing right to occupy, would be a wasting asset whose value would be relatively small at the date of death provided the original lease was for less than 21 years[2]; and

---

[1] *St Aubyn v AG* [1952] A.C. 15: the case was concerned with the application of the reservation of benefit provisions in the estate duty legislation. These provisions were, of course, very largely incorporated into the IHT legislation by FA 1986.

[2] See **2–12** and **14–11** below.

(b) the interest given away (typically the encumbered freehold) would be a PET[3] and so the gift would be free of IHT provided that the donor survived by seven years. Further, it would be an appreciating asset: as the value of the retained interest fell so that of the gifted interest would increase. But that increase in value would, in any event, fall outside the IHT net.

THE *INGRAM* DECISION[4]

The facts

14–02 Lady Jane Ingram transferred landed property to a nominee in 1987; the following day (on her directions) he granted her a 20-year rent-free lease in the property and on the next day transferred the property (subject to the lease) to trustees who executed declarations of trust whereby the property was held for the benefit of certain individuals, excluding Lady Jane. The arrangements, all part of a pre-planned scheme, amounted to a classic shearing operation. Lady Jane died in 1989 and the Revenue issued a determination that, because of the reservation of benefit rules, the gifted property still formed part of her estate at her death.

The Revenue's claim

14–03 The Revenue argued that the grant of a lease by a nominee in favour of his principal was a nullity with the result that although it was accepted that the trustees took the property subject to the interest of Lady Jane (as per the abortive lease), that interest took effect by way of a leaseback. Hence Lady Jane's interest could only arise contemporaneously with the gift made to the trustees, thereby resulting in a reservation of benefit. Alternatively, and even if the nominee lease was effective, the same result would follow as a result of applying the *Ramsay* principle.

The approach of the House of Lords

14–04 Lord Hoffmann referred to the long history of the legislation in this area and noted that the decided cases showed that although its provisions prevent a donor from "having his cake and eating it", there is nothing to stop him from "carefully dividing up the cake, eating part and having the rest". He decided the appeal on the assumption that the lease granted by the nominee was a nullity, i.e. on the basis that the leasehold interest came into existence only at the time when the freehold was acquired by the trustees.

---

[3] Provided that it was gifted outright or settled on qualifying interest in possession or accumulation and maintenance trusts. Of course since March 2006 accumulation and maintenance trusts can no longer be established and inter vivos interest in possession trusts are generally not qualifying.

[4] *Ingram v IRC* [1995] 4 All E.R. 334; on appeal [1997] 4 All E.R. 395 (CA) revs'd; [1999] STC 37, HL.

The consequences of such a "contemporaneous carve-out" involved a consideration of the estate duty case of *Nichols v IRC*[5] which had concerned a gift by Sir Philip Nichols of his country house and estate to his son, Francis, subject to Francis granting him an immediate leaseback. Goff J., giving the judgment of the Court of Appeal, concluded that such an arrangement involved a reservation of benefit by Sir Philip:

" . . . we think that a grant of the fee simple, subject to and with the benefit of a lease-back, where such a grant is made by a person who owns the whole of the freehold free from any lease, is a grant of the whole fee simple with something reserved out of it, and not a gift of a partial interest leaving something in the hands of the grantor which he has not given. It is not like a reservation or remainder expectant on a prior interest. It gives an immediate right to the rent, together with a right to distrain for it, and, if there be a proviso for re-entry, a right to forfeit the lease. Of course, where as in *Munro v Commissioner of Stamp Division (NSW)*[6] the lease, or, as it then may have been, a licence coupled with an interest, arises under a prior independent transaction, no question can arise because the donor then gives all that he has, but where it is a condition of the gift that a lease-back shall be created, we think that must, on a true analysis, be a reservation of benefit out of the gift and not something not given at all."

In the event the *Nichols* case fell to be decided on the basis of the covenants given by the son in the lease in which he assumed the burden of repairs and the payment of tithe redemption duty, and which amounted to a reservation. The wider statement of Goff J. quoted above to the effect that a leaseback must *by itself* involve a reservation constituted the main authority relied upon by the Revenue (and the comment that the *Munro* case involved a "prior independent transaction" had subsequently been widely debated).

Lord Hoffmann unequivocally rejected this approach:

"It is a curious feature of the debate in this case that both sides claim that their views reflect the reality, not the mere form of the transaction, but the Revenue's version of reality seems entirely dependent upon the *scintilla temporis* which must elapse between the conveyance of the freehold to the donee and the creation of the leasehold in favour of the donor. For my part I do not think that a theory based on the notion of a *scintilla temporis* can have a very powerful grasp on reality . . . If one looks at the real nature of the transaction, there seems to me no doubt that Ferris J. was right in saying that the trustees and beneficiaries never at any time acquired the land free of Lady Ingram's leasehold interest."

The nominee lease

Given that no reservation was involved, even if the nominee lease was a nullity, **14–05** it was not strictly necessary for their Lordships to express any view on the validity of such an arrangement. Lord Hoffmann, however, indicated that he was of the opinion that such a lease was valid as a matter of English law for reasons given by Millett L.J. in the Court of Appeal. (Nominee leases are, in fact, widely used in practice.) It should, however, be appreciated that nothing in the speeches

---

[5] *Nichols v IRC* [1975] 2 All E.R. 120, CA.
[6] [1934] A.C. 61, PC.

affects the proposition that a man cannot grant a lease to himself[7] nor the position under Scots law.[8]

Ramsay[9]

14–06 Given the conclusion that a leaseback did not involve any reservation of benefit the question of the *Ramsay* principle being used to nullify the nominee lease did not arise, and neither Lord Hoffmann nor Lord Hutton expressed any views on this matter.

The meaning of "property" in FA 1986, s.102

14–07 Lord Hoffmann pointed out that s.102 is concerned with a gift of "property" and that term does not necessarily refer to something which has a physical existence such as a house, but is used in a technical sense and requires a careful analysis of the nature of what has been gifted. A landowner may, for instance, gift an unencumbered freehold interest in his house, in which case were he to continue to occupy that property (in the absence of a payment of full consideration and assuming that such occupation was more than on a de minimis level) then he would reserve a benefit. By contrast, he might retain a leasehold interest and only give away the encumbered freehold interest gifted. As Lord Hoffmann concluded, s.102 "requires people to define precisely the interest which they are giving away and the interest, if any, which they are retaining".

The use of shearing arrangements

14–08 The speeches demolished the argument that the creation of the lease and the gift of the encumbered freehold had to be independent transactions. The lease could be carved-out contemporaneously with the gift. Accordingly, a prior nominee arrangement is not necessary; the arrangement could be structured as a gift and leaseback. However, it was essential that all the relevant terms of the lease were agreed before the freehold gift was made so that it is clear that the proprietary interest retained was defined with the necessary precision. Further, it was thought that the lease should contain no obligations onerous to the landlord. The assumption of, for example, liability to carry out structural repairs on the part of the landlord might have been regarded as a collateral benefit conferred on the donor.

---

[7] *Rye v Rye* [1962] A.C. 496, HL.
[8] *Kildrummy (Jersey) Ltd v IRC* [1990] S.T.C. 657.
[9] The so-called "*Ramsay* principle" is derived from a line of cases starting with *Ramsay (WT) Ltd v IRC* [1982] A.C. 300. Broadly it enables the courts to excise artificial steps in a pre-planned tax saving scheme. See the authors', *Trust Taxation*, 2nd edn, 3.37 et seq.

It was no great surprise that amending legislation followed in FA 1999 which:

14–09

(a) reversed the *Ingram* decision in respect of gifts of interests in land made after March 8, 1999;

(b) but otherwise did not change the existing legislation.

It was a classic example of narrowly-targeted anti-avoidance legislation. The legislation extended the reservation of benefit provisions so that they apply if the following two conditions are met.

Condition 1: There must be a gift of an interest in land. In respect of this condition, note that the trigger for the application of this new legislation is a "gift" and that these rules are only concerned with gifts affecting land.[11] Hence a sale of the freehold land subject to a lease is not caught by reservation of benefit.

Condition 2: The donor must retain "a significant right or interest in relation to the land" or be party to a significant arrangement in relation to the land.

Looking back at the facts in *Ingram* it can be seen that both conditions are satisfied: the gift of the encumbered freehold satisfies Condition 1 whilst the retention of a lease satisfies Condition 2. Hence, from March 9, 1999 new *Ingram* arrangements in respect of land are ineffective so that on the death of the donor the gifted freehold interest will be taxed as part of his estate under the reservation rules.

Limitations on the ambit of the new legislation

Condition 2 is not met if:

14–10

(a) the donor pays full consideration for the retained right or interest; or

(b) the right or interest was obtained at least seven years before the gift. Hence in a very limited way *Ingram* schemes falling outside the reservation of benefit rules remain possible but only if the lease is carved-out and the taxpayer then waits at least seven years before gifting the freehold. In practice such long term planning has not, so far as the authors are aware, been undertaken.

It is also considered that the new legislation does not apply:

(a) if a property is divided so that A retains (say) the granny annex and gives away the main house; and

(b) if the retained interest is not significant, e.g. if A gives away land which surrounds his house whilst retaining a right of way to that house.

---

[10] See FA 1999, s.104 inserting new s.102A–C into FA 1986.
[11] *Ingram* schemes have been developed for chattels: see **Ch.20**.

14–11　As has been noted, a large number of *Ingram* schemes were carried out before March 9, 1999 and professional advisers need to be aware that as and when the donor dies the following problems may arise.

    (a) What value is to be attributed to the retained lease? Specifically did it give security of tenure/a right to enfranchise? A lease for more than 21 years may well mean that the donor has rights of enfranchisement or possession on expiry of the term which will increase the value of what he retains. Even if there is no right to enfranchise, the fact that the lease may be non assignable does not mean it has no value. What has to be valued is how much any hypothetical purchaser would pay to have rent-free occupation for the remaining term of years subject to the same covenants against alienation and the same covenants as to repair. IHTA 1984, s.160 provides that the value is the price which the property might reasonably be expected to fetch in a hypothetical sale if sold on the open market at that time. HMRC tend to raise two arguments in relation to *Ingram* schemes: that there is a special purchaser and that the lease has some marriage value. The donee clearly has an interest in purchasing the property and to that extent can be counted as a special purchaser. However, if the donee has no resources to fund that purchase this value has to be discounted to some degree. HMRC have in the past argued that a proportion of the vacant possession premium or marriage value should be allocated to the lease but these arguments should be resisted. The marriage value was lost on the initial transfer of value made by the donor when the freehold reversion was gifted and so increased the size of the transfer of value (normally a PET) made by the donor.

    (b) If, after death, the family wish to sell the property, bear in mind that the deceased donor merely owned a lease at death so that the CGT uplift will be limited to this asset. The freehold acquired by the family is likely to have a low base cost and will not benefit from the CGT main residence relief. In practice, *Ingram* schemes tended to be used where the donor was unlikely to move and where the donee would move in to the house after the death of the donor so that the house would never be sold.

14–12　Other problems may arise during the life of the donor: for instance if he wishes to sell the property and move (e.g. to a retirement bungalow) he will find that all he owns is a lease which may have a relatively low value. If the family are prepared to co-operate in selling the freehold, this may give rise to a CGT charge as noted above whilst an application of the proceeds of sale for the benefit of the donor may lead to the reservation of benefit rules applying. In some cases the lease retained may expire before the death of the donor.[12] If he wishes to continue in occupation of the property he must pay full consideration to avoid being caught by the reservation of benefit rules.[13]

---

[12] The most convenient arrangement would have been to reserve a lease limited to the life of the donor but that was made impossible by IHTA 1984, s.43(3), which treats the arrangement as a settlement with the donor/tenant as having an interest in possession.

[13] See FA 1986, Sch.20, para.6(1)(a) and see **2–08** above.

In most (if not all) cases the scheme will have been implemented more than seven years ago so that the PET of the freehold interest will have now become an exempt transfer.

IMPACT OF THE PRE-OWNED ASSET REGIME

The December 2003 Consultation Paper suggested that the Regime would not **14–13** apply to *Ingram* schemes since it referred to the charge being subject to "an exclusion for cases where the donor has expressly reserved a right to continued occupation when making the gift". Any celebrations were, however, premature and HMRC made it clear during the consultation exercise that whatever this proposed exclusion meant it was not intended to exclude *Ingram* schemes. The final legislation accordingly confers no special treatment on these schemes.

The para.3 charge will therefore apply given that:

(a) the donor is in occupation of land; and

(b) the disposal condition is met in respect of that land.

It is irrelevant that he is in occupation under a reserved lease. Curiously there is no let-out similar to that contained in FA 1999 reservation of benefit legislation if the freehold is gifted more than seven years after the grant of the lease.[14]

All that remains is to calculate the chargeable amount in relation to the land. In applying the para.4 rules the appropriate rental value must be apportioned using the formula:

$$R \times \frac{DV}{V}$$

given that the donor has not disposed of his entire interest in the land. This can best be understood by taking an example.

Example 14.1

In 1998, A retained a 20-year, rent-free lease in Blackacre and gave the encumbered freehold to his daughter. Assume that on the **"valuation date"** the value of the interest disposed of (the freehold) is £750,000 and the value of the "**relevant land**" (on the basis of a freehold with vacant possession) is £1.5. Assume further that the rental value (calculated in accordance with the provisions of para.5) is £15,000 p.a.

Applying the formula

R = £15,000

DV = £750,000

V = £1,500,000

So that the appropriate rental value is:

$$15,000 \times \frac{750,000}{1,500,000} = £7,500$$

---

[14] See **14–10** above.

A's chargeable amount is therefore £7,500 so that if he is a higher rate taxpayer he will suffer income tax of £3,000.

The benefit is taxed each year whilst A continues to occupy the land. "The valuation date" for *Ingram* schemes is April 6, 2005 and a revaluation will not be required until April 6, 2010. Of course, it is likely that the value of the gifted freehold (DV) will increase as the retained lease wastes away. Hence the freezing of values.

Chattels

14–14 As discussed in **Ch.20** *Ingram* schemes have also been employed for chattels and these were not affected by the anti-avoidance legislation in FA 1999 which was limited to land. POAT, however, will apply to such schemes and the calculation of the chargeable amount under para.7 will be arrived at in a similar fashion, in this case by applying the formula:

$$\frac{N \times DV}{V}$$

where N is the amount of the interest that would be payable for the taxable period if interest were payable at the prescribed rate on an amount equal to the value of the chattel at the valuation date. The prescribed rate of interest is the "official rate" which applies on beneficial loans to employees (currently 4.75 per cent).

PRACTICAL ADVICE

14–15 There are limited options open to the taxpayer who has effected an *Ingram* scheme.

Option 1—Pay the income tax charge

This will in effect be 40 per cent (for most individuals) of a full rent for the property,[15] but with a discount which reflects the value of the retained lease. In fact the DV/V valuation method may not truly reflect the value of the lease in the taxpayer's estate. In those cases where seven years have elapsed so that the PET of the freehold is outside the IHT net and the taxpayer (or his family) can afford to pay the tax this may be the most attractive option. Bear in mind the following when ascertaining the taxable benefit and therefore the income tax due.

(a) The rental value as at April 6, 2005 is arrived at on the assumption that one is letting with vacant possession. However, the house may be in need of

---

[15] It is generally thought unlikely that the payment of a market rent will be attractive. However, if the freehold interest is held in trust then opportunities for sheltering the income tax charge on such a rent may arise (e.g. if the beneficiaries include non-taxpayers). It will be important to ensure that the rent paid will be deducted from the appropriate rental value and this requires the payment to be made under a legal obligation (see **3–36**). Given that in *Ingram* arrangements the donor will be in occupation of the property under a lease which provides for only a nominal rent, the answer may be for him to execute a deed of covenant in favour of the donee. Such payments are not thought to be taxable in the hands of the donee (see also **14–17**).

modernisation and not easy to let. In these circumstances the rental value may be significantly reduced. In ascertaining the rent the valuer must assume that the donor pays all those expenses normally paid by the tenant and the donees bear the costs of repairs and buildings insurance. (The fact that this is not actually true does not matter—it is a hypothetical valuation.)

(b) The freehold reversion must also be valued at April 6, 2005 but this does not need to take into account marriage value. Any valuation should take account of the terms of the lease—i.e. that the lessee will be able to live in the property rent free. A typical *Ingram* scheme might be for 15 years, and so if the lease was granted in 1999 the lease will expire in 2014. The donor will have no right to occupy beyond that date. In these circumstances it appears that the freehold reversion may be discounted from the vacant possession value by something in the region of 25–35 per cent (but of course each case will depend on its own facts and it is important to obtain a professional valuation). The owner of the freehold reversion is not generally required under the terms of the lease to carry out any repairs which will increase the value of his interest and therefore the DV element.

If the taxpayer is in poor health and may not live more than (say) five years, paying the tax may be the most sensible option. As noted in **Ch.17**, it is generally possible for the donee to pay the income tax due without a reservation of benefit problem[16] and given that the donee will be the person who ultimately pays the inheritance tax if the donor elects, this may be the fairest solution.

Option 2—the donor ceases to occupy the property

If it is desired to retain the IHT advantage but not pay any income tax then this **14–16** affords one way out. Of course alternative accommodation will need to be found. Before surrendering the lease consider carefully any tax implications: e.g. if the freehold gift is accelerated will this amount to an associated operation? Often the lease is non-assignable so cannot be gifted to another member of the family. If the fag end of the lease is gifted to the freeholder or surrendered then the concern is that there has been a disposition of the unencumbered freehold by associated operations at the point of surrender which would be potentially disastrous in IHT terms. A slightly less radical alternative would be for the donor to occupy a smaller part of the property.

Example 14.2

Lady Ire effected an *Ingram* scheme over her large estate in 1998. The donee is her son. She is shocked by the POA charge. Rather than surrender her lease or elect she decides to move to the small gamekeeper's cottage at the entry to the estate. The son has now married and moves into the main house with his growing family.

In these circumstances HMRC accept[17] that the income tax charge is limited to the part she actually occupies rather than the whole of the property originally gifted.

---

[16] See correspondence with HMRC at A2.72. The donor will agree not to make the election.
[17] See correspondence with HMRC at A2.71.

Option 3—donor pays rent or equivalent

14–17 There are two ways in which the payment of rent might reduce the income tax charge. The first option is for the donor to assign her lease to someone other than the donee (if this is possible under the terms of the lease). The donor would no longer have any rights of occupation. In order to avoid a reservation of benefit the donor would then need to pay full consideration for her continued occupation for as long as she lives there. (See FA 1986, Sch.20, para.6.) Such arrangements might not involve paying the same rent as would be due under an assured shorthold tenancy. Instead the donor could agree to take on responsibility for repairs, etc. under a tenants repairing lease provided that constituted full consideration. Independent valuations should be obtained by the two parties.[18]

Who should the payment be made to? The person with the current right to occupy the property is the assignee of the lease and so payments should be made to that person. However, to avoid the POA charge under para.11(3) it is the "relevant property" (defined for these purposes as "the property disposed of") which must be subject to a reservation and then protected by the payment of full consideration. Unfortunately that does not seem to be the case if the payment is to the assignee of the lease. The alternative, of assigning the lease to the donee of the freehold, is not considered desirable given the risk that this will involve a substantial transfer of value under the associated operations provisions (see IHTA 1984, s.268).

The alternative option is for the donor (say Mrs X) to bring herself within para.4(1), Sch.15 and to make payments to the donees "in pursuance of a legal obligation . . . in respect of the occupation of the land." Note that the section does not refer to the payments being rent. At present under the terms of the lease the donor is under no legal obligation to pay for her continued occupation; she has a right to occupy anyway. However, she could *put herself* under such an obligation by covenanting with the donees that for as long as he occupies the property she will make payments under the deed of covenant. Such payments serve to reduce her POA charge. So if the appropriate rental value ascertained as if it were an assured shorthold tenancy is say £32,500 and she paid £30,500 under the deed of covenant, she would be chargeable to POA income tax on £2,000.

Entering into a deed of covenant is a gift by the donor because she has no need to do this, having a right to occupy under the lease. The payments she makes under the deed of covenant are therefore not taxable income in the hands of the donees: they are annual payments and outside the income tax net under ITTOIA 2005, s.727. Nor are the payments rent because no letting business has been run. The donees should self-assess on this basis.

This option depends on the donor being prepared to pay much larger sums over to the children. Instead of paying 40 per cent of the rental value to HMRC she is paying the rental value itself over to the *children*. It will save tax if the payments under the deed of covenant are not taxable but involves the donor in more outlay.

---

[18] On the full consideration "let-out", see **2–08**; **7–39** and **21–27** above.

Option 4—Election opt into the reservation of benefit rules

For the individual wishing to remain in occupation of the property and unable/ **14–18** unwilling to pay the income tax charge or sums under covenant the election is an option. There are two points to note.

(a) The person who will eventually end up suffering the IHT will be the donee.[19] Curiously enough there is no provision which requires that person to be notified of the making of the election: accordingly the eventual tax bill may come as something of a shock!

(b) It will potentially be a complete own goal if, having made the election, the donor then ceases to occupy the property. At that point he will make a deemed PET under s.102(4) and so will start the seven-year clock running all over again.

In considering the equity of the pre-owned assets charge the plight of taxpayers who have effected successful *Ingram* schemes is striking. Arrangements concluded perhaps 19 years ago are now subject to an income tax charge unless the invidious decision is taken to accept a future IHT charge or to leave one's home.

Option 5—Reverter to settlor relief

Prior to December 5, 2005 changes and the subsequent enactment of s.80 in FA **14–19** 2006, one option was for the donees to give their freehold reversion to a qualifying interest in possession trust for the donor reverter to each of them. There was no SDLT payable. The analysis then was that the carve-out done by the donor had ceased and the donor (Mrs X) was treated as owning the freehold reversion by virtue of her qualifying interest in possession in the same. Hence the para.11(1) ownership exemption applied. She also reserved a benefit in the property (the reversion) which she had gifted. The wording of s.102(3) of FA 1986 dealing with the position on her death is as follows:

> "If immediately before the death of a donor there is any property which in relation to him is property subject to a reservation then, to the extent that the property would not apart from this section, form part of the donor's estate immediately before his death, that property shall be treated for the purposes of the 1984 Act as property to which he was beneficially entitled immediately before his death."

Therefore if the freehold reversion was property in Mrs X's estate immediately before her death because she had a qualifying interest in possession in it, this displaced the reservation of benefit provisions. Despite having an interest in possession the value of property was not taxable on her death provided that it then reverted to the settlor donee(s). IHTA 1984, s.54 provided that if on the death of a person entitled to an interest in possession it reverted to the settlor (here the donees) the value of the settled property should be left out of account in determining the value of the property immediately before Mrs X's death. Note that it is only the *value* that was left out of account. The property is still comprised in her (Mrs X's estate) for all other inheritance tax purposes while she is alive.

---

[19] See **11–20**.

The reverter to settlor exemption is discussed further in **Ch.18** and rests on the distinction between the value of property in Mrs X's estate and the property comprised in it.

Such a course would until December 5, 2005 also have avoided the POA charge while she is alive because of the ownership exemption under para.11(1); as discussed in **Chs 7** and **18** this is no longer possible.

Option 6—Buying back the freehold

14–20 If the donor Mrs X has sufficient resources she could buy back the freehold reversion at market value. Then the entire relevant property (the land) becomes part of her estate again and there is no POA charge. The inheritance tax savings are preserved except that the donees now hold cash rather than the freehold interest. She has the appreciating asset in her estate.

If this course of action is followed the donor would have to pay SDLT on the purchase of the freehold reversion. There will also be capital gains tax for the donees to pay on the sale of the freehold interest (assuming it shows a gain) and, of course, it will not be possible to effect the transaction by leaving the purchase price outstanding as a debt since the debt would not be deductible from Mrs X's free estate.[20]

THE FUTURE OF *INGRAM* SCHEMES

14–21 It might be thought that the combination of inheritance tax changes and the POAT charge means *Ingram* schemes have no further place in estate planning. However, the carve-out principle is still relevant and *Ingram* schemes remain useful in the following circumstances:

(a) where the trust is an old-style interest in possession trust (e.g. set up before March 22, 2006 or the life tenant has a transitional serial interest), the present life tenant is not the settlor and the trustees have overriding powers of appointment and advancement, particularly where the settled property comprises a house occupied by the settlor;

(b) where the trust was set up by Will before or after March 2006 and the life tenant (whether the deceased's spouse or otherwise) has an immediate post death interest.

The scope for this planning is discussed at **15–09** onwards.

---

[20] See FA 1986, s.103.

CHAPTER 15

REVERSIONARY LEASES

BACKGROUND

The development of reversionary lease arrangements is closely linked to *Ingram* **15–01** schemes which were considered in the last chapter. In particular:

(a) the attraction for taxpayers in entering into these arrangements was the same: see **14–01**;

(b) like *Ingram* schemes reversionary leases involved a shearing operation or carve-out: see **14–01** et seq.;

(c) similar CGT problems would arise in the event of a sale of the property: see **14–12**. Hence they were ideal in cases where it was envisaged that the property would never be sold but would be retained within the family;

(d) as with *Ingram* schemes, reversionary lease schemes remain of value where the house is held in a qualifying interest in possession trust and the life tenant is someone other than the settlor. This is discussed further at 15–09 et seq.

Once it was clear that HMRC were going to challenge *Ingram* shearing arrangements, taxpayers and their advisers turned to the reversionary lease as an alternative. Specifically it appeared to offer an advantage over an *Ingram* shearing arrangement in that it was a single transaction. Whereas in *Ingram* arrangements it was necessary **first** to carve out a lease and **then** to gift an encumbered freehold reversion, reversionary leases were a single stage transaction involving merely the grant of a lease.

HOW THE REVERSIONARY LEASE WORKS

Example 15.1   **15–02**

Assume that Jasper owns Biddecombe Manor which he wishes to pass on to his eldest son, Rufus. He wishes to occupy the Manor for the rest of his life. It is inconceivable that the property will be sold outside the family. The "scheme" operates as follows.

(a) Jasper grants Rufus a long lease over the property (say 125 years) to take effect in 20 years time. Because the lease does not give Rufus occupation rights immediately it is known as a deferred or reversionary lease. The terms of the lease do not involve the payment of any rent nor do they impose onerous conditions on Rufus.

(b) Jasper can continue to occupy the property for the next 20 years because he remains the freeholder and the lease has not given Rufus an immediate right to occupy.

(c) The gift of the lease is a PET by Jasper and so free from IHT provided that he survives by seven years.

(d) The freehold interest (of diminishing value) remains in Jasper's estate and will be taxed accordingly on his death.

(e) Of course if Jasper is still alive at the end of 20 years and wishes to continue to occupy the property he will need to pay Rufus a market rent: otherwise he will have reserved a benefit in the lease gifted to Rufus.[21]

RESERVATION OF BENEFIT ANALYSIS

15–03 Jasper continues to occupy by virtue of his retained freehold property: he does not retain a benefit in the gifted property which is the reversionary lease. Like *Ingram* the arrangement is a horizontal carve-out: see **14–01**. This analysis has been accepted by HMRC.

HMRC originally considered that the legislation introduced in 1999 to stop *Ingram* arrangements also caught reversionary lease schemes and on that basis reversionary lease schemes effected from March 9, 1999 were caught by reservation of benefit and therefore not subject to POAT. This view was not shared by most practitioners and in a late change of heart HMRC finally announced on January 27, 2007:

> "For reversionary lease schemes entered into on or after 9 March 1999 HMRC had previously held the view that section 102A Finance Act 1986 would apply because the donor's occupation would be a "significant right in relation to the land". If that analysis were correct, the reservation of benefit rules would apply and there would be no income tax charge. However, HMRC now consider that where the freehold interest was acquired more than seven years before the gift, the continued occupation by the donor would not be a significant right, and contrary to its previously held view, section 102A cannot apply to the gift because of section 102A(5). If the donor grants a reversionary lease within seven years of acquiring the freehold interest, section 102A may apply to the gift depending on how the remaining provisions of that section apply in relation to the circumstances of the case.

> Bear in mind, however, that, whenever the freehold interest was acquired, a gift may be a gift with a reservation of benefit under section 102 FA 1986 if the lease contains terms beneficial to the donor. An example of this may be where the lessee covenants to pay the costs of maintaining the property.

> Where the GWR provisions do not apply it will nevertheless be regarded as a disposal of an interest in the relevant land under paragraph 3(2) of Schedule 15, and the charge

---

[21] For the full consideration let-out, see **2–08** and **7–38** above and FA 1986, Sch.20, para.6(1)(a).

to income tax will apply, calculated in accordance with the formula in paragraph 4(2), unless the donor elects into the reservation of benefit provisions."[22]

The above HMRC notice sets out one reason why reversionary leases are not caught by the FA 1999 legislation. In fact there may be two reasons as follows.

(a) The basic conditions in the legislation that have to be satisfied are first that the taxpayer disposes of an interest in land by way of gift (this Jasper in *Example 15.1* undoubtedly does when he grants Rufus the deferred lease). Secondly, he must retain "a significant right or interest or (be) party to a significant arrangement in relation to the land". Of course Japer retains his freehold interest—does that satisfy the second requirement?

(b) The short answer is that it all depends on the facts! By s.102A(5), "a right or interest is not significant [for the purposes of the second condition noted above] if it was granted or acquired before the period of seven years ending with the date of the gift". In the vast majority of cases persons wishing to enter into reversionary lease arrangements will do so in relation to property which they have owned for at least seven years. In such cases it is considered that the s.102A(5) let-out applies and the gifted lease is not property subject to a reservation.[23] It is on this basis that HMRC accept that there is no reservation of benefit.

(c) An alternative reason not mentioned by HMRC is based on s.102A(3) which excludes a right interest or arrangement which enables the donor to occupy the land "for full consideration in money or money's worth". If Jasper had originally purchased his freehold interest (whether or not within seven years of the date of the gift) for full consideration then this let-out should apply so that again the arrangement remains outside the amended reservation of benefit legislation.

That, of course, means that a reversionary lease granted within seven years of Jasper inheriting the property would be caught because neither of the let-outs would then be available. However, if Jasper was left an immediate post-death interest in possession in the property under the Will of his father a reversionary lease scheme is still possible even though he has not had the interest in possession for seven years or acquired the property for consideration. This is discussed at **15-09** et seq.

MISCELLANEOUS TECHNICAL POINTS

The precise arrangements involved in reversionary lease schemes gave rise to a number of uncertainties. **15–04**

(a) Could the period of deferral exceed 21 years? This might be desirable if Jasper were (say) in his mid–60s so that he could easily live for another 25 years. This involves the construction of s.149(3) of the Law of Property Act 1925 which provides:

---

[22] This view is now reflected in the amended guidance notes at A2.57.

[23] It may be noted that s.102A(5) provides for the right or interest not to be significant. Can it be said that Jasper is party to a significant arrangement (which is not protected). The authors do not consider that he is.

"A term [i.e. lease] at a rent or granted in consideration of a fine, limited to take effect more than 21 years from the date of the instrument purporting to create it, shall be void".

It is thought that a lease which does not involve the payment of any rent (or fine) is outside these provisions and will be valid.

(b) If the lease is granted for a term in excess of 300 years then when it vests in interest the tenant is entitled to call for the freehold interest: see s.153 of the Law of Property Act 1925.

(c) Could the lease be made to vest on the **earlier** of 21 years from the date of grant and the death of Jasper (the freeholder)? If so, this would have an obvious attraction in reducing the value of the freehold interest in Jasper's estate. Some concern has been felt that this could convert the reversionary lease into a lease for life under IHTA 1984, s.43(3), but the authors do not accept this.

Capital gains tax

15–05 Advisers also gave some thought to alleviating the capital gains tax position on the leasehold interest if the property were ever sold. A few arrangements had been structured so that both the freehold and the lease were held within a single settlement (albeit in different funds) with the intention of taking advantage of the principal private residence relief available to trustees.[24] The capital gains tax planning became much more difficult after the inheritance tax changes on March 22, 2006 and more or less impossible after the transitional period had expired on October 5, 2008. The result is that a capital gains tax charge cannot easily be avoided in respect of either *Ingram* or reversionary lease schemes.

Example 15.2

Edwin settled his house (owned for 10 years) into a qualifying interest in possession trust for himself in 2005. He is deemed to continue owning it for inheritance tax purposes and there is no transfer of value.

In June 2007 he decides to embark on some inheritance tax planning. The trustees therefore grant a 199-year reversionary lease to a nominee to vest in 10 years and then terminate Edwin's interest in possession in the lease which they hold on interest in possession trusts for his son George. Edwin therefore

---

[24] See TCGA 1992, s.225. This extends the CGT exemption to a residence which is settled property provided that the trustees satisfy the conditions as to ownership. The relief requires a claim by the trustees and is available if and to the extent that the conditions as to residence are satisfied by one or more beneficiaries who are entitled to occupy the house under the terms of the settlement. Any notice of election between two or more residences has to be signed jointly by the trustees and the beneficiary. It is not necessary that the beneficiary has an interest in possession in the entirety of the settled property for the trustees to claim relief on all the gain and it is possible for a house to be held by trustees for a number of beneficiaries with only one of them in occupation: in these circumstances s.225 still gives relief in respect of the entire gain. In *Sansom v Peay* [1976] 1 WLR 1073 it was accepted that when a beneficiary of the trust occupies trust property under discretionary powers given to the trustees, relief under s.225 is available to exclude the entire gain from charge.

retains an interest in possession in the freehold, but he is excluded from the reversionary lease fund.

Edwin, by virtue of FA 1986, s.102ZA, is deemed to make a gift of the underlying settled property on termination of his interest in possession in the lease (see **15–06** below). This is a PET by Edwin since George takes a qualifying interest in possession within the transitional period. Edwin purchased the property on the open market and in any event has owned it (either personally or as a qualifying interest in possession beneficiary) for more than seven years. Section 102A should not therefore apply so there is no reservation in respect of the reversionary lease. Only the freehold interest (of decreasing value) remains part of his estate for inheritance tax purposes.[25]

For capital gains tax purposes there is no disposal by the trustees of the property because the reversionary lease and freehold remain comprised in one settlement. Since Edwin occupies the property as his main residence (albeit by virtue of his interest in possession in the freehold) TCGA 1992, s.225 protects the trustees from a capital gain on both the freehold and reversionary lease interests even though George is not in occupation.

However, for POAT purposes the disposal condition is satisfied because Edwin disposed of an interest in land in 2005. Until 2007 the ownership exemption under para.11(1) applied to protect him from a POA charge. From June 2007, para.11(1) ceases to protect the reversionary lease. Hence POAT is payable from 2007/8.

If Edwin's interest in possession in the reversionary lease had been terminated **15–06** after October 5, 2008 and George had taken the lease outright this would have been a PET for inheritance tax purposes and the same inheritance tax and POAT treatment would have arisen as above. However, there would have been a part disposal of the property by the trustees for capital gains tax purposes (albeit protected from tax by main residence relief at that point) and George would acquire the reversionary lease at a relatively low base cost. On a subsequent sale of the whole property George is likely to make a chargeable gain: even if the property remains at the same value on the open market the leasehold interest will increase in value as the vesting day approaches. No principal private residence relief is available on George's reversionary lease unless he occupies the property as his main residence.

As set out at **15–09** below, both *Ingram* and reversionary lease schemes continue to present planning possibilities in the case of settled property even after March 22, 2006, since provided the settlor is not the life tenant of the trust in question, both reservation of benefit and POAT can be avoided. The capital gains tax problems, however, remain.

IMPACT OF THE PRE-OWNED ASSETS REGIME

It is considered that taxpayers such as Jasper in *Example 15.1*, who have entered **15–07** into reversionary lease arrangements will be subject to an income tax charge

---

[25] Note also the restricted wording of s.102ZA which is said to apply only for the purposes of s.102 and Sch.20 (i.e. not to the anti-*Ingram* legislation in s.102A-C). Accordingly it is arguable in such cases that there is no gift (merely a termination of the interest in possession) so that GWR cannot apply: see **15–12**.

under the Regime from April 6, 2005. The analysis is much the same as for *Ingram* schemes: see **14–13** et seq.

As with those schemes an apportionment will be necessary under Sch.15, para.4 of the appropriate rental value. The property gifted (the leasehold interest: DV in the formula) is likely to show a year-on-year increase in much the same way as the freehold reversion in *Ingram* schemes. Once again the fact that one only has to revalue every five years will generally be advantageous for the taxpayer.

However, there is one significant difference. As noted above, HMRC have now indicated in the guidance notes that reversionary lease schemes effected pre- and post- March 8, 1999 are within the POA charge because they do not fall foul of the reservation of benefit rules. In the case of *Ingram* schemes only those schemes effected prior to March 9, 1999 are subject to POAT. *Ingram* arrangements made after that date will generally fall foul of the reservation of benefit rules.[26]

PRACTICAL ADVICE

15–08 In essence, the practical advice to taxpayers such as Jasper who carried out a reversionary lease scheme before or after March 9, 1999 and who is therefore within the POA charge is much the same as for persons who have effected *Ingram* schemes and hence the comments at **14–15** et seq. will be relevant.[27] There is one point of difference. In the case of reversionary lease arrangements, the taxpayer retains the freehold interest, giving away a long lease which vests in possession in (say) 20 years time. Assuming that he is within para.3, i.e. that the arrangement does not involve a reservation of benefit, the taxpayer may wish to pay a full rent for his use of the land so as to avoid a POA charge (see Sch.15, para.4(1)). He may wish to make such payments under covenant. The difficulty is that the owner of the relevant land in this case appears to be the taxpayer and he cannot pay rent to himself. Hence if the deed of covenant route is to be pursued the donor will need to settle his freehold reversion (which gift will generally be protected from CGT by principal private residence relief) onto an interest in possession trust for himself. The "rent" payable under a legal obligation can then be paid to the trustees of the life interest trust. Of course after March 21, 2006 such new settlements will generally be chargeable transfers and unless the freehold reversion is worth less than the taxpayer's unused nil rate band an immediate inheritance tax charge will arise.

PLANNING POSSIBILITIES FOR REVERSIONARY LEASE SCHEMES

15–09 Despite the potential POA charge, both *Ingram* and reversionary lease schemes have a place in future inheritance tax planning. Before discussing this it is necessary to understand an inheritance tax change introduced in FA 2006, namely the insertion of the new s.102ZA into FA 1986, and the reservation of benefit provisions generally.

---

[26] Although see **14–10** for a few instances where the donor is not subject to reservation of benefit on a post-March 1999 *Ingram* scheme and therefore may be subject to POAT.
[27] It is thought that the same difficulties in respect of the "full consideration" exemption arise: see **14–17**.

Reservation of benefit generally

Rather surprisingly, neither s.102 nor Sch.20 (the reservation of benefit code) **15–10**
contains any definition of the word "gift". The 1984 Act has a definition in
s.42(1), but that is merely for the purposes of ch.III of Pt II of the Act (allocation
of exemptions). In the context of s.102 one might expect "gift" to mean "transfer
of value", and the word is used in that sense in subs.(5), which excludes various
exempt gifts from the gift-with-reservation rules. However, in the absence of any
specific provision for reservation of benefit, the word gift must be given its
ordinary meaning.[28]

Extension of "gift" to termination of an interest in possession

HMRC accept that prior to March 22, 2006 a termination by the trustees of a life **15–11**
interest was not a gift by the life tenant unless (possibly) the life tenant consented[29]
to such termination or (more likely) surrendered the interest himself. In other
words, on the inter vivos termination of a life interest in settled property, the
question whether the life tenant made a gift (or, in the words of s.102(1), "disposes
of property by way of gift") prior to the FA 2006 changes may have depended on
the way in which the interest was terminated.

Example 15.3

Under the Will of his father who died in 1999, A was life tenant of a house,
but the trustees had power, without A's consent, to terminate his interest and
transfer the house to his daughter. They did so in 1991, and A continued to
live there until his death in 1999. HMRC accept this was not a gift with
reservation. If, however, A had assigned or surrendered his life interest (for
instance because the trustees did not have the overriding powers to end his
interest), HMRC consider that A has made a gift "in the real world" and that
gift comprises the house. (It is far from clear that HMRC are right in this
view and the point is discussed further in *Trust Taxation* at 26.05.)

Changes in FA 2006

The "loophole" of a life tenant's interest being terminated by the trustees was **15–12**
used in a number of situations, including Will trusts where the surviving spouse
was left residue on interest in possession trusts and his interest was later
terminated (usually in the nil rate sum which was then held on discretionary
trusts). The surviving spouse could continue to benefit from the settled assets in
that trust but the property would not be taxed as part of his estate for inheritance
tax purposes so that if he survived for seven years the assets would pass onto the
next generation tax free.

---

[28] See IHTM 14315. See also the author's *Trust Taxation,* 2nd edn, 26.04 et seq.
[29] Although it is difficult to see how the giving of consent could be treated as a disposition of
property for the purposes of s.102(1); it is the subsequent advance by the trustees which is the
effective disposition.

All this changed following the amendments to FA 1986, s.102 inserted by FA 2006.[30] The termination of A's interest in possession after March 21, 2006 in Example 15.3 is now treated as a gift by A under FA 1986, s.102ZA. This section provides:

> "For the purposes of section 102 and schedule 20 the individual shall be taken...to dispose on the coming to an end of the interest in possession of the no-longer-possessed-property by way of gift."

The "no longer possessed property" is defined as "the property in which the interest in possession subsisted immediately before it came to an end...".

Hence the life tenant is deemed to make a gift for the purposes of the reservation of benefit rules. (Note that no attempt is made by the draftsman to change the reservation of benefit rules so that they are triggered by a transfer of value rather than by a gift.)

However, curiously s.102ZA does **not** treat the life tenant as making a gift for the purposes of s.102 A–C but only for the purposes of s.102 and Sch.20. Therefore it is possible for the trustees to implement *Ingram* schemes or alternatively carry out reversionary lease schemes even where the life tenant has not held the interest in possession for seven years. So long as A has made an adequate carve-out for general reservation of benefit purposes under s.102 purposes, the fact that the arrangement may be an *Ingram* scheme or otherwise caught by the s.102A legislation does not matter.

Example 15.4

A is the elderly life tenant of a trust set up by his father in 1985. He now wishes to reduce his estate for inheritance tax purposes. The trust owns a large country mansion worth £3m in which A lives.

In 2009 the trustees grant a reversionary lease to a nominee to take effect in, say, 17 years time and the reversionary lease is then appointed (by exercise of their overriding powers) to A's son. As a result of FA 1986, s.102ZA, A is deemed to have made a gift of the no longer possessed property. This involves a PET by A. The freehold interest is still held on interest in possession trusts for A. Either A has not made a gift for the purpose of s.102A or A has enjoyed a life interest for at least seven years so should be within the protection of s.102A(3). He is not a party to any arrangement given that it was the trustees who took away his interest. A reserves no benefit in the reversionary lease. He occupies by virtue of his interest in possession in the freehold which will decline in value.

15–13 A major advantage about carrying out a reversionary lease scheme within a trust structure is that no POA charge should arise provided that the person whose interest in possession is being (partially) terminated did not settle the property into trust and did not provide funds for the acquisition of the home by the trustees. In the above example, even if on termination of his interest in possession A has made a disposal of an interest in land for POAT purposes (which may be doubted) the value of what he has given away as life tenant has a small value being the right to receive rent after 17 years for the rest of his life.

15–14 In Example 15.4 the reversionary lease has to be appointed outright to the son (given that the transitional serial interest regime has now expired), otherwise A

---

[30] By s.156 and Sch.20, para.33(1)(2) and (4).

will be treated as making a chargeable transfer rather than a PET for inheritance tax purposes. Assuming that the son takes outright the inheritance tax and POAT advantages are the same as above, but there is a capital gains tax disadvantage since there is no main residence relief on the reversionary lease.[31] The result may be capital gains tax at 18 per cent on any gain on the reversionary lease when the property is eventually sold. On the other hand this may be viewed as preferable to 40 per cent inheritance tax in the entirety. The freehold interest retained by A the life tenant qualifies for main residence relief but of course is unlikely to show a gain.

As noted above, these arrangements are still relevant even if the qualifying **15–15** interest in possession arises after March 21, 2006 and even if the conditions in s.102A(3) are not satisfied (e.g. because the life tenant has not had a qualifying interest in possession in the house for seven years).

Where a husband leaves the family home to his spouse outright her options are limited in terms of inheritance tax planning if she wants to continue enjoying using the property. She can carry out a reversionary lease scheme inheritance tax effectively but faces a POA charge. By contrast if the husband leaves his spouse the family home in his Will on an IPDI trust, provided the trustees are given sufficient overriding powers, they can carve-out an interest which is retained by the spouse on the same IPDI trusts and they then appoint the valuable freehold interest or the long reversionary lease interest outright to the children. No POA issues arise.

It does not matter that the spouse has not had an interest in possession for seven years and has inherited the lease. Provided that the carve-out is effective for s.102 purposes this appears to be sufficient to avoid a reservation of benefit on termination of her interest in possession. Hence either an *Ingram* or a reversionary lease arrangement could be implemented. The spouse makes a PET and will hopefully survive seven years. The arrangement can be made over let properties as well as the main home. The main problem may be capital gains tax if there is a loss of main residence relief, but given the rate of 18 per cent this may be regarded as an acceptable price to pay.

Note, however, that where property is jointly owned so that the husband leaves **15–16** the wife only a share in the property, schemes such as *Ingram* and reversionary lease schemes are prevented. It is not possible to leave the surviving spouse an interest in possession in say half the house and then effect a reversionary lease scheme over that part!

---

[31] See **15–05** above.

CHAPTER 16

EVERSDEN SCHEMES

Background

16–01 *Eversden* arrangements were a prime target of the Regime with the Government intending that such schemes, in relation to both insurance bonds and the family home, should be caught. Indeed, the Paymaster General, Dawn Primarolo, may have had such planning specifically in mind when she talked about inheritance tax schemes involving the home being a "one-way bet" and having "no lasting effect" (see **1–06**).

It is certainly true that *Eversden* arrangements were often marketed on the basis that there was no real downside for the taxpayer. Unlike many of the other schemes involving the family home, such arrangements did not create "new" chargeable assets; there were generally no capital gains tax problems and there were few complications if the client wanted to move house. Moreover it was a scheme that most clients could understand, at least in principle, and it could be unscrambled relatively easily. The one limitation was that it only worked for married couples![32]

The facts of *Eversden*, the decision of the Court of Appeal and the amending legislation in 2003 preventing future *Eversden* planning are discussed at **2–13** et seq. In fact the inheritance tax changes introduced in FA 2006 stopped *Eversden* schemes anyway after March 21, 2006 because it is no longer possible to settle assets inter vivos on qualifying interest in possession trusts for the spouse.[33]

Eversden arrangements were first used mainly in relation to insurance schemes but became popular in relation to the family home after the decision in favour of the taxpayer in the High Court.[34] As with the home loan scheme discussed at **Ch.17**, demand was fuelled by the rise in house prices in recent years.

---

[32] The Civil Partnership Act had not come into force by the time the law had changed stopping *Eversden* schemes.

[33] Unless the spouse is disabled.

[34] [2002] STC 1109.

Who used these schemes?

The typical clients would be married with combined assets in excess of two IHT **16–02** nil rate bands. They would generally both be domiciled in the UK.[35] The house would usually be their most valuable asset but they may also have had some cash which they were prepared to put into trust provided they had the possibility of retaining access to the funds in the future.

Example 16.1

John and Emma are married and in their early 60s. They have equities worth about £300,000, an unmortgaged house in joint names worth around £800,000 and cash of about £200,000, in John's sole name. Their three children are all adult.

Eversden and insurance bonds

John was advised to transfer his cash (usually of an amount equal to his IHT nil **16–03** rate band) into an interest in possession trust for Emma. Emma took a qualifying interest in possession and therefore the transfer was spouse exempt. The trustees then invested the cash in an insurance bond, usually on the lives of both spouses and children with the intention of avoiding an IHT charge on the death of a spouse. The trustees were John's solicitors.

After six months, Emma's interest in possession over the bond was terminated (without her consent being required) and discretionary trusts arose. On the termination of her qualifying interest in possession Emma made a chargeable transfer of value but within her nil rate band so no inheritance tax was payable. John and his issue were members of the discretionary class of beneficiaries. The spouse Emma was sometimes excluded from benefiting from the insurance bond after termination of her interest in possession to avoid the possibility of her making a gift with reservation (see **16–18**).

The trustees could cash in up to five per cent of the bond each year without any income tax liability and could exercise their discretion to appoint the proceeds to John if he required funds.

By holding the assets in the bond structure, no income arose to be taxed on the **16–04** settlor under ITTOIA 2005, s.624,[36] and administration of the trust was easy. The settlor had the satisfaction of knowing that he had access to the cash at the trustees' discretion, yet the capital value of the bond would fall outside his and his wife's estates for IHT purposes. If Emma survived seven years she would have a full nil rate band available. If the bond was worth an amount in excess of her nil rate band then revocable qualifying interest in possession trusts for the children were often appointed (instead of a discretionary trust). Accordingly

---

[35] In order for the spouse/civil partner exemption under IHTA, s.18 to be fully available and therefore for FA 1986, s.102(5) to afford protection it was necessary for: (a) the recipient spouse/civil partner to be UK domiciled, (b) for both spouses/civil partners to be domiciled here, or (c) for both spouses/civil partners not to be domiciled here. Contrast this with the para.10 POAT exclusion for gifts between spouses/civil partners where the domicile of the recipient spouse/civil partner is irrelevant.

[36] Formerly TA 1988, s.660A.

Emma would then make a PET, not a chargeable transfer, when her interest ended.

16–05   The main disadvantage of such structures related to the inflexibility of the investment. Clients needed to have liquid assets to settle. The bond could be expensive to take out and generally could not be surrendered without a penalty. It was usually taken out with one company and problems could arise if the trustees later wanted to diversify.

16–06

Nevertheless, the scheme represented a relatively straightforward means of effecting IHT planning without the client feeling that he had lost control of the asset—precisely the sort of "have your cake and eat it" arrangements that the gifts with reservation rules were designed to stop.

Diagram of an "*Eversden* bond scheme"

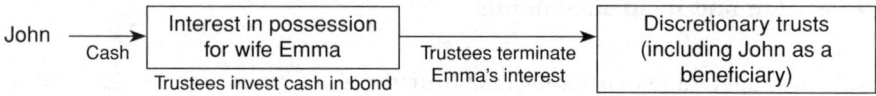

John — Cash → Interest in possession for wife Emma / Trustees invest cash in bond → Trustees terminate Emma's interest → Discretionary trusts (including John as a beneficiary)

EVERSDEN AND THE FAMILY HOME

16–07   Arrangements involving the family home were structured a little differently. Suppose that John transferred his half share in the family home on flexible qualifying interest in possession trusts for Emma. (All such interest in possession trusts were qualifying if established prior to March 22, 2006.) On termination of her interest in possession, one would want to avoid discretionary trusts arising since usually Emma would be making a chargeable transfer in excess of her nil rate band.

16–08   In addition, the comments of Lightman J. in *Eversden* at the High Court suggested that there could be IHT difficulties if discretionary trustees owned a share in a house, because of the implication that, at least in the case of any replacement property, the trustees had allowed the settlor into exclusive occupation and therefore conferred an interest in possession on her.[37]

16–09   Matters would generally therefore be arranged so that the spouse's interest in possession would be terminated only[38] in part—say as to 95 per cent—with her children then taking revocable interests in possession conferring rights of occupation (albeit they might choose not to exercise such rights).

---

[37] See further **16–14** where Lightman J.'s comments are set out and discussed.
[38] Such termination might occur automatically after a fixed initial period or be at the discretion of the trustees—there were pros and cons of each option.

Diagram of an "*Eversden* house scheme"

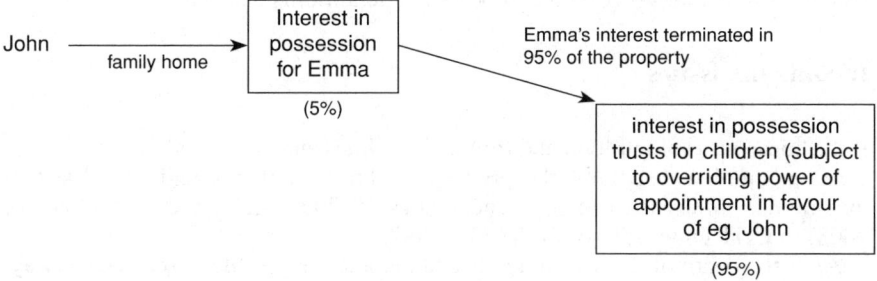

Capital gains tax issues

For CGT purposes, principal private residence relief was generally available **16–10**
under s.222 of the TCGA 1992 on the disposal of the house into trust by John.[39]
The termination of Emma's life interest by the trustees was not a disposal for
capital gains tax purposes since the property remained settled property within the
same trust. Similarly the beneficial interests could be rearranged within the trust
at any time without triggering a CGT charge.

On a sale of the house during John and Emma's lifetimes, there would be a
disposal by the trustees for capital gains tax purposes, but any gain arising on that
sale would qualify for principal private residence relief under s.225 of the TCGA
1992 because of the occupation of the property by a beneficiary of the trust. (The
capital gains tax treatment of trusts holding houses is discussed at **15–05**.)

In the above example, it was not necessary for Emma to have an interest in
possession in the entirety of the property for the trustees to benefit from principal
private residence relief.[40] That relief is available provided that she occupied the
house under the terms of the settlement (in this case by virtue of her 5 per cent
retained interest in possession).[41]

On the death of Emma, there would be a capital gains tax free market value
disposal and reacquisition by the trustees in respect of the portion of the house in
which her interest in possession subsisted.[42] There would be no CGT base cost
uplift on the balance but main residence relief would continue to be available if

---

[39] This assumes the donor had occupied the property as his main residence for the entire period of
his ownership bar the last three years and that the total area did not exceed half a hectare.

[40] See TCGA 1992, s.225.

[41] Although note that if Emma also owns a half share in her own right HMRC have been known to
argue that there is no PPR relief because she is occupying by virtue of her own beneficial share not
under the terms of the trust. The argument is that under the Trusts of Land and Appointment of
Trustees Act 1996 the trustees of the *Eversden* trust are not the trustees of the trusts of land but
trustees of a sub-fund holding the 50% beneficial interest and as such have no rights of occupation
themselves (see TLATA 1996, s.22). In these circumstances do the beneficiaries of the sub-fund trust
have rights of occupation? The position may be different depending on whether the beneficiaries of
the sub-fund are discretionary or interest in possession beneficiaries. It may be helpful to ensure that
the trustees of the *Eversden* trust are also registered as the legal owners of the property along with the
spouse.

[42] See TCGA 1992, s.72.

the house was sold within 36 months of Emma's death.[43] (In practice her five per cent interest in possession share was often left to John so that principal private residence relief would continue to be available until his death.)

Income tax issues

16–11 If the house was sold in John and Emma's lifetimes and cash or other investments were acquired with part of the proceeds, John as settlor would be subject to income tax on any trust income under ITTOIA 2005, s.624 and (until April 6, 2008) to CGT under s.77 of the TCGA 1992.

After the death of the settlor, gains and income are taxable in the normal way, i.e. income is taxed on the life tenants in their percentage shares and gains are taxed on the trustees at the rate of 18 per cent.[44]

PET on the clock

16–12 Once Emma's interest in possession has been terminated she made a transfer of value under IHTA 1984, s.52 and therefore needed to survive seven years for the full IHT savings to be secured. If it was decided to unravel the scheme because of the POAT Regime, the PET was still on Emma's clock. Hence the clients could not be placed in exactly the same position as they were in before any planning was done.

16–13 If Emma died within seven years of the termination of her interest in possession, the PET of (say) £380,000 (95 per cent of £400,000) would become chargeable and IHT payable. The tax has been triggered earlier than if no planning had been done (assuming that the spouse exemption would have been used on the first death). Usually this potential downside was covered by taking out seven-year term assurance on Emma's life to cover the possible failure of the PET.

Trusts of Land and Appointment of Trustees Act 1996

16–14 By retaining a five per cent interest in possession and, in practice, being in sole occupation with John, has Emma retained an interest in possession in the whole of the house? If so, that would make any concerns about reservation of benefit irrelevant.

This was an argument that HMRC sometimes raised in the context of both discretionary and interest in possession trusts, citing comments of Lightman J. in

---

[43] See TCGA 1992, s.223(2)(a).
[44] Since April 6, 2008.

Eversden[45] and s.12 of the Trusts of Land and Appointment of Trustees Act 1996 ("the 1996 Act") although the arguments were slightly different in each case

Discretionary trusts

In relation to discretionary trusts, HMRC's argument was that the trustees must **16–15** have taken the positive decision to allow a beneficiary to enjoy sole occupation of the property.

Interest in possession trusts

In relation to interest in possession trusts, HMRC sometimes argued that given **16–16** the provisions of ss.12 and 13 of the 1996 Act, a beneficiary who is excluded from occupation can have no interest in possession and that where a beneficiary occupies alone or jointly he has (respectively) either the entire beneficial interest or an equal beneficial share with the other occupant.

Analysis of s.12

There is nothing in ss.12 or 13 to suggest that where part of the land is held on **16–17** discretionary trusts and part is beneficially owned, the beneficial owner who does not pay a "compensatory" rent has an interest in possession in the entirety of the land even if he is one of the beneficiaries of the discretionary trust (in fact the provision for compensation in s.13(6)(a) is limited to payment to an interest in possession beneficiary who has been excluded from occupation by the trustees under s.13(1)). Nor does s.12 suggest that beneficial shares must be equal if beneficiaries have rights of occupation. It merely confers rights of occupation on an interest in possession beneficiary and permits the trustees to exclude one or more of them from occupation but it does not say that someone in occupation has

---

[45] Lightman J. commented as follows (see [2002] S.T.C. at para.27):

"On the sale of Beechwood (the property originally settled) the trustees held 5% of the net proceeds as bare trustees for the settlor and 95% on the trusts of the settlement. On receipt of the net proceeds of sale the trustees were legally obliged to pay over the 5% to the settlor. The trustees could not unilaterally decide to invest the 5% in any other property (whether alone or together with the remaining 95%) without the agreement of the settlor as beneficially entitled to the 5%. The trustees invested the full net proceeds of sale in the purchase of Meadows. In the absence of any evidence to the contrary, it is common ground that the trustees must be presumed to have acted lawfully and in accordance with their fiduciary duties (see e.g. *Billingham (Inspector of Taxes) v Cooper* [2001] EWCA Civ. 1041 at [32], [2001] STC 1177 at [32]). Accordingly it must be presumed that the trustees and the settlor agreed that the trustees should invest both the settlement's 95% of the net proceeds of sale and the settlor's 5% in the purchase of Meadows and the bond; and it must likewise be presumed (in the light of the law as it stood prior to the coming into force of the 1996 Act) that the trustees and the settlor agreed and intended that by virtue of her contribution of 5% of the purchase price the settlor should become entitled to a like right of occupation of Meadows as she had previously enjoyed in respect of Beechwood and that the purchase was made on this basis. This scenario entirely accords with the skeletal evidence before the commissioner, and most particularly the application of the settlor's money as 5% of the purchase price of Meadows (and the bond) and the subsequent occupation by the settlor of Meadows."

an interest in possession in the whole. In our example, as the children have rights of occupation, it is not thought that Emma retains an interest in possession in the whole property. It is the right to occupy rather than the fact of occupation which is determinative of whether there is an interest in possession.[46] In fact HMRC have not in practice pursued the interest in possession argument and in the authors' experience have accepted that pre-June 2003 *Eversden* schemes worked for inheritance tax purposes.

GWR implications of terminating Emma's interest

16–18 On the termination of her interest in possession Emma made a transfer of value for IHT purposes[47] which was normally a PET (if the children took qualifying interests in possession) and so free from IHT provided that she survived by seven years. It was accepted by HMRC , however, that (prior to March 22, 2006) she did not make a gift (so that the reservation of benefit provisions were not in point in the event that she continued to benefit from the settled property). Nor did she dispose of property so that the POA charge will not apply to her.[48]

THE ATTACK ON *EVERSDEN* SCHEMES: 2003 ONWARDS

16–19 There has been a three-pronged inheritance tax attack on *Eversden* schemes between 2003 and 2006 which makes future planning of this sort redundant. As far as pre-June 2003 schemes are concerned these can escape inheritance tax but will be subject to the POA charge.

The first attack came in 2003 and was targeted specifically at *Eversden* schemes. As discussed at **2–14**, as from June 20, 2003 it is no longer possible to avoid the gifts with reservation rules by granting an interest in possession to the settlor's spouse/civil partner and then terminating that interest. The effect of the legislation[49] is that on termination of the spousal interest in possession, the donor's disposal by way of gift is treated for the purposes of s.102 as having been made immediately after the spouse's interest came to an end.

Example 16.2

On August 21, 2003 Ben settles his house on qualifying interest in possession trusts for his wife Janet. Janet dies with the property passing to her children but Ben continues to live in the house. At the termination of Janet's interest in possession, Ben is treated as having disposed of the house by way of gift. Since he continues to occupy the property the gift infringes the reservation of benefit rules so that on his death (if he is still in occupation) the house will be taxed as part of his estate. If he moves out before his death his reservation of benefit has ceased and he makes a deemed PET.[50] Note that provided Janet's interest in possession is terminated prior to March 22, 2006, only Ben not Janet reserves a benefit. However, as Example 5.5

---

[46] See *Woodhall (personal representatives of Woodhall deceased) v IRC* [2000] STC (SCD) 558.
[47] IHTA 1984, s.52(1).
[48] The distinction between a gift and a transfer of value is considered in **15-11** and the effect of the amending legislation in FA 2006 is discussed at **15-12** et seq.
[49] IHTA 1984, s.102(5A)—(5C) inserted by FA 2003.
[50] Under FA 1986, s.102(4).

demonstrates, if Janet's interest in possession is ended after March 21, 2006, both Ben **and** Janet reserve a benefit, but under different anti-avoidance legislation!

What is the reservation of benefit position in relation to Ben? It does not matter that Janet's interest in possession ended on her death rather than as a result of the exercise of trustees' powers. The settlor is still alive, and therefore s.102(5A) applies. This is in contrast to the POAT Regime where the death of the donee spouse does not take away the protection of the spouse exemption.[51] Of course, if Ben dies before Janet's interest is terminated, s.102(5A) (and indeed POAT) will have no application.

The sort of arrangements made by Ben in *Example 16.2* may not have been **16–20** carried out in the context of IHT planning: Ben may, for instance, settle property on interest in possession trusts for Janet for asset protection reasons. If he does so, he needs to take care because if her interest is terminated the reservation of benefit rules will catch him if he then occupies the property or benefits from the trust. Furthermore, note that if the house is sold and the trustees hold cash or other intangibles then even if the spousal interest in possession has not been terminated Ben suffers a charge under the POAT Regime.[52]

Note that under the legislation the gift by Ben is only treated as being made on **16–21** the termination of Janet's interest for the purposes of the gifts with reservation rules. Thus he will not make an actual transfer of value at that time. Instead the transfer of value by Ben was made on the initial gift into trust for his wife and this was spouse exempt. IHT is charged on the death of the wife as if she had made a transfer of value equal to the value of the house in the normal way. Accordingly, if Ben ceases to benefit from the settled property before termination of Janet's interest in possession he has not made a deemed PET under FA 1986, s.102(4).

The second attack on *Eversden* schemes came in the form of FA 1986, **16–22** s.102ZA, introduced with effect from March 22, 2006. The loophole that made *Eversden* schemes possible was the fact that on termination of the spousal interest in possession by the trustees, the spouse was not treated as making a gift for reservation of benefit purposes and could therefore continue to benefit from the settled property. It would have made much more sense for *Eversden* schemes to have been stopped in 2003 by deeming the termination of the interest in possession to be a gift by the life tenant rather than trying to impose a retrospective reservation of benefit on the original settlor. In the event the Government eventually took this route as well in 2006 with the aim of preventing more widespread avoidance. Section 102ZA is discussed at **15–12**. Of course, it is not limited simply to terminations of a spousal interest in possession. Any termination of a qualifying interest in possession on or after March 22, 2006 will result in a deemed gift by the person whose interest in possession is being ended.

The practical effect of this is that if Janet's interest in possession ends after March 21, 2006, she is deemed for reservation of benefit to have made a gift of the underlying settled property. The result is that both she and Ben are treated as

---

[51] A gift on interest in possession trusts for the settlor's spouse is an excluded transaction unless that interest terminates inter vivos: see FA 2004, Sch.15, para.10(2)(c); 10(2)(b); and 10(3).

[52] See **Ch.6** (intangibles) and **Ch.5** (excluded transactions). Note the curious limitation on excluded transactions in that an interest in possession trust for the spouse is not excluded from the para.8 charge even while the spousal interest continues. So consider Ben's position: if the transfer of intangibles into a spousal interest in possession trust was made now, then if he can benefit from that trust he would still be caught by the POA charge even though no inheritance tax is saved. If the spousal interest in possession is ended during Ben's lifetime then Ben is caught by the reservation of benefit rules (due to s.102(5A)) and so there is no longer a POA charge!

reserving a benefit! *Example 5.5* sets this out in more detail. Note that s.102ZA can operate even though Ben set up the qualifying interest in possession trust for his wife before June 2003 provided that the termination of the interest in possession occurs after March 21, 2006.

16–23   The third attack on *Eversden* schemes was simply that from March 22, 2006 it was no longer possible to set up inter vivos qualifying interest in possession trusts for the spouse or civil partner. If the spouse does not take a qualifying interest in possession then s/he is not treated as beneficially entitled to the underlying settled property for inheritance tax purposes and no spouse exemption is available. If a gift of assets into an interest in possession trust is no longer spouse exempt under s.102(5) then the settlor is no longer protected from reservation of benefit. See examples at **5–13** onwards.

POST-EVERSDEN PLANNING

16–24   As noted in **Ch.2**, tax planners were not slow in responding to the anti-avoidance provisions in June 2003 and by November 2003 had begun to market "*Eversden* II" schemes. It was apparently rumours of these new schemes that finally prompted the Revenue to take a new approach to avoidance of the reservation of benefit provisions and to introduce the POA charge.

It is not felt by the authors that many of the post-*Eversden* schemes had merit, but partly for historical interest they are outlined briefly here. They tended to rely either on not terminating the spousal interest in possession (and thus avoiding the effect of s.105(5A)) or avoiding an initial gift of settled property to the spouse altogether. Some thought that the legislation was defectively drafted in relation to successive spousal interests in possession and gifts of undivided shares in property. The schemes have not survived the 2006 legislation. If they ever did work for inheritance tax purposes there will be a POA charge. Better estate planning options are now available which can avoid both reservation of benefit and POAT problems and these are discussed in **Ch.19**.

Scheme 1: Property not initially settled in favour of spouse by virtue of the gift

16–25   Under this scheme, H settled property on trust for himself for life, remainder to children. Prior to March 22, 2006, this was a qualifying interest in possession. H is excluded from the default trusts. There is no transfer of value at this point since H is treated under IHTA, s.49 as beneficially entitled to the settled property.

The trustees have overriding powers to end his interest. H assigns his interest to his wife (this is an exempt transfer). The trustees then (before 2006) exercised their overriding powers and trusts for the children took effect. The wife makes a deemed PET but the property does not **become** settled property by virtue of the gift to the spouse; it was already settled property. Reading subss.102(5A)(a) and (b) together it seems reasonably clear that the property must become settled property by virtue of the **initial** gift into the trust being for the spouse and therefore exempt.

HMRC could argue that there is a reservation of benefit on the basis that the initial transfer on interest in possession trusts for H is a gift by H albeit not a transfer of value. Of course, the Revenue's argument that the settlor makes a number of gifts into trust involving distinct interests was rejected in *Eversden* so that a gift of property into a qualifying interest in possession settlement cannot any longer be so divided (see **2–13**). The assignment by him to the spouse was a gift but an exempt gift and not within s.105(5A) for the reasons outlined above.

Scheme 2: Sale at an undervalue

This scheme involved a sale at an undervalue to avoid a disposal by way of gift. **16–26** HMRC regarded a sale at an undervalue as a gift to the extent of the undervalue.[53] The better view is probably that the property being disposed of by gift is the entire land but the same problem, i.e. that there has been a disposal by way of gift and therefore that the reservation of benefit rules apply, still arises.

Scheme 3: Avoiding a disposal of property by way of gift: unexercised option

A third scheme was that the taxpayer granted an option over the relevant asset to **16–27** either a nominee or, say, a trust for his benefit ("the First Trust"), on terms that the holder of the option was, within the next (say) 90 days, entitled to acquire the asset for a nominal sum. The asset would then be sold at its reduced market value into a trust ("the Second Trust"), under which the taxpayer's wife had a qualifying interest in possession, with remainders over on interest in possession trusts for the taxpayer's children. The wife's interest in possession would then be terminated and the option in due course allowed to lapse.

Alternatively, the option might be allowed to lapse before the wife's interest terminated. The idea was that there had been no gift as such to the Second Trust but a sale for full consideration taking into account the reduced value of the property.

The authors consider that the bona fides of the option, which was not intended to be exercised, would not stand up.

Scheme 4: Successive spousal interests in possession

A fourth scheme involved taking advantage of a perceived lacuna in the wording **16–28** of ss.102(5A)(c) and (d). The thinking was that:

(a) s.102(5A)(c), in referring to the "relevant beneficiary's interest in possession" appears to mean the spouse's initial interest in possession referred to in s.102(5A)(b); and

(b) s.102(5A)(d) provides that the conditions for the operation of ss.102(5A) are not satisfied if, on the "occasion on which that interest comes to an end" the spouse becomes entitled to another interest in possession in the same settled property.

Does "that interest" mean only the initial interest in possession of the spouse or does it include any successive interest in possession that the spouse takes? If the

---

[53] See discussion at **3–25** and IHTM 14316.

former interpretation is correct and the spouse was given two successive interests in possession such that s.102(5A)(d) applied then the condition in s.102(5A)(c) would not be satisfied when the first interest came to an end. The second interest in possession would not be caught by s.102(5A)(c) and therefore the gifts with reservation rules would remain disapplied by the spouse exemption in s.102(5)(a).

The authors never had a great deal of confidence in this approach. First, they considered that any court would be reluctant to uphold the schemes and would conclude that in s.102(5A)(c) "the relevant beneficiary's interest in possession" is not limited to the relevant beneficiary's initial interest but extends to any successive interest coming within s.102(5A)(d), with the result that the conditions in s.102(5A) are satisfied when the spouse's second interest in possession comes to an end, in which case s.102(5)(a) will not apply.

Even if the court accepted the existence of the lacuna, it would not be difficult for it to conclude that the arrangement in question failed to take advantage of it. Although it may be possible in theory to arrange for successive interests (it is not entirely clear what the closing words of s.102(5A)(d) contemplate: they effectively replicate and appear to be modelled on the closing words in IHTA 1984, s.53(2)), the court would be mindful of the fact that the sole purpose for inserting successive interests was to oust s.102(5A) and the authors would not be surprised if, in those circumstances, it was not prepared to accept the interests were genuinely successive.

Scheme 5: Gift of an undivided share in land

16–29 This scheme had the most merit. The basis for it is that a gift of an undivided share in land (to which FA 1986, s.102B applies) is not caught by the anti-avoidance provisions in s.102(5A)–(5C). This is because s.102C(2) states that:

> "an interest or share disposed of is not subject to a reservation under . . . s.102B(2) above if . . . the disposal is an exempt transfer by virtue of any of the provisions listed in s.102(5) above".

It is not clear that s.102C(2) requires that the availability of the spouse exemption under s.102(5)(a) is to be read as subject to the exception in s.102(5A).[54] On that basis, a person could before 2006 settle a share of his home upon qualifying interest in possession trusts for his wife for life with remainder to his children and occupy the house without reservation of benefit problems on the basis that s.102C(2) does not incorporate s.102(5A). The courts might well argue that the opening words of s.102(5A): "subsection 5(a) does not prevent this section from applying", nevertheless mean that s.102(5A) is incorporated into s.102C.

In any event the POA charge combined with the 2006 inheritance tax changes made all the above schemes, whatever their merits, redundant.

---

[54] Although the same point arguably applies in relation to gifts of interests in land under s.102A, given the fact that s.102B takes priority over s.102 but s.102 takes priority over s.102A (see s.102C(6) (7)) it might be thought that in relation to *Eversden* schemes this route will only work on gifts into trust for the spouse of undivided shares.

The purpose of the POA Regime is to ensure that "unacceptable" inheritance tax **16–30** schemes now have a downside—an income tax charge must be paid in exchange for preserving the IHT savings. *Eversden* schemes were certainly the sort of "have your cake and eat it arrangements" that the Government had in mind and in the authors' view are caught by the legislation. It is the very simplicity of *Eversden* schemes that has made them more vulnerable to attack under the Regime.

While new *Eversden* schemes were stopped from June 20, 2003, any arrangements already completed before that date are subject to the POA charge. (See **5–12** et seq for a series of examples on *Eversden* planning.) By contrast, the home loan scheme has still not been stopped by specific IHT legislation and even the 2006 inheritance tax changes have failed to close down the scheme altogether. The biggest deterrent to the home loan scheme appears to be SDLT. Furthermore as we explain in **Ch.17**, Sch.15 appears altogether less successful in imposing an income tax charge on home loan arrangements.

The effect of Schedule 15 on *Eversden* schemes involving the family home

In *Example 16.1*, John gave his interest in the house to Emma. John and Emma **16–31** continued to occupy the house. Emma's interest in possession was terminated as to 95 per cent. The trust was set up prior to June 20, 2003.

The requirements of para.3 of the Regime are prima facie met since:

(a) John continues in occupation of the house, and

(b) the disposal condition is met since he owned an interest in the house after March 17, 1986 and has disposed of the property.

Is there an exclusion?

Can John successfully contend that he made a disposal by way of an excluded **16–32** transaction and is therefore out of the POA charge?

Paragraph 10(1)(c) provides that in relation to the disposal condition the disposal of any property is an excluded transaction if it was a disposal by way of gift "by virtue of which the property became settled property in which his spouse . . . is beneficially entitled to an interest in possession". Note that this let out does not cover sales,[55] although presumably a sale at an undervalue would still be treated as a gift for the purposes of the exclusion to the extent of the undervalue with the balance being covered by the non-exempt sale provisions (see **3–25**).

When John made the disposal it was therefore an excluded transaction. However, para.10(1)(c) is more in the nature of a "safe harbour" than a total exclusion. Thus the disposal ceases to be an excluded transaction if the interest in possession of the spouse has come to an end otherwise than on death. In the

---

[55] See **5–11**.

above example, Emma's interest in possession was terminated while she is alive, and therefore John (not Emma) is subject to the para.3 income tax charge.

16–33   Note that if Emma now died, John would continue to be subject to the income tax charge because the interest did not terminate on her death. Contrast the position if Emma's interest in possession came to an end only on her death—in those circumstances the disposal remains an excluded transaction and there is no income tax charge.

This, of course, differs from the reservation of benefit position under s.102(5A) of the FA 1986: if John had made the disposal into trust on or after June 20, 2003, he is not protected from the reservation of benefit charge if Emma's interest terminates on her death although curiously while Emma's interest in possession continues, if the trust holds intangibles, John is subject to the POA charge. Hence before Emma's death he is subject to POAT and after her death he is not subject to POAT (because he is subject to a reservation of benefit).

16–34   In the first edition of this book the authors expressed the view that para.10(1)(c) protection might be available not only where the initial gift is into a trust where the spouse has an interest in possession but also where the settlor set up a trust say for himself for life and then to his spouse, and the spouse subsequently takes an interest in possession in settled property. HMRC have now explicitly stated in the guidance notes that their view is that the spouse needs to take the interest in possession from the start.[56] None of the other exceptions or indeed the para.11 exemptions would be applicable in the case under consideration.

Options in relation to the family home

16–35   What did most taxpayers do who entered into *Eversden* schemes involving the family home and what options remain open to them? There are a number of possibilities.

Option 1—avoid termination of the spousal interest in possession

16–36   If the spouse interest (in *Example 16.1* Emma's interest) had not been terminated by the time POAT was introduced the structure was often left in place with the spousal interest in possession intact. Nothing should now be done to end that interest in possession since this will be deemed a gift by the spouse (and therefore cause her reservation of benefit problems) as well as produce POAT problems for the settlor (in our example John).

If the settlor dies, then the spousal interest can at that point be terminated (in part) by the trustees. The POA charge will not apply to the spouse because she has not made a disposal of land[57] and it cannot apply to the settlor because he is dead. However, on the termination of the qualifying interest in possession the spouse must be excluded from the property in which her interest has ended otherwise reservation of benefit problems arise for the spouse (in the above example Emma). It would, however, be possible to do the sort of carve-out discussed at **15–12**.

---

[56] See A2.10.
[57] See **15–11**.

What happens if Emma dies with her interest in possession unrevoked? POAT can then never apply to the settlor because the exclusion in para.10 protects him permanently once the spouse has died. The spouse might want her share to pass back to the settlor on revocable interest in possession trusts to avoid an IHT charge on her death. This will be a transitional serial interest even if Emma dies after October 2008 because Emma took a qualifying interest in possession prior to March 2006 and her widower can take a qualifying interest in possession on her death. Can the trustees then carry out IHT planning at that point, terminating the settlor's interest without a reservation of benefit if he continues in occupation?

Prior to March 2006 this was possible, if the original gift into trust was made prior to June 20, 2003. The fact that the spousal interest and then the settlor's subsequent interest terminated after June 20 would not appear to have lost the settlor the original protection of s.102(5)(a). However, if the settlor's interest in possession is terminated after March 22, 2006 then he is deemed to make a gift for reservation of benefit purposes under s.102ZA irrespective of the fact that his initial gift into trust was spouse exempt. That subsequent deemed gift is not protected from reservation of benefit by the original spouse exemption. In these rare circumstances however it would be possible to do a carve-out of the sort discussed at **15–12** and the settlor should not be subject to reservation of benefit or POAT. Of course, this is long-term planning and depends on the settlor surviving the termination of his interest in possession (which he takes on the death of his spouse) by seven years.

Option 2—appointing back the house to the settlor or spouse

Suppose Emma's interest in possession has been terminated in 95 per cent of the **16–37** trust fund. Should the trustees appoint the house back to the settlor John or to Emma to avoid the POA charge? The authors' view is that the house should be appointed outright to the spouse rather than to the settlor. If the house is appointed back to the settlor there is a greater risk of a double IHT charge on the value of the house if the spouse dies within seven years of her PET.

Assume that Emma's interest in possession was terminated as to 95 per cent **16–38** prior to March 22, 2006 and the children now have revocable interests in possession as to 95 per cent. If the trustees revoke the children's interests and appoint back the 95 per cent to John and advance the whole property out (95 per cent to John outright and the 5 per cent retained by Emma to her outright), then the reverter to settlor exemption should be available so that the children are not treated as making PETs.[58] The trust has ended but there should not be any CGT payable because main residence relief is available under TCGA 1992, s.225.

However it must be remembered that Emma has already made a PET on the **16–39** termination of her interest in possession. There is potentially a double IHT charge if the property is appointed back to John outright and Emma dies within seven years of the PET.

Example 16.3

(1) John gave his house on trust for his spouse Emma in 2000. Her interest in possession was terminated as to 95 per cent in 2001 and the trustees

---

[58] See ss.53(3) (4) of the IHTA 1984 and **Ch.18**.

now hold that share on revocable qualifying interest in possession trusts for the children.

In 2009 the trustees revoke these interests and appoint the property back to John outright. No PET is made by the children. John no longer faces a POA charge because he is protected under the ownership exemption in para.11(1)(a). Note that if John was appointed an interest in possession in 2007 (which would be a qualifying interest in possession being a transitional serial interest) this would not protect him from a POA charge (see para.11(11) (12) and **7–24**). It is necessary for John to take outright for the ownership exemption to be available.

(2) Emma dies in 2007. The PET (the 2001 termination of her interest in possession) becomes chargeable. John dies in 2008. The full value of the property is taxed on his death. IHT has been paid twice on the same asset (albeit with some reduction in tax on the PET because Emma survived six years from making it).[59]

(3) Assume instead that John dies in 2005 after the property has been appointed back to him, leaving the property to Emma (i.e. he dies before her). There is no IHT on his death because of the spouse exemption. Emma then dies in 2007. Is relief available under the Double Charges Regulations?[60] The relevant regulation is reg.4. Although the property is back in Emma's estate she did not acquire the property from the transferee (the children) as is required under reg.4, para.3(a). She acquired it back from her husband. No double charges relief is due. The trust will be liable for IHT on the failed PET.[61] Emma's estate will be liable for any IHT due on the house.

(4) Suppose instead that the property is appointed outright to the spouse Emma rather than to the settlor John in 2009 when the children's interest in possession is ended. Reverter to settlor exemption is still available under IHTA 1984, s.53(4) to avoid a PET by the children. If the settlor dies before Emma there is no inheritance tax payable anyway. If Emma the spouse dies before John the settlor and before 2008 then the PET becomes chargeable but there is no further inheritance tax payable on her death because the house can pass back to John and will be spouse exempt. However, on John's death, inheritance tax will be payable with no allowance for the inheritance tax on the PET made by Emma. On the other hand, if Emma left her share in the house to her children on her death, double charges relief *would* be available on her death. In effect, there is one lot of inheritance tax and the property remains outside John's estate for inheritance tax purposes. Assuming the house does not increase in value significantly during the seven-year period after the PET, **the most *IHT* efficient** course would therefore be to appoint the house back to the spouse Emma and ensure that in her Will for the next seven years Emma leaves it to her children (or on trust for them with the settlor spouse as a discretionary beneficiary under an overriding power of

---

[59] Consider also the availability of quick succession relief: see IHTA 1984, 141.
[60] See SI 1987/1130 in **Appendix I**.
[61] The trustees should ensure that they retain sufficient assets in the trust to protect themselves against any liability for such tax.

appointment). However, does such an approach mean that POAT thereafter applies to the settlor (John)? In earlier editions of this book we suggested it might do so because the house is now owned by Emma outright and thus her interest in possession has ended. Paragraph 10(1)(b) provides an exclusion where property is transferred outright to a spouse initially. Paragraph 10(1)(c) gives protection where the house is transferred on continuing interest in possession trusts for the spouse. We suggested that the protection in para.10(1)(c) was lost if the spouse then took outright. However, HMRC now accept that in these circumstances the transaction remains excluded and John is not subject to a POA charge if Emma takes the property outright.[62]

Conclusion

In these circumstances appointing the property outright to the spouse avoids a **16–40** POAT charge but also minimises the risk of a double IHT charge if the spouse dies within seven years of the original PET.

There is no harm though in keeping the existing trust in place if the spousal interest in possession has not been ended. No POAT issues arise for the settlor. If Emma (the spouse) dies having retained the qualifying interest in possession there are long-term IHT advantages in ensuring that the house is appointed back to John (the settlor) on *interest in possession trusts* rather than to him *outright*. The reason is that John will not be subject to a POAT charge and the interest in possession he takes will qualify as a transitional serial interest.

This gives the trustees more flexibility in effecting future IHT planning by use of carve-outs. Such flexibility is lost if the property is appointed to the settlor outright.

Option 3—pay the income tax charge

In some cases the settlor was ill and therefore it was worth preserving the IHT **16–41** advantages and, if necessary, paying the income tax charge on an *Eversden* scheme. In these circumstances what tax will John pay? Assume the value of the house is £800,000. The rental value of the house is £25,000. John is charged on:

$$\frac{\pounds25,000 \times (DV)}{(\pounds800,000) \, (V)}$$

The unknown figure above is DV—what is the value of the interest disposed of by John? Despite the decision in *Arkwright*,[63] it appears that HMRC have not conceded the principle that IHTA 1984, s.161(4) has no application and that the value of a half share in a house owned by spouses is not necessarily a **mathematical one-half of the vacant possession value of the property**. In any event, there is nothing comparable to s.161 in Sch.15 and so the general principles of valuing a share (involving a discount) will apply.[64]

---

[62] See A2.09.
[63] [2004] EWHC 1720 (CH); [2004] STC 1323.
[64] See A2.77

If, say, the value of John's interest (DV) is discounted to £340,000 the chargeable amount on which he would pay income tax is £10,625, giving rise to a tax liability (for a 40 per cent tax payer) of £4,250 pa. In the circumstances this might be thought an acceptable price to pay to preserve the IHT advantage. However, the settlor cannot change his mind after January 31, 2007 and opt into the reservation of benefit rules.

16–42   Where the settlor is ill, likely to move out, can limit his occupation to a discrete part or become non-resident or the amount of income tax is relatively small and/ or the children are prepared to pay it[65] then it may be best to keep the structure in place.

Option 4—making the election

16–43   Should John make an election under para.21? (It is the settlor not the spouse who needs to make the election because he is the one liable to the charge.) Generally no. *Eversden* schemes are relatively easy to unravel. Making an election poses the same potential problems on double charges as mentioned above if the property is appointed back to the settlor and the spouse dies within seven years. However, there are two further significant disadvantages involved in making an election.

1.   The property remains part of the children's estate for IHT purposes. Remember that an election does not in any way alter the property law consequences of what has happened.

2.   There is an IHT charge on the property on the death of the settlor before the spouse. This could pose severe cash flow difficulties for the spouse.

16–44   The effect of the election is that the settlor has reserved a benefit in the property: it is not back in his estate for any other purposes. In these circumstances there can be no spouse exemption available on his death. The property is deemed to be comprised in his estate on death by virtue of s.102(3) of FA 1986.[66] But it is not actually comprised in his estate so does not pass under his Will. Hence if the children's interest in possession continues there is no spouse exemption. Even if the settlor elected and by the time the settlor had died the trustees had appointed the property on interest in possession trusts to spouse, it cannot easily be said that the value transferred on the settlor's death is attributable to property which "becomes" comprised in the estate of the spouse on the settlor's death because it is already comprised in the spouse's estate.[67] The trustees would be better appointing the property back to the spouse or settlor outright.

---

[65] See correspondence with Revenue as to GWR issues where donee pays income tax at A2.72.

[66] Any IHT payable is the responsibility of trustees.

[67] For the spouse exemption to apply, then one would have to treat s.102(3) as deeming two things:
a)   that the settlor has the property in his estate for IHT purposes, and
b)   that the spouse does not have the property in her estate.
It may be possible to take the deeming provisions so far but HMRC do not agree.

It may be that the property is not in fact held on interest in possession trusts for **16–45** the children but is held by them outright or the trustees could advance it to them outright. Until March 22, 2006, the children could then, if they chose, settle the property on reverter to settlor trusts for John in which he took a qualifying interest in possession. As set out in **Ch.18**, this avoided the POAT charge until the law changed in December 5, 2005 and protected the property from an inheritance tax charge on John's death. Such an option is no longer available.

EVERSDEN ARRANGEMENTS AND INSURANCE BONDS

In Example 16.1,[68] John settled £200,000 on interest in possession trusts for **16–46** Emma. The trustees invested the cash in a bond and Emma's interest was terminated with discretionary trusts arising from which John could benefit.

Suppose the bond is now worth £220,000. No encashments have been made but John is saving the bond for a "rainy day" when his pension ceases. He does not think he needs to worry about the bond—it is not land, he receives no benefit at the moment and it produces no income.

The difficulty is that para.8[69] will catch these arrangements. It provides that:

(a) where the terms of a settlement are such that any income rising from the property would be treated by virtue of s.624 of ITTOIA 2005[70] as the settlor's income, **and**

(b) where the trust holds intangible property (defined to include anything other than chattels and/or land) settled after March 17, 1986

then there is an income tax charge on the "chargeable amount". Paragraph 8 does contain an exclusion if the only reason why the trust is treated as settlor interested for income tax purposes is because the spouse has an interest.[71] However, any interest retained by the settlor, however remote, is sufficient to bring the trust within the scope of para.8. It does not matter that John has received no benefit from the trust and indeed that the settled property produces no income.

Paragraph 10 (excluded transactions) does not apply to exclude transactions **16–47** otherwise within the para.8 charge so even if the spousal interest has not been terminated, if the settlor can benefit from the settlement there is an income tax charge. So even those half way through *Eversden* schemes where the spousal interest has not yet been terminated will be caught by para.8.

Paragraph 9 imposes a relatively severe charge because it is calculated on the **16–48** basis of capital values rather than any actual income.[72] In the example the bond is worth £220,000. This will be treated as producing deemed or hypothetical income at the official rate of (currently) 4.75 per cent.[73] That produces £10,450 deemed income (probably taxed at 40 per cent in John's hands).

---

[68] See para.**16–03**, et seq.
[69] See generally **Ch.6**.
[70] Formerly TA 1988, s.660A.
[71] See FA 2004, Sch.15, para.8(1)(b).
[72] See further **Ch.6**.
[73] See **Ch.12**.

The trustees might encash the bond. That is a chargeable event which would trigger an income tax liability under ITTOIA 2005, s.461[74] on John. In those circumstances he can deduct (but not credit) that income tax against the £10,450,000 deemed income and he will then pay income tax on the lesser figure.

If the bond is retained it will have to be revalued at the start of each tax year. For most settlors an income tax charge based on a fixed percentage of capital value is likely to be unacceptable, particularly as it means annual valuations. Fortunately, there are greater opportunities to avoid the para.8 charge in relation to *Eversden* arrangements over bonds than there are over the home. Some of these are as follows.

Exclude settlor from benefit

16–49 If John, as settlor, is excluded from any benefit then there is no para.8 charge even if his spouse Emma still benefits. This is obviously not possible in all cases: for example, if the spouse has been excluded or has died. In the example, John is the member of a discretionary class of beneficiaries and he may also have a remainder interest in the settlement. If the trustees have an express power of exclusion they can exclude John and he can assign his remainder interest, e.g. to Emma. If the trustees do not have an express power of exclusion, then they will need to exercise their powers of appointment and exclude him under the terms of the appointment.

Move out of intangibles

16–50 Another option is for the trustees to move out of intangible property. There is no great magic about using the *Eversden* scheme with bonds—bonds were popular simply because such products did not generally produce an income tax liability for the settlor. However, if the trustees sell the bond and move into (say) let property, the trust is outside para.8 and the charge cannot apply. The settlor is not in occupation of the land so there is no para.3 charge. There may, of course, be tax payable on encashment by the bond.

Under this route both settlor and spouse can continue to benefit without POAT problems. Obviously the income produced by the letting will be taxable on the settlor under ITTOIA 2005, s.624 (formerly TA 1988, s.660A) but at least he is being taxed on actual rather than deemed income, and the amounts are likely to be significantly lower.

CONCLUSIONS

16–51 *Eversden* schemes involving bonds and family homes are subject to the POA charge. Unscrambling the scheme or waiting until the spouse dies may ultimately be the best course in relation to the home. For the insurance bond there are other options but they will often depend on the settlor being prepared to give up any possible benefit.

---

[74] Formerly TA 1988, s.547.

CHAPTER 17

HOME LOAN ARRANGEMENTS

SETTING THE SCENE

The home loan (or as it is sometimes called the "double trust") scheme was a **17–01** prime target of the Government when it introduced POAT. Although a "guesstimate", it has been suggested that as many as 30,000 of these schemes have been implemented. It was therefore the undoubted hope (and expectation) of the Government that the introduction of POAT would lead to taxpayers opting into the reservation of benefit provisions,[75] thus bringing scheme purchasers safely back into the IHT net. In fact surprisingly few elections have been made— apparently less than 5,000. Either home loans have been dismantled or other options have been pursued.

Unlike *Ingram* or *Eversden* schemes, no targeted inheritance tax legislation **17–02** has been enacted to stop home loans schemes: hence if a way round the POAT charge can be found they are still an attractive planning option. As noted at the end of this chapter and discussed further in **Ch.21**, a version of the home loan scheme is still being used in the case of transfers between spouses even after the inheritance tax changes in 2006: this does not involve trusts and can avoid a POAT charge. The main deterrent to the SDLT charge but the principle can be used to save inheritance tax in respect of other assets such as shares.[76]

But apart from SDLT and POAT there are three other reasons why inheritance tax planning is now less likely to be relevant to the family home: first the fall in house prices, secondly the introduction of the transferable nil rate band and thirdly the Conservative Party announcement that the nil rate band will increase to £1 million under a future Conservative administration. This means a couple may in the future be able to shelter up to £2m worth of assets before paying inheritance tax and it has undoubtedly reduced the incentive to consider complex or risky inheritance tax planning, particularly in relation to the family home.

As a matter of terminology it is proposed to call these arrangements "home loan schemes" rather than "double trust" schemes for the simple reason that whilst one trust has to be employed, the use of the second trust (to receive the benefit of the debt) was a matter of choice. If preferred the debt could have been given to (say) the taxpayer's daughter.

---

[75] These are considered in detail in **Ch.11**.
[76] The so-called "family debt scheme" is discussed in **21–30**.

17–03   There was no "single" home loan scheme: rather there were a number of variants. Also whilst many were sold as a package, others were bespoke.

WHO USED THE SCHEME?

17–04   The demand for the scheme was generated by the significant rise in house prices in the 1990s which was not accompanied by a corresponding increase in the IHT nil rate band. The result was that many individuals found that simply by virtue of owning a house, IHT would be payable on their death. The home loan scheme was a way of avoiding inheritance tax with apparently no significant downside or loss of flexibility. In particular the main residence capital gains tax relief was not jeopardised.

17–05   It is possible to present the following "profile" of a typical home loan client:

(a)   his house was worth at least £500,000 so that even if he had no other assets, IHT of over £50,000 would have been payable on his death;

(b)   he was in his 60s or early 70s and likely to survive for at least seven years since the scheme involved the making of a PET and hence, for its success, required seven-year survival. However, people who hoped to survive even three years were often prepared to enter into the scheme on the basis that at least some tax would be saved, particularly if the house continued to increase in value; and

(c)   it did not matter whether the property was freehold or leasehold but it was important that a disposal of the property would benefit from CGT main residence relief.[77] The existence of a mortgage on the property was a complicating factor.

Of course, other individuals used the scheme: persons in their early 40s (rather young to be engaged in heavy IHT planning) and persons who owned other substantial assets (and who thereby neglected the cardinal rule that using the main residence in any tax planning arrangement should always be the option of last resort). It is also fair to say that some elderly taxpayers who had no other inheritance tax planning options and might well die within seven years still entered into the scheme on the basis that "there was nothing to be lost".[78]

The structure of a typical home loan scheme

17–06   One of the difficulties in considering the effect of the pre-owned assets charge on home loan schemes is the variety of home loan schemes that have been carried out. This chapter will discuss a number of variants because the options for taxpayers in each case following the introduction of the POA charge were different.

---

[77]   As to the conditions for this relief, see TCGA 1992, ss.222–225.

[78]   In some cases the scheme was seen as a social accessory: "all my neighbours have one and therefore I want one!"

Example 17.1

Take for our typical taxpayer, Mischa, a widower aged 67 who owns a substantial property (worth £500,000 with no outstanding mortgage) in Rotting Hill. He wishes to leave all his assets in due course to his daughter, Sasha, who is married with young children. The house will benefit from full principal private residence relief for capital gains tax purposes and Mischa thinks that in a few years he might wish to relocate to Brighton and see out his days in the seedy glamour associated with that town.

Step 1: Mischa set up a life interest trust ("Trust 1") under the terms of which he was a life tenant with the right to enjoy the income of the trust or to enjoy the use of trust property. The trustees were given the usual modern flexible powers: e.g. to advance capital to Mischa or to terminate his life interest. The remainder beneficiaries of this trust were Sasha and her family. (Note that this was a qualifying interest in possession being set up prior to March 22, 2006.)

Step 2: Mischa set up a second trust ("Trust 2") for the benefit of Sasha and her family. As this trust received a gift from Mischa with a value in the region of £500,000 (the current value of his house) it was important:

(a) that Mischa was wholly excluded from all benefit under this trust; and

(b) that the gift made by Mischa qualified as a PET for IHT purposes— hence before March 22, 2006 the trust could be interest in possession or accumulation and maintenance in form it but not discretionary. Obviously the gift made by Mischa could be outright to his daughter Sasha if he so chose although this would be unusual. (If any home loan schemes are done after March 2006 the gift of the debt will now be outright because all gifts to inter vivos trusts will be chargeable transfers unless the beneficiary is disabled.)

Step 3: Mischa sold his house to the trustees of Trust 1; they did not have the cash to purchase the property so Mischa made them a loan to enable the transaction to proceed. In effect, the purchase price was left outstanding as a debt owed by Trust 1 to Mischa. (In some cases where a new house was being purchased Mischa might lend cash to the trustees of Trust 1 who would then purchase the new house.) It was the terms of the debt where the schemes tended to differ most markedly.

Step 4: The debt (i.e. the right to repayment in due course) is gifted by Mischa into Trust 2. Diagrammatically the position is as follows:

TRUST 1	TRUST 2
Owns property worth £500,000 and owes Trust 2 £500,000	Is owed £500,000 by Trust 1

TRUST 1	TRUST 2
Mischa is life tenant and hence can continue to live in the property. PPR relief will be available to the trustees under TCGA 1992, s.225	Mischa is excluded from all benefit—the beneficiaries are Sasha and her family

Miscellaneous technical points

17–07 The sale to the trustees of Trust 1 will now attract SDLT: prior to December 1, 2003 (i.e. in the (good old) days of stamp duty) duty could be postponed by resting in contract. This was not possible after November 30, 2003 so given that rates of duty are now 4 per cent above £499,999 the SDLT effectively killed off the home loan scheme for most taxpayers anyway after that date.

1. On Mischa's death the position is as follows:

    (a) he enjoys a qualifying pre-March 2006 interest in possession in Trust 1 and so is subject to IHT on the house (see IHTA 1984, s.49(1)). On these facts and if we assume no movement in the value of the property, because the debt will reduce the value of the house to nil, the result is that the net value of the property subject to IHT is nil (value of house exactly offset by debt owing)[79];

    (b) provided he has survived by seven years, the PET of the debt will be left out of account (i.e. it will be an exempt transfer); and

    (c) if Sasha was given an interest in possession in Trust 2 then her estate will include the value of that debt. Normally, therefore, her husband would be given a subsequent revocable life interest (with a view to taking advantage of the IHT spouse exemption). Alternatively, life insurance would be taken out to cover the risk of Sasha dying unexpectedly.

2. It was in the precise terms of the loan that the schemes varied so significantly:

    (a) in some cases it was an interest free demand loan;

    (b) in others it was interest free but repayable on the death of Mischa;

    (c) sometimes interest was payable and rolled up with the principal; in other cases the debt was indexed (e.g. by reference to a property index);

    (d) in some cases the loan was structured as a relevant discounted security but repayable on demand and in other cases as a relevant discounted security repayable only on the death of Mischa; and

    (e) one arrangement involved the use of a tripartite loan agreement between Mischa and the two sets of trustees, thereby avoiding the necessity for a separate assignment of the debt by Mischa. This might avoid certain capital gains tax problems on repayment of the debt to Trust 2 (given that the trustees of Trust 2 would not otherwise be the original creditor). This arrangement is discussed further in the context of the family debt scheme between spouses in **Ch.21**.

    In some cases the trustees of Trust 1 incurred no personal liability for the debt. It could only be satisfied out of the assets of the Trust Fund and the

---

[79] Generally the debt was not charged on the house in order to avoid problems with s.103 of FA 1986. For confirmation that the trustees' liability reduced the value of the trust fund which was treated as Mischa's property under IHTA 1984, s.49, see *St Barbe Green v IRC* [2005] STC 288.

trustees were not permitted to make distributions until the loan had been discharged. In other cases the trustees of Trust 1 did incur personal liability and the Trust Fund of Trust 1 was not specifically made subject to any lien.

HMRC's approach to home loan schemes

HMRC became aware of the existence of such schemes in the early years of this **17–08** century but so far no case has been litigated. The guidance notes (see A2.60) (after some initial hesitation) now confirm that HMRC will challenge those schemes where the debt is repayable on demand but in general will accept those schemes where the debt is repayable only on the settlor's death. This is on the basis that by failing to call in the loan before the death of the donor he has reserved a benefit in the debt by associated operations. The result (if this argument is correct) is that the debt is taxed as part of the settlor's estate on his death and the inheritance tax savings nullified.[80]

HMRC's arguments analysed

The argument is that by failing to call in the loan, the trustees of Trust 2 have **17–09** conferred a benefit on the settlor because he has thereby been able to continue living in his house (which otherwise would have to be sold to pay off the debt). One counter-argument to this is that many such on demand loans were structured so that if the trustees of the debt trust required repayment of the debt before the final repayment date (usually specified to be on a date equal to the likely life expectancy of the donor) they would only have been entitled to receive the face value of the loan and would have forfeited any rolled up interest. In other words the trustees of Trust 2 did much better for their beneficiaries if they waited until the donor's death. Are the trustees of Trust 2 required to act to their positive detriment in order to avoid a reservation of benefit problem for the donor?

The donor derives no benefit from the loan itself. If he derives benefit at all, it is from occupation of the house, which, on the basis of cases such as *St Aubyn v AG (no 2)*[81] should be regarded as property separate from the gift. In other words the benefit of occupying the house does not derive from the gifted property.

HMRC would therefore have to argue that the gift of the loan and the failure **17–10** to call it in such that the donor can continue to occupy the property are associated transactions. But is para.6(1)(c) of Sch.20 wide enough to deem the failure to call in the debt so that the donor continues to occupy the property (the associated operation) a benefit to the donor in the property disposed of (the gift of the loan)? If, as is thought, the benefit enjoyed from the associated operation must entrench in some way upon the possession of the actual gifted property in order for there to be a reservation of benefit, then it is arguable there is no problem even if the debt is repayable on demand. The benefit enjoyed by the donor is arguably not the failure to call in the loan as such but the occupation of the house and this does not in itself entrench on the gift of the loan. (The counter argument is that the

---

[80] Further it is arguable that the taxpayer is also subject to the POA charge: see **17–15** and A2.60.
[81] [1952] AC 15.

occupation of the house entrenches upon the gift because the trustees have failed to convert their debt into cash.)

17–11   Trusts provide all sorts of indirect benefits for donors which are not regarded as involving a reservation of benefit to the donor. For example, one might argue that a trust set up for the settlor's children and which pays their school fees, leads to a benefit being conferred on the parent donor which involves a reservation of benefit but HMRC do not argue this. Not all benefits remotely linked to the gift can be said to fall within the reservation of benefit rules.

17–12   It is by no means clear that HMRC are correct in their view particularly when the loan was structured so as to ensure that the trustees of the debt trust received far more if the loan was left outstanding until after the donor's death than if it was called in beforehand. Even where the debt was simply interest free and repayable on demand it is by no means clear that there is a reservation of benefit. No taxpayer has chosen to litigate this issue when the point has been raised by HMRC. A similar point crops up in relation to carve-outs and trusts and also in relation to insurance arrangements. For example, if a life tenant settlor has an income interest but the trustees have power to terminate his interest and do not do so, is a collateral benefit conferred on the life tenant? The point is discussed further at **Ch.19**.

Compliance issues for taxpayers

17–13   Even if there is a reservation of benefit in the debt, this does not necessarily mean that there is no POAT charge. The relevant property is the house and the donor has satisfied the disposal condition by the transfer into the interest in possession trust. Whilst the para.11(1) exemption applies the donor's estate is still reduced by an excluded liability so that the POA charge applies. Even if the donor has reserved a benefit in the debt, reservation of benefit property does not form part of the donor's estate for inheritance tax purposes while he is alive so that the debt as an excluded liability reduces the value of his estate.[82]

In summary:

(a) some home loan schemes may not work to save inheritance tax but there could still be an income tax charge under the POAT Regime;

(b) HMRC have so far challenged some home loan schemes and no taxpayer has chosen to litigate but the authors are aware that they have accepted that other schemes "worked";

(c) a taxpayer may decide to pay the income tax charge and preserve his inheritance tax savings. If he then discovers that there are no inheritance

---

[82] The effect of reserving a benefit in property is not that it is treated as part of the taxpayer's estate while alive but simply that it is taxed on the taxpayer's death. So under s.102(4) if the reservation of benefit ceases while he is alive the legislation does not say he is treated as ceasing to own it but rather deems a PET to arise (this is why a cessation of reservation of benefit in a discretionary trust is also a deemed PET). If the reservation of benefit ceases because of the donor's death then under s.102(3) the donor at the point immediately before death is deemed to own the reserved benefit property as part of his estate; this wording confirms that up to that point reserved benefit property is not part of his estate. As we will see this gives raise to both difficulties and opportunities. "Excluded liabilities" are provided for in Sch.15, para.11(6) and (7): see **17–47** below.

tax savings he is likely to feel aggrieved but he is unlikely to be able to recover the income tax paid[83];

(d) in the light of all this the taxpayer may decide to unravel the scheme.

This chapter now examines the following. **17–14**

1. Does POAT apply to home loan schemes?

2. Assuming it does, what options are now open to affected taxpayers?

3. What is the effect of making an election?

4. How best should the scheme be unravelled?

DOES POAT APPLY TO A HOME LOAN SCHEME?

The requirements of para.3 are met since: **17–15**

(a) the individual (Mischa: see *Example 17.1* above) occupies land; *and*

(b) the disposal condition is met given that he owned an interest in that land after March 17, 1986 and that he disposed of the property otherwise than by an excluded transaction.

There are five possible arguments against a POAT charge. In the authors' view **17–16** the second, fourth, fifth and sixth ones are the most likely to succeed.

1. The sale to Trust 1 was a transaction such as might be expected to be made at arm's length between unconnected persons: see para.10(1)(a). If it was such a transaction Sch.15 does not apply.

2. The sale to Trust 1 is a non-exempt sale: see para.4(4). If so, the imputed rent and therefore the tax charge will be nil (see para.4(2)).

3. The loan is not an "excluded liability".

4. The loan is an excluded liability but does not "affect" the house (see paras 11(6), (7)). If it is not such a liability the full value of the house is treated as comprised in the estate and the POA Regime does not apply (see para.11(1)(a)).

5. The charges do not apply when the house is sold and the trust holds cash or other intangibles.

6. The POA charge does not apply if the settlor lent cash to the trust, it then purchased a house occupied by the settlor. A loan of funds is not a provision of funds for the purpose of contribution condition and the disposal condition is not satisfied. The fact that the settlor subsequently assigned the debt to another trust does not seem to matter. See **3–11**, Example 3.3(d), **7–20** and *Example 7.14*.

Each of these arguments will be examined in turn.

---

[83] See **13–07**.

First argument: Is it an arm's length transaction?

17–17 The authors do not consider that the sale to Trust 1 would be protected as an excluded transaction.[84] It was a sale of Mischa's whole interest in the property but was it "a transaction such as might be expected to be made at arm's length between persons not connected with each other"? The sale has a number of features not present in a commercial sale (notably the deferment in the payment of the price/financing the arrangement by a vendor loan).[85]

Second argument: Is it a non-exempt sale?

17–18 A non-exempt sale is defined (in Sch.15, para.4(4)) as a sale of the individual's "whole interest in the property for a consideration paid in money in sterling or any other currency" which is not an excluded transaction: i.e. it is a sale at an undervalue. Mischa is certainly selling his whole interest to Trust 1 at an undervalue[86] but has consideration been paid? The answer may depend upon the particular scheme used: in cases where the consideration for the sale is satisfied by a sterling loan it is certainly arguable that because nothing remains payable under the land contract and the purchase price has been satisfied by the acceptance of a debt the requirement is satisfied.

17–19 What is the result if the non-exempt sale rules do apply? Given that the sale price will be equal to the then value of the house, "the appropriate proportion" will be nil (see the formula in para.4(4)).

Using Mischa as an example:

$$MV = £500{,}000$$

$$P = £500{,}000$$

Hence

$$\frac{MV - P}{MV} = \frac{0}{500{,}000} = 0$$

If that appropriate proportion is then applied to find the appropriate rental value (under para.4(2)) DV will be nil and so the rental value will be nil. See **3–25** for further comments on non-exempt sales. In previous editions of this book the authors suggested that one difficulty with this analysis was that the home loan scheme may well satisfy the contribution as well as the disposal condition in that an element of bounty has been "provided" to the trustees of Trust 1 which has enabled them to purchase the property. In that event the non-exempt sale provisions would give no relief. However, HMRC have now accepted that a loan is not the provision of consideration and does not satisfy the contribution condition. (See A2.05 and for further consideration of loans see **3–12**.) On that

---

[84] See Sch.15, para.10(1).

[85] An alternative way of viewing the home loan arrangement would be to see it as satisfying the contribution condition given that the loan is used to discharge the trustees' obligation to pay the purchase price. Arguably bounty has been "provided": see **3–10**. In that event the exclusion in para.10(1)(a) would not give protection from the POA charge anyway because this paragraph only affords an exemption from the disposal not the contribution condition.

[86] See **17–17**.

basis there is no POAT due because even though the disposal condition is satisfied the actual charge is nil.

Third argument: Is the debt an "excluded liability"?

As has been discussed elsewhere,[87] POAT will generally not apply if the property **17–20** is comprised in the individual's estate. Given that Mischa in our example is the life tenant of Trust 1 (which owns the property), it will form part of his estate for IHT purposes.[88] Doubtless realising that this would exclude the home loan scheme from the Regime, the draftsman of the POA legislation introduced the concept of an "excluded liability".[89] This is defined in para.11(7) as follows:

" a liability is an excluded liability if

    (a) the creation of the liability, and

    (b) any transaction by virtue of which the person's estate came to include the relevant property or property which derives its value from the relevant property or by virtue of which the value of property in his estate came to be derived from the relevant property were associated operations, as defined by s268 IHTA 1984."

Under para.11(6) if the value of Mischa's estate is reduced by an excluded liability "affecting" any property, that property is not to be treated as comprised in his estate. This provision is intended to operate in the following way. Assume that the value of the house is now £550,000 and the debt remains £500,000.

    (a) To the extent that the value of the property exceeds the amount of the excluded liability (£550,000 - £500,000) the exemption from the Regime in para.11(1) operates. This is consistent with the general scheme of the legislation since £50,000 will be included in Mischa's estate for IHT purposes; and

    (b) As to the amount of the excluded liability (£500,000), the Regime applies (in percentage terms to 90 per cent of the value of the house).

The above assumes, however, that the value of the excluded liability to be taken is the face value of the debt: see **7–20** for a consideration of whether it is the face value or the discounted value that is to be used.

The definition in para.11(7) limits an excluded liability to one where the **17–21** creation of the liability and any transaction by virtue of which the person's estate came to include relevant property. Arguably Mischa's estate included the property when it was sold to Trust 1, since it then became comprised in his estate under IHTA 1984, s.49(1). Given that Mischa had owned the house for a number of years, it might be said that selling the property to the trust did not affect Mischa's inheritance tax position (there was certainly no transfer of value at that time). However, even if the liability was a subsequent event wholly unconnected with Mischa's original acquisition of the property, the definition of an associated operation is in the authors' view wide enough to cover the debt.

---

[87] See **Ch.7** and Sch.15, para.11(1).

[88] See IHTA 1984, s.49.

[89] See **7–19** for the meaning of an "excluded liability".

Specifically, it does not matter that the creation of the debt was not in contemplation when the house was originally purchased. The operations can still be associated.

The meaning of associated operations

17–22 Operations are associated under IHTA 1984, s.268 if one of two heads is satisfied. Head (b) provides that where any two operations are effected with reference to the other they are associated. In this case the original purchase of the house by Mischa (the transaction by which it became comprised in his estate) was not done with reference to the creation of the debt because the purchase occurred many years earlier.

17–23 However, Head (a) provides that operations are associated if they affect the same property or one of which affects some property and the other of which affects property which represents directly or indirectly that property. The question in Mischa's case is whether these operations are over the same property: does the debt affect the house or represent the house? It is not charged on the house and it is not clear that it represents indirectly the house. The house is still there. On the other hand the debt would not have arisen if the house had not been sold and the debt is derived from the value of the house.

17–24 For IHT purposes, the operations need to form *part of a disposition* by associated operations and in the light of *Macpherson v IRC*[90] and *Reynaud v IRC*,[91] it is thought that a series of associated operations which are not connected in terms of intention cannot be part of a single disposition for inheritance tax purposes even under Head (a). One might also argue that the purchase of the house might be an associated operation but is not a *relevant* associated operation because it was not at that point intended to confer a gratuitous benefit—see *Reynaud* where the Special Commissioner said that an associated operation is relevant only if it is part of the scheme contributing to the reduction of the estate. However in that case the point was that it was the **second** associated operation which contributed nothing to the diminution of the estate which had *already* occurred.

In fact, one could argue in the context of the home loan arrangement that neither the creation of the debt nor the purchase of the house as such diminish the settlor's estate. What diminishes his estate is the gift of the debt. So it may be that neither of the operations listed in para.11(7) are in fact relevant even if associated!

17–25 However, the difficulty is that para.11(7) merely refers to associated operations under IHTA 1984, s.268 and an operation can be associated without being relevant for IHT purposes. For the purposes of the POA charge it is the association that is important and it is thought that the test of relevance does not apply.

Fourth argument: If the debt is an excluded liability does it affect the value of the relevant property— namely the house?

17–26 There is only a problem under POA if the liability "affects" the property and it might be argued that the property is only affected if the debt is charged on the

---

[90] [1988] STC 362.
[91] [1999] STC (SCD) 185.

property or otherwise impacts on its nature or value. So if the debt was given outright to an individual or a company, it would not affect the property unless secured.

Example 17.2

Cate lends cash to a wholly owned company (interest free) which purchases her house. She retains the debt. The company's liability is an excluded liability within the para.11(7) definition but since that liability does not affect the house, the excluded liability rule does not apply. Cate has made a disposal of the property which is not an arm's length excluded transaction. The company shares and loan are in her estate and derive their value from the house. Therefore the value of the relevant property is in her estate and no POA is due.

If Cate sells the house to an interest in possession trust for herself and gives away the loan (as would normally happen in a home loan scheme) then is the house "affected" by the debt? In the authors' view the answer is yes.

In almost all cases the liability is unsecured. However, in many home loan **17–27** schemes the trustees are expressly made liable only in their capacity as trustees and in that capacity have specific recourse to the assets comprised in Trust 1: i.e. against the house. The trustees have a lien over the trust fund. It is therefore difficult to argue that the house is not in some way "affected" by the liability.

In some home loan schemes the trustees are personally liable and there is no specific recourse to the assets comprised in Trust 1. It may then be argued more strongly that the property is not affected by the liability although the trustees would still have a right of recourse to the assets of the trust and therefore arguably the property is still affected by the liability.

Fifth argument: It cannot apply to intangibles

In some cases the house will by now have been sold and the trustees of Trust 1 **17–28** will merely hold cash and securities, i.e. intangibles. In these circumstances if the settlor retains a qualifying interest in possession and the settled property is subject to debt owed to the children or to another trust, HMRC will argue that the para.9 charge applies, i.e. the intangibles charge. However, for the reasons outlined in **6–11**, the authors consider that the settlor has not "provided" any of the settled property to Trust 1 (other than possibly £10) and therefore the charge cannot apply once the house has been sold.

Conclusion on the applicability of the POAT Regime

What might have seemed obvious—that the Regime will catch home loan **17–29** schemes—turns out on consideration to be much less certain. Of course, it will be surprising if the Regime does not apply (given that such schemes were a principal target) and it is likely that the legislation will be amended in the future if it proves to be defective. Nevertheless, there is sufficient doubt to mean that some taxpayers may take the view that they will self-assess on the basis that POA income tax is not due. If they do this then they would want to put full disclosure of their reasons in the white space of the tax return so that the Inspector was made aware of any "insufficiency" and the taxpayer is protected from a discovery assessment. Taxpayers should not take this option unless they are prepared to argue the point out with HMRC and ultimately be prepared to pay the income tax if they lose.[92]

OPTIONS OPEN TO TAXPAYERS

17–30   If the POAT Regime does apply to taxpayers who entered into a home loan scheme (and as indicated above there are a number of reasons why it might not do so), what are their options now? The table at the end of this chapter summarises the main options. Any discussion can only be of a general nature given that so much will depend on the particular scheme adopted by the taxpayer but the following general points should be noted. It is assumed in all cases that the home loan scheme was effected prior to March 22, 2006.

Option 1: Pay the income tax and/or consider repaying (part of) the loan

17–31   Before taking any decision, the taxpayer should calculate the POA income tax charge that will be payable if he does nothing <u>and</u> the Regime applies. This means obtaining a market value for the house as at April 6, 2005; identifying the amount of liability and obtaining a rental value of the house at that time. There is then no need to carry out any further valuations until April 6, 2010. Rental values are currently low and therefore the income tax charge may not be as large as feared, particularly if a discounted valuation for the excluded liability is taken. If the property has a high capital value but needs modernisation then the rental value may be relatively low.

Example 17.3

A, a higher rate taxpayer, effected a home loan scheme in 2003. The house is now worth £1 million with a rental value of £40,000. The loan's face value is £800,000 but its commercial value given that it is not repayable until A's death is £400,000.

A's income tax charge for the year 2005/6 (and thereafter until the tax year 2010/11) will be £40,000 reduced by the amount of property still in his estate. If the value of the excluded liability is £800,000 this means that 80 per cent of the market rent is the deemed benefit, i.e. £32,000 = income tax of £12,800.

If the value of the excluded liability is £400,000 then only 40 per cent of the rent is taken as the taxable benefit, i.e. £16,000 giving an income tax charge of £6,400. If part of the loan is paid off during the five years then a revaluation of the loan is made (and POAT reduced accordingly), but the land is not revalued.

The authors consider that the correct view is that the excluded liability is £800,000 and this point has been agreed with HMRC.[93]

---

[92]   See **Ch.13**.
[93]   See A2.59

A may decide to pay the annual income tax charge. This will be particularly attractive where he is likely to move out of the house soon or become non-UK resident or he is in ill health and does not think that he will live long.

One point to bear in mind is that if the annual rental value of A's land is less than **17–32** £5,000 (£10,000 for a married couple) the de minimis exemption applies and A is not subject to POA income tax at all.[94]

In order to reduce the annual taxable benefit A might be able to repay part of **17–33** the debt owed to the Debt Trust. For example, by adding cash to the Property Trust so that the trustees repay enough of the debt to reduce the taxable benefit to within the de minimis levels. In Example 17.3, for instance, if the debt was reduced to £125,000 the benefit enjoyed by A reduces to £5,000.

Any inheritance tax savings are preserved but A has to find funds to repay the debt. Those monies would need to be paid by A into Trust 1 for the trustees of that trust to effect partial repayment of the debt owed to Trust 2.

A disadvantage of repayment is that it may trigger an income tax charge on the children's trustees (Trust 2) to the extent of any profit realised if the loan is a relevant discounted security or has provided for interest to be rolled-up. Moreover since March 22, 2006, any addition of funds to either the Property or the Debt Trust is a chargeable transfer by A.

Could the donees, who stand to benefit from any IHT savings, pay the income tax on A's behalf? Does this cause a reservation of benefit problem?

This question was asked of HMRC and the correspondence is contained at A2.72. HMRC have confirmed (both in relation to home loan and other schemes) that there is no reservation of benefit if the donee puts the donor into funds to pay the income tax liability on schemes undertaken before the Regime was introduced provided that the income tax is not paid out of the property originally given by the donor.

Option 2: Unscrambling the scheme

There are a variety of ways in which a home loan scheme could be unscrambled. **17–34** Much will depend on how the debt was structured.

(a) Unscrambling scheme if loan note not an RDS— assignment of the debt

For the debt that is not a relevant discounted security it may be possible to **17–35** unscramble the entire arrangement.

The basic scheme involves the benefit of the debt being assigned to the settlor (or settlors if a married couple effected the scheme) and aims to qualify for double charges relief in the event that one of them dies within seven years of the gift of the debt.

---

[94] For de minimis, see **Ch.9**.

Stage 1

17–36 If the benefit of the debt is transferred to the children outright by the trustees of Trust 2 who assign it back to the settlor(s) each child will make a PET. To avoid this, the trustees of Trust 2 (the children's trust) appoint the capital value of the debt to the children (who already have interests in possession) contingent on their being alive in (say) 21 days. During the 21-day period the children assign their benefits under that appointment to the settlor(s). (Note that the children retain their existing qualifying interests in possession which will terminate only when the contingency is met after 21 days.) So far as the children are concerned this assignment will not have adverse tax consequences since:

(a) for IHT the assignment is of a reversionary interest (viz a future interest under the settlement) which is excluded property[95];

(b) for CGT purposes the disposal is of an interest under a settlement on which, as a result of TCGA 1992, s.76(1), no chargeable gain accrues unless Trust 2 is non-UK resident.

The making of the appointment by the trustees will not have any tax consequences. There will, of course, be consequences when the condition is satisfied.

Stage 2

17–37 At the end of 21 days the settlor(s) becomes absolutely entitled to the debt which is then owed by the property trustees (Trust 1) to the settlor(s). The Children's Trust (Trust 2) has ended as a result of the appointment. Although the children's qualifying interests in possession have terminated there is no charge because of reverter to settlor relief. This relief is still available even after March 22, 2006 provided the settlor(s) take absolutely. The debt is not at this point written off. If the settlor were to die within seven years of having entered into the home loan scheme the position (after Stage 1 and Stage 2 have been effected) is as follows:

(a) he is taxed on the value of the house in Trust 1 less the value of the debt which is owing by those trustees. Hence any tax charge will be limited to the growth in value of the property above the amount of the debt;

(b) in addition the benefit of the debt is in his free estate and accordingly taxed. However, reg.4 of the 1987 Double Charges Regulations will prevent there being a charge on both the failed PET of the debt and on the debt itself which is comprised in the settlor's estate.[96]

17–38 The end result is that the scheme has been unscrambled and whilst the settlor has obtained no IHT advantage he has not suffered any IHT double charge.

The tax consequences of Stage 2 are as follows.

(a) The children's interests in possession in Trust 2 have ended with the absolute vesting of the trust property in the settlor. This does not involve

---

[95] For the definition of excluded property, see IHTA 1984, s.48(1)(3).

[96] Note, however, that relief will not be available unless the gifted property is received back from the original transferee: hence problems may arise if the debt trust was originally A-M in form or if the interests in possession were originally held by different beneficiaries.

the children in making a PET because of the availability of reverter to settlor relief.[97]

(b) On the ending of the debt trust no CGT charge will arise provided that the debt falls within TCGA 1992, s.251(1) (which provides that no chargeable gain arises on its disposal).[98]

Diagrammatically this unscrambling arrangement is as follows.   **17–39**

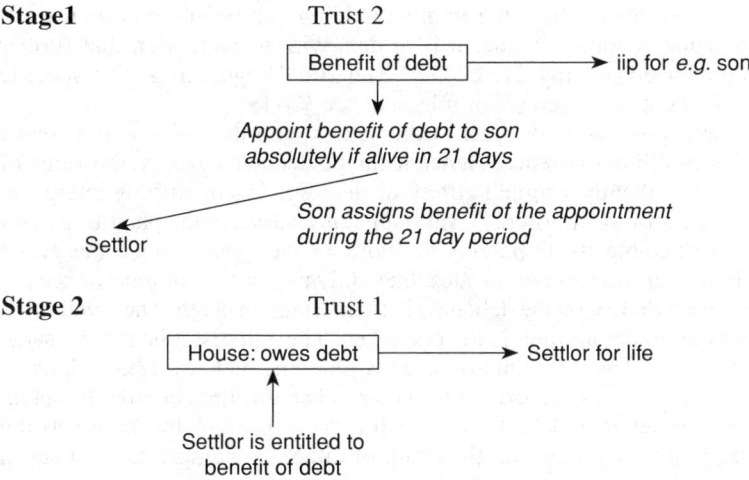

Stage1   Trust 2

Benefit of debt ⟶ iip for *e.g.* son

Appoint benefit of debt to son
absolutely if alive in 21 days

Son assigns benefit of the appointment
during the 21 day period

Settlor

Stage 2   Trust 1

House: owes debt ⟶ Settlor for life

Settlor is entitled to
benefit of debt

The structure can then be collapsed. Before March 22, 2006 this could have been   **17–40** done by (i) the settlor releasing the debt to the trustees of Trust 1 and (ii) the trustees subsequently appointing the house—free of debt—to the settlor absolutely.[99] From March 22, 2006 it is arguable that the release of the debt owed by the trustees of Trust 1 (who hold the house) is a chargeable transfer for inheritance tax purposes although the authors consider that this is wrong: the release of a debt is not an addition of property to the trust but has merely made the settled property, in which the existing interest in possession subsists, more valuable. However, HMRC do not take this view. On that basis even after seven years the debt should not be written off in favour of the trustees of Trust 1. The trustees should first advance the house to the settlor subject to the charge and only then should the debt be written off. In order to avoid SDLT the settlor must take on no personal liability for the debt.

So far as the POA charge is concerned once the debt is back in the settlor's   **17–41** estate even if it remains outstanding the excluded liability (viz the debt which affects the house) does not reduce the value of the settlor's estate so that the POA charge will not apply.[100]

---

[97] See IHTA 1984, s.53(3), and on reverter to settlor trusts generally see **Ch.18**.

[98] This is where the various schemes differ: if the debt had been assigned to the trustees of Trust 2, for instance, so that they are not the original creditors then any gain (and, of course, it may not be standing at a gain) may be chargeable. If the debt is a relevant discount security, its transfer may trigger an income tax charge.

[99] For SDLT beware FA 2003, Sch.16, para.7.

[100] Sch.15, para.11(6). It is thought that for these purposes the settlor's estate must be looked at "in the round": viz as the aggregate of the settled property and his free estate (contrast the approach adopted in *St Barbe Green v IRC* [2005] STC 288).

17–42 The problem of the double charge can best be illustrated by an example. Suppose the children do not assign their interests in the debt to the settlor but simply write it off and the settlor dies within seven years of the original gift of the debt. In that event the PET the settlor made becomes chargeable and inheritance tax is due on it. However, the house is now fully chargeable to inheritance tax since the debt has ceased to exist. So in effect the family could end up paying inheritance tax twice on the same economic value. It is to deal with this situation that further relief was announced on July 21, 2005.[101] The 2005 Regulations give specific relief where the debt is written off or released: see **17–45**.

17–43 If the children give the debt back to the settlor who then dies within seven years, the debt is still in existence. Hence it can be deducted against the value of the house provided that the original gift of the debt was to a qualifying interest in possession trust for those children.[102] Although it is an asset of the parents' estates which becomes taxable if the parents die within seven years, since the gifted property is now back within their estates, they only pay one lot of inheritance tax either on the failed PET or on the debt now in their estates at death. The calculation that produces the higher amount is the one taken. The end result is that the same inheritance tax is paid as if the inheritance tax planning had never been done. If the home loan scheme was carried out by a married couple then in order to obtain double charges relief it will be necessary for them to leave the house to the children <u>rather than each other</u> on the death of either of them in the first seven years from the original gift.

(b) Unscrambling scheme if loan note is an RDS—write off of debt

17–44 If the loan note is an RDS then the above method of unscrambling may involve income tax charges for the debt trustees if the RDS shows a profit on assignment. In some cases it has been structured in such a way as to avoid a profit arising.[103] However, if income tax is a problem then unscrambling is likely to involve the following steps.

(a) Vary the Debt Trust so that only adults are beneficiaries.

(b) The trustees with the concurrence of the beneficiaries release or write off the RDS. After March 22, 2006 a release of the debt in favour of the trustees of Trust 1 may be considered a chargeable transfer rather than a PET by the children.

---

[101] See **Ch.12** and Inheritance Tax (Double Charges Relief) Regulations SI 2005/3441; reproduced in **Appendix I**.

[102] See reg.4 and reference to transferee in reg.4(3). The debt must come back from the original transferee (deemed to be the children who take qualifying interests in possession) in order to obtain double charges relief.

[103] For instance, if the RDS is limited to the value of the trust assets and the house has not increased in value since the assignment of the debt then there will be no taxable profit. A commercial valuation of the RDS should be undertaken. If only repayable on the death of the taxpayer any taxable profit is likely to be small.

The analysis of these steps is as follows.

(a) Although a breach of trust the release is voidable rather than void and thus unable to be upset as the beneficiaries have all concurred in it. It is possible that minor beneficiaries who have been excluded may bring proceedings later.

(b) The release avoids an income tax charge on the RDS interest accrued to date.

(c) The release of the RDS means that there is no liability affecting the property with the result that Sch.15 no longer applies (para.11(1)).

(d) The POA charge between April 6, 2005 and the date of release may be avoided by the £5,000 de minimis exemption (Sch.15, para.13) if the release is effected before the notional rent exceeds £10,000 (when husband and wife have jointly entered into the scheme so that two £5,000 exemptions are available).

(e) Once the release is effected, the property will be fully eligible for the spouse exemption on the death of the settlor and any other "normal" inheritance tax saving measures.

(f) Prior to March 22, 2006 the children made a PET resulting in the termination of their qualifying interests in possession equal to their share in the value of the debt. They needed to survive seven years. For write offs occurring after that date HMRC consider that the children make chargeable transfers if the write off of the debt is in favour of the trustees of Trust 1.

17–45 What happens if the settlor fails to survive seven years from the date of the original gift? Originally there was a risk of a double charge to inheritance tax on the value of the property where the debt was released rather than assigned back to the settlor. However, double charges relief is available under the 2005 Inheritance Tax Regulations (2005/341)[104] if the original donor dies within seven years of the gift of the debt and the following conditions are satisfied:

(a) the disposal or contribution condition is satisfied and the donor has made a transfer of value as a result of which a third party becomes entitled to the benefit of the debt owed to the deceased;

(b) before the donor has died the debt is wholly written off or released;

(c) the donor dies on or after April 6, 2005;

(d) on the donor's death, the house (or substitute property) is included in the donor's estate.

The Regulations calculate (i) the inheritance tax due on the donor's death ignoring the gift of the debt and (ii) the inheritance tax due on the donor's death including the PET but ignoring the value of the house. The higher charge is taken.

Example 17.4

A enters into a home loan scheme. He sells his house to the trustees of Trust 1 for £1m and gives away a debt of £1m to his children in 2003 but since it

---

[104] Set out in **Appendix I**.

is only repayable on his death the commercial value is £800,000. In 2005 the children write off the debt. He dies in 2007 when the house is worth £1.4m leaving everything to his spouse. HMRC will tax the PET of £800,000. If his spouse later dies the house is chargeable in full.

However, if A had left his house to a discretionary trust with his spouse remaining in occupation then HMRC would have taxed the house on his death but ignored the gift of the debt. On the spouse's death no further tax would have been payable.

The regulations only give relief if the entire outstanding debt is written off. Partial releases will not be sufficient. Moreover, as noted above it is rare for the debt to be written off now anyway because of the inheritance tax problems this may cause after 22 March 2006.

Option 3: Election

17–46 This is the route the Government has offered as a way of avoiding the POA income tax charge. However, despite Government assurances, the effect of the election is far from clear. This was discussed **Ch.11** and is considered further below.[105]

Option 4: Pay rent under a legal obligation by setting up a deed of covenant

17–47 The taxpayer uses the let-out in Sch.15, para.4(1) and makes payments under a legal obligation equal to the appropriate rental value in respect of his occupation. Note that the legislation does not refer to payment of *rent* as such. The taxpayer could therefore enter into a deed of covenant and agree to pay to the property trustees a sum equal to the market rent of the property for so long as he remains in occupation. The sums paid do not suffer income tax in the hands of the recipient trustees. Otherwise the structure remains unchanged.

   In connection with this arrangement note:

   (a) that it is considered that payments under the deed are not rent: they are voluntary payments outside the income tax net[106];

   (b) because the payments are to the Property Trust in which the payer has a life interest prior to March 22, 2006, there was no transfer of value for IHT purposes. After that date such payments made under any new covenant are chargeable transfers unless they can be paid out of surplus income in which case they are exempt[107];

   (c) if the payments are not rent (viz not paid as consideration for the occupation of the property) CGT principal private residence relief will not be affected.[108]

---

[105] See **17–53** et seq.
[106] See ITTOIA 2005, s.727.
[107] See IHTA 1984, s.21.
[108] See generally *Sansom v Peay* [1976] 3 All ER 375.

Option 5: Reverter to settlor trust

This involved reorganising the Property Trust in an attempt to preserve the inheritance tax savings but to avoid an income tax charge. The use of this arrangement to avoid a POAT charge was arguably stopped by FA 2006, s.80, although the position is not free from doubt in some cases (see below). However, even if such planning still works for POAT purposes if done after March 22, 2006, it will involve immediate chargeable transfers for inheritance tax purposes. **17–48**

The restructuring could be complex but essentially involved the following.

1. The settlor surrendered his life interest in the Property Trust to his children so they became entitled to qualifying interests in possession. He was excluded as a beneficiary of the Property Trust; he paid a market rent for his continued occupation.

2. The Children's Trust then appointed the benefit of the debt (owed to it by the Property Trust) to the Property Trust which now had the same beneficiaries. Alternatively the Children's Trust wrote off the debt.

3. Subsequently, the Property Trust then appointed the house to the children absolutely (the house of course was free of debt and so SDLT was not in point).

4. The children then decided to resettle the house (free of debt) on a new third trust being a reverter to settlor trust for the settlor under which he took a qualifying interest in possession (Third Trust).[109] The idea was to ensure that the ownership exemption in para.11(1) was available to protect the settlor from a POA charge.

Note the following. **17–49**

1. If a child died within seven years of settling the house into the Third Trust his failed PET became chargeable.[110]

2. The new structure was vulnerable to legislative changes. These came in the form of an announcement that with effect from December 5, 2005 where property had ceased to be comprised in the settlor's estate and then became comprised in it again by being settled in a qualifying interest in possession trust the settlor was not protected from a POA charge. The ownership exemption was in effect disapplied. This change was enacted in FA 2006, s.80 and is discussed in **Chs 7, 8** and **11**.

However, curiously s.80 would appear not to catch those reverter to settlor trusts where the house remained held on interest in possession trusts for the settlor throughout and the trustees simply advanced the debt to the children who then resettled it on reverter to settlor trusts for the settlor. In these circumstances the excluded liability continues but no longer reduces the value of the settlor's estate given that under the reverter to settlor trust the debt forms part of his estate. The relevant property held on reverter to settlor trusts is not the house but the debt and the debt was never originally

---

[109] It will be appreciated that this restructuring could only be contemplated if the children were adult and were independently advised.

[110] Note the general advantage and pitfalls of reverter to settlor trusts in **Ch.18**.

part of the settlor's estate at all. Hence the ownership exemption is not disapplied under s.80.

3. The new reverter to settlor trust could only hold the house or other real estate rather than cash or equities, otherwise the children faced a POA charge. Children could not occupy the house.

4. HMRC could challenge the arrangement on the basis that it involves unacceptable tax avoidance, was circular and the children were not really the settlors.

5. The appointment of an RDS to the Property Trust or to the children was likely to cause income tax problems if it showed a profit.

As noted above, such reverter to settlor arrangements are not possible after March 21, 2006 given the inheritance tax changes.

Option 6: Reorganise the Property Trust

17–50 A less radical option was to restructure the Property Trust alone. The Trustees would terminate the settlor's interest in say 75 per cent of the Trust Fund which then became held on revocable qualifying interest in possession trusts for settlor's children. (Again this planning was not feasible once the period for creating transitional serial interests had expired on October 5, 2008.) The appointment in favour of the children was revocable. The settlor was not wholly excluded from future benefit.

Full CGT principal private residence relief continues to be available on the basis of the settlor's occupation of the property as a beneficiary of the trust.

The POA charge applies to the settlor but only on that portion of the rental value attributable to his interest retained and with the possibility of limiting the size of the share so that the benefit falls within the £5,000 de minimis exemption.

On the 75 per cent share now held for the children, it is arguable that a benefit has been reserved by the settlor and so under Sch.15 para.11(3) the POA charge is inapplicable. Reserved benefit property is not affected by the "excluded liability" provisions which do not apply to para.11(3). Hence the POA charge does not apply on the 75 per cent share.[111]

17–51 The above analysis depends on the settlor being treated as having reserved a benefit in the 75 per cent share. On the settlor's death what happens? The reservation of benefit rules treat the settlor as beneficially entitled to the property at that time. Nothing is included in the legislation to deal with the valuation of that property and it is therefore thought that general principles will apply and that it is only the net value of the property which is included in his estate.[112]

17–52 Bear in mind that the children enjoy interests in possession in 75 per cent of the property and in general terms have a right to occupy it.[113] Of course they may not exercise that right and it is not thought in such a case that the settlor would be treated as having an interest in possession in the entirety. Of course the position

---

[111] This of course involves applying the reservation of benefit let-out to part only of the relevant property. It also involves apportioning the excluded liability between the retained and appointed funds.

[112] See further in the context of the election, **17–54**.

[113] See TLATA 1996, s.12.

would be strengthened if the settlor made a "compensating payment" to the children to reflect his sole occupancy.[114] This would be sensible: the settlor does not want to be treated as having an interest in possession in the whole because otherwise he suffers a POA charge on the whole Trust Fund.

Option 7: Change the nature of the settled property

If the settlor ceases to occupy the house, e.g. it is let or the property is sold and the trustees then hold intangibles, no POA charge should arise. The para.4 change on land does not apply to let property and the para.9 charge on intangibles should not apply to home loan schemes, given that the relevant property has not been "settled".[115]

MAKING THE ELECTION

The mechanics involved in the making of an election have been considered in **Ch.11**. In the case of home loan schemes a key matter to bear in mind is the time limit: for a scheme in existence on April 6, 2005 which is within the POA charge, the deadline was January 31, 2007 (subject only to the point made in **Ch.11** that the necessary regulation had not been passed[116]). After that date HMRC consider that it will not be possible to elect although as explained in **Ch.11** the authors consider that a later election is not only possible but necessary to be valid. The effects of making the election are considered below but the intention behind the legislation is clear: by electing the taxpayer shall bring himself within the IHT reservation of benefit rules so that on his death the property occupied will be taxed as part of his estate.

17–53

Does the s.102(3) condition apply?

The legislation[117] provides as follows:

17–54

  (a) if an election is made the POA Regime shall not apply;

  (b) s.102(3) and (4) of FA 1986 shall apply;

  (c) s.102(3) deals with the situation where on the death of the taxpayer there is property in which he has reserved a benefit and provides that, for the purposes of the IHT charge, the taxpayer is to be treated as beneficially entitled to that property immediately before his death; and

  (d) however, s.102(3) only applies to the extent that the property "would not, apart from this section, form part of the donor's estate immediately before his death".[118]

---

[114] See TLATA 1996, s.13.
[115] See **6-11**.
[116] See **11-13**.
[117] Sch.15, para.21(2)(b).
[118] Curiously this limitation on the operation of s.102(3) is not included in s.102(4), which imposes a deemed PET when a reservation ceases inter vivos.

17–55 When the election is made and s.102(3) applies does the restriction continue to apply, i.e. where the taxpayer makes the election can his executors in due course successfully argue that because he had a qualifying interest in possession the property already formed part of his estate at death so that a charge to IHT will not arise under the reservation of benefit rules? The wording in s.102(3) does not impose any restriction for excluded liabilities.

The first argument is as follows.

17–56 The draftsman has throughout the Regime expressly adopted the IHT legislation to give effect to the Regime. Where an election is made, the legislation simply provides, without stating anything more, that the property in question (i.e. the land) is to be treated as property subject to a reservation and ss.102(3) and 102(4) are to apply. Had it been intended that s.102(3) were to be read as though important words had been excised from it, one would have expected the draftsman to provide as much. In the absence of express provision, it is hard to justify applying s.102(3) one way under the normal rules and another way when the taxpayer elects for it to apply under the Regime. On that basis making an election has no adverse inheritance tax effect.

The counter-argument in favour of HMRC which was outlined in earlier editions of this book was as follows:

17–57   (a) para.21(2)(b) provides that, if the election is made, the chargeable proportion of the property is to be treated as property subject to a reservation; and

   (b) s.102(3) shall apply.

However, the amendments made in FA 2006, s.80 (to stop reverter to settlor schemes) expressly state that the chargeable proportion of the property is to be treated as property subject to a reservation of benefit and s.102(3) shall apply *but only so far as the chargeable person is not beneficially entitled to an interest in possession.* On that basis, the additional words in italics seem to reinforce the argument above that making an election has no adverse effect for inheritance tax purposes because the reservation of benefit provisions are disapplied by s.102(3) and the taxpayer is simply treated as holding an interest in possession in the property with a deduction for the debt.

17–58 The IHT 500 form hardly helps because it refers to an election in respect of the land—there is no suggestion that the election is in respect of the debt itself which would make more sense in the context of home loan schemes.[119]

What value is included in the taxpayer's estate if s.102(3) applies?

17–59 A further problem in considering the effects of the election is as follows: s.102(3) provides that the taxpayer is to be treated as beneficially entitled to the property in which he has reserved a benefit immediately before his death. Nothing is said about how that property is to be valued but presumably normal IHT principles

---

[119] See further **11–22.**

apply.[120] It is therefore thought that liabilities affecting the property (e.g. the debt owed by the trustees of Trust 1) fall to be deducted and it is only the net value which falls into the IHT net. In practice this may result in a relatively small value being clawed into the IHT net.[121] This argument would be strengthened if the property were to be made subject to an express charge for the amount owed (see IHTA 1984, s.162(4): "*a liability which is an incumbrance on property shall, so far as possible, be taken to reduce the value of that property*").

Summary

There are two arguments that the election protects the chargeable person from a **17–60** POA charge but has no adverse effect for inheritance tax purposes. The first is that the taxpayer continues to be treated as holding a qualifying interest in possession in the house, the reservation of benefit provisions are therefore disapplied, and the debt is still deductible. Alternatively the taxpayer is treated as reserving a benefit in the home but the debt is deductible against that reserved benefit property.

If either analysis is right it may be concluded that there is no IHT cost in making the election. However, there is one respect in which this is not so, for under the GWR rules, the ending of a reservation inter vivos is treated as a PET, without regard to beneficial entitlement (FA 1986, s.102(4)). Accordingly a deemed PET would technically occur if the settlor(s) ceased to benefit from the settled property, e.g. if his interest in possession was ended and he moved out of the property.

Double charges relief

Under the original terms of Sch.15 the election could result in double tax. This **17–61** was because the gift of the debt to the Children's Trust was a PET and yet the election resulted in the full value of the property (without deduction for the debt) being in the estate of the settlor.[122] This potential double charge was addressed by reg.6 of SI 2005/724.[123]

Further considerations flowing from the election

There is a question mark over whether the spouse exemption will apply to the **17–62** extent of the debt or only the net value of the property will attract the spouse

---

[120] The wording used is similar to that in IHTA 1984, s.49 which treats an interest in possession beneficiary as being "beneficially entitled to the property in which the interest subsists". Again nothing is said expressly about liabilities but in practice they have always been allowed so that the net value of the trust fund is taxed. This was accepted as correct in *St Barbe Green v IRC* [2005] STC 288.

[121] HMRC consider that personal liabilities of the taxpayer cannot be offset against the value of reservation of benefit property. The point discussed in the text is quite different and goes to the question of how to value the reservation property.

[122] This, of course, assumes that the defects identified above in connection with the election are wrong.

[123] See further **Ch.12** where the regulation is considered in detail.

exemption. The authors consider that full spouse exemption should be available on the basis that the deceased's share in the house becomes comprised in the survivor's estate as IHTA, s.18 requires. This is so even if the value of the debt equals or exceeds that of the house. If this is wrong then the effect of the election for married couples is that there will be an accelerated inheritance tax charge on the death of the first rather than the last spouse.[124]

17–63   An election can only be made if tax under Sch.15 is otherwise chargeable. This, inter alia, precludes an election if the notional rent attributed to the settlor is less than £5,000 per year. It also precludes election if in fact no income tax is due because the POA Regime does not apply to home loan schemes anyway.

17–64   If an election is made it cannot be revoked after the deadline for an enquiry into the tax return has ended or the death of the settlor if earlier.

17–65   If an election is made, bear in mind that the children still have the debt in their estates. The result is that the children may suffer an inheritance tax charge if they die. This is of course the normal result of the GWR legislation.[125]

Property schemes today

17–66   Old style home loan schemes in respect of the taxpayer's dwelling house will not be entered into today in the same form as previously: first, because of the very real risk of a pre-owned assets charge, secondly, because of the SDLT charge (rates up to four per cent and no more resting in contract) and thirdly because of the 2006 changes to the inheritance tax treatment of trusts. However, other possibilities remain (see **Ch.21**).

Variants of a home loan between spouses are discussed at **21–30**.

SUMMARY OF HOME LOAN SCHEME OPTIONS

17–67

Options	Advantages	Disadvantages
Option 1: Unscramble RDS scheme Debt Trust assigns debt to children contingent on surviving 21 days and children assign remainder interest to settlor. No further POAT once excluded liability comprised in settlor's estate. Property Trust advance the property out to the settlor(s) subject to the debt but without the settlor taking on any liability.	1. Settlors back in original tax position but only after 7 years. Original PET may become chargeable but double charges relief available. 2. No POA income tax charge once debt in settlor's estate compliance issues, etc avoided.	1. IHT savings lost but future less controversial; IHT planning may still be possible. 2. Children must be adult and agree. 3. Care needed to avoid SDLT. 4. Possible capital gains tax and income tax issues on assignment of debt.

[124] For HMRC's view on the availability of the exemption, see A2.90.
[125] See **2–23**.

Options	Advantages	Disadvantages
Option 2: Pay income tax/do nothing	1. IHT savings preserved.	1. Compliance issues on valuation but only every 5 years.
	2. Taxable benefit may be within de minimis exemption. Otherwise income tax payable unless taxpayer takes view that debt does not cause POA problem because not an excluded liability or is fully protected as a non-exempt sale.	2. Election time limit missed unless de minimis excludes benefit from charge.
	3. No disturbance to current structure.	3. May end up with no IHT savings and income tax payable if HMRC successfully argue reservation of benefit.
	4. Client may die, become non-resident or move out in which case no need to argue point anyway, i.e. family circumstances may change. Trustees may sell house.	4. Annual income tax charge may erode IHT savings.
	5. Defers decision until more information is available and there may be further changes in legislation. Future action can still be taken.	
	6. Settlor may become non-resident later or die. Preserves flexibility on IHT planning.	

Options	Advantages	Disadvantages
Option 3: Election	1. No POA. 2. IHT savings arguably preserved due to defective legislation. 3. No continuing compliance issues once election made. 4. No double charge if death within 7 years.	1. Fiscal uncertainties e.g. as to whether spouse exemption available on first death of married couple. 2. Defective legislation may eventually be corrected by Revenue and IHT savings lost. 3. Structure remains in place with debt still outstanding. Scheme not unravelled. Future IHT planning options very restricted. 4. Debt remains part of donee's estate for inheritance tax purposes.
Option 4: Move out and let/sell home or go non-resident	1. Preserves IHT position. 2. No POA. 3. Sensible if parents have another home or intend to move abroad soon. No major legal restructuring required.	1. Major disruption to lifestyle. 2. Settlor pays tax on rent received if home let and income from securities. 3. No point if settlor has to rent elsewhere. 4. Restriction on principal private residence relief after 3 years of absence.
Option 5: Settlor enters into deed of covenant agreeing to pay oroperty trustees fixed sums for his occupation under legal obligation for as long as he occupies	1. No POA. 2. IHT savings preserved. 3. Arguably no income tax on payments under deed of covenant. 4. No major restructuring required.	1. Compliance— disclosure, valuations needed. 2. Payments under covenant must actually be made and may be taxable as rent. However, after expenses this may be less than paying the POA income tax. 3. Covenant payments are chargeable transfers after March 21, 2006.

Options	Advantages	Disadvantages
Option 6: Reorganise property trust Parent settlors reserve benefit and trustees appoint revocable interest in possession trust to children as to (say) 75% subject to charge in favour of family trust. Home still held in one trust. Debt remains in Family Trust.	1. POA payable only on 25%. 2. IHT savings may be preserved. 3. Parents can benefit from 75% fund in future if needed. 4. CGT principal private residence relief preserved.	1. Parents may be treated as having interest in possession in whole and therefore POA not saved. 2. Technical IHT analysis difficult— parents have reserved a benefit but value in what they have reserved is still reduced by the charge. Not possible to do after October 5, 2008 because children cannot take qualifying interests in possession. 3. Difficult if married couple. No spouse exemption so IHT on first death if deduction argument wrong. 4. Current debt structure remains in place. 5. Compliance issues on valuation of 25% in parents' estates— continuing POA valuation every 5 years needed.

CHAPTER 18

REVERTER TO SETTLOR TRUSTS

18–01 Reverter to settlor trusts were very popular until 2006. They were seen as a tax efficient way of providing for an elderly relative and were also regarded as a means of maximising principal private residence relief in an era of rising house prices. However, during the course of 2005, as the scope of the POA legislation became clearer, they were used for more controversial purposes as a way round the POA charge. Two blows were struck against reverter to settlor trusts: the first was the Government announcement that with effect from December 5, 2005 legislation would be passed to prevent reverter to settlor trusts being used as a way of avoiding POAT. This was enacted as FA 2006, s.80. The second blow came in the form of the wide-ranging IHT changes introduced in FA 2006, Sch.20, which generally prevented inter vivos trusts being set up with a qualifying interest in possession except for disabled trusts. Although trusts can still be used to give a relative some financial security in a tax efficient way and so as to maximise private residence relief, the options are more limited and do not generally involve reverter to settlor trusts.

This chapter first discusses the pre-2006 tax treatment of reverter to settlor trusts before considering the effect of the FA 2006 changes.

WHAT IS A REVERTER TO SETTLOR TRUST?

18–02 A trust which attracts the IHT reverter to settlor relief involves the following ingredients.

(a) The trust fund is held on a qualifying interest in possession trust (note that property held in a discretionary trust can never benefit from reverter to settlor relief although it could have done so if the trust had been converted into an interest in possession trust before March 22, 2006). This means the trust must either have been an interest in possession trust prior to March 22, 2006 or the beneficiary taking the interest in possession is disabled so that the interest is a qualifying interest in possession.

(b) On the termination of the qualifying interest in possession (whether during the lifetime of the beneficiary or on his death) the trust fund reverts to **either**:

(i) the settler; **or**

(ii) the settlor's spouse/registered civil partner during his lifetime; **or**

(iii) the settlor's widow or widower/surviving civil partner within two years of his death.

(c) The reverter could be absolutely or (prior to October 6, 2008) on interest in possession trusts. After October 5, 2008 the trust property must revert absolutely to the settlor or spouse/civil partner/widow, etc. in order for reverter to settlor relief to be available.

I   The Tax Position Prior to March 22, 2006

Inheritance tax position

IHTA 1984, ss.53(3) and 54(1) provided that IHT was not chargeable on the **18–03** termination of an interest in possession (whether on the death of the beneficiary or otherwise) if, when the interest came to an end, the property in which the interest subsisted reverted to the living settlor. Additionally, reverter to settlor relief applied where the settled property reverted to the spouse or civil partner of the settlor while the settlor was alive or to the widow/widower or surviving civil partner of the settlor within two years of his death.[126]

The result, if these conditions were satisfied, was that:

(i) IHT was not chargeable if the interest in possession ended during the lifetime of the beneficiary[127]; and

(ii) on the death of the beneficiary the value of the settled property was left out of account in determining the value of his estate immediately before his death.

Example 18–1

Angela set up a trust in 2000 for her father Fred for life reverter to Angela absolutely on the death of Fred or on earlier termination of Fred's interest. The trust owned the house in which Fred lived as his main residence. Fred died in 2005 and the property passed back to Angela.

(i) The creation of the trust was a PET by Angela.

(ii) There was no IHT on the death of Fred as the property then reverted to Angela.

(iii) If, instead, the property had reverted to Angela's spouse while Angela was alive or to her widower within two years of her death, there would still be no IHT payable on the ending of Fred's interest.

(iv) However, if Angela died while Fred was still alive, the trust fund had to revert to Angela's widower within two years of her death in order to secure the relief.

---

[126] See IHTA 1984, s.53(4) and s.54(2).

[127] Hence the ending of the interest in possession was not a potentially exempt transfer: see IHTA 1984, s.53(3); 53(4).

18–04 The exemption was often used when children wanted to provide for their parents or for other elderly relatives. In the above example, CGT principal private residence relief was available to the trustees if the house was sold during Fred's lifetime. This would not have been available if the house had been owned by Angela and she simply allowed Fred to live there under licence. The reverter to settlor relief could also be useful where a settlor wanted to make provision for a minor child but wished to ensure that if the child died before becoming absolutely entitled, the funds would revert to him. Additionally, the trust was sometimes used in a matrimonial context where one spouse wished to provide for a former spouse but wanted to retain a long-term interest in the assets being transferred. Finally, the exemption was sometimes used in the context of "s.102B sharing arrangements" to deal with the problems that arose if the donee moved out.[128]

18–05 The exemption was only applicable at the point when the settled property reverted to the settlor. Thus if property was settled on trust for A for life, then to B for life with a reverter to the settlor, C, there was no IHT on the death of B when the property reverted to C but there would have been IHT (subject to the availability of any other reliefs, such as the spouse exemption) on the death of A when it passed in trust for B.

Restrictions

18–06 The IHT relief was *not* available if:

(i) the settlor (or spouse/widow/widower, etc. as the case may be) had acquired a reversionary interest in the property for a consideration in money or money's worth. This restriction was extended to catch the situation where the settlor acquired the reversion as a result of transactions "which include a disposition for such consideration (whether to him or another) of that interest or of other property";[129]

(ii) the relief depended upon a reversionary interest having been transferred into a settlement on or after March 10, 1981.[130]

The first qualification was designed to prevent tax being avoided in the following way.

Example 18–2

Assume that Sol settled property on trust for Bill for life some time ago remainder to Bruce. Bill is elderly. The property settled is worth £500,000 and Bruce's reversion is worth £200,000. But for the above qualification the tax that would otherwise have been payable on Bill's death could have been avoided by the settlor Sol purchasing Bruce's reversion for £200,000 with the result that on Bill's death no charge would have arisen (thanks to the reverter to settlor relief) and the £200,000 would have reached Bruce free of tax.

[128] See Example 18.3.
[129] IHTA 1984, s.53(6); 54(3).
[130] IHTA 1984, s.53(5) and see s.54(3).

The second qualification was designed to counteract the sort of planning that proved successful in *IRC v Fitzwilliam*.[131]

Reservation of benefit and reverter to settlor trusts

By retaining a reversionary interest in his settlement did the settlor reserve a benefit? In general the answer was no: the interest retained involved a carve-out, i.e. the settlor retained his interest in reversion and merely gave away the immediate enjoyment of the settled property (the interest in possession).[132]   **18–07**

If, however, the trustees had power to appoint the settled funds back to the settlor at any time (i.e. to bring the interest in possession to an end), then the carve-out argument was less persuasive: see the statements of Lightman J. in the *Eversden* case confirming that a settlor reserved a benefit when he was an object of his discretionary trust.[133]

The remainder interest would have had some value in the settlor's estate because it was not excluded property.[134] However, if the interest could be defeated by the exercise of overriding powers of appointment its value was likely to be nominal. In any event, the planning was obviously done on the basis that the settlor would survive the life tenant. FA 2006 did not change the reservation of benefit rules in so far as they affected the settlor of a reverter to settlor trust.

From the perspective of the life tenant the position was slightly different. Suppose he had previously owned the property but given it to X who then later settled it on trust for that life tenant (the original donor) reverter to X. In these circumstances the life tenant reserves a benefit in the property originally given away under the general principles of FA 1986, s.102. However, it was not taxed under the reservation of benefit rules provided the interest in possession continued until his death.[135] The property was comprised in his estate albeit that the value was ignored. As a result reverter to settlor trusts were seen as a way of preserving a "sharing" arrangement when the donee had ceased to occupy the property.   **18–08**

Example 18–3

Cynthia lived in Blueberry Villas with her daughter, Jane. She gave Jane a 50 per cent share in the property relying on FA 1986, s.102B(4) to avoid a reservation of benefit (this is a "sharing arrangement"). However, Jane unexpectedly married at the age of 45 and moved out. Cynthia was thereupon treated as having reserved a benefit in Jane's share. But if Jane then settled her 50 per cent share on reverter to settlor trusts giving Cynthia a life interest, then because the property was comprised in her estate (as the result of s.49(1)) it was outside the reservation of benefit rules (see FA 1986, s.102(3))

---

[131] [1993] S.T.C. 502 and see further the authors', *Trust Taxation*, 2nd edn, 29.07.

[132] This was confirmed in an HMRC letter to the Law Society dated May 18, 1987. See also *Re Cochrane* [1906] 2 I.R. 200.

[133] The whole concept of a carve-out in reverter to settlor trusts is difficult to reconcile with the decision of the Court of Appeal in *Eversden* that there is only a single gift to the interest in possession beneficiary.

[134] See IHTA 1984, s.48(1)(b).

[135] FA 1986, s.102(3).

even though because of the reverter to settlor relief its value was left out of account when on her death it reverted to Jane.[136]

It might be thought that the distinction between property being comprised in the estate of the deceased life tenant but its value not being taxed is wafer thin but it is a distinction carefully drawn in a number of places in the IHT legislation: for instance, in relation to a business attracting 100 per cent relief (the business assets are in the estate but are untaxed) and in the context of the estate duty exemption for the surviving spouse which is carried over into IHT by IHTA 1984, Sch.6, para.2.

Failed PET

18–09 If the settlor died within seven years of making the settlement, he made a failed PET. In calculating the transfer of value, the value (if any) of his reversionary interest was taken into consideration.

Example 18–4

In February 2000 Alan settled property worth £100,000 on interest in possession trusts for his mother Mischa, remainder to him. His mother had a life expectancy of 10 years. Alan died two years after the settlement was made. At the date of the settlement Alan's reversionary interest was worth £20,000 and therefore the loss to his estate in making the transfer into trust was £80,000. By the time A died, however, his reversionary interest was worth £40,000. On his death he was taxed on the value of the reversionary interest (£40,000) and on the failed PET of £80,000.

A settlor-interested trust

18–10 The settlor retained an interest in the settlement for the purposes of income tax (see ITOIA 2005, s.624) and (until April 6, 2008) capital gains tax (see TCGA 1992, s.77), and therefore he (rather than the trustees or life tenant) was subject to tax on any settlement income and (prior to April 6, 2008) trust gains. Reverter to settlor trusts were therefore commonly used to hold property which produced neither income nor chargeable gains, e.g. a family home which was occupied by the life tenant or an insurance bond.

Capital gains tax before March 22, 2006

18–11 On the life tenant's death, *if the trust then ended*, the property was deemed to be disposed of at no gain no loss and the normal death uplift did not apply. The settlor would therefore receive back the trust assets without a CGT charge but

---

[136] See FA 1986, s.102(3) which taxes reservation of benefit property on the death of the donor unless the property forms part of his estate immediately before his death. Because of his life interest it does form part of his estate but because of the reverter to settlor relief the value is untaxed. The position would be different on an inter vivos termination of the life interest since s.102(4) does not deem the property to be part of the person's estate immediately before termination but simply deems a PET to arise.

(broadly speaking) at a base cost equal to the market value of the assets when he first put them into trust.[137]

For this reason it was normally preferable to ensure that on the death of the life tenant, the settlor became entitled to an interest in possession with the trustees having power to advance him capital. This still secured the IHT reverter to settlor relief but meant that the death uplift was available for CGT purposes when the life tenant died.[138] (It is this aspect that has created a problem for existing reverter to settlor trusts which continued after October 6, 2008.)

Example 18–5

In 1999 Kindly purchased a pleasant riverside flat for his mother which he settled on trusts under which she had an interest in possession and subject thereto on the following (alternative) trusts.

(i) For Kindly absolutely: when his mother dies and the property reverts to Kindly, IHT is avoided but there is no uplift in the CGT base cost of the flat so that if it has increased in value and is now sold by Kindly the gain will be taxable (see TCGA 1992, s.73(1)(b)).

(ii) For Kindly on interest in possession trusts: IHT reverter to settlor relief was available. Normal CGT death uplift applies (see TCGA 1992, s.72, which does not contain a restriction similar to that in s.73). Some doubt had been expressed as to whether reverter to settlor relief was available where the property reverted to the settlor on interest in possession trusts rather than absolutely but the HMRC Manual confirmed (at IHTM 16121) that relief was due (and this was still the case if the reverter took place prior to October 6, 2008 because the settlor could take a qualifying interest in possession under the transitional serial interest rules).[139]

(iii) For Kindly's wife either absolutely or on interest in possession trusts: provided that Kindly was alive when the interest in possession of his mother ends, IHT relief was available under the pre-March 2006 old rules in both cases (and continues to be available in both cases if his mother dies before October 6, 2008). For CGT purposes the death uplift was available in both cases (TCGA 1992, s.73(1)(b) only excludes the uplift if the property reverts absolutely to the 'disponer' and there is no similar restriction on reverter to spouses of the settlor).

(iv) The same results as in (iii) followed if the property passed to Kindly's widow (either absolutely or on interest in possession trusts) within two years of his death. For CGT purposes the death uplift was (and continues to be) available.

Note that if the property was sold during his mother's life the trustees were entitled to principal private residence relief under TCGA 1992, s.225. It did not matter, for this purpose, what trusts (if any) took effect after the termination of mother's interest in possession. However, if the trust ended on his mother's death

---

[137] TCGA 1992, s.73(1)(b), which applies if the settlement ends on the death of the interest in possession beneficiary.

[138] TCGA 1992, s.72: there is no logic in the different CGT treatment of a continuing trust which is thought to result from a legislative oversight.

[139] This is no longer the case if the reverter to Kindly occurs after October 5, 2008.

so that the settlor took outright there was no capital gains tax on the mother's death but on a later disposal by Kindly there was no possibility of principal private residence relief unless Kindly had gone to live there. The trustees' period of ownership could not be counted and Kindly acquired the property at the original base cost.

Putting a house in the trust

18–12 A reverter to settlor trust was often used to obtain principal private residence relief on what was effectively a second home of the settlor.

> ### Example 18–6
>
> Eric wanted to purchase a property for the use of his mother. In 2005 he settled cash on interest in possession trusts for his mother, reverter to himself. The trustees purchased the property. On the death of his mother in February 2006 there was no charge to IHT as a result of the reverter to settlor exemption.[140]
>
> If the house had been sold during the mother's lifetime (while she was in occupation or within three years of her ceasing to occupy it) principal private residence relief under s.225 of TCGA 1992 would have been available to the trustees, and no chargeable gains would be assessed on the settlor, Eric, under TCGA 1992, s.77. This was advantageous since if Eric had bought the property personally then unless he was also in occupation, no principal private residence relief would have been available on the sale.[141]

POA regime prior to December 5, 2005

18–13 The POA Regime affected reverter to settlor trusts in two ways. First, HMRC considered that the POA charge could apply to the settlor if the trust fund included intangibles.[142] Secondly, reverter to settlor trusts were sometimes used as a way of avoiding the POA charge.

Dealing with the first point, in the case of Eric and his mother (see Example 18–6 above), there was no charge on Eric under the POA Regime. Eric was not in occupation of the property and so the land charge had no application[143] despite the fact that he had either satisfied the disposal condition (if he settled the house) or the contribution condition (if he provided the trust with funds to purchase the house). If Eric moved into the property with his mother, then he would reserve a benefit and so still be outside POA.[144]

Assume, however, that Eric's mother moves into a nursing home and the trustees sell the house. At that point the trust holds intangibles (cash) and all the other conditions for the para.8 charge to apply are satisfied.[145] If Eric wished to keep the trust going to provide income for his mother (although he derives no

---

[140] See IHTA 1984, s.53(3).
[141] Relief for dependent relatives was abolished in 1988: TGCA 1992, s.226.
[142] FA 2004, Sch.15, para.8.
[143] FA 2004, Sch.15, para.3.
[144] See FA 2004, Sch.15, para.11(3).
[145] FA 2004, Sch.15, para.8.

income tax benefit from this since it is taxed on him) the trustees should invest in assets other than intangibles (for instance, in let land) so that he is not subject to a POA charge.

Example 18–7

If the cash from the sale of the house is (say) £1m, the chargeable amount for POA purposes for the whole year in 2006 at five per cent is £50,000. Assume the cash is held by the trustees for one month before being reinvested in land. The chargeable amount for the taxable period of one month is £4,166. This falls within the POA de minimis exemption and therefore Eric pays no tax. If, however, the taxable benefit was (say) £6,000 for the month, then tax is charged on Eric as follows. Assume also that the cash produces income (e.g. £1,000 in the relevant month), and that Eric is a 40 per cent taxpayer.

Trust income

£400 income tax under ITTOIA 2005, s.624

POA Regime charge

Chargeable amount is
£6,000 less £400 = £5,600 × 40% = £2,240
Total income tax liability is £2,640 (£2,240 + £400)

In these circumstances there was no benefit to Eric in keeping the trust going and it was preferable to appoint him an interest in possession to take effect immediately on the sale of the house. If an interest in possession was appointed to Eric before October 6, 2008 it was a transitional serial interest. After that date the trust had to be ended in favour of Eric or his wife for reverter to settlor relief to be available. If Eric is appointed an interest in possession after October 6, 2008 then his mother was treated as making a chargeable transfer for inheritance tax purposes. No reverter to settlor relief is available.

Reverter to settlor trusts were also used to avoid the POA charge.   **18–14**

Example 18–8

Clara carried out an *Ingram* scheme in 1998 giving the freehold reversion of her house to her daughter Rose. As a result of the introduction of the POA charge on April 6, 2005, Rose settled the freehold reversion in 2005 on interest in possession trusts for her mother Clara with reverter to Rose. In these circumstances the entire property (freehold and lease) formed part of Clara's estate under FA 2004, Sch.15 para.11(1) so that there was no POA charge. Provided that on Clara's death the settled property (the freehold interest) reverted to Rose, relief was available from inheritance tax on Clara's death.[146] The analysis was different if Clara's interest in possession was ended during her lifetime. In these circumstances there was a deemed PET because her reservation of benefit ceased and FA 1986, s.102(4) was not displaced. Hence Clara's interest in possession had to continue until her death if IHT protection was to be maintained.

---

[146] The fact that there is no inheritance tax payable on Clara's death does not prevent the property from being part of her estate while she is alive nor displacing FA 1986, s.102(3) (gifts with reservation) on her death.

18–15 Apart from their use in providing for aged relatives and to circumvent the POA charge, reverter to settlor trusts were used in the following situations.

(i) As part of a property purchase arrangement: assume that Dad retained a lease and sold the encumbered freehold of his main residence for full market value. This was outside the POA charge as the result of para.10(1).[147] Funds for its purchase were settled by the children on a reverter to settlor trust for Dad's remainder to them. Provided that the trust was appropriately drafted, the CGT death uplift would apply on Dad's death. (Of course, the entire property could have been bought by such a trust if the children had sufficient funds.)

(ii) As part of post-death planning: on Dad's death his half share in the family home was left in his will to his daughter Clara to use up his nil rate band. She settled that interest on reverter to settlor trusts for her Mum (the other beneficial owner, who is in occupation of the property). Main residence relief or death uplift (as appropriate) would then be available on the share held in trust.

(iii) As part of a marketed IHT avoidance scheme: Jim gave his house to his son reserving a shorthold tenancy (on commercial terms) to permit his continued occupation. At the end of that tenancy the son settled the property on a reverter to settlor trust giving Jim an interest in possession. This type of arrangement involved exploiting the distinction between property and value in order to circumvent the POA/GWR rules.

II   The IHT Position from March 22, 2006

The IHT relieving sections

18–16 Sections 53(3) and (4) and 54(1) and (2) are not themselves amended by FA 2006. However, the revised IHT legislation on settlements affects reverter to settlor trusts in two ways.

Existing trusts

18–17 In order to obtain reverter to settlor relief for existing trusts the property must revert to the settlor or his spouse either absolutely or on qualifying interest in possession trusts so that they become "beneficially entitled". The interest in possession must be a "qualifying" interest and in the case of interests arising after March 21, 2006 means that the interest in possession must either be an IPDI; a disabled person's interest; or a transitional serial interest.[148] The only qualifying interest in possession which is of relevance is the TSI.

---

[147] FA 2004, Sch.15, para.10(1) provides that this will be an excluded transaction given that Dad is disposing of his whole interest in the property apart from the rights reserved under the lease.

[148] IHTA 1984, s.49(1A).

Hence if the settlor is to obtain reverter to settlor relief on existing trusts it is necessary to satisfy one of two conditions:

(i) either the settlor (or his spouse/civil partner if the settlor is still alive or had died two years previously) must take *absolutely* on the ending of the interest in possession; or

(ii) the settlor/(or spouse/civil partner if settlor alive or died two years previously) must take on an interest in possession which is a TSI. This was only possible if the interest in possession arose before October 6, 2008.

Example 18–9

Eric settled a house on interest in possession trusts for his mother in February 2005. The intention behind the trust was CGT planning.[149] His mother is still alive but in poor health in July 2006. The settlement was drafted so that on his mother's death the property would revert to Eric on interest in possession trusts so as to obtain the base cost uplift for CGT purposes. For reverter to settlor relief to apply, Eric's interest in possession had to arise before October 6, 2008. It was then a TSI. After that date there has been an IHT charge on his mother's death when the continuing trusts will be subject to the relevant property regime. If the trusts had provided for Eric or his spouse to take absolutely on the termination of his mother's interest (or if they are so amended) then reverter to settlor relief is available whenever the mother's interest ends. However, the CGT death uplift will then be lost if Eric takes outright (although not if his spouse or civil partner takes outright).

The definition of a TSI can present problems

In the above example, if the mother died and the trust property passed to her **18–18** widower on interest in possession trusts the spouse exemption is available. The widower takes a transitional serial interest. However, on the death of the widower, *unless* the property reverts to Eric or his spouse absolutely (if Eric has died already then it needs to revert to Eric's widow within two years of his death) there is an IHT charge. Note even if the widower died before October 6, 2008 when Eric took an interest in possession, that interest did not qualify as a transitional serial interest (so no reverter to settlor relief was available) because it was not the first interest that arose after the termination of the mother's interest. For the same reason, if the mother's interest had been replaced before October 6, 2008 during her lifetime (e.g. by an interest in favour of her spouse) so that Eric did not take outright or on interest in possession trusts at the point mother's interest ends, Eric will have to take absolutely on the death of the second life tenant. Otherwise there is no reverter to settlor relief.

---

[149] Either to secure principal private residence relief on a sale of the property during the lifetime of the mother or the death uplift.

Conclusions on inheritance tax

18–19 All existing reverter to settlor trusts should be reviewed. From October 6, 2008 the settlor (or his spouse/civil partner) must take absolutely on the death of the life tenant or on the inter vivos termination of his interest if reverter to settlor relief is to be available. In these circumstances, if the settlor takes outright, the capital gains tax uplift will be lost. There is no change to the reservation of benefit rules. Hence in *Example 18–9* even if mother had originally given the property to Eric there is no reservation of benefit if her life interest ends on her death although there would be a deemed PET under FA 1986, s.102(4) if her interest ended during her lifetime.[150]

The position of new trusts

18–20 New trusts which will qualify for reverter to settlor relief cannot be established on or after March 22, 2006 except in very limited circumstances because few trusts can be set up in which the life tenant enjoys a qualifying interest in possession.[151]

Accordingly reverter to settlor relief on new trusts is limited to the following circumstances:

(i) if B (the beneficiary who takes the interest in possession) has a disabled person's interest; or

(ii) if B has a transitional serial interest (not strictly a new settlement but the variation of an existing trust); or

(iii) if B becomes entitled on or after March 22, 2006 to an immediate post death interest (an IPDI). In these circumstances the settlor was the testator (who gave B the IPDI by his will) and so reverter relief can only be available if the settlor's surviving spouse or civil partner becomes absolutely entitled to the property as a result of B's interest ending within two years of the testator's death.

III The POA Position from December 5, 2005

18–21 As discussed above, reverter to settlor relief was seen as a way round the POA provisions. Such arrangements should now be reviewed. FA 2006, s.80 amended the POA legislation with effect from December 5, 2005 so that the interest in possession of Clara in *Example 18.8* that example is ignored and the property is not treated as part of her estate for the purposes of the POA legislation. Accordingly, from December 5 she is within the POA charge. The inheritance tax protection for Clara has not been directly attacked but a POA charge imposed. FA

---

[150] As a result of s.102ZA of FA 1986 (inserted by FA 2006) even if the mother had not given the property to Eric for him to settle, if her life interest is terminated on or after March 22, 2006 there is a potential reservation of benefit problem since the mother is deemed to have made a gift and so must be excluded from any ongoing benefit.

[151] See IHTA 1984, s.54(2A).

2006, s.80 potentially affects all reverter to settlor trusts whenever set up although the income tax charge only applies from December 5, 2005 onwards.

The amending legislation[152] inserted new sub-paras 11(11) and (12) into para.11 of FA 2004, Sch.15 as follows: **18–21**

"(11) Sub-paragraph (12) applies where at any time –

    (a) the relevant property has ceased to be comprised in a person's estate for the purposes of IHTA 1984, or

    (b) he has directly or indirectly provided any consideration for the acquisition of the relevant property,

and at any subsequent time the relevant property or any derived property is comprised in his estate for the purposes of IHTA 1984 as a result of section 49(1) of that Act (treatment of interests in possession).

(12) Where this sub-paragraph applies, the relevant property and any derived property –

    (a) are not to be treated for the purposes of sub-paragraphs (1) and (2) as comprised in his estate at that subsequent time, and

    (b) are not to be treated as falling within sub-paragraph (5) in relation to him at that subsequent time.

(13) For the purposes of sub-paragraphs (11) and (12) references, in relation to the relevant property, to any derived property are to other property –

    (a) which derives its value from the relevant property, and

    (b) whose value, so far as attributable to the relevant property, is not substantially less than the value of the relevant property.".

This change goes much further than had been indicated in the pre-Budget Press Release of December 5, 2005. It does not affect just reverter to settlor trusts but as discussed in **Ch.7** can affect any trust set up at any time on or after March 18, 1986 even where the settlor is entitled to an interest in possession where property was comprised in someone's estate, it left his estate and then he acquired a qualifying interest in possession in the property again. **18–22**

In relation to reverter to settlor trusts the taxpayer can obviously make an election into reservation of benefit. How then will inheritance tax be charged on the taxpayer's death? Consider *Example 18–8* above. Clara is entitled to a qualifying interest in possession in the freehold interest. On her death, s.102(3) (reservation of benefit) is displaced because she has an interest in possession. The election does not change this. **18–23**

In addition s.54(1) would normally disapply any inheritance tax charge on the death of Clara because the settled property has reverted outright to the settlor Rose. However, if an election into reservation of benefit is made, then Sch.15, paras 21(2)(b)(iii) and 22(2)(b)(iii) provide that for POA purposes reverter to settlor relief is <u>not available</u> where the person is beneficially entitled to an interest in possession in the property. Hence on the death of Clara the freehold interest <u>is</u> taxed as part of her estate for inheritance tax purposes, not because she has reserved a benefit but because she has a qualifying interest in possession and the

---

[152] See also **Chs 7** and **8** for a discussion of the para.11(1) ownership exemption and the effect of s.80 on foreign domiciliaries, and **Ch.11** for discussion of FA 2006, s.80 and the election. See also A2.119 et seq.

settled property is deemed to be part of her estate. In these circumstances if the settled property reverts outright to Rose although no reverter to settlor relief is available on Clara's death (and therefore an inheritance tax charge may arise) there is still no capital gains tax uplift because the property reverts to the original disponer, Rose. Hence if Clara elects, Rose could suffer the worst of all worlds: an inheritance tax charge on Clara's death and a capital gains tax charge when Rose later comes to dispose of the freehold based on the original acquisition cost of the trust. In many cases the freehold interest may not have increased in value significantly from the original value when it was settled if the trust was effected after 2005 to avoid POAT. The alternative is that Clara does not make the election under Sch.15 and instead pays income tax (or Rose puts Clara in funds to pay the income tax).

IV Comments and Conclusions

18–24 Reverter to settlor relief has been severely curtailed. The sort of arrangement discussed above where Dad leaves his house in his will to his only daughter who then settles it on trust for Mum will no longer attract relief. Such a trust now involves the making of a chargeable transfer for IHT purposes by the daughter and Mum does not have a qualifying interest in possession. However, it may be that reverter to settlor relief is not necessary in these circumstances. It is likely that Dad's share in the house is within his nil rate band. Accordingly, if the daughter then settles that share on an inter vivos trust for her mother, giving her an entitlement to occupy the property, although a chargeable transfer no inheritance tax will be payable (assuming the daughter has made no other chargeable transfers).

On the death of the mother, there is still no inheritance tax payable if the trust continues because her entitlement to occupy the property or enjoy its income is ignored for inheritance tax purposes.[153] Further, the trustees may benefit from principal private residence relief so the trust might still be thought worthwhile. Although there is no uplift on mother's death this does not generally matter if principal private residence relief is available. Even if the settlor becomes absolutely entitled there is a deemed disposal by the trust at market value and any past principal private residence relief will reduce the chargeable gain. The daughter acquires the property at market value. By contrast, if the mother has a qualifying interest in possession which terminates in favour of the daughter (settlor) absolutely then the daughter simply acquires that property at base cost and all past principal private residence relief accruing during the ownership of the trustees is lost.

---

[153] The relevant property regime applies and tax may be charged if the trust ends at that time (an exit charge) although the value of the settled property means that this is unlikely since it will be covered by the IHT nil rate band.

Example 18–10

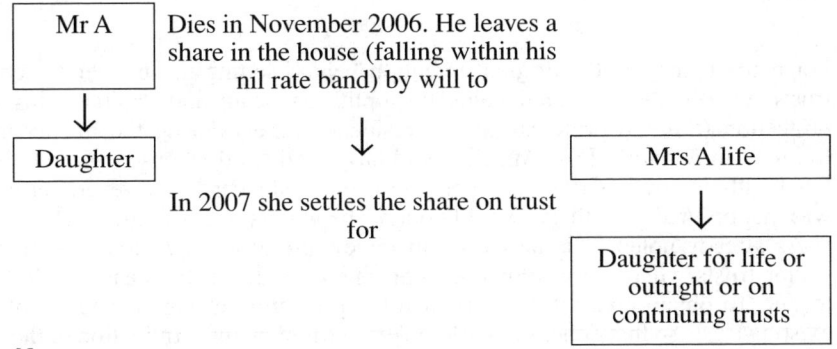

Mr A	Dies in November 2006. He leaves a share in the house (falling within his nil rate band) by will to

↓

Daughter

In 2007 she settles the share on trust for

Mrs A life

↓

Daughter for life or outright or on continuing trusts

Notes

1. The gift by daughter of her interest in the land is a chargeable transfer as opposed to a PET. Since the gift is within her nil rate band this generally makes little odds.

2. If the house is worth more than the nil rate band at the 10-year anniversary then inheritance tax will be payable but only on the excess above the nil rate band and at a maximum rate of 6 per cent. If Mrs A dies within the first 10 years and the trust is ended, there is no inheritance tax charge even if the house is worth more than the nil rate band at that point.

3. Principal private residence relief for capital gains tax purposes is available if Mrs A is in occupation of the property as her main residence: see TCGA 1992, s.225.

4. It does not matter if the daughter or her spouse does not survive Mrs A in terms of the IHT position on Mrs A's death. On Mrs A's death there is no inheritance tax charge because her life interest is ignored for inheritance tax purposes (it is not qualifying).

5. On Mrs A's death there is no base cost uplift for capital gains tax purposes. She does not have a qualifying interest in possession. On disposal of the house by the trustees, however (whether on a deemed disposal if the trust ends and the daughter takes the house outright or on an actual disposal if the house is sold by the trustees), they are entitled to principal private residence relief. Hence capital gains tax will not be a problem.

6. If the daughter dies then she may be treated as having reserved a benefit in the property so that inheritance tax is payable.

7. There is no POA charge unless the daughter occupies the house or the trust fund comprises intangibles and even then only if the daughter does not reserve a benefit. The position is the same as before the 2006 changes. Section 80 is not a problem.

8. Does it matter if Mrs A previously gave the interest in the house to Mr A which is now left to the daughter and which before March 22, 2006 the daughter settled for Mrs A? Is Mrs A subject to POA because of s.80? No, because the transaction between Mr and Mrs A is excluded for POA purposes. In any event Mrs A's interest in possession is not a qualifying interest in possession so would not be caught by s.80.

The best of both inheritance tax and capital gains tax worlds—planning points

18–25 For many taxpayers the original intention behind setting up reverter to settlor trusts was to obtain capital gains tax uplift on death and capital gains tax protection (through principal private residence relief) during the life tenant's lifetime. In *Example 18–1* Angela could have retained the house in which Fred lived without any inheritance tax problems on Fred's death. However, her hope was that on Fred's death she would obtain a capital gains tax uplift.

As already noted, it is necessary to review pre-March 22, 2006 reverter to settlor trusts where the settlor does not take outright on the death of the life tenant. To obtain continued inheritance tax protection change the terms of all existing trusts so that either the settlor takes outright on the termination of the life tenant's interest in possession or (to avoid capital gains tax problems) the settlor's spouse or civil partner takes outright since then the base cost uplift is available as well as continued inheritance tax protection. If the settlor is worried about divorce then one option would be for the trustees to appoint the spouse an absolute interest but revocable at any time before the life tenant's death. Then if they divorce before the life tenant dies the spousal interest can be revoked.

18–26 In some cases the settlor will not be married and therefore using the spouse (or civil partner) will not be an option. Is there any way of obtaining both capital gains tax advantages and inheritance tax protection? Of course the taxpayer may decide that inheritance tax protection is not very useful anyway because the life tenant has few other assets and the house falls within his nil rate band. The figures always have to be calculated before a decision is taken: is it better to pay 40 per cent inheritance tax on the entire value (but starting at a high threshold of £325,000 if the life tenant has no other assets and made no other relevant gifts) or to pay capital gains tax at 18 per cent on the gain.

One option might be to trigger the gain while the settlor is alive if the asset held in trust is a house qualifying for principal private residence relief. If the house is sold while the trust continues then principal private residence relief is available. If this is not felt to be desirable another option might be to emigrate the trust. This will trigger a deemed disposal and reacquisition under TCGA 1992, s.80, but no chargeable gain on the trustees because of PPR relief. The trustees have then rebased the asset. Only gains arising since emigration will be taxed on the settlor when the life tenant dies. Of course, the trust could be immigrated after one complete tax year of non-residence if the family wanted to keep matters straightforward.

18–27 Suppose the trust property does not qualify for principal private residence relief, e.g. it is let land or farmland? Or maybe it does qualify for principal private residence relief but the trustees cannot engineer a disposal while the life tenant is alive. Another option in relation to land might be to engineer a *Crowe v Appleby* arrangement under which the settlor becomes entitled to 95 per cent of the property outright for inheritance tax purposes in order to secure reverter to settlor relief but five per cent is retained in trust so as to stop outright entitlement of the whole by the settlor for capital gains tax purposes. [154]

---

[154] For further details see the authors' *Trust Taxation*, 2nd edn, 29.37.

PART IV: PLANNING IN PRACTICE: PROACTIVE PLANNING

What can still be done to mitigate or avoid the imposition of Inheritance Tax? This Part considers the possibilities in the light of the Pre-Owned Assets charge and the Government's antipathy to "schemes".

CHAPTER 19

TAX PLANNING GENERALLY

In retrospect the tax planning opportunities available before December 10, 2003, **19–01** resemble a "golden age": by contrast the current opportunities and, equally significant, the judicial and political climate suggests that those who wish to avoid inheritance tax legitimately will find life much tougher. Nevertheless there are a number of options which can be considered by those wanting to avoid IHT. The caveats and comments set out at the start of **Ch.21** apply equally here. For planning involving family homes see separately **Ch.21**; for planning involving chattels see **Ch.20** and for planning involving foreign domiciliaries see **Ch.24**.

Considering capital tax planning opportunities in the wake of the POA Regime is only part of the story and the introduction of the POA charge needs to be seen as part of a wider picture which should be taken into account in effecting future tax saving exercises.

BACKGROUND

The Changes of December 10, 2003

The changes announced in the Chancellor's Autumn Statement, delivered rather **19–02** late on December 10, 2003, dealt a severe blow to capital tax planning in that:

(a) the pre-owned assets regime was announced with retrospective (or at least retroactive) effect which struck at the heart of schemes designed to circumvent the reservation of benefit rules[1]; and

(b) restrictions on CGT hold-over relief were introduced which, above all, destroyed the basis of *Melville* schemes which had become an essential adjunct to much lifetime IHT planning[2];

---

[1] See **1–06**, et seq.

[2] See the restrictions on CGT hold-over relief in ss.165 and 260 of the TCGA 1992, introduced by FA 2004, s.116. "*Melville* schemes" enabled the CGT that would otherwise have been payable on lifetime gifts to be held over by utilising a discretionary trust under which the settlor was interested. A new scheme became popular after the December 2003 changes. Taxpayers avoided paying capital gains tax on gifts by use of options (which exploited anti-avoidance legislation in TCGA 1992, s.144ZA) but this too was stopped in the pre-Budget Report of December 2004.

(c) further changes announced in December 2003 restricted principal private residence relief where a previous hold over relief claim had been made over the house.

A duty of disclosure

19–03 The introduction of a requirement that marketed tax schemes in relation to financial and employment products should be disclosed to HMRC (with effect from August 1, 2004, subject only to transitional provisions) represented a radical step into the unknown.[3] Exasperation in Government circles with the scale, growth and success of tax saving schemes (notably in the area of income, capital gains and corporation tax) appears to have driven ministers to seek early disclosure of such arrangements, doubtless with an eye to producing appropriate anti-avoidance legislation that much sooner. For the present, IHT schemes are not generally subject to disclosure, but as explained in **Ch.13** it should be remembered that if a scheme is devised which involves avoidance of POA income tax it will need to be disclosed if the other conditions on disclosure are satisfied.

Ramsay and the construction of taxing statutes

19–04 Tax saving schemes—especially artificial pre-packaged schemes—not only infuriate ministers, they also present problems for the judiciary in deciding how the tax legislation is to be applied. For instance, should CGT loss relief be given in a case where, by a manipulation of the wording of the legislation, a loss appears to have arisen albeit that, in economic terms, the taxpayer has suffered no loss (although he will doubtless have paid substantial fees to the scheme promoters!). The so-called *Ramsay* principle was developed in an attempt to limit the effectiveness of the pre-planned scheme by excising artificial steps and attempting to look at the transaction in the real world. The scope of the doctrine has waxed and waned over the years and has recently taken a new turn with a spate of cases.[4]

The changes in FA 2006

19–05 As explained in **Ch.2**, significant chances in the IHT treatment of settlements were introduced with effect from March 22, 2006. Broadly speaking all new settlements fall within the relevant property regime and are therefore subject to 10 yearly and exit charges, whilst on creation the settlor makes an immediately chargeable transfer. Existing settlements benefit from transitional provisions: accordingly an interest in possession in existence on March 22, 2006 remains "qualifying" (so that the beneficiary is treated as the beneficial owner of the settled property[5]) but if that interest is replaced then that new interest is not

---

[3] See FA 2004, ss.307–318, the Tax Avoidance Schemes (Prescribed Descriptions of Arrangements) Regulations 2004; Tax Avoidance Schemes (Promoters and Prescribed Circumstances) Regulations 2004 and the Tax Avoidance Schemes (Information) Regulations 2004. The rules have been extended: see FA 2008, s.116 and SI 2007/3104.

[4] See further the authors' *Trust Taxation*, 2nd edn, 3.35 et seq.

[5] IHTA 1984, s.49(1).

qualifying so that the settlement falls into the relevant property regime and the original beneficiary makes a chargeable transfer.[6] The changes mean that the use of settlements in IHT planning schemes initially declined (e.g. in the family debt scheme the debt was formerly settled but it is now given outright) and alternatives to family trusts have been sought. In fact the alternatives (such as limited partnerships, cell companies, purpose trusts, foundations, close companies, bare trusts and employee benefit trusts) all raise significant practical problems. In some cases (for example foundations), it may not always be clear what type of beast one is dealing with—at least for taxation purposes. The particular constitution of each foundation (a creature of statute) varies hugely—and not only from country to country.[7] In some cases they could be regarded as corporate structures and in other cases as settlements for tax purposes.[8] Although some of the above vehicles may be appropriate in certain circumstances they do not easily deal with succession problems. For example, the donor may want flexibility as to how his property should be held in the future: he may not want to commit himself to vesting property in a particular beneficiary now. A trust is still the best way of providing for flexibility. Although the Government has sought to attack trusts by introducing a raft of taxation changes, their non-tax advantages remain. Trusts can provide for the younger and more vulnerable members of a family; they can be used to ensure that great wealth is not split and possibly dissipated between individual members of a family but held within one trust in a controlled and orderly way. This can be particularly useful for a large family company. No other vehicle is as simple and effective in achieving these aims. In fact the taxation disadvantages associated with trusts really centre round the entry charge (of 20 per cent for IHT purposes). If this can be avoided, then the 6 per cent charges every 10 years are usually manageable, especially if there is no IHT on the death of a beneficiary. Unlike partnership or company structures, once the property is in a trust, the persons for whom it is held can be altered without capital gains tax or IHT implications. Trusts have a body of case law regarding enforceability and accountability which may be lacking in relation to other vehicles.[9] A gradual realisation of the continuing advantages of trusts has therefore led to advisers looking again at ways of avoiding the entry charge.

STOPPING THE SCHEMES—THE GOVERNMENT'S RESPONSE

There is now a willingness—certainly on the present Government's part—to stop **19–06** tax saving schemes by whatever means are necessary. References to fighting fire with fire and that those who play with fire must expect to get burnt abound. The rhetoric is, of course, designed to seize the moral high ground and to provide a justification for measures that in another age might have been rejected on the grounds of "not playing the game" or, more importantly, as being retrospective. Such issues are rarely understood, however, and there is a general perception that anyone who avoids tax is damaging the community (taking a shovel to the cash

---

[6] There is an exception if the new interest in possession arises on the death of the beneficiary and is in favour of his spouse or civil partner. It is then a qualifying interest (a transitional serial interest).

[7] See, for example, the new foundation introduced by Jersey law.

[8] For further commentary on Foundations see *Trust Taxation*, 2nd edn, **17–05**.

[9] For a detailed commentary on the FA 2006 changes, see the authors' *Trust Taxation*, 2nd edn, especially **Ch.16**. See also **Ch.2** and at **2–31** and **7–06** of this book for further comments.

that should be in the Exchequer). Thus when retrospective changes were made to the CGT treatment of offshore trusts in 2003, the principle at stake was lost amid the condemnation of the actions of the wealthy few in establishing the offshore structures in the first place. The general climate that can be seen are in the Paymaster General's comments quoted above at **1–06**. Her attitude was encapsulated once again in the Finance Committee debates in July 2005 when the Shadow Chief Secretary to the Treasury suggested that relief should be given for the potential double inheritance tax charge on home loan schemes where the debt is released.[10] The Paymaster General responded:

> "Call me a cynic, but I have a horrible feeling that the sudden desire to unwind is prompted by the discovery of a way to replan. I also think that election is a good and fair answer for all taxpayers."[11]

Where does this leave the professional adviser charged with doing his best to mitigate a client's IHT liability? If all that is involved is taking advantage of statutory exemptions for their intended purpose he may feel that this will not be attacked by future legislation: more aggressive tax planning, however, may well (when discovered) provoke the wrath of an easily enraged Exchequer. This needs to be discussed with clients, given that the response of Government may be to leave the taxpayer in a worse position than if he had done nothing. The Pre-Owned Assets charge on *Ingram* schemes is a particularly striking illustration.[12] The easy assumption of some ministers that schemes can be undone (unravelled) because they lack substance is normally far from being the reality. As we have seen in relation to past schemes, there may be real problems about the double charges that can arise if a scheme is now unravelled.

19–07   In the past, the Government has sought to stop IHT planning by changing the IHT legislation with effect from the date of the announcement. So schemes that had been completed prior to the announcement were home and dry. This approach has not changed in the IHT context, but the Government can now impose a pre-owned assets income tax charge for those who have engaged in planning it deems "unacceptable." The result is that while the IHT savings are preserved, the annual income tax charge until death makes the scheme suddenly rather expensive! An example of this is in relation to reverter to settlor schemes[13] where in December 2005 the Government announced changes that prevented the ownership exemption from protecting the taxpayer from a POA charge.[14]

SAFE PLANNING

19–08 Using the basic IHT exemptions and reliefs (annual exemption, small gifts and PETs) is hardly exciting but it is safe. Making larger gifts is obviously still possible provided that the donor retains no benefit or interest in the gift. Make sure both husband and wife use their annual exemptions. More interesting is the normal expenditure out of income exemption which, the courts have decided, has a wider application than had originally been thought to be the case. For a taxpayer

---

[10] See **Ch.17** for further discussion.
[11] She eventually executed a U-turn: see **Appendix I**–A7.
[12] See **14–13** et seq.
[13] Discussed in **Ch.18**.
[14] See FA 2006, s.80, discussed at length in at **7–24**, **8–19**, **11–25**, **18–21** and **23–14**.

in his 50s with substantial surplus earnings it is to be recommended as a way of controlling the growth in value of his estate.[15] Moreover the normal expenditure out of income exemption is one way of settling property into trust without a 20 per cent charge on the excess over the nil rate band. The expenditure must:

a. be part of the normal expenditure of the donor;

b. be made out of income (taking one year with another);

c. leave the donor with sufficient income to maintain his usual standard of living.

Note that the exemption is not suitable for death bed planning where the donor knows he is terminally ill! To be "normal" the donor must intend to make regular gifts out of surplus income each year. If he dies unexpectedly and his executors can demonstrate his commitment to make these gifts then they can be exempted.

Example 19.1

A calculates that he will have surplus income of £150,000 pa (after tax) from his directorship with Quango Inc. He therefore determines to settle this sum each year into a trust for his children and grandchildren. Note:

a. there is no need to report the payments each year since they are not chargeable transfers even though they are gifts into a relevant property trust;

b. the gifted sum is taxed as income of Mr A in the year it is received by him and the surplus he has available to give is calculated after taking account of income tax and normal (non-capital) expenditure;

c. the GWR rules are capable of applying so Mr A must not benefit in the settled property (although he can be a trustee);

d. there is no 20 per cent inheritance tax entry charge even though he exceeds his nil rate band in the third year. Of course, there are 10 year and exit charges on the settlement.[16]

Family maintenance

Another option which should be considered, particularly in the context of death **19–09** bed planning, is IHTA 1984, s.11. This provides that certain dispositions are not transfers of value, i.e. that even though they reduce the estate of the disponer they are ignored. The scope of s.11 has been considered in two recent cases: *Phizackerley v IRC* [2007] STC (SCD) 328 (in the context of the non deductibility of debts under FA 1986, s.103), and *McKelvey v RCC* [2008] STC (SCD) 944. Section 11(3) exempts a disposition in favour of a dependent relative which is

---

[15] See IHTA 1984, s.21 and see *Bennett v IRC* [1995] STC 54 and *McDowell v IRC* [2004] STC (SCD) 362. However, gifts made under the normal expenditure out of income exemption are potentially within the POA Regime. It would seem that many insurance schemes may be considered "safe" given that the Revenue has suggested that, despite arguments to the contrary, the Regime will not apply to them: see **Ch.22**.

[16] Consider whether the use of pilot trusts would be beneficial.

"reasonable provision for his care or maintenance". Reasonable imports an objective standard. It is possible to use this exemption to make gifts to a trust for a dependent relative but care is needed that the capital is needed for his care or maintenance.

Example 19.2

Ruth has been diagnosed with terminal cancer. She is concerned to provide for her elderly mother who she suspects will need to go into a nursing home. Accordingly she gifts her mother two investment properties which can be sold to pay nursing home fees as and when needed. Although she dies within seven years the gifts are not failed PETs to the extent that they involve *"reasonable provision for (the mother's) care or maintenance"* and are protected from an IHT charge under IHTA 1984, s.11(3).[17]

Using the nil rate band

19–10 More standard planning simply involves giving away the unused nil rate band of a couple every seven years. Over time significant sums can be placed in trust.

Example 19.3

Sid settles investment properties on trusts for his children. Note the following points.

  a. To avoid an immediate IHT charge he ensures that the value transferred falls within his nil rate band; he may do this by use of a *Melville* scheme[18] or by transferring some of the properties to his wife or civil partner so they can then each set up a trust. Alternatively he just limits the value that is settled into trust.

  b. CGT hold-over relief under TCGA 1992, s.260 is available to postpone any CGT charge provided that the trust is not "settlor-interested" (hence neither Sid, his wife / civil partner, nor any dependent child can be capable of benefitting under the trust).

  c. At the end of seven years the chargeable transfer drops off his cumulative total and he can repeat the exercise: he is better off setting up a new trust rather than adding to the existing trust since future 10-year anniversary charges are then reduced.

  d. As noted above Sid's wife / civil partner could carry out a similar exercise and they could be joint settlors. It does not matter if they settle property into the same trust since the trust will be taxed as two separate trusts for IHT purposes with each trust having a separate nil rate band (IHTA 1984, s.44).

19–11 Business property (as defined) and farming can attract IHT relief at 100 per cent irrespective of the value of the enterprise. This is a striking valuation relief and should be safeguarded at all costs. Do not, for instance, depress the value of

---

[17] See *McKelvey v RCC* [2008] STC (SCD) 944.
[18] See **19–17**.

business property by raising mortgages against it[19] and do not rush into inter vivos tax planning given that full relief will be available on death.[20]

RUNNING THE RISK

Suppose there is a loophole in the legislation—which may or may not be intended—do you exploit it? This is the area of risk where a health warning should certainly be given to clients. A good example is the reverter to settlor scheme. Originally these were seen as a way round the the POA Regime but became vulnerable when the Government introduced anti-avoidance legislation with effect from December 2005.

19–12

One practical point about future legislation is to note that it can be made to impact upon a continuing state of affairs (doubtless in a "retroactive" way) but that a "done deal" is far more difficult to attack without imposing a blatantly retrospective tax charge.[21]

The authors feel that the following arrangements—considered in detail elsewhere—can be considered "safe":

(a) sharing arrangements for the family home[22];

(b) cash gifts and the seven-year "window"[23];

(c) commercial sales (equity releases)[24]; and

(d) trust reorganisations.[25]

Savings can also be obtained by the use of deeds of variation and flexible wills.[26]

"NON-APPROVED" TAX PLANNING ARRANGEMENTS

Some more controversial planning arrangements include the following:

19–13

● settled gifts and derived property;

● rental arrangements;

● *Melville* arrangements;

● purchasing an interest in possession;

● family debt schemes.

---

[19] See IHTA 1984, s.162(4).

[20] A good example is a gift by a farmer of his farmland and retention of the farmhouse. On his death, because the house will no longer be a farmhouse, relief will not be available: see *Rosser v IRC* [2003] STC (SCD) 311.

[21] For the distinction between retrospectivity and retroactivity, see **1–22** et seq.

[22] **Ch.21-05**

[23] **Ch.23**.

[24] **Ch.21**.

[25] **Ch.15**—and see in particular 15-12.

[26] See the authors' *Trust Taxation*, 2nd edn, Chs 30 and 31.

Settled gifts and derived property

19–14   Under FA 1986, para.5(1), Sch.20, where the property becomes settled by virtue of the gift, paras 2 to 4, Sch.20 do not apply. Hence settled cash gifts can fall foul of the reservation of benefit rules if the property comprised in the settlement represents or is derived from the gifted cash. In addition, if the settlement comes to an end, the property then comprised in the settlement which now passes to someone other than the donor is treated as comprised in the original gift: see para.5(2). Curiously, however, para.5 does not contain tracing provisions to deal with the position when the beneficiary who has received the settled property sells it and uses the proceeds to buy further property in which the donor reserves a benefit.

> ### Example 19.4
>
> A settles shares on trust for, inter alia, his son. The trustees hold the shares for some years and then sell them and invest in pictures. The pictures are then advanced to the son and the trust is ended. If A derives some benefit from the pictures, e.g. they hang on his walls, then para.5(2) applies and he is treated as reserving a benefit. (A would therefore need to pay full consideration for his use of the chattels in the normal way to avoid a reservation of benefit.) However, if the son sells the pictures and then buys a house in which A lives, the reservation of benefit provisions do not apply. However, one would need to consider the POA provisions which use the words "*property directly or indirectly applied*" so that the house which A now occupies may satisfy the condition in para.3 with the result that the POA charge may arise. If, however, the son sold the chattels and bought shares, paying all the dividends to A, neither POA nor reservation of benefit would be in point.

Rental arrangements

19–15   Section 102B(3)(a) provides that there is no reservation in cases where there is a gift of an undivided share in land and the donor "*does not occupy the land*". Accordingly even if the donor otherwise benefits from the gift there is no reservation of benefit.

> ### Example 19.5
>
> Assume that Q owns a beneficial 50 per cent share in a let industrial property which he gives to his daughter. She continues to pay him all the rent on the property. In cases such as this, s.102B is the governing section (specifically s.102 and s.102A cannot apply) and hence there is no reservation of benefit. Further there is no POA charge on let property. Note that there must be a gift of a **share** in the land.
>
> Alternatively, assume that R retains a 50 per cent share in a let property settling the other 50 per cent share onto trusts under which he can benefit. Again there is no reservation of benefit. But if the property was sold and the trust invested the proceeds in a share portfolio, the s.102B protection would be lost and under the tracing rules in FA 1986, Sch.20 the gift would be of the shares in which R has now reserved a benefit.

However, if R had set up a trust under which he retained a life interest (albeit non **19–16** qualifying) with no right to receive the capital it may be argued that the right to income from the property in the settlement does not involve a reservation since it amounts to a "carve-out", i.e. (and as in the case of discounted gift plans) it is a right which R never gave away. In this case, there is no reservation of benefit even if the land is eventually sold and the trust invests the sale proceeds in shares. Of course, in these circumstances a POA charge under FA 2004, Sch.15, paras 8 and 9 would operate once the trust held intangible property such as cash and shares. This option is therefore generally limited to situations where the donor wishes to give away let property but to retain all the rental income. There may, of course, be capital gains tax problems given that no hold-over relief is available on a gift of the let property into a settlor interested trust and principal private residence relief would not normally be in point. The powers of the trustees should be suitably circumscribed. Hence there should be no power to advance or appoint capital to R.

Melville schemes revisited

A major problem caused by FA 2006 is that the settling of more than the settlor's **19–17** nil rate band involves an immediate IHT charge at 20 per cent on that excess. *Melville* schemes had been developed in order to avoid a CGT charge on a gift of property: they involved a settlement on discretionary trusts for which hold-over relief was available but with the value settled being kept low (by the retention first of a "settlement right" and subsequently a settlement interest) so as to avoid an IHT charge. Hence the settlor would have a right to require the assets to be transferred back to him if he survived a minimum period and such right was an asset of his estate which prevented any significant loss from arising. This was on the basis that the settlor paid inheritance tax on the loss in value of his estate which was minimal. Restrictions on CGT hold-over relief into settlor-interested trusts in 2003 put an end to these CGT saving arrangements. Note, however, that although settlement powers are not regarded as "property" for inheritance tax purposes later *Melville* schemes had emerged (involving the retention of a beneficial interest) which meant that they still worked for inheritance tax purposes.

In considering the scheme discussed in Example 19.6 it should also be borne in mind that FA 2006 provides that the estate of a taxpayer does not include the value of any interest in possession.[27]

Two scenarios

Shortterm has been diagnosed with six months to live. He borrows £1m charged **19–18** against his main residence and undertakes a *Melville* scheme. He dies four months later. The aim is to ensure that the borrowing reduces the value of his house and the borrowed cash is given away in such a form so as to avoid the need to survive seven years.

Generous wishes to settle £1m on trusts benefitting his grandchildren but wishes to avoid a 20 per cent IHT entry charge on the excess above his nil rate band. He also undertakes a *Melville* scheme: after four months he surrenders his right to income.

---

[27] See IHTA 1984, s.5(1): (1A) inserted by FA 2006.

Example 19.6

Y settles £1m into a trust which is discretionary over income (or someone else has entitlement to income) for a period of [three months] after which if Y is still alive he enjoys a right to income for 90 years. Consider:

- the trust falls into the relevant property regime;

- it is settlor-interested and so hold-over relief is not available (hence Y should settle cash or assets not showing a substantial gain);

- the retained contingent right to income is a reversionary interest which is not excluded property and must be valued for the purposes of calculating the fall in value of Y's estate (see IHTA 1984, s.48(1)(b));

- when the interest (i.e. the right to income for 90 years) vests in Y it ceases to be part of his estate;

- POA and GWR issues. This works well for death bed planning but a POAT charge is likely to arise unless the trust invests in let property.

Summary—what is in Y's estate?

At the start £1m.

Then a reversionary interest being the contingent right to an income for 90 years. This is not excluded property and is believed to be worth close to £1m.

When that right vests Y has a non-qualifying interest in possession which is not included in his estate for IHT purposes. *Hence £1m has disappeared out of Y's estate!*

Purchasing an interest in possession

19–19   Can advantage be taken of the fact that an interest in possession does not form part of the beneficiary's estate in other ways?

Example 19.7

Under the Bloggs Discretionary Trust Willie is given a non-qualifying interest in possession. He sells this—for its actuarial value of £100,000—to his father who promptly dies. His father has entered into a commercial transaction and the interest in possession is not part of his estate.

The tax saving may be £40,000 provided that the non-gratuitous exemption in IHTA 1984 s.10 is available. It is important that there is no power for the trustees to terminate the interest in possession, otherwise it is commercially valueless. Hence Willie's interest in possession must not be capable of being overridden by the trustees without the consent of the holder for the time being of that life interest.

19–20   *The Family Debt Scheme* is discussed in detail at **21–30**.

19–21   Planning for foreign domiciliaries is discussed in **Ch.24**.

CHAPTER 20

CHATTEL ARRANGEMENTS

Background

For some taxpayers, chattel collections (or even the ownership of individual **20–01** items) raise the spectre of a substantial IHT liability on death. Hence there has been a demand for an arrangement under which the chattels can be given away (whether outright or into trust for children and issue) whilst at the same time leaving the taxpayer able to continue to use and enjoy them. In recent years two main "schemes" have been employed to meet these requirements.

Ingram schemes

In simple terms the arrangement blessed by the House of Lords[11] is applied to **20–02** the chattels: viz the taxpayer retains a lease which enables him to continue to possess the chattels and gifts the "freehold" interest. Doubt was originally expressed in some quarters as to whether a land shearing operation was capable of applying to chattels but HMRC accepted that such arrangements were possible.[2] Of course the "*Ingram* scheme" was reversed by legislation in FA 1999 but that legislation was expressly limited to land and interests in land.[3]

---

[1] See **14–02**.

[2] See *Taxation*, October 16, 2003 (Nicholas Brown). In the particular case the chattels in question were individually valued at under £6,000 but collectively had a value of £750,000. A lease for 17 years was retained and on the death of the taxpayers there was 7 years left to run on the lease: the PET of the assets (subject to that lease) occurred more than 7 years before the deaths and so was an exempt transfer. The value of the remainder of the lease was then worth £13,000 and the collection of chattels £1,380,000. The Revenue initially argued that unlike land it was not possible to create different interests in chattels with the result that there had been a gift of the entire interest in the chattels with a contractual arrangement (not involving the payment of full consideration) permitting their use and which amounted to a reserved benefit. See now IHTM 14314 and the Guidance Notes at A2.54.

[3] In the Press Release of March 1999 announcing the blocking of *Ingram* arrangements, it was stated that "if no action were taken, the [*Ingram*] decision would jeopardise a large part of the tax base. As the decision affects only gifts involving land, the changes to the gifts with reservation rules are limited to such gifts. However, the operation of these rules will be closely monitored and the Government will not hesitate to act to prevent any tax avoidance through other gifts."

Gifts and commercial leaseback

20–03 This alternative arrangement has been widely used for a number of years. The designated chattels are gifted to the donee and then leased back by the donor who pays full consideration for his continued use: hence the reservation of benefit rules are inapplicable.[4] In the case of land (to which a similar exemption applies), the amount of the required commercial rent will frequently be beyond the means of the taxpayer. In the case of chattels, however, there is no ready market in rentals and no standard type of agreement. In practice, experts are engaged by both donor and donee to negotiate a full value for the enjoyment of the chattels. Arrangements are entered into under which there is payment of a relatively small rent (perhaps 0.75 per cent of the value of the chattels each year) with the donor/lessee also being made responsible for insuring and maintaining the chattels in question (which will often include the provision of a suitable security system). Similar negotiations are necessary to agree the level of any rent reviews.[5] The agreement is often made non-assignable by the donor. Some agreements contain price adjuster clauses.[6]

20–04 As with land, HMRC attach importance to the parties having the benefit of independent advice—see comments in a letter to Law Society dated May 18, 1987 in relation to land:

> "Whether an arrangement is for full consideration will of course depend on the precise facts. But among the attributes of an acceptable arrangement would be the existence of a bargain negotiated at arm's length by parties who were independently advised and which followed the normal commercial criteria in force at the time it was negotiated."

HMRC commented in the same letter in relation to chattels: "it would be difficult to overturn an arm's length commercial arrangement entered into by parties who were independently advised."

The CGT dimension

20–05 In both arrangements it was important to bear in mind the CGT consequences of disposing of the chattel (or an interest in it). There is a general exemption for chattels which are individually worth £6,000 or less,[7] whilst if the item is a wasting asset then gains are exempt without limit. A wasting asset is one with a predictable useful life of 50 years or less and includes yachts, caravans, washing

---

[4] See FA 1986, Sch.20, para.6(1)(a): actual enjoyment of a chattel "if it is for full consideration in money or money's worth" is disregarded in applying the reservation of benefit rules.

[5] See generally *Christie's Bulletin for Professional Advisers*, Autumn 1995 (Manisty) and Autumn 1998 (McCall).

[6] An alternative approach suggested by Christopher McCall QC in his article in *Christie's Bulletin* in Autumn 1998, vol.3, no.3 was for the donor to warrant for himself and his estate that the rent he pays is full consideration for the purposes of para.6, Sch.20 and to covenant that at the end of the term if so required he will make good any shortfall which the donee is able to establish by reference to the warranty. The covenant is made under deed.

[7] TCGA 1992, s.262(1): note that there are special rules for sets: TCGA 1992, s.262(4). In the case of more valuable chattels the gift could be into a trust taking advantage of hold-over relief under TCGA 1992, s.260(2)(a) provided that the value is limited to the donor's available IHT nil rate band (so as to avoid an immediate IHT charge).

machines, animals and all plant and machinery, the latter term to include, in HMRC's view, such assets as antique clocks and watches, certain vintage cars and (generally) shotguns.[8]

Impact of the POAT Regime

Stated objectives

The December 2003 consultation paper made it clear that a main target of the new charge was chattel schemes: it referred to tax being charged at a specified percentage of capital value in cases where there was no market evidence of an appropriate rent as in the case of "art or antiques". **20–06**

Ingram schemes

The charge under para.6[9] will apply (in essence the analysis is much the same as in the case of *Ingram* arrangements affecting the land: see **14–13**). Hence the options open to the taxpayer are much the same. And the same difficulties arise in connection with chattels as set out in that chapter in relation to land regarding payment of rent or full consideration. **20–07**

> #### Example 20.1
>
> In 2003 Andrew effected an *Ingram* scheme over chattels under which the "freehold" interest in chattels was gifted to an interest in possession trust for his daughter Charlotte. He is now caught by the Regime.
>
> If he surrenders the leasehold interest, this may be an associated operation with the result that a large transfer of value equal to the full market value of the chattels (less the value of the earlier transfer) is now made.[10] What happens if instead Andrew assigns his leasehold interest to another member of the family? At that point he would need to pay full consideration for his continued use of the chattels in order to avoid a ROB. However, as noted above, full consideration can often be relatively low, for example one per cent of the value of the asset. Does this then protect Andrew from a POA charge by virtue of para.11(5)(d)?
>
> The concern is that "the relevant property" for the purposes of para.11(3) is the property disposed of, i.e. both the leasehold and freehold interests. Does he reserve a benefit in respect of the freehold interest as a result of assigning his lease and continuing to use the chattels? To be sure of the para.11(5)(d) protection he would need to surrender the lease to the freeholder

---

[8] *Tax Bulletin*, October 1994 and February 2000: TCGA 1992, s.44.

[9] See **Ch.4**, above. Note that para.6(2)(b) refers to a disposal of all **or part** of his interest in the chattel and para.6(4) treats the creation of a new interest out of an existing interest as the disposal of part of the existing interest. The authors are not aware of reversionary leases being used for chattels.

[10] For associated operations, see **17–22**. Note also that such a surrender may be viewed as the addition of property to Charlotte's settlement and thereby causing Andrew to make an immediately chargeable transfer with (arguably) the surrender creating a relevant property settlement. Given that the lease ceases to exist it is difficult to see what property could be included in such a settlement but HMRC may seek to argue that a proportion of the value of the chattels is so compromised.

and pay him full consideration and as noted above this may cause IHT problems[11] or (perhaps) pay full consideration to both freeholder and leaseholder (which may still be cheap!).

20–08 Hence paying full consideration may not let him off the POA charge. Could Andrew instead make payments in pursuance of a legal obligation to the owner of the chattel for his use and possession of the chattel within para.4(1)? If he does not assign or surrender the lease the only way he can put himself under a legal obligation is to enter into a deed of covenant. The amounts involved may be substantial.

Example 20.2

The encumbered freehold value of the chattels is now £1 million. The market value without the lease is £1.5 million. The appropriate amount is 4.75 per cent x £1.5 million = £71,250. £71,250 x 1/1.5 = £47.750. Tax on £47,750 at 40% = £19,000 pa.

Andrew enters into a deed of covenant with the trustees of Charlotte's trust under which he agrees to pay £50,000 being "the appropriate amount". Arguably such amount is not taxable in the hands of the recipient trustees.[12]

Gift and leaseback arrangements

20–09 It is considered that POAT does not apply for the following reasons:

(a) the para.6 charge does not apply if the relevant property falls within para.11(5): see para.11(3); and

(b) para.11(5) includes (inter alia) property which would fall within the reservation of benefit rules "but for s.102C(3) of, and para.6 of Sch.20 to, the 1986 Act." The latter provision deals (inter alia) with full consideration arrangements in relation to the enjoyment of chattels.[13]

Whatever the original intention (as manifested in the December Consultation Paper), it has subsequently been accepted by HMRC that there should be consistency between the treatment of land and chattels and full consideration arrangements work.

Current attitude of HMRC

20–10 A number of gift and leaseback schemes are under consideration by HMRC, which is concerned to ascertain whether full value has been paid in "rent". Bear in mind that if it can be shown that there is **any** element of undervalue the

---

[11] The problem of the scope of the reservation of benefit protection from the POA charge arises in other areas: see for instance **14–17**.

[12] See **14–17** for a consideration of the use of deeds of covenant.

[13] The wording of para.11(5) is unsatisfactory in running together s.102C(3) with para.6 given that the former provision is concerned with occupation of land in hardship cases (dealt with also in para.6(1)(b)), whereas para.6 deals with other matters such as full consideration. It is therefore considered that "and" must be read disjunctively and this has now been confirmed by HMRC in the guidance notes. See A2.41.

protection of Sch.20, para.6(1)(c) will be lost and the taxpayer will have reserved a benefit in the chattels. The pre-owned assets charge will not therefore apply.[14] HMRC have queried some gift and commercial leaseback arrangements on the basis that if there is no real market in letting country house chattels they do not have to accept a rate agreed by expert valuers. Instead, in the absence of a "real world market", HMRC have suggested that a Canadian Court of Appeal case[15] provides some useful guidance as to what should be adopted as constituting full consideration and argue that full consideration is in reality the return that the donee would obtain if he invested an amount equivalent to the cash value of the chattels on deposit or in government securities. This would obviously equate much more to the fixed rate return of five per cent set out in para.7 of Sch.15.

However, the case of *Youngman* was concerned not with full consideration but **20–11** with benefits to the taxpayer. The shareholder was living in a house built by his company and was paying full market rent for his occupation. The market rent was below the rate of return the company could have obtained from investing the cash. The judge held that in determining the value of the benefit to the taxpayer one should take the *cost* of providing that benefit to the company into account. Hence free market rent was not in all circumstances the sole indicator of real value.

In the case of chattel arrangements one is concerned not with benefits as such to the donor but with whether he has paid full consideration which is a very different test. Furthermore in the Canadian case the company had used its own cash to build a unique residential property for the taxpayer while in chattel gifts and leases the donee is simply being given an existing asset which he is likely to want to retain within the family anyway.

Alternatives

As noted in **Ch.5**, chattel schemes will not be subject to a POA charge where **20–12** there is a disposal of the chattel or the contribution condition has been satisfied in an excluded transaction within para.10. The only exclusions likely to be relevant to chattels are paras 10(1)(a) and 10(2)(c).

Paragraph 10(1)(a) provides that the sale of chattels is an excluded transaction if it is a sale of the taxpayer's whole interest in the property at full market value except for any right expressly reserved by him over the property.

Example 20.3

Edward owns a valuable picture which shows little gain. He carves out a lease for himself and then sells (rather than gives) the chattel subject to this lease to his son at full market value. The transaction is a sale not a gift so will not be caught by reservation of benefit and that such a transaction will be excluded from the POA charge under para.10(1)(a). Note that if there is any undervalue element one moves into the problems posed by non-exempt sales.[16] There is no stamp duty payable (compare the position with land).

Edward does not need to worry about what constitutes full consideration, he pays no rent and is not caught by the POA income tax charge. However,

[14] Para.11(5)(a).
[15] *Youngman v The Queen* [1991] 90 DTC 6322.
[16] For further discussion, see **3–25**.

Edward must not have given the cash to his son in order to enable the son to purchase the chattel from him, otherwise he is in breach of the contribution condition.

20–13 An alternative option is to use the cash let-out in para.10(2)(c).

Example 20.4

Edward gives cash to his son in 1997. His son uses the cash to buy a picture which his father puts on his wall. He pays no rent. Edward is not in breach of the ROB provisions nor does he satisfy the contribution condition because the gift was made prior to April 6, 1998. Alternatively Edward could give cash to the son and then wait seven years before using any chattels purchased with the cash.

20–14 Another option is to consider whether *shared* use and possession of the chattels might be possible.

Example 20.5

Luke and Charlotte jointly use a holiday home which contains chattels owned by Luke. He gives a half share in those chattels to Charlotte. For IHT purposes there is no similar statutory relief for chattels from the reservation of benefit provisions as that contained in s.102B(4) for land. The analysis would presumably be that Luke's use of the chattels was in consideration of allowing Charlotte the same level of use. In these circumstances it would probably be unwise for Luke to give Charlotte more than 50 per cent. The alternative analysis is that the gift of a part share in chattels is more in the nature of a carve-out and that the donor has the right to continue using them anyway.

20–15 A part owner of a chattel does not have the same rights as a part owner of land or a shareholder of a company. The only relevant legislation is s.188(1) of LPA 1925 which states:

> "Where any chattels belong to persons in undivided shares, the persons interested in a moiety or upwards may apply to the court for an order for the division of the chattels or any of them, according to a valuation or otherwise, and the court may make such an order and give any consequential direction as it thinks fit."

No cases have been decided under s.188 but it is thought that this justifies a discount in valuation of a half share.[17] There is no reason to think that the co-owner of such chattels necessarily has rights of use and possession in the same way as an owner of land under TLA 1996.

Practical advice

20–16 (a) Consider what steps should be taken to deal with the para.6 charge in the case of *Ingram* chattel schemes. It will not usually be attractive to pay the charge (apart from the cost, the valuation difficulties and expenses are likely to be considerable), although in a case where the gift of the freehold

---

[17] See *Christie's Bulletin*, Summer issue 2005.

(the PET) has been made more than seven years ago (so that there is an accrued IHT benefit) it ought to be considered. This will be especially so if the taxpayer is in poor health so that paying for a few more years use of the chattels may be sensible. In some cases the taxpayer may be prepared to give up possession or use of the chattels so that the Regime will not apply.

It has been suggested that the donor could exercise the election for the reservation of benefit rules to apply and then bring the reservation to an end by paying full consideration for the use of the chattels within FA 1986, Sch.20, para.6(1).[18]

(b) In the case of existing and new gift and leaseback arrangements, make sure **20–17** that arguments can be adduced to defend the level of rent paid (in particular make sure that the terms of the lease—and especially the level of rent— have been reviewed periodically). Bear in mind that different types of assets command may different levels of rent. For example, items which have some utilitarian purpose such as furniture or table silver both of use in a contemporary domestic context may command a higher rent than other less readily hireable or purely decorative items such as pictures or sculptures. Equally contemporary art may command a higher fee than (say) eighteenth-century art because it has a larger commercial rental market. Vintage motor cars, in particular, may well command a high return since there is a thriving market in the hire of these.

(c) Finally, alternative arrangements, particularly sales, may be worth **20–18** considering.

---

[18] HMRC accept that the full consideration let-out can apply in these circumstances: see A2.89.

CHAPTER 21

PLANNING INVOLVING THE FAMILY HOME

Introduction

21–01 In retrospect, the tax planning opportunities available for family homes before December 10, 2003 (the announcement of POAT) resemble a golden age: by contrast the current climate makes lifetime planning with the family home much more difficult. Equally, as noted in **Ch.17**, the introduction of the transferable nil rate band combined with the possible increase in the nil rate band to £1 million if the Conservatives gain office at the next election has reduced the appetite and perceived need for schemes involving the family home. Clients do not want to embark on expensive IHT planning which may involve payment of SDLT and/or POAT if on their deaths no IHT will be payable anyway!

21–02 Any professional adviser should always exercise caution before advising his client to carry out inheritance tax planning with the family home. As far as possible any such planning should take advantage of the statutory exemptions and reliefs since these are less likely to be attacked or changed. The adviser should then explore some of the options discussed in **Ch.19** which involve other assets before looking again at the family home. More aggressive tax planning may well (when discovered) provoke the wrath of an easily enraged Exchequer. It is relatively easy for any government to change the POA legislation so that income tax can be imposed on an "unacceptable" tax scheme. The fate of past schemes (*Ingram, Eversden,* reversionary lease schemes, home loan schemes) has been discussed in **Chs 14 to 17**.

Summary of options

21–03 The taxpayer who wants to embark on IHT planning in relation to the family home will typically have much of their wealth tied up in that asset and it will be unmortgaged. They may be single or married. Ideally they will have good pension provision although it is possible that in the future they may need to release the equity in their home to fund nursing care, etc. The authors consider that it is unwise for IHT planning to be considered on the family home where the client is under the age of 65 unless they are in obvious ill-health. Any client needs to appreciate that such planning will result in some loss of flexibility. Planning at too young an age can be dangerous: people's circumstances may change in unforeseen ways. Is the price of the inheritance tax saving worth paying? It is important that all the practical disadvantages are explained to the client.[1] The adviser should consider the following points in assessing the pros and cons of any scheme involving the family home.

- Possible loss of capital gains tax main residence relief. However, capital gains tax is charged at 18 per cent on any chargeable gain as opposed to IHT at 40 per cent on value above the nil rate band threshold.

- Lack of flexibility—can the client move? Can he access the equity of the house easily in the future and is he likely to need to sell the house to pay for care home fees? What are his other resources?

- Does the scheme depend on the donee agreeing to stay in the house; what happens if donee and donor later fall out?

- Is the donor married or in a civil partnership? What happens if the donor dies within seven years of any PET: will the couple be worse off?[2]

- Does the scheme involve an immediate or ongoing cost such as payment of SDLT or interest on loans?

- Are the POAT and GWR positions adequately protected or is there a likelihood of retrospective legislation? It is probable that the inheritance tax savings will be secure but a POAT charge may well be imposed on a scheme deemed unacceptable.

- What happens if the donor's personal circumstances change, e.g. he marries or divorces? Will he then need to use the capital of the house?

- Does the donor have to move out at some point in the future? Does he understand this? Where will he go?

- Are the donees in a relatively stable position? There is no point in saving IHT if the donee then loses the gifted sums in a divorce. How old are the donees? Is a trust desirable?

Options for the family home (taking the "safest" first) are as follows: **21–04**

1. payment of full consideration for occupation of the property;

2. co-ownership arrangements;

3 borrowing on the security of the property;

4. reversionary leases;

---

[1] For an example where this was not done see *Wolff v Wolff* [2004] STC 1633: parents had carried out a reversionary lease scheme which was later set aside for mistake on the basis that they were unaware that they would have to move out of the house when the lease took effect.

[2] See *Re Griffiths (Deceased): Ogden & Anor v Trustees of the RHS Griffiths 2003 Settlement & Ors* [2008] STC 776. In 2003, Ronald Griffith, then aged 73, made two transfers of amounts which, in total, slightly exceeded his IHT nil rate band. In February the following year, he made a further PET, this time of substantial value (£2.6m). In the autumn of 2004, he was diagnosed with lung cancer and died the following April. As a result the PETs failed, resulting in a substantial IHT liability. He was survived by his slightly younger wife and, looking at the matter from an IHT perspective and with the benefit of hindsight, it could be said that it would have been better for him to have done nothing leaving all the assets to his spouse who could then (on the basis that she was a better life) make lifetime PETs. The executors of Mr Griffiths' estate were successful in applying to the court to have the February 2004 gift set aside on the grounds of mistake.

5. trust carve-outs;

6. equity release schemes;

7. family debt scheme.

CO-OWNERSHIP ARRANGEMENTS

21–05 During the consultation period on the POA charge, it became apparent that the Government was anxious not to disturb "genuine" house sharing arrangements, which have always qualified for protection from the reservation of benefit rules provided that certain conditions are satisfied.

Example 21.1

An elderly mother living with her daughter has given a share in the property to daughter. Will mother be caught by the Regime in respect of the gifted share? Generally the answer is no. The principle is that since such arrangements are "approved" for inheritance tax purposes, they will not be subject to a pre-owned assets income tax charge.

Since co-ownership arrangements have statutory protection, in appropriate circumstances they offer a valuable IHT planning tool.

Inheritance tax position pre-March 1999

21–06 The IHT treatment of co-ownership arrangements is not entirely straightforward. Prior to March 9, 1999, the Revenue considered that the following ministerial statement ("the Hansard Statement") governed the position:

"It may be that my Hon Friend's intention concerns the common case where someone gives away an individual share in land, typically a house, which is then occupied by all the joint owners including the donor. For example, elderly parents may make unconditional gifts of undivided shares in their house to their children and the parents and the children occupy the property as their family home, each owner bearing his or her share of the running costs. In those circumstances, the parents' occupation or enjoyment of the part of the house that they have given away is in return for similar enjoyment of the children of the other part of the property. Thus the donors' occupation is for full consideration.

Accordingly, I assure my Hon Friend that the gift with reservation rules will not be applied to an unconditional gift of an undivided share in land merely because the property is occupied by all the joint owners or tenants in common, including the donor".[3]

---

[3] Statement of Mr Peter Brooke, Minister of State, Treasury Standing Committee G; Hansard, June 10, 1986, col.425.

This is a somewhat puzzling statement.[4] The parents' occupation is surely by virtue of their owning a share in the property: the children are not "allowing" them to live there. The statement also implies that the house is divided into discrete parts so that the parents' use of the children's part is in return for the parents letting the children use their part. In reality, the parents have the right to occupy the entire property as the owners of an undivided share. Presumably the "full consideration" referred to in the above statement is intended to be that "I will let you use my 50 per cent of the house in consideration for you allowing me to use your 50 per cent". This is the basis of the supposed 50 per cent ceiling in the size of the gift.

However, this arrangement is in the nature of a carve-out—the parents' right to occupy the entire property is derived from the interest they have retained and does not amount to a reservation in the gifted share. This carve-out argument was considered in the *Eversden* case at first instance (of course the taxpayer was not in joint occupation and therefore could not rely on the full consideration argument or on the *Hansard* statement). The Special Commissioner and Lightman J. appeared to accept it, at least in relation to the original property, although the latter did not agree there was a carve-out in relation to the replacement property.[5]

If the carve-out argument is right, then full consideration is irrelevant and the **21–07** precise interest doesn't matter since even a 5 per cent retained share would confer the right to occupy the property in its entirety. In correspondence between the Law Society and the Revenue in 1987, the Revenue accepted that an arrangement would not necessarily be jeopardised simply because it involved a gift of an unequal share in the home. However, that statement made it clear that the owners had to remain in joint occupation and that the donee should not pay the donor's share of running costs. It was also seen as important that the donee occupied as the family home. The position was substantially altered by the "anti-*Ingram*" legislation in 1999.

Position post-March 8, 1999

For gifts of undivided shares in land from March 9, 1999, the position is regulated **21–08** by FA 1986, s.102B. In general the gift of an undivided share in land will involve a reservation of benefit in cases where the donor continues in occupation (see s.102B(2)). Subsection 102B(4), however, gives relief from this charge under the reservation of benefit rules in the following circumstances:

1. the donor disposes by way of gift on or after March 9, 1999 of an undivided share of an interest in land;

2. the donor and the donee occupy the land; and

---

[4] 4 This perhaps understates the position! "Wholly misconceived" might be more appropriate with the authors being of the opinion that a gift of a share followed by continued occupation by the donor had no need of any ministerial exemption. Instead it falls within the shearing principles accepted by the House of Lords in *Ingram*: viz that the donor has retained a defined interest in land (like a lease only in this case an undivided share) to which his continued occupation can be attributed. The change in the law in 1999 was intended to make it clear that the basic shearing arrangement in relation to land was caught by the amended reservation of benefit rules in FA 1986, s.102A.

[5] For the facts of the case, see **2–13** and **Ch.16** et seq

3. the donor does not receive any benefit, other than a negligible one, which is provided by or at the expense of the donee for some reason connected with the gift.

Occupation

21–09 Note that there is no requirement for occupation by the donor and donee as *the family home*. Further, there is no reference to full consideration as the basis for the exemption, so it is thought that the donor is able to give away more than a 50 per cent interest.

> **Example 21.2**
>
> (1) Judith, now widowed, lives in the family home at Sandbanks. Her married daughter lives in South London and comes to stay with Judith with her two young children most weekends and for holidays. Judith gives the daughter a 50 per cent share in the house.
>
>   (i) It is thought that s.102B(4) will apply given that both occupy the property. The daughter comes and goes as she pleases; leaves possessions in the property; has her own bedrooms, etc. From her point of view it is like owning a second home.
>
>   (ii) What is the daughter's CGT position assuming that she owns a house in South London? Which is to qualify as her principal private residence (consider the use of the election under TCGA 1992, s.222(5))?
>
> (2) Some years ago Ben gave a one-third share in his home to his daughter Sheila who lives at home and looks after him. He now gifts a further one-third share to his son, an airline pilot who spends most of his time in New York but who stays with Ben ("treats the place like home") when he is in the UK (on average six weeks a year). It is considered that both gifts are protected by s.102B(4).

HMRC give a wide meaning to "*occupation*" for the purpose of the para.3 POAT charge.[66]

21–10 HMRC are known to dislike arrangements where the donor gives away (say) 90 per cent of the property and retains 10 per cent, and are likely to investigate carefully the third condition set out above—i.e. has the donor received any connected benefits from the donee? That in turn will involve scrutinising how expenses have been split between them.

Expenses

21–11 Under both *Hansard* and s.102B there has been some misunderstanding of precisely how the running costs should be split. A cursory reading of the *Hansard* statement might suggest that running expenses should be split in proportion to the *beneficial* interests that each has in the property. However, "his share of the

---

[6] See generally **3-02** et seq.

running costs", as the Revenue subsequently confirmed in 1987, is referring to the donor and donee's *actual* expenses incurred. Thus if there is a 90/10 beneficial split in the property, the donee arguably should not pay 90 per cent of the expenses but instead no more than the expenses he has actually incurred; where donor and donee live together full time, this will generally mean a 50 per cent split.

For instance, HMRC's view is that just because a person owns 90 per cent of a property, it does not mean that he uses 90 per cent of the gas, electricity and water, and if the donee agrees to pay 90 per cent of those expenses he is therefore conferring a benefit on the donor. The focus is on what collateral benefits, if any, are being provided by the donee in connection with the gift. HMRC do not seem to distinguish between capital and living expenses although it may be argued that repair bills should fairly be split in proportion to ownership of the property. The concern is the potential width of "benefit" to the donor. Assume, for instance, that Bob has always occupied his house with his unmarried son Bill and had paid all the property expenses. He now gives Bill a share in the property (say 60 per cent) and Bill takes over 60 per cent of the property bills. Nothing else changes in their relationship, Bob continues living in the property (as before) but is now relieved of the worry of paying 60 per cent of the property bills. This sort of arrangement prompts the following conclusions:

(a) Bob must not receive a benefit (however small) from Bill which is in some way connected with the gift;

(b) there is nothing in the IHT legislation or in common sense to suggest that if Bill does not pay a share of expenses the gift of the 60 per cent is in any sense a "sham"; accordingly

(c) it will be sensible to err on the side of caution—better for Bob to overpay (or even pay all expenses!) than for there to be a risk that he is in receipt of a benefit. Quite often Bob will be content to do this: it was, after all the arrangement prior to the gift! It may also represent sensible IHT planning for Bob to deplete his estate in this way.

Example 21.3

In 2000, Barry gave 50 per cent of his house to his son, David, who lives in a flat in town during the week but spends most weekends at the property. Are the donor and donee both "occupying" the land? This is a question of fact and degree but a person may be in occupation of more than one property. If David pays 50 per cent of the outgoings but is using the property less than Barry, arguably a benefit is being conferred on Barry by David in connection with the gift and s.102B(4) is not satisfied so that the gift is caught by the reservation of benefit rules.

The correct course is for Barry (as donor) to pay at least the share of the outgoings reflecting his *actual* use. So as he is there more often than David, one would expect him to pay a significantly greater share of the running costs. Indeed to be safe, he may want to consider paying almost all the outgoings, including capital expenditure on the property.

POAT position

21–12 Prima facie POAT can, of course, apply to co-ownership arrangements because there has been a disposal of an interest in land and the donor continues to occupy the property. Thus, the basic disposal and occupation conditions in para.3, Sch.15, FA 2004 are satisfied.

However, para.11(5)(c) provides a rather tortuous exemption. If property "would fall to be treated as property which is subject to a reservation of benefit" but for s.102B(4), such a disposal is protected from a POA charge. Since s.102B(4) can only apply to, and therefore protect, post-March 8, 1999 arrangements, the legislation also provides that a gift made before March 9, 1999 will not be subject to the POA Regime if had it been made on or after that date it would have qualified for s.102B(4) protection.

Thus, if in *Example 21.3* we assume that the gift had been made in 1997 then Barry would not be subject to a charge in respect of the gift, whilst David continues in occupation because para.11(5)(c) gives protection. What is slightly odd about this is that if this particular gift had been made in 1997 it might not have had *Hansard* protection given that the donee was not occupying as his family home, albeit it would qualify for s.102(B)(4) protection if made now. The POA Regime does not seem to distinguish between the different conditions required under *Hansard* as opposed to s.102(B)(4) and it may be, in the light of the comments in **21–07** above, that HMRC does not, in practice, require occupation as a *family home* in relation to pre-March 1999 arrangements. Of course, if the pre-1999 gift was *not* protected under *Hansard* or on the basis of the carve-out argument then there would be a reservation of benefit so that there will be no POAT anyway (see Sch.15, para.11(5)(a)).[7]

Sales of part

21–13 It is somewhat odd that *gifts* of part falling within s.102B(4) are protected from the POA charge but that sales of part at *full* value are not so protected (albeit that such transactions are not gifts and therefore are not subject to the gifts with reservation rules).[8]

Sales of part at an *undervalue* are gifts as to the undervalue and may still qualify for protection from the reservation of benefit rules under s.102B(4) and therefore protection from charge under the POAT Regime.

Cash gifts

21–14 What happens if Barry does not give an undivided interest in the land to his son but instead gives him cash? For example, suppose Barry gives cash of £100,000 to David and together they buy a house worth £200,000, owning it in equal shares and both living there. Section 102B(4) is not satisfied because Barry has not satisfied the first condition—he has not made a gift of an undivided share in land.

---

[7] The authors believe that HMRC did not appreciate that the 1999 legislation differed from the 1986 statement in any significant respect.

[8] See **2–06**.

He has, however, not made a gift with reservation unless the cash gift was conditional on David using it to purchase the property (and then it may be analysed as a gift of a share in the property rather than cash so that s.102B(4) can apply). Does Barry then have a POAT problem? He has satisfied the contribution and the occupation conditions and therefore prima facie is caught by para.3. He is not directly protected under the para.11(5)(c) exemption as he does not have s.102B(4) protection. Paragraph 11(8), however, provides that in determining whether any property falls within para.11(5)(c) in a case where the contribution condition is met, para.2(2)(b) of Sch.20 FA 1986 (exclusion of gifts of money from the GWR tracing rules) is to be disregarded. The consequences of this deeming appear to be as follows:

(a) FA 1986, Sch.20, para.2(2)(b) is disapplied;

(b) accordingly a gift of cash falls within the general "tracing" rule in FA 1986, Sch.20, para.2(1): viz if the donee ceases to have possession and enjoyment of the gifted property (the cash), then any property which that donee received in substitution for the cash (the share in the purchased property) shall be treated as having been comprised in the original gift instead of the cash;

(c) if the original gift had been of an undivided share in land then s.102B(4) protection will be available if the relevant conditions are met.

In this situation if the donee ceases to occupy the property so that the POA protection of para.11(5)(c) is lost, the gift is not caught by the reservation of benefit rules and the POA charge will apply.

Donee moves out[9]

In considering whether a sharing arrangement is appropriate for a particular **21–15** taxpayer it should be remembered that if either of the requirements of s.102B(4) are broken then the basic GWR charge under s.102B(2) will operate. From the date of the breach there is a reservation of benefit (one way of looking at the position is to say that although the donor has reserved a benefit in the gifted share, the reservation of benefit rules will not apply to him whilst the donee occupies the property and he receives no benefit from the donee).

Example 21.4

Sally gives a 50 per cent share in her Reading house to her daughter Shula who is aged 18 and studying at the university. After obtaining her degree in media studies Shula moves out to take up a well paid job in London. The IHT/POA consequences are as follows:

(a) Sally no longer has the protection of s.102B(4) because sub-section (a) is no longer satisfied;

---

[9] Although s.102B(4) refers to the need for both donor and donee to occupy the property it is not thought that IHT problems will arise if it is the donor who ceases to occupy (e.g. he may move into a nursing home). In this situation because the donor is not in occupation of the gifted property there is no reservation of benefit: see FA 1986, s.102B(3)(a). Nor will there be a POA charge.

(b)   accordingly the gifted share is property subject to a reservation and the usual charging provisions in FA 1986, s.102(3) and s.102(4) apply;

(c)   because Sally is caught by the reservation of benefit rules the POA charge does not apply (para.11(5)(a)).

21–16   As the above example shows it is important that a gift is only made when it is likely that the joint occupation of the property is going to be long term. Otherwise the position can end up in a mess. It is not, for instance, true to say that Sally is back where she started as a result of falling foul of the reservation of benefit rules: all that these do is to bring the gift back into her estate either to be taxed at death or to form the subject of a lifetime PET. Accordingly should she wish to sell the property in a few years then not only would Shula be entitled to 50 per cent of the proceeds but full CGT main residence relief will not be available on Shula's share.

Reorganising the arrangement

21–17   In cases where the donee intends to cease to occupy so that the spectre of a reservation of benefit is looming, consider the following restructuring options.

(i) Donor pays a "full consideration" for his occupation of the whole property

21–18   In these circumstances he would not be subject to the reservation of benefit rules because he would have the protection of FA 1986, Sch.20, para.6; nor would he be subject to the POAT Regime which gives protection under para.11(5)(d).[10] There are, of course, difficulties in determining what would be full consideration for these purposes given that the donor is already entitled to occupy the property as a co-owner. Does he pay the rent that a lodger would have to pay to share with him or does he have to pay 50 per cent of the full market rent he would have to pay if the property were let with vacant possession? The former is likely to be much lower than the latter! In practice it is understood that HMRC consider that full consideration in this situation is the appropriate percentage (based on the size of the share given away) of the rent for the whole property.

(ii) Donee settles gifted share on a reverter to settlor trust

21–19   An alternative strategy prior to the December 5, 2005 changes would have been for the donee to have settled the gifted share in the property on a reverter to settlor trust for the donor for life. The tax treatment of these trusts is considered in **Ch.18**, but the pre-owned assets tax protection was stopped from this date and the FA 2006 changes effectively destroyed the use of such trusts.

Practical issues

21–20   There are a number of practical issues that should always be considered before entering into co-ownership arrangements. For example, what happens if the donee marries someone whom the donor does not like? The spouse may then move in with donee. Or suppose that the donor wishes to sell and move somewhere smaller, does he have sufficient funds from his retained share to re-house himself?

---

[10]   See **Ch.7**.

Example 21.5

Sebastian's one substantial asset was Flyte Hall, an Edwardian property worth £1m. His son, recently divorced, lived with him and as the arrangement was likely to be permanent Sebastian gave him a 90 per cent share in the property. Unfortunately the son died in a motor accident shortly afterwards leaving Sebastian devastated. The son was intestate and his share in the property passed to his young children who live in London with their mother. Sebastian died shortly afterwards.

(i) *Death of the son*: IHT will be charged on 90 per cent of Flyte Hall. One of the problems that Sebastian was struggling with when he died was how to raise the money to pay the tax either in whole or on the instalment basis. It is always important in entering into a sharing arrangement to consider not just the IHT position of donor but also of donee.

(ii) *Death of Sebastian*: because he has continued to live in the Hall after the son's death the reservation of benefit rules will result in the entire property being taxed on his death. Double charges relief may be available if he died within seven years of his original gift.

A particular concern is whether a gift of a share to one child will disadvantage **21–21** any other children. Assume that Barry has given a share in his house to his youngest son David. Suppose he made the gift in September 2009 and that share is worth £330,000. That is in excess of his nil rate band but covered by two years' annual inheritance tax exemptions. However, if Barry dies within seven years of the gift, although David suffers no extra inheritance tax as donee, John, Barry's other son, who has been left the rest of Barry's estate will find that the benefit of the nil rate band has been allocated entirely against David's gift and John suffers 40 per cent inheritance tax on the estate.

Other problems can arise where the house increases in value faster than the **21–22** rest of the estate or the remaining estate has to be used to pay nursing home fees. Suppose Barry gives David a 90 per cent interest in the house and retains 10 per cent. The 90 per cent share is worth £285,000 and the 10 per cent share £31,000. Barry's other investments such as cash and equities are worth around £300,000 at the time of the gift. He leaves all these to John by Will. Unfortunately within three years of the gift Barry becomes ill and has to move into a nursing home. (Barry will not fall within the reservation of benefit rules given that he no longer occupies the property.) David remains in the property but all the liquid assets of Barry are used to pay the nursing home fees. Three years later Barry dies and his remaining investments are by then worth only £150,000. In addition, John has to pay tax at 40 per cent. He receives significantly less than David.

Who is the donee?

An outright gift of an undivided share is the most common, but assume that Barry **21–23** would prefer to settle an interest in the property for the benefit of David (perhaps because David is a spendthrift). Prior to March 22, 2006 a gift into a flexible life interest trust for David fell within the protection of s.102B(4) on the basis that, as life tenant, David was treated as owning the property in the settlement (by virtue of IHTA 1984, s.49(1)) and hence is the donee. The flexibility given to the trustees and which enabled them to terminate David's interest in whole or part gives Barry protection against David seeking to raise money on his interest. From March 22, 2006 this option is no longer available unless the donee is disabled. David is not treated as taking a qualifying interest in possession and therefore the donee is the trustee not the child in occupation. Even if the child is appointed a trustee it is not thought that this is sufficient to enable the co-ownership exemption to be available.

Second homes

21–24 In cases where it is desired to gift a share in a second home which it is considered will be protected by s.102B(4) provided that both donor and donee occupy the property, a problem which frequently arises is the CGT charge on the disposal. To deal with that problem the gifted share may be put into a non-settlor interested trust (in order to obtain the benefit of CGT hold-over relief under TCGA 1992, s.260(2)(a)) and after (say) three months appointed out to the intended donee (again with the benefit of holdover relief). The difficulty with this arrangement is reconciling it with the wording of s.102B(4) since the donee will not be the original donee of the gift but the trustees. Hence it is considered that s.102B(4) will not afford protection so that the share settled by the donor will be caught by the reservation of benefit rules and taxed as part of his estate when he dies.

Example 21.6

(1) A gives a large share in his house to his son B and occupies it with B. B subsequently gives part of that share to his adult children who are not in occupation. In these circumstances is A still protected from reservation of benefit under s.102B(4)? Both donor and donee still occupy the land so the basic conditions in s.102B(4) are satisfied.

(2) In 2002 A gave a share in his home to his wife on interest in possession trusts in an *Eversden* type arrangement.[11] The wife occupies the property. Soon after her interest in possession is terminated but she continues to occupy the property. The disposal is no longer an excluded transaction for POA purposes. Can A successfully argue that his wife still occupies so therefore he falls within the protection of s.102B(4) and therefore para.11(5)(c)? It is thought not. Section 102C(2) provides that such a gift is not subject to a reservation of benefit when it is a spouse-exempt gift and therefore one cannot argue that para.11 provides protection because the property would not fall to be treated as property subject to a reservation "but for s.102(B)(4)". The property was not subject to a reservation of benefit because of s.102(5)(a), which is specifically excluded from protection for POA purposes.[12]

---

[11] For *Eversden* arrangements, see **Ch.16**.
[12] See para.11(5)(b).

Co-ownership arrangements may be regarded as one of the safer lifetime **21–25** inheritance tax planning options provided that the donee continues to occupy the property and the various family and practical issues mentioned above can be resolved. The result is that the donor can avoid both the reservation of benefit rules and a POA charge. It is also of some comfort that these exemptions under both the IHT legislation and the POAT Regime are unlikely to be removed: in effect co-ownership has been given statutory protection. The one area that is vulnerable to future change is gifts of a majority share, for example where the donor gives a 90 per cent interest away. Hence the cautious may wish to limit their gifts to a 50 per cent share in the property.

Finally bear in mind that the relief is for shared occupation and shared **21–26** ownership: it is crucial that the donor retains an interest in the property. Give away a 90 per cent share and GWR/POA problems may be avoided: give away a 100 per cent share and the reservation of benefit rules will catch the donor. Similarly a gift of cash used to purchase a 100 per cent interest in the home occupied by the donor results in a POA charge. By contrast if the donor also purchased a share and there is joint occupation then there is no POA charge.

FULL CONSIDERATION ARRANGEMENTS

The POA Regime does not apply to full consideration arrangements in relation to **21–27** gifts of land and chattels.[13] This follows a let-out for GWR purposes in FA 1986, Sch.20, para.6(1)(a), which prevents a reservation of benefit where the land or chattels are being occupied or used for full consideration in money or money's worth.

Hence a donor is free to give away his house (or chattels) and continue living in the house (or using the chattels) without a reservation of benefit or POAT problem provided he pays full consideration. Bear in mind that if it can be shown that there is any element of undervalue, the protection of Sch.20, para.6(1)(c) will be lost and the taxpayer will have reserved a benefit in the chattels.[14] Moreover the donor must continue paying full consideration not only for the first seven years after the gift but until his death or until he ceases to occupy the property!

HMRC attach importance to the parties having the benefit of independent **21–28** advice: see comments in their letter to the Law Society dated May 18, 1987 in relation to land:

"Whether an arrangement is for full consideration will of course depend on the precise facts. But among the attributes of an acceptable arrangement would be the existence of a bargain negotiated at arm's length by parties who were independently advised and which followed the normal commercial criteria in force at the time it was negotiated."

---

[13] FA 2004, Sch.15, para.11(5).
[14] See **Ch.20** for a discussion of the full consideration exemption in relation to chattels.

HMRC commented in the same letter in relation to chattels:

> "It would be difficult to overturn an arm's length commercial arrangement entered into by parties who were independently advised."

Unlike the POAT charge in para.4 it is not necessary for the payment to be under any legal obligation or under any formal arrangement. Nor is it a requirement that the consideration must be taxable as rent. The authors have seen examples where the donor has paid the equivalent of full consideration on an ad hoc basis, e.g. by improving the property, paying capital repairs. This is still sufficient to obtain the POAT and reservation of benefit protection. The difficulty may come in proving that the donor is in fact paying full consideration for his occupation throughout the relevant period and also in tracking down what the donor has paid. Merely paying council tax and outgoings such as electricity will not be sufficient. However, if the gifted property is in poor condition it may not require the donor to pay much to ensure that the full consideration requirement is met. HMRC accept that full consideration can constitute not merely rent under an annual shorthold tenancy but also an upfront lump sum in exchange for say a seven-year full repairing lease. For a landed estate this may be a better option.

The CGT dimension

21–29 Bear in mind the CGT consequences of disposing of a house (or an interest in it). The donee will not be able to obtain PPR relief in the future unless he occupies it.

THE FAMILY DEBT SCHEME

21–30 More aggressive planning is the following arrangement, a variant of the home loan scheme, between spouses.

Example 21.7

- Tobias owns commercial properties which show a large unrealised capital gain. He can no longer carry out a *Melville* scheme[15] but wishes to give the properties to his grandchildren.

- He sells the properties at market value to his wife Ruth. The purchase price for the properties is left outstanding as a debt owed by Ruth which is repayable on the last of them to die. That debt is given by Tobias to his grandchildren. (Note that the properties can be sold for less than market value but should not be sold for more if the debt is to be fully allowable.)

- The tax consequences are as follows.

  (i) SDLT is payable by Ruth on the consideration payable for the purchase of the commercial properties.

---

[15] This was a scheme which allowed assets pregnant with gain to be settled into a discretionary trust with no inheritance tax payable (because the loss to the transferor's estate was minimal) and with capital gains tax hold over relief. From December 5, 2003 such schemes were blocked with hold-over relief no longer being available on gifts to settlor-interested trusts.

(ii) There is no capital gains tax payable by Tobias on the disposal of the properties to his wife because under TCGA 1992, s.58, the sale is treated as taking place at no gain no loss.

(iii) The POA Regime will not apply because the transfer is to a spouse (the fact it is a sale not a gift does not matter).[16]

(iv) For inheritance tax purposes, the properties are part of Ruth's estate but subject to a debt in favour of the grandchildren.[17] On Ruth's death the properties can pass to Tobias if he is still alive subject to the debt. On the last of Tobias and Ruth to die, the debt is repayable. Tobias has made a PET of the debt and so provided that he survives seven years there is no inheritance tax. There is no reservation of benefit provided the debt is not made repayable on demand.[18] There will be a substantial discount on the PET of the debt given that it is not repayable until the last of them to die.

(v) There may be capital gains tax or income tax repercussions on the eventual repayment of the debt, depending on how the arrangement is structured.

(vi) The income arising from the commercial properties is paid to Ruth but may be taxed as Tobias' under the settlement provisions.

A variant of this scheme involves a sale of the family home between spouses. **21–31** Although the property continues to be occupied by Tobias, the transfer to his wife is an excluded transaction for POA purposes (see para.10(1)(b)) and (provided the spouse/civil partner is domiciled here or neither of them are domiciled here) outside reservation of benefit (FA 1986, s.102(5)). The scheme can also be adapted for other assets such as equities pregnant with gain or shares in private companies. Here the POA position is less vulnerable to change (because POA can never apply to intangibles which are not settled) and there is only stamp duty at 0.5 per cent.

Since the 2006 legislation, normally the debt must be given outright to the **21–32** children or grandchildren and not on trust in order to avoid an immediately chargeable transfer. On the other hand if the parents are worried about the children divorcing and the loan being an asset of their estates, they can take some comfort in the fact that until the last of Tobias and Ruth to die, the debt cannot be called in. Watch FA 1986, s.103, and do not implement the scheme where there have been gifts by the purchasing spouse to the vendor spouse.[19] Take care where the asset being sold is jointly owned: it is important that the house or other property is not sold for more than its market value, otherwise the debt will not be deductible.

It is also important to ensure that if (in the above example) Ruth dies first and **21–33** the assets pass back to Tobias subject to the debt the terms of the debt do not involve Tobias taking on any personal liability, otherwise the deduction will not

---

[16] If the asset sold was shares rather than land then stamp duty would be at 0.5% and there would be no possibility of POA since the charge does not apply to intangibles which are not settled.

[17] It is of course critical that the debt is IHT deductible (e.g. on Ruth's death) and hence FA 1986, s.103 needs to be borne in mind.

[18] See **17–08**.

[19] See *Phizackerley* v *RCC* [2007] STC (SCD) 328.

be available on his death. It is generally easier if the debt is not made interest bearing.[20] That means the inheritance tax savings will be limited to the current value of the asset sold.

REVERSIONARY LEASE SCHEMES

21–34 Reversionary lease arrangements are discussed in **Ch.15**. It is now accepted by HMRC that they can be done without triggering a reservation of benefit problem. However, in most cases POAT will mean they are not feasible. Where they are useful is in the context of trust carve-outs and this is discussed in detail in **Ch15**. As noted there, these arrangements are still relevant even after October 5, 2008. For example, where a husband leaves properties to his spouse outright her options are limited in terms of inheritance tax planning if she wants to continue enjoying any benefits. She can carry out a reversionary lease scheme inheritance tax effectively but faces a POA charge. By contrast, if the husband leaves the spouse properties on an IPDI trust, provided the trustees are given sufficient overriding powers, they can carve-out an interest which is retained by the spouse on the same IPDI trusts and they appoint the valuable freehold interest or the long reversionary lease interest outright to the children. No POA issues arise. Spouse makes a PET and will hopefully survive seven years. The arrangement can be made over let properties as well as the main home. In practice, the main problem may be capital gains tax if there is a loss of main residence relief, but given the rate of 18 per cent this could be regarded as an acceptable price to pay.

selling the family home/borrowing on the family home

21–35 One of the (many) curious features about the POA Regime is the approach taken to sales of land and chattels. Unlike the reservation of benefit legislation, the POA Regime can apply even when no gift has been made. Any disposal of land which the disponer continues to occupy can, in principle, be caught unless it comes within a specific exemption.

Example 21.8

Rose and Emily, two sisters, have lived together for some years. Rose alone owns the house worth £800,000. She decides to sell for full consideration a half share in the property to Emily. (She may want the cash to supplement her lifestyle or may wish to give it away, to Emily or to other relatives.) Emily pays £400,000 for a 50 per cent share in the property.

(i) Despite the fact that Rose has not made Emily a gift nor made a transfer of value for inheritance tax purposes, she is prima facie caught by the POA Regime. A disposal of the property has been made and Rose continues in occupation. By contrast, if Rose had given away a half share to Emily, she would not have a POA charge as a result of the protection of para.11(5)(c) (incorporating the "sharing arrangements" in FA 1986, s.102B(4)).

---

[20] This avoids income tax problems on the interest and also problems later if the scheme has to be dismantled, e.g. on the divorce of the spouses.

(ii) The fact that Emily has paid full consideration for her share does not help Rose: the sale is not protected under para.10(1)(a) because it is not a sale of her whole interest in the land.

(iii) The pre-owned assets charge cannot be reduced under the non-exempt sale provisions because these require a transfer of the whole interest in land.

In the March 2005 Regulations,[21] reg.5 provides for certain exemptions from POA where there are sales of part at full value, namely: **21–36**

(a) an exemption for commercial sales of part (see reg.5(1)(a)); and

(b) certain other sales but only if carried out before March 7, 2005.

Example 21.9

Mary needs to raise cash on her home. After taking financial advice she enters into an equity release scheme with Rest Assurance Inc to whom she sells a 40 per cent share of the property. Under the general terms and conditions Mary is entitled to go on living in the property for the rest of her life. Mary is exempted from any POA charge by reg.5.

There is also an exemption for connected person disposals provided that (a) it was such as might be expected to have been made at arm's length between persons not connected with each other and either the disposal was for a consideration not in money or in the form of readily convertible assets or the disposal was made before March 7, 2005. The upshot is that unless the sale to a connected person occurred before March 7, 2005 Rose in the above example is caught by the POA charge. Accordingly, she will pay income tax on any interest generated by the cash of £400,000 plus a POA charge on the appropriate rental value. The cash of £400,000 is also part of Rose's estate for IHT purposes and similarly a half share in the property is part of Emily's estate.

Borrowing

By contrast if Rose raised the cash by borrowing from Emily the POAT regime does not apply because there has been no disposal of land and the cash borrowed has not funded the acquisition of the property. Emily could lend to Rose on the basis of an equity linked loan, fully secured on the house. On repayment of the loan, the increased value is likely to be subject to income tax in the hands of Emily as interest rather than capital gains tax but the loan should be deductible in Rose's estate. Watch s.103: if Rose has made any gifts to Emily or intends to leave her property in her Will then the debt may not be allowable for inheritance tax purposes. **21–37**

---

[21] SI 2005/724: see **Appendix I**.

Sales of whole for full consideration

21–38 What are arguably more controversial arrangements do not appear to be caught by the POA Regime. The starting point for any planning depends on using the exclusion given in para.10(1)(a). This provides a complete protection from the POA charge if the disposal is:

> "of his whole interest in the property except for any right expressly reserved by him over the property either by a transaction made at arm's length with a person not connected with him or by a transaction such as might be expected to be made at arm's length between persons not connected with each other."

The disposal need not be for cash: it can be an arm's length exchange of property.

21–39 One option that has been used in the past (and is still available) is for the whole house to be sold by the individual to a member of his family for full market value. The purchaser can then allow the vendor to live there free of charge. There is no gift, so the reservation of benefit provisions do not apply. The cash is part of the vendor's estate for inheritance tax purposes and he can, if he wishes, give it away in due course. This apparently simple transaction does, however, pose a number of problems. Whilst acceptable for IHT purposes, there are difficulties if the purchaser does not have sufficient cash to pay the purchase price. If the purchaser borrows from a bank and the vendor then gives cash to the purchaser to pay off the mortgage then the contribution condition is satisfied and a POA charge arises. In those circumstances, the purchaser might want the vendor to agree to leave the purchase price outstanding as a long-term loan.

In order to ensure that the para.10(1)(a) exclusion applies, the terms of the loan must be the same as those offered by any bank or building society, i.e. it should be on normal terms, interest bearing with interest being paid not rolled up, secured and with the usual deposit paid. It has to be shown that the whole arrangement is a transaction *"such as might be expected to be made at arm's length between persons not connected with each other"*.

21–40 SDLT will be payable by the purchaser who also may end up suffering capital gains tax on eventual sale of the property because the vendor who occupies it does not own it. In the past the problem could be solved by the purchaser settling the house on reverter to settlor trusts but this is no longer feasible.[22]

Sale of freehold reversion subject to a lease

21–41 Given the difficulties involved in finding sufficient cash to pay for the whole property, an alternative arrangement involves the taxpayer first carving-out a lease for himself for a fixed term (or possibly for life) at a nil or nominal rent, and then selling the freehold interest (subject to that lease) for full market value. There is no gift by the vendor, and therefore the disposal is not caught by FA 1986, s.102A. However, he has devalued the freehold reversion by carving-out the lease in his own favour. In the case of a 15-year lease one might expect the freehold value to be devalued by as much as one-half.

Such an arrangement is acceptable for IHT purposes, although it is important to ensure that the proper price is paid so that there is no element of bounty. The

---

[22] As a result of the 2006 changes in the IHT treatment of settlements see **Ch.18**.

valuations are difficult, not least because the transaction is not a common one. One problem is that there will be a loss of marriage value; the value of the freehold subject to the lease and the value of the lease are together unlikely to be equal to the vacant possession value. Should the purchaser pay for the marriage value as well as for the freehold reversion? If so, that would cause a problem under the POA Regime since it is not the sort of transaction that would be made between parties at arm's length: see para.10(1)(a)(ii).

If, instead, the vendor sells the reversion for a price equal to the value it has in the hands of the purchaser and he pays nothing for loss of marriage value, the vendor's estate has been diminished for IHT purposes. However, such a transaction not be a transfer of value if there was no intention to confer a gratuitous benefit on the purchaser.[23] Even if the vendor has made a transfer of value, he has not made a gift within the meaning of FA 1986, s.102(1) or s.102A(1). The question that remains is whether such a transaction can qualify for para.10(1)(a)(ii) protection from the POA charge. In a commercial transaction between unconnected parties (such as an equity release scheme) it would be common for the vendor to receive no payment for the loss of marriage value. **21–42**

When fixing the price for the encumbered freehold interest, account should be taken of the terms of the lease to be retained (i.e. the terms of the lease should have been agreed and considered by the valuers). Whilst there is some debate as to whether a lease for life or a lease for a term of years should be granted. The better view is that a lease for life should be avoided because of s.43(3) of the IHTA 1984: it is hard to argue that such a lease has been acquired for full consideration (although this seems to be accepted by HMRC in the IHT Manual). **21–43**

The capital gains tax problems mentioned above are still an issue. If the property is sold, the vendor will obtain principal private residence relief in respect of the lease which he retains but the purchaser will find that the freehold reversion is an appreciating asset in his estate which will not qualify for relief.

Funding the purchase price

Despite the reduced purchase price, difficulties can remain: suppose a purchasing child has insufficient cash to fund the purchase? Perhaps he cannot borrow from his bank and security on the property itself is of limited value because the child only owns the reversion and receives no rent. Can the vendor safely give cash to his child to enable the child to fund the purchase? The reservation of benefit substituted property rules do not apply to non-settled cash.[24] This would, however, cause POA problems. The contribution condition has been satisfied because consideration, namely cash, has been provided by the vendor for the acquisition of an interest in the land that he occupies.[25] **21–44**

---

[23] IHTA 1984, s.10.
[24] Sch.20, para.2(2)(b), assuming that the gift of cash was not made conditional on the purchase of the freehold reversion by the child.
[25] Of course, the normal limitations on the scope of the contribution conditions apply: for instance, if there had been an outright gift of cash before April 6, 1998 the POA charge is excluded.

Conclusions

21–46 IHT planning involving sales of the house (or chattels) to members of the family is still possible even under the POA Regime, but considerable care is needed to ensure that a charge to tax is avoided. HMRC not will accept that sales of freehold reversions subject to a retained lease are within the protection of para.10(1)(a) without clear valuation evidence of commerciality, and great care must be taken if the purchase money is given away. SDLT will increase the costs and CGT issues remain a problem if the vendor wishes to move.

CHAPTER 22

INSURANCE-BASED ARRANGEMENTS

There are a wide variety of arrangements involving insurance policies held in **22–01** trust which, in one form or another, avoid the reservation of benefit provisions by relying on the carve-out principle.[1] It is beyond the scope of this discussion to consider all these arrangements, but the following comments should provide some guidance. It should be noted, however, that the technical analysis provided by HMRC in relation to insurance products is far from satisfactory and seems hard to reconcile with the tax treatment under the POA Regime of other assets. For HMRC's approach to insurance based arrangements, see A2.133 et seq.; A2.47; A2.61 and A2.78–A2.81.

Qualitative carve-outs

Under one arrangement a policy is held by trustees on trusts to hold certain rights **22–02** under the policy for the settlor absolutely and other rights on trust for other beneficiaries. For example, under a critical illness policy, the trustees would hold the critical illness benefit on trust for the settlor absolutely and the death benefit on trust for his family. This is thought to be effective to avoid a reservation of benefit.

So far as the POA charge is concerned, the requirement under para.8 is that:

(a) the terms of a settlement, as they affect any property comprised in the settlement, are such that the settlement is a settlor-interested settlement (note, however, that a trust which can benefit the spouse of the settlor but not the settlor is not settlor-interested for the purposes of the POA Regime); and

(b) that property includes any property which is intangible property settled by the settlor or representing such property.

For this purpose, "settlement" and "settled property" have the same meanings as for IHT. Property held on trust for a person absolutely is not settled property for IHT purposes.

What is the settled property for this purpose? On one construction, it is the **22–03** insurance policy, which is the property comprised in the settlement. On that analysis, such arrangements are within para.8. On another construction:

(a) the rights held on trust absolutely for the settlor are not settled property; and

---

[1] The carve-out principle is discussed in the context of *Ingram* schemes: see **Ch.14**.

(b) the rights held on trust for the other beneficiaries are settled property but are not held on settlor-interested trusts.

It is the latter construction which HMRC have indicated they will adopt in discussions with the Association of British Insurers.[2] Although this is consistent with the IHT treatment of such arrangements, so far as the Regime is concerned it is arguable that the insurance policy as a whole is the relevant property for the purpose of para.8 and one cannot separate out the critical illness part from the remaining settled property.

An alternative construction is that even if the critical illness is "settled property" this is the only part of the trust property to which s.624 applies and therefore to which the Regime could apply.[3] The death benefits are held in a separate fund from which the settlor is excluded. Therefore the POA charge cannot apply to the death benefits. (In some unusual cases the settlor's estate can benefit from the death benefits and in these circumstances it may be that the settlor has not reserved a benefit but HMRC may apparently argue that there is a POA charge.)

Quantitative carve-outs: immediate drawdown

22–04 Under another arrangement (often marketed as "discounted gift schemes")[4] the settlor's entitlement is defined quantitatively, e.g. he makes a gift into settlement with certain "rights" being retained by him. The retained rights may comprise the right to receive a fixed portion of the trust fund if he is alive on the prospective payment date. Alternatively, there may be a series of single premium policies maturing on successive anniversaries of the initial investment date if the settlor is alive then. In the first case the other beneficiaries get what is left of the trust fund after the payments made to the settlor. In the second case until the settlor's interest in the fund vests, the trust assets are held on trust for the beneficiaries.

Although this is thought to be effective for reservation of benefit purposes (based on the carve-out principle), it would seem to be caught by para.8 because there is no segregation of the rights under the policy: the only intangible property is the policy. It appears, however, that HMRC propose to treat such arrangements in the same way as qualitative carve-outs.

22–05 HMRC's analysis is based on the idea that the trustees hold the settlor's retained rights on bare trust for the settlor. A bare trust is not a settlement for IHT purposes and provided that the settlor is excluded from all other benefits in the policy the Regime does not apply. Alternatively HMRC suggest that the settlor's retained rights may be held on trust but should be construed as being held in a separate trust. Again no charge arises. Even if there was a charge arising (for example because the retained rights are in fact part of the same trust) HMRC state: "any charge under [the Regime] would apply by reference to the value of the rights held on trust for the settlor, not by reference to the value of the underlying life policy".

If this is correct then presumably the same analysis could apply to any property held under reverter to settlor trusts. In **Ch.18** it is suggested that the settlor of a

---

[2] See A2.47.

[3] See **6–04** for a detailed discussion of sub-funds. Of course, property held in trust for the settlor absolutely is part of his estate for IHT purposes and so outside the para.8 charge (see para.11(1)(b)).

[4] See further **22-06** below.

reverter to settlor trust could be caught by POAT Regime if the trust holds intangibles. However, if it is correct that the settlor's interest is not settled at all or if it is settled is in a different trust or alternatively only that interest is valued for the purposes of the POA Regime, then there is no POA problem. HMRC seek to distinguish reverter to settlor trusts holding (for example) stocks and shares from reverter to settlor trusts holding insurance policies and argue that the settled property cannot be segregated in relation to stocks and shares. [5]

Discounted gift plans and the *Bower* case

The essence of a discounted gift plan is that the settlor makes a gift into settlement **22–06** but with certain rights in the settled property being retained. Typically the rights retained may be in a series of single premium policies maturing on successive anniversaries of the creation of the settlement or to future capital payments if the settlor is alive at the prospective payment date.

Diagrammatically the position is as follows:

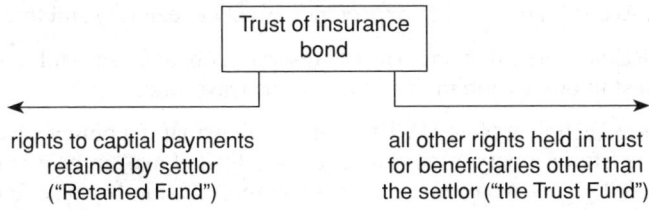

The arrangement is viewed as a "carve-out" or a "shearing arrangement" so provided that the rights retained by the settlor are sufficiently clearly defined and that he is excluded from all benefit in the Trust Fund there is no reservation of benefit.[6]

One of the attractions of the discounted gift plan lies in the "discount". The **22–07** transfer of value made by the settlor when establishing his trust is the fall in value of his estate and in calculating this it is necessary to arrive at a value for the rights that he retains in the Retained Fund (e.g. to five per cent capital payments out of the trust each year for as long as he lives). This will depend on such factors as age, health and sex and on the size of the capital payments that he will receive. The question therefore is what is the value of the Trust Fund, taking into account the existence of the Retained Fund? For instance, if A, a healthy 70-year old, put £500,000 into a discounted gift plan reserving a right to five per cent annual withdrawals of capital over the next 20 years[7] (if he is then alive) a substantial

---

[5] In theory though there should be no difference. What one is looking at in each case is the interest of the settlor under the trust and if the interest of the settlor in a life policy can be segregated so too can the interest of the settlor in stocks and shares. The current approach is to treat reverter to settlor trusts as within the para.8 charge.

[6] The arrangement involves a *chose in action* (viz rights under an insurance bond) which are not capable of separate transfer, i.e. unlike land where a settlor can retain a leasehold interest and transfer only the encumbered freehold, in this case the entire bond must be held in trust but with the rights under it split into a retained fund (for the settlor) and a settled fund (from which he is excluded). On the need for precision in defining the gifted property, see the speech of Lord Hoffmann in the *Ingram* case: [1999] STC at p.40.

[7] To avoid an income tax charge on the excess see *Sugden v Kent* [2001] STC 158.

discount will be in order. If it is of (say) 40 per cent then the transfer of value made by A is reduced to £300,000. If, however, A had been uninsurable when the scheme was effected then the retained rights would be worth less and therefore the transfer of value much larger.

The Bower Case[8]

22–08 Mrs Bower, aged 90, purchased a discounted gift bond for £73,000. The bond was held in trust under which Mrs Bower retained a five per cent life annuity (equivalent to withdrawals totalling £304.16 per month). She died approximately five months after taking out the policy. It was accepted that she had made a failed PET equal to the premium paid less the value at the time when the policy was taken out of her right to the life annuity. The sole issue was what value should be attributed to her retained rights. Note especially the following points.

  a. Medical reports indicated that when Mrs Bower took out the policy, her age should be loaded and treated for life expectancy purposes as being 103. Accordingly, her life expectancy was between two and three years.

  b. HMRC accepted that she had not reserved a benefit and did not enjoy an interest in possession in the whole of the trust fund.

  c. In their Technical Note HMRC took the view that if a policy was taken out on the life of a person with an age (or adjusted age) in excess of 90, the reserved rights would have a nil or nominal value because genuine life insurance would not be available in such cases. Further, as any buyer of the reserved rights would wish to lay off the mortality risk by taking out such cover, its absence rendered the rights effectively valueless.

  d. In arriving at the price to be paid by a buyer for Mrs Bower's retained rights, a reduction would be made for the expenses of purchase (for instance, legal expenses and possibly the cost of a further medical examination).

  e. HMRC argued that a purely nominal value of £250 should be attributed to the rights, largely because of the inability to lay off the mortality risk by taking out genuine life cover. This argument was rejected by the Special Commissioner who concluded:

"It seems realistic in this case to say that the buyer need not necessarily be of the risk-averse category who would lay off the mortality risk and then run fairly conventional discounting calculations, but might more appropriately be a speculator."

22–09   This approach was rejected by Lewison J.:

"In asking whether the sale in the open market contemplates that a sale must take place in "some sort of conventional market manner", it is not at all clear to me that the Special Commissioner appreciated that the hypothetical sale takes place in the real world. He was of course not wrong in saying that he was entitled to consider other possible purchasers, and I do not consider that the possibility of other possible

---

[8] [2008] STC (SCD) 582: *revs'd* [2009] STC 510.

purchasers is necessarily precluded. There must, of course, be an assumed buyer in order to give effect to the statutory hypothesis that the sale takes place.

But although the Special Commissioner was, in my judgment, entitled to consider possible purchasers, he was not entitled to invent them. The assumption of a buyer in order to give effect to the statutory hypothesis in addition tells you nothing about the price which the buyer is assumed to have paid. If in the real world an asset is worthless, the statutory hypothesis does not make it valuable. It is not, in my judgment, lip service to the hypothesis, as Mr Bretton argued, in those circumstances to ascribe a nominal value to an asset. On the contrary, it is the necessary consequence of a finding of fact that an asset is not commercially, as opposed to legally, saleable coupled with the assumption that a sale must be assumed to have taken place. In my judgment, therefore, Mr Ewart QC is correct in saying that at this point in his decision the Special Commissioner went wrong in law."

The Special Commissioner valued the retained rights at £4,200 as being the price **22–10** that he considered a speculator would pay. He arrived at this figure as follows:

i   he started from a "ceiling" calculation of £7,800 which had been arrived at by the insurance company on the basis of the life expectancy of a 103 year old; taking the number of monthly payments she might be expected to draw (2.5 years worth) and then discounting that sum to an equivalent present value by applying a 4.5 per cent interest rate, but allowing no deduction for the expenses of the buyer;

ii he then reduced that figure by one-third to allow for mortality risk; the inaccuracy of the life expectancy tables; the lack of competing purchasers; doubts about the medical opinions; and discounting for time;

iii finally he deducted £1,000 for estimated legal expenses in acquiring the retained rights.

He accepted that this method was very much based on the particular facts of the **22–11** particular case and that his approach *"of simply reducing the price by a 1/3 deduction from a ceiling figure might be much less tempting with a longer life expectancy"*.

This was scathingly rejected on appeal:

"In paragraph 37 he described his figure as being "little more than uninformed, but hopefully realistic, guesswork". Thus, the Special Commissioner himself acknowledged that there had been no evidence before him about how a price payable by a speculator might be calculated. Nevertheless, he went on to produce what he described as "my calculation and valuation". The Special Commissioner's method of calculation and valuation is not one that had been put forward by anyone and not put by him to any of the witnesses or parties for comment. This in itself was a breach of the rules of natural justice. But more important for present purposes is that it was not based on the evidence before the Special Commissioner. It flowed from the Special Commissioner's erroneous conclusion that he was required or entitled to populate the real market in which the hypothetical sale took place with hypothetical speculators who did not share the characteristics of real buyers."

Death of taxpayer

22–12 When the taxpayer dies the right to payments under the terms of the Retained Fund ceases. Does this mean that there is no IHT charge (in effect that the discounted amount is wholly free from charge)? HMRC's current practice is to treat the Retained Fund as valueless but it is far from clear that this is correct. The issue is whether the valuation exercise is to be performed *immediately before death* taking into account only factors known at that time or with the benefit of hindsight (i.e. with knowledge of the deceased's imminent demise). If the former method were to be adopted then a reduction in value as a result of the death under IHTA 1984, s.171 would not seem appropriate given that what is coming to an end on death is "any interest".[9]

The POA dimension

22–13 The introduction of the POA income tax charge in FA 2004 (with effect from April 6, 2005) led to concerns that discounted gift trusts were settlor-interested trusts which, because they contained intangible property, fell within the para.8 charge. Surprisingly, however, the position was not viewed in this light by HMRC who developed further the analysis adopted for reservation of benefit by concluding that the Retained Fund had not only been carved-out and retained by the settlor but that the rights in it were held on bare trust for the settlor. Hence the para.8 charge did not apply to this fund[10] and nor did it apply to the Trust Fund given that the settlor could not benefit under it.[11] It is thought that this argument is deeply flawed since there is no separate property in the Retained Fund: rather a single asset is held in trust and the settlor is entitled to certain benefits from that asset. However, many discounted gift arrangements have been established in reliance on this HMRC statement.

Impact of the FA 2006

22–14 The future of these plans was thrown into doubt as a result of the changes in the IHT treatment of settlements. The preferred trusts of the Trust Fund had been flexible interest in possession so that the creation of the trust was a PET. From March 22, 2006, however, it is no longer possible to create qualifying interests in possession[12] so that such a trust will involve an immediately chargeable transfer by the settlor. Accordingly, if the (discounted) value transferred exceeds the settlor's available IHT nil rate band, tax at 20 per cent will be payable on the

---

[9] The correct valuation procedure was considered in *Arkwright (PR of Williams decd) v IRC* [2004] STC (SCD) 89. See further Oliver L.J. in *Fetherstonehaugh v IRC* [1984] STC 261 at 268 who commented (in an obiter dicta) that:

"*The occasion of the deemed transfer of value is, it is true, related to the moment before the death of the deceased but there is nothing in the statute to suggest that the valuation is to be conducted on the basis that the impending demise of the deceased is a known factor which the hypothetical valuer is to take into account.*"

[10] Because it is not *a settlement* for IHT purposes.
[11] The analysis is found in the POA guidance notes.
[12] There are only restricted exceptions which are not relevant in this context.

excess. Further, the settlement so created will be subject to anniversary and exit charges and some concern was raised that for this purpose the value to be taxed would include the rights in the retained fund. Such fears appear to be ill founded, however, since HMRC considers:

a. that the same approach to that adopted for POA will be followed, i.e. the Retained Fund will be treated as a bare trust and so as a separate settlement and not therefore aggregated with the Trust Fund;

b. for the purpose of imposing the 10-year charge it will be necessary to value the insurance bond on the basis of what would a purchaser pay for it given that certain rights have been reserved to the settlor (in the form of the Retained Fund). Hence the normal discount will apply.

The main impact of the 2006 legislation has been in limiting the value of the discounted gift to £325,000 (or relevant nil rate band), which is necessary if an immediate IHT charge is to be avoided. For the majority of taxpayers who purchase discounted gift plans that ceiling will not be a problem. For those wishing to invest more there is the possibility of the Trust Fund being held on a bare trust for one or more individuals. This would mean that the transfer of value would then be a PET and so the nil rate band restriction overcome.

Eversden-based arrangements

Eversden-based arrangements involving insurance products are within para.8 and HMRC have indicated that such arrangements are among the targets of the POA charge.[13]　　　　　　　　　　　　　　　　　　　　　　　　　　　　**22–15**

Gift and loan arrangements

Under some arrangements the settlor effects a policy and settles it on trust for the benefit of others. He then makes an interest-free loan repayable on demand to the trustees. The settlor is excluded from the settlement. The trustees use the loan to purchase more policies and make partial surrenders each year to pay off the loan. HMRC accept that such an arrangement is not within para.8 because any benefit accruing to the settlor from the repayment of the interest-free loan will arise to him as a creditor, not under the terms of the settlement (*Jenkins v IRC*[14] had initially been quoted by HMRC to refute this view). No funds have been provided or settled on trust.　　　　　　　　　　　　　　　　　　　　　　　　　　　　**22–16**

Personal pensions

It is common for an individual to settle a personal pension on trusts under which the pension rights are held absolutely for the individual and the death benefit is held on discretionary trusts for his family. HMRC will treat such arrangement in　　**22–17**

---

[13] For a detailed discussion, see **Ch.16**.
[14] [1944] 2 All E.R. 491. See 2004 SWTI, p.2160.

the same way as qualitative carve-outs (i.e. that there is no charge under the POA Regime).[15]

Partnership death benefits

22–18 It is common for partners in a firm to take out policies on their own lives or else a single policy payable on a partner's death. The policies are held on discretionary trusts for all the partners with the intention that on the death of any partner his fellow partners are put in funds to purchase the deceased partner's share in the business. The deceased partner will generally wish to remain a beneficiary of the policy taken out in case he leaves the partnership. In that case the policy on his life can be assigned back to him because it is no longer of use to the other partners.

Strictly, such arrangements appear to be within para.8 and HMRC have confirmed this at the end of **Appendix 1** of the guidance notes.[16] In particular the "no-bounty" defence will not be available because the definition of "settlement" for these purposes is the IHT definition, not the income tax definition (see **6–01**). Such policies are not within the GWR rules because the arrangement is on commercial terms. Hence there is no protection under para.11(3). As noted in **Ch.6**, similar arrangements are also often set up by shareholders in a private limited company. They too will be caught under para.8. It is possible that if the policy is a term policy and the life assured is in good health then the taxable benefit will be within the de minimis provisions but the taxpayer will still have to go to the trouble of obtaining annual valuations.

If the life policy is one which automatically reverts to the settlor if the settlor leaves the partnership (or business) but the trustees have retained no discretions exercisable in favour of the settlor, presumably the taxpayer could argue that his interest is held under some form of bare trust (as in the qualitative arrangements mentioned above) and hence there is no POA charge. It is not known if HMRC take this view.

What would be desirable would be for HMRC to agree that all commercial arrangements are outside the Regime.[17] After all such arrangements will not be caught by GWR nor by the income tax settlement code in ITTOIA 2005 so it is perverse that the Regime (designed to stop circumvention of the GWR provisions) should apply.

Double taxation

22–19 If para.8 does apply and charges are imposed under the insurance policy "chargeable events" legislation, the tax paid under the chargeable events legislation reduces the chargeable amount under the Regime.[18] However, tax charges on chargeable events (e.g. on the surrender of a policy) are likely to arise after most of the charges imposed under the Regime so that this will be of little, if any, comfort.

---

[15] See A2.80.

[16] See A2.63.

[17] The let-out in para.10 for commercial sales of whole in relation to houses and chattels does not apply to intangibles. It does not appear that an exemption from the Regime is in prospect: see A2.78.

[18] See **6–1**.

Pre-18 March 1986 policies[19]

Some life policies were taken out prior to the introduction of the GWR legislation on March 18, 1986. Hence the settlor was often included as a discretionary beneficiary because there was no need at that time to worry about the GWR rules. The difficulty is that premiums have continued to be paid on such policies post March 17, 1986. In these circumstances FA 1986, s.102(6) gave an exemption from the GWR provisions for premiums that were within the original amount payable under the contract or increased at a pre-arranged rate, say under a cost of living increase option. The life policy could not, however, be varied.

22–20

Are premiums paid post March 17, 1986 on a policy taken out before March 18, 1986 within the Regime? If so, how are such policies to be valued for the purposes of assessing the charge—does one apportion between the premiums paid pre- and post- March 1986? It is not even clear how the life policy itself should be valued in these circumstances. There is no reason why the surrender value should be taken. The settlor could, of course, be excluded from the policy to avoid a problem under the Regime.

In any event, it might be argued that there is no problem under the Regime because the payment of the premiums does not in itself add property to the settlement; it merely maintains the value of the settled property, i.e. the life policy itself. Paragraph 8 refers to property settled or added to a settlement after March 17, 1986. If the settlor pays the premiums to the life policy company direct rather than to the trustees arguably he is not caught. HMRC disagree with this analysis.[20] *"The proportion of the value of the policy which is attributable to post March 18, 1986[21] premiums will be subject to the income tax charge although that presumably will increase year by year as more premiums are paid."* It may well be that the notional benefit on the policies attributable to post March 17, 1986 premiums will fall within the de minimis exemption anyway.

22–21

---

[19] For further commentary, see A2.81.

[20] However, see *Taxation* June 30, 2005, p.359, where it is stated that HMRC confirm that such a policy is indeed within the POA Regime.

[21] Presumably this should read post March 17, 1986.

CHAPTER 23

CASH GIFTS

SETTING THE SCENE

23–01   ***Example 23.1***

Jason has lived abroad for many years and plans to return home. In 2000, he gave his daughter, Laos, £250,000 which she used later to purchase a Suffolk property ("the Crow's Nest"). On his return to England in 2002, Jason occupies the property with Laos.

Reservation of benefit

23–02   Jason has made a gift to his daughter and now occupies the property purchased: is he caught by the reservation of benefit rules in FA 1986? The relevant provisions are as follows.

(a) Section 102(1) of the FA 1986 provides that there is a gift with reservation if an individual disposes of any property (here the cash) by way of gift and either: (a) possession and enjoyment of the property is not bona fide assumed by the donee, or (b) at any time in the seven years prior to the donor's death the property is not enjoyed to the entire exclusion of the donor and of any benefit to him by contract or otherwise.

(b) Paragraph 6(1)(c) of Sch.20 to the FA 1986 is also relevant. This provides that in determining whether any property which is disposed of by way of gift is enjoyed to the entire exclusion of the donor and of any benefit to him by contract or otherwise, a benefit which the donor obtained by virtue of any associated operations of which the disposal by way of gift is one shall be treated as a benefit to him by contract or otherwise.

(c) Associated operations are defined by s.268 of the IHTA 1984 to mean any two or more operations of any kind being: (a) operations which affect the same property or one of which affects some property and the other or others of which affect property representing that property or (b) any two operations of which one is effected with reference to the other or with a view to enabling the other to be effected or facilitating its being effected.

(d) Finally Sch.20, para.2 ("substitutions and accretions") deals with substitutions but the paragraph does not apply if the property is a gift of cash.[1]

Has Jason reserved a benefit in the cash gifted?

Prima facie it does not appear that there is any reservation of benefit in the cash **23–03** itself because the cash has gone and Sch.20 provides no tracing provisions for outright gifts of cash. There is no direct link between the benefit received (donor living in the property) and the gift of cash. The benefit to Jason of occupying the house does not arise from the gift of cash unless that gift was in some way made conditional on being used to purchase a property.

The property gifted (i.e. the cash) has been enjoyed to the entire exclusion of Jason provided that the gift had not been made **conditional** on being used to purchase the property: otherwise there is a risk that the gift is in fact of an interest in land or alternatively (and more likely here) that Jason is treated as receiving a benefit in the cash gifted because it was made on the basis and on the understanding that he should be allowed to continue in occupation. (The benefit does not need to come from the gifted asset as such if it arises out of the gift.) So, HMRC might argue that Laos is estopped from denying Jason's occupation once the gift has been made, because he had made the gift under an agreement that she would use the funds to purchase the property and so she is estopped from changing her mind later.

Position of Jason

In this case, however, it seems difficult to argue that the gift of cash was in reality **23–04** a gift of the Crow's Nest. On the basis of estate duty cases such as *Sneddon v Lord Advocate*[2] (gift of cash used to purchase shares three days later) and *Potter v Inland Revenue*[3] (gift from donor of cash expressed to be to enable the donee to purchase shares), the subject-matter of the gift was nevertheless the cash not the property purchased, and this is important in the context of reservation of benefit. The fact that the money was given for a particular purpose does not mean that the gift was subject to a legally enforceable condition.

Effect of the associated operations rule

It is not thought that the associated operations rule will affect the conclusion: **23–05** either the arrangement involves a reservation in the gifted property or the reservation of benefit provisions are inapplicable.

---

[1] para.2(2)(b). Note also that different rules apply if the original property disposed of by the gift is not cash or is cash which "becomes settled property by virtue of the gift": Sch.20, para.2(2)(a). The rules affecting settled gifts are in para.5 which treats the gift as being of property comprised in the trust fund from time to time. There is therefore no exemption for settled cash gifts.

[2] 2 [1954] A.C. 257.

[3] [1958] S.L.T. 198.

It might be argued that the gift of cash and the purchase of the freehold are associated transactions in that the gift of cash was made at least with reference to the subsequent purchase and questions of estoppel and conditional gifts are not relevant. But is para.6(1)(c) of Sch.20 wide enough to deem the benefit from the associated operation (the purchase) to be a benefit to the donor in the property disposed of (the gift of cash)? If, as is thought, the benefit enjoyed from the associated operation must entrench in some way upon the possession of the actual gifted property in order for there to be a reservation of benefit, then associated operations do not cause an additional reservation of benefit problem. The benefit enjoyed (i.e. the occupation of the house) does not in itself entrench on the gift of the cash. Put another way, the point is that HMRC may be able to establish that Jason has received a benefit from the associated operation made by his daughter (namely the purchase of the property) but they also have to show that the gifted property (i.e. the cash) is not enjoyed to the entire exclusion of any benefit to Jason. Unless the cash gift was conditional or Laos was estopped from using the cash in any other way, Jason does not enjoy a benefit from the cash as such. The purchase of a property by Laos combined with her allowing him to live there benefits him but this is still not a benefit from the cash itself which has been spent.

Approach of HMRC

23–06 In the IHT manual[4] HMRC accept that the tracing rules do not apply to an absolute gift of a sum of money. This is qualified in two ways:

(a) if the absolute cash gift is itself subject to a reservation then the sum of money will be taxable; and

(b) "a gift which initially seems to be of cash may in reality be a GWR, by associated operations, of other property". The example given involves A giving £100,000 cash to B which B uses to buy A's residence (worth £100,000) in which A continues to reside. HMRC comment that "this is a GWR, by associated operations, of the residence".

As already noted, it is difficult to see how the associated operations rules can be used to re-characterise a gift as being of property rather than of cash. Of course, the specific example involves a circular arrangement in which the actual cash may never have changed hands. The weakness of the argument appears underlined by the subsequent comments (under the heading "What to do").

> "You will not normally raise any enquiries to see if a gift which appears to be of cash may be a gift, by associated operations, of other property. Only ask questions if there is a positive reason for doing so, *e.g.* where
>
> the gift is of an odd amount, such as £49,563.15, which suggests it may be related to a purchase by the donee,
>
> or
>
> there is specific information that the gift was related to the acquisition by the donee of property, especially if the acquisition is from the donor."

---

⁴ See IHTM14372.

"An absolute gift of cash is not subject to the inheritance tax reservation of benefit provisions unless the donor retains a benefit in the cash itself. For example, A, while a partner in a business, withdraws capital from his capital account and gifts this to B, who then lends the partnership an equivalent cash sum. That sum is still on loan to the partnership when A dies. The cash sum is treated as a gift with reservation."[5]

Despite the example cited in the manual, HMRC appear to take a more circumspect position in the guidance notes:

"where an absolute gift of cash may later be used by the recipient to purchase property occupied or enjoyed by the donor, for example, the application of the reservation of benefit rules to this property is precluded unless the transaction can be shown to be a gift with reservation of benefit by associated operations, of the purchased property."

So there is no categoric statement that the associated operations must necessarily apply where cash is used to purchase a house for the donor to live in. Equally HMRC apparently have not given up the idea that the associated operations could be invoked in certain circumstances although the authors have never seen them take this point in practice.

Conclusion on the IHT position

In conclusion, it does not follow that all benefits referable to a gift will come **23–08** within s.102. It is not sufficient to take the situation as a whole and find that the donor has continued to enjoy substantial advantages which have **some relation** to the gifted property. Each advantage must be considered separately to determine whether it is a benefit within the statute.[6] In the authors' view outright cash gifts to an individual will rarely be caught by the reservation of benefit rules.

IMPACT OF THE PRE-OWNED ASSET REGIME

Given that Jason's gift is not caught by the reservation of benefit rules, it will fall **23–09** within the POAT Regime so that he will suffer an income tax charge from April 6, 2005. The following points may be noted.

(a) Paragraph 3 applies given that Jason is in occupation of the property and that the contribution condition is met.

(b) If Laos had provided some of the purchase price for the "Crow's Nest", para.4(2) will require an apportionment of DV to determine such part of the value of the relevant land as may be attributed to the consideration provided by Jason.

(c) Although Jason is not in sole occupation, no allowance appears to be made for this in fixing the rental value of "Crow's Nest".

---

[5] A2.38.

[6] *Oakes v Stamp Duties Commissioner of New South Wales* [1954] A.C. 57 at 72; and see *St Aubyn v AG* [1952] A.C. 15.

23–10 If the facts are varied so that Jason made the gift to his daughter in March 2000 and only returns to England in April 2007 when he occupies the property for the first time, then as a result of FA 2004, Sch.15, para.10(2)(c),[8] the pre-owned asset charge will not apply.

The introduction of this seven-year defence (which occurred when the legislation was amended at Committee Stage in 2004) is somewhat curious—the explanation for its introduction presumably being the need to impose some limit on the operation of the contribution condition.[9] Of course the seven-year period echoes:

(a) the PET period in the IHT legislation: once the donor has survived his gift by this period it is exempt. In the same way a donor is free to enjoy the use of property purchased with his gifted cash once that period is up; and

(b) in the anti-*Ingram* legislation there is no reservation if the carve-out is effected at least seven years before the interest in land is given away.[10]

In fact the POAT Regime designed to catch cash gifts is more limited than perhaps HMRC originally anticipated. Only outright cash gifts made after April 5, 1998 are caught by the Regime even if occupation of the property purchased with the gifted money took place soon after the original gift.

23–11 Accordingly if Jason had made the cash gift in March 1998 and then in 2002 took up occupation no POA charge is due even though he occupied the property within seven years of the cash gift.

Curiously para.10(2)(c) refers to outright cash gifts "to the other person" and in the authors' view could include gifts of cash into settlement.[11] As noted above, such gifts are generally caught by the reservation of benefit provisions anyway because the tracing provisions apply but there may be circumstances in which a cash gift into settlement is exempt from the reservation of benefit provisions and also from the POA charge.

Example 23.2

In 2002 Perseus settles cash on old-style qualifying interest in possession trusts for his spouse and he can also benefit under the trust. As noted previously[12] such a transaction cannot be excluded because para.8 transactions can never be excluded transactions within para.10. Hence Perseus is subject to a POA charge.

In 2006, in order to avoid a POA charge on Perseus the trustees then purchase a house with the cash and terminate the spousal interest in

---

[7] See **5–21**.

[8] The arrangement is an excluded transaction.

[9] See *Taxation*, May 6, 2004, p.13 (Bruce Sutherland).

[10] See **14–10**.

[11] Contrast the wording in para.10(2)(e) which refers expressly to a gift to an *individual*. The Independent Taxation Manual comments that *"a gift is not an outright gift if it is subject to conditions or if it could revert to the donor in any circumstances whatsoever"*.But see also A2.10—HMRC do not accept this. See **Ch 5**.

[12] See **Chs 5** and **6**.

possession. The property is initially rented out but then in 2010 Perseus occupies the house.

The POA analysis is that the transaction is not excluded under para.10(2)(b) because of the proviso in para.10(3) but it could be excluded under para.10(2)(c) as an outright gift of money to a person. Hence provided Perseus does not occupy the property within seven years of the gift of cash he is protected from a charge under the Regime.

Example 23.3

What would be the position if Perseus gave the cash to the trustees in March 1998, the spouse took a qualifying interest in possession initially which is later terminated and Perseus occupies the house purchased with the cash in say 2000? It is believed that there is still no POA charge. There has been an outright gift of cash prior to April 1998, albeit into settlement. The reservation of benefit rules do not apply.[13] It does not matter that Perseus goes into occupation within seven years provided the gift was made more than seven years before the POAT Regime came into force.

Options for taxpayers

What are the options for Jason in *Example 23.1* if he is caught by the POA charge, e.g. because the cash gift was made on or after April 6, 1998 and he occupies the purchased property within seven years?   **23–12**

Election

Jason could elect for the reservation of benefit rules to apply[14] in order to avoid   **23–13** the income tax charge. He should consider whether it will then be advantageous to pay full consideration for his occupation (calculated on the basis that it is not "exclusive") in order to cause the reservation to come to an end.[15] Obviously this will depend on what (if anything) Jason can afford to pay and the calculation of the benefit under para.3 (on which he will suffer up to 40 per cent in income tax) as against "full consideration" under the Sch.20 rules.

Reverter to settlor trust

Prior to March 22, 2006 Laos could have settled the property on qualifying   **23–14** interest in possession trusts for Jason remainder to her; then Jason would have been protected from a POA charge by virtue of para.11(1)(a) (ownership exemption) and the value of the trust fund would not form part of his estate for inheritance tax purposes on his death assuming Laos survived him.[16] However, Laos then could not occupy the property (because she had made a disposal herself

---

[13] But for a different reason—the transfer is spouse exempt—see **Ch.16**.
[14] See **Ch.11**.
[15] This will result in Jason making a deemed PET under FA 1986, s.102(4): see **11–29** et seq.
[16] See further **Ch.18**.

for POA purposes). Such reverter to settlor arrangements are discussed in **Ch.18** but are no longer feasible following the inheritance tax changes in 2006. In any event, even existing arrangements will generally no longer protect Jason from a POAT charge following the changes effective from December 5, 2005. (See **Chs 7** and **18** and FA 2006, s.80).

Cash gifts—shared occupation

23–15 Suppose Jason gives Laos cash to purchase a house. Laos and Jason eventually pool resources and jointly buy a house for their joint occupation. In these circumstances there is no POA charge (see para.11(8)). The conclusion is that if people are going to live together it is preferable that they do not give away cash sufficient to enable the donee to purchase **all** the land but only sufficient cash to ensure that each party has an undivided share in the land. In these circumstances there will be no charge under the Regime and no reservation of benefit.

Improvements

23–16 Cash gifts still have a place in tax planning provided the cash is not used to acquire an interest in land. Further, there is nothing to stop the cash being used by the donee to improve land already acquired.

Example 23.4

Martin gives £200,000 to his son from the sale proceeds of his house. He then immediately moves in to a house next door to his son which is owned by the son already and the son uses most of the cash to improve the house so that it is suitable for Martin's occupation. In these circumstances neither reservation of benefit nor POAT will be a problem.

CHAPTER 24

FOREIGN DOMICILIARIES AND ESTATE PLANNING

This chapter discusses one particular aspect of a foreign domiciliary's affairs: **24–01** namely ways of mitigating his IHT exposure, taking into account pre-owned assets income tax and taking into account the changes to the taxation of foreign domiciliaries that came into effect from April 6, 2008.[1] The basic IHT regime for foreign domiciliaries has been outlined in **Ch.8**. The main IHT risk for the foreign domiciliary is if he acquires valuable UK property.

The impact of pre-owned assets income tax on foreign domiciliaries has already been discussed in **Ch.8**. As noted there, foreign domiciliaries have the benefit of special reliefs contained in para.12 and the exemptions in para.11 are also of relevance to them. It should be remembered that POAT only applies to UK residents so any non-resident, wherever domiciled, is outside the scope of the tax and does not need to consider it further (unless they plan to return to the UK).

Example 24.1

Petros is a famous actor, domiciled by origin in the UK but resident in Monaco. He spends his time in a number of different countries, but rarely in the UK. He has no definite intention to settle permanently in any particular place and therefore retains his UK domicile. For many years he has owned a £10m house in London. He stays there when he returns to the UK for assignments and which his children also like to use it. He wishes to avoid IHT. There is nothing to stop him granting a reversionary lease over the property to his children and continuing to occupy the property by virtue of his retained freehold. The reservation of benefit rules are thus avoided and while he is non-resident, POAT does not apply.[2] The gift of the lease is a PET.

foreign domiciliaries and poat

There are three main ways in which the POA regime can be a problem for the **24–02** foreign domiciliary living in the UK.

First, HMRC have now indicated that where a trust funded by the settlor has **24–03** lent money to a company which owns the house then the company shares are worth less than the value of the house and the loan does not derive its value from

---

[1] For a more detailed discussion of the general effect of those changes on foreign domiciliaries, see Chamberlain and Whitehouse, *Trust Taxation*, 2nd edn (2008) and note 11 in **Ch.8**.
[2] See **Ch.15** for further details.

the house. This can mean a POA charge on the difference between the value of the company shares subject to the debt and the house even though company shares and loan may be in the settlor's estate.[3]

24–04 Secondly, many foreign domiciliaries purchased UK homes prior to March 22, 2006 using two qualifying interest in possession trusts—one holding the debt and the other holding the house subject to the debt. The idea was that although the debt was an excluded liability within para.11(7), it did not reduce the value of the settlor's estate for POA purposes because he had a qualifying interest in possession in the trust holding the debt (see para.11(6)). Nevertheless the debt did reduce the value of the house for inheritance tax purposes. The debt was a foreign asset held in an excluded property trust and therefore not chargeable to IHT. Such structures already in existence may not be affected but after March 21, 2006 it is not possible to create an inter vivos debt trust with a qualifying interest in possession.

24–05 Thirdly, and most seriously, FA 2006, s.80 has had an adverse effect on foreign domiciliaries where a trust is or has been a qualifying interest in possession trust. For many years a foreign domiciliary who wished to own, e.g. a house in London, was advised to establish a trust which owned all the shares in an offshore company which in turn owned the house. The rationale was that the relevant asset for IHT purposes was the shares in the company which would be held in an excluded property settlement. There then arose a protracted controversy concerning the possible exposure of the foreign domiciliary to a charge to income tax under what was then Sch.E (now ITEPA 2003, ss.97–113) by reason of the benefit of the occupation conferred upon him if he was an actual or a shadow director of the company. The *Dimsey*,[4] *Allen*[5] and *Deverell*[6] cases exacerbated this problem and accordingly new structures were developed which are discussed below. However, s.80 can prove a problem for foreign domiciliaries with UK houses, although in practice an election into the reservation of benefit provisions may not be disadvantageous.[7]

foreign domiciliaries and the family home—the options

The foreign domiciliary is generally concerned to avoid IHT on the home he occupies in the UK and possibly also his UK pictures and furniture. His overseas assets can easily be protected from IHT by means of a trust provided such trust is set up before he becomes deemed domiciled here. UK houses are more difficult since by definition they are not excluded property. The obvious solution is to own the property through a non-UK company. This provides complete IHT protection but raises capital gains tax and income tax issues. This section looks at this and other options on the family home.

---

[3] See **Ch.7** for further discussion on whether this view is correct. A loan by the settlor to a company or trust which then purchases a house from a third party would not appear to satisfy the contribution condition so the transaction is not caught by POAT anyway. See **Ch.3** and in particular **3–11** et seq. See also **7–20** Example 7.8(e).

[4] *R v Dimsey* [2001] S.T.C. 1520.

[5] *R v Allen* [2001] S.T.C. 1537.

[6] *Secretary of State for Trade & Industry v Deverell* [2001] Ch. 340.

[7] See **8-19**.

Previous options—offshore "home loan" arrangements

Prior to March 22, 2006 these involved two trusts. The foreign domiciled settlor **24–06** funded the first trust, which was often discretionary, which in turn funded a company wholly owned by that trust. The company lent the funds to a second trust, under which the foreign domiciliary had an interest in possession and which used the funds to purchase the house. The loan, which was secured on the house, was left outstanding interest-free and repayable on demand.

Diagrammatically the position was as follows:

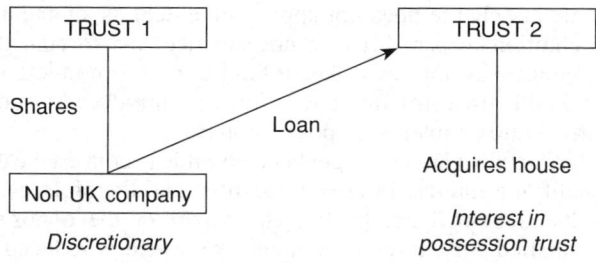

It will be noted that the house is no longer owned by a company so that the **24–07** shadow director problem no longer applies. An alternative structure was for the discretionary trust to lend the cash by way of a specialty debt to the interest in possession trust with no formal charge taken over the house and no company involved. This was thought to make the loan non-UK situated (and in any event both debtor and creditor are non-UK resident) but in order to ensure the IHT deductibility of the debt by the interest in possession trustees, the interest in possession trust must hold no other property.[8]

Assume that the company (or discretionary trust) lent to the interest in possession trust £1,500,000 all of which the trust used to purchase the house and that 10 years later, when the foreign domiciliary died, the house was worth £2,000,000. For IHT purposes the value of the property would be reduced by the debt owed to the company and so worth only £500,000. The debt was a non-United Kingdom situs asset and so was excluded property in the hands of the discretionary trustees. The net result was to take the amount of the debt outside the scope of IHT. In many cases the foreign domiciliary and his spouse had successive life interests in the property, so that if the foreign domiciliary's spouse survived him any charge on the excess value of the property on his death was deferred until the death of his spouse. Alternatively any exposure to UK tax on the excess was covered by insurance arrangements.

The POA Regime adversely affected the tax effectiveness of some of these **24–08** arrangements. Although both the para.12(2) basic relief and the settled property para.12(3) relief will operate in respect of the shares in the company (or the debt if it was held directly by the trustees and was non-UK situs), neither of these reliefs is available in respect of the house, because it is situated in the United Kingdom and is not excluded property. If the foreign domiciliary has a qualifying interest in possession in the house, the para.11(1) ownership exemption will prima facie be available but only to the extent that the value of the house exceeds the "excluded liability" of, returning to the above example, £1,500,000. The

---

[8] See IHTA 1984, s.162.

effect (given that it seems clear that the debt is indeed an excluded liability) is that the first £1,500,000 of the house will be within the POA Regime and be subject to annual income tax charges.

24–09 However, Sch.15, para.11(6) provides that there is a POA charge on the debt only "*where the value of someone's estate for the purposes of IHT is reduced by an excluded liability affecting any property*". Accordingly, if the discretionary trust holding the debt was converted into a qualifying interest in possession trust, the effect was that the debt was now part of the foreign domiciliary's estate for IHT purposes so that the value of his estate was not reduced. Although the debt is excluded property and so outside the inheritance tax net at death, nevertheless the POA income tax charge does not apply to the debt as an excluded liability because the condition in para.11(6) is not satisfied: the foreign domiciliary's estate is not reduced by the debt. Accordingly, foreign domiciliaries quickly amended their double trust structure once POA was introduced by converting the discretionary trust into an interest in possession trust.[9]

24–10 Since March 22, 2006 it has no longer been possible to convert the discretionary trust into a qualifying interest in possession trust and therefore a discretionary trust holding the debt will not be treated as part of the donor's estate and para.11(6) is satisfied—the foreign domiciliary's estate is reduced by the debt even though he reserves a benefit in the debt owned by the discretionary trust. Reserved benefit property is not treated as part of a person's estate: it is merely taxable on death. Hence a debt in which the foreign domiciliary reserves a benefit where he does not have a qualifying IIP is one that reduces his estate and the POA charge[10] can apply. Moreover those foreign domiciliaries who converted their debt trust into a qualifying interest in possession trust prior to March 22, 2006 found themselves potentially within FA 2006, s.80 (the anti-reverter to settlor trust legislation), i.e. back within a POA charge from December 5, 2005. There were arguments against this latter point. For example, the loan might not satisfy the contribution condition even though derived from a trust funded by the settlor because nothing has been "provided" for the acquisition of the land.[11]

In any event, even if s.80 did apply, it could be argued that an election into reservation of benefit may have no adverse inheritance tax effect if the house is sold by the time the foreign domiciliary dies. All that happens is that the reserved benefit property is excluded property at the date of his death and therefore outside IHT. Alternatively the effect of the election in these circumstances appears to be to give the taxpayer the benefit of the deduction for the debt.[12]

---

[9] Note that the value of the house in the property trust is still reduced by the debt so that property in the taxpayer's estate is reduced in value. However, the reduction is then comprised in his estate by virtue of the interest in possession in the debt trust. Overall therefore there is no reduction in value of his total estate because of the debt. It is not considered appropriate in this case to consider the two trusts in isolation (contrast the approach of Mann J. in *St Barbe Green v IRC* [2005] STC. 288).

[10] See **Ch.18**.

[11] See **7-20**.

[12] See **Ch.12**.

Current options for the foreign domiciliary

What are the alternatives now? The foreign domiciliary can obviously implement **24–11** the planning open to any UK domiciliary over his UK property.[13] However, he has other options.

Direct ownership

This is simple. The risk of IHT may be mitigated by taking out term assurance which is written in trust or taken out offshore. If the taxpayer is married then the inheritance tax liability is likely to arise only on the second death and term assurance may be cheap. Perhaps the taxpayer will rely on having sufficient warning of his death to transfer the house into an offshore company moments before death (albeit with an SDLT charge) so that at death he owns only non-*situs* property. This would depend on him not being UK deemed domiciled at death. This also avoids the capital gains tax problems associated with holding a house in trust from April 6, 2008 which are discussed below. If he eventually leaves the UK as anticipated, the house is likely to be sold and the IHT problem disappears.

Alternatively he can always charge the house with commercial debt and keep his cash offshore. This house is not subject to IHT. Watch FA 1986, s.103.

Ownership through a company

In some cases it is still worthwhile for a foreign domiciliary to purchase a house **24–12** in the UK through a company which is owned by a trust, particularly if he is non-UK resident or is likely to remain in the UK for only a few years. A company provides complete inheritance tax protection. The company should probably be funded by way of share capital rather than loan from the trustees to avoid any POA problem. The main immediate risk is income tax due to the shadow director charge but this can be minimised with careful management.[14] One way round the s.106 shadow director income tax charge is for the company to incur no cost in the acquisition of the property. This would mean that the foreign domiciliary buys the house and then gives it to a wholly owned company. However, there is SDLT[15] payable and there is a concern that the gifted land remains in his estate for IHT because of the reservation of benefit provisions. Furthermore if the company shares are sold by the foreign domiciliary the gain involved is likely to be substantial (albeit not chargeable unless remitted) because of the gift of the

---

[13] See **Ch.2**.

[14] Unfortunately the legislation which exempted foreign houses held in a company from any risk of income tax did not apply to UK houses (see ITEPA s.100A 2003). The risk is that the occupation may be taxable as a benefit in kind under ITEPA 2003, ss.97–113. This normally results in tax on notional earnings each year equal to 4.75% (the official rate of interest) of the cost to the company of providing a house worth over £43,937.50 (s.106 and see also s.105, ITEPA 2003). Hence a house costing £1 million could mean an assessable benefit of £57,812 annually on the foreign domiciliary and income tax (at 40%) of £17,575. This may well be more than the market rent for the property, so that even if the foreign domiciliary pays a market rent of say £50,000 this will not wholly eradicate the charge although it will reduce the taxable benefit.

[15] FA 2003, s.53.

house. If the company sells the house then there is no main residence relief and the foreign domiciliary who is UK resident at that point is chargeable on an <u>arising</u> basis in respect of any gain realised by the company where it arises on the disposal of a UK asset. Even if the company shares are gifted to a trust a substantial gain would be realised on the settlement of the shares and eventually taxed on the foreign domiciliary.[16]

24–13   The other problem since April 6, 2008,[17] where the company is held in trust, is capital gains tax under TCGA 1992, s.87, on the benefit of the settlor beneficiary's occupation. The house will not qualify for main residence relief given it is held by a company. The result is that on a disposal of the house or company shares, the foreign domiciliary could be charged under TCGA 1992, s.87 by reference to the benefit of his past occupation if he is still UK resident at the date gains are matched.[18] The remittance basis will not protect him because the benefits have been received here.

Example 24.2

H occupies a UK house but it is owned in an offshore company which in turn is owned by a trust. He has no inheritance tax exposure. He is treated as receiving a taxable benefit for CGT purposes equal to rent-free occupation of (say) £50,000 pa, but there is no tax charge as long as the trust makes no gains on or after April 6, 2008.

In 2017/18 the company sells the house realising gains of £1.05 million. Assume most of the gains accrued post April 5, 2008 and therefore all of these gains are potentially taxable on him. H has received benefits of £500,000 in the UK since April 2008. He now pays capital gains tax because the gains can be matched to the past benefits under TCGA 1992, s.87B and he is UK resident at that time.

If, however, the trustees make a capital distribution of £1m to him in 2018 in the same tax year as the sale and he keeps this capital abroad then the trust gains are matched to capital payments made in the same year as the gains are made, before being matched to earlier capital payments. In 2017/18 he has therefore received total benefits in that year alone of £1,050,000 of which £50,000 was received in the UK. He therefore pays tax on the remittance basis but only on £50,000 benefits. The earlier benefits received here remained unmatched and untaxed.

If the trust realises further gains in future tax years those gains (if not matched to capital payments made in the same year) can be taxed on him by reference to the earlier benefits if he is UK resident at the date of matched.

24–14   In summary, if H can ensure that no gains are realised at a time when he is UK resident or that they are matched to capital payments made to him abroad, then he can receive UK benefits without significant capital gains tax liabilities and have IHT protection on his UK house. There is no POAT because para.12(3) protects the shares and para.11(3) protects the house (the latter via the derived reserved benefit exemption—see **Ch.8**). The position becomes more complicated when the trust holds more than one asset. The timing of capital payments can be important.

[16]   See s.809T as inserted by Sch.7, FA 2008.
[17]   Prior to that date s.87 did not apply to tax foreign domiciliaries.
[18]   See **Ch.12** of Chamberlain and Whitehouse, *Trust Taxation*, 2nd edn.

Example 24.3

Assume as above that the trustees hold a UK house through a company. The house is occupied by H who therefore receives taxable UK benefits. The trustees sell the company in 2010/11 for a gain of £1m. All the gain realised on the disposal accrued pre-April 6, 2008; the trustees have made a rebasing election[19] to ensure that all such gains are not chargeable on foreign domiciliaries. The trustees should not make a cash distribution to H abroad in 2010/11. If they do, they are "wasting" tax free gains on a capital distribution that would not be taxed on H anyway because he receives it abroad and does not intend to remit it.

If they do not make any distributions to him in that tax year all of those £1m gains (deemed to accrue pre-April 2008) would then be matched to the earlier capital payments of £500,000 (i.e. the occupation of the house) and no tax is payable on H even though the capital payment was received after April 5, 2008. £500,000 gains are carried forward to be matched against future capital payments. However, since these gains are also pre-April 2008 gains they are not taxed on H in the future.

Hence it is better to match pre-April 2008 gains accrued on an election to capital payments received in the UK by the foreign domiciliary because no tax is then paid and match post-April 2008 election gains to capital payments received outside the UK.

Double trust schemes

24–15 Can these be implemented after March 22, 2006? Obviously no qualifying interest in possession trust can be created so if the relevant property trust holds the UK house it must either do so directly and minimise 10-year inheritance tax charges by use of debt or hold the house through a company (which increases the capital gains tax risks under s.87 from April 6, 2008). POA issues must also be considered.

Inheritance tax issues of double trust schemes

24–16 What is the reservation of benefit position on the death of the foreign domiciliary who has funded the purchase of the house? Does the foreign domiciliary reserve a benefit in the UK house and if so can the debt be deducted against the value of the house?

Example 24.4

Lilian—a foreign domiciliary—wishes to purchase a house in the UK. In 2007 she settles US $1m into a debt trust (excluded property and no entry charge). The debt trust will be a relevant property settlement whether or not Lilian takes an interest in possession.

Lilian's father settles $10 on a House Trust. Debt Trust then lends the cash to House Trust. House Trust (which is also a relevant property settlement) uses the borrowings to buy the house. The house will be subject to 10-year

---

[19] See FA 2008, Sch.7, para.120.

charges, but the debt will be deductible in calculating the inheritance tax charge on those occasions. On Lilian's death is there a reservation of benefit from her occupation of the house? She is not the settlor of the House Trust (since she has not given the $10) and the loan is not in itself a gift by her. It is thought that the reservation of benefit provisions should not apply.

24–17 The above example envisages Lilian settling funds into a cash trust which then lends to a house trust funded with say £10 by someone else and the house trust purchases the house direct. Main residence relief is obtained so there is no s.87 problem until the house trust makes chargeable gains.

Since there is no initial gift by Lilian to the house trust, the problem raised by FA 1986, para.5(4), Sch.20 cannot apply to cause any reservation of benefit problem in respect of the house. In any event the cash trust rather than Lilian is making the loan so para.5(4) should not apply anyway even if she funded the house trust with £10. One then avoids any reservation of benefit issue and the result is that on Lilian's death the house is not subject to inheritance tax (because she cannot take a qualifying interest in possession in it and there is no reservation of benefit). The only inheritance tax charges are the 10-year anniversary charges which can be predicted and therefore minimised by further borrowing.

POA issues of a double trust scheme

24–18 This scheme works for inheritance tax purposes but has a POA risk in that if one views the loan from the cash trust to house trust as a contribution, Lilian is within the POA charge in respect of the house which does not have the protection of para.11(3)—reservation of benefit. Nor does it have the protection of para.11(1) any longer since her interest is not a qualifying interest in possession. However, it may be argued that a loan to purchase a house does not satisfy the contribution condition even if it is interest free.[20] If that is right, POA is not a problem.

24–19 The second option is for Lilian deliberately to bring herself into the reservation of benefit rules to obtain POA protection under para.11(3), but then argue for the inheritance tax deduction of the debt on her death (as well as on any 10-year anniversary of the trust). This could be done by Lilian settling say £10 cash into house trust and then lending the house trust the balance of the purchase price and assigning the loan to a separate cash trust. The concern then is that the reservation of benefit is only in the net equity of the property and so only that element is protected by para.11(3). On the other hand one could presumably argue that the loan element itself was reserved benefit property given that Lilian is a beneficiary of the cash trust and this loan does derive its value from the relevant property (the house). The issue would then arise as to whether the loan is deductible for GWR purposes against the value of the house on the death of Lilian.[21]

[20] See **Ch.7**.
[21] See **Ch.17** (home loan schemes) for further discussion.

One risk with such structures following April 6, 2008 changes is Sch.4B (transfer **24–20** of value linked to trustee borrowing), which can now apply to foreign domiciliaries. Schedule 4B ought not to be in point provided the borrowing is applied directly in the house purchase for the house is an ordinary trust asset.

However, any trust structure now involves a consideration of capital gains tax issues for the foreign domiciliary. If the property is owned personally, capital gains tax will not normally arise due to main residence relief. If the property is owned in the trust, the inheritance tax savings must be worthwhile to justify the capital gains tax and POA risks and it is not clear that they are.

The use of a trust will avoid or at least defer CGT on UK situated assets but can complicate the remittance rules greatly. Instead of looking at the gain on the actual foreign asset and determining whether that gain has been remitted it is necessary to compute all the stockpiled gains of the trust.

Example 24.5

An offshore trust owns a portfolio of shares and a UK house occupied by B, a foreign domiciliary. The trust sells the shares at a gain and reinvests the proceeds. B pays tax on the gain even though nothing has been distributed to him because the trust gains are matched to his capital benefits deriving from the occupation of the house (s.87B). The remittance basis provides no protection because B has received benefits in the UK.

Compare the position if B (a foreign domiciliary) owns a UK house which qualifies as his main residence. There is no capital gains tax on sale (due to main residence relief) and no tax charge on the benefit of his occupation. The main tax problem is that he will pay inheritance tax on his death but, as noted above, this could be dealt with by insurance.

CHAPTER 25

AGRICULTURAL PROPERTY RELIEF AND BUSINESS PROPERTY RELIEF

25–01 The two reliefs are similar and overlap but the following distinctions are worthy of note.

    a.   APR is given in priority to BPR (IHTA 1984, s.114(1)).

    b.   Differences exist in the treatment of woodlands, crops, livestock, deadstock, plant and machinery, and farmhouses, etc. When APR does not apply, consider whether BPR is available (it can apply to any part of the value transferred not relieved under APR: e.g. the hope value of agricultural land).

    c.   Formerly APR was only available on property situated in the UK, Channel Islands and Isle of Man, whereas BPR was not so restricted. FA 2009 changed this, allowing APR and Woodlands relief for property in the EEA.

    d.   In the *Tax Bulletin* 1994, p.182, the then Inland Revenue commented that:

> "Where agricultural property which is a farming business is replaced by a non-agricultural business property, the period of ownership of the original property will be relevant for applying the minimum ownership condition to the replacement property. Business property relief will be available on the replacement if all the conditions for that relief were satisfied. Where non agricultural business property is replaced by a farming business and the latter is not eligible for agricultural property relief, s114(1) does not exclude business property relief if the conditions for that relief are satisfied.
>
> Where the donee of the PET of a farming business sells the business and replaces it with a non-agricultural business the effect of s124A(1) is to deny agricultural property relief on the value transferred by the PET. Consequently s114(1) does not exclude business property relief if the conditions for that relief are satisfied: and, in the reverse situation, the farming business acquired by the donee can be "relevant business property" for the purposes of s113B(3)(c)."

"Agricultural property" is defined by s.115(2) which, for convenience, may be **25–02** divided into three parts:

a. "in this chapter 'agricultural property' means agricultural land or pasture" ("*Limb 1*");

b. "and includes woodland and any building used in connection with the intensive reading of livestock or fish if the woodland or building is occupied with agricultural land or pasture and the occupation is ancillary to that of agricultural land or pasture" ("*Limb 2*");

c. "and also includes such cottages, farm buildings and farmhouses, together with the land occupied with them, as are of a character appropriate to the property" ("*Limb 3*").

The Antrobus litigation

a. HMRC conceded that Cookhill Priory was a farmhouse. **25–03**

b. The Special Commissioner decided[1] that it was of a character appropriate to the property so that it constituted agricultural property and qualified for APR.

c. However, APR is only given on the "agricultural value" of agricultural property. "Agricultural value" is defined in s.115(3) as follows:

"For the purposes of this Chapter the agricultural value of any agricultural property shall be taken to be the value which would be the value of the property if the property were subject to a perpetual covenant prohibiting its use otherwise than as agricultural property."

It was agreed that the market value of Cookhill Priory was £608,475 but HMRC contended that the agricultural value was only £425,932.50 (i.e. a discount of some 30 per cent on the market value.) The taxpayer considered that there was no discount on market value.

Finding in favour of HMRC the Lands Tribunal subsequently decided[2]:

a. that the covenant under s.115(3) prohibited the use of the property otherwise than as "agricultural property";

b. under the s.115(2) definition "agricultural property" includes a farmhouse and Cookhill Priory would only qualify if it was a farmhouse. This had been conceded by HMRC "but only in the particular circumstances of Miss Antrobus' occupation of the house and land" and in particular her active farming of the 123 acres of freehold agricultural land and the 6.54 acres of leased land;

---

[1] See *Lloyds TSB* (PRs of Antrobus deceased) v IRC [2002] STC (SCD) 468.
[2] See *in the matter of a notice of reference between Lloyds TSB Private Banking plc (as PRs of Antrobus deceased) and Peter Twiddy (IR Capital Taxes)* decision dated October 10, 2005.

c. the taxpayers argued that the property would remain a farmhouse if purchased by someone who carried on a farming business on the land even though he might spend little time in the business.[3]

Thus they would have been unaffected by the s.115(3) covenant since they would have complied with it and as they will be the highest bidders in the market the agricultural value would therefore be equal to the amount which the highest bidder would pay.[4]

This was rejected by the Tribunal in the following terms:

"A farmhouse is the chief dwelling-house attached to a farm, the house in which the farmer of the land lives. There is, we think, no dispute about the definition when it is expressed in this way. The question is: who is the farmer of the land for the purpose of the definition in section 115(2)? In our view it is the person who lives in the farmhouse in order to farm the land comprised in the farm and who farms the land on a day to day basis. It is likely, although it may not necessarily always be the case, that his principal occupation will consist of farming the land comprised in the farm. We do not think that a house occupied with a farm is a farmhouse simply because the person living there is in overall control of the agricultural business conducted on the land; and in particular we think that the lifestyle farmer, the person whose bid for the land is treated by the appellant as establishing the agricultural value of the land, is not the farmer for the purposes of the provisions." (See further the *McKenna* case below.)

d. it considered that the following factors supported this conclusion:

   i   the "character appropriate" test which supports the idea of the farmhouse being "the dwelling of a working farmer who requires a suitable house to support his working life";

   ii   the deletion of "mansion house" from the definition of agricultural property in 1975;

   iii the other elements of the definition "cottages and farm buildings" support the idea of a working farm;

---

[3] The so-called "lifestyle farmer". Giving expert evidence for the taxpayers Mr Clive Beer commented that:

"There were at least three ways in which a lifestyle buyer could carry on a farming business without prior experience and without spending much time at the farm. Firstly, the land could be farmed with the assistance of one or more employees, for example a farm manager, or through a contract farming arrangement. Secondly, the land could be farmed in partnership with an active local farmer. Thirdly, the new owner could come to a share-farming arrangement, whereby the landowner would grow grass or other crops for sale to a local livestock farmer, whose cattle or sheep would eat down the crop which he had bought in situ. Whichever of these methods was adopted by the lifestyle farmer, the farmhouse would continued to be occupied by him and used as agricultural property."

[4] Mr Beer accepted that the open market value would fall to be discounted for any actual or potential non-agricultural uses of the property to which additional value might be attributable (e.g. any value attributable to sporting rights; development potential or mineral rights). It appears that there were no such factors present in this case.

e. HMRC were "not wrong" to in treating the s.115(3) covenant in relation to farmhouses as equivalent to the standard planning AOC for the purposes of establishing values[5];

f. the conclusion that a farmhouse for s.115(2) purposes was limited to a property occupied by a full-time working farmer meant that the agricultural value under s.115(3) had to be decided on the basis that the covenant would not be satisfied by a "lifestyle" farmer. Accordingly the Tribunal accepted that the 30 per cent deduction in value proposed by HMRC was appropriate[6];

g. at the end of its decision the Tribunal considered the value which the property would have *"on the assumption that our interpretation of the legal position is incorrect and that the demand from the lifestyle farmer may be taken into account in calculating its agricultural value"*. On this basis it concluded that the relevant discount would be only 15 per cent thereby giving an agricultural value for the property of £517,203.75.[7]

The McKenna case[8]

Mr McKenna died on January 29, 2003 and his wife, Lady Cecilia, on June 16, **25–04** 2003. Since 1997 they had been the joint owners of the Rosteague Estate. This comprised a substantial Grade II* house (Rosteague House); some 187 acres (of which around 52 were foreshore and 110 agricultural land); various farm outbuildings and a cottage, stable flat and lodge. The estate had originally been purchased by Mr. McKenna in 1945 as a second home and only occupied as the main home on his retirement in 1984. Initially the land was tenanted but in 1984 the tenancy was surrendered and thereafter it was contract farmed under a succession of agreements with different contractors. A land agent, acting for the McKennas, was responsible for the management of the land, the farming activities and dealing with the contractors. He purchased a property on the estate and hence was on the spot to supervise and manage the farming operation. At the date of death, Mr McKenna was aged 91 and had suffered from ill health since 1997. After his death Lady Cecilia, who was aged 92 and who had suffered from ill health since a heart seizure in 1998, entered a nursing home. The Special Commissioner decided the following:

---

[5] The "agricultural occupancy condition" (AOC) in a planning permission provides that "the occupation of the dwelling shall be limited to a person solely or mainly working, or last working, in the locality in agriculture or in forestry, or a widow or widower of such a person and to any resident dependents" (see DoE circulate No.11/95 para.45).The Tribunal considered that in some respects the terms of the AOC were less restrictive than those of the s.115(3) covenant.

[6] There was a dearth of comparable evidence. Three AOC properties were of no assistance and the only comparable used comprised a farm in which there had been an agreement as to agricultural value (a 33.4% discount).It involved a seven-bed house and 217.69 acres of land.

[7] The Tribunal considered that there would still be a discount over the open market value of the property since (1) the lifestyle farmer would be buying the property together with all the land whereas (ii) a higher price would be obtained by someone who brought the house and part only of the land and who was not subject to the s.115(3) covenant.

[8] *Arnander & Ors (Exors of McKenna dec'd) v RCC* [2006] STC (SCD) 800.

a. Rosteague House was not a farmhouse.[9]

She made the following general comments on the meaning of "farmhouse" in IHTA 1984, s.115(2):

i. that the wording of the legislation makes it clear that the agricultural land is paramount: other things must be either ancillary or of a character appropriate to the land;

ii. there is nothing to suggest that every farm must have a farmhouse: the reference in s.115(2) is to farmhouses generally;

iii. she adopted the definition given in the *Rosser* case[10] as "a dwelling for the farmer from which the farm is managed" and accepted that the Land Tribunal conclusion in *Antrobus II* that "the farmer of the land is the person who farms it on a day to day basis rather than the person who is in overall control of the agricultural business conducted on the land" was a "helpful principle";

iv. the status of the occupier of the property is not the test: rather it is the purpose of the occupation which is relevant;

v. whether a building is a farmhouse is a matter of fact to be decided on the circumstances of each case and according to ordinary ideas of what is appropriate in terms of size, content and layout in the context of the particular farm buildings and the area of land farmed.

On the particular facts of the case, she concluded that it was the land agent who was responsible for the management of the farming operation (albeit as agent for the McKennas). Hence "*the purpose of Mr. McKenna's occupation of Rosteague House was not to undertake the day to day farming activities. In any event, ... Rosteague House was larger, grander, more elaborate and more expensive than was required for the reduced farming purposes for which it was in fact used. Its size, content and layout, taken in conjunction with the farm buildings and the particular area of farm being farmed points to the conclusion that it was primarily a rich man's residence rather than a farmhouse*".[11]

b. On the basis that, if it was a farmhouse, was it of a character appropriate? Again the Special Commissioner decided that the requirements for relief were not met. Following the criteria that she had identified in Antrobus she added a further factor: the relationship between the value of the land and

---

[9] The sale particulars (the estate was sold for in excess of £3m after the McKennas' deaths) described the house as follows:

"long hall, dining room, library, study, drawing room, flower room, main foyer and stairs, cloakroom, rear hall, kitchen, staff sitting room, back kitchen, seven bedrooms, three bathrooms, sewing room, laundry room, staff flat, detached lodge, cottage, music room, garage, gardens, range of outbuildings".

There was no mention of it being a farmhouse!

[10] [2002] STC (SCD) 311 at para.53.

[11] At para.92.

the profitability of the land.[12] She concluded that the return from agriculture (a profit of £6,820 in 1998 falling to a loss of £7,975 in 1994) "would not provide a living income for a person who paid over £3m for the whole estate and so would not attract demand from a commercial farmer".[13]

c. Was the property occupied for the purposes of agriculture throughout the period of two years ending with the death of the owners?[14] Whilst this issue did not have to be decided given the Special Commissioner's decision in (i) and (ii), she concluded that "it is clear that neither Mr. McKenna nor Lady Cecilia were able to engage in farming matters throughout the period of two years ending with the relevant dates of death".[15]

Conclusions

Whilst the *McKenna* case will undoubtedly make it difficult for a "lifestyle" **25–05** farmer to obtain relief on the house which he occupies, the following matters should be borne in mind.

A. The relationship between farming income and the value of the property has not been fully explored. Is the test that a house can only be a farmhouse if it is capable of being maintained out of the farming profit? (This, of course, begs the question maintained to what standard?) Or is it that the house will only qualify if "required" by the actual farming operation carried on?[16]

B. The position of the land agent is also in need of further consideration. Once it is accepted that the land can be farmed by employees, including a farm manager, answerable to the owner, then drawing the line between that situation and the facts in *McKenna* is difficult. If Mr McKenna had dealt directly with the contractor would that have made a difference? Arguably yes, since there is nothing in the decision to suggest that contract farming per se will prevent APR being available.

The conacre case: *McCall and Keenan (PRS of McClean Deceased) v RCC* [2008] STC (SCD) 782; affd [2009] STC 990.

---

[12] From the evidence of comparables it was clear that Rosteague was at the "top end" of the size of a Cornish farmhouse and that a house of that size would generally have more land. It only came into use as a farmhouse in 1984 (so the historical association is weak) whilst lack of repair went, she considered, to value rather than character.

[13] At para.113.

[14] See IHTA 1984, s.117(a).

[15] At para.119

[16] It might be thought that if the purpose of relief is to prevent farms having to be sold to pay IHT then, provided that the occupier of the property is the farmer, a precise link should not be made between farming income and property values. Bear in mind that the same test will be applied even if the property is not sold and so may deny relief when it is retained within the family. Note the similar issue in CGT main residence relief concerning what area of land is required for each owner of the property.

25–06   The deceased let 33 acres of farmland which she had inherited from her husband in 1983 under grazing agreements to local farmers.[17]

The land was zoned for development and when the deceased died, although the agricultural value was only £165,000, its market value was £5.8m.

Two preliminary matters should be noted.

1. There is no doubt that APR was available in respect of the agricultural value of the land. The issue was limited to the availability of business property relief on the enhanced value (i.e. on the difference between the market value and the agricultural value).

2. The letting arrangements were arranged on behalf of the deceased (whose mind rapidly deteriorated after the death of her husband) by her son-in-law. The Special Commissioner accepted that it remained her business.

So far as the availability of business property relief was concerned, he decided (and the NI Court of Appeal agreed) as follows.

1. The activity of tending the land undertaken by Mr Mitchell (the son-in-law) coupled with the annual letting of the land was just enough to constitute a business. The Special Commissioner concluded that around 100 hours per annum was spent in weed control, fence maintenance, litter and damage control and drainage and water works.

2. But the business consisted wholly or mainly of the holding of investments so that (as a result of IHTA 1984, s.105(3)) business property relief was not available. He concluded:

"The activities of the business do not involve the cutting of the grass and the feeding of it to the cattle but simply making the asset available so that the cattle may live and eat there: the income arises substantially from the making available of the asset not from the other activity associated with it or from selling separately the fruits of the asset: that is the business of holding an investment, and it was the main activity of this business. It was not like a "pick your own" fruit farm where after months of weeding, fertilising, spraying and pruning, customers are licensed to enter to take the produce and pay by the pound for what they take away: in the business of letting the fields there was less in preparatory work, the fields were let for the accommodation of the cattle as well as for the grazing and the rent was paid by the acre rather than by the ton of grass eaten: it was not a business consisting of the provision of the grass but of the provision of the (non exclusive) use of the land."

The courts did not accept that the correct analysis of a grazing licence was that it involved the business of selling a grass crop.

25–07   It is suggested that the following points of general interest emerge from this decision.

1. It is thought that the decision is significant in relation to arrangements in England and Wales. These take a variety of forms: for instance, the grazing licence which may if it grants exclusive possession amount to a short-term

---

[17] Although there was much discussion of local letting arrangements in Northern Ireland (especially "conacre" or "agistment" arrangements) the agreements in this case were essentially the same as those employed in England and Wales: for instance, the lettings were for the period during which grass was growing, April 1 to November 1. Hence it is thought that the case is of general significance.

business tenancy. An alternative, for which the CLA provide a precedent, is a profit à prendre under which the grazier is allowed to put cattle on the land to take the grass. What precisely was the arrangement in this case? Girvan L.J. explained the nature of the agistment arrangement as follows:

"The use by Northern Ireland landowners of conacre and agistment arrangements with other farmers is common even though such arrangements have been criticised as unsatisfactory arrangements which do not assist in good land management practices. The fact that such arrangements are common is in part due to their traditional use in Northern Ireland, in part due to a fear on the part of both landowners and graziers and conacre tenants of creating agricultural tenancies with potential adverse legal consequences and in part due to the desire of landowners to retain a degree of control over the land during the period of the contract. What appears clear from the old Irish authorities is that an agistment contract confers on the grazier only a right to graze and not possession of the land in law. They do not create a tenancy. Such an arrangement partakes of the quality of the profit à prendre but one which by way of exception to the normal rules does not require to be created by deed. Such an arrangement bears a close comparison to a contractual licence."[18]

He further commented that the absence of a full and exclusive right of occupation of the land for the grazier and the existence of a right by the owner to enter the land during the period of the agistment did not prevent the business being regarded as the holding of an investment.

2. The fact that the deceased did not qualify for business property relief will be important when, as in this case, the land has hope value. It may also be significant, however, in considering whether any house occupied can be a farmhouse: if the correct analysis is that the grazing agreement involves the holding of an investment, then it is difficult to see how the property can be a farmhouse[19];

3. If only a part of the farmland is subject to a grazing agreement and the bulk of the farm is in hand, then on the basis of the "wholly or mainly" test in s.105(3) it is thought that business property relief will be available on all the land.

If grazing agreements do not attract business property relief, thought should be given to alternative arrangements such as a partnership agreement with the grazier.[20]

RELEVANT PROPERTY TRUSTS AND BPR / APR

It is not uncommon for relevant property settlements to be set up in order to hold **25–08** business or agricultural property attracting valuation reliefs for IHT.[21]

---

[18] At para.[16].
[19] For a consideration of the meaning of farmhouse, see the *McKenna* case.
[20] Of course, no problem would arise if the owner put his own cattle on the land or harvested and sold the grass, but that is a completely different arrangement.
[21] Business property relief is given by IHTA 1984, Pt IV, **Ch.1** and Agricultural Property Relief by IHTA 1984, Pt IV, **Ch.2**.

Typically the trust may hold shares in the family trading business. In such a case, the following should be noted.

- If the property qualified for relief at 100 per cent the value transferred into the trust will be nil although an IHT return is still necessary under s.216 since the general rule is that every transferor who is liable for inheritance tax on the value transferred by a chargeable transfer or who **would be so liable** if inheritance tax were chargeable on that value must deliver an account. The requirement for an account if there "would be" liability covers chargeable transfers within the nil rate band and chargeable transfers that qualify for business property relief or agricultural property relief. See, however, the following.

- The trustees must then satisfy the normal requirements (for instance the two-year ownership requirement under s.106 or the occupation requirement under s.117) if they are to be entitled to either business or agricultural property relief. Subject to that, normal reliefs will be due in the case of both anniversary and exit charges.[22]

- The legislation is not, however, straightforward in a case where the business or agricultural property is sold by the trustees and the cash received is then distributed to beneficiaries.

Example 25.1

1. A settles property qualifying for 100 per cent business property relief in 2000. In 2006 the business is sold and the cash distributed amongst the beneficiaries. It might be thought that the IHT exit charge in 2006 will be nil on the basis that the value of the property originally settled was, after relief, nil. However, IHTA 1984, s.68 (which deals with the rate of tax before the first 10-year anniversary) provides that the rate is calculated by reference to *"the value, immediately after the settlement commenced, of the property then comprised in it"*.[23]

   Accordingly it is the value ignoring business or agricultural relief which must be taken and hence the distribution of cash may attract an exit charge.[24]

2. If, however, the business property remained in the settlement beyond the first 10-year anniversary, is then sold and the proceeds paid out to beneficiaries, the IHT position is as follows:

   a. there will be no 10-year charge (since BPR at 100 per cent is then available);

   b. the rate of tax charged on the distribution of the cash after sale of the business will be calculated by reference to appropriate fraction of

---

[22] IHTA 1984, s.103(1); s.115(1).

[23] IHTA 1984, s.68(5)(a).

[24] If the trustees had distributed the business property when it attracted relief at 100% no problem would then arise given that although tax would be chargeable on the basis of the value of the property originally settled the charge will be on a nil value.

the rate at which it was last charged rather than by reference to the value of the property in the settlement at the last 10-year anniversary.[25]

Assuming, therefore, that the only property in the settlement qualified for relief at 100 per cent so that the rate of tax previously was 0 per cent, the rate of the exit charge will be nil.

Finally, bear in mind that one result of the 2006 changes in the IHT treatment of settlements is that once the property has been in the settlement for the qualifying period (two years under s.106)[26] business relief will be available and changes in the form of the settlement (for instance if the trustees appoint an interest in possession) will not affect the position: specifically it will not cause a new two-year qualifying period to commence.[27]

BPR: ASSETS HELD OUTSIDE A QUALIFYING COMPANY

Assume that A is a beneficiary in a discretionary trust set up by his father which **25–09** owns 26 per cent of the shares in his family trading company. A himself owns 25 per cent of the shares and land which is used by the business. On A's death:

- his shareholding attracts 100 per cent relief;

- the land does not obtain relief.

BUT if immediately before A's death the trustees appointed him an interest in possession in the trust he would be treated as controlling the company (see IHTA 1984, s.269).

RECENT CASES AND OTHER BPR DEVELOPMENTS

Nelson Dance Family Settlement v RCC [2008] STC (SCD) 792 aff'd [2009] STC 802

In 2002, Nelson Dance settled property forming part of his farming business on **25–10** to discretionary trusts. This transfer did not involve either the transfer of his entire business nor any part of that business (i.e. it amounted to a transfer of mere assets). He died within seven years of the transfer. The Special Commissioner

---

[25] IHTA 1984, s.69(1).

[26] A similar period applies for agricultural property relief under s.117 if the land is occupied by the trustees for the purposes of agriculture (for the purpose of this provision if the trustees allow a beneficiary—such as the life tenant—to farm the land that this requirement is met). Alternatively agricultural property relief may be due once the land has been owned by the trustees for seven years provided that it was occupied (for instance by a tenant) for agricultural purposes throughout that period.

[27] The only situation where this problem can still arise is if the trustees of a relevant property settlement were to appoint a disabled person an interest in possession within IHTA 1984, s.89B(1)(c). Because that person is treated as beneficially entitled to the property (see IHTA 1984, s.49(1); (1A) (b)) he will need to satisfy a fresh qualifying period before relief is available; see, generally, *Burrell v Burrell* [2005] STC 569.

had to decide on a preliminary point whether the original transfer into the discretionary trust qualified for business property relief.[28]

He decided, contrary to the unanimous views of the text book writers on the subject, that it did[29]

and his decision has been upheld in the High Court. The relevant arguments are as follows.

1. Business property relief is given when the whole or part of the value transferred by a transfer of value is attributable to the value of any relevant business property.[30]

2. Throughout the IHT legislation, value transferred means the fall in value of the transferor's estate.

3. In the context of business property relief, IHTA 1984, s.110 requires liabilities incurred for the purposes of the business to be deducted in arriving at the net value of that business.[31]

4. As can be seen from the above, there is nothing to say that the value transferred must be attributable to the transfer of the whole business or indeed a part of the business.

5. That is only relevant to the definition of "relevant business property" and it is a function of s.105 so list property capable of being relevant business property (hence, for instance, s.105(1)(a) is dealing with the situation where a taxpayer is a sole trader or typically a partner in a partnership).

25–11 The following points of significance emerge from the decision.

1. It provides a classic example of the need to construe the provisions of the legislation as a whole rather than focusing on words used in a particular section. It provides an object lesson to all text book writers!

2. The decision is significant in allowing individual assets to be stripped out of a business: for instance, in the case of a mixed business where there is concern that the investment aspect may become predominant, it will be possible to remove sufficient of the investment assets to ensure that the "wholly or mainly" test in s.105(3) continues to be met. Say that if the business is predominantly one of house building but has, over the years, acquired a number of tenanted properties. These properties may be stripped out. Likewise if a business has accumulated a substantial cash reserve which it has been keeping for business purposes (as in the *Brown* case[32]) then this, it appears, may be distributed with the benefit of relief.

3. That is not to say, however, that the decision does not throw up difficulties. Certainly the claw back rules in IHTA 1984, s.113A assume that any gift will be of either the business or part of the business. Hence in the *Dance* case, the fact that extra tax is in point given that Mr Dance died within

---

[28] The transfer attracted agricultural property relief but only on the agricultural value of the relevant land which had substantial development potential.

[29] See, for instance, *Dymond* at 24.710; *McCutcheon* at 14-19 and *Foster* at G1.11.

[30] IHTA 1984, s.104(1).

[31] See Dymond at 24.750.

[32] [1996] STC (SCD) 277.

seven years of the chargeable transfer into the discretionary trust means that these provisions have to be considered and it would seem, because the transferee does not own an interest in a business, that no relief will be due so that a full additional tax charge will arise.[33]

Executors of Piercy Deceased v RCC [2008] STC (SCD) 858 and property development companies

Did shares in the deceased's company qualify for BPR or did the company's **25–12** business consist wholly or mainly in the making or holding of investments? The following background facts may be noted:

- the company had been established for property development and had large holdings of land for which it received substantial amounts of rent;

- although, for corporation tax purposes, it was generally classified as trading, HMRC considered this to be irrelevant, contending that the receipt of substantial rents meant that business property relief was not available since the activities of the company fell foul of s.105(3) in involving mainly the holding of investments.

The Special Commissioner concluded, however, that the business of the company involved marshalling sites for development with a view to selling the finished developments. Accordingly, land was held as trading stock and even though it produced a rental income, there was no evidence that it had been appropriated as an investment. Note the following.

- The reference in s.105(3) to a land dealing company (the shares in which do not qualify for business property relief) does not affect building companies: *"the only type of land dealing company whose shares fail to qualify for the relief is of some sort of dealing or speculative trader that does not actually develop or actually build on land."*

- A company can only conduct the business of holding investments if it has got some investments! In this case, whilst some land was retained, it had not been appropriated as an investment. For instance, there was land in Islington which had been earmarked by the company for residential development but it was blighted by rail links and so the company had built poor quality limited life industrial workshops on this land (let on short-term leases) but with the continuing intention of knocking down these units once residential development became possible. The Special Commissioner concluded that this land had never become appropriated as an investment (incidentally, had it been so appropriated the corporation tax returns of the company over a number of years should have been quite different and, contrary to the arguments of HMRC, the Special Commissioner concluded that this was a case where the two taxes "go hand in hand").

- It is hard to know quite why HMRC decided to take this case given that property development companies invariably tend to hold a land bank in this way, comprising parcels of land which are only developed over a period of time. The decision appears to accord with the statement of the

[33] There are anomalies in the calculation of the charge in cases such as this: specifically the cumulative total of the taxpayer is not adjusted.

Chief Treasury Minister in 1996: "relief should not be denied to a genuine building company which holds properties as stock as opposed to investments". There was no evidence that the business as a whole was becoming more focused on lettings and dealings. As the Valuation Manual confirms, the question is whether the business is holding the properties as genuine stock in trade awaiting development and in this respect all aspects of the business must be considered and its assets and sources of income or gains over a reasonable period.[34]

- The position might be different in the case of other traders: for instance, a farmer would hold the farmland as capital of the business and so were any of it to be rented to third parties it may then be viewed as an investment so resulting in the "mainly" test in s.105(3) being relevant (the same would be true of the caravan site operator receiving a licence fee for the use of his capital land).

General comments on property development companies

25–13 Property development companies need to consider whether there are any other impediments to BPR. One point is whether the company is carrying out property development or property dealing—the latter is an excluded activity and will not qualify for relief. Unfortunately the distinction between property development and property dealing is not always clear—similar problems used to arise in the context of capital gains tax and the old reinvestment relief. For a company to be carrying out development activities, generally the character of the land or building should be changed and improved in some way. Merely applying for planning permission and carrying out some redecoration would not be sufficient. Building infrastructure on the land or reconstructing the inside of a building prior to sale usually would constitute development. The difficulty is in determining how much work has to be done to the land before it becomes development not dealing.

However, if the company merely fails to develop one area of a large development, e.g. due to planning difficulties and then sells on, this would not in itself make the company a dealing company if its other activities were clearly development. Buying a property and reselling it in the same state (or reselling it in units) or regearing leases and putting in a better tenant to increase the value of the land prior to resale might be dealing but even this should not jeopardise the company's overall status if it is merely one part of the company's portfolio (or the planning difficulties were unexpected). It is sensible where land is sold on without development to obtain evidence from the directors of their original intentions and retain external evidence of how the land had originally been marketed, e.g. were there particular factors in the local development plan that had changed and made the planning permission different and less profitable than originally anticipated? This is not uncommon for commercial property where disputes arise about the level of infrastructure required.

Another question is the value restriction for BPR set by s.110 which requires one to establish the assets and liabilities used or incurred for the purposes of the business—see the difficult decision of *Hardcastle & Another v IRC [2000] STC*

---

[34] *FPH Finance Trust Limited v IRC* 1944 26 TC 131.

(SCD) 321, which gave guidance on the meaning of net liabilities incurred for the purposes of the business.[35]

Can commercial contracts and buildings which are stock in trade (and constitute the major value of many property development businesses) fail to qualify for relief on the basis of *Hardcastle* in that they are merely "the fruit" produced by the tree rather than the tree itself. It is thought that HMRC do not apply the decision in this way and certainly the point was not raised in *Piercy*.

THE "WHOLLY OR MAINLY" TEST[36]

This determines whether relief is due on "mixed" business (the two leading cases **25–14** are the Special Commissioner's decision in *Farmer* and the Court of Appeal decision in *Stedman*). The exclusion from relief is for a business which is *mainly* one of holding investments (e.g. property letting). Because the test is "all or nothing" a business involving the holding of investments may attract relief (even on those investments) provided that this is not the main activity. HMRC have been reviewing their approach to mixed business and it may be that some which formerly obtained relief will not get relief in the future. Consider:

a.   a hotel business;

b.   a bed and breakfast business;

c.   furnished holiday lettings and note:

   ii.   owners of UK furnished holiday lettings are deemed to be carrying on a *trade* for income tax and CGT purposes (e.g. loss relief, pension limit and CGT roll-over). By FA 2009 that treatment is extended to the property in the EEA; **but**

   ii.   the special treatment of FHL ends from 2010/11. The income will thereafter be taxed as income from a property letting business;

   iii. what steps taxpayers may take before April 6, 2010; for instance to take advantage of CGT roll-over by replacing the current property or, even if they wish to keep the property, extracting CGT entrepreneurs' relief (e.g. by putting the property into trust);

   iv.   there have never been special rules for IHT (i.e. FHL are not deemed to attract BPR) and HMRC recently withdrew the section in the IHT Manual implying that relief would be due if the owner provided personal services. Normally FHL will fall foul of s.105(3), i.e. they will merely involve the holding of an investment;

d.   car parks;

e.   markets and marinas.

---

[35] There it had been held that trading losses did not reduce the assets on which relief was available because they were incurred not for the purposes of the business but arose out of the running of the business.

[36] Whether there was a simple business (to which the "wholly or mainly" test applied) or two separate businesses, see *Brander (PR of the 4th Earl of Balfour) v RCC* [2009] TC 69.

25–15 These are as capable of applying to gifts of business and agricultural assets as to gifts of any other assets. There is no blanket exclusion which applies. However, the following may be noted.

Full consideration let-out

25–16 Take the case where the father farms land and decides to take the son into partnership, giving him (say) a 50 per cent interest in the land and an accompanying 50 per cent share of all profits. In such a case, there may be no element of gift (it may be a commercial bargain) or the full consideration let out in FA 1986, Sch.20, para.6 may apply so that there is no reservation of benefit in that gift.

It involves looking at the matter in the round and saying that the benefits in the form of profits should be consistent with the contributions that father and son make in the form of capital and labour. With this in mind the sharing arrangements should stack up commercially.[37]

Illustrations

25–17 IHRM provide a number of useful examples of the operation of the GWR rules in the area of businesses and companies including the following.

Example 25.2[38]

Father and son have been in partnership together since 1980 sharing profits equally. The land is owned by the father and occupied by the partnership rent free without any formal tenancy agreement. In 1989 the father gives the land to the son but the partnership continues to occupy it on the same basis. At the same time the profit sharing ratio is adjusted in favour of the son.

Provided the increase in the son's share of profits represented full consideration in money or money's worth for occupation of the land, FA 1986, Sch.20, para.6(1)(a) will apply and this will not be a GWR.

The father is in effect occupying the land through the partnership and this prima facie constitutes a reservation. However, HMRC accept that the let-out in para.6(1)(a) may be satisfied by an appropriate upward adjustment (in lieu of rent) reflected in the donee's share of the partnership profits. The circumstances of the case must determine what is "appropriate" having regard to what might be agreed under an arm's length deal between unconnected persons.

Example 25.3[39]

A, who is a partner, withdraws capital from his partnership capital account and gives it to B. B then lends the partnership an equivalent cash sum.

This is a reservation. Though the partnership may pay B a commercial rate of interest for the loan, this payment will not prevent the loan being a reservation. (This is a rare example of a benefit being reserved in a cash gift.)

---

[37] See also *Dymond's Capital Taxes* at 9.300 and *AG v Boden* [1912] 1 K.B. 539.
[38] See IHTM 14341.
[39] See IHTM 14336.

Example 25.4[40]

A, a farmer, retires and gives his farmhouse, lands and farming assets to his son, but A continued to live in the farmhouse rent free until his death.

The donor's continued residence in the farmhouse constitutes a reservation so far as that particular property is concerned, but the reservation does not extend to the remainder of the gifted land and farming assets.

Example 25.5[41]

A gives all the shares in his family company to B, it being part of the agreement that B would appoint A to the Board of Directors, a salaried position entitling him to a company car and other fringe benefits.

This would be regarded as the reservation of a benefit to the donor "by contract or otherwise".

Example 25.6[42]

A husband and wife each own 50 per cent of the issued capital of a limited company. The company owns the freehold property in which they live. The spouses transfer their shares into a settlement for their grandchildren. They continue to live in the house rent-free until the husband's death.

This is not a GWR. The continued occupation of the property is not referable to the gift.

Example 25.7[43]

A farmer, on taking his son into partnership, makes a gift to him of a share of all the partnership assets including the land. They then share the profits and losses in the same proportion as they own the partnership assets at commencement. The farmer dies 10 years later.

This is not a GWR. The son has taken possession and enjoyment of the partnership share gifted to him in the form of his share of profits. The father's share of profits is referable to his own partnership share, not the share gifted. (Note that the analysis is not that full consideration is being paid to prevent the GWR provisions from applying but that there was no reservation in the first place. This may have implications for the POA charge[44] although if the gift is analysed as of a partnership share (a *chose in action*) rather than of each and every partnership asset (including land) it should not give rise to problems in practice.)[45]

Shared occupation

Broadly speaking if Dad gives his son a share in his land which they both occupy **25–18** and Dad receives no benefit, other than a negligible one, from his son, which is

---

[40] See IHTM 14334.
[41] See IHTM 14334.
[42] See IHTM 14334.
[43] See IHTM 14332.
[44] See **25–16**.
[45] See A2.108.

for some reason connected with the gift, then there is no reservation in the gifted property.[46]

Application of relief if there is a reservation

25–19 Business (and agricultural) property which is caught by the reservation of benefit rules is treated as comprised in the donor's estate for IHT purposes at his death if the reservation is continuing. Alternatively, if the reservation ceases inter vivos he makes a PET.[47]

In both cases, relief may be available to reduce the value of the property subject to charge.[48]

The requirements are complex but two sets of conditions need to be satisfied:

(a) *at the time of the gift* the property has to qualify for relief either as relevant business property or as agricultural property[49]; and

(b) *at the time of the tax charge* the property has to satisfy a number of conditions, the basis of which is the concept of a notional transfer by the donee.[50]

In deciding whether the business property relief ownership condition is met,[51] ownership by the donor prior to the gift is treated as ownership by the donee[52] and if the donee dies before the donor (or before the reservation of benefit charge), his personal representatives or his beneficiaries under his Will or intestacy are treated as if they were the donee.[53]

In general, if the conditions are met the rate of relief is then decided by reference to the notional transfer by the donee. This is, however, subject to the qualification that whether certain stocks and shares are relevant business property is to be decided on the basis that they remained owned by the donor.[54]

(This has the effect of preventing aggregation with other property of the donee: however, the restriction is of reduced importance given the availability of 100 per cent for minority shareholdings.) Similar rules apply in the case of agricultural property relief: for instance, ownership and occupation by the donor before the gift is treated as that of the donee and in the case of the occupation condition, occupation by the donor **after** the gift is also treated as that of the donee.[55]

25–20 Take the example of Dan who gives his farm (which he has owned and farmed for many years) to his son Phil. Dan continues in occupation until his death 18 months later. The analysis is as follows.

(a) Dan has made a gift which is caught by the reservation of benefit rules and which will be subject to IHT on his death.

---

[46] See FA 1986, s.102B(4). See **Ch.22** for a detailed consideration of this exemption.
[47] This is the effect of FA 1986, s.102(3) and s.102(4).
[48] See FA 1986, Sch.20, para.8 and see IHTM 25381 et seq.
[49] See FA 1986, Sch.20, para.8(1).
[50] See FA 1986, Sch.20, para.8(1A)(b).
[51] See IHTA 1984, s.106.
[52] See FA 1986, Sch.20, para.8(2)(a).
[53] See FA 1986, Sch.20, para.8(5).
[54] See FA 1986, Sch.20, para.8(1A)(a).
[55] See FA 1986, Sch.20, para.8(2).

(b) At the time of the gift the property qualified for agricultural property relief.

(c) At the time of Dan's death, Phil is treated as making a notional transfer of value and has satisfied the ownership/occupation requirement for agricultural property relief to be available.

Reasonable remuneration

A question that frequently arises in the context of a gift of shares in the family business is whether the donor can safely continue to be remunerated for working in the business or whether such payment gives rise to a reservation of benefit. The views of HMRC were published in letters dated February 19, 1987 and May 18, 1987. They make the key point that *"the continuation of reasonable commercial arrangements in the form of remuneration and other benefits for the donor's services to the business entered into prior to the gift would not, by itself, amount to a reservation provided that the benefits were in no way linked to or affected by the gift".*[56]   **25–21**
IHTM 14395 gives the following illustration:

Example 25.8

The donor transfers shares in an unquoted company into a settlement of which she is trustee (but not a beneficiary). She is entitled to retain remuneration for her services as director of that company.

The continuation of reasonable commercial arrangements governing the remuneration of any other benefits for the donor's services in the company entered into before the gift would not, by itself, amount to a reservation, provided the benefits were in no way linked to or affected by the gift.

On the other hand, if, as part of the overall transaction, including the gift, new remuneration arrangements are made, consider whether the new package amounts to a reservation "by contract or otherwise".

IMPACT OF THE PRE-OWNED ASSETS CHARGE

There are no provisions in FA 2004, Sch.15 that deal specifically with businesses   **25–22**
and farms. Accordingly, the application of the Regime depends on general principles.

In considering the application of the Regime it will be important to identify the property gifted. For instance:

(a) a gift of shares will only be a problem if the para.8 charge is in point (i.e. because the shares become held in a settlor interested trust); and

(b) a gift of a partnership share, as for instance when a father gives part of his capital account to his son, in a case where land is a partnership asset is a

---

[56] The problems posed by this statement are many: what for instance is "reasonable" in the context of remuneration? Why must the arrangements pre-date the gift if the rationale for the statement lies in the commerciality of the services? Note that FA 1986, Sch.20, para.6(1)(a) is limited to land and chattels but does the donor receive a benefit within FA 1986, s.102(1)(b) if the consideration represents no more than a fair commercial payment for his services?

gift of the share (*chose in action*) and not of an interest in land. Again, therefore, there will only be a problem if the para.8 charge could apply.[57]

In cases where the full consideration let-out prevents the reservation of benefit rules from applying to land and chattels, the pre-owned assets charge is equally inapplicable.[58]

Default election

25–23 If the Regime would otherwise apply, the election is available to the taxpayer to opt into reservation of benefit.[59]

As a result:

(a) no income tax will be payable, **and**

(b) the asset may attract business or agricultural property relief on the death of the taxpayer or earlier cessation of the reservation.[60]

---

[57] See A2.108.

[58] See Sch.15, para.11(5)(d). See **Ch.7**.

[59] See **Ch.11** for a consideration of the election.

[60] See **25–10** et seq.

APPENDIX I: STATUTORY MATERIAL

Gifts with a reservation

84   Charge to income tax by reference to enjoyment of property previously owned
(1) Schedule 15 (which contains provisions imposing a charge to income tax by reference to benefits received in certain circumstances by a former owner of property) has effect.
(2) That Schedule has effect for the year 2005–06 and subsequent years of assessment.

SCHEDULE 15

CHARGE TO INCOME TAX ON BENEFITS RECEIVED BY FORMER OWNER OF PROPERTY

Introductory

1.   In this Schedule:

"IHTA 1984" means the Inheritance Tax Act 1984 (c.51);

"the 1986 Act" means the Finance Act 1986 (c.41);

"chattel" means any tangible movable property (or, in Scotland, corporeal movable property) other than money;

"excluded transaction" has the meaning given by para.10;

"intangible property" means any property other than chattels or interests in land;

"interest in land" has the same meaning as in Ch.4 of Pt 6 of IHTA 1984;

["ITTOIA 2005" means the Income Tax (Trading and Other Income Act 2005][1];

"land" has the same meaning as in IHTA 1984;

"prescribed" means prescribed by regulations;

"property" has the same meaning as in IHTA 1984;

"regulations" means regulations made by the Treasury under this Schedule;

"settlement" and "settled property" have the same meanings as in IHTA 1984.

---

1   Definition of "ITTOIA 2005" inserted by ITTOIA 2005 s.882 Sch.1 paras 629, 653, with effect from April 6, 2005.

[2.— (1) For the purposes of this Schedule whether a person is connected with another person is determined in accordance with section 993 of the Income Tax Act 2007.

(2) But for those purposes sections 993 and 994 of that Act are to be read as if in those sections—

(a) "relative" included uncle, aunt, nephew and niece, and

---

1   This paragraph substituted by Income Tax Act 2007 s.1027 Sch.1 paras 456, 482, with effect for income tax purposes from 6 April 2007 and corporation tax purposes for accounting periods ending after 5 April 2007.

Land

3   (1) This paragraph applies where—

(a) an individual ("the chargeable person") occupies any land ("the relevant land"), whether alone or together with other persons, and

(b) the disposal condition or the contribution condition is met as respects the land.

(2) The disposal condition is that—

(a) at any time after 17th March 1986 the chargeable person owned an interest—

(i) in the relevant land, or

(ii) in other property the proceeds of the disposal of which were (directly or indirectly) applied by another person towards the acquisition of an interest in the relevant land, and

(b) the chargeable person has disposed of all, or part of, his interest in the relevant land or the other property, otherwise than by an excluded transaction.

(3) The contribution condition is that at any time after 17th March 1986 the chargeable person has directly or indirectly provided, otherwise than by an excluded transaction, any of the consideration given by another person for the acquisition of—

(a) an interest in the relevant land, or

(b) an interest in any other property the proceeds of the disposal of which were (directly or indirectly) applied by another person towards the acquisition of an interest in the relevant land.

(4) For the purposes of this paragraph a disposition which creates a new interest in land out of an existing interest in land is to be taken to be a disposal of part of the existing interest.

(5) Where this paragraph applies to a person in respect of the whole or part of a year of assessment, an amount equal to the chargeable amount determined under paragraph 4 is to be treated as income of his chargeable to income tax.

4   (1) For any taxable period the chargeable amount in relation to the relevant land is the appropriate rental value (as determined under sub-paragraph (2)), less the amount of any payments which, in pursuance of any legal obligation, are made by the chargeable person during the period to the owner of the relevant land in respect of the occupation of the land by the chargeable person.

(2) The appropriate rental value is—

$$\frac{DV \times R}{V}$$

where—

R is the rental value of the relevant land for the taxable period,

DV is—

(a) in a case falling within paragraph 3(2)(a)(i), the value as at the valuation date of the interest in the relevant land that was disposed of as mentioned in paragraph 3(2)(b) by the chargeable person or, where the disposal was a non-exempt sale, the appropriate proportion of that value,

(b) in a case falling within paragraph 3(2)(a)(ii), such part of the value of the relevant land at the valuation date as can reasonably be attributed to the property originally disposed of by the chargeable person or, where the original disposal was a non-exempt sale, to the appropriate proportion of that property, and

(c) in a case falling within paragraph 3(3), such part of the value of the relevant land at the valuation date as can reasonably be attributed to the consideration provided by the chargeable person, and

V is the value of the relevant land at the valuation date.

(3) The "rental value" of the land for the taxable period is the rent which would have been payable for the period if the property had been let to the chargeable person at an annual rent equal to the annual value.

(4) The disposal by the chargeable person of an interest in land is a "non-exempt sale" if (although not an excluded transaction) it was a sale of his whole interest in the property for a consideration paid in money in sterling or any other currency; and, in relation to a non-exempt sale, "the appropriate proportion" is—

$$\frac{MV - P}{MV}$$

where—

MV is the value of the interest in land at the time of the sale;

P is the amount paid.

(5) Regulations may—

(a) in relation to any valuation date, provide for a valuation of the relevant land or any interest in the relevant land by reference to an earlier valuation date to apply subject to any prescribed adjustments, and

(b) in relation to any year of assessment, provide for a determination of the rental value of the land by reference to any earlier year of assessment to apply subject to any prescribed adjustments.

(6) In this paragraph—

"the taxable period" means the year of assessment, or part of a year of assessment, during which paragraph 3 applies to the chargeable person;

"the valuation date", in relation to a taxable period, means such date as may be prescribed.

5 (1) For the purposes of paragraph 4 the annual value of the relevant land is the rent which might reasonably be expected to be obtained on a letting from year to year if—

(a) the tenant undertook to pay all taxes, rates and charges usually paid by a tenant, and

(b) the landlord undertook to bear the costs of the repairs and insurance and the other expenses (if any) necessary for maintaining the property in a state to command that rent.

(2) For the purposes of sub-paragraph (1) that rent—

(a) is to be taken to be the amount that might reasonably be expected to be so obtained in respect of a letting of the land, and

(b) is to be calculated on the basis that the only amounts that may be deducted in respect of services provided by the landlord are amounts in respect of the cost to the landlord of providing any relevant services.

(3) In this paragraph "relevant service" means a service other than the repair, insurance or maintenance of the premises.

Chattels

6 (1) This paragraph applies where—

(a) an individual ("the chargeable person") is in possession of, or has the use of, a chattel, whether alone or together with other persons, and

(b) the disposal condition or the contribution condition is met as respects the chattel.

(2) The disposal condition is that—

(a) at any time after 17th March 1986 the chargeable person had (whether alone or jointly with others) owned—

(i) the chattel, or

(ii) any other property the proceeds of the disposal of which were (directly or indirectly) applied by another person towards the acquisition of the chattel, and

(b) the chargeable person disposed of all or part of his interest in the chattel or other property otherwise than by an excluded transaction.

(3) The contribution condition is that at any time after 17th March 1986 the chargeable person had directly or indirectly provided, otherwise than by an excluded transaction, any of the consideration given by another person for the acquisition of—

(a) the chattel, or

(b) any other property the proceeds of the disposal of which were (directly or indirectly) applied by another person towards the acquisition of the chattel.

(4) For the purposes of this paragraph, a disposition which creates a new interest in a chattel out of an existing interest in a chattel is to be taken to be a disposal of part of the existing interest.

(5) Where this paragraph applies to a person in respect of the whole or part of a year of assessment, an amount equal to the chargeable amount determined under paragraph 7 is to be treated as income of his chargeable to income tax.

7 (1) For any taxable period the chargeable amount in relation to any chattel is the appropriate amount (as determined under sub-paragraph (2)), less the amount of any payments which, in pursuance of any legal obligation, are made by the chargeable person during the period to the owner of the chattel in respect of the possession or use of the chattel by the chargeable person.

(2) The appropriate amount is—

$$\frac{DV \times N}{V}$$

where—

N is the amount of the interest that would be payable for the taxable period if interest were payable at the prescribed rate on an amount equal to the value of the chattel as the valuation date,

DV is—

    (a)   in a case falling within paragraph 6(2)(a)(i), the value as at the valuation date of the interest in the chattel that was disposed of as mentioned in paragraph 6(2)(b) by the chargeable person or, where the disposal was a non-exempt sale, the appropriate proportion of that value,

    (b)   in a case falling within paragraph 6(2)(a)(ii), such part of the value of the chattel at the valuation date as can reasonably be attributed to the property originally disposed of by the chargeable person or, where the original disposal was a non-exempt sale, to the appropriate proportion of that property, and

    (c)   in a case falling within paragraph 6(3), such part of the value of the chattel at the valuation date as can reasonably be attributed to the consideration provided by the chargeable person, and

V is the value of the chattel at the valuation date.

(3) The disposal by the chargeable person of an interest in a chattel is a "non-exempt sale" if (although not an excluded transaction) it was a sale of his whole interest in the chattel for a consideration paid in money in sterling or any other currency; and, in relation to a non-exempt sale, "the appropriate proportion" is—

$$\frac{MV - P}{MV}$$

where—

MV is the value of the interest in the chattel at the time of the sale;

P is the amount paid.

(4) Regulations may, in relation to any valuation date, provide for a valuation of the chattel or any interest in the chattel by reference to an earlier valuation date to apply subject to any prescribed adjustments.

(5) In this paragraph—

"the taxable period" means the year of assessment, or part of a year of assessment, during which paragraph 6 applies to the chargeable person;

"the valuation date", in relation to a taxable period, means such date as may be prescribed.

Intangible property comprised in settlement where settlor retains an interest

8   (1) This paragraph applies where—

    (a)   the terms of a settlement, as they affect any property comprised in the settlement, are such that any income arising from the property would be treated by virtue of [section 624 of ITTOIA 2005]¹ (income arising under settlement where settlor retains an interest) as income of a person ("the chargeable person") who is for the purposes of [Chapter 5 of Part 5]¹ of that Act the settlor,

(b) any such income would be so treated even if [section 625(1) of ITTOIA 2995 (settlor's retained interest)]¹ did not include any reference to the spouse [or civil partner]² of the settlor, and

(c) that property includes any property as respects which the condition in sub-paragraph (2) is met ("the relevant property").

(2) The condition mentioned in sub-paragraph (1)(c) is that the property is intangible property which is or represents property which the chargeable person settled, or added to the settlement, after 17th March 1986.

(3) Where this paragraph applies in respect of the whole or part of a year of assessment, an amount equal to the chargeable amount determined under paragraph 9 is to be treated as income of the chargeable person chargeable to income tax.

---

1   Words substituted by ITTOIA 2005 s. 882 Sch.1 paras 629 and 653, with effect from 6 April 2005.

---

2   Words inserted by Tax and Civil Partnership Regulations (SI 2005/3229) regs 175 and 179, with effect from 5 December 2005.

9   (1) For any taxable period the chargeable amount in relation to the relevant property is N minus T where—

N is the amount of the interest that would be payable for the taxable period if interest were payable at the prescribed rate on an amount equal to the value of the relevant property at the valuation date, and

T is the amount of any income tax or capital gains tax payable by the chargeable person in respect of the taxable period by virtue of any of the following provisions—

(a)   [section 461 of ITTOIA 2005]¹,

(b)   [section 624 of that Act]¹,

(c)   sections 720 to 730 of the Income Tax Act 2007.]²

(d)   section 77 of the Taxation of Chargeable Gains Act 1992 (c. 12), and

(e)   section 86 of that Act,

so far as the tax is attributable to the relevant property.

---

1   Words substituted by ITTOIA 2005 s.882 Sch.1 paras 629, 653, with effect from 6 April 2005.
2   Sub-para.(c) substituted by Income Tax Act 2007 s.1027 Sch.1 paras 456, 482, with effect for income tax purposes from 6 April 2007 and corporation tax purposes for accounting periods ending after 5 April 2007.

(2) Regulations may, in relation to any valuation date, provide for a valuation of the relevant property by reference to an earlier valuation date to apply subject to any prescribed adjustments.

(3) In this paragraph—

"the taxable period" means the year of assessment, or part of a year of assessment, during which paragraph 8 applies to the chargeable person;

"the valuation date", in relation to a year of assessment, means such date as may be prescribed.

Excluded transactions

10   (1) For the purposes of paragraphs 3(2) and 6(2) (the disposal condition), the disposal of any property is an "excluded transaction" in relation to any person ("the chargeable person") if—

(a)   it was a disposal of his whole interest in the property, except for any right expressly reserved by him over the property, either—

    (i)   by a transaction made at arm's length with a person not connected with him, or

    (ii)   by a transaction such as might be expected to be made at arm's length between persons not connected with each other,

(b)   the property was transferred to his spouse [or civil partner][1] (or where the transfer has been ordered by a court, to his former spouse [or civil partner][1]),

(c)   it was a disposal by way of gift (or, where the transfer is for the benefit of his former spouse [or civil partner][1], in accordance with a court order), by virtue of which the property became settled property in which his spouse [or civil partner][1] or former spouse [or civil partner][1] is beneficially entitled to an interest in possession,

(d)   the disposal was a disposition falling within section 11 of IHTA 1984 (dispositions for maintenance of family), or

(e)   the disposal is an outright gift to an individual and is for the purposes of IHTA 1984 a transfer of value that is wholly exempt by virtue of section 19 (annual exemption) or section 20 (small gifts).

(2) For the purposes of paragraphs 3(3) and 6(3) (the contribution condition) the provision by a person ("the chargeable person") of consideration for another's acquisition of any property is an "excluded transaction" in relation to the chargeable person if—

(a)   the other person was his spouse [or civil partner][1] (or, where the transfer has been ordered by the court, his former spouse [or civil partner][1]),

(b)   on its acquisition the property became settled property in which his spouse [or civil partner][1] or former spouse [or civil partner][1] is beneficially entitled to an interest in possession,

(c)   the provision of the consideration constituted an outright gift of money (in sterling or any other currency) by the chargeable person to the other person and was made at least seven years before the earliest date on which the chargeable person met the condition in paragraph 3(1)(a) or, as the case may be, 6(1)(a),

(d)   the provision of the consideration is a disposition falling within section 11 of IHTA 1984 (dispositions for maintenance of family), or

(e)   the provision of the consideration is an outright gift to an individual and is for the purposes of IHTA 1984 a transfer of value that is wholly exempt by virtue of section 19 (annual exemption) or section 20 (small gifts).

(3) A disposal is not an excluded transaction by virtue of sub-paragraph (1)(c) or (2)(b), if the interest in possession of the spouse [or civil partner][1] or former spouse [or civil partner][1] has come to an end otherwise than on the death of the spouse or former spouse.

---

1   Words inserted by Tax and Civil Partnership Regulations (SI 2005/3229) regs 175, 179, with effect from 5 December 2005.

Exemptions from charge

11 (1) Paragraph 3 (land), paragraph 6 (chattels) and paragraph 8 (intangible property) do not apply to a person at a time when his estate for the purposes of IHTA 1984 includes—

(a) the relevant property, or

(b) other property—

(i) which derives its value from the relevant property, and

(ii) whose value, so far as attributable to the relevant property, is not substantially less than the value of the relevant property.

(2) Where the estate for the purposes of IHTA 1984 of a person to whom paragraph 3, 6 or 8 applies includes property—

(a) which derives its value from the relevant property, and

(b) whose value, so far as attributable to the relevant property, is substantially less than the value of the relevant property,

the appropriate rental value in paragraph 4, the appropriate amount in paragraph 7 or the chargeable amount in paragraph 9 (as the case may be) is to be reduced by such proportion as is reasonable to take account of the inclusion of the property in his estate.

(3) Paragraphs 3, 6 and 8 do not apply to a person at a time when—

(a) the relevant property, or

(b) any other property—

(i) which derives its value from the relevant property, and

(ii) whose value, so far as attributable to the relevant property, is not substantially less than the value of the relevant property,

falls within sub-paragraph (5) in relation to him.

(4) Where any property which falls within sub-paragraph (5) in relation to a person includes property—

(a) which derives its value from the relevant property, and

(b) whose value, so far as attributable to the relevant property, is substantially less than the value of the relevant property,

the appropriate rental value in paragraph 4, the appropriate amount in paragraph 7 or the chargeable amount in paragraph 9 (as the case may be) is to be reduced by such proportion as is reasonable to take account of that fact.

(5) Property falls within this sub-paragraph in relation to a person at a time when it—

(a) would fall to be treated by virtue of any provision of Part 5 of the 1986 Act (inheritance tax) as property which in relation to him is property subject to a reservation,

(b) would fall to be so treated but for any of paragraphs (d) to (i) of subsection (5) of section 102 of the 1986 Act (certain cases where disposal by way of gift is an exempt transfer for purposes of inheritance tax),

(c) would fall to be so treated but for subsection (4) of section 102B of the 1986 Act (gifts with reservation: share of interest in land), or would have fallen to be so treated but for that subsection if the disposal by way of gift of an undivided share of an interest in land had been made on or after 9th March 1999, or

(d) would fall to be so treated but for section 102C(3) of, and paragraph 6 of Schedule 20 to, the 1986 Act (exclusion of benefit).

(6) Where at any time the value of a person's estate for the purposes of IHTA 1984 is reduced by an excluded liability affecting any property, that property is not to be treated for the purposes of sub-paragraph (1) or (2) as comprised in his estate except to the extent that the value of the property exceeds the amount of the excluded liability.

(7) For the purposes of sub-paragraph (6) a liability is an excluded liability if—

(a) the creation of the liability, and

(b) any transaction by virtue of which the person's estate came to include the relevant property or property which derives its value from the relevant property or by virtue of which the value of property in his estate came to be derived from the relevant property,

were associated operations, as defined by section 268 of IHTA 1984.

(8) In determining whether any property falls within sub-paragraph (5)(b), (c) or (d) in a case where the contribution condition in paragraph 3(3) or 6(3) is met, paragraph 2(2)(b) of Schedule 20 (exclusion of gifts of money) is to be disregarded.

(9) In sub-paragraphs (1) to (8) "the relevant property" means—

(a) in relation to paragraphs 3 and 6—

(i) where the disposal condition in paragraph 3(2) or 6(2) is met, the property disposed of,

(ii) where the contribution condition in paragraph 3(3) or 6(3) is met, the property representing the consideration directly or indirectly provided,

(b) in relation to paragraph 8, the relevant property within the meaning of that paragraph.

(10) Property is not to be treated as falling within sub-paragraph (5)(b) at any time in a case falling within section 102(5)(h) of the 1986 Act unless the property remains subject to trusts which comply with the requirements of paragraph 3 (1) of Schedule 4 to IHTA 1984.

[(11) Sub-paragraph (12) applies where at any time—

(a) the relevant property has ceased to be comprised in a person's estate for the purposes of IHTA 1984, or

(b) he has directly or indirectly provided any consideration for the acquisition of the relevant property,

and at any subsequent time the relevant property or any derived property is comprised in his estate for the purposes of IHTA 1984 as a result of section 49(1) of that Act (treatment of interests in possession).

(12) Where this sub-paragraph applies, the relevant property and any derived property—

(a) are not to be treated for the purposes of sub-paragraphs (1) and (2) as comprised in his estate at that subsequent time, and

(b) are not to be treated as falling within sub-paragraph (5) in relation to him at that subsequent time.

(13) For the purposes of sub-paragraphs (11) and (12) references, in relation to the relevant property, to any derived property are to other property—

(a) which derives its value from the relevant property, and

(b)   whose value, so far as attributable to the relevant property, is not substantially less than the value of the relevant property.]¹

---

1   Words in sub-para.(9) substituted and sub-paras (11), (12) and (13) inserted by Finance Act 2006 s.80, with effect for the part of the year 2005–06 beginning with 5 December 2005 and for 2006–07 and subsequent years of assessment.

Chargeable person resident or domiciled outside the United Kingdom

12   (1) This Schedule does not apply in relation to any person for any year of assessment during which he is not resident in the United Kingdom.

(2) Where in any year of assessment a person is resident in the United Kingdom but is domiciled outside the United Kingdom, this Schedule does not apply to him unless the property falling within paragraph 3(1)(a), 6(1)(a) or 8(1)(c) is situated in the United Kingdom.

(3) In the application of this Schedule to a person who was at any time domiciled outside the United Kingdom, no regard is to be had to any property which is for the purposes of IHTA 1984 excluded property in relation to him by virtue of section 48(3)(a) of that Act.

(4) For the purposes of this paragraph, a person is to be treated as domiciled in the United Kingdom at any time only if he would be so treated for the purposes of IHTA 1984.

Exemption in cases where aggregate notional annual values do not exceed £5,000

13   (1) This paragraph applies where, in relation to any person who would (apart from this paragraph) be chargeable under this Schedule for any year of assessment, the aggregate of the amounts specified in sub-paragraph (2) in respect of that year does not exceed £5,000.

(2) Those amounts are—

(a)   in relation to any land to which paragraph 3 applies in respect of him, the appropriate rental value as determined under paragraph 4(2),

(b)   in relation to any chattel to which paragraph 6 applies in respect of him, the appropriate amount as determined under paragraph 7(2), and

(c)   in relation to any intangible property to which paragraph 8 applies in respect of him, the chargeable amount determined under paragraph 9.

(3) Where this paragraph applies, the person is not chargeable for that year of assessment under any of the following provisions—

(a)   paragraph 3(5) (land),

(b)   paragraph 6(5) (chattels), or

(c)   paragraph 8(3) (intangible property).

Power of Treasury to confer further exemptions by regulations

14   Regulations may confer further exemptions from the charges to income tax imposed by paragraphs 3, 6 and 8.
Valuation

15   Except as otherwise provided by this Schedule, the value of any property shall for the purposes of this Schedule be the price which the property might reasonably be expected to fetch if sold in the open market at that time; but that price shall not be assumed to be reduced on the ground that the whole property is to be placed on the market at one and the same time.

Changes in distribution of deceased's estate

16   Any disposition made by a person ("the chargeable person") in relation to an interest in the estate of a deceased person is to be disregarded for the purposes of this Schedule if by virtue of section 17 of IHTA 1984 (changes in distribution of deceased's estate, etc.) the disposition is not treated for the purposes of inheritance tax as a transfer of value by the chargeable person.

Guarantees

17   Where a person ("A") acts as guarantor in respect of a loan made to another person ("B") by a third party in connection with B's acquisition of any property, the mere giving of the guarantee is not to be regarded as the provision by A of consideration for B's acquisition of the property.

Persons chargeable under different provisions by reference to same property

18   (1) Where, in any year of assessment, a person ("the chargeable person") is (apart from this paragraph) chargeable to income tax both—

  (a)   under paragraph 3 (land) or paragraph 6 (chattels) by reason of his occupation of any land or his possession or use of any chattel, and

  (b)   under paragraph 8 (intangible property) by reference to any intangible property which derives its value (whether in whole or part) from the land or the chattel,

he is to be charged to income tax under whichever provision produces the higher chargeable amount in relation to him.

   (2) Where sub-paragraph (1) applies, only the amount under the paragraph under which he is chargeable is to be taken into account in relation to the chargeable person for the purposes of paragraph 13(2).

Relationship with Part 3 of Income Tax (Earnings and Pensions) Act 2003

19   Where, in any year of assessment, a person is (apart from this paragraph) chargeable, in respect of his occupation of any land or his possession or use of any chattel, to income tax both—

  (a)   under this Schedule, and

  (b)   under Part 3 of the Income Tax (Earnings and Pensions) Act 2003 (c. 1),

the provisions of that Part shall have priority and he shall not be chargeable to income tax under this Schedule, except to the extent that the amount chargeable under this Schedule exceeds the amount to be treated as earnings under that Part.

Regulations

20   (1) Regulations under this Schedule may—

   (a)   make different provision for different cases, and

   (b)   include transitional provisions and savings.

   (2) Any power conferred by this Schedule to prescribe a rate of interest includes power—

   (a)   to prescribe different rates in relation to property of different descriptions, and

   (b)   to prescribe a rate by reference to a rate specified in the regulations.

Election for application of inheritance tax provisions

21   (1) This paragraph applies where—

   (a)   a person ("the chargeable person") would (apart from this paragraph) be chargeable under paragraph 3 (land) or paragraph 6 (chattels) for any year of assessment ("the initial year") by reference to his enjoyment of any property ("the relevant property"), and

   (b)   he has not been chargeable under the paragraph in question in respect of any previous year of assessment by reference to his enjoyment of the relevant property, or of any other property for which the relevant property has been substituted.

   (2) The chargeable person may elect in accordance with paragraph 23 that—

   (a)   the preceding provisions of this Schedule shall not apply to him during the initial year and subsequent years of assessment by reference to his enjoyment of the relevant property or of any property which may be substituted for the relevant property, but

   (b)   so long as the chargeable person continues to enjoy the relevant property or any property which is substituted for the relevant property—

   (i)   the chargeable proportion of the property is to be treated for the purposes of Part 5 of the 1986 Act (in relation to the chargeable person) as property subject to a reservation, and

   (ii)   section 102(3) and (4) of that Act shall apply.

   (3) In this paragraph, "the chargeable proportion", in relation to any property, means—

$$\frac{DV}{V}$$

where DV and V are to be read in accordance with paragraph 4(2) or 7(2), as the case requires, but as if—

   (a)   any reference in paragraph 4(2) or 7(2) to the valuation date were a reference—

   (i)   in the case of property falling within subsection (3) of section 102 of the Finance Act 1986, to the date of the death of the chargeable person, and

   (ii)   in the case of property falling within subsection (4) of that section, to the date on which the property ceases to be treated as property subject to a reservation, and [(iii) in the case of property in which the chargeable person is beneficially entitled to an interest in possession, to the date of his death or (if his interest comes to an end on an earlier date) that earlier date, and][1]

(b) the transactions to be taken into account in calculating DV included transactions after the time when the election takes effect as well as transactions before that time.

(4) For the purposes of this paragraph a person "enjoys" property if—

(a) in the case of an interest in land, he occupies the land, and

(b) in the case of an interest in a chattel, he is in possession of, or has the use of, the chattel.

---

1 Words in sub-para.2(b)(i) inserted, sub-para.(2)(b)(ii) substituted, sub-para.2(b)(iii) inserted, and sub-para.3(a)(iii) inserted by Finance Act 2006 s.80, with effect for the part of the year 2005–06 beginning with 5 December 2005 and for 2006–07 and subsequent years of assessment.

22 (1) This paragraph applies where—

(a) a person ("the chargeable person") would (apart from this paragraph) be chargeable under paragraph 8 (intangible property) for any year of assessment ("the initial year") by reference to any property ("the relevant property"), and

(b) he has not been chargeable under that paragraph in respect of any previous year of assessment by reference to the relevant property or any property which the relevant property represents or is derived from.

(2) The chargeable person may elect in accordance with paragraph 23 that—

(a) the preceding provisions of this Schedule shall not apply to him during the initial year and subsequent years of assessment by reference to the relevant property or any property which represents or is derived from the relevant property, but

(b) so long as the conditions in sub-paragraph (3) are satisfied—

(i) the relevant property and any property which represents or is derived from the relevant property shall be treated for the purposes of Part 5 of the 1986 Act (in relation to the chargeable person) as property subject to a reservation[, but only so far as the chargeable person is not beneficially entitled to an interest in possession in the property concerned][2],

[(ii) section 102(3) and (4) of that Act shall apply, but only so far as the chargeable person is not beneficially entitled to an interest in possession in the property concerned, and][2]

[(iii) if the chargeable person is beneficially entitled to an interest in possession in the property concerned, section 53(3) and(4) and 54 of IHTA 1984 (which deal with cases of property reverting to the settlor etc) shall not apply in relation to the chargeable proportion of the property.][2]

(3) The conditions referred to in sub-paragraph (2)(b) are—

(a) that the relevant property or the property which represents or is derived from the relevant property remains comprised in the settlement, and

(b) that any income arising under the settlement would be treated by virtue of [section 624 of ITTOIA 2005][1] as income of the chargeable person.

---

1 Words in sub-para.3(b) substituted by ITTOIA 2005 s.882 Sch.1 paras 629, 653, with effect from 6 April 2005.

2 Words in sub-para.2(b)(i) inserted, sub-para.(2)(b)(ii) substituted, and sub-para.2(b)(iii) inserted by Finance Act 2006 s.80, with effect for the part of the year 2005–06 beginning with 5 December 2005 and for 2006–07 and subsequent years of assessment.

23   (1) In this paragraph—

"election" means an election under paragraph 21 or 22;

"the relevant filing date" means 31st January in the year of assessment that immediately follows the initial year within the meaning of paragraph 21 or (as the case requires) paragraph 22.

(2) The election must be made in the prescribed manner.

[(3) The election must be made on or before—

(a)   the relevant filing date, or

(b)   such later date as an officer of Revenue and Customs may, in a particular case, allow.][1]

(4) Where the chargeable person can show reasonable excuse for the failure to make the election on or before the relevant filing date, the election must be made on or before such later date as may be prescribed.

(5) The election may be withdrawn or amended, during the life of the chargeable person, at any time on or before the relevant filing date.

(6) Subject to sub-paragraph (5), the election takes effect for the purposes of inheritance tax from the beginning of the initial year within the meaning of paragraph 21 or (as the case requires) paragraph 22 or, if later, the date on which the chargeable person would (but for the election) have first become chargeable under this Schedule by reference to the property to which the election relates.

1   Sub-para.(3) substituted for original sub-paras (3) and (4) by Finance Act 2007 s.66. This amendment is deemed to have come into force on 21 March 2007.

80 Restriction of exemption from charge to income tax

(6) If-

(a) paragraph 11 of Schedule 15 to FA 2004 ceases, in consequence of the amendments made by this section, to apply to a person in relation to any property, and

(b) that person dies before the day on which this Act is passed without making an election under paragraph 21 or 22 of that Schedule in relation to that property,

his personal representatives (within the meaning of IHTA 1984) may make any election under paragraph 21 or 22 of that Schedule that he might have made.

(7) If-

(a) in consequence of the amendments made by this section a person makes an election under paragraph 21 or 22 of Schedule 15 to FA 2004,

(b) that person dies before the day on which this Act is passed, and

(c) an amount of inheritance tax would (but for this subsection) fall due before that day,

that amount is to be treated instead as falling due at the end of the period of 14 days beginning with that day.

III THE CHARGE TO INCOME TAX BY REFERENCE TO ENJOYMENT OF PROPERTY PREVIOUSLY OWNED REGULATIONS: SI 2005/724

The Treasury, in exercise of the powers conferred upon them by paragraphs 1, 4(5) and (6), 7(2), (4) and (5), 9(1) and (3), 14 and 20 of Schedule 15 to the Finance Act 2004[1], and the Commissioners of Inland Revenue, in exercise of powers conferred upon them by section 104 of the Finance Act 1986[2], make the following Regulations:

Citation and commencement

1. These Regulations may be cited as the Charge to Income Tax by Reference to Enjoyment of Property Previously Owned Regulations 2005 and shall come into force on 6th April 2005.

Prescribed valuation date

2. In paragraph 4 (chargeable amount in relation to land), paragraph 7 (chargeable amount in relation to chattels) and paragraph 9 (chargeable amount in relation to intangible property) of Schedule 15 to the Finance Act 2004 the valuation date in relation to a taxable period is 6th April in the relevant year of assessment or, if later, the first day of the taxable period.

Prescribed rate of interest

3.—(1) In paragraphs 7(2) and 9(1) of Schedule 15 to the Finance Act 2004 the prescribed rate is the official rate of interest at the valuation date.

(2) In this regulation, "the official rate of interest" has the meaning given in section 181 of the Income Tax (Earnings and Pensions) Act 2003[3].

Valuation and rental value

4.—(1) The valuation of land or any interest in land for the purposes of paragraph 4 of Schedule 15 to the Finance Act 2004 and a chattel or any interest in a chattel for the purposes of paragraph 7 of Schedule 15 to the Finance Act 2004 is—

(a) before the first five-year anniversary, by reference to the first valuation date, and

(b) thereafter, by reference to the valuation date at the last five-year anniversary.

(2) The rental value of land for the purposes of paragraph 4 of Schedule 15 to the Finance Act 2004 is determined in relation to a year of assessment—

(a) between the end of the first taxable period and the first five-year anniversary, by reference to the annual value in relation to the first year of assessment in which paragraph 3 of Schedule 15 to the Finance Act 2004 (land) applied, and

(b) thereafter, by reference to the rental value for the year of assessment commencing at the last five-year anniversary.

(3) Subject to paragraph (4), in this regulation—

"five-year anniversary" means the fifth anniversary of 6th April in the year of assessment in which paragraph 3 (land) or paragraph 6 (chattels) of Schedule 15 to the Finance Act 2004 first applied to a person in relation to the relevant land or chattel or any interest in the relevant land or chattel, and subsequent anniversaries at five-year intervals;

"first valuation date" means the date on which paragraph 3 or paragraph 6 of Schedule 15 to the Finance Act 2004 first applied to a person in relation to the relevant land or chattel or any interest in the relevant land or chattel.

(4) If there is no valuation date at a five-year anniversary, the date on which paragraph 3 or paragraph 6 of Schedule 15 to the Finance Act 2004 next apply to the person in relation to the relevant land or chattel, or any interest in the relevant land or chattel, shall be treated as the date on which, and being in the year of assessment in which, paragraph 3 or paragraph 6 of that Schedule first applied to that person in relation to that land, chattel or interest.

Exemptions

5.—(1) Paragraph 3 (land), paragraph 6 (chattels) and paragraph 8 (intangible property) do not apply to a person in relation to a disposal of part of an interest in any property if—

(a) the disposal was by a transaction made at arm's length with a person not connected with him;

(b) the disposal was by a transaction such as might be expected to be made at arm's length between persons not connected with each other for a consideration not in money or in the form of readily convertible assets; or

(c) the disposal was made before [date].

(2) In this regulation "readily convertible asset" has the meaning given in section 702 of the Income Tax (Earning and Pensions) Act 2003[4].

Avoiding double charge

6.—(1) This regulation provides for the avoidance, to the extent specified, of double charges to tax arising in the circumstances specified (in paragraph (2)) for the purposes of paragraph (d) of section 104(1) of the Finance Act 1986 (being circumstances which appear to the Board to be similar to those referred to in paragraphs (a) to (c) of that subsection).

(2) The specified circumstances are—

(a) a person makes a transfer by way of gift of property representing the proceeds of the disposal of relevant property by virtue of which property becomes comprised in a settlement,

(b) the transfer is or proves to be a chargeable transfer,

(c) the person dies on or after 6th April 2005 and within seven years of the transfer,

(d) the person made an election under paragraph 21 of Schedule 15 to the Finance Act 2004 (election for application of inheritance tax provisions) in relation to the relevant property,

(e) the relevant property—

    (i) is by virtue of section 102(3) of the Finance Act 1986 treated for the purposes of the Inheritance Tax Act 1984 as property to which the person was beneficially entitled immediately before his death, or

    (ii) ceased to be property subject to a reservation and became the subject of a potentially exempt transfer by virtue of section 102(4) of the Finance Act 1986, and

(f) the chargeable proportion of the relevant property—

    (i) is comprised in the estate of the person immediately before his death within the meaning of section 5(1) of the Inheritance Tax Act 1984 and the value attributed to it is transferred by a chargeable transfer under section 4 of that Act, or

    (ii) is property transferred by the potentially chargeable transfer to which sub-paragraph (e)(ii) applies, value attributable to which is transferred by a chargeable transfer.

(3) Where this regulation applies, there shall be calculated, separately in accordance with sub-paragraphs (a) and (b), the total tax chargeable as a consequence of the death of the person—

(a) disregarding so much of the value transferred by the transfer of value to which paragraph (2)(a) refers as represents the proceeds of the disposal of the relevant property to which (2)(f) refers, and

(b) disregarding so much of the value transferred by the transfer of value to which paragraph (2)(f) refers as is represented by property to which (2)(a) refers.

(4) Where the amount calculated under paragraph (3)(a) is higher than the amount calculated under (3)(b)—

(a) only so much of that higher amount shall be payable as remains after deducting, as a credit, from the amount comprised in the higher amount which is attributable to the value of the property to which paragraph (2)(f) refers, a sum (not exceeding the amount so attributable) equal to so much of the tax paid—

    (i) as became payable before the person's death, and

    (ii) as is attributable to the value disregarded under paragraph (3)(a), and

(b) so much of the value transferred by the transfer of value to which paragraph (2)(a) refers as is attributable to the property to which paragraph (2)(f) refers shall (except in relation to chargeable transfers which were chargeable to tax, when made by the person, for the purposes of an occasion which occurred before the person's death on which tax was chargeable under section 64 or 65 of the Inheritance Tax Act 1984 (charge at ten year anniversary and charge at other times in relation to settlements without interests in possession)) be treated as reduced to a nil amount for all the purposes of the Inheritance Tax Act 1984.

(5) Where the amount calculated under paragraph (3)(a) is less than the amount calculated under paragraph (3)(b) the value of the property to which paragraph (2)(f) refers shall be reduced to a nil amount for all the purposes of the Inheritance Tax Act 1984.

(6) In this regulation, "relevant property" and "the chargeable proportion" have the meanings given in paragraph 21 of Schedule 15 to the Finance Act 2004.

EXPLANATORY NOTE

(This note is not part of the Regulations)

These Regulations are made pursuant to Schedule 15 of the Finance Act 2004 (c.12) which provides for an income tax charge in relation to the benefit enjoyed by taxpayers in certain circumstances from continuing to enjoy assets they formerly owned.

Regulation 1 provides for citation and commencement.

Regulation 2 prescribes the valuation date.

Regulation 3 prescribes the rate of interest to be used to determine the monetary benefit of assets enjoyed.

Regulation 4 makes provision for a five yearly rather than an annual valuation of land and chattels.

Regulation 5 provides for exemptions from the charge.

Regulation 6 makes provision for the avoidance of a double charge where an inheritance tax charge also arises.

IV INCOME TAX (BENEFITS RECEIVED BY FORMER OWNER OF PROPERTY) (ELECTION FOR INHERITANCE TAX TREATMENT) REGULATIONS: SI 2007/3000

The Treasury, in exercise of the power conferred by paragraph 23(2) of Schedule 15 to the Finance Act 2004, make the following Regulations:

Citation and commencement

1. These Regulations may be cited as the Income Tax (Benefits Received by Former Owner of Property) (Election for Inheritance Tax Treatment) Regulations 2007 and shall come into force on 14th November 2007.

Manner in which election to be made

2. An election under paragraph 21 or 22 of Schedule 15 to the Finance Act 2004 (power to elect for inheritance tax treatment of pre-owned assets) is to be made in writing on the form designated IHT 500 in the Schedule to these Regulations.

19 October 2007

SCHEDULE

Form IHT 500

Regulation 2

HM Revenue & Customs

Election for Inheritance Tax to apply to asset previously owned

Fill in this form if you are chargeable to Income Tax on the benefit you receive from property you previously owned but want to elect for the property to be treated as part of your estate for Inheritance Tax purposes.

You should read the notes IHT501 as you fill in this form. Please provide information for all sections, inserting 'not applicable' where appropriate.

About the person making the election

Title

Unique Taxpayer Reference (UTR)

Surname

National Insurance number

First name(s)

Address

Date of birth *DD MM YYYY*

Postcode

HMRC Income Tax office

HMRC Income Tax office reference

About the property subject to the election

The property is:

an interest in land ☐   a chattel ☐   intangible property ☐

Description of the property

IHT500   Page 1   HMRC 10/07

371

Name(s) of the legal owners of the property

Details of disposal(s) or contribution(s)

What is the nature and extent of your interest in the property?

Is the property conditionally exempt from Inheritance Tax or Capital Gains Tax on an earlier event?

Yes ☐   No ☐

If 'Yes', please provide details

Name(s) of anyone else who receives a benefit from the property

The election

I elect that the property specified above is to form part of my estate for Inheritance Tax purposes under the provisions of paragraphs 21 to 23, Schedule 15 to the Finance Act 2004.

Signature of person making the election

Date *DD MM YYYY*

☐☐ ☐☐ ☐☐☐☐

Capacity

The election applies from the year of Assessment beginning on

6 April ☐☐☐☐

When you have completed this form send it to:

Pre-owned Assets Section
HMRC Inheritance Tax
PO Box 38
Castle Meadow Road
Nottingham
NG2 1BB

Document Exchange: **DX 701201 Nottingham 4**.

Probate and Inheritance Tax helpline:
0845 30 20 900.

For further guidance go to:
www.hmrc.gov.uk/poa/index.htm

V THE INHERITANCE TAX (DOUBLE CHARGES RELIEF) REGULATIONS: SI 1987/1130

The Commissioners of Inland Revenue, in exercise of the powers conferred on them by section 104 of the Finance Act 1986,[1] hereby make the following Regulations.

Citation and commencement

1. These Regulations may be cited as the Inheritance Tax (Double Charges Relief) Regulations 1987 and shall come into force on 22 July 1987.

Interpretation

2. In these Regulations unless the context otherwise requires—

"PET" means potentially exempt transfer;

"property" includes part of any property;

"the 1984 Act" means the Inheritance Tax Act 1984;[2]

"the 1986 Act" means Part V of the Finance Act 1986;

"section" means section of the 1984 Act.

---

1   1986 c 41.
2   1984 c 51.

Introductory

3. These Regulations provide for the avoidance, to the extent specified, of double charges to tax arising with respect to specified transfers of value made, and other events occurring, on or after 18 March 1986.

Double charges—potentially exempt transfers and death

4.—(1) This regulation applies in the circumstances to which paragraph (*a*) of section 104(1) of the 1986 Act refers where the conditions ("specified conditions") of paragraph (2) are fulfilled.

(2) The specified conditions to which paragraph (1) refers are—

(*a*) an individual ("the deceased") makes a transfer of value to a person ("the transferee") which is a PET,

(*b*) the transfer is made on or after 18 March 1986,

(*c*) the transfer proves to be a chargeable transfer, and

(*d*) the deceased immediately before his death was beneficially entitled to property to which paragraph (3) refers.

(3) The property to which paragraph (2)(*d*) refers is property—

(*a*) which the deceased, after making the PET to which paragraph (2)(*a*) refers, acquired from the transferee otherwise than for full consideration in money or money's worth.

(*b*) which is property which was transferred to the transferee by the PET to which paragraph (2)(*a*) refers or which is property directly or indirectly representing that property, and

(*c*) which is property comprised in the estate of the deceased immediately before his death (within the meaning of section 5(1)), value attributable to which is transferred by a chargeable transfer (under section 4).

(4) Where the specified conditions are fulfilled there shall be calculated, separately in accordance with sub-paragraphs (*a*) and (*b*), the total tax chargeable as a consequence of the death of the deceased—

(*a*) disregarding so much of the value transferred by the PET to which paragraph (2) (*a*) refers as is attributable to the property, value of which is transferred by the chargeable transfer to which paragraph (3)(*c*) refers, and

(*b*) disregarding so much of the value transferred by the chargeable transfer to which paragraph (3)(*c*) refers as is attributable to the property, value of which is transferred by the PET to which paragraph (2)(*a*) refers.

(5)(*a*) Whichever of the two amounts of tax calculated under paragraph (4)(*a*) or (*b*) is the lower amount shall be treated as reduced to nil but, subject to sub-paragraph (*b*), the higher amount shall be payable,

(*b*) where the amount calculated under paragraph (4)(*a*) is higher than the amount calculated under paragraph (4)(*b*)—

(i) so much of the tax chargeable on the value transferred by the chargeable transfer to which paragraph (2)(*c*) refers as is attributable to the amount of that value which falls to be disregarded by virtue of paragraph (ii) shall be treated as a nil amount, and

(ii) for all the purposes of the 1984 Act so much of the value transferred by the PET to which paragraph (2)(*a*) refers as is attributable to the property to which paragraph (3)(*c*) refers shall be disregarded.

(6) Part I of the Schedule to these Regulations provides an example of the operation of this regulation.

Double charges—gifts with reservation and death

5.—(1) This regulation applies in the circumstances to which paragraph (*b*) of section 104(1) of the 1986 Act refers where the conditions ("specified conditions") of paragraph (2) are fulfilled.

(2) The specified conditions to which paragraph (1) refers are—

(*a*) an individual ("the deceased") makes a transfer of value by way of gift of property,

(*b*) the transfer is made on or after 18 March 1986,

(*c*) the transfer is or proves to be a chargeable transfer, (*d*) the deceased dies on or after 18 March 1986,

(*e*) the property in relation to the gift and the deceased is property subject to a reservation (within the meaning of s 102 of the 1986 Act),

(*f*) (i) the property is by virtue of s 102(3) of the 1986 Act treated for the purposes of the 1984 Act as property to which the deceased was beneficially entitled immediately before his death, or,

(ii) the property ceases to be property subject to a reservation and is the subject of a PET by virtue of section 102(4) of the 1986 Act, and

(*g*) (i) the property is comprised in the estate of the deceased immediately before his death (within the meaning of section 5(1)) and value attributable to it is transferred by a chargeable transfer (under section 4), or

(ii) the property is property transferred by the PET to which sub-paragraph (*f*)(ii) refers, value attributable to which is transferred by a chargeable transfer.

(3) Where the specified conditions are fulfilled there shall be calculated, separately in accordance with sub-paragraphs (*a*) and (*b*), the total tax chargeable as a consequence of the death of the deceased—

(*a*) disregarding so much of the value transferred by the transfer of value to which paragraph (2)(*a*) refers as is attributable to property to which paragraph (2)(*g*) refers, and

(*b*) disregarding so much of the value of property to which paragraph (2)(*g*) refers as is attributable to property to which paragraph (2)(*a*) refers.

(4) Where the amount calculated under paragraph (3)(*a*) is higher than the amount calculated under paragraph (3)(*b*)—

(*a*) only so much of that higher amount shall be payable as remains after deducting, as a credit, from the amount comprised in that higher amount which is attributable to the value of the property to which paragraph (2)(*g*) refers, a sum (not exceeding the amount so attributable) equal to so much of the tax paid—

(i) as became payable before the death of the deceased, and

(ii) as is attributable to the value disregarded under paragraph (3)(*a*), and

(*b*) so much of the value transferred by the transfer of value to which paragraph (2)(*a*) refers as is attributable to the property to which paragraph (2)(*g*) refers shall (except in relation to chargeable transfers which were chargeable to tax, when made by the deceased, for the purposes of an occasion which occurred before the death of the deceased on which tax was chargeable under section 64 or 65) be treated as reduced to a nil amount for all the purposes of the 1984 Act.

(5) Where the amount calculated under paragraph (3)(*a*) is less than the amount calculated under paragraph (3)(*b*) the value of the property to which paragraph (2)(*g*) refers shall be reduced to nil for all the purposes of the 1984 Act.

(6) For the purposes of the interpretation and application of this regulation section 102 of and Schedule 20 to the 1986 Act shall apply.

(7) Part II of the Schedule to these Regulations provides examples of the operation of this regulation.

Double charges—liabilities subject to abatement and death

6.—(1) This regulation applies in the circumstances to which paragraph (*c*) of section 104(1) of the 1986 Act refers where the conditions ("specified conditions") of paragraph (2) are fulfilled.

(2) The specified conditions to which paragraph (1) refers are—

(*a*) a transfer of value which is or proves to be a chargeable transfer ("the transfer") is made on or after 18 March 1986 by an individual ("the deceased") by virtue of which the estate of the transferee is increased or by virtue of which property becomes comprised in a settlement of which the transferee is a trustee, and

(*b*) at any time before his death the deceased incurs a liability to the transferee ("the liability") which is a liability subject to abatement under the provisions of section 103 of the 1986 Act in determining the value transferred by a chargeable transfer (under section 4).

(3) Where the specified conditions are fulfilled there shall be calculated, separately in accordance with sub-paragraphs (*a*) and (*b*), the total tax chargeable as a consequence of the death of the deceased—

(*a*) disregarding so much of the value transferred by the transfer—

    (i) as is attributable to the property by reference to which the liability falls to be abated, and

    (ii) as is equal to the amount of the abatement of the liability, and

(*b*) taking account both of the value transferred by the transfer and of the liability.

(4)(*a*) Whichever of the two amounts of tax calculated under paragraph (3)(*a*) or (*b*) is the lower amount shall be treated as reduced to nil but, subject to sub-paragraph (*b*), the higher amount shall be payable,

(*b*) where the amount calculated under paragraph (3)(*a*) is higher than the amount calculated under paragraph (3)(*b*)—

    (i) only so much of that higher amount shall be payable as remains after deducting, as a credit, from that amount a sum equal to so much of the tax paid—

        (*a*) as became payable before the death of the deceased, and

        (*b*) as is attributable to the value disregarded under paragraph (3)(*a*), and

        (*c*) as does not exceed the difference between the amount of tax calculated under paragraph (3)(*a*) and the amount of tax that would have fallen to be calculated under paragraph (3)(*b*) if the liability had been taken into account, and

    (ii) so much of the value transferred by the transfer to which paragraph (2)(*a*) refers—

        (*a*) as is attributable to property by reference to which the liability is abated, and

        (*b*) as is equal to the amount of the abatement of the liability,

shall (except in relation to chargeable transfers which were chargeable to tax, when made by the deceased, for the purposes of an occasion which occurred before the death of the deceased on which tax was chargeable under section 64 or 65) be treated as reduced to a nil amount for all the purposes of the 1984 Act.

(5) Where there is a number of transfers made by the deceased which are relevant to the liability to which paragraph (2)(*b*) applies the provisions of this regulation shall apply to those transfers taking them in reverse order of their making, that is to say, taking the latest first and the earliest last, but only to the extent that in aggregate the value of those transfers does not exceed the amount of the abatement to which paragraph (2)(*b*) refers.

(6) Part III of the Schedule to these Regulations provides examples of the operation of this regulation.

Double Charges—chargeable transfers and death

7.—(1) This regulation applies in the circumstances specified (by this regulation) for the purposes of paragraph (*d*) of section 104(1) of the 1986 Act (being circumstances which appear to the Board to be similar to those referred to in paragraphs (*a*) to (*c*) of that subsection) where the conditions ("specified conditions") of paragraph (2) are fulfilled.

(2) The specified conditions to which paragraph (1) refers are—

(*a*) an individual ("the deceased") makes a transfer of value to a person ("the transferee") which is a chargeable transfer,

(*b*) the transfer is made on or after 18 March 1986

(*c*) the decreased dies within 7 years after that chargeable transfer is made, and

(*d*) the deceased immediately before his death was beneficially entitled to property to which paragraph (3) refers.

(3) The property to which paragraph (2)(*d*) refers is property—

(*a*) which the deceased, after making the chargeable transfer to which paragraph (2)(*a*) refers, acquired from the transferee otherwise than for full consideration in money or money's worth,

(*b*) which was transferred to the transferee by the chargeable transfer to which paragraph (2)(*a*) refers or which is property directly or indirectly representing that property, and

(*c*) which is property comprised in the estate of the deceased immediately before his death (within the meaning of section 5(1)), value attributable to which is transferred by a chargeable transfer (under section 4).

(4) Where the specified conditions are fulfilled there shall be calculated, separately in accordance with sub-paragraphs (*a*) and (*b*), the total tax chargeable as a consequence of the death of the deceased—

(*a*) disregarding so much of the value transferred by the chargeable transfer to which paragraph (2)(*a*) refers as is attributable to the property, value of which is transferred by the chargeable transfer to which paragraph (3)(*c*) refers, and

(*b*) disregarding so much of the value transferred by the chargeable transfer to which paragraph (3)(*c*) refers as is attributable to the property, value of which is transferred by the chargeable transfer to which paragraph (2)(*a*) refers.

(5)(*a*) Whichever of the two amounts of tax calculated under paragraph (4)(*a*) or (*b*) is the lower amount shall be treated as reduced to nil but, subject to sub-paragraph (*b*), the higher amount shall be payable, (*b*) where the amount calculated under paragraph (4)(*a*) is higher than the amount calculated under paragraph (4)(*b*)—

    (i) only so much of that higher amount shall be payable as remains after deducting, as a credit, from the amount comprised in that higher amount which is attributable to the value of the property to which paragraph (2)(*d*) refers, a sum (not exceeding the amount so attributable) equal to so much of the tax paid—

        (*a*) as became payable before the death of the deceased, and

        (*b*) as is attributable to the value disregarded under paragraph (4)(*a*), and

    (ii) so much of the value transferred by the chargeable transfer to which paragraph (2)(*a*) refers as is attributable to the property to which paragraph (3)(*c*) refers shall (except for the purposes of an occasion which occurred before the death of the deceased on which tax was chargeable under section 64 or 65) be treated as reduced to a nil amount for all the purposes of the 1984 Act.

(6) Part IV of the Schedule to these Regulations provides an example of the operation of this regulation.

Equal calculations of tax—special rule

8. Where the total tax chargeable as a consequence of death under the two separate calculations provided for by any of regulation 4(4), 5(3), 6(3) or 7(4) is equal in amount the first of those calculations shall be treated as producing a higher amount for the purposes of the regulation concerned.

Schedule and saving

9. The Schedule to these Regulations shall have effect only for providing examples of the operation of these Regulations and, in the event of any conflict between the Schedule and the Regulations, the Regulations shall prevail.

SCHEDULE

Regulation 9

INTRODUCTORY

1 This Schedule provides examples of the operation of the Regulations.
  2 In this Schedule:

"cumulation" means the inclusion of the total chargeable transfers made by the transferor in the 7 years preceding the current transfer;

"GWR" means gift with reservation;

"taper relief" means the reduction in tax provided under s 7(4) of the 1984 Act, inserted by para 2(4) of Sched 19 to the 1986 Act.

3 Except where otherwise stated, the examples assume that: tax rates and bands remain as at 18 March 1987;

the transferor has made no other transfers than those shown in the examples;

no exemptions (including annual exemption) or reliefs apply to the value transferred by the relevant transfer; and

"grossing up" does not apply in determining any lifetime tax (the tax is not borne by the transferor).

Part I

Regulation 4: Example

Jul 1987	A makes PET of £100,000 to B.	
Jul 1988	A makes gift into discretionary trust of £95,000.	Tax paid £750
Jan 1989	A makes further gift into same trust of £45,000.	Tax paid £6,750
Jan 1990	B dies and the 1987 PET returns to A.	
Apr 1991	A dies. His death estate of £300,000 includes the 1987 PET returning to him in 1990, which is still worth £100,000.	

First calculation under reg 4(4)(*a*)

Charge the returned PET in A's death estate and ignore the PET made in 1987.

		Tax
Jul 1987	PET £100,000 ignored	NIL
Jul 1988	Gift £95,000	
	Tax £1,500 less £750 already paid	£750
Jan 1989	Gift £45,000 as top slice of £140,000	
	Tax £13,500 less £6,750 already paid	£6,750
Apr 1991	Death estate £300,000 as top slice of £440,000	£153,000*
	Total tax due as result of A's death	£160,500

*In first calculation the tax of £153,000 on death estate does not allow for any successive charges relief (under s 141 IHTA 1984) that might be due in respect of "the returned PET" by reference to any tax charged on that "PET" in connection with B's death.

Second calculation under reg 4(4)(*b*)

Charge the 1987 PET and ignore the value of the returned PET in A's death estate.

		Tax
Jul 1987	PET £100,000. Tax with taper relief	£2,400
Jul 1988	Gift £95,000 as top slice of £195,000	
	Tax £34,000 less £750 already paid	£33,250
Jan 1989	Gift £45,000 as top slice of £240,000	
	Tax £20,000 less £6,750 already paid	£13,250
Apr 1991	Death estate £200,000 as top slice of £440,000	£111,000
	Total tax due as result of A's death	£159,900

*Result**

First calculation gives higher amount of tax. So PET reduced to nil and tax on other transfers is as in first calculation.

Part II

Regulation 5: Example 1

Jan 1988	A makes PET of £150,000 to B.	
March 1992	A makes gift of land worth £200,000 into a discretionary trust of which he is a potential beneficiary. The gift is a "GWR".	Tax paid £19,500
Feb 1995	A dies without having released his interest in the trust. His death estate valued at £400,000, includes the GWR land currently worth £300,000.	

First calculation under reg 5(3)(*a*)

Charge the GWR land in A's death estate and ignore the GWR.

		Tax
Jan 1988	PET (now exempt)	NIL
Mar 1992	GWR ignored	NIL
Feb 1995	Death estate £400,000	
	Tax £144,000 less £19,500 already paid on GWR*	£124,500
	Total tax due as result of A's death	£124,500

---

*Credit for the tax already paid cannot exceed the amount of the death tax attributable to the value of the GWR property. In this example the tax so attributable is £108,000 (ie 144,000/400,000×300,000). So credit is given for the full amount of £19,500.

Second calculation under reg. 5(3)(*b*)

Charge the GWR and ignore the GWR land in the death estate.

		Tax
Jan 1988	PET (now exempt)	NIL
March 1992	GWR £200,000	
	Tax £39,000 less £19,500 already paid	£19,500
Feb 1995	Death estate £100,000 (ignoring GWR property) as top slice of £300,000	£48,000
	Total tax due as result of A's death	£67,500

Result

First calculation yields higher amount of tax. So the value of the GWR transfer is reduced to nil and tax on death is charged as in first calculation with credit for the tax already paid.

Part II

Regulation 5: Example 2

Apr 1987	A makes gift into discretionary trust of £150,000	Tax paid £9,500
Jan 1988	A makes further gift into same trust of £50,000.	Tax paid £10,000
Mar 1993	A makes PET of shares valued at £150,000 to B.	
Feb 1996	A dies. He had continued to enjoy the income of the shares he had given to B (the 1993 PET is a GWR). His death estate, valued at £300,000, includes those shares currently worth £200,000.	

First calculation under reg 5(3)(*a*)

Charge the GWR shares in the death estate and ignore the PET.

		Tax
Apr 1987	Gift £150,000. No adjustment to tax as gift made more than 7 years before death	NIL
Jan 1988	Gift £50,000. No adjustment to tax as gift made more than 7 years before death	NIL
Mar 1993	PET £150,000 now reduced to NIL	NIL
Feb 1996	Death estate including GWR shares £300,000. No previous cumulation	£87,000
	Total tax due as result of A's death	£87,000

Second calculation under reg 5(3)(*b*)

Charge the PET and ignore the value of the GWR shares in the death estate.

		Tax
Apr 1987	Gift £150,000. No adjustment to tax as gift made more than 7 years before death	NIL
Jan 1988	Gift £50,000. No adjustment to tax as gift made more than 7 years before death	NIL
Mar 1993	GWR £150,000 as top slice of £350,000 (ie previous gifts totalling £200,000+£150,000)	£75,000
Feb 1996	Death estate (excluding GWR shares) £100,000 as top slice of £250,000 (the 1987 and 1988 gifts drop out of cumulation)	£43,000
	Total tax due as result of A's death	£118,000

Result

Second calculation yields higher amount of tax. So tax is charged by reference to the PET and the value of the GWR shares in the death estate is reduced to NIL.

Part III

Regulation 6: Example 1

Nov 1987	X makes a PET of cash of £95,000 to Y.
Dec 1987	Y makes a loan to X of £95,000.
May 1988	X makes a gift into discretionary trust of £20,000.
Apr 1993	X dies. His death estate is worth £182,000. A deduction of £95,000 is claimed for the loan from Y.

First calculation under reg 6(3)(*a*)

No charge on November 1987 gift, and no deduction against death estate.

		Tax
Nov 1987	PET ignored	NIL
May 1988	Gift £20,000	NIL
Apr 1993	Death estate £182,000 as top slice of £202,000	£39,800
	Total tax due as result of X's death	£39,800

Second calculation under reg 6(3)(*b*)

Charge the November 1987 PET, and allow the deduction against the death estate.

		Tax
Nov 1987	PET £95,000. Tax with taper relief	£600
May 1988	Gift £20,000 as top slice of £115,000. Tax with taper relief	£3,600
Apr 1993	Death estate (£182,000-loan of £95,000) £87,000 as top slice of £202,000	£32,300
	Total tax due as result of X's death	£36,500

Result

First calculation gives higher amount of tax. So debt is disallowed against death estate, but PET of £95,000 is not charged.

Part III

Regulation 6: Example 2

Aug 1988	P makes a PET of cash of £100,000 to Q.	
Sept 1988	Q makes a loan to P of £100,000.	
Oct 1989	P makes gift into discretionary trust of £98,000.	Tax paid £1,200
Nov 1992	P dies. Death estate £110,000 less allowable liabilities of £80,000 (which do not include the debt of £100,000 owed to Q).	

First calculation under reg 6(3)(*a*)

No charge on August 1988 PET, and no deduction against death estate for the £100,000 owed to Q.

		Tax
Aug 1988	PET ignored	NIL
Oct 1989	Gift £98,000	
	Tax (with taper relief) £1,920 less £1,200 already paid	£720
Nov 1992	Death estate £30,000 as top slice of £128,000	£9,000
	Total tax due as result of P's death	£9,720

Second calculation under reg 6(3)(*b*)

Charge the August 1988 PET, and allow deduction against death estate for the £100,000 owed to Q.

		Tax
Aug 1988	PET £100,000. Tax with taper relief	£1,800
Oct 1989	Gift £98,000 as top slice of £198,000	
	Tax (with taper relief) £28,100 less £1,200 already paid	£26,900
Nov 1992	Death estate £30,000–£100,000 (owed to Q)	NIL
	Total tax due as result of P's death	£28,700

Result

Second calculation gives higher amount of tax. So the PET to Q is charged, and deduction is allowed against death estate for the debt to Q.

Part III

Regulation 6: Example 3

1 May 1987	A makes PET to B of £95,000.	
1 Jan 1988	A makes PET to B of £40,000.	
1 Jul 1988	A makes gift into discretionary trust of £100,000.	Tax paid £1,500
1 Jan 1989	A makes PET to B of £30,000.	
1 Jul 1989	B makes a loan to A of £100,000.	
1 Dec 1990	A dies. Death estate £200,000, against which	
	deduction is claimed for debt of £100,000 due to B.	

First calculation under reg 6(3)(*a*)

Disallow the debt and ignore corresponding amounts (£100,000) of PETs from A to B, starting with the latest PET.

		Tax
1 May 1987	PET now reduced to £65,000	NIL
1 Jan 1988	PET now reduced to NIL	NIL
1 Jul 1988	Gift into trust £100,000 as top slice of £165,000	
	Tax £25,000 less £1,500 already paid	£23,500
1 Jan 1989	PET now reduced to NIL	NIL
1 Dec 1990	Death estate £200,000 as top slice of £365,000	£98,000
	Total tax due as result of A's death	£121,500

Second calculation under reg 6(3)(*b*)

Allow the debt and charge PETs to B in full.

		Tax
1 May 1987	PET £95,000. Tax with taper relief	£1,200
1 Jan 1988	PET £40,000 as top slice of £135,000	£12,000
1 Jul 1988	Gift into trust £100,000 as top slice of £235,000	
	Tax £41,000 less £1,500 already paid	£39,500
1 Jan 1989	PET £30,000 as top slice of £265,000	£15,000
1 Dec 1990	Death estate £100,000 as top slice of £365,000	£53,500
	Total tax due as result of A's death	£121,200

Result

First calculation yields higher amount of tax. So the debt is disallowed and corresponding amounts of PETs to B are ignored in determining the tax due as a result of the death.

Part III

Regulation 6: Example 4

1 Apr 1987	A makes gift into discretionary trust of £100,000.	Tax paid £1,500
1 Jan 1990	A makes PET to B of £60,000.	
1 Jan 1991	A makes further gift into same trust of £50,000.	Tax paid £8,000
1 Jan 1992	Same trust makes a loan to A of £120,000.	
1 Jun 1994	A dies. Death estate is £220,000, against which deduction is claimed for debt of £120,000 due to the trust.	

First calculation under reg 6(3)(*a*)

Disallow the debt and ignore corresponding amounts (£120,000) of gifts from A to trust, starting with the latest gift.

		Tax
1 Apr 1987	Gift now reduced to £30,000. No adjustment to tax already paid as gift made more than 7 years before death	NIL
1 Jan 1990	PET £60,000 as top slice of £90,000	NIL
1 Jan 1991	Gift now reduced to NIL. No adjustment to tax already paid	NIL
1 Jun 1994	Death estate £220,000 as top slice of £280,000 (the 1987 gift at £30,000 drops out of cumulation)	£77,000
		£77,000
	Less credit for tax already paid £1,500+£8,000	£9,500
	Total tax due as result of A's death	£67,500

Second calculation under reg 6(3)(*b*)

Allow the debt and no adjustment to gifts into the trust.

		Tax
1 Apr 1987	Gift £100,000. No adjustment to tax already paid as gift made more than 7 years before death	NIL
1 Jan 1990	PET £60,000 as top slice of £160,000. Tax with taper relief	£12,000
1 Jan 1991	Gift £50,000 as top slice of £210,000 Tax (with taper relief) £16,000 less £8,000 already paid	£8,000
1 June 1994	Death estate £100,000 as top slice of £210,000. (The 1987 gift drops out of cumulation. No credit for tax paid on that gift.)	£37,000
	Total tax due as result of A's death	£57,000

Result

First calculation yields higher amount tax. So the debt is disallowed and corresponding amounts of gifts into trust are ignored in determining the tax due as a result of the death.

Part IV

Regulation 7: Example

May 1986	S transfers into discretionary trust property worth £150,000. Immediate charge at the rates then in force.	Tax paid £13,750
Oct 1986	S gives T a life interest in shares worth £85,000. Immediate charge at the rates then in force.	Tax paid £19,500
Jan 1991	S makes a PET to R of £20,000.	
Dec 1992	T dies, and the settled shares return to S who is the settlor and therefore no tax charge on the shares on T's death.	
Aug 1993	S dies. His death estate includes the shares returned from T which are currently worth £75,000, and other assets worth £144,000.	

First calculation under reg 7(4)(*a*)

Charge the returned shares in the death estate and ignore the October 1986 gift. Tax rates and bands are those in force at the date of S's death.

		Tax
May 1986	Gift into trust made more than 7 years before death. So no adjustment to tax already paid but the gift cumulates in calculating tax on other gifts	NIL
Oct 1986	Gift ignored and no adjustment to tax already paid	NIL
Jan 1991	PET of £20,000 as top slice of (£150,000+£20,000) £170,000	£8,000

	Tax
Nov 1993 Death estate £219,000 as top slice of £239,000	
Tax £56,500 less £19,350 (part of tax already paid)*	£37,150
Total tax due as result of S's death	£45,150

*£19,350 represents the amount of the death tax attributable to the value of the returned shares, and is lower than the amount of the lifetime tax charged on those shares. So credit against the death charge for the tax already paid is restricted to the lower amount.

Second calculation under reg 7(4)(*b*)

Charge the October 1986 gift and ignore the returned shares in the death estate. Tax rates and bands are those in force at the date of S's death.

	Tax
May 1986 Gift into trust made more than 7 years before death. So no adjustment to tax already paid but the gift is taken into account in calculating the tax on the other gifts	NIL
Oct 1986 Gift of £85,000 as top slice of £235,000 Tax (with taper relief) £7,100 less £19,500 already paid	NIL*
Jan 1991 PET of £20,000 as top slice of £255,000	£10,000
Aug 1993 Death estate (excluding the returned shares) £144,000 as top slice of £249,000 (£85,000+£20,000+£144,000)	£57,000
Total tax due as a result of S's death	£67,000

*Credit for the tax already paid restricted to the (lower) amount of tax payable as result of the death. No repayment of the excess.

Result

Second calculation gives higher amount of tax. So tax is charged as in second calculation by excluding the shares from the death estate.

VI   THE INHERITANCE TAX (DOUBLE CHARGES RELIEF) REGULATIONS: SI 2005/3441

The Commissioners for Her Majesty's Revenue and Customs, in exercise of the powers conferred by section 104 of the Finance Act 1986(a), and now exercisable by them(b), make the following Regulations:

Citation, commencement and interpretation

1.—(1) These Regulations may be cited as the Inheritance Tax (Double Charges Relief) Regulations 2005, and shall come into force on 4th January 2006.

(2) In these Regulations—

"the Commissioners" means the Commissioners for Her Majesty's Revenue and Customs;

"the debt" means the debt mentioned in regulation 3(2);

"the relevant property" has the meaning given in regulation 3(6).

General

2.—(1) These Regulations apply in the circumstances specified in regulation 3.

(2) They apply for the purposes of paragraph (d) of section 104(1) of the Finance Act 1986 (which refers to circumstances appearing to the Commissioners to be circumstances similar to those referred to in paragraphs (a) to (c) of that provision).

(3) To the extent specified in regulation 4, these Regulations apply for the avoidance of double charges to tax.

Circumstances in which these Regulations apply

3.—(1) These Regulations apply where conditions A to D are met.

(2) Condition A is that an individual ("the deceased") enters into arrangements ("the arrangements") under which—

(a) the disposal condition or the contribution condition is met as respects the relevant property, and

(b) the deceased makes a transfer of value as a result of which a third party becomes entitled to the benefit of a debt ("the debt") owed to the deceased.

(3) Condition B is that, before the deceased's death, any outstanding part of the debt is wholly written off, waived or released, and the write-off, waiver or release is made otherwise than for full consideration in money or money's worth.

(4) Condition C is that the deceased dies on or after 6th April 2005.

(5) Condition D is that—

(a) on the deceased's death, the transfer of value treated as made immediately before the deceased's death included the relevant property (or any property then representing the relevant property), and

(b) as a result of the deceased's death, the transfer of value referred to in paragraph (2)(b) has become a chargeable transfer.

(6) In these Regulations "the relevant property" means property which, immediately after the carrying out of the arrangements, falls within the definition of "the relevant property" given in paragraph 11(9) of Schedule 15 to the Finance Act 2004(a).

(7) In paragraph (2)(a) "the disposal condition" and "the contribution condition" are to be construed in accordance with Schedule 15 to the Finance Act 2004.

Avoidance of double charge: amounts to be calculated

4.—(1) Where these Regulations apply, amounts A and B must be calculated separately.

(2) Amount A is the total tax chargeable as a consequence of the death of the deceased, but disregarding the value transferred represented by the relevant property (or by any property which, at the time of the death, represents the relevant property).

(3) Amount B is the total tax chargeable as a consequence of the death of the deceased, but disregarding the value transferred by the transfer of value specified in regulation 3(2)(b).

(4) The total tax chargeable is reduced to amount A or to amount B (whichever is the greater).

VII WRITTEN MINISTERIAL STATEMENTS OF 7 AND 8 MARCH 2005 (DEALING WITH THE CONTENTS OF THE REGULATIONS) AND OF 21 JULY 2005 DEALING WITH RELIEF FROM DOUBLE CHARGES

(i) Schedule 15 Finance Act 2004: Pre-Owned Asset Regulations

The Paymaster General (Dawn Primarolo): Schedule 15 Finance Act 2004 provides for an income tax charge on the benefit that taxpayers gain, in certain circumstances, from the continuing enjoyment of assets they formerly owned. The primary legislation leaves some matters—the operative date for valuations, and the rates of return which apply for purposes of the Schedule—to be specified in secondary legislation. They also allow regulations to provide for assets to be valued less frequently than annually. More generally, they enable regulations to make further exemptions from the charge set out in Schedule 15.

The Inland Revenue issued a consultative document on 18 August 2004 ("Taxation of Pre-Owned Assets: Further Consultation") seeking views on the matters to be covered by regulations. There was a full and constructive response and I am grateful to all who took part. We propose to make regulations as follows, having regard to the responses received.

Valuation date

As proposed in our consultation document, the valuation date for a tax year will be 6 April in the year or, if later, the beginning of the "taxable period" for which the asset in question first becomes chargeable.

The "prescribed rate"

The "prescribed rate" (to be applied to the values of chattels and intangible assets when quantifying the cash value of the benefit enjoyed) will be equal to the "official rate" of interest, as defined in section 181 of the Income Tax (Earnings and Pensions) Act 2003. The rate is currently 5 per cent.

Valuations at extended intervals

Regulations will provide, broadly, that land and chattels will be valued every five years. That is to say, a valuation will be made as prescribed in the primary legislation for the first tax year in which a particular asset becomes chargeable under Schedule 15. That valuation will also be used in any of the four succeeding years in which a charge arises.

If a charge arises in the fifth year after the first chargeable year, a fresh valuation will be made which will apply in the next four succeeding years, and so on for years ten, fifteen and subsequent five-year anniversaries. If no charge arises for the fifth year, or any later five-year anniversary, no valuation need be made until the next tax year (if any) for which a charge arises, and a fresh series of five-yearly valuations will start from that year.

Valuations will be carried forward in cash terms without adjustment (e.g. for indexation against asset price inflation, as the enabling power would permit).

Equity release

Schedule 15 provides exemption for any case where the former owner continues to enjoy an asset they have sold, so long as they have disposed of their whole interest in it (apart from the right of continuing enjoyment) and have done so either at arm's length or on arm's length terms.

It became clear in consultation that this was not sufficient to accommodate all open-market equity release transactions, under which homeowners often sell only a part share in their property. I made clear last autumn that regulations under Schedule 15 would cover the full range of bona fide equity-release schemes with arms' length providers, while continuing to bear down on schemes aimed at avoidance. With that in mind, we do not in general think it is appropriate to provide exemption for sales of a part interest which are made otherwise than at arm's length. If one member of a family needs to raise cash, and another member of the family is willing and able to provide it, there are other and more straightforward ways of structuring this than adopting the form of an equity release transaction.

The point was however made in consultation that some intra-family part disposals can arise from patterns of behaviour adopted for good family or business reasons, for example where a child moves in to care for an aged parent and acquires an equitable interest in their shared home as a corollary of that, or where younger members of a family take over the active role in a family partnership, and in doing so acquire an interest from the partners who preceded them. And we also accept that any cases where asset owners have already sold a part interest within their family are unlikely, given the law as it stood at the time, to have chosen that approach primarily for tax avoidance purposes.

Bringing together these different considerations, the regulations will extend the existing exemption (described above) to all sales done at arm's length where they involve the whole or a part of the vendor's interest in their asset. They will extend this exemption to any part sale, even if not at arm's length, so long as it was made before today and on arm's length terms. And this will also apply to future disposals if they are made for a consideration other than money or readily realisable assets.

Regulations to this effect will be made shortly, in time to take effect from the commencement of the new charge on 6 April. The Inland Revenue will also be publishing their guidance on the interpretation and operation of Schedule 15: it will be announced and made available on *www.inlandrevenue.gov.uk*

HM Treasury

7 March 2005

(ii) Pre-Owned Asset Regulations—Relief from Double Charges

The Paymaster General (Dawn Primarolo): This statement announces regulations under section 104 Finance Act 1986 to provide relief from double inheritance tax (IHT) charges in situations caught by the pre-owned assets provisions at Schedule 15 Finance Act 2004, and is in addition to extended relief from income tax under Schedule 15 which I announced in a written statement on 7 March.

The pre-owned assets legislation in Schedule 15 provides for taxpayers to make an election so that they do not have to pay income tax in respect of a pre-owned asset but instead have the asset treated as part of their estate for IHT purposes. If the taxpayer dies within the next few years after making the election there is a possibility of two IHT charges on the same underlying asset value.

In particular, many taxpayers have used a "double trust" structure: one trust is created to buy the settlor's asset in exchange for an IOU, and this IOU is gifted into a second trust to take it out of the settlor's taxable estate. If the settlor dies within seven years, the estate will be liable to IHT on the IOU; and if they have made an election under Schedule 15

Finance Act 2004, their estate will be also liable on the underlying asset. It is clear from responses in consultation that this prospect is preventing some people from making an election which they would otherwise find attractive.

The regulations will eliminate this double IHT charge so that people who wish to make an election under Schedule 15 can be assured that only one IHT charge will be due whatever the timing of their death.

The Regulations will be announced and made available on the Inland Revenue's website (*www.inlandrevenue.gov.uk.*)

HM Treasury

8 March 2005

(iii) Pre-Owned Asset Regulations—Relief from Double Charges

The Paymaster General (Dawn Primarolo): This is to announce regulations under section 104 Finance Act 1986 to provide relief from double inheritance tax charges in situations caught by the pre-owned assets provisions at Schedule 15 Finance Act 2004.

Double inheritance tax (IHT) charges can arise in certain circumstances when taxpayers who have used IHT avoidance schemes re-arrange their affairs in response to the income tax charge on "pre-owned assets" introduced by Schedule 15, Finance Act 2004

My statement of 8 March 2005 announced regulations to provide relief from double charges where taxpayers have made an election to disapply the pre-owned asset income tax charge under paragraph 21, Schedule 15

Comparable double charges can arise where taxpayers do not make this election, but instead dismantle their previous arrangements so that the pre-owned asset income tax charge is no longer due. In particular, many taxpayers have used a "double trust" scheme; this involves selling a valuable asset to one trust in which the vendor retains an interest, in exchange for an IOU, and then giving the IOU to a second trust. The gift is a potentially exempt transfer for IHT purposes, and the value of the IOU will be chargeable if the scheme user dies within seven years of implementing the scheme. If in the meantime the scheme has been reversed, so that the full value of the asset originally sold is back in the scheme user's ownership at the time of their death, that value will also be subject to IHT.

I am satisfied that scheme users can have legitimate non-avoidance reasons for arranging their affairs in this way, and the regulations already made will therefore be extended to provide relief from double charges which arise from their doing so. They will cover cases where

- a deceased person has made a gift of a debt owed to them;

- the gift was chargeable to IHT or becomes so chargeable (by virtue of the donor's death);

- the donor dies within seven years of the gift and on or after 6 April 2005;

- the debt was entered into as consideration for the purchase of an asset owned by the donor, or to provide funds for such a purchase;

- the full value of that asset, or of property derived from it, is also chargeable to IHT as part of the donor's estate at death.

In those circumstances, relief will be given so that tax will be due only on the more valuable of the two chargeable assets mentioned.

The regulations will be made as soon as practicable and made available in HM Revenue and Customs' website (*www.hmrc.gov.uk*).

HM Treasury

21 JULY 2005

APPENDIX II: MATERIAL USED BY HMRC

I   POAT: HMRC GUIDANCE NOTES (2008 VERSION)

Contents

1. Outline of the charge to income tax

1.1 The circumstances in which the charge applies

A2.01 Section 84 of the Finance Act 2004 gave effect to the provisions of Schedule 15 of that Act. The schedule provides for a charge to income tax on benefits received by a former owner of property. Broadly it applies to individuals (the chargeable person) who continue to receive benefits from certain types of property they once owned after 17 March 1986 but have since disposed of. The schedule has effect for the tax year 2005–06 and subsequent years.

The property within the scope of the charge can be grouped into three headings:

- land;
- chattels; and
- intangible property.

If the chargeable person has either disposed of any property within these headings by way of gift or, in some circumstances, sale, or contributed towards the purchase of the property in question and they continue to receive some benefit from the property they are potentially liable to the charge. The benefit may be occupation of the land, use of the chattel or the ability to receive income or capital from a settlement holding intangible property.

The preceding paragraph may suggest that every instance where an individual may have disposed of, or made a contribution to the purchase of, the relevant property will come within the scope of the charge. However, there are several types of transactions relating to land and chattels that are excluded from the scope of the charge. There are also provisions exempting the relevant property from the charge where the property is subject to a charge to inheritance tax or where specific protection from inheritance tax is given by legislation.

If the income tax charge applies the Schedule contains provisions enabling the taxable benefit to be calculated. In the case of the occupation or use of land and chattels the calculation of the taxable benefit will be determined to a large extent by the proportion which the value of the chargeable person's original interest in, or contribution to, the purchase, bears to the current value of the property.

The following sections provide more detail on the conditions required for the charge to arise, where the transaction may be excluded or where the property is exempted, and how the benefit is calculated. All references to "this Schedule" refer to Schedule 15 unless otherwise specified. References to "the charge" refer to the charge to income tax arising under Schedule 15.

1.2 What property is affected?

A2.02 The conditions required for the charge to apply are virtually identical where the property in question is land or chattels but they differ slightly in respect of intangible property.

1.2.1 Land and chattels

A2.03 The charge applies where the chargeable person occupies any land or uses or possesses any chattels, either alone or with other persons, and either the "disposal condition" or the "contribution condition" is met. Paragraphs 3 and 6 of this Schedule define the conditions.

The disposal condition

The disposal condition will apply if the chargeable person, at any time after 17 March **A2.04** 1986, owned relevant land or chattels, or other property whose disposal proceeds were directly or indirectly applied by another person towards the acquisition of the relevant land or chattels, and then disposed of all or part of their interest in the relevant land or chattels (or other property). If the disposal was an excluded transaction (*see* 1.3.1) the disposal condition will not apply.

Note that the disposal condition will apply to the chargeable person's occupation or use of property even if that property was never actually owned by them. If they gave away other property (apart from cash) to another person who sold such property and used these proceeds to purchase the relevant land or chattel the disposal condition is satisfied, unless it qualifies as an excluded transaction.

A disposition that creates a new interest in land or in a chattel out of an existing interest is taken to be a disposal of part of the existing interest.

The contribution condition

The contribution condition will apply if the chargeable person, at any time after 17 March **A2.05** 1986, provided any of the consideration given by another person for the acquisition of an interest in the relevant land or chattel, or for the acquisition of any other property the proceeds of the disposal of which were directly or indirectly applied by another person towards an acquisition of an interest in the relevant land or chattel. As with the disposal condition, if the provision of the consideration qualifies as an excluded transaction, this condition will not apply.

It can be seen that the contribution condition can apply not only where the contribution provided by the chargeable person is directly used to purchase the relevant land or chattel but where the contribution is indirect too. If they provided all or part of the consideration (e.g. a cash gift) for the purchase of property by another person, who then sold the property and used the proceeds to purchase the land occupied, or the chattel used, by the chargeable person, the contribution condition is satisfied, unless it qualifies as an excluded transaction (*see* 1.3.1).

HMRC do not regard the contribution condition set out in Sch.15 para.3(3) as being met where a lender resides in property purchased by another with money loaned to him by the lender. Our view is that since the outstanding debt will form part of his estate for IHT purposes, it would not be reasonable to consider that the loan falls within the contribution condition [and therefore not reasonably attributable to the consideration (Sch.15 para.4(2) (c)], even where the loan was interest free. It follows that the "lender", in such an arrangement, would not be caught by a charge under Schedule 15.

1.2.2   Intangible property

In contrast to the provisions relating to land and chattels there is only one condition to be **A2.06** met for the charge to apply. Paragraph 8 of this Schedule defines the condition.

The charge extends to intangibles that are or represent property settled or added by the chargeable person to a settlement after 17 March 1986 on terms that any income arising from the settled property would be treated under s.624 of the ITTOIA 2005 (income arising under a settlement where the settlor retains an interest) as income of the chargeable person as settlor and any such income would be so treated even if subsection (2) of that section did not include any reference to the spouse of the settlor. In other words, a charge under para.8 is not triggered where s.624 applies only because the settlor's spouse rather than the settlor has retained an interest. The settlor in this case is, of course, the chargeable person. For example if A sets up a trust for his wife on marriage and he is excluded from all benefit there is no possibility of paragraph 8 applying. However, if he sets up a trust where his wife receives the income but he can benefit if she dies then para.8 could potentially apply subject to any relevant exemptions. In this context "settlement" has the same meaning as it does for inheritance tax purposes. The definition of "settlement" can be found in s.43(2) of the Inheritance Tax Act 1984. The fact that there is no element of bounty does not matter.

Intangible property means assets such as stocks and securities, insurance policies and bank and building society accounts. The provisions of this paragraph do not apply to land and chattels included in a settlement.

1.3　When the charge does not apply

A2.07　There are a number of situations where a charge to tax under Schedule 15 will not arise. Certain transactions are excluded from the charge and there are also exemptions from the charge where certain conditions are met.

1.3.1　Excluded transactions (Sch.15 para.10)

A2.08　The concept of excluded transactions has no application to intangible property. They only serve to exclude from the income tax charge certain transactions relating to land and chattels.

For the purposes of the disposal conditions relating to land and chattels, the disposal of any property is an excluded transaction in relation to the chargeable person if:

- it was a disposal of their whole interest in the property, except for any right expressly reserved by them over the property, either:

  (i) by a transaction made at arm's length with a person not connected with them, or

  (ii) by a transaction such as might be expected to be made at arm's length between persons not connected with each other.

The exclusion clearly only applies to sales of the entire interest in the property at full market value although the words "except for any right expressly reserved" would envisage the sale of a freehold reversion subject to a lease but only if it was on arm's length terms.

A2.09　Concern was expressed that sales of a part share of property to commercial providers of equity release schemes would not qualify as an excluded transaction and an individual would be subject to the charge if he remained in occupation of the land. This concern was recognised in the Regulations to the charge which specifically exempted from the charge disposals of part of an interest in any property by a transaction made at arm's length with a person not connected with the chargeable person. Furthermore, the exemption is extended to disposals of a part share to anyone provided that they were made on arm's length terms and either took place before 7 March 2005, or took place on or after that date for a consideration not in the form of money or assets readily convertible into money.

- The property was transferred to their spouse or civil partner, or former spouse or civil partner where the transfer has been ordered by a court.

- The disposal was by way of gift (or in accordance with a court order for the benefit of a former spouse or civil partner) by virtue of which the property became settled property in which his spouse or civil partner or former spouse or civil partner is beneficially entitled to an interest in possession. The spouse or civil partner must take an interest in possession from the outset. It is not an excluded transaction, however, if the interest in possession of the spouse or civil partner or former spouse or civil partner has come to an end other than on their death. In cases where the spouse or civil partner or former spouse or civil partner has become absolutely entitled to the property, we would accept that the benefit of the exclusion is not lost.

- The disposal was a disposition falling within s.11 of the Inheritance Tax Act 1984 (disposition for maintenance of family).

- The disposal is an outright gift to an individual and is for the purposes of the Inheritance Tax Act 1984 a transfer of value that is wholly exempt by virtue of s.19 (annual exemption) or s.20 (small gifts).

For the purposes of the contribution conditions relating to land and chattels, the provision by the chargeable person of consideration for another's acquisition of any property is an excluded transaction in relation to the chargeable person if: **A2.10**

- The other person was their spouse or civil partner, or former spouse or civil partner where the transfer has been ordered by a court.

- On its acquisition the property became settled property in which their spouse or civil partner or former spouse or civil partner is beneficially entitled to an interest in possession. The spouse or civil partner must take an interest in possession from the outset. It is not an excluded transaction, however, if the interest in possession of the spouse or civil partner or former spouse or civil partner has come to an end otherwise than on their death unless the spouse or civil partner or former spouse or civil partner has become absolutely entitled to the property.

- The provision of the consideration constituted an outright gift of cash by the chargeable person to the other person (in this context the "other person" means the person referred to in paras 3(3) and 6(3)) and was made at least seven years before the earliest date on which the chargeable person occupied the land or had possession or use of the chattel As the earliest date the conditions can be met is 6 April 2005, any provision of consideration by way of an outright gift of cash made before 6 April 1998 will be an excluded transaction.

- The provision of the consideration is a disposition falling within s.11 of the Inheritance Tax Act 1984.

- The provision of the consideration is an outright gift to an individual and is for the purposes of the Inheritance Tax Act 1984 a transfer of value that is wholly exempt by virtue of s.19 or s.20.

1.3.2   Exemptions from the charge (Sch.15 para.11)

Property in the estate (para.11(1)) exemption **A2.11**
The charging provisions in Schedule 15 relating to land, chattels and intangible property do not apply to a person at a time when their estate for the purposes of the Inheritance Tax Act 1984 includes the relevant property, or other property which:

- derives its value from the relevant property, and

- whose value so far as attributable to the relevant property, is not substantially less than the value of the relevant property.

Where their estate includes property which derives its value from the relevant property and whose value, so far as attributable to the relevant property, is substantially less than the value of the relevant property:

- the appropriate rental value of the relevant land, or

- the appropriate amount in respect of the chattel, or

- the chargeable amount in relation to the relevant intangible property must be reduced by such proportion as is reasonable to take account of the inclusion of the property in their estate.

For example if Mr B transfers his house to a company wholly owned by him, then provided there are no loans to the company one can say that the value attributable to the company is not less than the value of the house. But if Mr B gave the house to a company which was owned 25 per cent by his wife then the value of the 75 per cent shares he holds would be substantially less than the value of the house. If he has lent money to the company and the company holds the house we take the view that the company's value is less than the house unless (possibly) the loan is charged on the house.

Gifts with reservation para.11(3) exemption

A2.12 The charging provisions also do not apply to a person at a time when, for IHT purposes, the relevant property or property deriving its value from relevant property falls within the Gifts with Reservation provisions set out in Finance Act 1986.

The provisions of Schedule 15 are also disapplied if the property:

- would fall to be treated as subject to a reservation but for any of ss.102(5)(d) to (i) of the Finance Act 1986 (certain cases where disposal by way of gift is an exempt transfer for purposes of inheritance tax). But where s.102(5)(h) is in point, Sch.15 is disapplied only when the property remains subject to trusts complying with the requirements of Sch.4 para.3(1) of the Inheritance Tax Act 1984 (maintenance funds);

- would fall to be treated as subject to a reservation but for subsection (4) of s.102B of the Finance Act 1986 (gifts with reservation: share of interest in land), or would have fallen to be so treated if the disposal by way of gift of an undivided share of an interest in land had been made on or after 9 March 1999. This refers to situations where the chargeable person transfers a share (usually 50%) of their property to the donee and both the donee and the chargeable person continue to occupy the property, paying their share of household expenses; or

- would fall to be treated as subject to a reservation but for s.102C(3) of, and para.6 of Sch.20 to, the Finance Act 1986 (exclusion of benefit). This refers to situations where the chargeable person continues to use or occupy the property but pays full consideration in money or money's worth, or where they leave the property but have to move back at a later date due to an unforeseen change in their circumstances and are unable to look after themselves because of age or infirmity.

A2.13 Where the contribution condition relating to land or chattels applies, para.2(2)(b) of Schedule 20 (which excludes gifts of money from the provisions that apply where property is substituted for the original gift) should be disregarded. For example, if A gives cash to his son and they buy a home jointly and live together then while they live together, the POAT charge will not apply.

A2.14 Schedule 15 also contains provisions for the chargeable person to elect that the relevant property that would otherwise be subject to the charge be treated as property subject to a reservation for the purposes of the Inheritance Tax Act 1984. If the election is made no charge under the Schedule will apply. Full details of these provisions are given in Part 3 of these notes.

Excluded liability

Where at any time the value of a person's estate for the purposes of the Inheritance Tax **A2.15**
Act 1984 is reduced by an "excluded liability" affecting any property, only the excess of
the value of the property over the amount of the excluded liability can be treated as
comprised in their estate for the purposes of this schedule.

A liability is an excluded liability if:

- the creation of the liability; and

- any transaction by virtue of which the person's estate came to include the relevant
  property or property which derives its value from the relevant property or by virtue
  of which the value of the property in their estate came to be derived from the
  relevant property, were associated operations, as defined by section 268 of the
  Inheritance Tax Act 1984.

The "amount" of the excluded liability will be the face value of the debt, including any
rolled up interest or accrued indexation where this has been allowed for under the terms
of the agreement. For the purposes of computing the charge under this Schedule, it will be
sufficient for the debt to be revalued taking into account outstanding interest, or accrued
indexation, at the five-yearly valuation dates. Any reduction of the debt resulting from a
repayment can be taken into account as it occurred, and may be reflected in a revised
computation of the tax in the relevant year and subsequently.

1.3.3 Residence or domicile outside the United Kingdom (Sch.15 para.12)

No charge to tax under this Schedule can arise in relation to any person for any year of **A2.16**
assessment during which they are not resident in the United Kingdom.

If a person is resident in but domiciled outside the United Kingdom in any year of
assessment, the provisions of this Schedule will only apply to land, chattels or intangible
property situated in the United Kingdom.

In applying this Schedule to a person who was at any time domiciled outside the United
Kingdom, no regard should be had to any property which is for the purposes of the
Inheritance Tax Act 1984 excluded property in relation to them by virtue of s.48(3)(a) of
that Act.

A person is to be treated as domiciled in the United Kingdom at any time if they would
be so treated for the purposes of the Inheritance Tax Act 1984. Hence the deemed domicile
rules will apply for the purposes of this income tax charge.

1.3.4 De minimis exemption (Sch.15 para.13)

An exemption from charge under this Schedule applies where in relation to any person in **A2.17**
a year of assessment (Example 1), the aggregate of the amounts specified below in respect
of that year do not exceed £5,000 (Example 2). Those amounts are:

- in relation to any land to which paragraph 3 applies, the appropriate rental value as
  determined under paragraph 4(2)—*see* 2.1 below;

- in relation to any chattel to which paragraph 6 applies, the appropriate amount as
  determined under paragraph 7(2)—*see* 2.2 below; and

- in relation to any intangible property to which paragraph 8 applies, the chargeable
  amount determined under paragraph 9—*see* 2.3 below.

Example 1

The £5,000 is based on the chargeable amount for the year. So if a person is chargeable throughout the whole tax year and the annual benefit is calculated at £5,000 or less they do not have to declare the benefit on their income tax return. If a person is chargeable for only part of the year, say they only become chargeable for the last six months of the year where the full annual benefit would be £8,000, their exposure for the last six months is half that and the benefit of £4,000 would be covered by the de minimis. Where two people are equally chargeable for the whole year in respect of the same property, for example a property with an annual rental value of £8,000, their benefit would be £4,000 each and would be covered by the de minimis. (On the death of one, you should consider former ownership of the property, and the terms of occupation, in deciding whether the whole or a half of the rental value is chargeable on the survivor.)

Example 2

A person is chargeable under para.3 for a benefit from land with an annual value of £4,000 and under Para 6 for a benefit from a chattel with an annual value of £3,000. The aggregate benefit is £7,000 and therefore not de minimis. If, in this example, an annual rental of £4,000 is paid to obtain the aggregate benefit, although the net benefit is £3,000 it is not de minimis because the annual open market rental value exceeds £5,000 and therefore the amount of the benefit (£3,000) would need to be declared. A person cannot avoid the tax charge by paying an annual rent to bring himself below £5000.

The de minimis is set against the annual benefit for intangible property after deduction of any tax paid under the headings of para.9(1) of Sch.15.

Example 3

A person benefits from a settlor interested trust where the benefit is calculated to £7,000 (N). The fund generates income on which tax of £3,000 (T) is payable. The net amount of the benefit (N-T) is £4,000 and is de minimis.The amount of £5,000 does not represent a nil-rate band, therefore where the aggregate chargeable value exceeds £5,000 it is subject to the charge in full. When a taxpayer is chargeable for only part of a year, the £5,000 exemption is not pro-rated.

Where the de minimis exemption under para.13 is not exceeded the transferor cannot make an election because he is not chargeable to income tax under Sch.15.

1.3.5 Changes in the distribution of a deceased's estate (Sch.15 para.16)

A2.18 Any disposition made by the chargeable person in relation to an interest in the estate of a deceased person is disregarded for the purposes of this Schedule if under s.17 of the Inheritance Tax Act 1984 the disposition is not a transfer of value by the chargeable person for IHT purposes. All dispositions covered by s.17, including disclaimers and variations where the provisions of s.142(1) of the Inheritance Tax Act 1984 apply, will be exempted from the charge by para.16 of this Schedule [see **Appendix 1** example].

For the purposes of this paragraph "estate" has the same meaning as it has for the purposes of the Inheritance Tax Act 1984.

1.3.6　Guarantees (Sch.15 para.17)

Where a person ("A") acts as a guarantor in respect of a loan made to another person ("B")　**A2.19**
by a third party in connection with B's acquisition of any property, the mere giving of the
guarantee is not regarded as the provision by A of consideration for B's acquisition of the
property.

2　How to calculate the benefit subject to the charge

Where the provisions of paragraphs 3 (land), 6 (chattels) and/or 8 (intangible property)　**A2.20**
apply to a person in respect of the whole or part of a year of assessment, an amount equal
to the chargeable amount specified by the Schedule is treated as income of theirs
chargeable to income tax.

Unless stated otherwise, the approach to valuing property for the purposes of Schedule
15 follows the rule for Inheritance Tax set out in s.160 of the IHTA 1984. In other words,
it is the price that the property might reasonably be expected to fetch if sold in the open
market at that time, without any scope for a reduction on the ground that the whole
property is to be placed on the market at one and the same time (see para.15 of this
Schedule).

The valuation date for property subject to the charge is 6 April in the relevant year of
assessment or, if later, the first day of the taxable period.

When valuing relevant land or a chattel it is not necessary to make an annual revaluation
of the property. The property should rather be valued on a five-year cycle. Before the first
five-year anniversary the valuation of the property will be that set at the first valuation
date. Thereafter the valuation at the latest five-year anniversary will apply.

The "relevant land" for the purposes of para.4(5) is the land currently occupied by the
chargeable person. Therefore, where a valuation has been carried out in respect of a charge
arising under Sch.15, and within the five-year cycle the subject property is sold and a
smaller less valuable property is purchased for occupation by the chargeable person, then
a new valuation will need to be carried out which will be used for the remainder of that
five-year cycle.

The five-year anniversary is the fifth anniversary of 6 April in the first year of assessment
in which the provisions of this Schedule relating to land or chattels apply to the chargeable
person. The first valuation date is the date on which the provisions of this Schedule
relating to land or chattels first applied to the chargeable person. If there is an interruption
in the person's use or occupation of the property and the year of a five-year anniversary is
not a taxable period, the year in which the provisions of this Schedule are applied again
will be treated as the next five-year anniversary.

Example

A is first chargeable to Schedule 15 on 6th April 2005. A valuation is obtained then.
He becomes non-UK resident for three years from 6th April 2006 to 6th April 2009.
The charge does not apply during this period. He returns to the UK on 7th April 2009.
A new valuation is made then and this is the start of the next five year anniversary.

2.1　Land (Sch.15 paras 4 & 5)

The chargeable amount in relation to the relevant land is the appropriate rental value, less　**A2.21**
the amount of any payments which the chargeable person is legally obliged to make
during the period to the owner of the relevant land in respect of their occupation.

The appropriate rental value is:

$$R \times \frac{DV}{V}$$

R is the rental value of the relevant land for the taxable period.
DV is:

- where the chargeable person owned an interest in the relevant land, the value as at the valuation date of the interest in the relevant land that was disposed of by the chargeable person or, where the disposal was a non-exempt sale, the "appropriate portion" (see final paragraphs of this section below) of that value;

- where the chargeable person owned an interest in other property, the proceeds of which were used to acquire an interest in relevant land, such part of the value of the relevant land at the valuation date as can reasonably be attributed to the property originally disposed of by the chargeable person or, where the original disposal was a non-exempt sale, to the appropriate portion of that property;

- if the contribution condition applies, such part of the value of the relevant land at the valuation date as can reasonably be attributed to the consideration provided by the chargeable person.

V is the value of the relevant land at the valuation date.

The "rental value" of the land for the taxable period is the rent which would have been payable for the period if the property had been let to the chargeable person at an annual rent equal to the annual value. The annual value is the rent that might reasonably be expected to be obtained on a letting from year to year if:

- the tenant undertook to pay all taxes, rates and charges usually paid by a tenant; and

- the landlord undertook to bear the costs of the repairs and insurance and the other expenses, if any, necessary for maintaining the property in a state to command that rent.

The rent is calculated on the basis that the only amounts that may be deducted in respect of the services provided by the landlord are amounts in respect of the cost to the landlord of providing any relevant services. Relevant service means a service other than the repair, insurance or maintenance of the premises. In other words, if the landlord provides other relevant services, for example the maintenance of the common parts in a block of flats, that are reflected in the rent then the cost of providing those services may be deducted from the rent.

The regulations do not specify the sources from which the required valuations should be obtained. However we would expect the chargeable person to take all reasonable steps to ascertain the valuations, as they would do if, for example, they were looking to let a property on the open market.

A2.22   Paragraph 4(4) introduces the concept of a "non-exempt sale" for a disposal which is a sale of the chargeable person's whole interest in the property for cash, but which is not an excluded transaction as defined in paragraph 10. The "appropriate proportion", which is relevant for ascertaining the "appropriate rental value in para.4(2), can be determined using the formula:

$$\frac{MV - P}{MV}$$

Where MV is the value of the interest in land at the time of the sale and P is the amount paid.

Example

A sells his house to his daughter for £100,000. It is worth £300,000. He lives in the house. In these circumstances we would say that only two thirds of the value of the house is potentially within the charge to POAT. However, since he made a gift of that two thirds we would accept that he is protected under para 11(5)(1) reservation of benefit from a charge on that two thirds. Note that if he sold part of his house to his daughter at an undervalue then the non-exempt sale provisions would not apply. So in the above example if he sold half his house to his daughter for £100,000 and that half share was in fact worth £300,000, although he would have reserved a benefit in two thirds of that half share, the £100,000 cash would be subject to POAT.

2.2 Chattels (Sch.15 para.7)

The chargeable amount in relation to any chattel is the appropriate amount, less the amount of any payments that the chargeable person is legally obliged to make during the period to the owner of the chattel for the possession or use of the chattel by the chargeable person.　　**A2.23**

The appropriate amount is:

$$N \times \frac{DV}{V}$$

N is the amount of the interest that would be payable for the taxable period if interest were payable at the prescribed rate on an amount equal to the value of the chattel at the valuation date. The prescribed rate is the official rate of interest at the valuation date. The official rate has the meaning given in section 181 of the Income Tax (Earnings and Pensions) Act 2003.

Example

In 2005/6 A was caught by Sch.15 in respect of an earlier disposal of chattels. The chattels were worth £1,000,000 at the relevant valuation date on 6th April 2005. He will be treated as receiving a taxable benefit of 5 per cent (the prescribed rate in 2005/06) x £1m = £50,000.

Note that the charge is computed differently from land and while any rental payments made to the owner will reduce the amount on which he is chargeable, the fact that he pays a market rent for their use does not prevent an income tax charge arising. Hence if he pays £10,000 rent he will still be taxable on a £40,000 benefit. Tax is due on 31 January 2007 unless A elects.

The provisions for ascertaining DV, V and defining a "non-exempt sale" and the "appropriate proportion" in relation to chattels that are similar to the provisions relating to land (*see* 2.1 above).

2.3 Intangible property (Sch.15 para.9)

The chargeable amount in relation to the relevant property is N minus T.　　**A2.24**

N is the amount of the interest that would be payable for the taxable period if interest were payable at the prescribed rate on an amount equal to the value of the relevant property at the valuation date. The prescribed rate is the official rate of interest at the valuation date. The official rate has the meaning given in s.181 of the Income Tax (Earnings and Pensions) Act 2003.

T is the amount of any income tax or capital gains tax payable by the chargeable person in respect of the taxable period by virtue of any of the following provisions:

- ss.547, 660A (now s.624 of the Income Tax (Trading and Other Income) Act 2005) or 739 of the Income and Corporation Taxes Act 1988,

- ss.77 or 86 of the Taxation of Chargeable Gains Act 1992

so far as the tax is attributable to the relevant property.

Example

Mr A is the UK resident and domiciled settlor of a non-resident settlor interested settlement. (You should assume that Mr A has not reserved a benefit in the settled property nor has an interest in possession in the trust and is therefore subject to the POAT charge.)

The settlement comprises "intangible" property of cash and shares with a value of £1,500,000 at the valuation date. In the tax year 2005/06 the trustees receive income of £60,000 which is chargeable to income tax on Mr A under s.624. A further £150,000 Capital Gains are realised which are deemed to be Mr A's gains by virtue of s.86 of the TCGA 1992. In these circumstances £24,000 income tax is payable on the £60,000 and £60,000 in CGT on the £150,000. The tax allowance (T) against the potential Schedule 15 charge is therefore £84,000. The chargeable amount (N) is 5 per cent (the prescribed rate in 2005/06) x £1,500,000 = £75,000. Since the tax allowance is greater than the chargeable amount, a charge under Sch.15 will not arise.

2.4   Avoidance of double charge to income tax

A2.25   The Schedule contains two provisions to avoid a double charge to income tax arising if the provisions of this Schedule apply.

- If the chargeable person is subject to the charge under more than one provision of this Schedule, i.e. if they were chargeable under para.3 in respect of land they occupied and also under para.8 (intangible property) if the land was owned by a company whose shares had been owned by them and had been settled on trusts of which they were a potential beneficiary, the charge will only apply to the provision that produces the higher amount of tax. If this amount does not exceed the de minimis limit no tax will be payable—the lower amount is disregarded completely.

- If the chargeable person occupies land or possesses or uses a chattel and is chargeable to income tax under the provisions of this Schedule **and** under the benefits code of Part 3 of the Income Tax (Earnings and Pensions) Act 2003, the provisions of Part 3 have priority. Tax will only be chargeable under this Schedule on any amount that exceeds the amount treated as earnings under Part 3.

3   The election into inheritance tax

3.1   The effect of the election

A2.26   Paragraphs 21 and 22 give the chargeable person the option of electing that any relevant property that would otherwise be subject to the charge be treated as subject to a reservation for the purposes of Part 5 of the Finance Act 1986. If an election is made the property will not be subject to the charge under this Schedule but will instead be subject to a charge to inheritance tax on their death. The charge to inheritance tax will be incurred unless the occupation or use (of property otherwise within this Schedule) ceases permanently (and is not recommenced) at least seven years before their death or (in the case of land or chattels) the chargeable person pays full consideration for use of the relevant property. If the person is already paying full consideration for use of the land or chattels before making an election and then elects we accept that there is no deemed PET at that point. However, if the person ceases to pay full consideration in the seven years prior to death and is still in occupation of the property the effect of the election is that they will be subject to an inheritance tax charge on their death.

In the case of a couple who are married or in a civil partnership who jointly owned a property and who are both caught by the provisions of this Schedule, if they both wish to have it treated as property subject to a reservation, they must both make an election. An election by one cannot affect the other. Hence one of them may instead choose to pay the income tax charge in respect of their share, whilst the other may elect for a GWR under para.21.

3.1.1 Land and chattels (Sch.15 para.21)

This paragraph applies where the chargeable person is potentially chargeable for any year **A2.27** of assessment by reference to their enjoyment of any land or chattels for the first time. Enjoyment refers to occupation of the land and possession or use of the chattel in question.

The chargeable person may elect that the relevant property, or property substituted for it, shall not be subject to the charge but so long as they continue to enjoy it, the chargeable proportion of the property will be treated as property subject to a reservation and ss.102(3) and (4) of the Finance Act 1986 will apply.

The "chargeable proportion" means:

$$\frac{DV}{V}$$

Where DV and V are the values detailed in 2.1 of these guidance notes. The valuation dates to be used in these circumstances are:

- in the case of property falling s.102(3) of the Finance Act 1986, the date of death of the chargeable person; and

- in the case of property falling within s.102(4) of the Finance Act 1986, the date on which the property ceases to be treated as property subject to a reservation.

When calculating DV the transactions to be taken into account should include transactions after the time when the election takes effect as well as before that time.

3.1.2 Intangible property (Sch.15 para.22)

This paragraph applies where the chargeable person is potentially chargeable for any year **A2.28** of assessment by reference to any relevant intangible property for the first time.

The chargeable person may elect that the relevant property, or property which it represents or is derived from, shall not be subject to the charge but, provided certain conditions are met, it will be treated as property subject to a reservation and ss.102(3) and (4) of the Finance Act 1986 will apply. The conditions are:

- that the relevant property, or property which it represents or is derived from, remains comprised in the settlement; and

- that any income arising under the settlement would be treated by virtue of s.624 ITTOIA (formerly s.660A of the Taxes Act 1988) as income of the chargeable person.

3.1.3 Withdrawal of election

A2.29 Whether it relates to land, chattels or intangible property the election may be withdrawn or amended during the life of the chargeable person at any time on or before the relevant filing date (*see* 3.3). If the election is withdrawn the property will be subject to the charge from the tax year 2005–06 or the year on which they would have first become chargeable under this Schedule.

3.2 How to elect

A2.30 The election must be made on form IHT 500. Guidance on how to complete the form, together with the form itself, can be found elsewhere on this website.

3.3 When to elect

A2.31 The election must be made on or before "the relevant filing date", or "such later date as an officer of Revenue and Customs may, in a particular case, allow".

If the chargeable person was subject to income tax from the initial year of the charge, the relevant filing date is 31 January 2007. If they become subject to the charge in a later year of assessment, the relevant filing date is 31 January in the year of assessment immediately following, e.g. if they first became subject to the charge during the year 2007-08, the relevant filing date will be 31 January 2009.

The election takes effect for inheritance tax purposes from the date on which the chargeable person would have first become chargeable under this Schedule but for the election. The earliest year it can take effect is the year beginning 6 April 2005.

3.4 Circumstances in which a late election will be accepted

An event beyond the chargeable person's control

A2.32 In general, we will accept a late election if the chargeable person can show that an event beyond their control prevented them from sending us the election by the relevant filing date. If the chargeable person was able to manage the rest of their private or business affairs during the period in question, we are unlikely to accept that they were genuinely prevented from delivering the election on time.

Examples of situations that we may consider as an event beyond the chargeable person's control include those where:

- an election was posted in good time but an unforeseen event disrupted the normal postal service and led to the loss or delay of the election;

- the chargeable person's financial records or other relevant papers were lost through fire, flood or theft and the information necessary for the completion of the election could not be replaced in time for it to be completed by the relevant filing date;

- the chargeable person was so seriously ill that they were prevented from dealing with the election before the relevant filing date and from that date to the time the completed election is sent in.

If an illness involves a lengthy stay in hospital or convalescence the chargeable person is expected to have made arrangements for completing and sending in the election on time.

But there may be circumstances where this is not possible and we may accept these as a valid reason.

The serious illness of a close relative or partner will be regarded as a valid reason for a delay in electing only if:

- the situation took up a great deal of the chargeable person's time and attention during the period from the relevant filing date to the date the completed election was sent in; and

- steps had already been taken to have the election ready on time;

- a close relative or partner died shortly before the relevant filing date and the necessary steps had already been taken to have the election ready on time.

Other circumstances

There may be cases where, given the overall circumstances, we will accept a late election **A2.33** even where the chargeable person cannot show that the reasons for the late election were beyond their control. Essentially, this will be where the chargeable person can show that they were unaware—and could not reasonably have been aware—that they were liable to an income tax charge under this Schedule, and elected within a reasonable time of becoming so aware.

It is likely that such cases will involve a number of relevant features. The chargeable person or their agent should send with their late election a full explanation of the factors that they wish to be taken into account, which may cover (but need not be limited to):

- the nature of the transaction that led to an income tax charge arising;

- when the transaction was put in place;

- the advice the chargeable person received at the time the transactions were put in place and, if later, when this Schedule came into force;

- the circumstances in which they became aware of their liability to an income tax charge under this Schedule;

- any other notable features.

We will only accept a late election where the chargeable person can show that their failure to elect by the relevant filing date is not a result of:

- their taking active steps to avoid both an income tax charge under this Schedule and an inheritance tax charge by virtue of the Gift with Reservation provisions;

- the wish to avoid committing to either an income tax charge or an election before the 31 January deadline in order to have longer to see which will be the most beneficial course of action.

Changes to HMRC guidance

Where HMRC makes changes to its guidance - for example, because we consider that a **A2.34** charge to income tax under Schedule 15 arises from particular transactions that we did not previously regard as giving rise to a charge - we will accept late elections in those cases where the taxpayer can show that they elected as soon as practicable after becoming aware of our revised view.

Changes to the law

Where a change in the law results in a charge arising from particular transactions that did not previously give rise to a charge, we will accept late elections in those cases where the taxpayer can show that they elected as soon as practicable after becoming aware of the change.

3.5   Liaison with other parts of HMRC

A2.35   When we receive a late election, we will consider if sufficient information has been provided to explain why the chargeable person did not elect on time. If it has not, we will write to the chargeable person or their agent for more details.

In all cases, we will also contact the chargeable person's income tax office and let them know we have received a late election. Whether we are then able to make a decision on the election may depend on whether or not they have opened an enquiry into the chargeable person's Self Assessment affairs, or whether they intend to do so as a result of the late election (or a combination of the election and other factors).

If there is an ongoing enquiry, or it is intended to open one, then we may not make a decision on a late election until the enquiry is concluded, in case information comes to light during the enquiry that is material to that decision. We may, though, make a decision at an earlier time if the chargeable person's income tax office is satisfied that no further information will be forthcoming that could affect it.

3.6   If we refuse to accept a late election

A2.36   There is no right of appeal against the refusal to accept a late election, although a taxpayer may seek to challenge such a refusal by way of judicial review. If we do refuse to accept a late election, we will explain our reasons for doing so.

If the chargeable person is unhappy about how we have dealt with their case, they may write to the Customer Service & Complaints Manager at:
HMRC Inheritance Tax

Ferrers House
PO Box 38
Castle Meadow Road
Nottingham
NG2 1BB

If, having taken that step, the chargeable person remains unhappy, they can contact the Adjudicator's Office with any complaints at:

The Adjudicator's Office
Haymarket House
28 Haymarket
London
SW1Y 4SP

The chargeable person can at any time ask their MP to refer their complaint to the Parliamentary Ombudsman. The Ombudsman will normally expect the complaint to have already been considered by HMRC and by the Adjudicator.

4 HMRC's approach to certain issues

This section of the guidance looks at the HMRC's approach to certain practical issues regarding the pre-owned assets charge under this Schedule.

Examples of how we view particular situations can be found in **Appendix 1** to the guidance material.

4.1 Domicile/residence issues

A2.37

Schedule 15 does not apply to a person who is not resident for income tax in the United Kingdom in the year of assessment. To be regarded as resident in the United Kingdom you must normally be physically present in the country at some time in the tax year. You will always be resident if you are here for 183 days or more in the tax year. If you are here for less than 183 days, you may still be regarded as resident for the year under other tests. If you consider that residency is an issue for you, and one that has not been previously agreed with HMRC, you may wish to consult leaflet IR20 which discusses the position in more detail. The person's domicile in this case is immaterial.

A person's domicile becomes material if that person is resident for income tax purposes in the United Kingdom for any year of assessment. If the person is resident in, but domiciled outside, the United Kingdom, only relevant property situated in the United Kingdom will be subject to the charge. As the treatment of domicile for the charge is the same as that for inheritance tax, a person's domicile under s.267 of the Inheritance Tax Act 1984 as well as that under general law is relevant.

A person is deemed domiciled in the United Kingdom under this section if:

- they were domiciled on or after 10 December 1974 in the United Kingdom and within the three years immediately preceding the relevant time; or

- they were resident for income tax purposes in the United Kingdom in not less than 17 of the 20 years of assessment ending with the year of assessment in which the relevant time falls.

The relevant time for the purposes of the charge will be the first day of the year of assessment in question.

Paragraph 12(3) of the schedule provides that if any property situated outside the United Kingdom became comprised in a settlement when the person settling the property was domiciled outside the United Kingdom it will not be subject to the charge. Even if that person becomes domiciled in the United Kingdom at a later date this property will remain excluded from the charge.

Paragraph 12(3) provides that a charge under this Schedule shall not arise in relation to property regarded as excluded by virtue of s.48(3) of the IHTA 1984. We do not regard this provision as having an impact on paragraph 11 in determining whether there is derived property in the taxpayer's estate, or GWR property in relation to him (see foreign domiciliary example in appendix).

If the person adds property, wherever situated, to the settlement after they became domiciled in the United Kingdom the additional property would be subject to the charge if it falls within the provisions of paragraphs 3, 6 or 8 of the schedule. If applicable the general exclusions and exemptions would still be available, as they would be for any United Kingdom situated property where the person is domiciled outside the United Kingdom.

4.2   Tracing and contributions

A2.38   An absolute gift of cash is not subject to the inheritance tax reservation of benefit provisions unless the donor retains a benefit in the cash itself. For example, A, who is a partner in a business, withdraws capital from his capital account and gifts this to B, who then lends the partnership an equivalent cash sum. That sum is still on loan to the partnership when A dies. The cash sum is treated as a gift with reservation under s.102(3) of the Finance Act 1986. But the provisions in para.2 Sch.20 of the FA 1986 that enable the reservation of benefit provisions to apply to property that is substituted for the original gift do not apply where the original gift is of cash (para.2(2)(b)).

Thus, where an absolute gift of cash may later be used by the recipient to purchase property occupied or enjoyed by the donor for example, the application of the reservation of benefit rules to this property is precluded, unless the transaction can be shown to be a gift with reservation of benefit, by associated operations, of the purchased property.

These "tracing" rules do not apply to the application of the income tax charge under this schedule. The arrangement referred to above would satisfy the contribution condition of para.3(3) of this schedule if the contribution was made on or after 18 March 1986. The income tax charge would then apply unless the provision of consideration was an excluded transaction (para.10(3)(2)) or it fell within one of the exemptions from the charge in para.11. For the purposes of the latter paragraph and more particularly subparas 11(5)(b), (c) and (d) the restriction on the tracing of cash gifts normally imposed for inheritance tax purposes does not apply when considering whether there is an exemption from the income tax charge (para.11(8) Sch.15).

4.2.1   House sharing

A2.39   Where people enter into an arrangement whereby they contribute to a shared property (land & buildings) owning venture and whereby they intend to and do in fact share the occupation of and the expenses arising from the occupation of the property **broadly equally**, it is not the intention of Sch.15 to the FA 2004 to levy an income tax charge on any part of that arrangement. Such circumstances are generally covered by s.102 B (4) of the FA 1986, which is made applicable to Sch.15 by para.11(5)(c). However, if the situation is that the contribution made by each person is not commensurate with their respective enjoyment of the property and/or the expenses were shared unequally, the circumstances may fall to be scrutinised in the context of Sch.15 to the FA 2004. In such circumstances, a charge to income tax may well result.

4.3   Reasonable attribution

A2.40   Paragraphs 3(2)(a)(ii) and 3(3) relating to land and 6(2)(a)(ii) and 6(3) relating to chattels apply where the chargeable person has either disposed of property and the proceeds of this disposal were used to acquire the relevant property, or where the chargeable person has contributed any of the consideration (directly or indirectly) to acquire the relevant property. Where these provisions apply it is necessary to calculate the proportion of the value of the relevant property that can be reasonably attributed to the property originally disposed of or to the consideration provided. How should this proportion be calculated?

Each case will turn on its own facts and the value of the land disposed of and its ultimate sale price, the consideration provided and the independent financial resources of the recipient will all have to be taken into account when making a reasoned judgement as to the value reasonably attributable.

For example, the disposal condition in para.3(2)(a)(ii) would be met if the chargeable person transferred land to another ("X"), who later sold the land and used the proceeds to purchase a second property which the chargeable person occupies. If the land was valued at £100,000 at the date of transfer, sold for £300,000 and the new property purchased for £150,000, we would consider it reasonable to treat the whole value of the new property to be attributable to the property originally disposed of. If the value of the new property exceeds the proceeds received from the sale of the original property the proportion of the value reasonably attributable to the original property will be reduced. The value reasonably attributable to the new property cannot exceed the final value of the property originally disposed of.

If in the above example X used the sale proceeds to buy another property (Blackacre) which the chargeable person did not occupy but also used his own resources to buy a house (Whiteacre) which the chargeable person did occupy then we will not treat the value of Whiteacre as attributable to the property originally disposed of unless X had borrowed on the security of Blackacre.

If X purchases Whiteacre for £200,000 and half the purchase price (say £100,000) comes from the sale proceeds of the original land given to him and half comes from his own resources we would argue that half the value of Whiteacre was attributable to the property originally disposed of. Note that the reasonable attribution is not limited to the £100,000 originally put into Whiteacre but is half the value of Whiteacre at the relevant valuation date.

4.4   Full or part consideration

If the chargeable person's occupation of the relevant land, or enjoyment of the relevant chattel, is for full consideration in money or money's worth, i.e. a full market rent is paid by them for their continued occupation/enjoyment, their occupation/enjoyment is not a reservation of benefit for inheritance tax purposes (para.6(1)(a) Sch.20 of the Finance Act 1986). This treatment is extended to the income tax charge under this schedule by virtue of para.11(5)(d). Any arrangement or transaction entered into on or after 18 March 1986 where the chargeable person pays full consideration for their enjoyment or occupation of the relevant asset will not be subject to the income tax charge. **A2.41**

If the consideration paid by the chargeable person is less than full consideration, or if they initially pay a full consideration but, over time, this falls below market rates, the asset in question will be treated as subject to a reservation of benefit from the date the chargeable person ceased to pay full consideration. There will be no income tax charge under this schedule provided that the provisions of para.11(5)(a) apply.

4.5   Sales at undervalue

The application of para.4(4) in respect of land to which the disposal conditions of para.3(2) applies by virtue of a "non-exempt sale" is restricted to sales of the whole interest in the property. If there is a sale of part only of the chargeable person's interest in the relevant land, no account can be taken of the consideration actually paid by the purchaser (for an example *see* 2.1 above). **A2.42**

As the consideration must be paid in sterling or another currency this sub-paragraph will not apply if the consideration took another form, i.e. if one item of land was exchanged for another. Example: X exchanges his house valued at £800,000, for Y's property valued at £200,000 (Y's property in this example could be taken to mean land, a business, a right, in fact any property other than cash). X continues to live in his former property. Under the provisions of paragraph 4(4) the value of Y's property is not regarded as consideration to be taken into account, and X will be subject to a POA charge on £200,000. On X's death there will be a GWR in respect of a three-quarter share of his former property, and his estate for IHT purposes will include the £200,000 from Y.

4.6   Occupation/possession

Land

A2.43   Paragraph 3 of the schedule applies where the chargeable person occupies any land that they had either both previously owned and disposed of, or contributed to its acquisition. In this context "occupation" is construed quite widely. For example, the chargeable person would be regarded as in occupation not only if they were resident in the relevant property but also if they used it for storage or had sole possession of the means of access and used the property from time to time (*see* **Appendix 1**). The chargeable person would not be regarded as occupying a property from which they receive rental payments from the person(s) actually in occupation.

If the person's occupation or use of the property is only very limited in its nature or duration it may not come within the provisions of para.3. Each case will ultimately be decided on the facts and circumstances relating to it. However, in line with the HMRC's Interpretation of inheritance tax and gifts with reservation—RI 55 (November 1993)—some examples can be given of limited occupation that will not bring the chargeable person within para.3. These include:

- a house which is the owner's residence but where the chargeable person subsequently stays with the other person for less than one month each year or, in their absence, stays for not more than two weeks each year;

- social visits, excluding overnight stays by the chargeable person as a guest of the owner. The extent of the social visits should be no greater than the visits that may be otherwise be expected if the chargeable person had never previously owned the property, or made a contribution to its acquisition;

- a temporary stay for some short term purpose, for example, while the chargeable person convalesces after medical treatment, or they look after the owner while they are convalescing, or while the chargeable person's own home is being redecorated;

- visits to a house for domestic reasons, for example baby-sitting by the chargeable person for the owner's children;

- a house together with a library of books which the chargeable person visits less than five times in any year to consult or borrow a book;

- land which the chargeable person uses to walk their dogs or for horse riding provided this does not restrict the owner's use of the land.

More significant use of the property may bring the chargeable person within the scope of paragraph 3. Examples are:

- a house in which the chargeable person stays most weekends or for more than a month each year;

- a second home or holiday home which the chargeable person and the owner both then use on an occasional basis;

- a house with a library in which the chargeable person continues to keep their own books, or which they use on a regular basis, for example because it is necessary for their work.

Chattels

Similar considerations apply to the possession or use of previously owned chattels when **A2.44** the application of para.6 is contemplated. Very limited or occasional use of the chattel in question will not incur an income tax charge under this schedule.

For example, a car used to give occasional lifts (i.e. less than three times a month) to the chargeable person will not be liable to the charge. But if the chargeable person is taken to work every day in the car it is likely an income tax charge will be incurred.

4.7 "Substantially less"

Where any relevant property is included in the chargeable person's estate for inheritance **A2.45** tax purposes, or is subject to the inheritance tax reservation of benefit provisions, the value of that property is exempt from the charge (*see* 1.3.2). If other property that derives its value from the relevant property is included in the estate or is subject to a reservation of benefit the charge will not apply either. However, if the value of that derived property that can be reasonably attributed to the relevant property is "substantially less" than the value of the relevant property, only that proportion of the value of the relevant property that can be reasonably said to be included in the estate is exempted from the charge.

The term "substantially less" is not defined by the legislation but by analogy with the Capital Gains Tax taper relief rules we would regard a reduction of value of less than 20 per cent as not substantially less for the purposes of this Schedule. If the circumstances of a particular case suggest that the "substantially less" provision should be triggered by a reduction of more or less than 20 per cent, it will be judged on its individual merits.

Where the value of the property in the estate is substantially less than the value of the relevant property the appropriate rental value of any land, and the appropriate chargeable amounts relating to chattels or intangible property, for the purposes of this Schedule will be reduced by a reasonable proportion to take into account the property in the estate.

4.8 Double charges

The regulations relating to the income tax charge (SI 2005/724) include provisions to **A2.46** avoid a double charge to inheritance tax where the chargeable person elects that the gift with reservation provisions apply to the relevant property. A double charge may arise where the chargeable person makes a gift of property that is a potentially exempt transfer for inheritance tax. If that property is then liable to the income tax charge they may decide to make an election that the property is subject to the inheritance tax reservation of benefit provisions. If they then die within seven years of the original gift a double charge to inheritance tax will arise—firstly on the original transfer that must now be aggregated with the death estate and secondly on the property subject to the reservation.

The provisions to avoid double charges effectively retain the charge on the transfer that produces the higher overall amount of inheritance tax and reduce the other transfer to nil. The application of these provisions may best be illustrated using an example.

Mr G entered into a lifetime loan scheme (or double trust scheme as it may be known) in June 2003. He sold his house to a trust fund of which he is the life tenant for £500,000. The trustees do not pay the purchase price but give Mr G an IOU instead. Mr G then makes a gift of the IOU (the outstanding purchase price) to a second trust for the benefit of his children. He remains in occupation of the property and, as the outstanding debt reduces the value of the house for inheritance tax purposes to nil (see 1.5.2 and "excluded liability"), he is liable to the income tax charge from 6 April 2005. To avoid paying the charge he makes an election under para.21 of Sch.15 that the house is subject to the gift with reservation provisions. Mr G dies in July 2007 and the house is valued at £750,000 at that date.

As the death occurred less than seven years after the original gift of the IOU it must be aggregated with Mr G's estate when calculating the inheritance tax liability. But the house is also chargeable on the death as a gift with reservation following the election. A double charge to inheritance tax would arise but for the double charges provisions which apply in this instance, as the gifted property (the IOU) represents the proceeds of the disposal of the relevant property (the house). The two potential charges should be considered in isolation. In these examples Mr G's estate is valued at £500,000 and the inheritance tax threshold at the time of writing of £285,000 is used.

Charge to tax using original gift		
Gift now taxable		£500,000
Estate		£500,000
Aggregate chargeable transfer		£1,000,000
Taxable gift	£500,000	
Less nil-rate band	-£285,000	
Excess	£215,000	
Tax @ 40%	£86,000	
Taper relief due @ 40%	(£34,400)	
Tax payable		£51,600
Taxable estate	£500,000	
Nil-rate band used against gift	£0	
Tax @ 40%		£200,000
Total inheritance tax payable		**£251,600**
Charge to tax using gift with reservation		
Estate		£500,000
Gift with reservation		£750,000
Aggregate chargeable transfer		£1,250,000
Less nil-rate band		-£285,000
Excess		£965,000
Total inheritance tax payable @ 40%		£386,000
(apportioned between estate and gift with reservation)		

In this scenario the charge to tax using the gift with reservation will be used and the charge using the original gift will be reduced to nil by the double charges provisions and disregarded.

Further regulations were made SI 2005/3441 to deal with the double charges that may arise where the taxpayer decides to dismantle a "double trust scheme" and return to the position they were in prior to that arrangement.

Example

Mrs X sells her house to a trust in which she has an interest in possession in exchange for an IOU from the trustees, which she then gifts to a second trust for the benefit of her children. The gift of the IOU is a potentially exempt transfer for IHT purposes and its value will be chargeable if the taxpayer dies within seven years of making it. The "double trust" arrangement is then dismantled e.g. by the cancellation of the IOU, so that the full value of the house will return to her estate and also be subject to IHT on her death. There is therefore the potential for a double charge.

Statutory Instrument 2005/3441, therefore extended the previous regulations by introducing the Inheritance Tax (Double Charges) Regulations 2005, to provide relief from the double charge that would otherwise arise in the above example. As in the previous example, tax is calculated on the basis of the failed PET, and again with the house as an asset of the death estate. Inheritance tax is then charged on whichever transfer produces the greater tax, and the other transfer is reduced to nil.

It should be noted that the double charges provisions will not always apply when a perceived double charge arises. In particular, if an election is made in respect of property subject to an "Eversden" type arrangement with the result that the life tenant has made a potentially exempt transfer and the settlor's estate includes property subject to a reservation, both charges to tax are unaffected by the double charges provisions. The provisions only apply where there is a double charge in respect of the same individual.

4.9   Insurance policies

There may be certain instances where schemes involving insurance policies fall within the **A2.47** scope of para.8 of the Schedule. However, the majority of the more common schemes should not be affected. Examples of those that might be caught can be found in **Appendix 1**.

Where a charge to tax under this Schedule arises, para.15 of this Schedule requires that the open market value of the policy at the relevant time should be used in establishing the chargeable amount determined under paragraph 9 (*see* 4.10 below).

4.10   Valuation

Paragraph 15 of this Schedule is taken from the wording of s.160 of the Inheritance Tax **A2.48** Act 1984. This provides that "Except as otherwise provided by this Schedule, the value of any property shall for the purposes of this Schedule be the price which the property might reasonably be expected to fetch if sold in the open market at that time; but that price shall not be assumed to be reduced on the ground that the whole property is to be placed on the market at one and the same time".

Schedule 1

Contents

- Land—straightforward gift or sale of whole
- Land—straightforward gift or sale of part
- Land—equitable interests
- Partnership interests
- Land—lease carve out (Ingram scheme)
- Chattels—lease carve out
- Land—settlement on interest in possession trust (Eversden scheme)
- Intangible property—Eversden scheme
- Land—reversionary lease scheme
- Land—death scheme involving a loan

- Land—lifetime scheme involving a loan (double trust scheme)
- Insurance policies
- Land—occupation
- Post-death variations of an estate
- Foreign domiciliaries—excluded property
- Reverter-to-settlor trusts http://www.hmrc.gov.uk/poa/poa_guidance5.htm - toptop

Land—straightforward gift or sale of whole

A2.49   As previously mentioned at 1.3.1 of this guidance, a disposal of property is an excluded transaction "if it was a disposal of his whole interest in property", coming within the provisions of para.10. As this wording makes clear, "his whole interest" is precisely that, and can for example be a half share, or a quarter share of the whole land if that share is all that he owns.

In 2000, Mr A conveyed his house to his daughter Miss B. He continues to live there.

- While Mr A remains in occupation the property is subject to a gift with reservation for inheritance tax, whether or not Miss B also lives there. The income tax charge will not apply by virtue of para.11(5)(a) of this schedule.

- If Mr A pays a full market rent to Miss B for his occupation the property will not be subject to a reservation by virtue of para.6(1)(a) Sch.20 Finance Act 1986 and the income tax charge will not apply by virtue of para.11(5)(d) of this Schedule.

- If the conveyance to Miss B was not a gift but a sale at full market value there will be no transfer of value for inheritance tax. The transaction is a disposal for the purposes of para.3(2) of this schedule but it is an excluded transaction by virtue of para.10(1)(a). An income tax charge will not arise under this schedule.

- If Mr A had carved out a lease of his property for himself, and sold the freehold reversion to Miss B, that disposal will be an excluded transaction by virtue of para.10(1)(a), provided that the sale was a transaction such as might be expected to be made at arms length between persons not connected with each other. If this provision has been met an income tax charge under this Schedule will not arise. The reversion is regarded as a distinct item of property, and the sale was of the entire interest in it. Mr A continued to occupy the house by virtue of his leasehold interest, which is a separate item of property. There is of course a "marriage" value for the two interests and a truly arm's length transaction must take account of this along with any other factors.

Land—straightforward gift or sale of part share

A2.50   In 2001, Mr A conveyed his house into the joint names of himself and his daughter Miss B. He continues to live there.

- If Miss B does not occupy the property the half-share gifted by Mr A is subject to a gift with reservation for inheritance tax. The income tax charge will not apply by virtue of para.11(5)(a) of this Schedule.

- If Miss B does not occupy the property but Mr A pays Miss B a full market rent for his occupation of her half-share, the half-share will not be subject to a reservation by virtue of para.6(1)(a) Sch.20 of the Finance Act 1986 and the income tax charge will not apply by virtue of para.11(5)(d) of this schedule.

- If Miss B does occupy the property with Mr A and they share the running costs of the property in the same proportion, the half-share will not be subject to a reservation by virtue of s.102B(4) of the Finance Act 1986 and the income tax charge will not apply by virtue of para.11(5)(c) of this schedule.

- If the conveyance to Miss B was not a gift but a sale at full market value there will be no transfer of value for inheritance tax. The transaction is, though, a disposal for the purposes of para.3(2) of this schedule. Furthermore, the transaction is not an excluded transaction under para.10(1). However, the Regulations provide that, as the sale took place before 7 March 2005, the income tax charge under this Schedule will not apply. If the sale had taken place on or after 7 March 2005 Mr A's occupation of the half-share would be subject to an income tax charge if the appropriate rental value exceeds the de minimis limit in para.13. There is a further exception that may apply if the sale was for a consideration not in the form of money or an asset readily convertible into money (see following examples).

- If the sale of a part share had been to a commercial provider of equity release schemes the income tax charge will not apply. This is so whether or not such a sale takes place on or after 7 March 2005.

Land—equitable interests

If Miss B acquired her interest in the property by way of an equitable arrangement rather **A2.51** than for cash—e.g. she had given up work to care for Mr A on the understanding that she would receive a share of the property in return—the income tax charge will not apply (reg.5).

In considering whether the conditions were satisfied, we would need information about how the essential elements of the transaction had been arrived at. We do recognise that there is a substantial body of case law dealing with the circumstances in which an interest in a house is acquired in consequence of a person acting to his detriment. The Ministerial Statement had these sorts of situations in mind and we would interpret reg.5 accordingly. In particular, we accept that the requirement that "the disposal was by a transaction such as might be expected to be made at arm's length between persons not connected with each other" would be interpreted with such cases in mind. Where the parties had sought separate advice and acted upon it or had obtained a court order confirming the property entitlement, that would reinforce the claim that the conditions were satisfied. But we would not expect parties to such an arrangement to have done this. We recognise that detriment that the acquirer can demonstrate he has suffered can provide consideration for the acquisition of the interest and prevent the transaction from being gratuitous.

Partnership interests

The treatment of a share of a partnership interest for Sch.15 purposes follows that applied **A2.52** for IHT purposes. In other words, we do not regard the partnership interest as transparent, and the disposal of a share is unlikely to give rise to a Sch.15 charge in any circumstances. http://www.hmrc.gov.uk/poa/poa_guidance5.htm - toptop

Land—lease carve out (Ingram scheme)

A2.53   Mr R transfers title to his property to a nominee who then grants Mr R a 20-year lease of the property at a peppercorn rent. The encumbered freehold reversion is then gifted to his son. Mr R continues to occupy the property.

If the transfer was effected on or after 9 March 1999 the property will be subject to a reservation of benefit for inheritance tax by virtue of s.102A of the Finance Act 1986. No charge to income tax will then arise under this schedule.

If the transfer was effected before 9 March 1999 the arrangement is not caught by s.102A of the Finance Act 1986 and will be subject to the income tax charge under para.3(2) of this Schedule. The value subject to the charge will be the value attributable to the property actually disposed of, calculated in accordance with the formula in para.4(2).

Chattels—lease carve out

A2.54   The provisions of s.102A of the Finance Act 1986 only apply to interests in land. If the subject matter of the scheme referred to above is chattels rather than land, therefore, the provisions of this section do not bite. The property will not be subject to a reservation for inheritance tax regardless of when the scheme was actually effected.

It does, however, represent a disposal by the chargeable person who will be subject to an income tax charge under para.6(2) of this Schedule. The value subject to the charge will be the value attributable to the property actually disposed of, calculated in accordance with the formula in para.7(2).

Land—settlement on interest in possession trust (Eversden scheme)

A2.55   Mrs T transfers 95 per cent of her property to a settlement for the benefit of her husband for his life. On his death the property passes to a discretionary trust, of which she is one of the potential beneficiaries. She remains in occupation of the property.

If the transfer was effected on or after 20 June 2003 the property will be subject to a reservation of benefit by Mrs T for inheritance tax by virtue of s.102(5A) of the Finance Act 1986 and the income tax charge will not apply.

If the transfer was effected before 20 June 2003 the property will not be subject to a reservation of benefit. If the interest in possession of Mrs T's husband continued until his death the property will not be subject to the income tax charge because, although the disposal condition in para.3(2) is met, the transaction is an excluded transaction by virtue of para.10(1)(c).

However if her husband's interest in possession ended during his lifetime the transaction will not be excluded because of para.10(3) and the property disposed of will be subject to the income tax charge. The value of the property will be determined by the formula in para.4(2).

Intangible property—Eversden scheme

A2.56   Intangible property may also be settled on Eversden-type scheme, i.e. the chargeable person settles cash on interest in possession trusts for their spouse or civil partner, which the trustees then invest in a bond. If the terms of the settlement fall within the definition in para.8 of this Schedule similar results to the scheme involving land referred to above apply.

For example, if the spouse or civil partner's interest in possession ends during their lifetime and the property is now held on discretionary trusts of which the settlor is one of the potential beneficiaries, the income tax charge will apply under para.8 if the settlement was effected before 20 June 2003. The charge will be calculated with reference to para.9 of this Schedule.

It should be noted that the excluded transaction provisions have no application with regard to intangible property so para.10(1)(c), which may have a bearing in respect of certain Eversden-type schemes involving land, has no relevance here.

If the settlement was effected on or after 20 June 2003 the property is subject to a reservation of benefit for inheritance tax by virtue of s.102(5A) of the Finance Act 1986 and the income tax charge will not apply.

Land—reversionary lease scheme

A reversionary lease scheme, typically, is an arrangement where a donor grants a long **A2.57** lease of his property for say 999 years to the proposed donee, and the lease does not take effect until some future date. An example of this would be where Mr V, who has owned his house since 1990, grants a 999-year lease to his daughter in 1998 but not to take effect until 2018. Mr V continues to occupy the property.

Such schemes entered into before 9 March 1999 are not gifts with reservation of benefit so long as the lease contains no terms that are beneficial to the donor (see example below), and the income tax charge will apply.

For reversionary lease schemes entered into on or after 9 March 1999 HMRC had previously held the view that section 102A Finance Act 1986 would apply to them because the donor's occupation would be a "significant right in relation to the land". If that analysis were correct, the reservation of benefit rules would apply and there would be no income tax charge. However, HMRC now consider that where the freehold interest was acquired more than seven years before the gift, the continued occupation by the donor would not be a significant right, and therefore, contrary to its previously held view, s.102A cannot apply to the gift because of s.102A(5). If the donor grants a reversionary lease within seven years of acquiring the freehold interest, s.102A may apply to the gift depending on how the remaining provisions of that section apply in relation to the circumstances of the case.

Bear in mind, however, that, whenever the freehold interest was acquired, a gift may be a gift with reservation of benefit under s.102 of the Finance Act 1986 if the lease contains terms beneficial to the donor. An example of this may be where the lessee covenants to pay the costs of maintaining the property.

Where the GWR provisions do not apply it will nevertheless be regarded as a disposal of an interest in the relevant land under para.3(2) of Sch.15, and the charge to income tax will apply, calculated in accordance with the formula in para.4(2), unless the donor elects into the reservation of benefit provisions.

Land—death scheme involving a loan

Mr and Mrs S own a house in equal shares as tenants in common. Under the Will of Mr S, **A2.58** assets not exceeding the "nil-rate band" for inheritance tax pass into a discretionary trust, of which Mrs S is one of the potential beneficiaries. The remainder of his estate passes to Mrs S. Following the death of Mr S in June 2005 his executors transferred his half share of the property to Mrs S and, in return, she executed a loan agreement equivalent to the value of the half-share. No inheritance tax is payable.

The income tax charge under this schedule will not apply here. As Mrs S did not own her husband's share at the relevant time and did not dispose of it the disposal conditions in para.3(2) do not apply. If she did not provide Mr S with any of the consideration given by him for the purchase of his half share the contribution condition in para.3(3) will not apply either. Even if she had provided him with some or all of the consideration the condition will still not apply as it would have been an excluded transaction under para.10(2)(a). In the final scenario, however, the debt would not be allowable for inheritance tax on the death of Mrs S by virtue of s.103 of the Finance Act 1986.

Land—lifetime scheme involving a loan (double trust or home loan scheme)

A2.59 There are a number of variants of this scheme—one of the more straightforward types is referred to in the Double Charges section of this guidance (*see* 4.8) —and the income tax charge under this Schedule will apply. (Guidance on whether the loan may be chargeable under the IHT reservation of benefit provisions is given at the end of this section).

As the chargeable person is usually still occupying the house as the life tenant of an interest in possession trust the exemption in para.11(1) of this Schedule would appear to prevent the charge from applying. However, the value of the property in the estate will be reduced by the debt now owned by the trustees of the second trust in the scheme. For example if the house is valued at £500,000 and the debt is valued at £400,000, only the net value of £100,000 is chargeable to inheritance tax. In this scenario the concept of excluded liabilities will apply—paras 11(6) and 11(7) of this Schedule (*see* 1.3.2). The exemption in para.11(1) is restricted to the value of the relevant property that exceeds the amount of the excluded liability—in this example £100,000. The remaining part of the house will be subject to the charge—in this example four-fifths of the appropriate rental value. If, in the above example, the debt is expressed as a percentage of the value of the house, the income tax charge would be payable on the same percentage of the rental value.

Reservation of benefit in the loan—HMRC's view

A2.60 The essence of many of these schemes involves the chargeable person(s) (the vendors) selling their home for full value to a newly formed trust (trust 1) with the sale proceeds left outstanding on loan. An IOU for the loan is gifted to a second trust (trust 2) for the benefit of the vendor's family. The vendor(s) continue to occupy the property under the terms of trust 1, and the loan is repayable to trust 2 on demand. HMRC's view on this is that since the loan was repayable on demand, there will be a GWR in respect of it, until such time as the trustees call in the loan. The reason for this is that if trust 2 had called in the loan, trust 1 would have been forced either to sell the home to repay the debt, or to seek finance from elsewhere. If the house were sold, then the vendor(s) would have been unable to occupy it under the terms of trust 1. In order to avoid the need for a sale, trust 1 would have had to find a third party willing to lend 100 per cent of the value of the property on the basis of a covenant by the trustees, and security over the house. Even if such borrowing could be obtained, which must be extremely doubtful, it would be prohibitively expensive. Trust 1 could only justify taking on such borrowing if they were financed by the vendor(s) (the life tenants) who would be benefiting from the property by residing in it. On the foregoing basis it is considered that the trustees of trust 2, in not calling in the loan, have enabled the vendor(s) to retain a significant benefit in it, and therefore that the debt was not enjoyed to the entire exclusion of any benefit to the vendor(s) by contract or otherwise. A variant of the scheme described above is where the terms of the loan provide that the debt is only repayable at a time after the death of the life tenant. Since, unlike the position with loans repayable on demand, the loan can not be called in by the loan trustees, it is generally thought that these schemes will not be caught as gifts with reservation.

If the loan is subject to a reservation of benefit this does not mean the vendor can avoid paying income tax. The reservation of benefit is in the loan not the house and he has still made a relevant disposal of the house which is subject to an excluded liability and which therefore reduces his estate. Reserved benefit property does not form part of someone's estate while he is alive (ss.102(3)(4) of the FA 1986). In these circumstances if A does not wish to pay the income tax charge the debt should either be appointed back to him or written off (in which case the excluded liability ceases to reduce the value of his estate and there is no income tax charge from the date the debt is written off or appointed back to him) or he should elect (in which case there is no income tax charge at all).

Insurance policies

The settlor effects a discounted gift scheme comprising a gift into settlement with certain **A2.61** "rights" being retained by them. The retained rights may, for instance, be a series of single premium policies maturing (usually) on successive anniversaries of the initial investment or on survival, reverting to the settlor, if they are alive on the maturity date, or the settlor carves out the right to receive future capital payments if they are alive at each prospective payment date. The gift with reservation provisions do not apply.

In the straightforward case where the settlor has retained a right to an annual income or to a reversion under arrangements, that right is not property within paragraph 8 as the trustees hold it on bare trust for the settlor. A bare trust is not a settlement for inheritance tax purposes. The settlor is excluded from other benefits under the policy and so this schedule does not apply.

There may be more complex cases where the settlor's retained rights or interests are themselves held on trust. But that would normally be construed as being a separate trust of those benefits in which the settlor had an interest in possession, and no charge to tax will arise under this schedule by virtue of para.11(1).

Even if, in less common cases, the para.11 provisions did not apply so as to exempt the case from charge completely, any charge under this schedule would apply by reference to the value of the rights held on trust for the settlor, not by reference to the value of the underlying life policy.

- The settlor effects a policy and settles it on trust for the benefit of others. He then makes a substantial interest free loan to the trustees, repayable on demand. The trustees use the loan to purchase more policies, and make partial surrenders each year to pay off part of the loan.

This arrangement is not a gift with reservation for inheritance tax. The settlor is not a beneficiary of the trust itself and the making of the loan does not constitute a settlement for the purposes of inheritance tax. No charge to tax will arise under this schedule.

Pension policies

Pension policies may typically provide pension and lifetime benefits for the scheme **A2.62** member, and other benefits that are payable on death at the discretion of the scheme trustees. It is considered that the pension and other lifetime benefits would either represent unsettled property or a trust separate from that on which the death benefits are held. In the arrangement described, both parts can be treated as mutually exclusive and therefore provided the scheme member could not benefit from the trusts governing the death benefits, a charge under this schedule will not arise.

A charge under Sch.5 will not arise in relation to approved pension arrangements or, from 6 April 2006, pension arrangements under registered schemes. Neither are such arrangements caught as GWRs, as HMRC's statement of practice 10/86 makes clear. Non-registered schemes do not fall within the statement of practice, and so may well come within Finance Act 1986, in which event, the same dispositions would not come within Sch.15.

Business trusts (or partnership policies)

A2.63   In some cases, policies are taken out on each partner's life solely for the purposes of providing funds to enable their fellow partners to purchase his/her share from the partner's beneficiaries on their death. The partner is not a potential beneficiary of his/her "own" policy. In such circumstances, a charge to tax under paragraph 8 of this schedule will not arise.

However, in many cases, the partner retains a benefit for themselves, for example they can cash in the policy during their lifetime for their own benefit. In such cases, even if the arrangement is on commercial terms so that it is not a gift with reservation for inheritance tax, the trust is a settlement for inheritance tax purposes and a charge to tax under para.8 will arise.

The valuation of a partner's, or settlor's, interest in a policy for the purposes of para.8 of Sch.15 should be his share of its open market value as at 6 April each year. That valuation will be relevant for determining the amount of charge for that year of assessment.

Where the policies are term assurances, in the vast majority of cases the policyholder will be in normal health, and therefore it is likely that the chargeable amount, as calculated under para.9 of Sch.15, will have little marketable value and will fall below the de minimis exemption in paragraph 13. Therefore, a policyholder in normal health at the valuation date may assume that he will survive beyond the term of the assurance, and complete his tax return accordingly. However, in circumstances where the policyholder has been advised that their state of health is such that it casts doubt on their survival to the end of the term of assurance (i.e. there becomes a realistic prospect of the policy paying out and therefore having a material market value), then consideration should be given to obtaining actuarial advice about the value of the policy.

Pre-18 March 1986 Policies settled on trusts

A2.64   A charge under Sch.15 does not arise where, before 18 March 1986, a life policy has been contracted and settled on trusts from which the settlor can benefit, even where premiums are paid after this date.

Land—occupation.

A2.65   Example 1: Mr A gives his house to his daughter in 1987. The disposal condition of para.3(2) has been met. He occupies the property along with his daughter, and later when she moves out, on his own. This was "relevant land" at all times since 1987, for the purposes of para.3(1), of Sch.15. It is protected from POAT throughout because it is subject to a reservation of benefit.

Example 2: Mr A sells his house and makes a cash gift to his daughter, who uses the money towards the purchase of a house of her own also using some of her own money. The contribution condition of para.3(3) is met. Within seven years of this gift he moves in with his daughter and occupies a self-contained part of the house, and has the means of access to the remainder of the property, and actually uses it from time to time, e.g. for storing furniture there. In these circumstances, the whole property is considered to be "relevant land" for the purposes of para.3(1). However, while he occupies with his daughter there is no POAT charge due to para.11(8). Had Mr A moved into occupation more than seven years after the cash gift, the provision of that consideration will be an excluded transaction, coming within para.10(2)(c) of Sch.15.

Example 3: The scenario is that of example 2, however Mr A does not have means of access to the rest of the house, and his access to the self-contained part is via an external door. He visits the rest of the house only when invited, e.g. for Sunday lunch. He stores no furniture there. In this example, only the self-contained part is "relevant land" for the purposes of para.3(1).

Post-death variations of an estate

Mrs W is bequeathed a house, which she occupies, under her husband's will. She **A2.66** completes a deed of variation within two years of her husband's death altering the terms of the Will so that the house passes to her son instead. The deed of variation is effective for inheritance tax purposes as the provisions of s.142(1) of the Inheritance Tax Act 1984 apply. Although she continues to occupy the house the income tax charge will not apply by virtue of para.16 of this Schedule.

The provisions of paragraph 16 will also apply if the deed of variation referred to above had merely changed Mrs W's absolute interest in the property to a life interest in possession, with her son as remainderman. If her life interest is terminated during her lifetime (but more than two years after her husband's death) and she continues to occupy the property the income tax charge will not apply provided that the deed of variation satisfied the provisions of s.142(1) of the Inheritance Tax Act 1984. In any event, if her life interest was terminated after 21 March 2006 and she continues to occupy the property the reservation of benefit provisions will apply (s.102ZA of the FA 1986 as amended by Finance Bill 2006).

Foreign domiciliaries—excluded property

An arrangement that is not uncommon is where a foreign domiciliary settles a trust which **A2.67** owns a UK house through a foreign registered company. The shares in this company (and any loan made to it) are excluded property, coming within the provisions of s.48(3) of the IHTA 1984. Paragraph 12(3) provides that Sch.15 will have no application to such assets. However in considering the application of paragraph 11 in respect of the house he occupies, the operation of para.12(3) does not mean that the shares (or any loan made to the company) are automatically disregarded in determining whether, for the purposes of paragraph 11, there is derived property which is in the taxpayer's estate or GWR property in relation to him. In these circumstances we would accept that the exemptions in paragraph 11 can apply to the foreign domiciliary.

Reverter-to-settlor trusts

Legislation introduced in the 2006 Finance Bill will, from 5 December 2005, prevent **A2.68** property gifted by the donor but still enjoyed by him as a beneficiary of a reverter-to-settlor trust from escaping an income tax charge under Sch.15.

Previously the donor could gift property that would then be settled back on him on trusts which allowed him to continue to enjoy the property, but which on his death would revert back to the settlor (the original donee). The property was (for trusts established pre-Budget 2006) treated as part of the donor's estate for IHT purposes, but on his death was excluded from a charge to IHT under ss.53 and 54 of the IHTA 1984, as it reverted back to the settlor (the original donee). A charge under Sch.15 would also not arise because the property was still regarded as part of the donor's estate for IHT purposes.

The new legislation will allow a Sch.15 charge to apply in situations where the former owner of an asset (or a person who contributed to its acquisition) enjoys the asset under the terms of a trust, and the trust property reverts to the settlor—or to the spouse or civil partner, widow, widower or surviving civil partner of the settlor.

A2.69   Question 1: Deeds of Variation

1.1   You will recall that the problem relates to the drafting of paragraph 16. This states *"any disposition made by a person ("the chargeable person") in relation to an interest in the estate of a deceased person is to be disregarded for the purposes of this Schedule if by virtue of section 17 IHTA 1984 the disposition is not treated for the purposes of inheritance tax as a transfer of value by the chargeable person"* . Section 17 provides that a variation or disclaimer to which s.142(1) applies is not a transfer of value.

1.2   The difficulty is that this wording and the Revenue statement in the guidance notes leaves the position ambiguous in certain cases where a spouse of the Deceased has effected a deed of variation. Suppose Mr X dies leaving his estate to his widow who within two years of Mr X's death enters into a deed of variation under which instead of taking her husband's estate absolutely, she decides to settle it on trusts under which she retains a continuing interest in possession with remainders over to her children. This would be a valid deed of variation for inheritance tax purposes, but will it qualify for favoured treatment under the POA Regime? Under s.49(1) of the IHTA the widow will, by virtue of her interest in possession under the new settlement, still be treated as owning her husband's estate with the result that she will not make a transfer of value.

1.3   On a narrow reading it is arguable that the deed is not a transfer of value by virtue of the protection under s.49(1) not by virtue of the protection under s.17 of the 1984 Act and therefore para.16 does not apply to protect the gift. This would matter if the widow's interest later ends but she continues to occupy the property in question.

1.4   We would argue that section 17 simply states that a variation or disclaimer to which s.142 applies is not a transfer of value anyway and the fact that the variation may not be a transfer of value for some other reason does not matter. Hence the variation is within s.142(1) (assuming all other conditions are met) and the widow is protected from a POA charge under para.16 irrespective of whether her interest in possession later terminates.

1.5   Is this though the Revenue view? You will understand that deeds of variation setting up a defeasible life interest trust for the spouse are extremely common and will have been done on a very extensive basis since 1986. We recall that in Consultation it was agreed that all deeds of variation falling within s.142(1) would be protected by para.16.

Answer

1.1   You are concerned here about the situation where an instrument of variation, which takes effect for IHT under s.142(1) of the IHTA, does not give rise to a transfer of value in any event. For example, Mrs X, who is entitled to her husband's estate under his will, within two years of Mr X's death, settles her absolute entitlement on trusts in which she retains a beneficial interest in possession. This is not a transfer of value for IHT purposes, even without the intervention of s.17 of the IHTA.

1.2   We would agree that s.17 applies to all disclaimers or variations that come within s.142(1), even if the variation may not be a transfer of value in any event. As a result, I can confirm that all instruments of variation to which s.142(1) of the IHTA applies will come within the protection afforded by para.16 of Sch.15. We will supplement the guidance at 1.3.5 to make this clear.

Question 2: Cash gifts A2.70

2.1   The position with cash gifts was discussed on several occasions. Suppose a cash gift is made by Jason to his son in January 1997. His son later buys a house and Jason then goes into occupation in March 1998. He satisfies the contribution condition and will be caught under the POA regime unless it is an excluded transaction. The cash gift is an excluded transaction under para.10(2)(c) if "*the consideration constituted an outright gift of money by the chargeable person* (here Jason) *to the other person and was made at least seven years before the earliest date on which the chargeable person met the condition in paragraph 3(1)(a)* " [our italics].

2.2   The chargeable person is Jason but the earliest date on which he could meet the condition in para.3(1)(a) is when the legislation comes into effect on 6 April 2005. Since the cash gift was made more than seven years before he satisfies the condition it would appear that he is protected from a POA charge despite the fact that he went into occupation shortly after the cash gift. In effect this would mean that such cash gifts made prior to 6 April 1998 will be protected from a POA charge under para.10(2)(c).

2.3   We are aware that Martin Haigh suggested this view was correct and that as a matter of policy the Revenue would not object if in effect only cash gifts post-April 1998 are within POA. However the guidance notes imply otherwise although the position is not explicitly stated. What view does the Revenue take on this point?

Answer

Having considered the matter further, we are content to accept that a person could not meet the condition in para.3(1)(a) or paragraph 6(1)(a) of Sch.15 before the legislation came into effect on 6 April 2005. On this basis, we agree that para.10(2)(c) has the effect of excluding from a charge under Sch.15 outright gifts of cash made before 6 April 1998. Again we will clarify the guidance on this point.

Question 3: Occupation A2.71

3.1   At the meetings last year, the meaning of occupation was discussed at some length and there is some helpful commentary on this in the guidance notes. However, it has not dealt with the position where someone gave away the whole land but now occupies only part of the gifted property.

3.2   The classic case is where mother has (say) carried out an Ingram scheme on a large estate comprising main house and lodge but then as she becomes elderly has moved out of the main house into the lodge. Her son moves into the main house and mother moves her furniture and possessions down to the lodge and genuinely does not occupy the main house. A less extreme example would be where someone gives away the whole of their house but then ends up living in the self-contained basement flat (a not uncommon scenario in London).

3.3   In these circumstances the disposal condition has been satisfied because the person owned an interest in "the relevant land" and has disposed of that interest and occupies "the relevant land". The charge appears to be in relation to the relevant land i.e. the whole amount gifted and there is no provision for pro rating just because someone is now occupying a small part of what they gave away.

3.4 At the meeting the Revenue said that if someone gave away the whole of an estate but in the end only reserved a benefit by occupying a small self-contained part they would only be subject to reservation of benefit on that part and suggested that the same approach would be adopted for pre-owned assets. Is this in fact the approach that you are going to take? Again many people need to know this in order to calculate their income tax liabilities.

Answer

3.1 As you say, our guidance notes, principally at para.4.6, set out our views on what constitutes occupation for the purpose of considering whether and to what extent a charge under Sch.15 arises. This general approach should be applied when considering what constitutes the "relevant land" where an owner has disposed of the whole property but may now be occupying only part of it.

3.2 Inevitably the facts of individual cases will be relevant in determining the extent of the land that is being occupied by a former owner. As we say at paragraph 4.6, we would construe "occupation" quite widely and believe it goes beyond residence or physical occupation. Thus, in a case where a former owner of property was residing in part of it and had possession of the means of access to the rest of it and used it from time to time, I think we would regard him as occupying the whole property for the purposes of para.3(1) of Sch.15. On the other hand, where a former owner of property occupies a self-contained part of it and has no access to the remainder which is occupied by others, it would seem reasonable to regard the "relevant land" for para.3(1) purposes as being confined to the self-contained part.

3.3 I am sure there is scope to expand the guidance on this topic, perhaps by including some examples in the Appendix. We will give this some thought.

A2.72 Question 4: Funding the POA Charge

Some people, particularly those who have carried out *Ingram* schemes, do not want to dismantle the scheme and lose the inheritance tax savings. The donee or other members of the family are prepared to put the donor in funds to pay the income tax each year in order to enable the donor to continue living in the house and to preserve the inheritance tax position. The question then is whether the reimbursement by the donee of the donor's income tax bill could be regarded as a reservation of benefit in respect of the original gifted property. We are talking here only about existing schemes which were carried out before the donor was aware of the possibility of a pre-owned assets charge. Hence the original gift was not in anyway conditional on the donee paying the donor's income tax liability.

It is thought that there is no reservation of benefit and the position is similar to the analysis on cash gifts. In order to avoid a reservation of benefit, in effect, three conditions must be satisfied:

1. Possession and enjoyment of the gifted property must be bona fide assumed by the donee. That limb is not in dispute - the donee enjoys the gifted property (the freehold reversion in the case of *Ingram* schemes) irrespective of whether or not the donee pays some cash to the donor to reimburse him for income tax. The original gift was not conditional on the donee paying the tax.

2. Section 102(1)(b) states that there is also a reservation of benefit if the actual property itself is not enjoyed to the entire exclusion or virtually to the entire

exclusion of the donor. Again the donor (assuming the particular scheme in question has been properly implemented) is excluded from the actual property gifted—say the freehold reversion or the loan or IOU of a double trust scheme.

3. The question then is whether the second limb of s.102(1)(b) is breached, i.e. the property has not been enjoyed to the entire exclusion of any benefit to the donor by contract or otherwise. Is the payment by the donee of the donor's income tax liability a collateral benefit conferred on the donor?

It is certainly of benefit to the donor that the donee pays the income tax liability. However, one surely needs to do more than simply identify the benefit which the donor has received from the donee. What one has to show is that the benefit actually entrenches in some way upon the donee's possession and enjoyment of the gifted property or is linked to the property. Otherwise any benefit that the donee gave to the donor in the future however unrelated to the gift would breach the rules.

So if a gift was made of the house now in such a way as to avoid the reservation of benefit provisions but the donee was under some obligation to pay the income tax charge, that might entrench upon the donee's possession and enjoyment of the gifted property and be a reservation of benefit but an undertaking made now by the donee to reimburse the donor for income tax in respect of a gift made some years ago would surely not be a problem.

4. Finally do the associated operations provisions incorporated by para.6(1)(c) alter this analysis: is this a benefit which the donor has obtained by virtue of associated operations of which the disposal by way of gift is one?

The benefit is not enjoyed as part of the arrangements under which the original gifted property was made. The gift of property was made before pre-owned assets regime was envisaged.

The view that there is no reservation of benefit seems to be borne out by the case law. In *Oakes v Commissioner of Stamp Duties for New South Wales* [1954] AC 57, the judicial committee said that it is necessary not merely to find that the settlor continued to enjoy substantial advantages which had some relation to the gifted property but one must consider the nature and source of each such advantage separately. It was specifically held there that the use of the income from the children's shares of the property for their maintenance and education during their minority may have been an advantage to the donor but did not impair or diminish the value of the gift of land to the children or their enjoyment of it.

In the light of this are you able to confirm that if the donee pays the POA income tax liability of the donor in relation to schemes effected prior to the announcement of the pre-owned assets income tax regime in December 2003 there would be no reservation of benefit for the donor?

Answer

I agree with all of your analysis save for a question mark on your paragraph 4. What you say is correct in the context of s.268(1)(b) of the Inheritance Tax Act 1984, which will be relevant in the great majority of cases. If, however, the source of the income tax monies was derived from the pre-owned assets it may be that s.268(1)(a) could be relevant and a GWR claim be possible.

III   POAT: CIOT/STEP COP 10 LETTER—
QUESTIONS AND ANSWERS (2006)

Contents

1. Valuation issues

Regulation 4 provides that in relation to land and chattels the valuation is by reference to the first valuation date and this valuation is used for a period of five tax years. This is favourable to taxpayers where the gifted land increases in value. For instance, in relation to existing Ingram and reversionary lease schemes, one takes the value of the gifted property as at 6 April 2005 even though the gifted interest (the DV) is likely to increase in value over the next five years. **A2.73**

However, the position is unclear where the property is sold and the taxpayer moves to a smaller house.

Example 1

A gave £300,000 to his son in April 2000. Son later uses all the cash to purchase a house and contributes none of his own funds. A goes into occupation of house in April 2002. He falls within the contribution condition and is subject to the POA charge from 6 April 2005. The house is worth £1 million on 6 April 2005. He pays income tax in 2005/6 by reference to the rental value of the house.

In 2007, Son sells house and buys a new one for £500,000 into which A moves. In these circumstances there seems to be no mechanism for assessing A to income tax on the rental value of the new house.

Does A continue to pay income tax on a hypothetical rental value of the original £1 million house until 2010?

Similar problems can arise if A moves into a discrete part of the house and only occupies that part, letting the remainder. If he has not done this by 6 April 2005 it would appear that his charge is not reduced for the next five years.

Question 1

Does HMRC interpret the legislation in this restrictive way or does it take the view that the relevant land for the purposes of para.4(5) is the land that the taxpayer actually occupies and therefore a new valuation is done when the taxpayer first occupies the smaller property or the smaller part? This is on the basis that a new taxable period then starts in which that property or part is the relevant property. The Regulations would then apply on the basis that the first day of such occupation is the first day of the taxable period.

HMRC answer to question 1

The "relevant land" for the purposes of para.4(5) is the land currently occupied by the chargeable person. A new valuation should be done when the occupation of that property starts, and we would intend that the new valuation should then be used for the remainder of that five-year cycle.

A2.74   Particular valuation problems arise in relation to the double trust or home loan schemes.

Example 2

B sells his house to a trust in which he retains an interest in possession ("the property trust") and the purchase price of £900,000 is left outstanding as a debt. B gives away the debt. Assume that B is caught by POA and that the debt is an excluded liability. The house is worth £1 million on 6 April 2005 and the debt is £900,000. Based on HMRC's example in the Appendix of the Guidance Notes, B pays income tax on nine-tenths of the rental value attributable to the house.

Question 2

Can HMRC confirm that this is the view taken, i.e. that where the debt is only a percentage of the value of the house the taxpayer pays income tax on the same percentage of the rental value?

There seems no express provision in para.11 to allow for a percentage reduction in the charge in the event that the property is subject to a debt but has some excess value. We assume from the example in the Appendix that HMRC interpret the interaction of paras 11(6) and (1) and in particular the words "to the extent that" to mean that if the value of the property exceeds the excluded liability by 10 per cent there is a 10 per cent reduction in the charge under para.4.

HMRC answer to question 2

We confirm that, where, as in Example 2, the debt is only a percentage of the value of the chargeable property, income tax is payable on the same percentage of the rental value. As you suggest, this follows from the interaction of paras 11(6) and (1). As far as subsequent valuation cycles are concerned, we would adjust the proportion of the rental value charged to reflect any adjustment to the value of the chargeable property.

A2.75   If the debt was reduced to £500,000 (by partial repayment or by writing off) then it would appear that B would pay income tax from that date on half the rental value of the property and that reg.4 does not prevent a reduction in the income tax charge on repayment of the debt even if this is done half way through the five year period. Half the value of the property is now deemed to be comprised in the person's estate under para.11(1) and there is no charge on this part.

Question 3

Can HMRC confirm that if the debt "affecting" the property is reduced for any reason the income tax charge reduces by the same proportion even if this reduction occurs during the five-year period?

Suppose in the above example the home loan scheme had been effected by a married couple H and W but only H later added the £500,000 to the property trust to enable the property trustees to repay part of the loan. Are we correct to assume that the loan is pro rated so that the excluded liability is reduced for H and W by £250,000 each rather than the repayment just reducing H's share of the excluded liability?

HMRC answer to question 3

We confirm that the income tax charge would be reduced by the same proportion by which the debt affecting the property was reduced. In view of the reference in para.11(6) to "at any time", we confirm that the charge would be reduced even if the reduction of the debt occurred during the five-year period.

Where the scheme had been effected by a married couple, H & W, we assume that the answer would depend on the precise terms of the property trust. But, assuming that the property is held by H & W equally, the addition by H of £500,000 to the trust would diminish his estate by £250,000 (an exempt transfer to W). On that basis, we would agree that the excluded liability for H & W would be reduced by £250,000 each.

Suppose that the house is sold by the property trust and the trustees then purchase a smaller property for say £600,000. The debt of £900,000 is not repaid but left outstanding and the spare cash of £400,000 is invested in intangibles to produce an income for B. On a literal reading of Regulation 4 it would appear that B still pays income tax on the market rental of the original property as at the April 2005 valuation (reduced by one tenth). **A2.76**

Question 4

We assume that HMRC consider that once a smaller property is purchased during the five year period, what is valued for the purposes of the POA charge under para.4 is indeed that smaller property. Please confirm.

HMRC answer to question 4

Assuming that the intangibles are held on the original trusts and that the debt of £900,000 is left outstanding, we agree that the smaller property would be within the charge under para.4 and that the intangibles would come within para.8.

In line with the answer to Q1, we would suggest that the paragraph 4 computation should be based on the value of the newer, smaller property with the intangible property being charged under para.8. The parts chargeable under paras 3 (as quantified in accordance with para.4) and 8 should then be arrived at by apportioning the loan rateably between the two components. However if the loan was originally secured specifically on the land, one would calculate the para.3 charge simply by reference to the value of the new, smaller property with the balance of the loan being charged under para.8.

A2.77 Suppose husband has given away his 50 per cent share in the home originally owned jointly with his wife. The gift was into an Eversden settlement and is now caught by POA. In these circumstances, professional surveyors consider that the 50 per cent share should be discounted and hence "the DV" figure be reduced.

Questions of valuation are not specifically addressed in the Guidance Notes but we assume that HMRC accept that, if professionally so advised, a discount for joint ownership would be appropriate for the DV figure.

Question 5

Can a standard percentage discount be agreed with HMRC in relation to jointly held interests?

HMRC answer to question 5

We agree that the 50 per cent share of the house chargeable under POA should be valued on normal open market principles for the purposes of ascertaining DV. This would imply a discount, but not sure that we can agree a standard discount in advance, any more than we would do for "normal" IHT purposes.

A2.78 There are difficulties in valuing settled insurance policies caught by para.8. For example, in their Guidance Notes HMRC take the view that life policies settled on a commercial basis by partners or shareholders for each other will be caught under POA if the settlor retains an interest. The settlor will often retain such an interest since there is usually a provision that the life policy will revert to the business owner if he leaves the business before death.

Question 6

(a) In these circumstances how does one value the intangible property?

(b) Would it be based on the surrender value of the life policy?

HMRC answer to question 6

Our current view is that a group policy taken out for the partners or shareholders is within the scope of the para.8 charge, because each partner, as settlor, is not excluded from benefit. This appears to be the case whether or not each partner can benefit on leaving the partnership and whether or not the only benefits that can accrue to a partner are those arising on the death of a partner. As far as valuation is concerned, we would expect the value of the policy to be its open market value at the relevant time, not its surrender value.

A2.79 The comments on life policies taken out by partnerships and other businesses contained at the end of the revised Guidance Notes seem to go directly against Government policy which is to encourage such arrangements (as illustrated by the relieving legislation introduced in FA 2003 s.539A for income tax purposes).

Question 7

Is HMRC considering an extra statutory concession to relieve such arrangements from the POA charge?

This would appear to be appropriate given that such arrangements are commercial with no donative intent and therefore outside the reservation of benefit provisions.

If the only interest of the settlor in the trust is that the life policy reverts to the settlor if he leaves the business before his death, do HMRC agree that the settlor's interest under such arrangement can be regarded as similar to his interest under discounted gift schemes and therefore outside the POA charge—see 8.1?

HMRC answer to question 7

An Extra Statutory Concession is not in view, as far as we are aware, and we do not think it is for us to comment on whether one would be appropriate. As far as the settlor's interest in the policy is concerned, we are doubtful that there is an exact analogy with Discounted Gift Schemes as you suggest. While this would depend on the terms of the policy concerned, it is not clear to us that the value of the settlor's contingent interest and the value of the interests of the surviving partners can be sufficiently distinguished in the way that we have agreed they can be for Discounted Gifts.

We should be grateful for some clarification of HMRC policy in respect of pension **A2.80** policies (whether retirement annuity or personal pension policies and whether approved or unapproved). Typically such policies provide that retirement benefits and other lifetime benefits such as a payment on demutualisation are held for the absolute benefit of the individual member with death benefits being held on discretionary trusts.

Question 8

HMRC takes the view that the analysis on such policies is similar to discounted gift schemes and that the retirement benefits represent separate unsettled property? See 8(a). Can HMRC confirm that the POA regime does not apply to such pension arrangements? Does their view change if the individual member can benefit from the discretionary trust over the death benefits?

HMRC answer to question 8

(a) As a general rule, the pension and other lifetime benefits for the scheme member and the benefits paid on death are mutually exclusive. On this basis, we would agree that an analogy can be drawn with discounted gift schemes so that the pension benefits would either represent unsettled property or a trust separate from that on which the death benefits are held.

(b) On the basis of the above, we would agree that the POA regime would generally not apply to pension arrangements, where the individual scheme member was not able to benefit from the discretionary trust governing the death benefits.

Valuation problems arise where a settlor takes out a life policy and writes it on trust pre-18 **A2.81** March 1986. The reservation of benefit rules did not apply then and so he is often a potential beneficiary. Suppose that for the last 20 years he has been paying the premiums on such policy. Section 102(6) of the FA 1986 provides an exemption from reservation of benefit in respect of premiums paid post-17 March 1986 where the policy was taken out before 18 March and the premiums increase at a pre-arranged rate. However, there has been concern that premiums paid post-17 March 1986 would appear to be within the POA Regime.

Question 9

(a) Do HMRC consider that such policies are caught? We would suggest that premiums paid since 17 March 1986 are not themselves additions to the settled property if paid direct to the insurance company but merely maintain the value of the settled property and therefore are not strictly within the wording of para.8.

(b) We understand from correspondence in Taxation that HMRC believe POA does apply and apportion the premiums between pre-18 and post-17 March 1986.

(c) In the light of the comment in (a) above will HMRC reconsider their views in respect of payments on such policies?

HMRC answer to question 9

In our view, it is correct to regard premiums paid after 17 March 1986 in respect of settled policies as additions to the settled property and so within paragraph 8 if the settlor is a potential beneficiary. As you suggest, the proportion of the settled property chargeable under paragraph 8 is arrived at by apportioning the premiums between those paid pre-18 and post-17 March 1986.

2. Home Loan or Double Trust Schemes

We have a number of specific queries on home loan schemes and would welcome clarification with regard to the following points.

A2.82   We welcome the provision for the avoidance of a double charge in the event of the GWR election being made. However, as discussed below, the election still has a number of uncertainties. Furthermore reg.6 is defective in a number of respects.

Firstly, it should not be limited to gifts into settlements (reg.6(a)(ii)) since in some cases the gift of the debt was outright to a child rather than into trust.

Secondly, reg.6 should not be limited to a gift of property representing "the proceeds of the disposal of relevant property".

Many schemes proceeded on the basis of taxpayers lending money to the trustees by a loan agreement and the trustees then using that money to buy the house. The loan does not represent the proceeds of the house. There should be relief in these circumstances.

Question 10

Will HMRC in practice apply Regulation 6 to relieve all home loan schemes from a potential double charge where the donor has died having made an election or is reg.6 being amended to cover the above points?

HMRC answer to question 10

We note your view that reg.6 of SI 2005/724 is not wide enough to cover all cases where a double charge may arise after the taxpayer has elected. At this stage, we cannot give an assurance that we will apply the regulation more widely than its terms indicate, but we will pass on your views on this point.

One of the ways that taxpayers are unravelling home loan schemes is to appoint the debt **A2.83** to the children who then assign it back to the settlor thus losing all inheritance tax benefits but at least ensuring (provided that the children took interests in possession under the original trust) that if the settlor dies within seven years of the original PET, there is relief under the Double Charges Regulations. (This course is often preferable unless double charges relief is to be given for the release of a debt.)

Although there is still an excluded liability in existence, the excluded liability does not appear to be relevant any longer in that it does not reduce the value of the parents' estates under para.11(6) albeit it affects the value of the house. The wording in para.11(6) refers "to the value of the person's estate" and we assume that this means the value of someone's total estate for inheritance tax purposes.

Therefore the fact that the loan continues to reduce the value of the house does not mean that the loan is caught under para.11(6).

Question 11

Is the analysis in 2.4 correct (a) in stating that there is relief under the Double Charges Regulations if the children assign the debt back to the settlor and the settlor dies within seven years of the original gift of the debt and (b) that para.11(6) is no longer in point once the assignment has been effected back to them because the debt no longer reduces the value of their estates?

HMRC answer to question 11

We agree with your analysis in para.2.4(a): the circumstances you have in mind seem to be covered by reg.4 of SI 1987/1130. As far as para.2.4(b) is concerned, we agree that para.11(6) would no longer be in point.

Paragraph 11(6) refers to "the amount of the excluded liability". We seek clarification as **A2.84** to whether this is the face value of the debt (including any rolled up interest or accrued indexation) or the commercial value of the debt.

Example 3

C entered into a home loan scheme. The house is worth £2 million and the debt is repayable on C's death, is linked to the RPI and has a face value of £1.9 million. Its commercial value is discounted due to the fact that it is not repayable until C's death. Allowing for the fact that the debt is linked to the RPI, its market value would be, say, £1.2 million but increasing.

In these circumstances the question is, whether the excess value which is treated as part of C's estate and therefore protected from the POA charge under para.11(1) is:

(i) £100,000;

(ii) £800,000; or

(iii) some other figure such as £100,000 less accrued indexation?

Question 12

What is HMRC's view regarding the amount of the excluded liability in the above scenario?

It would appear that the correct view is to take the commercial value of the debt as reducing the person's estate because in reality the property is "affected" by this amount of debt. Obviously the POA charge would become higher as the commercial value of the debt increased towards the end of the donor's lifetime and hence less property exceeded the value of the debt.

HMRC answer to question 12

In our view, the fact that para.11(6) refers to the "amount" of the excluded liability indicates that it is the face value of the debt, including any rolled-up interest or accrued indexation, that is relevant. In practice, we would only seek to adjust the value of the debt to take account of interest and indexation at the five-yearly valuation dates, though we would be prepared to allow any reduction of the debt resulting from any repayment be taken account as it occurred and to be reflected in a revised computation of tax in the relevant year and subsequently.

A2.85   A common scenario (both for foreign and UK domiciliaries) is where cash is settled into an interest in possession trust for the donor life tenant. The trustees then buy a house for the donor to live in using the gifted cash plus third party borrowings. Although not a home loan scheme, the legislation appears to affect such arrangements.

Example 4

E settles cash of £200,000 into an interest in possession trust for himself in 2003. The trustees purchase a property worth £500,000, borrowing £300,000 from a bank. There are other assets in the trust which can fund the interest but the borrowing is secured on the house which E then occupies.

In these circumstances, one would not expect a POA charge. There is no inheritance tax scheme since the property is part of E's estate and the borrowing is not internal. One would argue that E's estate still includes the house and therefore protection is available under para.11(1). The difficulty is that on one view the loan is an excluded liability within para.11(7) reducing E's estate, albeit it is a loan on commercial terms with a bank.

We would argue that the relevant property for the purposes of para.11 is simply the value of the property net of the commercial borrowing. As this is part of E's estate there is no POA charge.

Question 13

Is the above analysis correct?

HMRC answer to question 13

We agree with your analysis in paragraph 2.6.

A2.86   In those home loan schemes where HMRC considers that there is a reservation of benefit in the debt, it would appear that the taxpayer can still face a POA charge—because he has made a disposal of land which is subject to an excluded liability. The fact that he has reserved a benefit in the debt does not make the debt part of his estate such that the excluded liability can be ignored.

Question 14

Where there is a reservation of benefit in respect of the loan can HMRC confirm that they would not expect the taxpayer to pay both POA and IHT and that the inheritance tax charge would take priority?

HMRC answer to question 14

We agree with the analysis at 2.6. (Even if there is a reservation of benefit in the loan for IHT purposes, it is the land, not the loan, which is the relevant property for POA purposes and para.11 Sch.15 in particular. And although the loan may be property subject to a reservation for IHT purposes, it remains an excluded liability within paras 11(6) and (7) Sch.15 for the purposes of the POA charge.) As matters currently stand, there is no provision to disapply the charge that may arise under Sch.15.

Question 15 A2.87

Will any statement be issued by HMRC as to which home loan schemes of the various types seen they consider do not work for inheritance tax purposes?

Otherwise taxpayers may self-assess and pay the income tax charge, thinking to preserve the inheritance tax savings but be unaware of HMRC's view.

HMRC answer to question 15

We will shortly be issuing updated technical guidance that will include material to identify the circumstances in which we consider a reservation of benefit in the loan exists. Hopefully, this will give some indication to providers of schemes affected whether or not we consider their scheme to be one where a reservation of benefit in the loan exists. This in turn may make it easier for providers to help any clients (or ex-clients) who seek their assistance over completion of their tax return.

3. The Effect of the Election

In the case of a married couple who have sold their jointly owned house to the property A2.88 trust and given the debt to a second trust, it is assumed that one of them can elect to come within the gift with reservation rules and one can choose not to elect, i.e. it is not necessary for both to make the election.

Question 16

Will HMRC please confirm this point?

HMRC answer to question 16

As far as we can see, it is possible for one spouse and not the other to elect under para.21.

A2.89 There is some uncertainty about the effect of the election because para.21 does not as such deem there to be a gift for inheritance tax purposes but simply states that the property is treated as property subject to a reservation.

Furthermore in para.21(2)(b)(ii) it is stated that only s.102(3) and (4) are to apply and not specifically s.102(8) which brings in Sch.20.

We assume that the wording in para.21(2)(b)(i) referring to the property being treated as property subject to a reservation of benefit for the purposes of the 1986 Act does not limit the scope of the reservation of benefit provisions so that only s.102(3) and (4) apply.

Example 5

D effected a home loan scheme. He elects into reservation of benefit and then in April 2010 starts to pay full consideration for the use of his house. Has he made a deemed PET at that point (under s.102(4)) and is he protected from a reservation of benefit charge provided he continues to pay a market rent? We assume that HMRC take the view that para.21(2)(b)(ii) does not narrow the effect of para.21(2)(b)(i) and the let-outs in para.6 Sch.20 apply.

Question 17

(i) Please confirm that on making an election there is a reservation of benefit in the house and not the debt in respect of the home loan scheme and that, once an election is made, all the provisions relating to reservation of benefit in FA 1986 and in particular Sch.20 apply?

Please also confirm the position on deemed PETs in the example above where the person who elects is already paying full consideration.

(ii) Suppose A elects into GWR in respect of his home. The house is then appointed back to him absolutely (i.e. the arrangement, e.g. a home loan scheme, is unscrambled). In these circumstances the reservation of benefit has ceased but the house is back in their estates anyway. Is there a deemed PET under s.102(4) of the FA 1986?

HMRC answer to question 17

(i) We confirm that on making an election under para.21, there would be a reservation of benefit in the house, not the debt in respect of the home loan scheme. In our view, the reference to s.102(4) of the Finance Act 1986 in para.21(2)(b)(ii) envisages circumstances in which the property ceases to be subject to a reservation and there is nothing to suggest that these would not include circumstances in which the provisions of paragraph 6, Schedule 20 Finance Act 1986 would be in point.

(ii) By analogy with the view we have taken for "actual" gifts with reservation, we believe that the tax treatment for the purposes of Sch.15 would depend on whether or not the taxpayer starts to pay full consideration for the continued use of the house or chattel immediately on making an election or after a period of time. We think it would only be in the latter case that there would be a deemed PET under s.102(4) of the FA 1986.

(iii) In our view, the provisions of s.102(4) do, in terms, apply, by virtue of para.21(2)(b)(ii), when the taxable property is appointed back to the chargeable person. But the value of A's estate would not be decreased by this deemed PET. On that basis we do not regard the deemed PET by A has having any practical consequences for A, because it would have no value.

We seek clarification of the position on home loan schemes when both spouses elect and A2.90 one then dies.

Example 6

H and W have effected a home loan scheme. They both elect. On H's death his share in the house is worth £400,000 but is perhaps entirely subject to debt. His share passes to W but the value of her estate is not increased because H's share is subject to the debt. Hence the concern is that the effect of the election is to make H's share taxable immediately on his death by virtue of s.102(3) as to £400,000.

In our view it would appear that the spouse exemption is available on the first death since the deceased's share in the house passes to the surviving spouse under the terms of the property trust or otherwise becomes comprised in the survivor's estate as IHTA 1984 requires. This is so even if the value of the debt equals or exceeds that of the house.

Question 18

(a) Does HMRC agree with this interpretation? (See also Statement of Practice E13.)

(b) Is HMRC's view that:

1. full spouse exemption is available even if the debt equals the value of the house; or

2. full spouse exemption is available provided the spouse's estate is increased by even a small amount; or

3. spouse exemption is only available to the extent the value of the house exceeds the debt?

HMRC answer to question 18

In the circumstances outlined in Example 6, the starting point is the disposals of property that H & W have each made in order to effect a home loan scheme. If then they elect under para.21 and H then dies, we think the effect would indeed be to bring £400,000 into H's estate immediately before his death for IHT purposes by virtue of s.102(3) Finance Act 1986. As far as we can see, there is no scope for spouse exemption as regards this chargeable item as the property disposed of by H in setting up the home loan scheme did not become comprised in the estate of W. Nor, having regard to para.21(3) can we see any scope for reducing the amount charged under s.102(3) of the FA 1986 by the amount of the debt. Of course, H's estate for IHT purposes will also include his interest in possession in the property trust. We imagine this would consist of his share in the house, subject to the debt. Undoubtedly spouse exemption would be available, but only to the extent that the value of H's share in the house exceeded the debt.

As noted in 1.5 above there are technical difficulties if the property is sold after an election. A2.91 Assume that a smaller replacement property is acquired by the trustees but the debt is not repaid. Accepting that the replacement property will be within the para.3 land charge, what of the surplus cash which has been invested in intangibles?

Example 7

Suppose the taxpayer moves out of the home and has made an election. He purchases a smaller replacement house a week later. The balance of the proceeds is invested and he enjoys the income as life tenant.

Question 19

(a) Does a new election need to be made at that point under para.22 in relation to the intangibles part and/or under para.21 in relation to the smaller home?

(b) What happens if the time limits for making the election on the original property have passed?

HMRC answer to question 19

Paragraph 21(2)(a) states that when an election has been made the income tax charge won't apply to the taxpayer's enjoyment of the relevant property "or of any property which has been substituted for the relevant property". From the "any property" we take that to include not only property in the form of land and chattels but also intangible property even though that is subject to a separate paragraph for the election. The equivalent measure in para.22(2)(a) uses the phrase "or any property which represents or is derived from the relevant property". We think this difference is necessary as it may not be possible to "substitute" intangible property for other intangible property.

But we assume you can convert intangible property into something different and we think an election under para.22 would similarly cover cases where intangible property is converted into land or chattels and would otherwise be subject to an election under para.21. So as the paragraphs cover substitutions/derivations, we do not think we require a fresh election when the underlying property changes. In any event, if the taxpayer apparently has an interest in possession in the intangible property, would not para.11(1) be in point assuming a home loan scheme was not involved? As we would not be looking for a fresh election, we assume part (b) of the question is not relevant.

A2.92   It may be said that the deeming provision in s.660A(1) of the TA 1988 (now s.624 of the ITTOIA 2005) is irrelevant to interest in possession trusts where the settlor is life tenant given that there is no question of the income being taxed as that of any other person as envisaged in that provision.

Question 20

Does the para.8 charge apply to cash held in such a trust on the basis that this is a settlor interested trust to which s.660A of the TA 1988 (now s.624 of the ITTOIA 2005) is therefore applicable or does the fact that the settlor is the life tenant of this trust preclude the application of s.660A? This would obviously affect the election mechanism. This is relevant to home loan trusts now holding intangibles.

HMRC answer to question 20

We are not sure that we can see how the application of s.624 of the ITTOIA 2005, and therefore para.8 is explicitly precluded per se.

A2.93   ## Question 21

When an election is made on a double trust scheme, is this election in respect of the entire land or just the part subject to the debt? Can HMRC confirm the former is correct given that in para.21(3) the DV/V formulation would mean that the entire value of the land equals DV?

HMRC answer to question 21

It seems to us that the relevant property in terms of Sch.15 generally and specifically for the purposes of the election would be the land in its entirety.

The election mechanism does not satisfactorily deal with the position where part of the original gifted property is not within the regime and part is. **A2.94**

Example 8

Andrew gives his house on interest in possession trusts for spouse Emma in 2000. Her interest in possession is terminated in all but 20 per cent of the fund. Hence the gift ceases to be an excluded disposal in relation to 80 per cent.

Andrew decides to make an election rather than to pay the income tax charge. In these circumstances is the chargeable proportion 100 per cent (being the DV/V figure) or 80 per cent?

It is assumed the latter on the basis that Andrew is chargeable only by reference to his enjoyment of the 80 per cent not by reference to his enjoyment of 100 per cent (see wording in para.21(1)(a)). Hence "the relevant property" on which he can elect is only 80 per cent.

Question 22

Does HMRC agree with this analysis?

HMRC answer to question 22

We would agree that, in the circumstances set out in Example 8, the "relevant property" would be 80 per cent of it. The use of the formula DV/V, as ordained in para.21(3), would simply mean that all of the 80 per cent would be treated as the chargeable proportion.

Where a taxpayer is doubtful as to whether he is caught by the regime in the first place he can put full details of his arguments on the additional information pages of the return and presumably would then be treated as having made full disclosure and be protected from a discovery assessment. Of course, even if a taxpayer does obtain finality in one tax year, this will not prevent HMRC raising an enquiry in later years if the taxpayer continued to self assess on the basis that the regime does not apply to him. **A2.95**

Suppose HMRC does not enquire into the taxpayer's return for 2005/6. In 2006/7, he continues to self-assess on the basis that he is outside the regime; HMRC makes an enquiry and it is established that the taxpayer was wrong to self-assess on the basis that no income tax was due under the regime. Possibly a court case clarifies the position or there is a change in legislation which is deemed to have always had effect.

In these circumstances the taxpayer will have missed the deadline for making the election (he first became chargeable under the regime in 2005 and therefore needed to elect by January 31, 2007) and will have to pay income tax going forward or else try to unravel the arrangement.

Question 23

Will the taxpayer be able to make a late election in these circumstances?

HMRC answer to question 23

Whether the taxpayer is protected from a discovery assessment in the circumstances described will depend on whether the argument he presents is tenable and if not whether he could then be considered negligent in submitting an insufficient self assessment. Tenability would need to be judged against the practice generally prevailing at the time the return was made. We would consider that the taxpayer was bound by the time limit for that year of assessment for making an election regardless of whether HMRC made an enquiry relating to that year or a later year. It would be for the taxpayer to demonstrate that he had a reasonable excuse for failing to make an election in time.

In a situation where a court decision overturns the previous practice or legislation makes changes which is deemed to have always had effect, then the taxpayer would be protected for earlier years and he would be chargeable only from the time the change in practice or legislation was made. It would not be unreasonable to assume he would then have until the deadline for that year of assessment to make an election.

A2.96 Another difficulty arises if the taxpayer wrongly pays income tax on the basis that he was within the regime when in fact he was not. This is particularly pertinent in relation to home loan schemes where HMRC appears to accept that some work and some do not.

Question 24

What position will be taken by HMRC in these circumstances? Will the taxpayer (or his personal representatives) be able to make a claim for repayment of the tax paid under a mistake of law for six years from the date of overpayment?

HMRC answer to question 24

Providers of certain home loan or double trust schemes are already aware that HMRC takes the view that the gifts with reservation of benefit legislation applies to them. We will include in our guidance information about the circumstances in which we consider the GWR legislation applies.

If the taxpayer has made an excessive self assessment by virtue of error or mistake in his return then he can claim relief under s.33 of the Taxes Management Act 1970. The time limit for doing so is five years from the 31 January following the year of assessment to which the erroneous return relates.

4. Regulation 5 and Para.10(1)(a)—Equity Release Schemes

A2.97 The relief given in reg.5 seems unnecessarily restrictive as a matter of principle and we do not fully understand the Ministerial Statement or the Guidance Notes on this. It is suggested that where a child moves into the house to care for an aged parent and acquires an equitable interest in the shared home in consideration for providing caring services, the parent is protected from a POA charge under reg.5(b). However, such a disposal does not seem to be by way of a transaction at arm's length between persons not connected with each other. These are not normal commercial arrangements. It is difficult to put a value in advance or even retrospectively on what the services to be provided will actually be worth in terms of a share in the house.

Question 25

What evidence is required to satisfy reg.5(b)? It will be difficult to establish what would be regarded as an arms length transaction without a court hearing which would generally only occur in the event of a dispute.

HMRC answer to question 25

In considering whether reg.5(b) was satisfied, we would need information about how the essential elements of the transaction had been arrived at. We do recognise that there is a substantial body of case law dealing with the circumstances in which an interest in a house is acquired in consequence of a person acting to his detriment. The Ministerial Statement had these sorts of situations in mind and we would interpret Regulation 5 accordingly. In particular, we accept that the requirement that "the disposal was by a transaction such as might be expected to be made at arm's length between persons not connected with each other" would be interpreted with such cases in mind. We would not therefore expect the parties to have sought separate advice and acted upon it or to have obtained a court order confirming the property entitlement. We recognise that detriment that the acquirer can demonstrate he has suffered can provide consideration for the acquisition of the interest and prevent the transaction from being gratuitous.

Suppose that something that had not been a readily convertible asset and was therefore protected under para.5(1)(b) subsequently became a RCA under ITEPA. We are concerned that a transaction that was previously protected could now lose such protection.   **A2.98**

Question 26

What happens if the definition of readily convertible asset in ITEPA 2003 changes?

HMRC answer to question 26

If the definition of "readily convertible asset" in ITEPA 2003 were to change, I think we would need to review the appropriateness of reg.5(2). We are not aware that any such alteration is in prospect, however.

There are difficulties where land is held under one title but is physically discrete—for example, two fields. Suppose father sells one of the two fields to his son for full value and continues to farm in partnership over that field. Does father have a pre-owned assets problem?   **A2.99**

Question 27

Is the father protected under para.10(1)(a)? Can it be treated as a sale of whole if son becomes beneficially and legally entitled to the entire field even though father is selling only one of the fields?

HMRC answer to question 27

The first issue is what constitutes "the property" for the purposes of para.10(1)(a). We think it would be possible to regard each of the two discrete fields as "the property", so the disposal of one of them would be a disposal of the whole interest in that asset. As far as your example is concerned, a sale by father to son would be within para.10(1)(a)(ii) on the basis that father receives a full open market price for his land.

A2.100 It is not uncommon for taxpayers to enter into transactions whereby they carve out a lease for themselves and sell the freehold reversion at full market value. Indeed some commercial equity release schemes are structured along these lines. In earlier informal discussions HMRC appeared to agree that the wording in para.10(1)(a) did cover such arrangements but the Guidance Notes suggest there has to be a disposal of the taxpayer's entire interest without any reservation of a lease. The provisions on non-exempt sales of course use a different wording.

Question 28

Can HMRC confirm that a disposal of a taxpayer's whole interest in the property "except for any right expressly reserved by him over the property" as set out in para.10(1)(a) is intended to cover a transaction where F has carved out a lease for himself and sold the encumbered freehold reversion for full market value to his son? If so, will the Guidance Notes be amended to confirm this?

HMRC answer to question 28

In our view, para.10(1)(a) does cover the scenario you envisage in 4.4. We will amend the Guidance Notes.

5. Reversionary Lease Arrangements

A2.101 In the case of reversionary lease arrangements, the taxpayer retains the freehold interest giving away a long lease which vests in possession in (say) 20 years time. Assuming that he is within para.3, i.e. that the arrangement does not involve a reservation of benefit, the taxpayer may wish to pay a full rent for his use of the land so as to avoid a POA charge: see Sch.15 para.4(1). The difficulty is that the owner of the relevant land in this case appears to be himself and he cannot pay rent to himself.

Question 29

Does this mean that in the context of reversionary leases this part of the legislation is meaningless? To obtain relief under para.4, will the taxpayer have to transfer his freehold to an interest in possession trust for himself and pay rent to the trustees?

HMRC answer to question 29

We agree that it would be difficult for the taxpayer to pay rent to himself in order to avoid a charge under Sch.15. But, as you suggest, it would be possible to overcome the difficulty.

The Guidance Notes state that reversionary lease arrangements effected post 8 March **A2.102** 1999 are not caught because they are subject to a reservation of benefit. You will be aware that many advisers do not agree with this view. On the basis of HMRC's current advice there is no requirement for a taxpayer to self assess and pay the pre-owned asset income tax charge. If, however, it turns out that HMRC is wrong in their view that post 8 March 1999 reversionary lease schemes are caught by the reservation of benefit rules, pre-owned assets income tax would have been due.

Question 30

(a) If HMRC's views are successfully challenged in the courts will the taxpayer be subject to back tax, interest and penalties?

(b) We would hope that HMRC would not in these circumstances seek to collect income tax (and interest) in respect of past years but only in respect of future years.

(c) Will it be a requirement for all taxpayers who have done a reversionary lease scheme post-March 1999 to put this on their tax return in the white space and explain why they are not paying income tax?

HMRC answer to question 30

Our view on the IHT treatment of reversionary leases and, in particular, the application of s.102A of the Finance Act 1986 to them is under review at the moment. We will be issuing guidance as soon as we can.

6. Miscellaneous Problems

There are difficulties in determining whether both contribution and disposal conditions **A2.103** have been met in a single transaction and this can be relevant when applying the exclusions in para.10 and the exemptions in para.11.

Paragraph 3(2) provides that the disposal condition is met if the chargeable person owned an interest in the relevant land or "in other property the proceeds of the disposal of which were directly or indirectly applied by another person towards the acquisition of an interest in the relevant land."

Paragraph 3(3) refers to the contribution condition being met where the chargeable person "has directly or indirectly provided, otherwise than by an excluded transaction, any of the consideration given by another person for the acquisition of an interest in the relevant land or an interest in any other property the proceeds of the disposal of which were directly or indirectly applied by another person towards the acquisition of an interest in the relevant land."

Question 31

Is the correct analysis of the interaction between the disposal condition and the contribution condition as follows?

1. If the transferred property is itself the relevant land (i.e. is occupied by the donor) only the disposal condition is met.

2. If the transferred property is cash and that cash is used by the donee to buy the relevant land occupied by the donor, only the contribution condition is met. If HMRC agrees with this can the Guidance Notes be amended at 1.2.1 which suggest (we think wrongly) that the disposal not the contribution condition is breached if cash is given to the donee who then purchases a property for occupation by the donor.

3. If the transferred property is an asset other than cash, and the donee then sells that asset and uses the proceeds to buy the relevant land, both the disposal and the contribution conditions are met.

4. In such a case Sch.15 para.11(9)(a)(ii) means the relevant land is the relevant property for the purposes of para.11, so that the para.11 exemptions can apply if the other conditions in para.11 are met.

HMRC answer to question 31

Taking your four questions in turn:

- If the property disposed of by the chargeable person is the relevant land, we agree that only the disposal condition in para.3(2) is in point.

- If the chargeable person transfers cash, which is then used by the donee to acquire relevant land, we agree that it is the contribution condition in paragraph 3(3) that is in point, not the disposal condition. As you suggest, our guidance at paragraph 1.2.1 needs revising on this point.

- We agree that the contribution condition contemplates circumstances in which a chargeable person has indirectly provided consideration by way of a disposal of assets other than cash. Such a disposal might also meet the disposal condition, as you suggest.

- Paragraph 3 makes it clear that, for the purposes of either the disposal or the contribution conditions, the "relevant land" is the land occupied by the chargeable person. In a case where the contribution condition (paras 3(3) or 6(3), as appropriate) is in point, the "relevant property" for the purposes of the exemptions in para.11 is the "property representing the consideration directly or indirectly provided": We think this must mean provided by the chargeable person. Whether this is the "relevant land" must, we think, depend on whether paras 3(3)(a) or 3(3)(b) apply.

A2.104 The meaning of the "provision" of "consideration" in the context of the contribution condition needs to be clarified. On the basis of the case law the word provided suggests some element of bounty.

On this basis our view is that if there is a transfer of Whiteacre by A (or another asset) to his son at full market value which is then sold by son and the sale proceeds used to purchase Blackacre for A to occupy this is a breach of the disposal but not the contribution condition because it lacks the necessary element of bounty.

Similarly, the provision of a loan on commercial terms by A to his son to enable his son to purchase a house which A then occupies in our view does not fall within the contribution condition.

Question 32

Does HMRC agree with this analysis?

HMRC answer to question 32

Now confirmed that loans are not caught by the contribution condition.

Clarification is requested on the position where a house is owned by a company but the **A2.105**
company is funded by way of loan. The concern is over paras 11(1)(b) and 11(3)(b).

Example 9

B owns 100 £1 shares in X Limited and otherwise funds it by shareholder loan. (Or
the house is owned by a company held within an interest in possession trust for B and
again the funding for the purchase comes by way of loan from trustees to company.)
X Limited buys the house in which B lives. B prima facie falls within the para.3
charge. It would appear that para.11(1) protects him. The shares are not themselves
property which derive much value from the house because they are worth substantially
less than the house (see para.11(1)(b)(ii)) but the shares and the loan together are
comprised in B's estate and between them indirectly derive their value from the
house. On that basis para.11(1) does offer full protection.

Question 33

Do HMRC agree with this analysis or do they consider that the loan derives its value from
the contractual undertakings that oblige the borrowing company to repay?
    It would be odd if there is a POA problem when the company is funded by way of loan
but not if it is funded by way of share capital.

HMRC answer to question 33

In our view, the loan, albeit an asset of B's estate, is not property that derives its value from
the relevant property. However, our response to question 32 above would no doubt be
applicable here in appropriate circumstances.

How is the charge computed under para.9 when the settled property comprises say a **A2.106**
deposit account but also an overdrawn current account at 6 April in the relevant year? Is
the POA tax charge based simply on the value of the deposit account without deducting
the overdraft?
    The definition of relevant property is property which is or represents property which
the chargeable person settled. If A settles cash into trust retaining a remainder interest and
then the trust invests that cash unwisely e.g. in a hedge fund incurring losses which require
the trustees to borrow to settle, is it the net or gross value of the trust fund that is taken in
computing the POA charge?

Question 34

Can HMRC clarify the above?

HMRC answer to question 34

In our view, it is the net value of the trust fund as at 6 April in the relevant year that should
form the basis of the computation under para.9.

A2.107 The excluded transaction provision in para.10(2)(c) refers to an outright gift "to the other person" whereas the wording in para.10(2)(e) refers expressly to an outright gift to an individual. The word person must include trusts and companies. In our view para.10(2)(c) applies to settled gifts and gifts to individuals although of course cash gifts into trust will be caught by the tracing rules in schedule 20 and are therefore generally gifts with reservation if the donor can benefit from the trust and protected anyway under para.11(3).

Question 35

Does HMRC agree with this analysis?

HMRC answer to question 35

We think the "other person" referred to in para.10(2)(c) must be the person referred to in paras 3(3) and 6(3) as acquiring an interest in the relevant land, etc. We agree that such a person need not necessarily be an individual. But we are more doubtful that an "outright" gift of money could include a gift to be held on trusts.

Partnership issues

A2.108 The Guidance Notes suggest that a partnership is transparent for inheritance tax purposes. While this is true for capital gains tax purposes, as a matter of law a gift of a partnership interest is not a gift of the underlying assets within the partnership.

   We therefore do not understand the example given in **Appendix 1** which refers to C who gives his son D an interest in the partnership in return for D taking on the day to day running. In these circumstances why is there a disposal of land or chattels at all? There is a fundamental distinction between a firm's capital on the one hand and its individual assets on the other. C's proportionate interest in the capital may be equal to the value of the land or chattels but it is not an interest in the land or chattels itself and therefore he cannot dispose of that land (or the chattels) when he makes the gift of the partnership interest. See *Lindley on Partnerships* 17th Edn.

Question 36

Is HMRC treating partnerships as transparent for POA income tax purposes?

HMRC answer to question 36

We do not intend to treat partnerships as transparent for the purposes of Sch.5. We will amend the example in **Appendix 1** of the Guidance that you refer to.

A2.109 Certain questions arise in relation to the annual exemption.

Example 10

X carried out a home loan scheme. In June 2005 he dismantles the scheme. The benefit enjoyed for POA purposes from April to June is £4,000.

Question 37

Will HMRC confirm that:

(a) where the de minimis exemption under para.13 is not exceeded it is not possible for the transferor to make an election because he is not "chargeable to income tax"?

(b) the £5,000 exemption is not pro-rated when a taxpayer is chargeable for only part of the year?

HMRC answer to question 37

We confirm both (a) and (b) are correct.

In a number of circumstances it is possible for (say) the husband to be caught by POA **A2.110** charge because he has made a disposal but not a gift and the wife to be caught potentially by gift with reservation.

In these circumstances do they each have to pay full consideration to escape their respective charges?

> ### *Example 11*
>
> In 1998, H transfers some properties into a company he wholly owns in consideration of the issue of shares. He has breached the disposal condition. He gives the shares to his wife. In 2003, W gives the company shares to her sons and later both of them occupy one of the properties owned by the company. H and W are not directors of the company.
>
> In these circumstances, H might wish to pay rent under paragraph 4 and W might want to pay full consideration under para.6 Sch.20 in order respectively to avoid a pre-owned assets tax charge and a reservation of benefit situation.

Question 38

(a) Is it sufficient that they pay such rent under an assured shorthold tenancy from their joint account and are jointly and severally liable for the rent?

(b) Or does each person have to pay the full consideration separately?

HMRC answer to question 38

It seems to us that Example 11 is dealing with concurrent charges under two separate regimes: Sch.15, and s.102 of the Finance Act 1986. In our view, it is arguable that H and W each has to pay full consideration separately in order to meet the separate requirements of para.4(1) Sch.15 and para.6 Sch.20 to the Finance Act 1986.

In 1.3.1 of the Guidance Notes under the bullet points relating to the spouse having to take **A2.111** an interest in possession from the outset it is not clear whether, if the interest in possession of the spouse or former spouse has come to an end other than on their death, the transaction is not an excluded transaction from the outset or whether it becomes so from the time the interest in possession terminates. It must surely cease to be an excluded transaction only from the time the interest in possession terminates.

Question 39

Will HMRC please clarify this point and confirm that the transaction only ceases to be an excluded transaction from the date the spousal interest terminates and therefore it is only from that point onwards there is a POA charge. Furthermore para.10(3) states that a disposal is not an excluded transaction if the interest in possession of the spouse comes to an end otherwise than on death of the spouse. Suppose a spouse becomes beneficially entitled to the property absolutely e.g. if the trustees advance the property outright to her so she becomes absolutely entitled. In these circumstances does the excluded transaction protection end? Her interest in possession has ended but only because she has become absolutely entitled to the property.

HMRC answer to question 39

In view of the way in which para.10(3) is drafted, it is clear that the transaction ceases to be an excluded transaction only from the time that the interest in possession comes to an end otherwise than on the death of the (former) spouse.

As far as para.10(3) is concerned, we can see how it might be said that, where a spouse becomes absolutely entitled, the protection afforded by paras 10(1)(c) or 10(2)(b) is no longer available, particularly as the property in question would no longer be settled property. That would be a less than satisfactory result in our view, particularly bearing in mind the related provisions in paras 10(1)(b) and (2)(a). A more satisfactory approach might be to regard the interest in possession, which is not limited in terms to settled property as far as the reference in para.10(3) is concerned, as not coming to an end in these circumstances.

A2.112 4.6 of the Guidance Notes give some examples of what HMRC considers constitutes occupation and the helpful letter from Mr McNicol dated 22 April 2005 gives further explanation. However, we do not fully understand HMRC's comments in this area. Please could the following common scenarios be clarified so that the taxpayer can self-assess appropriately. This is particularly relevant in relation to holiday homes.

Question 40

(a) If there is a right to use a property throughout the year but it is not in fact used by the chargeable person, is it correct that there is no POA charge?

(b) If there is a right to use a property throughout the year and the chargeable person uses the property but it falls within the de minimis limits set out in the guidance notes, is it correct that there is no POA charge?

(c) If there is a right to use a property throughout the year and the chargeable person uses the property for say three months of the year there is a POA charge based on the whole year, even though others may have the right to use the property during that period (we are thinking particularly here of holiday homes)?

(d) If there is a right to or actual storage of items in the relevant property but the chargeable person never lives there and the property is occupied by someone else, is it correct that there is no occupation of land within Sch.15?

(e) Would the position of HMRC differ in (d) above if the property remained empty?

HMRC answer to question 40

Before dealing with your individual questions, we think it is worth reminding you of our view that occupation and use should be construed widely and are not confined to physical occupation.

(a) If there is a right to use, but no occupation or use (in the wider sense) by the chargeable person in the year, it is unlikely that there would be a Sch.15 charge.

(b) We are not sure we can confirm that no Sch.15 charge would arise in these circumstances. The examples of de minimis use given in paragraph 4.6 of the Guidance Notes do not contemplate (or, at least, do not assume) a right to use in the hands of the chargeable person for the rest of the year. If there is a right to use the property with even a small amount of use, the issue of how in fact the property was used for the rest of the year would need to be considered and whether this use also constituted use by the chargeable person.

(c) We would agree that a Sch.15 charge based on the whole year would arise.

(d) We think it is difficult to give an assurance that there is no occupation of land under Sch.15 by the chargeable person, if he is actually storing assets in the property. Particularly if he might have a right of access to these items, the circumstances might suggest that both the chargeable person and the person living in the property were using it.

(e) By saying that the property remains empty, we assume you are envisaging that no-one is living in it. On that basis, if the chargeable person is storing items there, it seems clear that he is using the property for the purposes of Sch.15.

The position on non-exempt sales is unclear. It is our view that there is no POA charge **A2.113** because the cash element paid is excluded under the computation in para.4 and the undervalue element is a reservation of benefit anyway and therefore exempted from POA under para.11(3).

If there is a part exchange at an undervalue with a cash adjustment, i.e. Y transfers Whiteacre worth £800,000 to X in exchange for Greenacre worth £200,000 and X also pays Y cash of £500,000, if at 6 April 2005 Whiteacre is worth £800,000 (i.e. total consideration is paid by X of £700,000) we assume that POA is payable only on £200,000. The cash element is excluded under para.4 and the undervalue element is excluded under the reservation of benefit provisions.

Question 41

Is the above analysis correct?

HMRC answer to question 41

We broadly agree with this analysis. (We have assumed that, in order for this question to arise at all, Y continues to occupy Whiteacre after the transfer.)

In more detail, we would regard Y's disposition as one partly by way of gift (as to £100,000) and partly by way of sale (as to the remaining £700,000). In the circumstances envisaged, the proportion of the value of Whiteacre disposed of by way of gift would be treated as property subject to a reservation, thus remaining in Y's estate for IHT purposes and so, by virtue of para.11(3), disapplying para.3 to that extent. And, again in the circumstances envisaged, the disposition by way of sale would not be an excluded transaction and thus would be a non-exempt sale for the purposes of para.4(2) and (4).

We then need to apply this analysis to the provisions of para.4 that determine how the chargeable amount is to be calculated and, in particular the R x DV/V formula in para.4(2). First, we assume that, in this example, the relevant land would consist of seven-eigths of Whiteacre and, for any taxable period, V, in para.4(2), would be the value of seven-eigths of Whiteacre at the appropriate valuation date. Looking at DV, we agree that, in applying the formula at para.4(4) to arrive at the "appropriate proportion", P would be limited to the cash element of the consideration. Thus, in your example, (MV—P)/MV would be (£700,000–£500,000) / £700,000, or 2/7.

In order to calculate the chargeable amount for a taxable period, let us assume that at the valuation date seven-eigths of Whiteacre is worth £875,000 (the whole being worth £1,000,000) and the rental value (R) is £38,500. The appropriate rental value, as prescribed in para.4(4) would therefore be £38,500 x (2/7 x £875,000) / £875,000: in other words, £11,000.

(More simply, the calculation is £38,500 x 2/7.)

7. Foreign Domiciliaries

A2.114 Paragraph 12(3) states that no regard is to be had to excluded property. In a case where a trust settled by a foreign domiciliary) owns a UK house through a foreign registered company the shares in the company (and any loan to the company) are excluded property. Concern has been expressed that since para.12(3) says that no regard is to be had to these assets, this in turn means that the shares and loan have to be ignored in applying para.11 and in particular cannot be taken into account in determining whether there is derived property which is in the taxpayer's estate or GWR property in relation to him (which the shares and loans otherwise are). We think that this argument is misconceived but it has been advanced.

Question 42

Can HMRC confirm that it agrees para.12(3) does not operate in this way and that para.11 can still work to protect the UK house or underlying assets owned by the offshore company in these circumstances?

HMRC answer to question 42

We agree with what you say in paragraph 7.1 about the interaction between paras 12(3) and 11.

8. Scope of the Para.8 Charge

A2.115 In addition to the points raised on valuation, we note that on insurance schemes involving for example quantitative carve outs (for example where the settlor taxpayer is the remainderman in the settlement as in a reverter to settlor trust) the settlor is treated as being outside the POA charge. This is on the basis that his interest in the trust property is either held on bare trust or on a separate trust.

Question 43

Will HMRC confirm that reverter to settlor trusts holding other assets are also outside the para.8 charge?

HMRC answer to question 43

If you are suggesting that reverter to settlor trusts are outside the scope of ss.624 and 625 of the ITTOIA 2005, we would be interested to see the reasoning put forward in support of this proposition. In the insurance schemes you mention, which we have agreed do not fall within the said ss.624 and 625 and therefore are outside the scope of para.8, the interests held on trust for the settlor are, as you suggest, carved out of the gift and retained by him. In our view, such schemes are not analogous with reverter to settlor trusts.

Question 44 A2.116

There is a potential problem about the wording in para.22(3): if income is treated as income of the chargeable person by virtue of s.660A then due to para.22(3)(b) it shall be treated as property subject to a reservation. Income could be taxed under s.660A (now s.624 of the ITTOIA) if only a spouse could benefit and that would not normally bring para.8 into play in the first place although this exclusion is not carried forward once an election is made.

So if someone elects on intangibles and then he but not his wife is excluded from benefiting under the settlement does this mean that the conditions in para.22(3) are satisfied and hence that he is still treated as having a reservation of benefit? Or does para.22(2)(b)(ii) (which says ss.102(3) and (4) shall apply) mean that if he ceases to reserve a benefit in the property himself the effect of the election falls away so that there is a deemed PET then, even if the conditions in para.22(3) are prima facie satisfied because his wife can still benefit?

HMRC answer to question 44

We lean towards your first interpretation of the effect of para.22(3)(b). If someone is in a position to make an election under para.22(2), he or she must be someone who is (or would be) chargeable under para.8 for that year of assessment. Clearly, the condition in para.22(3)(b) would also be met at that time. It does seem that this condition would continue to be met until such time that both the chargeable person and his or her spouse (or civil partner) were excluded from benefit. At that point, a PET would be deemed to have arisen by virtue of para.22(2)(b)(ii).

IV CORRESPONDENCE WITH HMRC ON ELECTIONS (October 2006)

A2.117 There is some uncertainty about the actual effect of the election because para.21 does not as such deem there to be a gift for inheritance tax purposes but simply states that the property is treated as property subject to a reservation. Schedule 15 provides for what happens if the person ceases to benefit from the elected property but does not provide for what happens if the property actually comes back into a person's estate.

In the COP 10 letter we asked (at question 17) what happens if A makes the election in respect of his home on a home loan scheme (or indeed any other type of Inheritance Tax Scheme). The house is then appointed back to him absolutely i.e. the arrangements are unscrambled. The reservation of benefit has ceased because the house is back in his estate and you confirmed that even if there was a deemed PET under s.102 (4) of the FA 1986, appointing the property back to A would have no immediate practical inheritance tax consequences because it is back in his estate anyway. This accords with how the reservation of benefit rules on actual gifts work. (See answer to question 17.)

As you will be aware, many people are unravelling schemes but also wish to make the election in order to avoid an income tax charge from 6 April 2005. If once the property is back in their estates the effect of the election ceases to apply for all inheritance tax purposes (in the same way that a reservation of benefit on gifted property would cease if it was transferred back to the donor) then spouse (and charities) exemption is available. If the election is made and the scheme is not unravelled, spouse exemption is not available.

I am therefore requesting confirmation that HMRC apply the Sch.5 of the FA 2004 legislation on elections in the same way as the reservation of benefit legislation on an actual gift. So even though HMRC would produce the election on any death, on being shown evidence that the property had been appointed back and the scheme entirely unravelled, the election would then be ignored for inheritance tax purposes. Spouse exemption is then available. If that approach is indeed the one HMRC adopts, does it matter if the election is made before or after the scheme is unravelled?

Response from HMRC Capital Taxes Nottingham: Pre-owned assets and elections

A2.118 I can confirm that we do believe that the Sch.15 to the FA 2004 legislation on elections should be applied in the same way as the reservation of benefit legislation on an actual gift. As I suggested when you originally raised this question with me on the phone, s.102(3) of the Finance Act 1986 only has practical force in relation to property that is subject to a reservation immediately before death and only to the extent that it would not form part of the estate in any event.

On that basis, if evidence is produced that property, in respect of which an election under the Sch.15 legislation had been made, has been appointed back to the estate, we would ignore the existence of the election for the purpose of determining the IHT estate on death.

On your supplementary question, we do not consider the timing of the election to be material. Even if it were made after the unscrambling, the chargeable person would still have been chargeable for the period up to the unscrambling, thus enabling the requirements of paras 21(1) or 22(1), as appropriate, to be met.

CIOT Note January 2007

Finance Act 2006 s.80: need for POAT election

Finance Act 2006 s.80 amended the income tax charge imposed by the 2004 Finance Act **A2.119** on pre-owned assets. Unfortunately a drafting error means it has a wider impact than was intended.

The s.80 amendment took effect when it was announced on 5 December 2005. PBR05 on that date is headed "pre-owned assets and reverter-to-settlor trusts". The text of PBR05 makes it clear that reverter to settlor trusts are those where the trust property reverts to the settlor or his spouse after termination of another beneficiary's interest in possession. Sections 53 and 54 of the Inheritance Tax Act 1984 are specifically referred to, those being the sections which exempt the trust from the Inheritance Tax otherwise payable on the termination of the beneficiary's interest in possession. For ease of reference it is convenient to refer to that beneficiary as the life tenant and his interest as the life interest.

The drafting error is that the amendment made by s.80 applies not only to trusts where the life tenant is another beneficiary but *also to those where the life tenant is the settlor himself.*

Where s.80 applies it removes the exemption from the pre-owned asset charge otherwise applicable where the taxpayer is treated as beneficially entitled to the relevant property for the purposes of inheritance tax. Loss of the exemption is thus in point in any case where the life interest vested in the settlor arose before 22 March 2006 or where the settlor takes an interest in possession after 21 March 2006 and is disabled within the meaning of s.89 of the IHTA 1984. The effect, on the widest view, is that any such life interest exposes the settlor to pre-owned assets tax. Strictly this is only avoided where the asset was settled land or chattels which have at all times subsequently been retained in the trust.

As will be apparent this is an absurd result. The whole point of pre-owned assets tax is to tax assets which a settlor or donor enjoys despite them not being in his estate for inheritance tax purposes. By definition it is not a tax on property to which a settlor or donor is treated as beneficially entitled as such property is fully subject to Inheritance Tax in his hands.

As will be seen from the attached correspondence HMRC contends that s.80 does not **A2.120** apply if the life-interest of the settlor has subsisted **at all times** since the inception of the trust. Please note though that there is an exception to this point mentioned below. HMRC has said that this view will be included in revised POAT guidance. On this basis, the difficulties identified above only arise where the initial trusts were discretionary or conferred interests in possession on other beneficiaries. But such scenarios are by no means uncommon, particularly in relation to non domiciliaries who are resident in the UK. A typical case where a non domiciliary would be caught would be where before 22 March 2006 he became entitled to an interest in possession in a UK house owned by a discretionary trust which he had created. Such interest could have arisen either by express appointment prior to the purchase of the house or as a result of SP 10/79.

HMRC has confirmed that the effect of s.80 can be removed by making an election, and that the cost of making the election is merely to disapply the reverter to settlor reliefs in ss.53 and 54 of the Inheritance Tax Act 1984. It is true that s.80 has conferred the right to make an election and it is also the case that in most cases the sole effect of the election is indeed to disapply ss.53 and 54. *For this reason an election should be considered urgently in all cases where the settlor did not have an interest in possession when the trust was created but has been appointed one subsequently.*

A2.121   The purpose of this note is to draw attention to the fact that if an election is to be made, then subject to the de minimis exemption mentioned below, it must be made on or before 31 January 2007, i.e. the end of this month. STEP and CIOT are pressing HMRC to introduce amendments to reverse the unintended effect of s.80 as described above. But there is no certainty such amendments will be introduced and an election should therefore be seriously considered.

As the amendments made by s.80 took effect only on 5 December 2005, the amount potentially chargeable to POAT for 2005–06 may be modest. Should the taxable benefit fall within the de minimis exemption, which is £5,000 per taxpayer, no tax is due for 2005–06 and an election will only be needed for 2006–07. It is not possible to make an election on 31 January 2007 if the taxable benefit is under £5,000. However, this gives the taxpayer another year to consider his options. An election would then need to be made by 31 January 2008 (assuming the de minimis charge does not also apply for the full year 2006–07).

A2.122   An election may not be appropriate where the settlor is non-domiciled and the asset giving rise to the pre-owned asset charge is land or chattels owned through an offshore company. In such cases an election could expose the land and chattels, and assets representing them to IHT. Specialist advice should therefore be sought. Such cases are comparatively rare because, as indicated above, on HMRC's view s.80 is only in issue if the settlor did not have an interest in possession when the trust was created but only acquired one subsequently. But if the settlor has by now acquired a deemed UK domicile, s.80 potentially impacts on such cases where the land or chattels owned by the company are foreign situs as well as where they are UK situs. (Where the foreign situated land or chattels are owned direct by the trustees then they should be protected from POAT under para.12(3) even if the trust was initially discretionary.)

A2.123   As a final point, it should be born in mind that on one scenario s.80 can impact on a trust in which the settlor has had a life interest since inception. This is where the trust has been funded by an advance from another trust of which he was settlor but has not at all times had an interest in possession. In those cases too, election should be considered.

Correspondence between CIOT/STEP and HMRC on this point is attached to this note.

CORRESPONDENCE BETWEEN HMRC AND STEP/CIOT FROM SEPTEMBER TO DECEMBER

Questions from STEP/CIOT

A2.124   Section 80 amends FA 2004 Sch.15 para.11. The amendments apply where the relevant property is comprised in a person's estate for the purposes of IHTA 1984 s.49 and previously one of two conditions has been met. These conditions are set out in new para.11(11) as follows:

(a) the relevant property has ceased to be comprised in the person's estate for inheritance tax purposes; **or**

(b) the person has directly or indirectly provided any consideration for the acquisition of the relevant property.

If at any subsequent time the relevant property or derived property is in his estate for the purposes of s.49 of the IHTA then the effect of s.80 is to provide that for POAT purposes (but for no other) the settlor is not treated as having an interest in possession or having reserved a benefit in the property.

The potential difficulty with paras 11(11) and 11(12) is that they do not distinguish between reverter to settler trusts and *any* trust set up between March 1986 and 22 March 2006 where the settlor has a qualifying interest in possession and would in that event be subject to inheritance tax on his death.

These difficulties arise because paras 11(11) and 11(12) catch not only those transactions where land has been given away and ceased to be comprised in the settlor's estate and then comes back into his estate (condition (a) above). They also catch transactions where a settlor contributed funds or property to a trust and the trust (or an underlying company) has then used those funds or property representing them to buy the relevant property i.e. the land which is now occupied (condition (b) above). There is nothing in the words about "any subsequent time" which suggests that under (b) the property had first to cease to be comprised in his estate before being caught by this provision. Indeed if that was the case the words in (a) would be redundant.

Are the following cases caught by POAT from 5 December 2005 (the date the change **A2.125** came into effect)?

1. In 1987, A sets up an interest in possession trust for himself into which he gifts his house. If the house is still held by the trustees now there is no POAT charge because nothing has left his estate. However assume that the house has since been sold but he retains an interest in possession. The trust holds a mixture of investments and another house that A occupies. Is para.11(11) (b) satisfied on the basis that A has provided consideration for the acquisition of the land which land has subsequently become comprised in his estate.

   A would then have to pay POAT on all the investments from 5 December 2005 for the foreseeable future even though they are prima facie chargeable to IHT in the event of his death. POAT may be due on the new house as well.

2. B is a foreign domiciliary (not deemed domiciled) who before 22 March 2006 set up a discretionary trust into which he transferred cash. He remains a beneficiary of the trust. The trust then funds a company which buys a house (and B will pay income tax under s.739 in respect of any UK income). The trust was before 22 March 2006 converted into an interest in possession trust. If there is UK land or there are UK chattels occupied or used by B which are held by the trustees through the company within the interest in possession structure he is now subject to POAT on such property or chattels. (If B is deemed domiciled here then the charge would also apply to non-UK property or chattels occupied or used by him). Even if one reads "subsequent time" to mean some time must elapse between the date when the gift is made and the date the property comes back into B's estate this would still not protect B in this example because the trust was originally discretionary.

3. In June 2006, C, a disabled person, sets up a trust for himself that qualifies as a disabled person's interest within s.89B. C puts in cash and the trustees invest in equities or a house that C occupies. C will pay POAT.

A simple amendment that would deal with the problem is to state that s.80 should not apply where the person with the qualifying interest in possession is the settlor. Is this in contemplation?

HMRC response

As I understand your concern, it is that the new para.11(11)(b) in Sch.5 to the FA 2004 **A2.126** will catch someone who has settled, say, cash on interest in possession trusts for themselves (either before 22 March 2006, or afterwards if it is a "disabled person's interest") and subsequently occupies property bought by the trustees; or where the property they settled initially has been sold and replaced by other property, while the settlor has retained their interest in possession.

The new paragraph refers to the chargeable person "directly or indirectly [providing] any consideration for the acquisition of the relevant property", and goes on to require that, "at any subsequent time", the relevant property is comprised in the settlor's IHT estate by virtue of their having an interest in possession in it.

In our view, the words "at any subsequent time" should be read as meaning that a POA charge will arise where the consideration leaves the donor's estate, *as a result of which that estate is reduced*, and later property acquired with such consideration becomes comprised in it again because of their interest in possession. This is consistent with the reasons for Schedule 15.

A2.127 We do not, therefore, consider that there will be a charge in the scenarios numbered 1 and 3 in your letters, because the assets transferred into trust and any derived assets have always been in the settlor's estate for IHT purposes. We believe that also applies if, in your second scenario, B set up an interest in possession trust from the outset before Budget Day. The taxpayer should self-assess on the basis that no POAT is due and there is therefore no need to put anything about POAT on the tax return or for him to make the election where the settlor has retained an interest in possession throughout and settled the cash or property directly into trust himself (rather than through any other funding vehicle such as another trust). This is because no POAT charge arises under s.80 FA 2006.

A2.128 In summary we do not consider that s.80 has any implications for:

- a settlement of cash on interest in possession trusts for oneself made before 22 March 2006, or made by a disabled person on or after that date, after which the trustees purchase a property in which the settlor resides; or

- the settlement of a house in the same way, which is subsequently sold by the trustees and replaced by other investments or another property.

That remains our view, on the basis that the words "at any subsequent time" mean that new para.11(11)(b) Sch.15 to the FA2004 will only be relevant where:

- the consideration in question leaves the donor's estate, as a result of which that estate is reduced; and

- later, property acquired with such consideration becomes comprised in the estate once more by virtue of an interest in possession.

A2.129 We do not agree that this interpretation makes para.11(11)(a) redundant, since that relates to cases where the disposal condition is met and para.11(11)(b) to cases where the contribution condition is met.

A2.130 We accept that a POA charge may arise where someone set up a discretionary trust that has subsequently been converted into an interest in possession trust for the benefit of the settlor (scenario 2 in your example). However, it remains possible in those circumstances to elect out of the charge. So, take the following example:

- H settles a property on discretionary trusts before 22 March 2006;

- also before that date, the trust is converted into an interest in possession trust for H's benefit, with remainder to his wife, W;

- a POA charge therefore arises because of s.80 but H elects.

As we see it, the effects of the election are:

- the chargeable proportion of the property will be treated as subject to a reservation, but only so far as H is not beneficially entitled to an interest in possession in the property (para.21(2)(b)(i), Sch.15 to the FA 2004), i.e. not at all;

- s.102(3) and (4) of the FA 1986 will apply, but only so far as H is not beneficially entitled to an interest in possession in the property (para.21(2)(b)(ii)), i.e. not at all; and

- the reverter-to-settlor exemptions in s.53(3) and (4) and s.54 of the IHTA will not apply to the actual interest in possession (para.21(2)(b)(iii)).

We do not, therefore, consider that the election affects the availability of spouse exemption on H's interest in possession on his death – or on its termination during his lifetime. That is because, as we have just noted, the election will not cause s.102(3) and (4) FA 86 to apply because of H's interest in possession, so there will be no deemed PET.

CIOT/STEP comment

In the light of the above it will be necessary for practitioners to review urgently all those **A2.131** trusts where the following conditions are satisfied:

1. they were funded between March 1986 and March 2006;

2. at the date of funding, the settlor settled funds or property on discretionary trusts or on interest in possession trusts for someone else but before 22 March 2006 he acquired an interest in possession in the settled property.

In these circumstances the UK resident and UK domiciled person (domiciled in the UK under general law) will need to **elect by 31 January 2007** but on HMRC's analysis there is no additional inheritance tax payable and the same reliefs and exemptions will be available as would have been due prior to the election.

If the conditions at 1 and 2 above are satisfied, the foreign domiciliary (*whether or not* **A2.132** *deemed domiciled here now*) who is resident in the UK and established his trust before he became domiciled here will need to elect by 31 January 2007 if the trust holds directly any UK situated intangibles or the trust directly or through a company holds UK real property that he occupies or UK chattels that he uses and he does not want to pay POAT. (An excluded property trust that holds intangibles through an offshore company structure will not be caught by s.80 in any event because para 8 does not apply to the underlying assets of a company and para.12(3) protects the offshore company shares). The settlor who is deemed domiciled here but was not domiciled here when he set up the trust will also need to consider an election on foreign situated land or chattels occupied or used by him where this is held in an offshore company owned by a trust assuming he does not want to pay POAT. However, there are a number of complexities.

Specialist advice should be sought as to the inheritance tax effects of such an election. In general terms an election will increase a foreign domiciliary's inheritance tax bill on his death where the UK situated property is owned by a company and he has an interest in possession in the shares. Otherwise the effect of making an election on UK situated property is likely to be broadly neutral.

EXTRACT OF LETTER FROM HMRC TO ABI SEPTEMBER 2004

A2.133 At the meetings we have had with you, you raised certain points which you wanted clarified. Except where otherwise stated, statutory references are to Sch.15.

Analysis of carve outs, etc

You were concerned that where trustees hold a policy of assurance, under the terms of which certain benefits have been retained by the settlor/proposer whilst the remaining benefits enure for others, the current provisions of para 8 are such that an income tax charge would be imposed on the settlor. This concern was based on the premise that the property comprised in the settlement is an indivisible chose in action, being the contract with the insurance company held by the trustees. You asked that we set out our views on why that approach to this draft legislation is in our eyes misconceived; these are as follows.

'Settlement' and 'settled property' for the purposes of Sch.15 mean the same as in IHTA 1984; see ss.43(1) and (2) of that Act.

A2.134 There are two relationships in being. The first is that between the company and the trustees, and is purely contractual. So far as the company is concerned that gives rise to an indivisible chose in action to which the company is one party. That is of no relevance to the current income tax/IHT issues. The material relationship is that between the trustees and the beneficiaries. The trustees possess the legal interest in the chose in action. They hold certain interest in the chose on the terms of a trust that falls into the IHTA 1984 s.43(2) definition of settlement for the benefit of persons other than the settlor. Those are the interests which are the property comprised in the settlement within the meaning of paragraph 8. Other interests, those retained by the settlor, are held by the trustees on a bare trust for him. A bare trust is not within the definition of settlement at all, and property so held cannot come within the ambit of para.8.

So in the simple case where the settlor has retained a right to an annual income under arrangements which are not subject to the 'gifts with reservation' (GWR) legislation, that right which is enforceable against the trustees is not property within para 8, being a bare trust. If the company is not providing the income to the trustees for them to pass on, then that would give rise to an action by the trustees against the company under the chose in action they hold.

There may be more complex cases where the settlor's retained rights or interests are themselves held on trust. But that would normally be construed as being a freestanding trust of those benefits in which the settlor had an interest in possession, which would fall within the exemption in para.11.

In the straightforward case where the settlor has retained a right to an annual income or to a reversion under arrangements which are not subject to the GWR legislation, that right is not property within para 8 as the trustees hold it on bare trust for the settlor. The settlor is excluded from other benefits under the policy and so Sch.15 has no application.

Even if the para.11 provisions did not apply so as to exempt the case from charge completely, any Sch.15 charge would apply by reference to the value of the rights held on trust for the settlor, not by reference to the value of the underlying life policy.

Interest free loans

You asked whether a settlor who made an interest-free loan to a settlement of which he **A2.135** was not a beneficiary would be treated as having an interest in the settlement for the purposes of TA 1988 s.660A.

The making of the interest-free loan to the trustees does not in itself constitute a 'settlement' for the purposes of Sch.15 (which adopts the IHT definition of settlement); and so in the case of a trust with a typical settlor-exclusion clause, the fact that the settlor has made an interest-free loan will not *per se* be caught by para.8 of Sch.15.

For completeness, in *Jenkins v CIR* (26 TC 265) the Court of Appeal found that the making of an interest-free loan brought the settlement within what is now s.660A...

In the *Jenkins* case, the dispute was about whether certain income received by the trustees of the settlement could be assessed on the settlor under the provisions of FA 1938 s.38(4). That provision contained an extended definition of retaining an interest in income that is in similar terms to the definition of retaining an interest in property or derived property found in s.660A(2).

The effect of the decision in *Jenkins* was that a settlor who has made an interest-free loan to his/her trust has brought himself or herself within the scope of s.38(4), and by implication s.660A (albeit that there would be no charge unless income actually arose to the trustees).

But, as explained in the second paragraph above, the *Jenkins* case does not affect the fact that the trusts in question are not caught by Sch.15.

Commercial (or partnership) policies

You were concerned to establish whether policies of this sort are caught by Sch.15 and **A2.136** suggested that TA 1988 s.660A(9) might apply.

That provision relates specifically to income consisting of 'annual payments made by an individual'. There are no such payments here because there is no income arising from the trust at all: but even if there were, we do not see that it could have that character.

Separately we have been considering whether the doctrine in *CIR v Plummer* (]1979] **A2.137** STC 793) might operate so that even though the arrangements are set up under a trust umbrella the arrangements would not constitute a settlement for TA 1988 s660A purposes where there is no element of bounty for the settlor.

However, in a formal trust if there is no specific exclusion clause excluding the settlor and spouse then the settlor retains an interest in the 'settlement'. So if the settlor, or his or her spouse, is named as a possible beneficiary of the trust holding the partnership policy, there is no doubt that the settlor retains an interest.

We have to go no further than the legislation itself to see if the settlor retains an interest in the trust, per s.660A(1). That subsection and (2) together are sufficient to bring the income into charge. The rest of s.660A is about exclusions, which are not relevant to the main point.

There is no mentioned of 'bounty' in the legislation. It has derived purely from case law and our view is that it is needed only to prove that there is a 'settlement' (i.e. to include 'arrangement') in the wider sense of s.660G.

INDEX